FRIENDS ACADEMY LIBRARY
11112

P9-CCJ-640

700 SCIENCE EXPERIMENTS FOR EVERYONE

700 SCIENCE EXPERIMENTS FOR EVERYONE

REVISED AND ENLARGED EDITION

COMPILED BY UNESCO

Foreword by Gerald Wendt

Originally published as
UNESCO SOURCE BOOK
FOR SCIENCE TEACHING

DOUBLEDAY & COMPANY, INC., GARDEN CITY, NEW YORK

ISBN: 0-385-05275-8 TRADE
0-385-06354-7 PREBOUND
Library of Congress Catalog Card Number 64–10638

Printed in the United States of America
30

Contents

Introduction

Science is perhaps unique as a subject in the curriculum of schools all over the world. This uniqueness results from the variety of materials and experiments necessary for its effective teaching. Most other subjects can be learned if ordinary tools are available, such as pencil, paper, blackboard, textbooks and a few supplementary aids. These are also essential for the teaching of science but, if they are the only tools, science becomes a dull and uninteresting subject.

If it is to be learned effectively science must be experienced. It must be learned and not learned about. Science is so close to the life of every boy and girl that there is no need to confine its study to the reading of textbooks or listening to lectures. Wherever you may go in the world, science is an intimate part of the environment—living things, the earth, the sky, air and water, heat and light and forces such as gravity. No teacher need ever be without first-hand materials for the study of science.

Good science teaching must be based on observation and experiment. There can be no substitute for these. But performing experiments and learning to make close observations require special facilities, and these are lacking in many parts of the world, especially at the elementary and early secondary levels. As a result, science teaching suffers a severe handicap in these regions. It is often believed—though erroneously—that to introduce laboratory teaching, even at the elementary level, requires elaborate equipment made by commercial manufacturers. Such materials are prohibitively expensive for most elementary and early secondary teaching, and in many parts of the world are quite unobtainable because they are not manufactured locally and cannot be imported because of the cost.

At the close of the second world war, many schools in many countries had been destroyed. As these schools began to revive, there was a great need for science equipment; for these countries had a tradition of basing science teaching on observation and experiment. To meet this need, Unesco sponsored the production of a small volume entitled *Suggestions for Science Teachers in Devastated Countries*. This book was written by Mr. J. P. Stephenson (science master at the City of London School; member of the Royal Society Committee for Co-operation with Unesco, United Kingdom). While it proved very useful for the devastated areas, it has had a phenomenal success in regions where previously there had been little or no equipment. Emphasizing the making and use of equipment from simple materials, the book has filled a great need in those countries where teachers are just becoming aware of the necessity for first-hand science experiments even at the lowest levels of instruction. It has gone through several editions and has been translated into French, Spanish, Chinese, Thai and Arabic.

Over the past few years, Unesco has sent many science teaching experts on field missions into areas where the need for the production and use of simple equipment is acute. These experts have had opportunities to make and try out the materials and experiments suggested in the Stephenson book. They have also had opportunites to go further in discovering other materials and devising new experiments, more suitable for tropical regions for which the Stephenson book was not originally intended. The work of these field experts, together with the Stephenson book, has produced an array of simple equipment and science experiments which needed to be assembled and described in one volume. This need has provided the impetus for the production of the present *700 Science Experiments for Everyone*.

Due acknowledgment of the source of the material brought together in this book will be found on pages 9 and 10.

Believing that science and the scientific method of problem solving should play a significant role in any modern educational scheme, Unesco offers this book in the hope that it will assist science teachers everywhere in their important work. The point of view taken is that science is most effectively taught and learned when both teacher and pupils practise the skills of problem-solving by engaging in group and individual study. The devising of experiments and the improvising of simple equipment for carrying them out should form no small part of such study. Thus, the present includes instructions for the making of many pieces of simple apparatus from materials usually found in almost any region. It also proposes a wide array of science experiments from which a teacher may select those most suitable for providing the observations upon which effective learning may be based.

These improvisations should not in any manner be regarded as makeshifts. The experiments and the exercise of constructing the apparatus are in the best traditions of science teaching. Many of the great masters of science have used such improvised apparatus and many of the great discoveries have been made with improvised equipment.

No claim for completeness is made for this book. The array of available materials has made it difficult to decide exactly what should be included. But it is hoped that these pages will serve as a guide, and as a stimulus to teachers and pupils to define their own science problems and then to improvise (from things that may be locally available) the necessary equipment for experimenting.

Acknowledgments

Science is universal and knows no boundaries. This great store of human knowledge has been gleaned from a reluctant nature by workers of many lands. It is altogether fitting and proper that this *700 Science Experiments for Everyone* should be a compilation of the work of experienced science teachers from many countries. It is through the sharing of experience that science teaching can be improved and enabled to move forward.

To give credit to all who have contributed to the making of this volume would be quite impossible. Much of the material included has its origin buried deeply in the past and has come to be a part of a common heritage of science teachers everywhere. Among those whose direct contributions have made this volume possible mention should first be made of Mr. J. P. Stephenson of the City of London School. To him and his collaborators we are indebted for the use of a large part of the material from the earlier Unesco publication *Suggestions for Science Teachers in Devastated Countries*. The impact of this little volume on science teaching has been world-wide and it is already considered a classic in the literature of science education.

Credit and appreciation are also due to: Dr. Glenn Blough of the University of Maryland and Dr. Paul Blackwood of the United States Office of Education, Washington, D.C., for permission to use parts of two bulletins on teaching elementary science, of which they were co-authors; the National Science Teachers' Association of the United States, Mr. Robert Carleton, secretary, and through them, to Mr. Guy Bruce of the Newark Teachers' College, for generous permission to use material from the series entitled *Science Teaching Today;* and the New York State Department of Education which granted permission to use material from the two volumes of their publication, *The General Science Handbook,* Volumes I and II.

Since the first appearance of the *700 Science Experiments for Everyone* in December 1956, many valuable comments and suggestions have been received, and reviews have appeared in journals in all parts of the world. This has led to minor revisions being made in each of the reprints. The first edition in English was reprinted eleven times, and the French edition is in its fourth impression. Translations have been published in seven other languages, while fourteen additional translations are in preparation.

The following were among the contributors of useful suggestions: Dr. F. J. Olsen of the Department of Education, University of Queensland, Australia, and a former President of the Australian Science Teachers' Association; Dr. W. Llowarch of the University of London Institute of Education and Dr. Vida Risberg, a former Unesco specialist in science teaching to the Philippines.

Note on the second edition

In this revised edition, note has been taken of further suggestions received from all parts of the world. Based on these, fifty new experiments have been added to the text, including new sections on 'Electricity and Chemistry', 'Optical Projection', and an extension to the section on 'Gravity'.

A chapter on recent tendencies in science teaching with special emphasis on physics has been added and the appendixes have been modified. The list of publishers has been replaced by a list of textbooks useful for a science teachers' library. The list of periodicals has also been brought up to date.

Grateful thanks are due to the following for their generous help. Suggestions for the book list were contributed by: M. A. Dolmazen (France); Dr. R. Eddy, Dr. I. Freeman, Dr. E. S. Obourn, and The National Science Teachers Association (USA); Mr. Silin (USSR). Many other useful suggestions and experiments were given by Mr. Bernacer (Spain), Mr. N. Dikwel (Holland), Mr. J. M. Cros (Honduras), Mr. Figved (Bandung), Mrs. Haggis (Ghana), Mr. Risan (Norway), and the World Federation for the Protection of Animals. The Educational Services Inc. (Washington, D.C.) and the Charles Heath Company also gave their kind permission to include in the text some of the ingenious experiments from the Physical Sciences Study Committee course.

J.P.S.

To begin with

A Few Words to Boys and Girls about This Book

It is probably only a legend that the idea of gravitation hit Sir Isaac Newton's mind when a falling apple hit his head. But the truth is that the simplest experiment, or even such an accident, can be an eye-opener when you are interested in the world around you. When the great Greek scientist, Archimedes, was puzzling about why some objects float on water and others sink, it is quite possible that the underwater lightness of his own body in the bathtub gave him the first hint of the answer. Certainly Charles Darwin's thinking out of the theory of evolution was the result of very careful observation of the plants and animals that he collected, including shells and fossils. These pioneers were all amateurs who had no elaborate apparatus to work with, and no textbooks either. That is the way science began.

You can begin your understanding of science that way too, and have a wonderful time exploring. The world we live in is as interesting as ever. In fact, with modern inventions now added, it is much more so. You do not need to wait for someone to explain the science behind the automobile engine, television, rocket flights in space, the development of new fruits and vegetables, or the causes of disease. You can investigate these ideas yourself.

Of course, you must begin at the beginning if you want to understand. But all the complex products of modern science are only combinations and developments of a few basic principles that govern the world. You can convince yourself and your family and friends that they are true by many easy experiments that you can do at home with common materials from the kitchen, the garage, or a nearby store. This book is intended to help you to do it.

You will be teaching yourself science, getting ready to join a science club or to take part in a school or county science fair. Then you will find the science textbooks easy to understand when you get to them. Best of all, you will be in the habit of having ideas and of trying them out, which is the common trait of all inventors and research men from Edison to Einstein. That trait is the source of almost all human progress, from the invention of the wheel and the sailboat to placing a man-made moon in an orbit around the earth.

This book is not a chemistry kit or a physics kit and does not need one. It is an idea kit. It describes hundreds of experiments that you can do for yourself, lists the simple things and materials that you need for them, and suggests what to do. The directions are brief and simple.

During each experiment you will draw your own conclusions about what it means or proves—and it's a good idea to write down your measurements and your conclusions in a special notebook. If your mind is as healthy and active as your muscles are, you will probably have many questions after each experiment—and you should write them down too. Some of them will be answered by the experiments that follow. For others you will want to look up the answers in an elementary science textbook in your school or library.

Often when you think about an experiment you may discover that you have different things around the house that will serve the same purpose.

Or you may think of other ways to prove the same thing. All the better. Certainly you will think of other experiments to do that are not in the book. Very good, because the experiments in this book are designed to start you thinking. One thing they will do: they will convince you that experimenting in science is fun and that thinking about science is exciting.

In the front pages of the book you will find a few suggestions for teachers, because this book was originally written for teachers in some countries where the schools do not have modern laboratories or perhaps have no laboratory at all. But these sections are not for you—not at the start at least; you can come back to them later. You will also find a list of tools, materials, and supplies that will be needed if you do all the experiments. But neither is this the place to start; you can find or get the materials as you need them.

The experiments begin with Chapter III on page 41, and the first chapters deal with botany, zoology, mineralogy, and astronomy. Start with them, if you like, or start with the experiments on air in Chapter VII on page 76. This is the first of ten chapters on common materials—like air, water, and solids—and on energy—including heat, light, and electricity—which introduce the science of physics. When you have done these experiments you will understand many things in nature and about modern machines that have seemed mysterious and you will be able to explain them to your friends.

One more thing about this book: Science is international, the same all over the world. It is studied in every country and in every language. This book was prepared by an agency of the United Nations (the United Nations Educational, Scientific, and Cultural Organization, usually called UNESCO from its initials) for use in all of them. As the *UNESCO Source Book for Science Teaching* it has been translated not only into the languages of Europe, such as French and Spanish, but also into many Asian languages, such as Arabic, Tamil, Hebrew, and even Chinese. So the experiments you do are being done at the same time by the students in South America, Europe, Asia, and Africa. Their languages and customs are different, but their experiments and their science are the very same as yours.

This English-language edition was prepared not only for the United States, but for all the countries that speak English, including England and Canada as well as Australia, New Zealand, India, South Africa, and many smaller ones. So it must be mentioned here that there are a few slight differences in spelling and in the use of some words between the United States and the other English-speaking countries. The United Nations have formally adopted the British, rather than the American forms. So you will find, for instance, that "color" is spelled "colour" in this book, and "aluminum" is "aluminium." These are not errors; they are just British English. What we call a "can" is called a "tin" in England, and a "flashlight" is a "torch." But these differences are very rare and they will not confuse you.

Now the book is yours, get going and have fun learning science.

GERALD WENDT
Former Head, Division of Science Education, UNESCO

The purposes of this book

There are many places in the world where both facilities and equipment for science teaching are at present inadequate. Such places are to be found in areas that are more advanced in the applications of science, as well as in other regions. This volume has been produced to help the trend of upgrading science instruction in schools and training colleges everywhere by basing it more and more on observation and experiment.

The basic purposes may be summarized as follows:

1 To provide a basis for better instruction in methods of teaching science in teacher-training institutions.
2 To provide a useful source of learning experiences and materials for science teachers in the elementary and secondary schools.
3 To provide a manual which may be used as a partial basis of instruction in science teaching methods for workshops and courses for the in-service training of teachers.
4 To provide a basis for the assembling of a loan collection of teaching kits containing simple equipment for science.

To provide some suggestive materials for science clubs and for other amateur science activities.

To provide a model or pattern so planned and developed that it can easily be adapted to science teaching conditions in many countries and translated into the national language.

SUGGESTED USES FOR THIS BOOK

In teacher-training institutions

Young teachers in training do not learn the methods of effective science teaching merely by listening to lecturers in colleges; they must have some contact in their training period with the many problems to be met later in the classroom. The teaching of science must have special consideration above and beyond what is usually given in a general methods course—this because science is unique as a subject in the school curriculum as using specialized materials, equipment and methods of approach. If the standards of science instruction are to be raised, such a special course in the techniques of teaching it must be in the curriculum of every teacher-training college.

A large part of a course in the methods of teaching science should be devoted to the practical or laboratory phase in which young teachers are given instruction in the devising, designing and construction of simple laboratory equipment from materials available in the community where they will teach. Only through such training will they be stimulated to base their teaching on observation and experiment.

In this practical course, the young teacher should find the opportunity to construct many pieces of equipment to carry out to his first teaching assignment. He might even be encouraged to begin the assembly of a nucleus of teaching kits.

A source book for science teachers

Many teachers who have not had an opportunity to study science appear to be afraid to teach it. In many cases this fear of the subject arises because they do not know how to assemble apparatus or to marshal the specialized learning experiences required. This book can be used by such teachers as a source of instruction for making the simple equipment needed and as a source of a variety of learning experiences for teaching almost any topic in the curriculum. In this way the teaching can be improved and enriched.

This book should also help to create and maintain a higher level of interest in science on the part of the pupil. Every child is by nature an experimenter. He is curious about why things happen and likes to try out his ideas. Even outside the school, children are constantly experimenting. Many young people will like helping to construct apparatus and to test the ideas proposed in their classroom experiences.

Pupil committees may be used in the building of many of the pieces of apparatus suggested as well as in assembling them into useful kits to be used in later experiments. If there is a workshop in the school, the teacher may co-operate by letting pupils make science equipment as special projects.

As a basis for workshop study conferences in science teaching

The workshop study conference is now a well-established and widely used device for the training of teachers in service. Such conferences have been held for science teachers in many parts of the world. It is only through them that teachers now teaching can be influenced to improve their practices and change their present conditions.

This book can serve as a useful basis both for instruction in methods of teaching science and for a laboratory practice where teachers are given instruction in the simple techniques of making improvised apparatus. They might then be encouraged to begin the training of other teachers in the area.

To provide the basis for assembling a loan library of simple science teaching kits

While the ideal situation would be for every school to assemble the simple equipment needed for teaching the various science units, this may not always be feasible because of lack of funds or time. Another scheme is to assemble kits of simple equipment for doing experiments. Each kit is assembled in a durable box with a hinged cover that latches securely. The kits are then stored in a central school and loaned out to teachers in the schools of the neighbourhood in much the same way as library books are loaned. Each kit also contains a list of the materials in the box as well as directions for doing the experiments.

The plan operates in this way. Assume that kits have been assembled and stored in a centrally located school. Perhaps the teachers in that school would take responsibility for keeping the kits in good order and making the necessary records. A card should be made out for each kit. Now let us suppose that a teacher in school X is planning to teach a unit on magnetism during the next week. She goes to the school where the kits are kept and fills out a card stating when she will need the kit on magnetism and when she will return it. The teacher in charge takes her card and then notes on the kit card, her name, the school and the dates. The kit is then issued to the teacher, and she takes it to her classroom for use. At the end of the unit the materials are carefully checked against the list and any breakage noted. The kit is then returned to the depository.

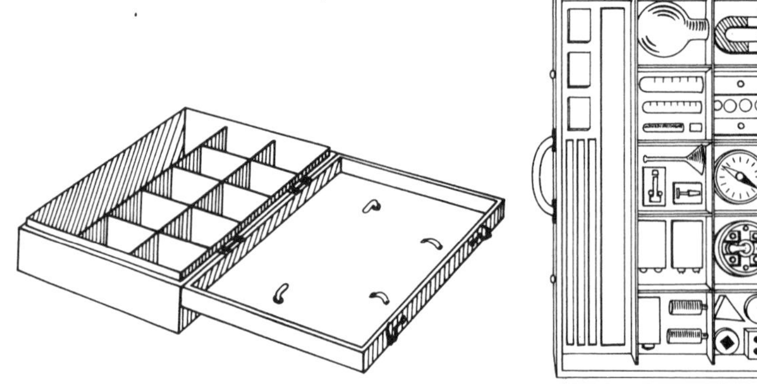

A project for assembling a library of simple equipment kits might be undertaken in several ways. One way would be to have the boxes made according to the pattern suggested above, by boys in a vocational school. The kits might be assembled at a central place or the project could be made co-operative by having each teacher, with her class, assume responsibility for assembling and making the necessary materials for one teaching kit.

Another plan might be worked out in which students in training at a teacher-training college could be assigned projects of assembling the kits for schools in a given locality.

As a source book for science club activities

Science club sponsors often find it a problem to provide worth-while projects and activities for club members. The many projects and experiments suggested in this book are appropriate for use by young people of all ages as science club projects.

To provide a model pattern of science materials and activities for many countries

The format of this book has been so planned, and the materials so selected as to make it adaptable to almost any local situation. The text materials and the simple line drawings can easily be reproduced.

TOOLS NEEDED FOR MAKING SIMPLE EQUIPMENT

Every school where elementary or general science is taught should be provided with some sort of work bench where simple equipment can be made. An old table can be used for this purpose. If no space is available for a work bench, a few rough boards cut to the right length may be placed on a school desk to prevent injury to the desk top. Such boards may be padded on the under side with cloth. A work bench will provide a place to hammer and saw. A good supply of old newspapers is always useful to put on the floor, especially if any painting is to be done.

Following is a basic list of tools that will be needed for the construction of simple equipment:

Hammers
Screwdrivers
Pliers
Small wood saw
Hack or metal saw
Small block plane
Wood chisel
Brace and bits
Gimlet

Metal shears
Round file
Triangle file
Flat file
Jack-knife
Metre stick
Glass cutter
Coping saw
Can opener (tin opener)

Cloth shears
Small table vice
Piece of heavy bench iron
Sandpaper
Paring knife
Steel wool
Leather punch
Soldering iron and solder
Wrenches

MATERIALS AND SUPPLIES

The materials needed for making simple equipment will vary from place to place and class to class. It is possible however to suggest a few basic materials and where they can be obtained.

From the home

Old pans of various sizes
Basins
Tablespoons and teaspoons
Cups and saucers

Dinner plates
Soup plates
Bottles, various shapes and sizes

Tin cans, various sizes with and without covers
Glass jars, various shapes and sizes

Garden tools
Hand tools
Ink bottles
Glass tumblers
Combs
Saltshakers
Soap
Old electric bulbs
Ink
Wire coat hangers
Fruit jars
Flower pots
Clothes pegs
Leather, soft, from old shoes
Milk bottles
Spools, wood
Old clocks
Razor blades
Old electrical appliances
Musical instruments
Cloth, various kinds
Fur
Newspapers
Paper bags
Used toothbrushes
Cork dinner-table mats
Plastic drinking cups
Aluminium and plastic tubes from old bird pens
Aluminium milk bottle caps

From the hardware shop

Nails—assorted sizes
Spikes—assorted sizes
Screws—assorted sizes
Bolts and nuts—assorted sizes
Screw eyes
Springs
Tape measure
Fishing-line
Staples—assorted sizes
Carpet tacks
Drawing pins
String and twine
Rope—small diameter
Mirrors
Glass jars—assorted sizes
Window glass
Washers
Hooks—assorted sizes
Torch batteries and bulbs
Sheet metal
Metal rods
Thermometers
Egg beater
Candles
Small wash-tub
Curtain rods
Magnetic compass
Kerosene lamps
Lamp chimneys
Lantern globes
Wire screening
Corks
Metal and plastic funnels
Rubber tubing
Metal tubing
Sewing, darning and knitting needles
Level
Sandpaper
Pulleys
Turnbuckles
Steel wool
Glue and household cement
Brass, copper and iron wire
Tools
Paint
Varnish
Flash lights
Hacksaw blades
Scissors
Shears
Metal and wooden balls
Dish pan
Oil cans
Oil
Tin and aluminium cups
Pyrex dishes and bottles
Small forceps
Tack puller
Sieve
Wicking for alcohol lamps
Asbestos mats
Battery jars
Pins
Block and tackle
Jack screw
Thermos bottles

From the automobile repair shop

Old rubber tyres
Old rubber inner tubes
Valves from inner tubes
Used storage batteries
Battery acid
Safety glass from old cars
Spark plug
Ammeter
Carburettor
Fuses
Curved reflectors from headlights
Fuel pump
Electric motor
Electric generator
Gears
Ball bearings
Springs from seats
Magnet from speedometer
Headlight lenses
Headlight bulbs
Tools
Metal tubing
Wire from old coils
Ignition coil
Engine
Rear view mirror
Wing mirror
Used oil

From the radio repair shop

Radio sets
Wire from old coils
Transformers
Old radio tubes
Electrical instruments
Coils
Transformer cores
Condensers
Rheostats
Solder
Metal plates
Plastic from old cabinets

From the food market

Ammonia
Baking powder
Baking soda
Bleaching powder
Blueing
Corn syrup
Epsom salts
Matches
Mineral oil
Paraffin
Beeswax
Sealing wax
Starch
String
Sugar
Paper bags
Table salt
Turpentine
Vinegar
Boards from boxes
Cardboard boxes
Wood boxes
Tin containers
Gelatine
Cooking oil
Lard
Seeds

From the lumber market

Asbestos sheets
Boards
Hardware
Insulating materials
Plywood
Press board
Rope
Paint
Varnish
Wire screening
Sawdust
Lime
Cement
Brick
Broken sewer pipes
Round dowel rod
Wood blocks and prisms

From the machine shop

Ball bearings
Gears
Sheet iron
Sheet brass
Sheet copper
Brass and iron rods
Iron filings
Scrap metal pieces

From the drugstore

Agar
Copper sulphate
Mineral oil
Saccharine
Hydrochloric acid
Nitric acid
Sodium hydroxide
Silver nitrate
First-aid kit
Cellophane
Beef extract
Drug capsule containers
Sheet rubber
Powdered sulphur
Boric acid
Manganese dioxide
Adhesive tape
Wood tongue depressors
Thermometers
Dyes
Ink
Iodine
Marble chips
Medicine droppers
Shaving mirrors
Glass tubes
Rubber stoppers
Medicine bottles and vials
Peptone
Sponges
Test tubes
Litmus paper
Potassium chlorate
Plaster of Paris

From the optical shop

Old cameras
Old eye-glass lenses
Lenses
Reading glass lenses

From the plumber and tinsmith

Scrap iron and lead pipe
Old taps
Sheet metal
Rubber suction cup

From the electrical shop

Dry batteries
Electric bulbs
Insulated wire
Switches
Lamp sockets
Insulation tape
Electric meters
Old electrical appliances
Miniature light sockets
Electric bell
Electric buzzer
Push buttons
Heating elements
Magnetic compass

From the toy market

Gyroscopes
Marbles
Small wagons
Ping pong balls
Mechanical toys
Coloured chalk
Steam engine
Steam turbine
Electrical toys
Rubber balloons
Toy musical instruments
Rubber balls
Plastic toys
Football pump adaptors

From the bicycle repair shop

Old bicycle wheels
Spokes from bicycle wheels
Inner tubes
Valves from tyres
A sprocket wheel
Bicycle pump
Rubber grips from handlebars
Bicycle lamp

From the textile market

Cloth—silk, cotton, woollen, and linen
Synthetic fabrics
Thread—cotton, silk, and linen

From the school

Cardboard
Blotters
Ink
Coloured chalk
Erasers
Burned-out electric bulbs
Paper
Oil
Chalk
Fuses
Paper towels
Pencils
Chalk boxes
Gummed labels
Rulers
Globes
Maps
Rubber bands

Miscellaneous materials

Mailing tubes
Cardboard
Blotting paper
Old watch and clock springs
Cigar boxes
Cigarette tins
Tin and aluminium foil
Old roller skates
Coal and charcoal
Telephone transmitters and receivers
Telephone magnetos
Magnetic iron ore (lodestone)
Tennis balls

Miscellaneous collections from the locality

Seeds and fruits
Leaves
Plants
Birds' nests
Rocks and minerals
Soils
Fossils
Insects

CHAPTER I

Some suggestions about the teaching of general science[1]

A. GENERAL SCIENCE

What is it?

In the primary school, children are seeking simple answers to their questions, which usually begin with: 'What is it?' First of all, science is *not* a lot of things it was once thought to be; not a series of object lessons about a piece of granite, an old wasp's nest, an acorn, or a tulip. It is not hit and miss like that, not learning the names of the parts of a grasshopper or a flower; not learning to identify 20 trees, 20 insects, 20 flowers or 20 anything else.

What is science, then? It is a study of the problems that are found wherever children live. More formally stated, it is a study of the natural environment—not merely pieces of chemistry and physics and biology and astronomy and geology. Its content is connected with those subjects but it is a study of problems that pop into curious children's minds as they live and grow from one day to the next, such as: What makes the wind blow? What's in a cloud? What's a stone made of? What does a bell do when it rings? How can a seed grow into a tree? What makes a rainbow? Anyone who has ever worked with primary school girls and boys knows that most of them are full of questions like this and like to know the answers to them. Well, finding the answers to such questions—that is science.

And it need not be too technical. The full explanation is not what the 10-year-old needs. He could not understand that. It is a foundation in simple terms of the how, the when, the where, and the what of the things that happen around him every day. That is his science. He doesn't need the technical terms, the formulas and the detailed explanations. Those will come later, but when he is 10 he chiefly needs to get satisfaction out of his tendency to be curious. He needs to have his curiosity broadened, his interests nurtured and his enthusiasms encouraged. That is the kind of science which fits him and with which he is able to deal.

Where is it?

Science in the primary school—where is it? It is everywhere that schoolchildren are: in the air they breathe, in the water they drink, in the food they eat. 'What's oxygen?', 'How do minerals get into water?', 'What's a vitamin?'

Science is in the things they see on their way to school: 'How does electricity make a street car move?', 'Why does my dog stick out his tongue when he pants in hot weather?', 'What makes the sky blue?'

Science is in their homes: 'What makes our doorbell work?', 'What makes lemons taste sour?', 'How does our furnace heat our house?'

Science is in the schoolhouse: 'How can the fire extinguisher put out a fire?', 'What made the rust in the drinking fountain?', 'Why did we all have to be vaccinated?'

Science, then, is all around the girls and boys we teach. They cannot help but see it. They will see more of it with a little help. They will get more interested in it with a little encouragement. They'll learn more about it with a teacher who sees the possibility of its use, and uses his teaching skill to help children learn about their environment.

What can it do?

It is generally true that a well-informed person is an interesting one, and some information regarding the environment is one of the pieces of equipment that go to make up an informed individual. That does not mean that you expect to pump your pupils full of facts that they can merely use to fill up blank spaces in

1. The materials for this chapter have been adapted with full permission of the authors and publishers from two booklets: *Teaching Elementary Science, Bulletin 1948, No. 4*, and *Science Teaching in Rural and Small Town Schools, Bulletin 1949, No. 5* of the Federal Security Agency, Office of Education, Washington, D.C. The authors were Dr. Glenn O. Blough and Dr. Paul Blackwood.

conversation. It means that you want to help them to come to learn generalizations or meanings which they can use in interpreting problems in their environment.

To illustrate: The members of the lily family have three sepals, three petals usually coloured alike, six stamens, one pistil, etc. A boy aged 10 can certainly live a full and well-rounded life without committing this to memory. But suppose he learns through an examination of many plants and many animals that 'Plants and animals are put into groups according to certain characteristics, and that knowing these characteristics helps you know the large group to which the living thing belongs'. This generalization can then be helpful in identifying animals and plants he sees, and make it possible for him to study their habits, to determine their helpfulness or harmfulness, and so on. He has become aware of this generalization through careful study and through observation, and by pressing together many small ideas into one large one. One aim in science, then, is to teach generalizations that can be used by pupils in interpreting the problems they come across in their daily living. The more nearly we can come to studying the problems that really make a difference in the lives of girls and boys the closer we are to having a science programme.

You don't want your girls and boys to grow up to be sloppy thinkers. The method by which science generalizations were originally discovered is the kind of thinking we hope they can be trained to achieve. We may call it a scientific way of getting the right answer. There is nothing brand-new about this idea. Probably you have been doing it for years in arithmetic and other subjects: defining the problem, suggesting several hypotheses, gathering evidence, drawing conclusions, checking conclusions. That does not mean that every time a problem comes up you get out these steps and make pupils climb them.

Actually, this scientific way of solving problems need not include these formal steps. For example: children want to know what makes a compass needle point north and south. You make sure that they state the problem as carefully as it needs to be stated, so that it asks exactly what children want to know. Then pupils say what they think makes the needle behave that way. Some explanations seem to make sense; some don't.

'How can we find out whose idea is right?' you ask. The pupils answer: 'Read our science books.' 'Ask Mr. Jackson, the physics teacher.' 'Do an experiment.' Then the pupils carry out their suggestions, discover an explanation, check it as carefully as they can by known authority, and they have solved the problem and can now make use of their knowledge. Simple, of course, and it is only the beginning of their introduction to a way of solving problems that, if properly used, is likely to produce good results. If they have intelligent guidance, pupils can make great strides in ability to solve problems in this manner. Contact with this way of problem solving cannot come too early in a child's school experience. It takes a long time to become an accurate solver of problems.

You want girls and boys to develop certain scientific ways of thinking as they work. For example: Things don't just happen; they happen because of natural causes, so don't be superstitious. Be open-minded toward the opinions of others. Regard your conclusions as tentative until you are sure. Look for reliable sources for evidence. Be willing to change your mind if you discover that you were wrong. Don't jump to conclusions. Be curious about things and don't be satisfied with a vague explanation. These are a few of the safeguards of scientific thinking that a carefully directed study of science can help pupils to attain. Again, the earlier the contact with this kind of thinking, the better.

Then, too, you want to broaden the interests of the girls and boys. They seem to be naturally curious about many of the things around them, but there's half a world of things they know nothing about, so they can't be curious about the things in it. A study of the stars may open up a new field of interest in the sixth form and for a few it may turn out to be a lasting interest. A study of how plants grow may stir up an interest in plant culture that would otherwise have remained buried. Studies of children's interests seem to show that children are interested in all aspects of their environment, not just in animal and plant life as was once supposed. Some pupils, however, appear to have more or less narrow interests and need help in seeing other possibilities. Many life-long interests were born early in a child's school experience; scientists often say that their interest in science began when they were still very young. With better science teaching in the primary school more such results might be obtained.

You also want to have your pupils grow in appreciation of the things around them. How do young children come to appreciate things? Little sermons about the beauties of nature won't help much. Vague talk about the beautiful butterflies, bees, and flowers won't be of much help either. While we are learning new ways of helping pupils to grow in their appreciation, let's try to teach them to see, to look closely, to examine carefully, and to discover by themselves what wonders there are in the world about them. In the common green leaf a manufacturing process goes on that man himself has not duplicated. He has learned that the raw materials used in the process are water and carbon dioxide, that the green colouring matter in the leaf is indispensable to the process, and that it cannot happen without the help of light. He can analyse the resulting process to the last molecule, but he himself cannot duplicate the process nor is he able to understand it completely. Furthermore, without this process life itself could not exist. As a child learns these truths, as he is helped to realize their significance, his appreciation grows, especially if working with an enthusiastic, intelligent, appreciative teacher.

These, then, are a few of the things that the study of science can do for the children in our schools if teachers of science are fully aware that these are the purposes, and are intent on seeing that science is taught in such a way that they are accomplished. Aims that remain planted in teachers' manuals without being used do not help children. But aims that are in the teacher's mind and in the minds of children as well, will help them. Such aims colour the selection of the subject, the method of teaching it, the activities selected, the method of evaluation, and everything else that is done in the classroom. Here, then, is a point for all science teachers to remember —decide what it is you hope to accomplish by teaching science, keep it in mind, keep checking to see that you are staying on the track, and keep evaluating to find out how closely you are coming to your goal. And, above all, let these purposes be as nearly as possible those of the pupils, and let pupils help with the plans for accomplishing these objectives.

Elementary science and nature study

There has been and still is controversy over whether a programme in science in the primary school should be called elementary science or whether the term nature study should still be used. Some schools have so-called nature study programmes that are excellent. They are teaching science in the broadest sense and have the most modern objectives in mind although continuing to use nature study as the name for their programme. In some other schools, the programme is called elementary science, but the philosophy under which it operates is antiquated and holds to the original, narrower, view of nature study. From this it appears that the name is not so important as is the content and the procedure actually used in the programme. The science programmes that take the best from the nature study idea and build upon it the best that we have learned in recent years are those that are most useful today. While the difference does not lie entirely in the name, programmes in elementary science are likely to be broader in scope and conform more nearly to modern needs than those called nature study.

To illustrate this point: the nature study idea stresses the study of an object such as a rock or tree rather than a broad problem concerning rock formation or forestry. It is likely to lay stress on identification of rocks and trees rather than use this as a means to an end. It is not likely to be concerned with the study of the problems of real concern in the lives of children or the whole field of science, but to deal rather with the study of plants and animals. Experience with children shows that they are interested in all phases of their environment. From this brief sketch of nature study ideas it appears that the original idea of nature study is being supplanted by a programme more suited to the needs of modern children. The world in which these boys and girls live today has changed greatly during recent years; so, too, must their programme of studies change.

From the nature study idea, however, we realize the importance of first-hand experience in observing life around us, not just reading and hearing about it. A nature trail that points out kinds of plants and animals, homes of animals, spots that show interrelationships among living things, relationships between living things and their environments, and special adaptations of these living things, is useful learning equipment. A nature trail, then, although it has its origin in the nature study idea has, if properly used, much to contribute to a more up-to-date science programme. Schools that are near a wood, near a park, or in the country are fortunate if they avail themselves of the opportunity to establish such a nature trail, or in some other organized way make use of this resource.

Camping experience is another source of first-hand information and appreciation which a modern elementary science programme might well include. The experience of building a camp fire, preparing sleeping quarters, getting pure drinking water, procuring and preparing food, and many other necessary activities are packed full of science. Again, how much science and what kind of science is learned depends on the point of view of the individual in charge.

In deciding whether or not your point of view is in line with pupils' needs, measure it in relation to the objectives discussed earlier in this section. These, along with the purposes of the total elementary programme, are the guides that point the way. Don't think that you have a modern science programme if you spend half the time covering walnuts with tinfoil and hanging them on a Christmas tree, pressing leaves, colouring robin pictures, or cutting paper snowflakes. Such activities do not achieve the objectives of even the most elementary science programme.

Science and the primary school programme

An elementary science programme that tries to exist without consideration of its relationship to the general primary school programme is bound to be ineffective. A science programme's right to exist as a separate subject must be challenged on the basis of its contributions in accomplishing the general objectives of primary education.

The general purposes of the primary school have been variously stated. Perhaps the most important is to help children to achieve the ideals, understanding, and skills essential for becoming good citizens. This involves giving them the basic skills of reading, writing and arithmetic, as fundamental tools for gaining information. In addition, it means giving them an opportunity to identify and understand social procedures and problems, to participate both in suggesting solutions and carrying out their suggestions, to develop their social sensitivity to the needs of individuals and groups. The elementary school should help children to recognize and practise a number of human relationship skills—co-operation, selection of leaders, group planning—provide conditions conducive to physical and mental health, and give the children information and skills for developing these traits. It should help them to develop wholesome interests for their leisure time. These are the general aims of a good primary school programme and no science programme can be effective without keeping them in mind.

The objectives for teaching elementary science must be adapted to these broader concepts of the primary school's purpose. How we teach science, what activities are most useful to children, how we help them plan and evaluate, all must be shaped in accordance with these objectives.

For example, how shall we teach science so that it will help children to be better citizens? If the teacher himself selects all the content, organizes it, decides how it is to be learned, and makes all other decisions, how are children to grow in ability to organize, to plan and work together? If we agree that being able to plan and work together is one of the attributes of a good citizen, we must make plenty of provision for children to plan and work together. There is a distinct difference between exercising leadership as a teacher and dictating from behind the desk. The teacher, as a leader, may take initial steps to create interest, open possible avenues of procedure, and then be a helper. Because of his experience he is able to exercise some guidance—but praise be to the teacher who has learned to be silent at the proper time! Children learn to be responsible citizens through being just that—silent—in science as in other school activities. The subject matter exists in large part for the purpose of developing this potentiality. So, in teaching science let us give opportunities for children to plan together, make decisions, make mistakes, decide how to rectify them, recognize their successes, set up new procedures and evaluate the results.

Do not tell children the answers to every question they may ask, or tell them always to read the answer. How do we gain information on science? By experimenting, by observing, by asking people who know, by reading, by looking at films, and in other ways. Again, how do pupils learn when to use these ways and when to depend on their results? They learn through practice in deciding, then through trying out their proposed plans and evaluating the effectiveness of their efforts. With practice, pupils grow in their ability to use the tools available for gaining knowledge—but this is true only if we help them. Every subject has here a definite contribution to make—if we give it a chance.

B. THE SCIENCE TEACHER

If we wait until all elementary teachers feel fully equipped to handle science we shall never get started. The most successful teachers of science in the primary school have said to themselves: 'I believe in the importance of including some science in my work. I don't believe my programme is complete without it. I don't know much science, but I know how children learn. I don't mind being asked questions that I can't answer because I know how to help children find answers.'

These teachers have many problems. They need to build background in science, to learn how to teach it, to find the necessary apparatus and other materials. But they have two essential pieces of equipment: they realize the importance of including science, and they know how children learn.

The following suggestions have been found useful by many such teachers:

1. Approach the teaching of science with confidence, not with the awe usually reserved for the first sight of a man from the planet Mars. It is not as unusual as you think. It is not so much different from teaching social studies, language, arts or arithmetic, in which most teachers feel at ease. It is not harder to teach; in fact, in some ways it is easier because it deals with concrete things and reaches the real interests of many children.

2. Don't expect to know the answers to all the questions children ask you. If you wait until you do, you'll never begin teaching science. Teachers tell children too much anyway. If you know children, and know how to help them learn, half your teaching battle is won. Don't be afraid to learn with children. Let them set up plans for finding the answers to their problems and then you act as a guide and learn with them. Of course you need to know some subject matter, but you don't need to be a science specialist. The next few items of advice will help you build up some science background.

3. After a unit or area of science study has been decided on, read some basic science textbooks on the learning level of the pupils you teach. Then get some good general science or biology textbooks (the kind used in secondary schools) and read them. Here you will find most of the science subject matter background essential for teaching young children.

4. Do some of the experiments suggested in these books so that you get the feel of the material. These elementary science experiments are not half as complex as you may think.

5. Do some of the 'things to do' that the books suggest—trips, observations, experiments, collections. To see is both to believe and to feel and it is much easier to get your pupils interested in and excited about the town's filtration plant if you have yourself seen how wonderful it is.

6. Talk with a secondary school science teacher near your school and enlist his help. Secondary science teachers can often give you teaching ideas, suggest experiments, and help provide materials and books. Science is their special field, and they are usually full of helpful ideas.

Remember that it is the unfamiliar that is likely to make you timid, so give yourself as much first-hand experience as you can with the science material. Following the preceding suggestions is almost sure to make you confident enough to tackle a new science topic.

7. Don't feel too handicapped because you lack materials. Children can bring from home almost everything you actually need. What they cannot produce, you can get at the market or hardware store (ironmongery), borrow from the secondary school science department, find in the schoolyard, get from the school janitor, or let the children themselves make. Expensive, complicated apparatus is worse than useless in the elementary science class. It is likely to be confusing and to draw attention to itself rather than to the problem at hand.

8. Let pupils experiment. Children like to learn in this way. Use some of the abler pupils in your class to gather materials and prepare the instruments.

9. Start your science by teaching the topic with which you feel most at home. This may be contrary to the belief of some persons that pupils should initiate all problems for study. That theory is open to question anyway. If some of your college science training, a personal hobby, or an interest of your own has given you background in some special field, using that knowledge or interest to determine your choice of topic may be your springboard for science teaching. Later it will be easier for you to follow children's leads. They can always enter into the planning even if the original idea comes from you as the teacher.

10. Make good use of the teachers' manuals that accompany your textbook in science. They are full of teaching ideas that have been tested and found good. They are often helpful even if you are not following the text which they have been prepared to accompany.

11. Keep track of your science material, your notes on teaching, your plans, etc. so that you can use them at a future time and so that other teachers may borrow them. A topic is easier the second time, especially if you have access to the material you used before.

12. Talk to other teachers about what things they have found successful, and be ready to share your experience with them. Such an exchange is often a great help.

C. HOW CHILDREN LEARN SCIENCE

Children learn science in a variety of ways, just as they learn anything else. They learn it more readily when they are interested in it, when they can see that it makes some difference to them, when it is graphic, involves some manipulation on their part, is not too hard but hard enough to make them think, and when it gives them the satisfaction of having found out something they wanted to know. This is not peculiar to science. It is true for arithmetic, languages, the arts, or any other subject. The activities selected by and for children should take these things into account. Keeping them in mind, let us then examine some of the ways in which children learn science.

Experimenting

Experimenting is one of the chief ways of learning science principles and generalizations. Experiments should be kept simple; the commonest material is often sufficient and almost always desirable; pupils are capable of originating their own experiments—often bringing the necessary material from home—and are usually enthusiastic about performing them.

Certain points should be borne in mind:

1. Experiments should be conducted so that they will cause pupils to think. An experiment in which the teacher tells the pupils everything obviously gives no food to growing minds.

2. Children should be conscious of the purpose of an experiment. It is often desirable to write the purpose on the board in a simple, direct form. This is easy when the experiment is done to solve a problem which the pupils themselves have raised. For example: the children arrive at school on a slippery winter morning. The janitor has scattered salt on the school steps to clear the ice. The children want to know what happens to the ice and why that happens. They decide to set up an experiment to discover the reason. They get the point of why they are experimenting and are therefore more likely to press the performance to an ultimately satisfying conclusion. Other experiments may arise from the textbook, but the plan of action should as far as possible be worked out by the pupils.

3. Careful planning is essential to successful experimenting. Appropriate materials must be assembled—by the children, if possible. A plan of procedure must be drawn up. The plan must then be accurately followed, to ensure that the results can be depended upon.

4. As far as possible, children themselves should perform the experiments. They may work as individuals or as groups, depending on the type of experiments and the amount of material available. Experiments involving use of fire or other possible dangers, or experiments of a complicated nature, if used at all, should be performed by the teacher.

5. Children themselves can often originate experiments to answer their questions. These are the most satisfactory from every point of view. Contrary to the belief of some teachers, experiments need not always be complicated, nor need they have been previously described in a science book—sometimes they are; sometimes they are not.

6. Experiments should be performed carefully, and according to the directions, either those from books or those originated by the class.

7. Pupils should critically watch what is really happening when they perform an experiment, so that their results will be more dependable. For example: suppose they are attempting to discover whether or not leaves of plants give off water. They set up the usual experiment of covering a plant with a glass jar and shutting off the soil from contact with the air in the jar. The next morning droplets of water are found on the inside surface of the jar. The children immediately decide that they have discovered the answer to the problem. But how can they be sure that the water did not come out of the air in the jar? They can't. But suppose they assemble another set of apparatus exactly like the first—a plant pot, a glass jar, soil, etc., but without a plant. The jars are placed side by side and observed. This time if water appears on the inside surface of the jar with the plant in it and does not appear on the other jar's surface, the water must have come from the plant leaves. Such a procedure of controlled experimentation is essential if experiments are to assume their full meaning as activities for children. In this connexion it is essential that the experiment be tried more than once before conclusions are drawn. (See also item 9.)

8. Simple apparatus is more appropriate than complicated material for use in experiments in the primary school. As has been previously pointed out, intricate pieces of apparatus borrowed from high school laboratories often detract from the real point of the experiment.

9. Pupils should exercise caution in drawing conclusions from an experiment.

They cannot prove anything from having performed an experiment once. They must regard their finding as tentative until more evidence—either from additional experiments or from authentic books—has been found. Results should be accurately and completely stated.

10. As many applications as possible to everyday-life situations and problems should be made from an experiment. This is a difficult step, but it is one of the most important reasons for studying science. When an experiment has been performed, only the first step in its usefulness has been taken. For example, after pupils have experimented with rusting iron they may want to see how things may be kept from rusting. An experiment is performed involving a wet, unpainted nail and a similar nail covered with a layer of paint. The experimenters note that the unpainted nail rusts and that the other one does not. Now in a real life situation how is this principle applied? In school? At home? On the way to school and elsewhere? The experiment was done to make the idea real. The applications must be made to see how important this idea is and how useful.

Helping children to learn through doing their own experiments is not a difficult job. Pupils should realize that they are experimenting, not to discover information for the first time, as is the case with scientists, but for the purpose of understanding scientific ideas.

Reading

Reading ranks high in the list of ways in which children learn science. Unfortunately, some courses in science deteriorate into reading periods to the exclusion of all other activities. However, reading is one of the ways to learn science and as such deserves thoughtful planning if it is to be an effective tool. Accurate material on the reading level of the various class members must be available, and there must be guidance to help pupils read it. The following considerations are important:

1. The science class is the best place for children to learn to differentiate between fact and fancy in their reading. That is, they should come to know that some books are written for pure enjoyment; others as sources of knowledge. They should learn to challenge the authenticity of what they read. They should learn to exercise care in drawing such conclusions about material; i.e. to check one fact in a reference with an authentic source does not necessarily indicate that the book is accurate. Finding an error on a printed page may be an enlightening experience. The pupil may learn the valuable lesson that just because something appears in print does not necessarily mean that it is accurate.
2. Reading should be done with a definite purpose in mind, i.e. to check a pupil's own conclusion, to find information, to find out how to perform an experiment, to answer a question or to solve a problem.
3. A variety of sources of reading material on a given topic is desirable. More information is obtained and different points of view are seen.
4. It is often necessary for science pupils to do individual reading as a type of simple 'research'. Under such circumstances careful note-taking is essential so that an accurate report may be given to the class.
5. The reading material should be appropriate. This is largely the responsibility of the teacher, but the help of the children is also desirable. Material which is too difficult, or too easy, or which is inappropriate because it does not answer the children's questions, is discouraging. Slow-learning pupils or pupils with reading difficulties need special attention in the selection of their reading materials.

Developing skill in reading and learning in science can go hand in hand. But reading is only one of the ways to learn science. To overemphasize it is to ignore some of the fundamental purposes of teaching science.

Before science can be learned, enjoyed, and made to function in the lives of girls and boys, it must leave the pages of a book and get into their daily experience in a graphic way. The textbook will serve as an excellent guide. Problems will be raised by the pupils and teacher together. Ways to solve the problem will be decided on by the group. Then, reading may be, and almost always is, an extremely useful method. The textbook will supply much of the needed information, although that does not mean: 'We shall open our book to page 18 and read to 24 and then talk about what we have read.'

Observing

Observing is another essential activity in all science teaching. Through the use of their senses children can come to experience many things. Feeling the texture of material or the heat from an electric wire attached to a dry cell, seeing cloud formations, seeing the changes in lengths of shadows, listening to birds, and many other similar activities are an important part of their science work. They make learning more vivid.

Children observe to determine the characteristics of things, to see the changes in growing things, to learn the habits of animals, and to see the results of experiments, but they must learn to do so with ever-growing accuracy and to report their observations carefully.

This ability to observe accurately and to report observations correctly is essential. Experimenting is a total loss without it; field trips and visual aids cannot be effective without it. Much may be learned from our daily surroundings if we can train ourselves to be more careful in our observations. Pupils who have experience with this method of learning early in their school experience have a running start on those who do not.

Taking field trips

Making excursions to solve problems and to give information and appreciation are important activities in elementary science. Trips to the park, the zoo, the telephone exchange, the sawmill, the airport, the water purification plant, the rice field and similar places within reach of the school are commonly made by teachers and pupils. These can result in a headache for the teacher, a mere holiday for the children and bad public relations for the school unless the trip is well planned and motivated.

Children should make excursions with definite purposes in mind—to answer questions that are best settled by first-hand observation of the kind trips furnish. They should be aware of the purpose of the trip and the person who is to act as guide should know in advance what the children want to see and learn; the teacher should make a preliminary trip to see the place for himself and talk with the guide. He should assist the guide in keeping the group together, making sure that there is plenty of opportunity to see and to ask questions.

Excursions should be an integral part of a subject being studied and not just something to do. Field trips can be of inestimable value to a science programme, or they can be a waste of time. It is probably safe to say that more time should be spent getting ready for an excursion, and gathering deductions from it, than on the actual excursion itself.

Using visual aids

Another way in which pupils learn science is to see it pictured either in motion or otherwise. Much has been said about the desirability of using visual aids in connexion with primary school science teaching. Without the use of some of the aids now available a science course is incomplete, but much depends on how the aids are used. Motion pictures and filmstrips are but one of the many useful helps. There are others equally important.

If motion pictures or filmstrips are used, here are a few essentials to be considered.

1. The selection of a film is as important as the selection of a book. Films designed for use at higher levels are generally useless for elementary pupils. Films should be selected which deal directly with the problem under consideration and which are prepared specifically for the levels at which they are being used.
2. Films should be previewed by the teacher and a committee of pupils to determine fitness for showing and to make proper preparation for use. Previewing a film helps to determine the purpose for which the film may be wisely used and when it is to be shown—at the beginning, middle or end of a unit of study, or at more than one of these places as the case may be.
3. The class should be prepared before seeing the film. Pupils should know what to look for in the film and know why they are seeing it.
4. The follow-up discussion of a film is essential. During such discussions, questions are asked, ideas clarified, and further explanations are made.
5. Efforts should be made to help pupils realize that the films are not shown as entertainment but for the purpose of learning.

Motion pictures and filmstrips are but one of the types of visual aids useful in primary school science. The use of pictures from magazines and similar sources is often overlooked. In many schools, teachers, pupils and parents have, in co-operation, assembled an excellent teaching collection of pictures. Pictures that show how animals grow, how they are adapted to their environment, where they live, and what they eat, are examples of such picture collections. Pictures that show how we use electricity, machines, lenses, various kinds of power, are other examples. The important thing to remember is that these collections should be made to illustrate certain important ideas and not be just a collection of pictures.

Models are often useful in making ideas clear, and they should be used chiefly for that purpose. There are many instances of model-making in elementary science classes which are almost entirely a waste of time. For example, at the primary school level, making a wax model of the parts of a flower is not very useful, since a detailed knowledge of flower structure is not essential at this level. On the other hand, quite difficult concepts about the solar system can be more easily understood by use of a model of the solar system. It will give an idea of the relative sizes, and of distances between its members, and help pupils to gain better conceptions of other ideas of size and space concepts with which children can begin to deal. The purpose of model making, like the construction of any other instructional aid, should be carefully considered. Building model weather instruments and making balancing toys are other construction activities that contribute to understanding by children.

Thus there are many types of activities through which pupils learn science. The selection of an activity depends on what is to be accomplished. Let it be activity for promoting understanding, interest, and appreciation and not just activity for its own sake. An activity should make a science principle or idea more graphic, more interesting, and give pupils a chance to participate with their minds as well as with their hands.

D. RESOURCES FOR TEACHING SCIENCE

We are continually being urged to use resources at hand to make our curriculum more vital and meaningful to girls and boys. Very often subject matter and methods of instruction make things near at hand seem foreign and far away, because we try to teach without relating them to the children's experiences. A list of all the possible resources in a rural area would be endless and no two regions would contain the same possibilities.

Resources of the type suggested here are useful in at least three ways: they inspire observing pupils to ask more questions; they serve as sources for finding the answers to the questions; and they serve to make the science concepts more real.

The resources

The following pages include some typical examples of local resources as well as suggestions for their use.

1. *A gravel pit or stone quarry* may be instructive for: learning how the surface of the earth has changed over a period of years; seeing an example of how man uses materials from the earth; learning how observations of geological materials help scientists learn about the age of the earth and changes in climate; seeing how machines are designed and used to serve man; finding fossils to use in a study of animals of the past.

Possible use: take a field trip to observe and gather materials; hear a talk by the owner telling about the place, how the materials are marketed, what safety precautions are used, etc.

2. *A wood near the school* may be instructive for: discovering changes that animals and plants make as the seasons change; studying habits of plants and animals; finding out where animals live; seeing how animal and plant life depend on each other; seeing how physical surroundings, such as moisture, temperature and amount of sunlight affect living things; finding examples of useful and harmful animals and plants; appreciating the wonders of nature; studying various phases of conservation.

Possible use: take a field trip to observe and collect materials; bring selected materials into the classroom.

3. *A burned-over area* (roadside, field, wood-lot) may be instructive for: discovering the effect of burning on plants and animals; studying the causes of the fires; arousing interest in ways of preventing such fires if they are harmful; learning ways of stopping such fires; observing how life starts again in such areas; noting over a period of time how long it takes to rehabilitate such an area; seeing the effects burning has on erosion of such an area.

Possible use: visit the area to examine results of fire; collect and examine materials damaged by fire.

4. *A nearby field* may be instructive for: finding evidences of erosion to see how it starts and how it may be prevented; noting various adaptations which plants make to their environment, such as leaf arrangements, root length and arrangement, and leaf texture; observing various kinds of insects to see how they are adapted to the environment, how they are useful or harmful, and how the harmful ones are being destroyed; observing (if the field is being cultivated) how plants are cared for to provide moisture; noting different amounts of moisture in high

and low parts of the field; seeing how the vegetation differs where there is more moisture.

Possible use: visit field to observe plants; dig some up and bring them back for further study; collect insects for closer observation and study; ask qualified adult to discuss problems of weed and insect control with class.

5. *A new building being constructed* may be instructive for: Seeing how electrical wiring is installed; seeing how building is insulated; seeing what different materials are being used; examining samples of soil dug from the basement and comparing it with garden soil; learning how sewage is disposed of.

Possible use: collect examples of building materials for study—electrical wires showing different kinds of insulation, rock wool and other kinds of insulating materials, samples of soil, etc.; talk with workmen who are wiring the house, installing plumbing, or doing similar types of work; observe the procedure for locating and drilling well if there is to be one; examine plumbing, cesspool and location and installation if indoor plumbing is to be used; if outdoor toilet is used, find out where it is located in relation to the water supply and why this location was selected.

6. *A saw mill* may be instructive for: Learning how trees are selected for cutting; finding out how young timber is protected; learning which kinds of trees are considered most valuable and why; observing the use of machines; learning how lumber is made and cured; observing changes in animal and plant life when an area has been cut over.

Possible use: visit the saw mill to observe the procedures; bring back samples of wood to see growth rings; walk through woods to observe how trees are being cut; examine various machines being used to observe how they help workmen.

7. *A farm* may be instructive for: Observing various ways of preserving and storing food; caring for animals; growing garden vegetables and flowers; observing the use of machines in house, field, barn, garden, orchard; observing how buildings and grounds are made free from fires and how accidents are prevented.

Possible use: visit farm to observe science applications; let pupils report examples of scientific facts and applications they have observed at home.

8. *A vegetable and flower garden* may be instructive for: Studying how plants get enough light, moisture and other essentials for growth; learning how ground is prepared for planting, how plants are transplanted, and how seeds are dispersed; studying how flowers are self- and cross-pollinated and how seeds sprout and grow; learning what kinds of soil are suitable for the growth of different kinds of plants and how the soil is tested; observing how plants store food and how plants change with the seasons.

Possible use: visit the garden to observe plants and methods of growth; make collections of seeds and fruits that show methods of dispersal; sprout seeds in the schoolroom to learn more about how plants grow; perform experiments with plants to see the effects of light, temperature and moisture in growth; plant a school garden (if practical) to learn more about how plants grow.

9. *An apiary* may be instructive for: Observing how bees are cared for; learning how hives are constructed and how prepared for cold weather; learning what happens when bees swarm and how they are handled safely, and how bees are helpful to man; observing bees at work and learning how life inside a hive goes on; seeing an example of social insects and of insects that are useful to man.

Possible use: visit apiary to observe various activities; talk with beekeeper to learn about bees and how they live; observe dead bees under a reading glass or microscope.

10. *A tree on the schoolground* may be instructive for: Observing seasonal changes, leaf arrangements, bud formation and growth; seeing bird life and nests and learning of the usefulness of birds.

Possible use: observe tree at intervals and discuss observations; cut small branches and study them more closely.

11. *An orchard* may be instructive for: Learning how plants are transplanted, sprayed and pruned; seeing relationship of plants to useful (bees), harmful (scales, aphids) and other insects; seeing an example of man's use of plants to supply food; observing the effect of sudden changes of temperature or other weather phenomena on plant growth.

Possible use: visit orchard to observe trees at different times of year; mark certain flowers and observe what happens as season progresses; collect and study insects and fruit damaged by insects.

12. *A creek or pond* may be instructive for: Observing kinds of plant life and the adaptations of stems, roots, leaves, flowers and fruit to moist environment; learning how animals are adapted for life in or near water and contrasting this with land animals; observing how these animals and plants change as seasons change; observing the food-getting and home-building habits of the animal life.

Possible use: visit area to observe science applications indicated above; collect specimens of plants and animals for further study.

13. *The roadside* may be instructive for: Observing animal homes and animal methods of food-getting and of caring for young; observing various forms of plant life to see adaptations to environment, such as methods of seed dispersal and changes under conditions of drought or excess moisture; studying relationships between plants and animals (plants and insects, for example); studying examples of erosion and methods of preventing it. If the road cuts through a hill, pupils can observe the difference between topsoil and subsoil, see the depth of the topsoil and understand more clearly the importance of saving it from being washed away.

Possible use: visit area to observe examples given above; collect samples of topsoil and subsoil, try to grow plants in each and note results; collect seed-dispersal specimens.

14. *People in the community.* There are other people in the community who can be of help. For example, many parents have travelled extensively; some are experts in animal husbandry; some are expert homemakers; some can contribute experiences about hunting, trapping and fishing. There is an electrician and a mechanic in nearly every community. People are usually pleased to be asked to help schoolchildren with their problems, and the practice of using adults in the community to help in school may be a beneficial practice to all concerned.

Using these resources

The value of any of these resources depends on how skilfully it is used. Each should be used for a definite purpose or purposes: to help solve a problem, to make a scientific principle more graphic, to increase appreciation of the usefulness and wonder of science. In preparing for a trip, the teacher and children should have clearly in mind a definitely stated problem or problems. The teacher and perhaps a small committee of pupils should first go to the place to be visited by the class, to determine its suitability and accessibility.

Whenever the pupils plan to seek information from someone in the community, make sure that he or she understands the purpose of the visit, and keeps explanations easy enough for them to understand.

Follow-up discussions to make use of the material should be carefully planned. Appropriate data should be used in solving the problem, and written records made of the findings whenever it seems likely that the children will have a use for the records.

Most schools are not yet making full use of the community resources available. We are likely to overlook many common things about us even though we say 'science is a study of the environment'. The science in our rural school is not necessarily being best taught where there is costly equipment. It is being best taught where children and teachers are aware that they are living in a world of science and that the materials for its study are near at hand.

E. FACILITIES FOR TEACHING SCIENCE

Few schools either in towns or rural areas are fortunate enough to afford a separate room for science teaching. Where elementary general science is a part of the curriculum, it is usually taught in an ordinary classroom where other subjects must also be taught. Science, however, is somewhat different from most other subjects in that it is not effectively learned by children unless they experience it. It is not sufficient to hear about science or to read about it. Children must observe and experiment if their science learnings are to be permanent.

Thus, if children are to experiment and observe science in their regular classroom, there are some problems which must be solved. In this section a few suggestions will be given to help the busy teacher provide some facilities in his classroom which will make the teaching of science more interesting.

Making a science corner in the classroom

Set aside a corner in the classroom and call it the Science Corner. If possible, secure one or two tables which may be used for experimenting and display. Perhaps the school custodian will help you build shelves underneath the table for storage of materials, supplies and equipment, as described in later chapters of this book. Encourage the pupils to bring in materials to display in the science corner. Some teachers have a little competition each week to see which pupil can bring in the item which is voted the 'Science Item of the Week'.

The Science Corner should be a place of activity and change. The materials brought in by the children should never be allowed to remain on the table so long that their interest value is lost.

Providing aquaria

Aquaria are a source of constant interest and provide a place where many important science phenomena may be observed. Directions for making and caring for aquaria will be found on page 58.

Cages for animals

Several types of animals can be kept in the classroom for observation. Some animals adjust to being caged better than others. Children may be encouraged to bring their pets to school for short periods of observation and study. Suggestions for building cages for animals will be found on page 54.

Setting up a weather station

In Chapter VIII, simple weather instruments are described. These can be made from materials available almost anywhere. Observing the weather changes from day to day is a source of interest and can form the basis for useful science lessons.

A science bulletin board

If children are encouraged they will constantly bring to school interesting things they have clipped from newspapers or magazines. The science bulletin board provides a place to display such materials, as well as drawings and other things prepared in science classes. A good place for the science bulletin board is just above the tables in the science corner. The bulletin board can be made from soft wood or plaster board.

Growing things

Small flower pots placed along a windowsill where there is plenty of light will provide ample space for growing seeds and small plants. If more space is desired for some experiences, shallow wood boxes may be obtained or made from old orange crates.

A museum shelf

Once children become interested, they are insatiable collectors. Some of the things they collect are bound to find their way to school. Such activities should be encouraged. One way to do this is to provide a museum shelf where collections or individual science items may be displayed.

CHAPTER II

How to make some general pieces of equipment

Wherever science teaching is based upon experiment and observation, there are certain pieces of apparatus that are used over and over again; such things as burners, tripods, flasks, aquaria, dip nets, etc. are almost indispensable in a science course. This chapter will be devoted to instructions for making pieces of equipment that are frequently used.

A. WEIGHING DEVICES

1 Simple 'spring' balance

Punch four holes in an old tin lid with a nail, spacing them equally round the circumference. Pass pieces of string through these holes and tie them together. Now attach this scale pan to a rubber band hung from a nail.

If weights are not available, it is possible to graduate the balance using known volumes of water poured from a measuring jar and by making marks on the supporting stick opposite the edge of the pan. Stones can then be found which will give the same extension and these should be marked for future use as weights. The use of coins for this purpose should also be investigated.

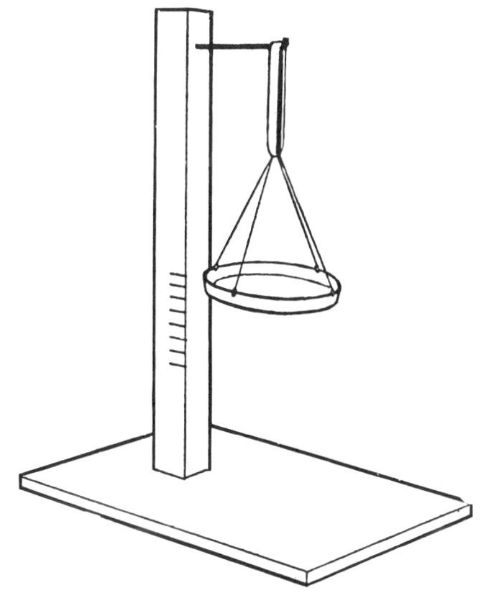

2 A serviceable spring balance

The quality of rubber deteriorates rather rapidly in unfavourable climatic conditions; a coiled steel spring is preferable. The pattern described has been found satisfactory. The coil is protected from damage by enclosing it in a tube. The reading is made at the bottom of the tube on a graduated wooden plunger.

First wind the spring (see Chapter XVIII, item 35), attach it by a screw eye to a piece of dowelling which will fit into the tube selected (bamboo or plastic). Fasten the other end of the spring by a wire staple to a wooden stick which will slide in the tube. Fix the dowelling to the top of the tube and insert into it a hook for suspending the balance. Screw another hook into the wooden plunger which can now be graduated.

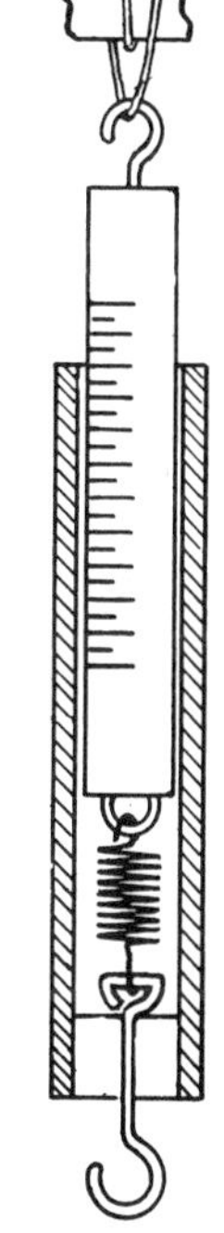

3 Spring balance for heavier loads

Fasten a chair or automobile cushion spring to a flat piece of wood that will serve as base to the instrument. As scale pan, use a large tin lid or plate. Fix this to the top of the spring. If it is not possible to use solder for this purpose, the scale pan can be secured by fine wire passed through double holes punched through it in convenient positions.

Attach two vertical laths to the base. These act as guides to the scale pan. Make graduations on these guides when loads of ½, 1, 2, etc., kilograms are placed on the scale pan. Wine bottles filled with water make suitable measures of litres, etc., and contain, of course, the equivalent weights in kilograms.

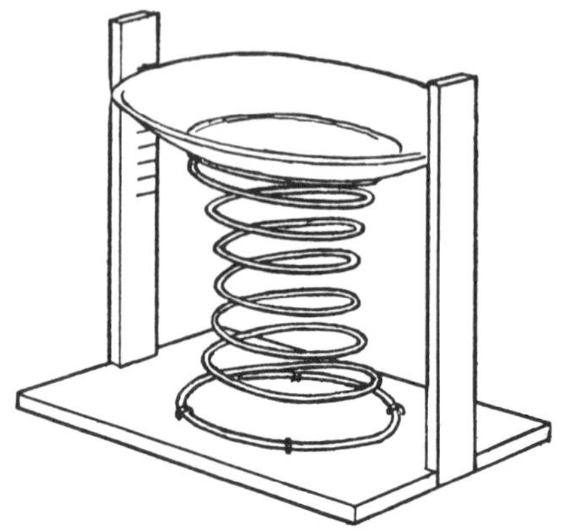

4 Steelyards

Either Roman or Danish steelyards can be improvised using short lengths of lead or iron water pipe as counter-weights and loops of wire as pivots.

The rod can be of either wood or metal; in the latter case notches can be filed on the underneath of the bar to indicate the balance points for various weights.

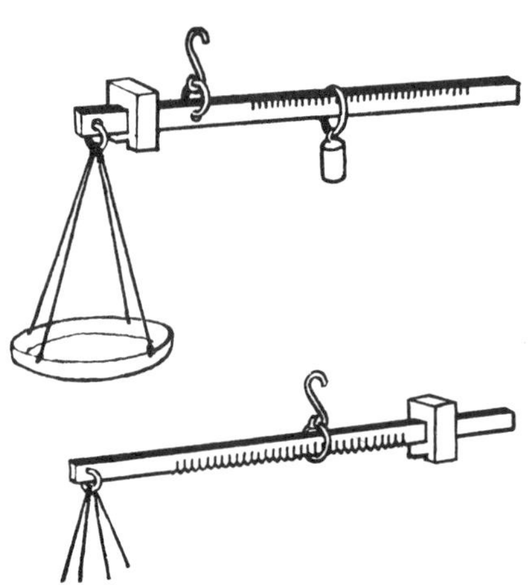

5 Laboratory steelyard

To make a steelyard weighing to 500 g use a wooden lath one metre long balanced on a strong sewing needle stuck through it 3 mm from its upper edge and 12 cm from one end. A disk of lead or anything suitably heavy can be used as counter-weight: if lead is used, a disk of it can be 'cast' in a tin lid.

A wire stirrup carrying a boot polish tin lid serves as scale pan and can be suspended 6 cm from the pivot.

A piece of U-shaped metal or two brass mirror plates separated by a wooden block will provide a suitable support.

Two sliders are needed, one weighing 50 g could be a piece of lead suspended by a copper wire: the other of 1 g weight could be in the form of a U resting on the top edge of the lath. The top edge can be calibrated in 6 cm divisions.

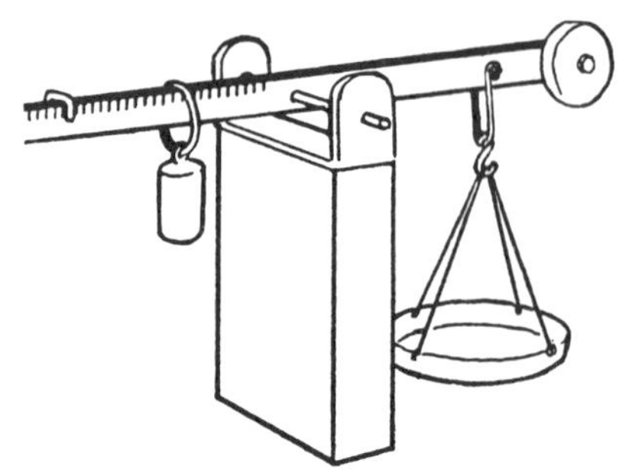

To use this apparatus, the nearest balance point is found by using the 50 g weight, and the final adjustment is made with the 1 g rider. No divisions are provided for this but the distance from the nearest mark can be quickly obtained by using a pair of dividers.

This balance is very quick in action and is satisfactory in use.

6 Clock spring balance

A sensitive balance for use between 0-1 g or 1-10 g is readily made using a piece of clock spring and a block of wood or cotton reel.

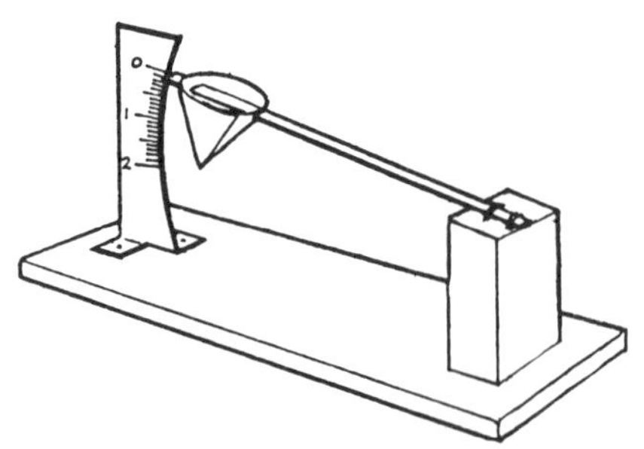

Fasten the wooden block or cotton reel down to a convenient base. Fix a piece of watch spring about 20 cm long to it and make a cardboard or paper conical pan. Fix the pan to the spring near the free end using sealing wax or cements suggested in Chapter XVIII. Use the free end as a pointer, and a postcard as a scale, and calibrate it by putting weights in the pan. The sensitivity depends on the spring used, but the scale is a reasonably open one.

7 **Simple steelyard** (reading to 100 g)

The pan is made from cardboard, and is shaped like a funnel. It is fixed to a beam made of a triangular-shaped lamina in plywood or 'perspex'.

The beam tapers from 2 cm at the extreme end to 5 cm near the pan. The pivot, which can be a strong darning needle, is driven through the beam at a point about 5 cm from the pan and 2 cm from the top edge. Some part of the beam or pan can be cut away to make it balance.

The pivot is supported in holes through a metal stirrup, and an outer stirrup serves to prevent the beam from slipping sideways. The top of the beam carries a U-shaped rider; notches are made in the beam using standard weights to calibrate it. Powdered solids can be weighed using a filter paper or a piece of paper folded into a similar cone.

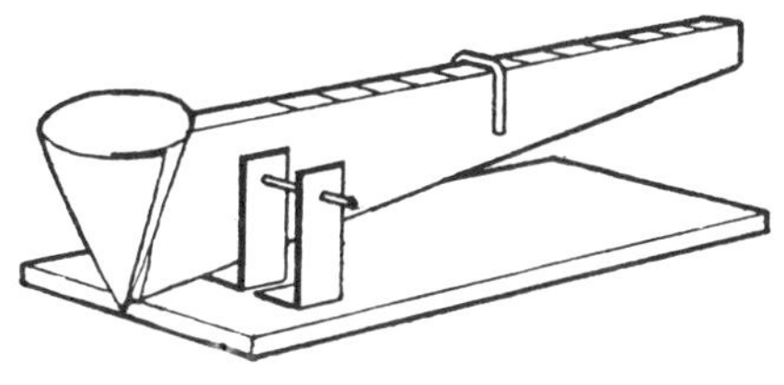

8 Soda straw balance

Obtain a small bolt (3 BA) which just fits inside the tube of a drinking straw, and screw it a few turns into one end. Determine roughly where this arrangement balances and punch a sewing needle through the straw to serve as a pivot. To ensure stability the hole should be made a little above the diameter of the straw.

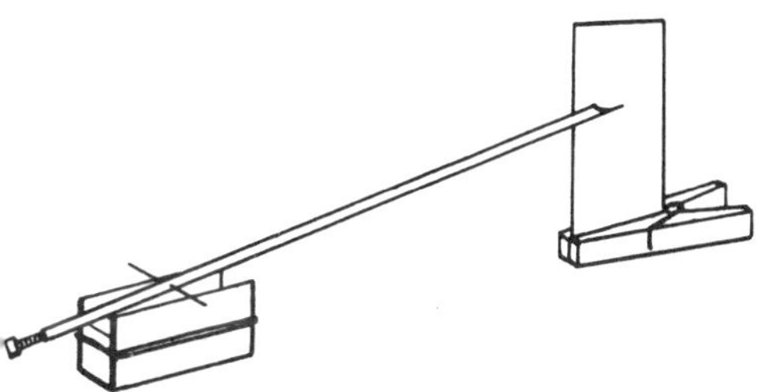

Cut away the other end of the straw to form a small scoop. When the needle is in place set it across the edges of two microscope cover slips (or two razor blades) held parallel by a block of wood and a rubber band. Adjust the bolt until the straw balances at about 30 degrees to the horizontal. Support a piece of card vertically behind the scoop using a clothes peg or another piece of wood and a thumb tack; this will serve as a scale.

Hang a hair or a small piece of tissue paper from the scoop and notice the deflection. To obtain quantitative readings the scale must be calibrated. Aluminium foil from cigarette packets is suitable for making small weights. A common gauge of foil weighs 5 mg for 2 sq. cm of area. Cut the foil into areas weighing 1 mg, 2 mg, etc., and place them in the scoop using a piece of copper wire bent to form tweezers. Record the positions of rest of the beam by making marks on the card. The sensitivity of the balance can be varied by adjusting the position of the bolt.

9 Zehnder's balance

This ingenious balance, which is very useful for demonstration experiments, can be constructed in a few minutes using pins, razor blade, cork and knitting needle.

The knitting needle is first pushed through the cork as eccentrically as possible along a line parallel to a diameter of the end of the cork.

Half cylinders are cut away from each end of the cork to produce the balance beams as shown.

The supporting pins are now pushed through the cork, and can rest on slips of glass glued to a strip of wood.

The sensitivity of the balance can be varied by adjusting the supporting pins.

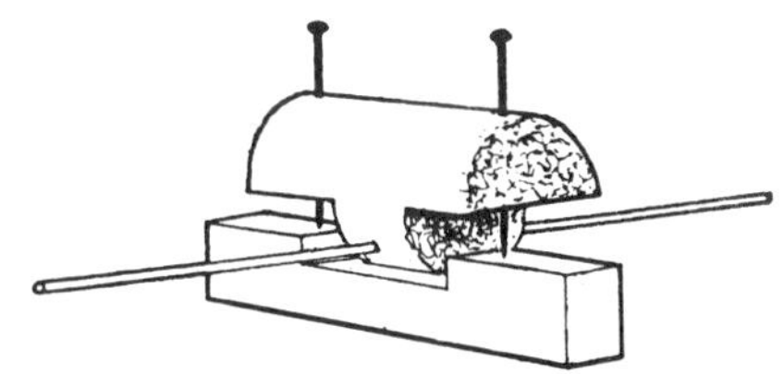

Experiments with the balance

1. A small rider of sewing thread or of the thinnest tissue paper, weighing about 2 mg and placed half-way along one arm, produces a turn of about 2 cm.
2. A slight formation of gas can be demonstrated by allowing the gas issuing from a small jet to impinge on the end of the beam.

3. Convection currents in air are shown by bringing a lighted match below the beam.

4. Since the balance-beam is an insulated conductor, it will show electrification. It can be charged by touching it with an electrified rod.

5. If the knitting needle is magnetized, it becomes a dip needle.

6. If the beam is magnetized and a wire spool is brought near to one of its poles, the balance becomes a galvanometer. For example, a thermocouple of iron-constantan can be connected to a coil of 22 turns of copper wire (1.5 mm thick). This, when warmed by a candle flame, produces a potential difference of only about 0.01 volt; nevertheless, the balance-beam detects the current flowing.

7. Projection. Small movements of the balance can be shown by using a beam of light reflected from a small strip of mirror attached to the beam. With this simple projection apparatus, thermo-electric currents can be demonstrated if the thermocouple mentioned above is merely warmed by the fingers.

10 A general utility equal-arm balance

Construct a base about 22 cm square from wood about 2 cm thick. Next make two uprights from wood 15 cm long by 6 cm wide by 2 cm thick and attach these near the centre of the base about 2.5 cm apart. They may be attached either with screws or by slotting the base and screwing the uprights to it. The top of each upright should be cut deeply enough with a thin saw to allow a razor blade to extend about 4 mm above the wood. The razor blades are wedged tightly in the slots.

The beam of the balance is made from a metrestick or similar length of wood with a thin finishing nail through its exact centre of balance. The nail rides on the razor blades.

To give stability to the beam, the supporting nail should be positioned a little above the geometrical centre.

11 A sensitive beam balance

The materials needed for this balance include a clothes peg, a knitting needle about 12 in. long, two pins or needles and a support such as a milk bottle or preserving jar.

The beam of the balance is made by passing the knitting needle through the hole in the spring of the clothes peg. The pivots for the beam are the two needles or pins placed one on either side of the clothes peg, slightly below the hole through which the knitting needle passes. The latter must project equally on either side of the clothes peg, and can be wedged in this position inside the spring by a small splinter of wood. The lower end of the clothes peg grips a pencil which serves as the pointer of the balance. The pans of the balance are made from two tin lids pierced at the circumference by the equally spaced holes through which threads are passed and tied together to form a loop from which they can be suspended from the beam. Once the scales are balanced it is advisable to make a nick with a file to prevent the loops slipping off the knitting needle. Finally a graduated scale is placed inside the bottle in such a way that the pointer swings in front of it.

The weights may be coins, crown corks, matches, etc., correlated to standard weights. If none of the latter are available two similar small bottles may be used, one in each pan, and known amounts of water poured into one of them from some graduated vessel. Failing all else an old novocaine tube used by dentists for local anaesthetic is graduated in cubic centimetres and may serve as a very small measuring cylinder. Fractional weights may be improvised by hanging a loop of wire from the beam.

B. SOURCES OF HEAT

1 A tin can charcoal burner

A large tin can at least 10 cm in diameter should be used. About 4 cm from the bottom mark off triangular windows around the can, as shown in the diagram. With a pair of shears cut along the sloping sides of each triangle to make the windows. Do not cut along the base line. Bend the triangular parts inward to form a shelf for the charcoal.

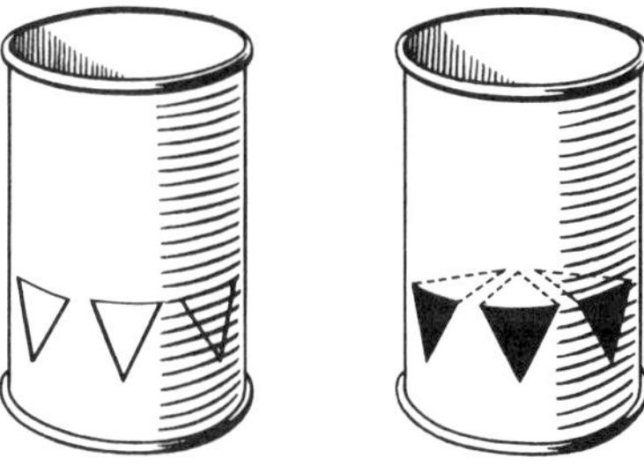

2 Methylated spirits burner

A simple burner can be made from an old boot polish tin. Though it is not essential, a metal tube can be soldered to the top and a twisted piece of wire makes a convenient handle. A piece of rag or cotton waste can be used for a wick.

3 An alcohol lamp from an ink bottle

Secure an ink bottle with a metal top which screws on. Punch a hole in the centre of the metal top with a nail. Enlarge the hole until it is about 8 to 10 mm in diameter by using a circular motion on a triangular file inserted in the hole. Smooth the opening by using some hard, round device. Cut a piece of metal about 2.5 cm wide and 4 cm long from a soft metal can or piece of sheet metal. Roll this into a tube on a piece of dowel rod or other round wood stick of suitable diameter to fit the opening in the top of the ink bottle. Insert the tube in the top and let it go about 1 cm into the bottle. The tube may be soldered around the joint with the top and along the seam. A wick may be made from cotton waste, a bit of cotton bath towel or from a bundle of strands of cotton string. Be sure to have enough wick to extend to the bottom of the bottle and cover it. Use denatured or wood alcohol.

In hot countries a cap should be made to cover the wick when the lamp is not in use. An old fountain pen cap may serve the purpose. If a brass rifle cartridge is available it can be used to make both the tube and the cap by cutting it with a hacksaw at a suitable place.

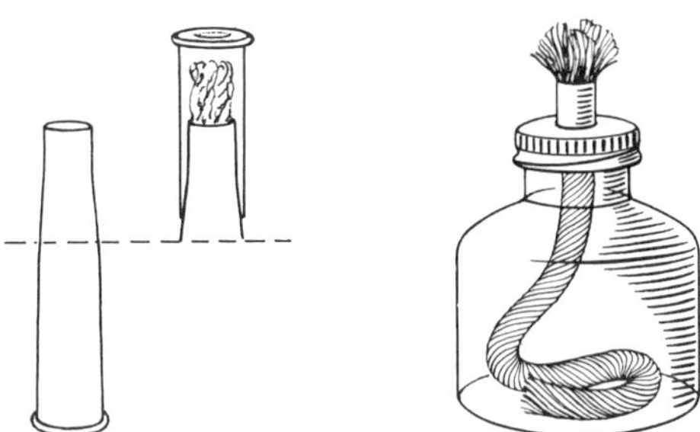

C. OTHER USEFUL THINGS

1 Demonstration vernier

Two pieces of tongued and grooved floor board about 1 m long can be used to make this apparatus. Saw 7 cm off the tongued board and glue it into the groove to provide an end stop. With indian ink or sawcuts, mark off graduations 5 cm apart along the whole length of the longer board. Use about 50 cm of the tongued board to provide the vernier slide. Graduate it by measuring 45 cm from one end and dividing this into ten equal parts, i.e. 4.5 cm each. The remaining piece of board can be used to provide brackets so that the apparatus will stand vertically on the bench.

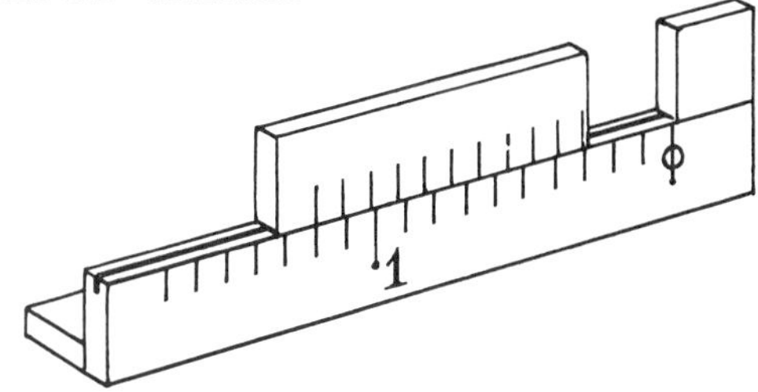

2 A simple tripod

A useful tripod can be made by cutting away the sides of a tin can. It is convenient to make two or three of these to suit different burners and for use as stands. Holes should be punched along the upper edge to let the products of combustion escape.

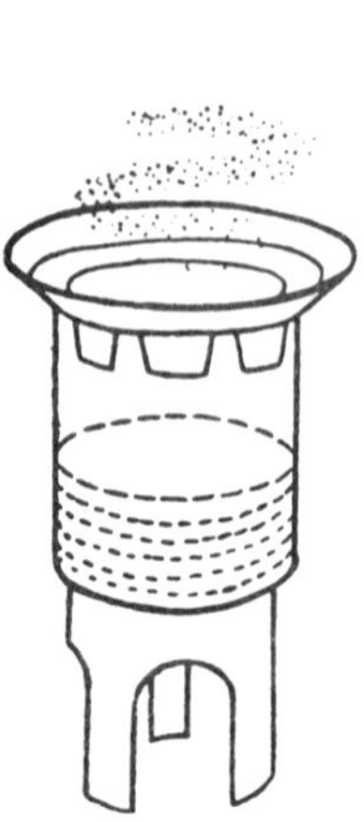

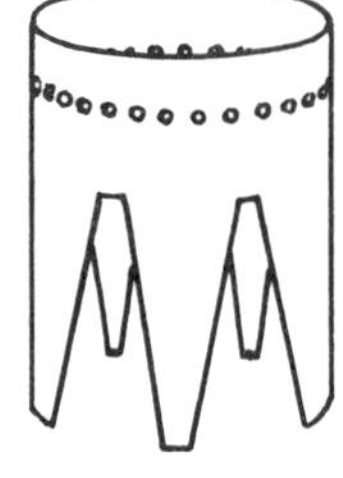

3 A steam bath

An evaporating dish and steam bath can be contrived from a saucer and a tin. Scallops are cut out of the top of the tin to allow the steam to escape.

4 Heater

Another form of heater can be made from an old oil tin. Iron wire is wrapped round a test tube and twisted to form a handle.

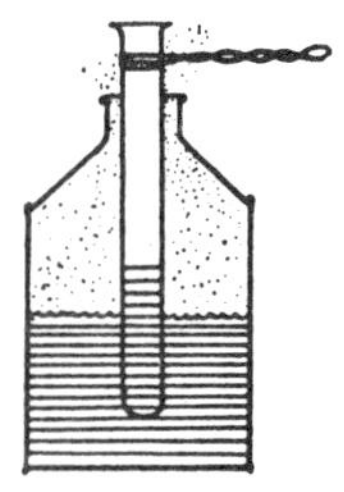

5 Steam supply for experiments in heat

A tin with a press-on lid may be used to make a steam can. Punch two holes in the lid and solder through them one long and one short pipe as shown in the diagram. The long pipe serves as a safety valve and the short one supplies steam to the experiment (through a rubber tube attached). When the tin leaks or becomes rusty the same lid may be transferred to a similar tin.

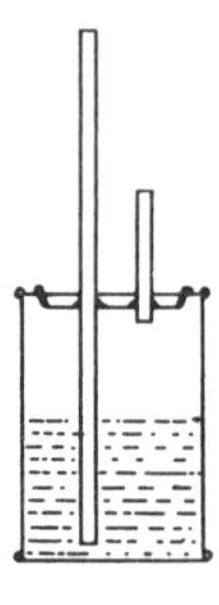

6 A simple calorimeter

Small soup tins can be found which fit loosely into a 1 lb. jam jar. If the top of the tin is cut off cleanly with a rotary type opener it serves as an excellent calorimeter.

The tin can be prevented from slipping into the jar either by a stout rubber band round the edge, or by cutting nicks in the rim and bending it slightly outwards. This form of suspension, and the low conductivity of glass and air contribute to its efficiency.

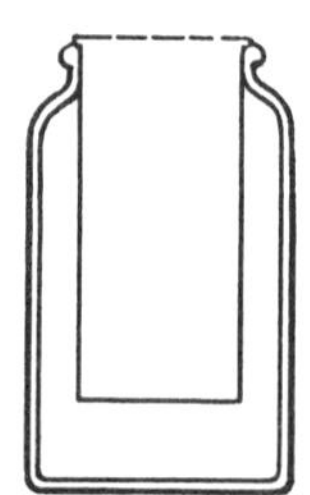

7 Distilled water

A kettle can be used to provide boiling water, which is then condensed in a jam jar fitted with a large cork and immersed in a pan of cold water. Rubber tubing, adhesive tape or clay can be used to make the joint.

8 An air oven

A large tin can be used as an air oven. A hole through the lid fitted with a cork holds a thermometer, and the saucer or dish rests on a wire gauze bridge placed inside the tin.

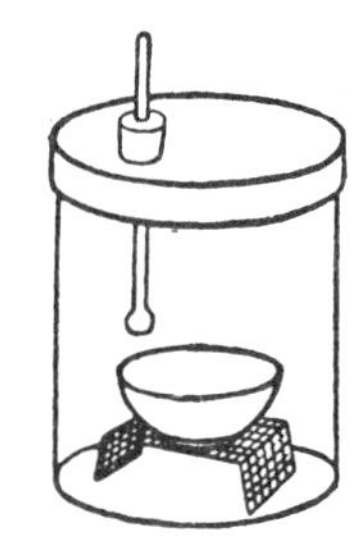

9 Liebig condenser (iron)

A piece of iron pipe such as is used for water or electric conduit can be used to make a metal condenser which is much more robust than a glass one. Inlet and outlet tubes are screwed or soldered to the sides. A one-hole cork fits each end and passes ordinary glass tubing.

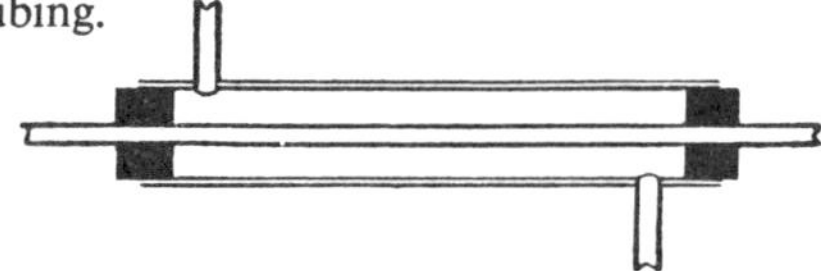

10 Filter

A plant pot with a plug of cotton wool in the bottom and a layer of sand a few inches deep makes a satisfactory filter for many purposes.

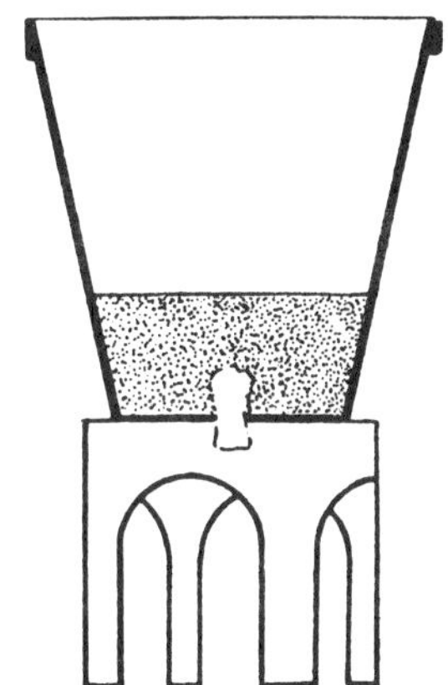

11 Filter pump

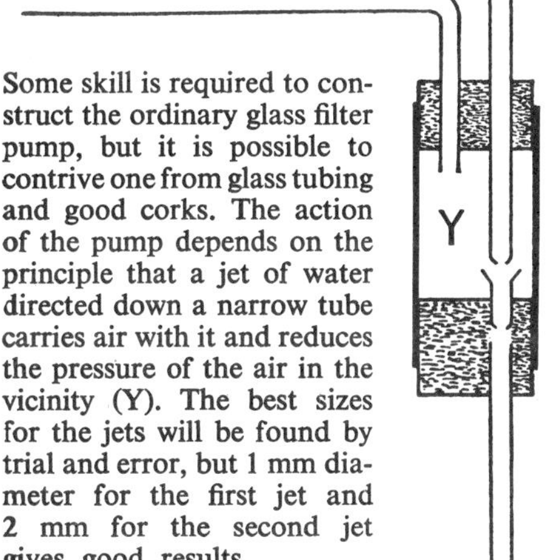

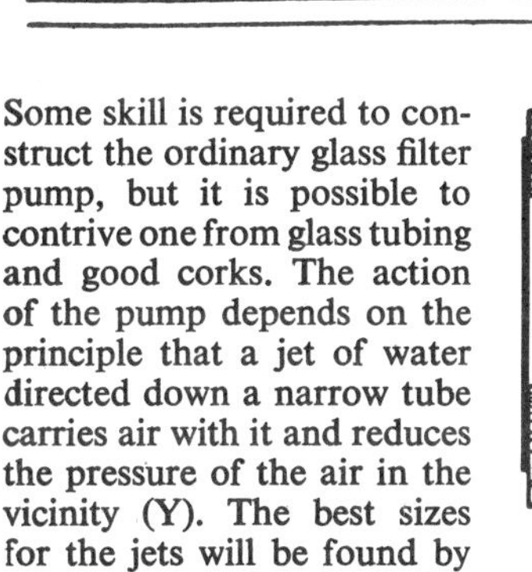

Some skill is required to construct the ordinary glass filter pump, but it is possible to contrive one from glass tubing and good corks. The action of the pump depends on the principle that a jet of water directed down a narrow tube carries air with it and reduces the pressure of the air in the vicinity (Y). The best sizes for the jets will be found by trial and error, but 1 mm diameter for the first jet and 2 mm for the second jet gives good results.

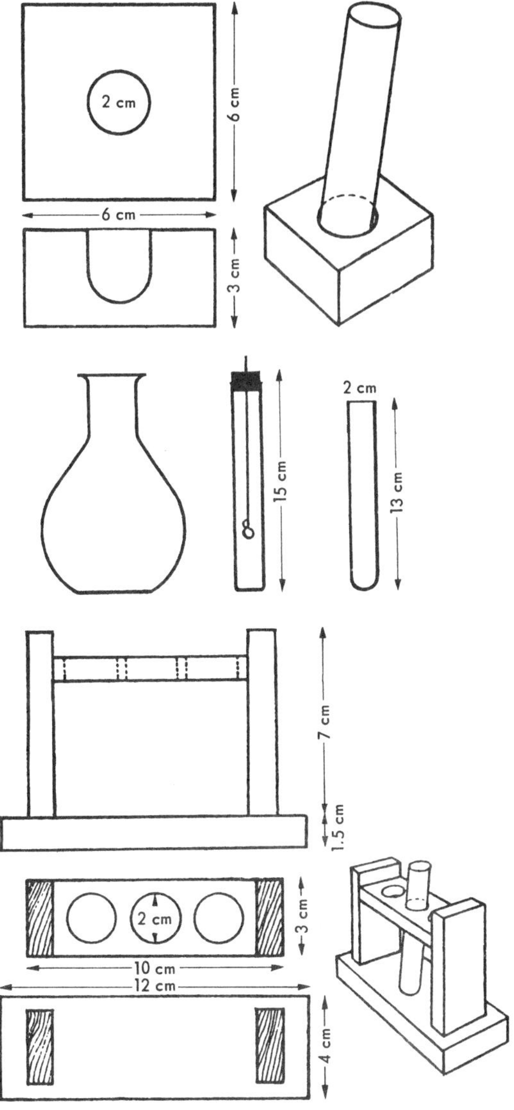

12 Apparatus for individual work in chemistry

Most of the experiments in elementary chemistry require some basic equipment such as beakers, test tubes, etc. The outfit described below will be found to include all that is usually required. The 150 cc Pyrex flask with a round neck can be used either as beaker, flask, or steam generator. An ordinary glass tube with a roll of wire gauze round it can be used as a combustion tube and does not break more often than the usual hard glass tube.

A specimen tube can be converted into a satisfactory small gas jar. Though not essential, a small test tube rack is convenient, and the small test tubes suggested have the advantage that they can be closed by the small fingers of children. A large tube with a wooden base is useful as a stock bottle for many other experiments. If running water is not available, a condenser is provided in the form of a large tin (500 cc) of water. The only difficult task is to make a water-tight joint for the outfall tube. This apparatus has been found very useful for junior class practical chemistry.

13 Containers from used electric bulbs

Used electric light bulbs can be made into containers that will substitute for flasks, beakers, test tubes and similar devices. With reasonable precautions these will stand considerable heat and handling. Any size electric bulb may be used. A variety of sizes will prove useful.

It is a wise precaution to wrap the bulb in an old towel or other piece of cloth while working with it. Begin by lifting the small metal button in the centre of the bulb top with a knife. Bend this up until it can be grasped with a pair of pliers. Raise this metal button by pulling upward on it with the pliers. This should expose the wire to which it is connected. Break the button away from the wire with a twisting motion. The hole in the centre of the black insulation should now be exposed. Carefully loosen and remove this insulation. It may be necessary to crack it into several pieces with the pliers. Be as careful as possible not to bend the brass shell. The next operation needs considerable care and you may break a few bulbs before developing enough skill. Hold the wrapped bulb firmly and use the top end of a file. With a quick motion puncture the bulb through the opening at the top. The glass rod which supports the bulb filament should drop into the bulb. Next use a round or rat-tail file to cut the jagged glass back at the neck. This can be done without cracking the bulb. The support rod and other material can be removed from inside the bulb which is now ready to use. If the brass shell which forms the top of the flask has been bent it can be re-shaped by inserting and rotating a piece of round wood of the proper diameter. The brass shell enables tight fits to be made with corks and rubber stoppers when needed in constructing a piece of apparatus.

14 Cutting a glass dish from a used electric bulb

The hemispherical bottom of an electric light bulb provides a useful glass dish; a soldering iron can be used to cut it off. Place the bulb on its side and make a scratch with a file somewhere along its line of greatest circumference. Support the soldering iron at an angle of 45° in a laboratory clamp so that the tip is the same height above the bench as the point of incision. Hold the bulb in both hands and, keeping it horizontal, bring the scratch into contact with the point of the soldering iron.

There will be a slight crack indicating the beginning of cleavage; the bulb, still held against the iron, should now be rotated on its axis to complete the cut. The sharp edge left by the cut can be removed by heating the rim in a gas flame.

In use these dishes are best supported on a wire ring with bearing points of asbestos fibre to prevent possible cracking along the wire. The remaining part of the bulb can be used to make a Voltameter.

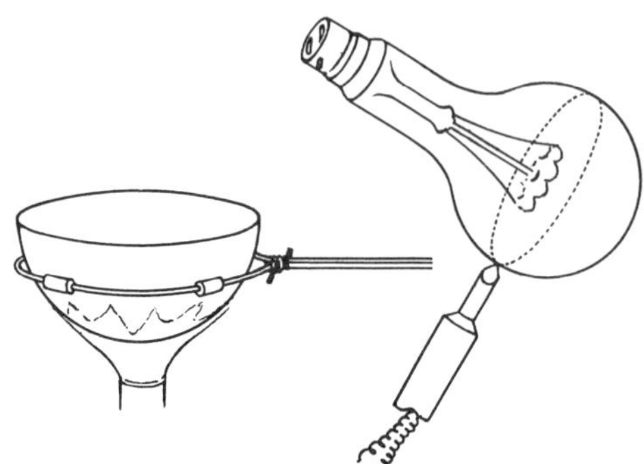

15 A measuring jar or graduate

Select several straight-sided glass jars of assorted sizes. Olive bottles are very useful for the making of graduated cylinders. Paste a strip of paper about 1 cm wide along the bottle to within about a centimetre of the top. Next secure a commercial graduated cylinder of about the same capacity as the bottle and measure out sufficient water to fill the bottle nearly to the top of the paper scale. Draw a line across the paper scale and mark under it the number of cubic centimetres of water poured in, say 50 cc or 100 cc. Next, if the bottle is of uniform diameter, divide the distance between the bottom of the bottle and the line into some convenient number of parts. Draw lines across the paper and label each division. For example, suppose that 50 cc of water were used: you might then divide the length of the bottle into five equal parts; the first line from the bottom would be marked 10 cc, then next 20 cc and so on. Each large scale division may next be sub-divided into smaller parts and lines placed across the paper scale. The graduated cylinder so constructed should be tested at several capacities by filling it to a certain level and then pouring the water into a commercial or standard vessel. Some of the lines may have to be moved slightly. When you have completed the test, you can make the scale permanent by covering it with a thin coat of melted paraffin, shellac, label varnish or plastic cement.

16 A test tube holder

A suitable test tube holder can be made by bending strong spring wire made of iron or brass into the shape shown in the diagram. Wire from a coat hanger works very well.

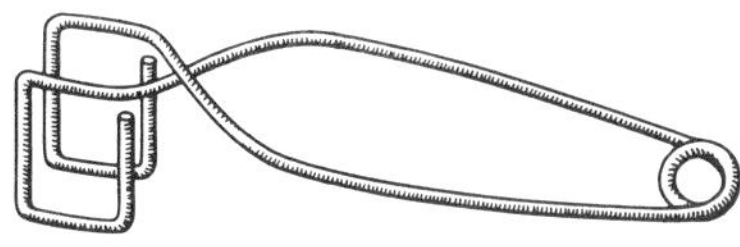

17 Laboratory tweezers

Very serviceable tweezers can be made from lengths of flexible strap iron used to put around boxes and crates for shipment.

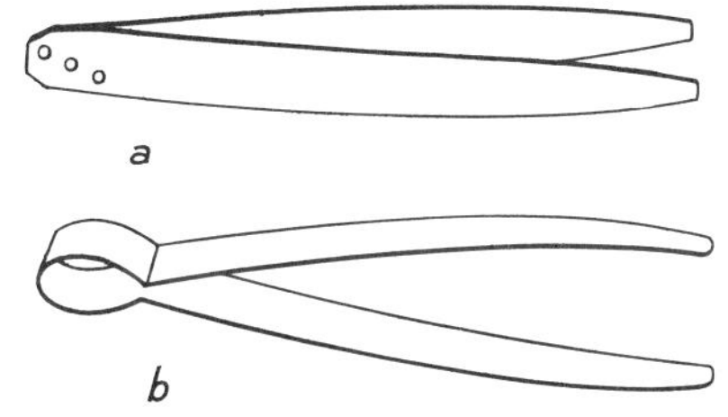

The tweezers shown are about 12 cm in length. The pair shown in diagram *a* can be made by brazing or riveting two pieces of strap iron together and then bending and cutting to the proper shape. Those in diagram *b* were fashioned from a single 26 cm length of strap iron. The round head was made by pinning the centre of the strip around an iron rod of suitable diameter. The sides were then cut and shaped to size.

18 A metal ringstand and rings

A useful ringstand and rings can be made from a flat curtain rod and the fixtures which clamp over electric bulbs to hold lamp shades. These are usually obtainable in hardware stores. The curtain rod is shaped as shown in the diagram.

The curtain rod consists of two pieces fitted to slide together so that they are adjustable for curtains of different width.

Attach each part of such a curtain rod to a suitable wooden base either with nails or screws. A triangular brace secured against the rod and attached to the base will make the ringstand stronger. This is shown in the diagram. The lamp shade fixtures are squeezed together and the prongs fitted into the slot on the inside of the curtain rod. The spring pressure is sufficient to hold the fixture at any height, making a very useful ring for the ringstand.

Another type of ring may be made by bending wire from a coat hanger into the proper shape and size.

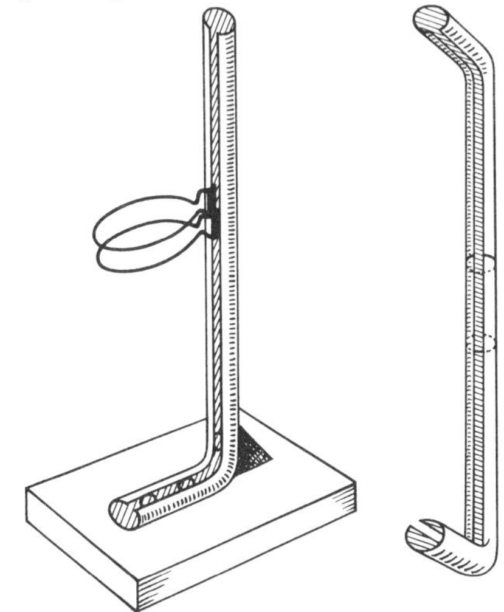

19 A wooden ringstand

The base for this ringstand is made from a piece of wood 40 cm long, 15 cm wide and 1 cm thick. A hole 1 cm in diameter is bored through the centre of the base. The upright is made from a piece of dowel rod 1 cm in diameter and 45 cm long. The dowel rod upright must fit very tightly in the hole made in the base. If dowel rod of this size is not available, another size may be used, but the hole in the base should be made accordingly.

20 Equipment support bar for ringstand

A useful equipment support bar for the above ringstand can be made from a piece of wood 18 cm long, 4 cm wide and 1 cm thick, together with four clothes pegs of the spring pincer type. The clothes pegs are attached to the bar as shown in the diagram. The clothes pegs at either end support equipment such as test tubes, and the two placed parallel nearer the centre clamp to the upright of the ringstand. Observe that the clothes peg on the right-hand end of the bar is set at an angle, after a suitable place has been levelled, as shown in the diagram. This makes it possible to support the test tube at an angle so that it may be heated without setting the wooden clamp on fire.

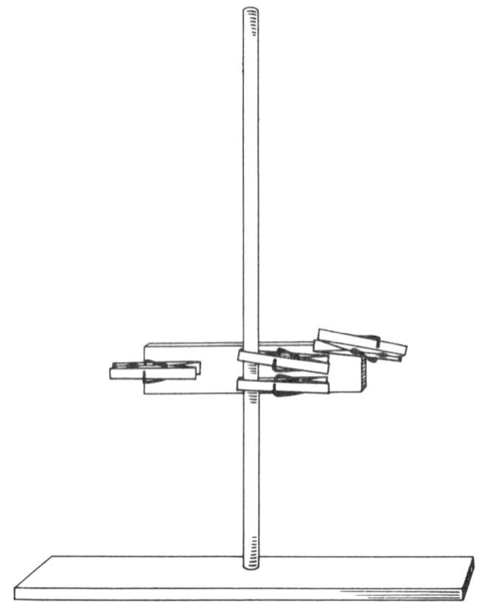

21 Iron pan

This is useful for many experiments in chemistry. The lid of a preserving jar is looped with galvanized wire. The free end of the wire is embedded in a piece of wooden dowelling rod, so that it can be supported in the left-hand clamp of the wooden stand.

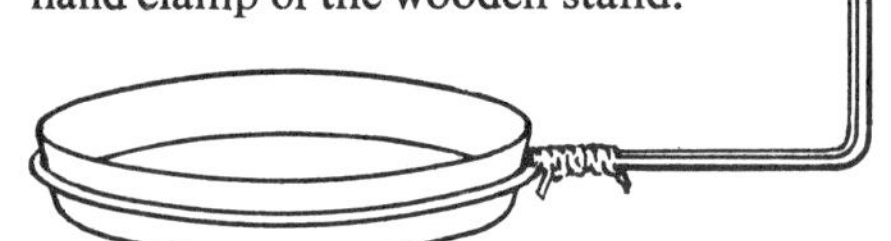

22 Automatic gas generator

This is a semi-micro Kipps apparatus. The solid reagent (zinc, marble, iron sulphide, etc.) is placed in a large test tube with holes in it, and the acid is contained in a jar or other receptacle. A series of holes is made in the bottom of the test tube using a blowpipe and playing a fine jet, one shot at a time, until the glass is pierced. Glass beads, or short lengths of glass tube placed vertically, are put on the bottom of the test tube to serve as a platform for the solid reagent. A rubber stopper with a glass tube through it is then inserted in the test tube and connected by rubber tubing to a glass nozzle. The outlet is closed by a clip or by pinching the tube with the fingers.

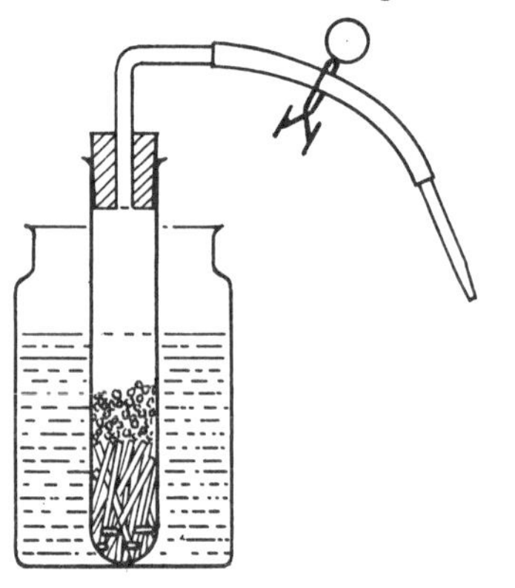

23 An electric device for cutting glass jars and bottles

A considerable number of pieces of useful equipment can be made from bottles, jugs, flasks, used electric bulbs and other things made of glass. It is often necessary to cut the top or bottom from such objects to adapt them to specific purposes. This piece of equipment will prove most useful for cutting such devices cleanly. After the cutting operation it is necessary to smooth sharp edges either with a file or by means of fire polishing.

Two wood uprights 20 × 7 × 4.5 cm are attached to a base of suitable size at a distance 15 cm apart.

Holes of suitable size to hold brass rods of 5 mm diameter are bored through the shorter dimension of each upright about 2 cm from the top. Through one upright a brass or iron bolt is put. Through the other a longer piece carrying a handle is placed. Notice that the drawing shows a set screw for the regulator.

A length of nichrome, or other wire of high electrical resistance suitable for the source of electricity (12 v, from a step-down transformer, 220-12 v, or 110-12 v) is attached to the ends of the rods by means of suitable nuts. The electrical circuit is shown in the drawing.

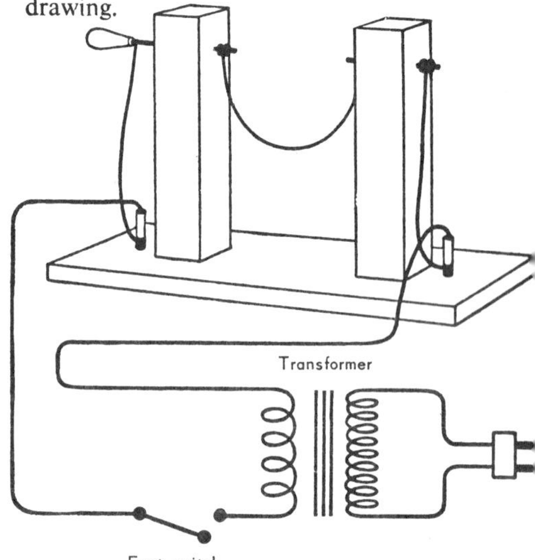

CHAPTER III

Experiments and materials for plant study

A. ROOTS

1 How to grow root hairs

Hairs can easily be seen on the roots of mustard seed grown on a damp flannel. Seeds placed on an earthenware dish standing in a soup plate containing water will produce very good specimens if covered by another plate to keep the air moist.

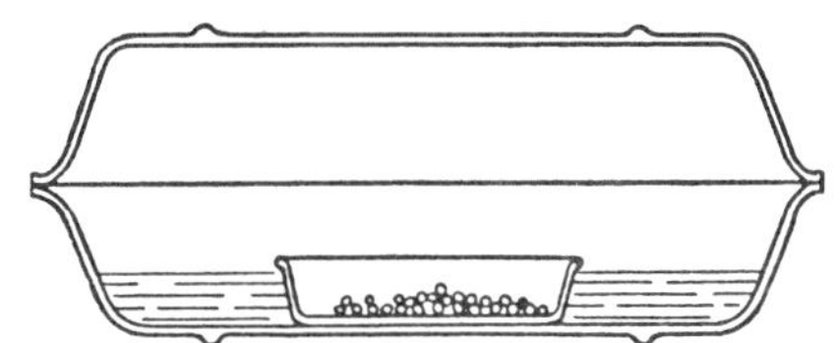

2 Observing root hairs

Study the root hairs with a hand lens and observe how they are constructed.

3 Testing whether roots absorb water and suspended solids

Three similar plants are inserted into test tubes containing 1, water; 2, red ink; 3, a suspension of congo red. After a few days 2 will be found to be coloured; 1 and 3 uncoloured, having absorbed only water.

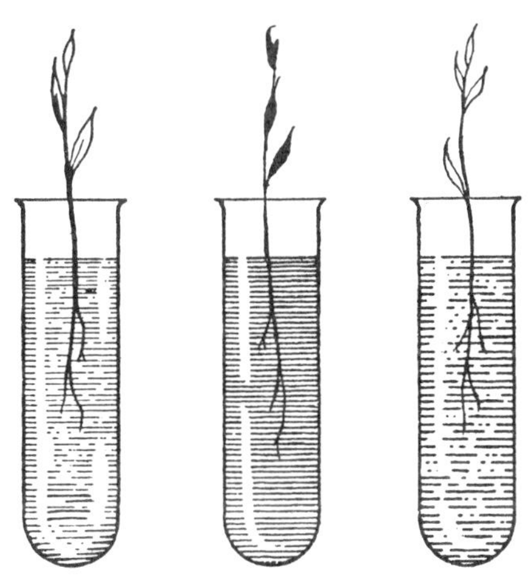

4 A simple osmometer

Remove the bottom from a small glass bottle about 2.5 cm in diameter. Fit a one-hole stopper tightly into the bottom and put a 50 cm length of glass tubing or a length of two soda straws through the hole.

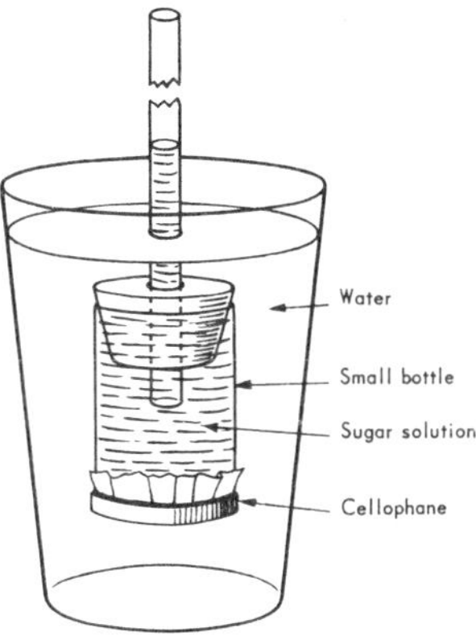

Place a piece of cellophane or parchment paper over the other end of the bottle and fasten it securely by winding with several turns of string or strong thread. Fill the bottle with a very concentrated sugar solution and replace the one-hole stopper being sure that no air bubbles remain inside the bottle. Clamp the osmometer in a glass of water and allow to stand a few hours.

5 A carrot osmometer

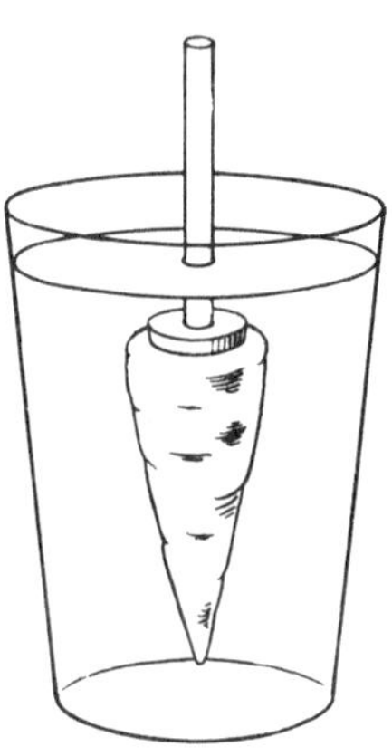

Select a carrot which has a large top and which is free of breaks in its surface. With a sharp knife or an apple corer cut a hole in the top of the carrot about 2 or 2.5 cm in depth. Be careful not to split the top. Fill the cavity with a concentrated solution of sugar. Insert a tightly fitting one-hole cork or rubber stopper which carries two soda straws pushed together or a length of glass tubing. Place in a jar of water for a few hours. If your cut in the top of the carrot has not been even it may be necessary to seal the cork in with some wax dripped from a burning candle.

6 An egg osmometer

Place some dilute hydrochloric acid or strong vinegar in a shallow dish, such as a saucer, to a depth of about one centimetre. Hold the large end of an egg in the acid until the shell has been eaten away on the end leaving the thin membrane exposed. Rinse the acid from the egg. With a sharp instrument work a small hole through the shell at the other end. Insert a soda straw or a length of glass tubing through the hole into the interior of the egg. Seal the opening around the tube with household cement or sealing wax. This must be absolutely tight. Place the osmometer in a glass of water and let it stand for a few hours.

7 The effect of gravity on roots

Cut several pieces of blotting paper about 8 cm square. Place these between two squares of glass. Place several radish or mustard seeds between the blotting paper and glass on each side and secure with rubber bands. Wet the blotting paper and then stand the apparatus upright in a shallow saucer of water. When the seeds have sprouted and the rootlets are about 1.5 cm long, turn the squares through 90° and allow them to remain undisturbed. Repeat the turning and observe the effect on the roots.

Another way to study the effect of gravity on roots is to sprout some seeds and select one that is straight. Pierce the seed with a long pin or needle and stick this into a cork. Place some damp cotton or blotting paper in a bottle. Put the cork and seedling in the bottle. Place the bottle in a dark cupboard and look at it every hour or so.

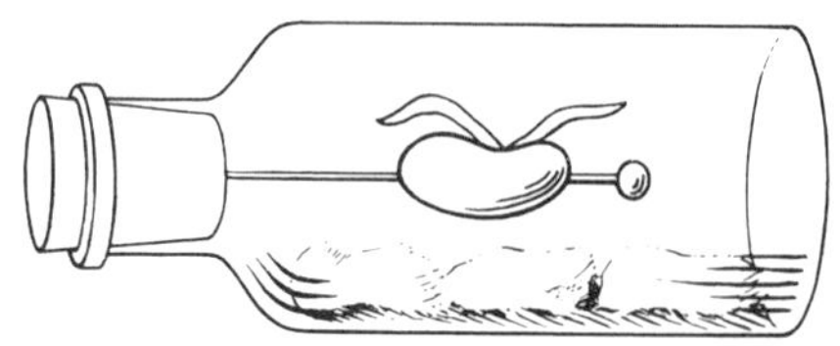

8 How are roots affected by water?

Grow some seedlings in one end of a glass dish or pan. When they are about 5 cm tall begin watering them on one side only and a little distance away from the nearest plants. Continue the watering daily for about a week and then dig away the soil and see if the watering has had any influence on the direction of growth of the roots.

9 Growing roots from different parts of plants

Secure a box of sand and place it away from direct sunlight. Wet the sand thoroughly and keep it moist. Plant the following things in the sand:

(a) Various bulbs.
(b) Cuttings of begonia and geranium stems.
(c) A section of sugar cane stem with a joint buried in the sand.
(d) A section of bamboo stem with a joint buried in the sand.
(e) Carrot, radish and beet tops each with a small piece of root attached.
(f) An onion.
(g) An iris stem.
(h) Pieces of potato containing eyes.
(i) A branch of willow.

B. STEMS

1 The effect of light on the growth of stems

(a) Plant some seeds that grow rapidly such as oats, radish, bean or mustard seeds in two flower pots. When the seedlings are about 2.5 cm high, cover one pot with a box that has a hole cut near the top. From time to time lift the box and observe the direction of growth. Turn the box so that light comes from a different direction and observe again after a few days.

(b) Put two light baffles in a long, narrow box as shown in the diagram, and cut a hole in the end. Plant a sprouting potato in a small pot that will fit in the box. Place the pot behind the farthest baffle from the hole. Cover the box and place in a window. Observe the direction of growth from time to time.

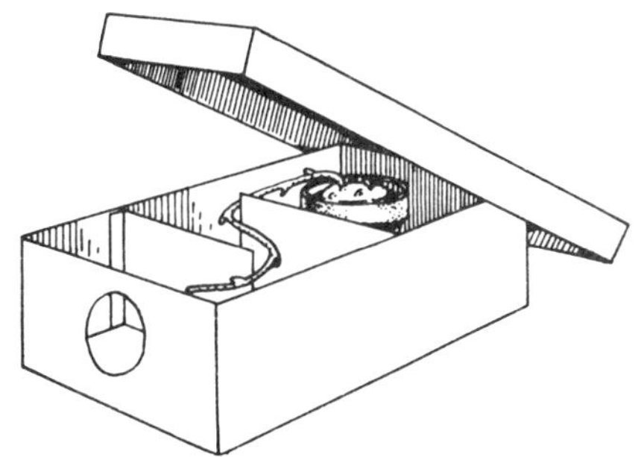

(c) Plant four flower pots with some fast-growing seeds as in (a) above. Keep the pots in a darkened room until the seedlings are about 2.5 cm high. Place one pot in a sunny window and observe the effect. Turn the plants away from the light and observe. Leave the pot in a place away from direct light for a few days and observe the results.

(d) Place each of the three remaining pots of seedlings in a different box. Cut a window in each box and cover each window with a different colour of cellophane such as red, yellow and blue. Place the three boxes containing the pots of seedlings in good light with the window facing the light. Observe any difference in the effect produced by different coloured light on the growth of stems.

2 Stems transport liquids

(a) Cut about 2 cm from the end of stems of celery and place them in cold water for about an hour to freshen. Next place the stems in dishes containing red ink and let them stand for several hours. Observe the stalks carefully. Cut them up into several short lengths and observe where the ink has moved upward in the stem. Try to pull some of the tubes out of the celery stems.

(b) Cut about 2 cm from the end of the flower stalks of white carnations. The cutting should be done with a sharp knife and under water. Place the stems with flowers in glasses containing different shades of food colouring or coloured ink. Observe after several hours.

(c) Split the stalk of a white carnation into three parts with a razor blade. Extend the split 8 or 10 cm up the stem and then wrap with tape to prevent further splitting. Spread the three sections out and place each in a vessel containing a different colour of ink or food dye. Observe the flower after a few hours.

(d) Put the cut ends of twigs or shoots of several kinds of trees in coloured ink and later cut them into short sections with a sharp knife. Observe the places where the colour has gone up in the stem.

(e) Plant seeds of common garden plants in flower pots. When the seedlings are 8 to 10 cm high and growing vigorously, cut the upper part of the stem off with a sharp knife. Soon drops of water will be seen where the cut was made.

3 Different types of stems

(a) *Monocots.* Secure stems of several plants such as bamboo, sugar cane and corn. Cut each of the stems crosswise with a very sharp knife or razor blade. Observe the similarities in the cut cross sections. Especially notice that the tubes or fibrovascular bundles are scattered throughout the pith on the inside of the stem.

(b) *Dicots.* Secure the stems of several plants or small trees such as willow, geranium, tomato, etc. Cut across each of these stems with a sharp knife or razor blade. Observe that just under the outside layer of the stem there is a bright green layer. This is the cambium layer. Also observe that the tubes or fibrovascular bundles are arranged in a ring about the central, or woody portion of the stem.

C. LEAVES

1 Types of leaves

Collect leaves from such plants as lilies, bamboo, sugar cane, corn, willow and geraniums. Observe that the monocots (lily, bamboo, corn, sugar cane) have the veins running parallel. Observe that leaves from dicotyledrous plants (willow, geranium, etc.) have branching venation.

2 Making leaf collections

Collect young leaves of as many varieties of plants as possible. Place several layers of newspaper or blotting paper on a firm, smooth board. Next arrange the leaves so they do not touch. Cover the leaves with other layers of newspaper or blotting paper. Place another board on top and then place several heavy stones or weights on the board. Keep the leaves in the press until they are thoroughly dried. When the leaves are removed from the press they may be neatly arranged on note book pages and secured either with Scotch tape or small sections of gummed labels. The name of the leaf and any other interesting material can be recorded on the note book page.

3 Making smoke prints of leaves

Smoke prints of leaves may be easily made by following the four steps shown in the diagrams.

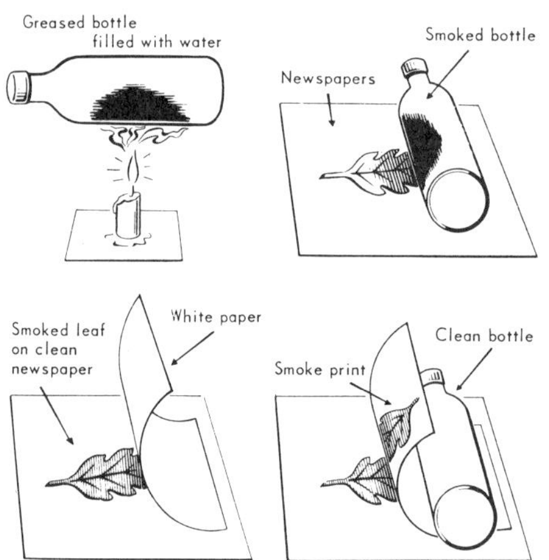

Cover the side of a smooth, round bottle with a thin layer of grease or vaseline. Fill the bottle with cold water and cork it tightly. Hold the bottle over a candle flame until it is covered evenly with soot. Place a leaf, vein side up, on a layer of newspaper and roll the sooty bottle over the leaf. Remove the leaf and lay it vein side up on clean newspaper. Cover the leaf with a sheet of white paper. Next, roll over the white paper and leaf with a clean round bottle or other roller.

4 Making spatter prints of leaves

Place the leaf on a sheet of white paper and flatten it with pins, thumb tacks, or a few small pebbles. Dip an old tooth brush in poster colour or Indian ink. Hold the brush over the paper and spatter the material from the tooth brush evenly around the leaf by carefully drawing the blade of a knife over the bristles. Do not use too much colour or ink. When the colour has dried remove the leaf.

A leaf print spatter box can be made as shown above (right). A piece of window screening is placed over a shallow box or frame. The spatter is made by dipping a tooth-brush in the colour and rubbing it over the leaf and paper which are secured to the bottom of the box. Try using white colour on various coloured papers.

5 Ink prints of leaves

Place a small quantity of printer's ink on a sheet of glass or a tile. Roll the ink into a thin even layer with a rubber roller. Place a leaf, vein side up, on several layers of news-paper and run the inked roller over it once. Carefully lift the leaf and place it, inked side down, on a sheet of white paper. After cover-ing with a sheet of newspaper roll with a smooth, round bottle. Again remove the leaf carefully and the print is finished.

6 Leaf silhouettes

Place a leaf on a sheet of white paper and hold it securely with thumb or finger. Press a piece

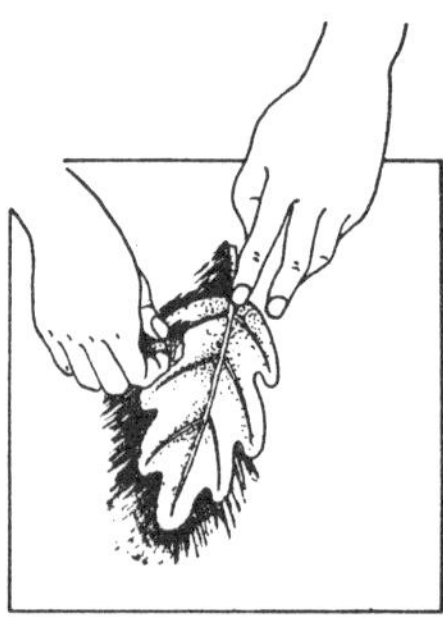

of natural or artificial sponge against an ink pad. With short, firm strokes, rub outward around the entire edge of the leaf as shown in the diagram.

7 Carbon paper leaf prints

Cover the vein side of a leaf with a very thin layer of lard or vaseline. Place the greased leaf vein side up on several layers of newspaper and cover with a sheet of carbon paper. Cover the carbon paper with another sheet of paper and rub across it several times with the side of a smooth pencil, to coat the leaf with material from the carbon paper. To make the final print place the leaf between two sheets of white paper and again rub with the pencil.

8 Studying leaf arrangements

Observe as many growing plants as possible by looking down on them from above. Draw sketches of the different patterns of leaf arrangement.

9 Growing leaves in the classroom

A sweet potato will produce dense foliage in the classroom if it is placed in water. Set the potato, root end down, in a glass or jar and keep the lower third covered with water. The potato may be kept in position by pressing three toothpicks or matches into its side and resting them on the rim of the jar.

The roots of carrots, beets and turnips contain much stored food. They will produce foliage if grown in water but will not develop into new plants. Remove the old leaves from the top and then cut off all the root except 5 to 8 cm. Place this portion in a shallow dish of water. A few pebbles placed in the dish will hold it upright.

Cut off a pineapple 3 to 5 cm below the base of the leaves, and set this portion in a shallow dish of water. The leaves will continue to grow for several weeks.

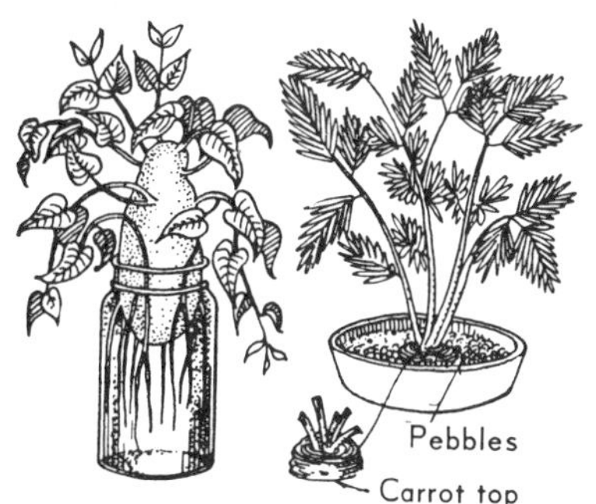

10 Leaves give off water vapour

Use two similar pots of soil, one with a small plant and the other without. Cover the soil in each pot with cardboard as shown in the diagram after watering. Invert glass jars over each pot as shown. Place the pots side by side in the sun and examine from time to time during the day.

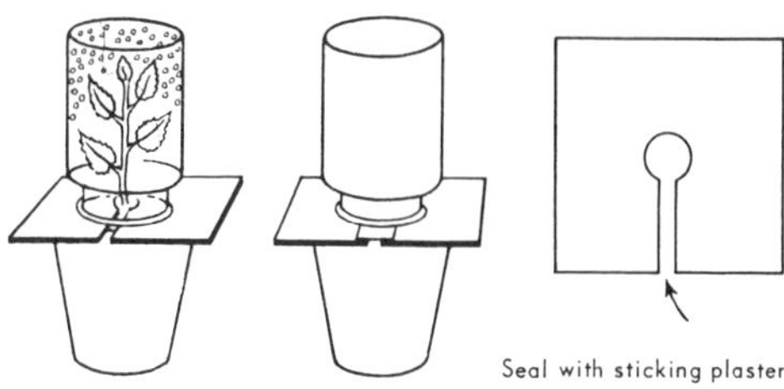

11 The structure of leaves

Borrow a microscope from another school, a doctor, or a hospital. Examine the underside of leaves and locate the breathing pores or stomata with the two little guard cells on either side.

Cut a very thin cross section of a leaf with a razor blade and look at the edge through the microscope. Locate the palisade layer, the epidermis and the spongy layer. You may be able to see a vein and a stomata opening into the spongy layer.

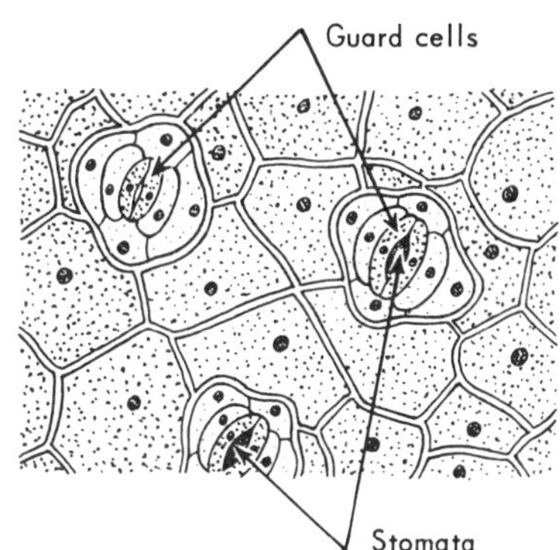

12 Green leaves make food for plants

Heat some alcohol in a jar over boiling water until it boils. Break several green leaves from a geranium or other plant which has been in the sun for several hours, and place them in the boiling alcohol until the chlorophyll has been removed. Quickly remove the leaves from the alcohol and put them in a basin of hot water. Remove a leaf from the water and spread it out on a piece of glass or tile. Cover the leaf with tincture of iodine and leave for several minutes. The deep blue colour is the test for starch which has been made by the leaf in the sunlight.

C. *Leaves*

13 Green leaves give off oxygen in sunlight

Place some water weed under a funnel in a beaker of water. Invert a test tube full of water over the tube of the funnel.

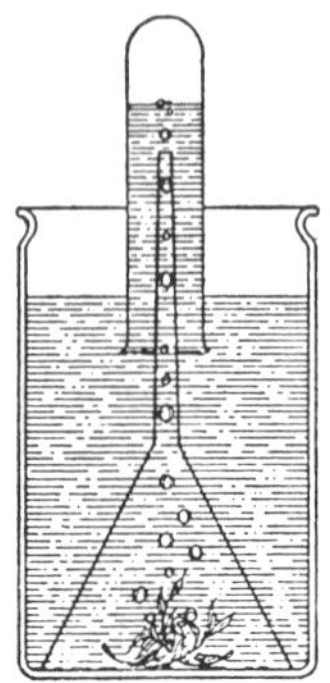

Leave the apparatus in strong sunlight. Bubbles of gas will be liberated from the weed and rise to the top of the test tube. In a short time the tube can be removed and the gas tested with a glowing splint.

14 Air can enter a plant through the leaf

Procure a leaf with a long stalk to it and seal it into a hole through a cork. Fit this with a side tube, and seal the cork into a flask containing water. Suck air from the side tube. Air bubbles will be seen to issue from the end of the stalk.

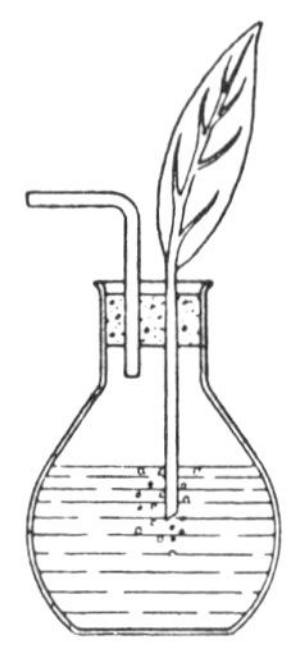

15 To show the respiration of a plant

Place the plant in a test tube held in a weighted wooden block. Put this in a bowl containing lime water and cover the plant with a jar. Keep the plant in a dark place for several hours, or examine next day.

The lime water will be milky showing that CO_2 was given off, and the rise in the level shows that a considerable amount of oxygen was taken in.

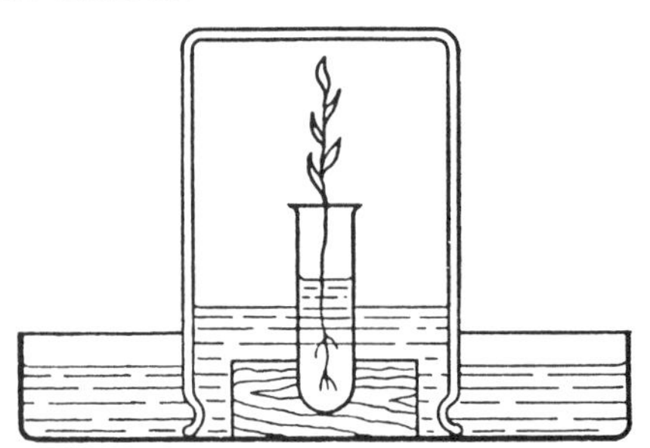

D. FLOWERS

1 Collecting and preserving flowers

Use the same method as described for leaves on page 43.

2 Studying the main parts of a flower

Examine specimens of large simple flowers such as tulips or lilies. Count the stamens and observe how they are arranged about the central pistil. Make large diagrams of the essential organs. Label the parts of the pistil (stigma, style and ovary). Label the parts of the stamen (filament and anther).

The end of the stalk on which the flower grows is called the receptacle. At the base of the receptacle there are usually leaf-like structures that enclose the bud. These are called sepals. Above the sepals there is usually a ring of brightly coloured petals called the corolla.

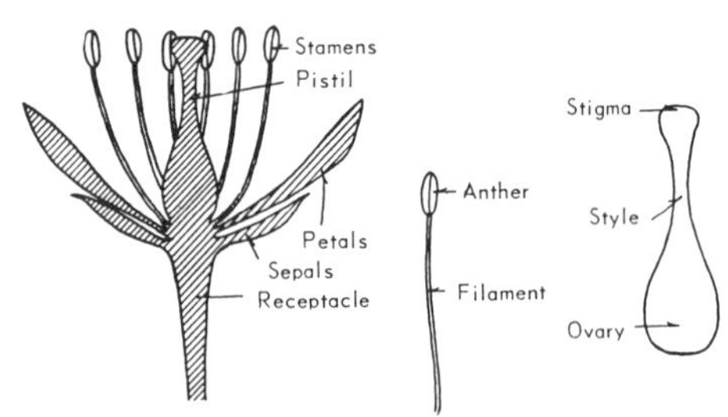

3 Dissecting simple flowers

Label each of five cards or pieces of paper with one of the following words: stamens, pistil, petals, sepals, receptacle. Dissect a flower carefully and place the parts neatly on the appropriate cards.

Some flowers can be pulled apart quite easily but a knife or scissors may be needed for others. If a sufficient number of flowers are available this exercise is most valuable as an individual pupil activity. Simple flowers with a single row of petals should be selected.

Pick up one of the stamens and rub the anther lightly across a piece of black paper. Traces of pollen will usually be seen.

Cut the ovary crosswise with a sharp knife and count the ovules or 'seed pockets'. Look for traces of seeds in the ovules.

4 Observing pollen grains from different flowers

Secure several flowers in which the pollen has formed on the stamens. Shake pollen from each flower on different pieces of black or dark paper. Observe each type of pollen with a magnifying glass and note any differences.

5 Germinating pollen grains

Make a strong sugar solution and place it in a shallow dish like a saucer. Shake pollen from several kinds of flowers onto the surface of the sugar solution. Cover with a sheet of glass and let it stand in a warm place for several hours. If the experiment is successful you will be able to see little tubes growing from the pollen grains. Use a hand lens.

6 Making a model of a simple flower

Using modelling clay, coloured paper and toothpicks make three-dimensional models representing the parts of a typical flower. This exercise is most valuable as an individual pupil activity and should fix firmly in mind the parts of a flower.

To make the flower-stalk roll a piece of modelling clay into the form of a cylinder 2 cm in diameter and about 5 cm long. Press one end firmly against a desk or table and push half a toothpick into the centre of the opposite end as shown in the diagram at *a*.

To make the sepals, cut a six-pointed star from green paper. Cut a hole in the centre at least 1 cm in diameter. Place the sepals in position on the stalk as shown at *b*.

From brightly-coloured paper, cut a corolla of petals. Cut a hole in the centre and set the corolla directly over the sepals as shown at *c*.

From modelling clay shape a pistil in the form of a small urn. Press this over the projecting toothpick to hold it in place, as shown at *d*.

Next, make stamens by putting bits of modelling clay on the ends of toothpicks. Push the toothpicks into the exposed circle of clay at the base of the pistil as shown at *e*.

When the flower model is finished, it can be made to look more realistic by stretching out the stalk with the fingers and bending over the flower head slightly.

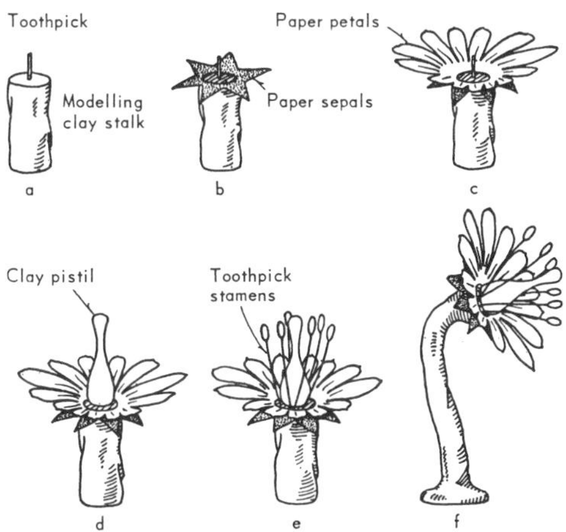

7 A field trip to observe flowers

Plan a field trip to observe flowers in bloom. If no interesting wildflowers can be found growing near the school, the trip can be planned to a private garden or park. Collect some flowers.

8 Observing the development of flowers into fruit

Collect specimens of flowers in different stages of maturity from newly opened buds to specimens in which the petals have fallen. Cut each ovary open and note the changes that take place during seed development.

Look over a quart of freshly picked peas or string beans and pick out the pods that are not completely filled. Open these and compare them with fully filled specimens. The abortive seeds are the remains of ovules that were not fertilized by pollen.

E. SEEDS

1 A useful way to grow seeds

Tie a piece of cloth over the mouth of an old potted meat jar. Allow extra cloth to hang down the sides and dip in about 2 cm of water contained in a jam jar. A sheet of glass placed over the top of the jar will keep the air moist. The seeds are placed on the cloth.

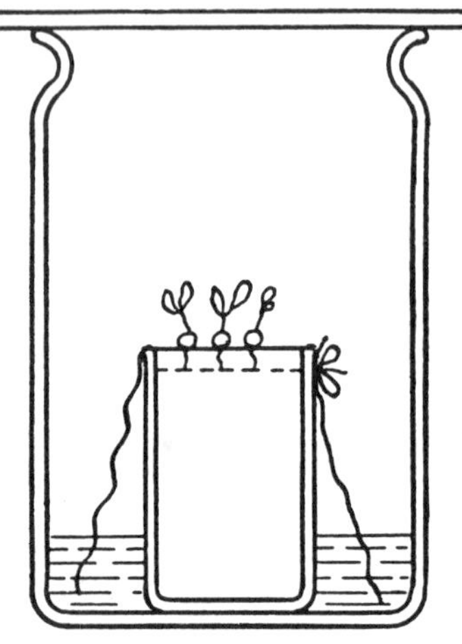

2 A 'rag doll' seed tester

Fold a square metre of muslin twice in the same direction. Near one end mark out eight or ten squares about 5 cm by 5 cm with a pencil. Number the squares and place ten seeds from each packet on each square. Fold the opposite end of the muslin over the seeds. Roll up the tester and tie it loosely with string. Saturate the tester with water. Keep it moist and in a warm place for several days. Then unroll it and see how many of each kind of seeds have germinated.

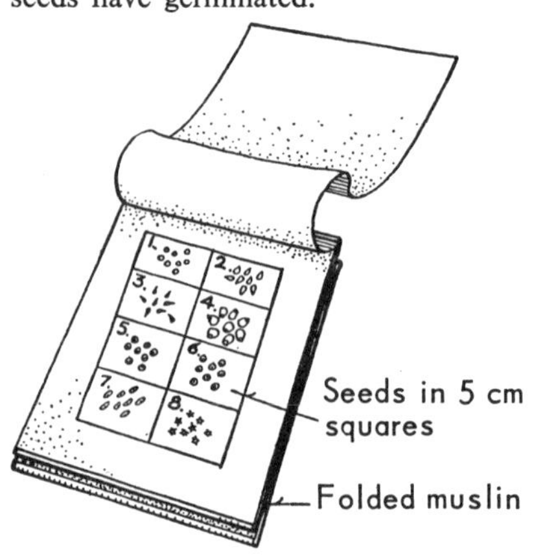

3 A tumbler garden

Grow various kinds of seeds in 'tumbler gardens'. Each pupil might grow a tumbler garden of his own and keep a day by day pictorial record of the development of the seedlings.

To make a tumbler garden cut a rectangular piece of blotter and slip it inside a drinking glass. Fill the centre of the glass with peat moss, cotton, excelsior, sawdust or some similar material. Push a few seeds between the outside of the glass and the blotter. Keep a little water in the bottom of the glass.

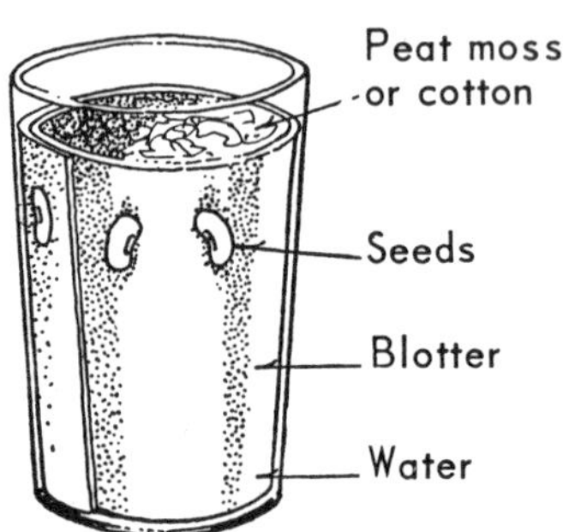

4 To study the conditions essential for the germination of seeds

In the diagram below *a* contains seeds on cotton wool with air, warmth, but no water; *b* has water, warmth, but no air, because a layer of boiled oil has been poured on top of the water; *c* has moistened cotton wool and air but is kept cool by having the test tube immersed in a freezing mixture.

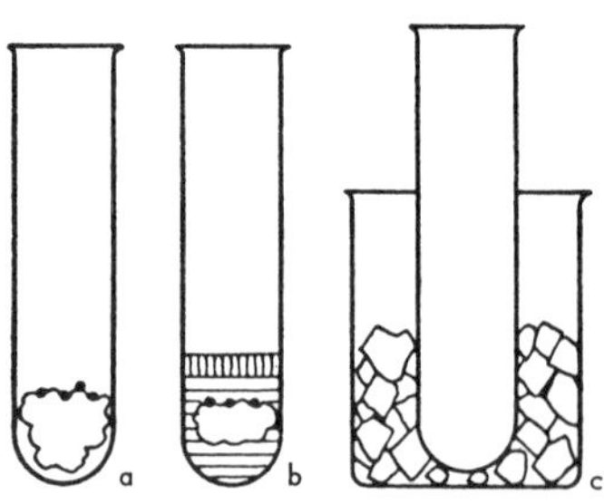

5 To show that growing seeds take in oxygen

Cork up one end of a tube, having first placed inside some damp cotton wool and some mustard seeds. Immerse the open end in dilute caustic soda solution and leave for a few days. The solution will rise up the limb. Removing the cork, and testing with a glowing splint that shows little or no oxygen remains.

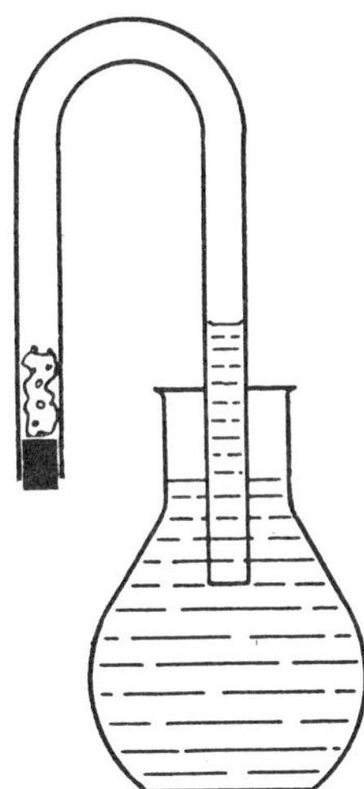

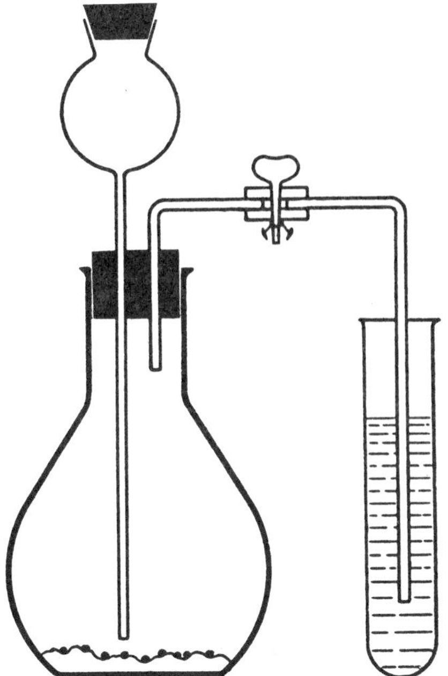

6 To study the structure of a seed

Soak seeds of bean, pea, pumpkin, sunflower, corn and other large forms. Remove the seedcoats and carefully cut the seeds open. Discover the parts that make up the seed. There is little point in teaching the botanical names of these parts though pupils may enjoy learning them. It is of more importance that pupils learn to recognize the part of a seed that is the young plant and the part that is stored food.

7 To test the gas given off when seeds germinate

Place some mustard seeds in a flask with some damp cotton wool, in the apparatus shown in the diagram, and allow them to germinate for a few days. Remove the cork carefully and pour water down the thistle funnel. Open the clip, and allow the displaced air to bubble through lime water. This becomes cloudy, showing the presence of carbon dioxide.

8 To show the direction of sprout growth in seeds

Soak pumpkin or other large seeds overnight and fasten three of them on needles as shown in the diagram. Fasten one with the tip pointing upward, one with the tip toward the side and the third with the tip pointing downward. Keep them in moist air and note the directions in which the sprouts grow.

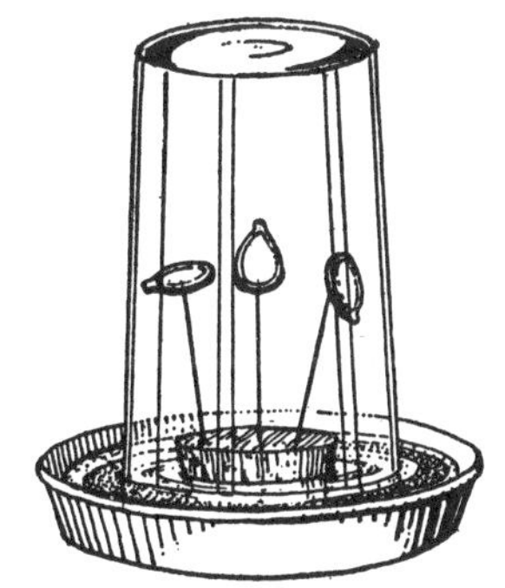

F. BACTERIA

1 Getting ready to grow bacteria

Secure two or three dozen shallow glass dishes. The glass coasters used to keep bed castors from marring floors will do. Cut 5 cm squares of window glass to make covers for the coaster dishes. These will serve very well for bacteria gardens. For beginning experiments slices of potato, carrot, or sweet potato will serve as soil upon which to grow the bacteria. Cut slices of these foods about 6 or 8 mm thick and large enough to fit easily into the dish.

In preparing gardens for bacteria care must be taken to keep everything clean. Wash the food slices thoroughly, wash and dry the dishes and their covers. Place dishes and covers on clean white paper. Be sure your hands are very clean. When all is ready lift the food slices into the dishes with toothpicks or wood splints. Tie the covers on as shown in the diagram. Place the dishes in a large pan and then bake them in an oven at about 110° to 120° C. for an hour. This should kill the bacteria inside the gardens.

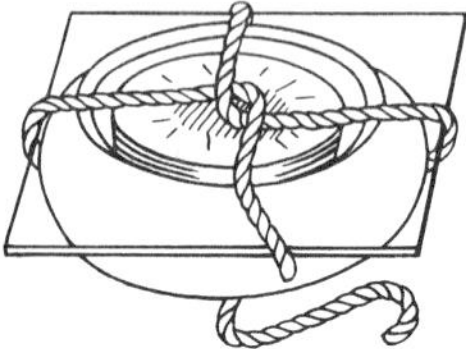

2 Planting bacteria gardens

When the bacteria gardens have cooled place them out on the table but do not raise the glass covers until you are ready to plant them. Toothpicks or small wood splints make good garden tools for planting bacteria gardens. Place 30 or 40 toothpicks in a covered can and bake them in an oven for an hour. This will kill most of the bacteria. When you remove one from the can use tweezers and only touch one toothpick.

Secure bacteria from as many sources as possible. The following will be suggested: (a) a piece of decaying or rotten fruit; (b) a decayed tooth; (c) dirty money; (d) dirt from under finger nails.

Touch the toothpick to the source of bacteria and then quickly raise the cover of a sterile garden. Rub the end of the toothpick over the potato slice and then replace the cover. Be sure to raise the cover as little as possible when planting the garden to keep out bacteria and moulds that are in the air. Tie the covers on tightly again and set the dishes away in a dark, warm place for a few days. When they are examined the bacteria will show as spots on the potato slice. Each spot is a colony of thousands of bacteria.

3 Another type of soil for bacteria gardens

Boil some rice or potatoes in a dish until well cooked. Drain and save the water. Use the water to prepare some gelatin, or agar. Add a pinch of salt and a little beef broth or a bouillon cube to the gelatin. Use the same type of dish and cover as was used above. Pour sufficient of the hot gelatin mixture into each dish to cover the bottom to a depth of 3 or 4 mm. Quickly replace the covers and let the dishes stand until the gelatin has hardened. Tie the covers on and sterilize in an oven. Allow the dishes to cool and the gelatin to reharden before removing from the oven. These bacteria gardens are planted and grown in the same way as the ones described above.

4 Making a transfer needle

A transfer needle which can be sterilized by heating in a flame is useful in working with bacteria. Secure a piece of soft wood about the size of a pencil for a handle. Push the sharp end of the needle well into the wood and use the eye end for contact with bacteria sources.

5 To study whether bacteria grow best where it is moist or dry

Use two sterile dishes. Inoculate each one by touching a sterile transfer needle to a bacteria colony growing in another dish. Smear the material on the needle across the gelatin in each of the two dishes. Quickly replace the covers. Label one dish dry and the other moist. Dry the first dish by placing it on a radiator but covered with a box. Place the one marked 'moist' in a dark warm place but where it will not dry out. Examine the two dishes for several days.

6 To study if bacteria grow better where it is warm or cold

Again inoculate two sterile dishes. Label one 'warm' and the other 'cold'. Place the first dish in a dark warm place and the second in a dark cool place. Examine the dishes each day for several days.

7 To study if bacteria grow better where it is dark or light

Inoculate two sterile dishes as before. Label one 'dark' and the other 'light'. Place the first dish in a dark warm place and the second in bright sunlight or where an electric bulb can shine on it all the time. Examine the dishes daily for a period of several days.

8 Where may bacteria be found?

Expose sterile bacteria dishes to as many of

the following conditions as you can. Label the dishes and set them away in a warm, dark place for a few days after which they should be examined.

1 Clean hands and dirty hands.
2 A dish cloth.
3 A garbage can.
4 Coughing.
5 Sneezing.
6 The bottom of your shoes.
7 A clean dinner plate.
8 A fly.
9 A cockroach.
10 Fur from a dog.
11 The air of the school room.
12 Souring milk.
13 A pencil point.
14 The air in a dirty street.
15 Stagnant water.
16 A rug or carpet.

9 Does sunlight kill bacteria?

Inoculate two sterile bacteria dishes from a dish where bacteria are growing. Place one dish in the open sunlight and the other in a warm dark place. After one dish has been in the sunlight for several hours place it in the dark warm place with the other dish. Examine the dishes each day for several days.

10 Do disinfectants kill bacteria?

Secure several types of commercial and household disinfectants. Inoculate as many culture dishes as you have samples of disinfectant and one dish in addition for a control. Rinse the soil in each inoculated dish with a different disinfectant. Pour off the excess. Label each dish. Replace the covers and set all the dishes including the control dish in a warm dark place and examine after a few days.

11 Observing where soil bacteria live

Dig up a clover, alfalfa or soy-bean plant. Carefully rinse all the soil from the roots and see if you can find the little white nodules on the roots. These are where the nitrogen fixing bacteria so important to soil fertility are found.

G. MOULDS

1 To secure different types of mould

(a) Secure an orange which has green mould on it and keep in a jar in a dark warm place.

(b) Place a piece of moist bread in a jar and expose it to the air. Leave for a few days in a dark warm place.

(c) Secure a piece of blue or Roquefort cheese in which there is mould. Place in a jar and keep in a dark warm place.

(d) Place a few dead flies in some stagnant water. In a few days they will become surrounded with a whitish growth of mould.

2 How to culture mould plants

Use either sterile dishes with potato slices or gelatin as those prepared for the experiments on bacteria. Transfer mould from each of the sources in Experiment 1 above to a sterile culture dish. Set the four dishes aside in a dark warm place. In a few days you should have pure cultures of each of the four types of moulds you have grown.

3 The structure of moulds

When the four pure cultures of mould have reached a vigorous state of growth examine each one with a hand lens. See if you can see the strands which make some moulds appear like spider webs. See if you can find little stalks with tiny black knobs on them. These are the spore cases. Thousands of spores are produced in each spore case which bursts when ripe. A new mould plant can develop from every spore if the conditions are right.

4 Do moulds need water for growth?

Place a spoonful of dry cereal such as rice or oatmeal in a sterile culture dish. Place a like amount of the same cereal cooked in another culture dish. Using a sterile transfer needle inoculate each sample with mould from a growing culture. Cover the dishes and label them. Set the dishes aside in a dark, warm place and observe each one after a few days.

5 Do moulds grow better where it is warm or cold?

Repeat Experiment 4. This time put one culture dish in a warm dark place and the other in a cold dark place. Examine the dishes after a few days.

6 Do moulds grow better where it is dark or light?

Repeat Experiment 4 above. This time leave one culture dish in a warm place where it receives light all the time. Place the other dish in a warm dark place. Examine the dishes after a few days.

H. YEAST

1 To show the effects of yeast on dough

Mix together some sugar, water and flour in the proportions to make a good bread dough. Divide the dough into two equal parts. Stir a half yeast cake in some water and mix this with one of the samples of dough. Put each sample of dough in a dish which has a label and set aside in a warm place. Observe after a few hours.

2 To test the effects of temperature on the activity of yeast

Make up a quantity of bread dough as in Experiment 1 above. Stir a yeast cake in water and thoroughly mix the yeast with the dough. Separate the dough into three equal parts and put in pans or jars. Label samples 1, 2, and 3. Place sample 1 in a refrigerator, sample 2 in a warm place, and sample 3 in a hot place. After a few hours examine each sample.

3 To show that yeast acts on sugar

Make a sugar solution in a jar either with brown or white sugar, molasses or honey. Thoroughly crumble a quarter of a yeast cake into a test tube of the sugar solution. Crumble another quarter yeast cake into a test tube containing the same amount of ordinary tap water. Keep both tubes warm. Observe the tubes from time to time and note any differences in them.

4 To study the gas produced when yeast acts on sugar

Place some clear lime water in a test tube and have a pupil exhale through a soda straw placed in the lime-water. Soon the lime-water will become milky which is a test for carbon dioxide gas. Next place some yeast in a solution of sugar water in a test tube. Fit a one-hole stopper to the tube and put a glass tube through the hole. Connect a rubber tube and another glass tube about 15 cm long to the stopper. Place the long glass tube in a solution of clear lime water. Let the tubes stand in a warm place for a while. Observe the lime water.

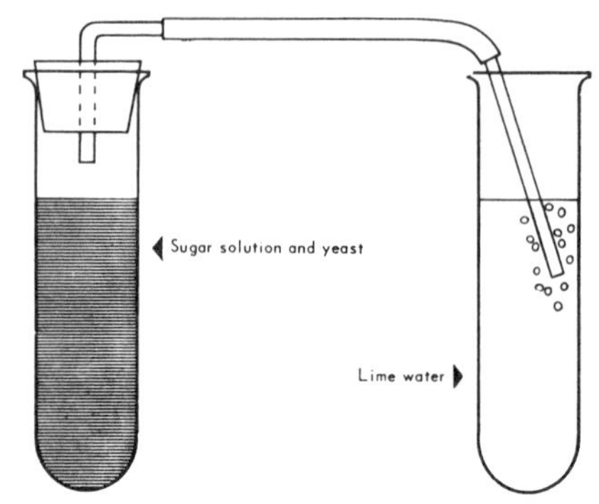

5 To observe yeast plants

Borrow a microscope from a college, a high school, a doctor or a hospital. Place a few drops of the sugar solution which contains yeast on a glass slide and observe it under the microscope. You will see many little oval-shaped cells each of which is a yeast plant. Perhaps you can see some that are carrying buds on them. This is the way that yeast plants reproduce.

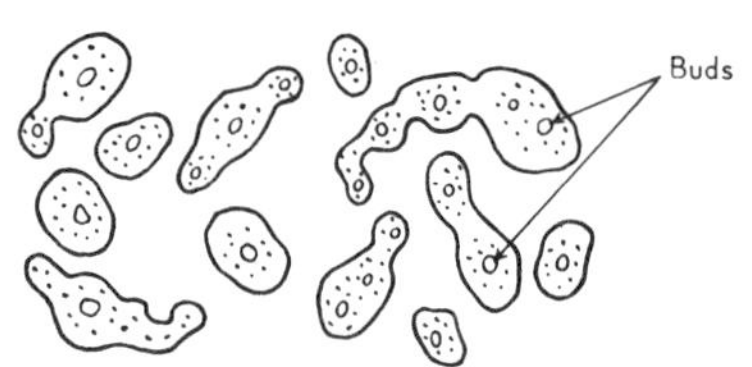

I. GROWING PLANTS WITHOUT SOIL

Some children may be interested in growing plants indoors without soil. This can be done but requires special materials and chemicals. A kit for such experiments has been made up and may be secured from Science Service, 1719 N Street, N.W. Washington D.C., U.S.A. for about $5.

J. SIMPLE GARDENING

Many children are interested in making home or school gardens. Each child should be encouraged to select and clear a small garden plot. After the ground has been spaded and prepared it should be marked off in rows. Such small vegetables as lettuce and radishes may be planted in alternate rows. Each pupil should draw a plan of his garden and mark on it where he has planted various things.

Plants may be started either at home or at school for later transplanting. For this wooden boxes about 10 cm deep will be needed. The boxes are filled to a depth of about 8 cm with good soil. Such seeds as tomato, cabbage, cauliflower and sweet peppers may be started indoors. By the time the lettuce and radish plants have matured, the plants grown indoors will be ready for transplanting into the outdoor garden.

Gardening activities will lead to many worth-while lessons on the growth and care of plants. Later in the year an exhibit of vegetables grown may be planned.

CHAPTER IV

Methods and materials for animal study

1 An insect collecting net

A useful insect net can be made from a round stick such as a broom or mop handle, some heavy wire and mosquito netting or cheese cloth. Bend a heavy piece of wire into a circle about 38 to 45 cm in diameter and twist the ends together to form a straight section at least 15 cm in length. Fasten this to the end of a broom or mop handle by lashing with a wire wrap or by means of staples. Cut a piece of mosquito netting or cheese cloth to form a net about 75 cm deep. Fasten this to the circular wire frame by stitching.

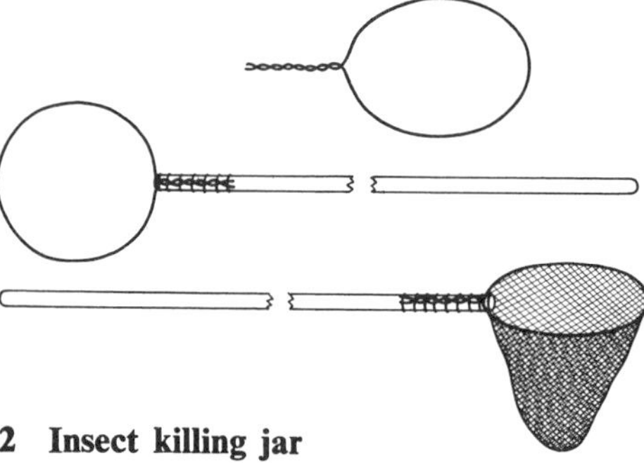

2 Insect killing jar

Secure a wide-mouth glass jar with a screw top or one which closes very tightly. Place a wad of cotton in the bottom and cover it with a round piece of cardboard or blotting paper which has several holes punched through it. When the jar is used saturate the cotton with carbon tetra-chloride (Carbona) or some available insecticide containing DDT. Place the piece of cardboard over the cotton and then put the insect in the jar. Close the jar tightly and leave until the insect has been killed. If moths or butterflies are being prepared be certain that the jar opening is large enough to prevent the tearing of the wings.

3 A stretching board for insects

A stretching board is essential when insects are being prepared for mounting. One can readily be made from a cigar box. Remove the cover from the cigar box and split it lengthwise into two equal parts. Attach these to the box again leaving a space about 1 cm wide between them. The body of the insect is placed in the slot and the wings are secured on the top by means of strips of paper held by pins into the soft wood but not through the wings. Sometimes a slight angle is desirable to the top pieces. This can be achieved by cutting the ends of the cigar box to a slight V form before attaching the sections cut from the cover. This is shown in diagram *b* below.

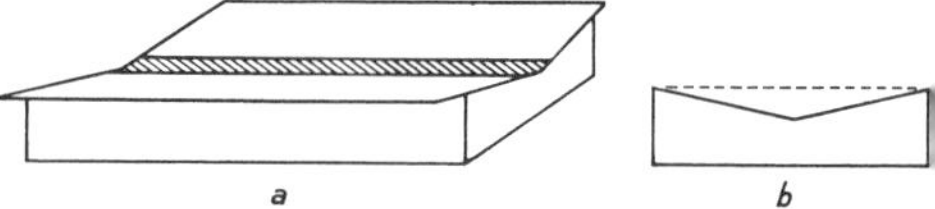

4 Mounting boxes for insect collections

Wood or cardboard cigar boxes make very useful and convenient housings for insect collections. After the insect has been removed from the stretching board a pin is placed through the body and is then stuck into the bottom of the box to hold the insect. The pins are arranged in an orderly fashion and may carry, near the top end of the pin, a small card upon which data about the insect are entered.

Cigar boxes may also be used to mount insects on cotton background. The cover is removed and the inside of the box filled with layers of cotton fluff. Next the insects are arranged on the fluff and then covered with glass or cellophane which is taped to the box making a permanent mounting. This type of mounting box is especially suitable for butterflies and moths or for displays in a school museum.

5 Cages for keeping animals in the science room

It is frequently desirable in elementary and general science to keep animals caged in the science room for short periods of observation. To carry out such activities effectively, suitable cages must be provided. These can be made from a variety of materials found in almost every locality.

One such cage is made from a wood box provided with a hinged cover and having a window covered by wire screening. Windows are also cut in three sides of the box. The side and back windows are covered with wire screen and a glass plate is fitted in the front window. This type of cage can be improved by a drawer which is fitted under the front glass window and which covers the entire bottom of the cage. This enables the cleaning of the cage without disturbing the animals to any great extent.

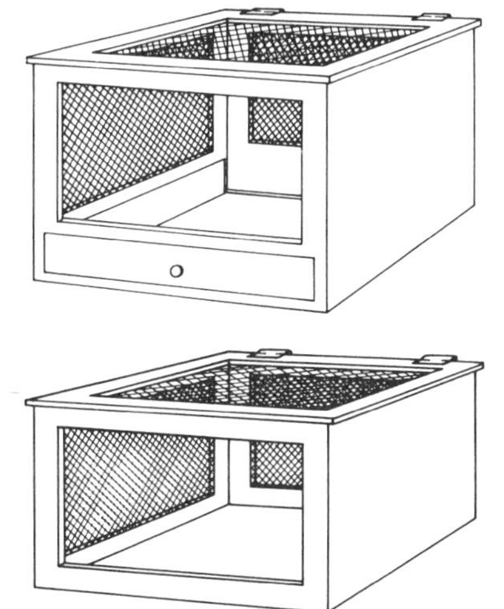

In tropical areas very useful cages can be made using bamboo splints or other wood in place of wire screening.

Providing food and water for caged animals is often a problem. Generally food and water containers should be kept up away from the floor of the cage. A convenient feeding trough for small animals may be made by cutting a section from an ordinary tin can and then attaching this to the side of the cage by means of wires as shown in the diagram. A watering device for such animals as mice, guinea pigs and hamsters can be made from a preserving jar inverted in a heavy dish or soup plate.

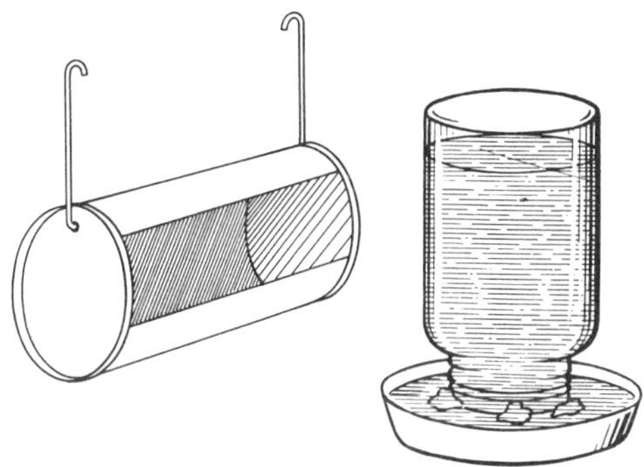

Regular feeding and watering of animals and regular cleaning of the cages are important, not only for the health and comfort of the animals but also for disciplined habits and a sense of responsibility in the pupils. Food and water must be changed daily and cages must be cleaned once a week.

6 A home-made wormery

A wooden box 30 cm by 30 cm by 15 cm fitted with a glass front is useful for studying the habits of earth-worms.

Fill the box nearly to the top with layers of (a) sand; (b) leaf mould; and (c) loam, padding down each layer before adding the next.

Place lettuce leaves, dead leaves, carrot, etc. on the surface soil, together with some worms.

Keep the contents damp and study the behaviour of the worms.

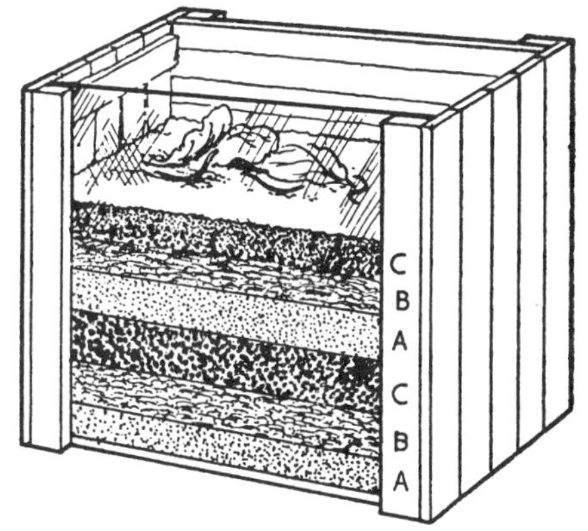

7 Studying life histories of insects

Cut large rectangular holes in the sides of a large cardboard container and cover them with muslin folded over at the edges and gummed or pasted into place. Make a large door by cutting along three sides of a rectangle and bending along the fourth side. Stick a tab of folded paper or cardboard to the front edge of the door to act as a handle. Leave the original bottom of the box intact, to give rigidity. (If cellophane is available a window can be made in the door or in one side of the box.) Put a loose piece of paper on the floor to facilitate cleaning out. Put moist soil into meat paste pots and put cut flowers into it, and stems and leaves of food plants. This is better than pots of water in which the insects may drown.

This cage is suitable for all stages of the life-histories of butterflies, and for moths if larger pots of soil are added, for pupation. The insects can be handled by means of a brush or small stick.

8 Providing for grasshoppers and stick insects

You can keep such insects in an inverted jam jar. They should be provided with a little foliage, which can be stood in a potted meat jar. To give the insect more room, and save it from drowning, the jar can rest on an inverted shoe box with the leaves projecting through what is now the top. Holes should be pierced in the shoe box to ensure a sufficient supply of fresh air.

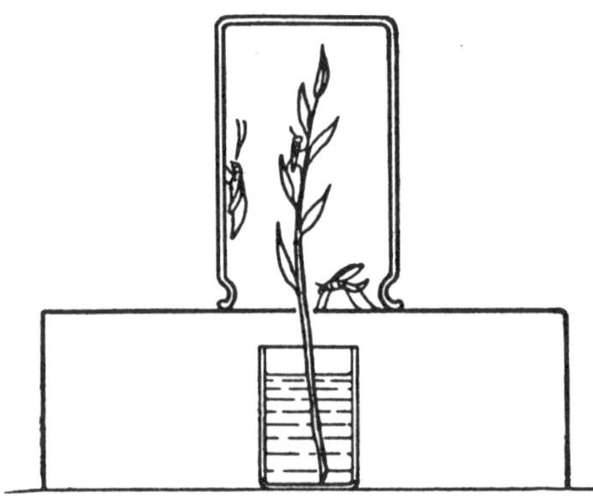

9 A jam jar vivarium for flies

A jam jar can be used to hold a blow fly for studying its life and habits. After the eggs have been laid on a piece of refuse, transfer the fly to another jar and place the eggs in a warm place in the sun or on a radiator. After a week has passed they will hatch out into gentles. In another week's time they will have become chrysalids. A little damp earth or moss introduced now will prevent them from drying up and the complete life cycle can be followed in a few weeks. Later, problems can be investigated. Do they sleep? How do they eat? What are the differences between male and female?

10 Observing spiders

Make use of the fact that many spiders cannot travel over water or a polished surface. Stand a plant in a pot in a bowl of water, or on a polished table. Put two or three sticks or strips of cardboard together, tie them into some sort of polygonal shape and lean this structure against the plant. Put an orb spinner on the plant and it will make a web.

If a few shelves can be removed from a cupboard a large spider such as Epeira diademata (female) can be persuaded to spin a web in it. Put some plants in pots in the cupboards with the spider, and close the door. After a few hours open the door. This will probably break the web, but if the door is now left open the spider will show no desire to escape but will spin another web. If enough insects are not caught, give her daddy-long-legs, caterpillars, moths or flies.

The process of web spinning may be watched, and dated and timed observations made on feeding and other habits.

A 'cobweb spider' can be kept in a large jam jar. A gauze over the top serves to keep in a fly which can be introduced occasionally. Eggs which are laid can be easily observed, as well as the interesting feeding habits.

11 Caring for frogs and toads

Frogs and toads may be kept in an old bird cage. Put in plants and soil, and an empty dish or two for water. Then put a bottle of water through the small door of the cage and fill the dish from it. Feed the frogs and toads on small earth-worms and flies.

Accurate observations can be made on respiratory mechanisms and rates, and on feeding habits. By shading the cage, changes in skin pigmentation can be observed.

Both frogs and toads need continuous shade and must not be kept in bright sunlight. Frogs must have sufficient water in the cage to enable them to swim, but when desired they can be transferred temporarily to a large tank to enable their swimming habits to be observed.

Tadpoles can be kept in glass jars but when nearing metamorphosis should be transferred to a shallow dish with a pile of stones in the middle. The small frogs are not easy to keep and it is better to let them go and keep older frogs as above.

(Galvanized vessels are *not* suitable for amphibia.)

12 Caring for rats

Black and white rats may be kept in old galvanized baths with strong wire-netting covers. The young rats will climb through the wire netting and use the top of it as a playground. They cannot get down if the wire-netting overhangs the sides of the bath by several inches and there is no other support. Put clean sand in the bath to a depth of at least 3 cm. This must be changed daily. It can be washed thoroughly in running water, air-dried and used again. Give the rats clean rags for nesting purposes. These should be boiled or discarded. Alternatively torn up newspaper may be used and renewed when the cage is cleaned every week.

Although rats will eat almost anything, they need a balanced diet. In addition to wheat (or bread) and/or crushed oats they need seeds such as lentils and linseed (or mixed parrot seed), milk or milk powder (except for nursing mothers and young rats which do better on liquid milk). They must also have greenstuff and fruit or fresh vegetables daily, a little salt, and vitamin supplement which may be in the form of seedlings of sunflower, peas, beans or wheat. A little meat twice a week is desirable.

One pair of rats will be enough to begin with, as they breed rapidly.

If well fed and sympathetically handled, they will become quite tame, and will not bite unless they are frightened. They should always be handled by the same people.

Do not attempt to lift a rat by the tail: to pick him up with one hand, lay the palm of the hand across his back and put the thumb and forefinger under his chin, supporting with the other three fingers. Alternatively and preferably cup the two hands round his body.

Observations can be made on habits and breeding. Records of growth can also be kept. Keep a special box in which to weigh the rats. A cardboard box with a deep lid is suitable. Make a number of small holes in the top for aeration. Put a few Helianthus seeds into the

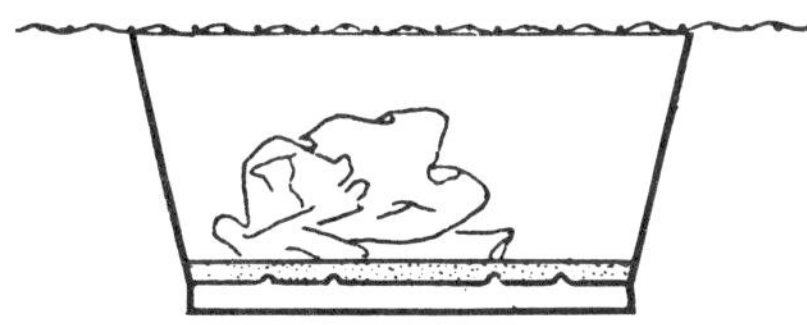

box, and when a rat enters put the lid on. Then weigh rat and box together and subtract the weight of the box. Simple experiments on diet can be done where weight can be used as a criterion. They should be weighed regularly; say, once a week.

Simple Mendelian experiments could be carried out with rats.

When a rat has to be killed for dissection this should preferably be done by enclosing it in a box or lethal chamber and passing in coal gas. Chloroform or ether may be used, but the liquid must not be allowed to cause pain by touching the animal, and there should be sufficient air to prevent suffocation.

Alternatively wrap the rat in a duster including both front legs, hold the head down and strike *very hard* behind the ears with a hammer or stout stick.

Drowning takes a long time and should not be used if it can be avoided. If it must be used, completely submerge a cage containing the rat and weigh it down.

No animal should be reckoned to be dead until stiffness (rigor mortis) has clearly supervened. Otherwise an animal which seems to be dead may later recover consciousness.

13 Making an observation nest for ants

An observation nest for the study of the life story of ants can easily be made as follows.

Make a wooden U from three 30 cm lengths of wood 1.5 cm square. Mount this vertically in a convenient wooden base. Now cut rectangles of glass 30 cm × 33 cm and clamp them on each side of the U with rubber bands or some sort of metal clip.

Make a well-fitting wooden lid to fit the top as shown in the diagram. Drill a 0.5 cm hole about 5 cm from the top of one of the sides and plug it with cotton wool.

The first thing to do in setting up the nest is to fill the space between the glass with soil. This should be taken from the field from which you get the ants themselves.

Pour sandy soil in the top and pat it down occasionally with a ruler until it is about level with the plugged hole.

Now for the ants; small black or red ants are the best for this purpose. They prepare their colonies under flat stones nearly everywhere.

Raise the flat stone and you will see the ants scurrying away. You will need two narrow necked medicine bottles with cotton wool stoppers, a gardening trowel, and a white sheet or large piece of paper.

Lay one of the bottles on the ground and guide the ants to the mouth until you have collected about a hundred: then close the neck with the plug of cotton wool.

Next you must find a queen. To do this dig rather deeply with the trowel and put the earth on the white sheet laid flat on the ground. As you break up the earth with the fingers you will notice one ant much larger than the rest. This is the queen which must be guided to the second bottle: some patience is required here.

To get the ants into an observation nest, fill a large tray with water and place an upturned dinner plate in the middle to form an island from which the ants cannot escape. Place the observation nest on the plate and release the ants either on the plate or straight into the top of the formicarium: once the queen is inside the others will follow through the doorway.

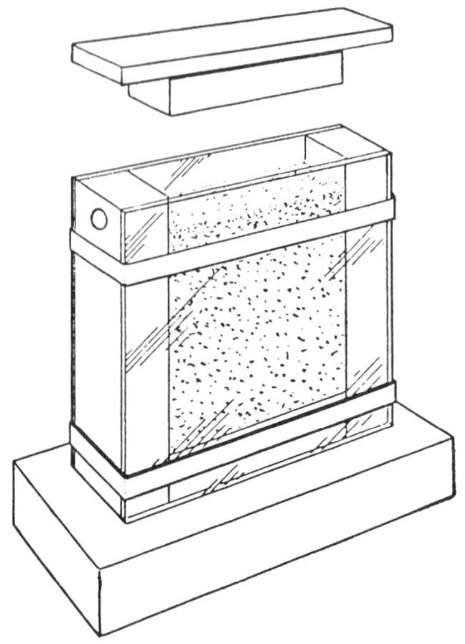

As ants don't like daylight, plug up the hole, fit a brown paper envelope over the case and remove the nest to its permanent home.

A little honey smeared on the glass just inside the door will provide plenty of food, and an occasional sprinkle of water with a fountain pen filler will keep the soil moist.

The exciting happenings inside the nest, the laying of the eggs, the grubs and the way the ants have of talking to each other by tapping each other on the head with their antennae, can all be studied in artificial light which does not disturb them, and as the tunnels must run parallel to the glass these things are all quite easily seen.

Experiments such as the removal and subsequent return of a few ants; the introduction of foreign ants, green flies, spiders, etc., are all most fruitful.

Once the nest is settled and the queen begins laying eggs the cotton wool plug from the doorway can be removed. Place the observation nest near a slightly open window and the ants will come and go freely for a whole year.

14 Making a jam jar aquarium

If a large glass tank is not available, practically any glass vessel can be used as a simple aquarium if it is well stocked with submerged water plants such as Elodea or Myriophyllum, to aerate the water. A 1 kg jam jar is quite suitable for keeping caddis larvae, pond snails, small crustacea and plants such as Elodea and Lemna minor, and will keep in properly balanced condition for months if carefully stocked. It is as bad to understock as it is to overstock. The aquarium should require no attention, but if a Dytiscus or other predaceous larva is kept it should be fed regularly on tadpoles. Three centimetres of clean sand will provide hibernating quarters for the caddises at the bottom of the jar, and a muslin cover will ensure that the caddis flies do not escape unobserved.

A diary should be kept, to record egg laying and other changes, as well as habits.

Such an aquarium can be made the basis for a simple study of the interrelationship between plants and animals in pond life.

For collecting pond and stream specimens a strong net can be made from a soup strainer if one is available. Its handle should be firmly bound to a stick, the tape being threaded through the handle repeatedly. The tape must be liberally smeared with rubber solution if available, and then tied tightly and the knot smeared too.

15 An aquarium for larger water animals

A glass aquarium 50 cm by 25 cm is of useful size. Old accumulator cells are suitable, but the glass is not very clear.

To prepare such an aquarium procure some fine silt from the bottom of a clear stream or pond and wash it carefully in running water. Cover the floor of the aquarium with it to a depth of about 2 cm. Plant a few reeds in this, weighting the roots with a stone or lead ring. Then put in a layer of coarse sand or gravel and some large stones to serve as hiding places for the water insects. Fill with a slow stream of water and allow to stand for a day or two until clear. Clean water plants should be introduced. There is no need for elaborate aerating arrangements if plenty of water weeds are present. If tap water is used some live food such as daphnia should preferably be added.

The animals can now be introduced with a few snails to keep the grass clean. Very little feeding will be necessary. Fish will eat the snails' eggs and enough small water organisms can be found in the average pond to supply other needs. If worms are used as food they should only be given once a week cut in pieces small enough to be eaten. Any unconsumed food should be removed immediately or fungi will grow and will infect the fish.

The aquarium must be covered with a glass plate or perforated zinc lid to keep out dust. If frogs or newts are kept, a floating piece of cork must be provided for them to sit on; the glass or zinc cover will then prevent their escape.

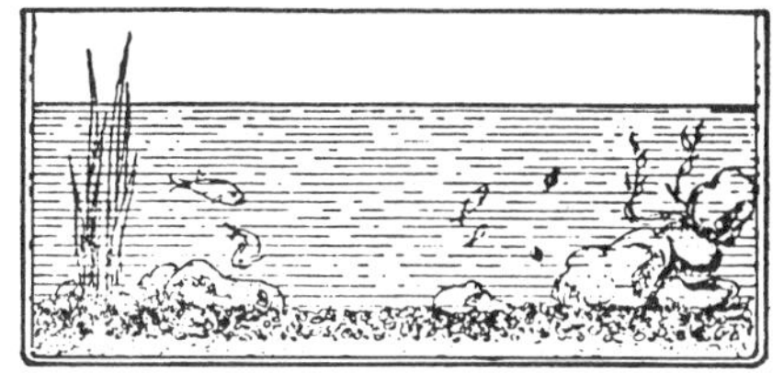

16 Observing the life cycle of fruit flies

Small glass jars make excellent habitats for fruit flies. Place a bit of ripe fruit in the bottom of the jar and make a paper funnel with a hole in the end to fit the mouth of the bottle. Place the bottle in the open; and when six or eight fruit flies have entered, remove the funnel and plug loosely with cotton wool. With this number of flies there should be both males and females. The females are larger with a broader abdomen. The males are smaller and have a black-tipped abdomen.

Soon eggs will be deposited, and in two or three days the larvae will hatch. A piece of paper may be placed in the jar for the larvae to crawl on when they are ready to pupate. The adult insects will come from the pupae. By adding newly hatched flies to another jar a new generation can be started.

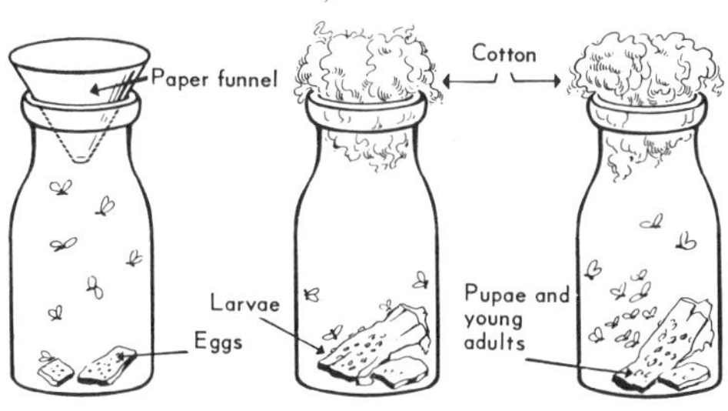

17 The incubation of chicken eggs

If electricity is available in your classroom a simple incubator can be made at a very low cost. Secure two cardboard boxes, one large and one small. Cut one end from the small box, and cut a 15 cm square window in a side of the large box. Next cut a slit in the top of the smaller box and suspend an electric lamp in it. There should be a long electric cord attached to the lamp.

Place the small box inside the larger one and pack crumpled newspaper between them on all sides. Be sure the open end of the small box fits against the side of the large box in which the window was cut. Place a thermometer in the box so that you can read it through the window. A glass plate is fitted over the window.

Now you are ready to begin to experiment. It is necessary to have a constant temperature of 103° F. (40° C.) night and day for 21 days. By using different bulbs and by changing the amount of newspaper you will be able after a few days to regulate your incubator to this temperature. A small dish of water should be placed in the incubator.

Now secure a dozen fertile eggs. Place the eggs in the incubator and leave them. At the end of three days remove one of the eggs and carefully crack it. Dump the contents into a shallow saucer. A three-day embryo will usually show the heart already beating. It may continue to beat for half an hour. Remove an egg every three days and observe the development of the embryo. Some of the eggs can be left for the full 21 days to see if any of them will hatch.

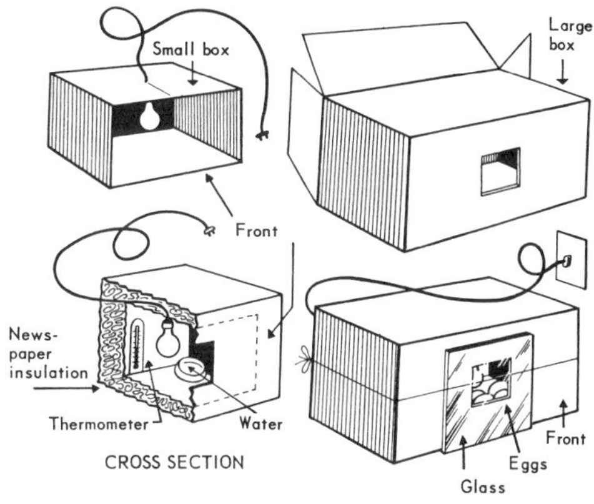

18 Snakes

Non-poisonous snakes can be brought into the classroom for observation. The diagram shows how a safe cage can be made for keeping a snake. The bottom should be covered with sand and gravel. A shallow pan of water should be placed in the cage. Some stones and a forked branch are also desirable. If snakes are kept in a glass tank, this must be protected from strong sunlight.

When a snake is observed outside it should be approached very quietly. If a snake is to be handled hold it securely just behind the head with one hand. Do not hold it too tightly. Support the rest of the body with the other hand. Snakes may be fed on earthworms, many kinds of insects, eggs or small bits of meat. A snake usually will not feed every day. Some will not eat at all in captivity. Often snakes do not eat for several weeks. If a snake does not eat it is best to let it go.

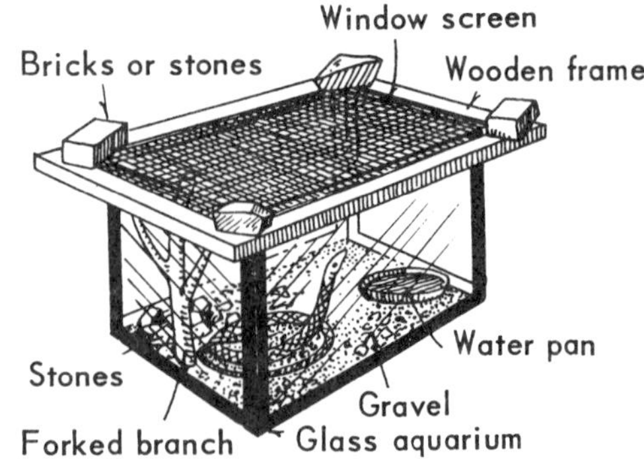

CHAPTER V

Experiments and materials for the study of rocks, soils, minerals and fossils

Rocks, soils, minerals and fossils are always of interest to children. Since samples are to be found in almost every environment, they can make a very important contribution to the teaching of science. The teacher should not feel it necessary to be able to name every specimen brought in by pupils; such classification and naming is the job of a trained geologist. Much can be learned about rocks and minerals without becoming involved with technical names. For additional information on rocks and minerals see Appendix C.

Some rocks are rough and gritty and appear to be composed of sand grains cemented together. *Sandstone* is a good name for such rocks. Another group of rocks appear to be made up of tiny flecks and crystals something like granite. These rocks may be called *granite-like* rocks. Other common rocks are *slate*, *limestone* and the soft, layered *shale* that often appears along the banks of streams. This simple vocabulary, while not technically complete, will serve very well for identifying and classifying most of the common rocks.

Rocks are generally classified into three great groups in accordance with the way in which they were formed.

1 *Sedimentary rocks* were formed under water from mud and silt deposited by rivers. These rocks often appear in layers. Examples are shale and limestone.

2 *Igneous rocks* were formed by the cooling of molten materials. Lava, quartz and mica are good examples of igneous rocks.

3 *Metamorphic rocks* were formed under great heat and pressure from both sedimentary and igneous rocks. Examples of this type are marble formed from limestone and slate formed from shale.

A. ROCKS AND MINERALS

1 Making a rock collection

A collection of the common rocks found in the community can be made by asking each pupil to bring in one piece of rock. Explain to the pupils that it will not be necessary to know the names of all the rocks. Similar specimens may be placed together on a table. Divide the collected rocks into groups based on differences of shape, colour and other characteristics. Try to find as many ways as possible of grouping the rocks.

2 Studying a single rock

Select a single rock and try to learn as much as possible about it from careful observation. If it is flat, it is probably a piece or layer from some sedimentary formation. Such rocks were formed by the hardening of sediments laid down millions of years ago. If the rock appears to be made of fine sand grains cemented together it is probably sandstone. If it is made up of larger pebbles cemented together, it is probably another sedimentary rock called *conglomerate*. If the rock appears to be rounded, it is probably the result of the stream action of water. Examine the rock with a magnifying glass. If it contains little flecks and crystals, it is a granite-like rock and was probably pushed up from deep in the earth long ago. Careful observation of several rocks in this manner will interest pupils in their further collection and study.

3 Making individual rock collections

Pupils should be encouraged to make their

own collection of rocks. Small pasteboard or cigar boxes will serve to keep the collections. The specimens may be kept separate by putting partitions in the boxes. As a pupil identifies the rocks in his collection, he should cut small pieces of paper or adhesive tape and fasten one to each rock. Place a number on each and then paste a list on the cover of the box. It is a good idea to have the collections kept small. Pupils may be encouraged to fill out their collections by trading samples with other pupils.

4 A study of broken rock

Break open several rock specimens. Compare the appearance of freshly broken surfaces with the weather-worn outside of the rock. The rocks may be safely broken by wrapping in a cloth, placing on a large rock, and striking hard with a hammer. The cloth wrapping will prevent small chips from flying off.

5 The test for limestone

You can test the rock samples to see if any are limestone by dropping lemon juice, vinegar or some other dilute acid on them. If any are limestone they will effervesce or bubble where the acid is placed on them. The bubbling is caused by carbon dioxide gas which is given off by limestone when in contact with acid. Marble, a metamorphic rock made from limestone, will also respond to this test.

6 Studying broken rocks with a magnifying glass

Study freshly broken rocks with a magnifying glass and try to find crystals of different minerals. The crystals of different minerals will differ in size, shape and colour.

7 Examining sand with a magnifying glass

Examine a small amount of sand with a magnifying glass or under the low power of a microscope if there is one available. The nearly colourless crystals are those of a mineral called *quartz* which is the commonest mineral on earth. Crystals of other minerals can often be found in sand. See if you can find any others.

8 The meaning of 'rock' and 'mineral'

Develop the meaning of these two terms through a study of the specimens collected. A rock is usually regarded as mineral matter found in the earth in large quantities. Most rocks are mixtures of minerals although some kinds consist of a single mineral. A mineral is a substance found naturally in the earth which has a definite chemical composition and a set of specific and characteristic properties.

9 A field trip to a rock quarry

The quarry should be visited by the teacher in advance. Observe how the rock is removed. If the rock is sedimentary, observe the layers. Collect rock samples to take back to the classroom for study. Look for fossils of any plants or animals. A field trip may also be planned to an exposed rock cut or ledge and to a coal mine if there is one nearby.

10 Mounting rock and mineral samples

Samples of rocks and minerals can be mounted neatly for a collection by making a base from plaster of Paris. The white powder is mixed with water to form a thick paste. This paste is put in a tin can cover about 1 cm deep which has been lined with wax paper or greased. Before the plaster hardens the small rock or mineral sample is pressed far enough into the surface so that it is held firmly but so that it can be seen well. The name of the material can be printed on the white base and then the base can be coated with clear shellac or varnish.

B. ARTIFICIAL ROCKS

1 Cement and concrete

Secure a small bag of Portland cement. Have the pupils mix it with water and put it in tin can covers, paper cups, or small pasteboard boxes until it hardens. Study its appearance and its properties. Break a piece of cement and study it. Mix the dry cement with about twice as much sand or gravel. This will form concrete. After adding water and mixing thoroughly place it in moulds. Allow these to harden several days. Again study the appearance and the characteristics of these samples.

2 Plaster of Paris

Secure some plaster of Paris and mix a small amount with water. It must be worked rapidly or it will harden while being mixed. Place the mixture in moulds and let it set until very hard. Study the appearance and properties of the samples.

3 Collections of building materials

Collect samples of all the different types of rock or mineral building materials available in your locality such as marble, granite, slate, limestone, brick, cement, plaster, etc. These may be added to your collection after proper labels have been attached to the samples.

C. ELEMENTS AND COMPOUNDS

1 A collection of elements

Obtain a table of the elements and make a collection of samples of as many as you can. You should be able to obtain samples of the following: iron, aluminium, zinc, tin, copper, lead, gold, silver, mercury, sulphur. See Appendix C.

2 A collection of common chemical compounds

Collect samples of as many common chemical compounds as you can. The following are suggestions: salt, sugar, starch, soda, copper sulphate, bleaching powder, plaster of Paris, rubber, wool, cotton, etc.

D. MAKING A MODEL VOLCANO

Secure from a chemical supply house 500 g of ammonium bichromate, 125 g of magnesium powder and 30 g of magnesium ribbon. The total cost of these materials will be about $2.50 and will provide from 30 to 40 volcanic eruptions.

Have the children collect some ordinary clay. Use a board for a base and with the clay, build a volcanic cone about 30 cm high and 60 cm in diameter at the base. Push a piece of broomstick down into the tip of the cone to a depth of 5 to 7 cm.

On a piece of paper pour out enough of the ammonium bichromate to fill the hole in the cone about twice. Do not grind up the crystals. The lumps work better. Mix a little magnesium powder with the bichromate crystals and carefully stir with a pencil.

Pour about half of the mixture into the cone of the volcano. Cut a 7.5 cm length of magnesium ribbon and push one end into the mixture in the cone. Let the other end stick out the top for a fuse. Light the magnesium ribbon with a match and step back. If the eruption does not take place the first time wait a few moments, insert another fuse and try again. After the eruption has occurred, but while the material left in the cone is still hot, pour in the remainder of the mixture, and you will have a second eruption.

E. SOIL

1 Types of soils

Secure samples of soil from as many places as possible and place in glass jars. Try to get examples of a sandy soil, a loam soil, a clay soil, a soil rich in decayed matter or humus. Have the pupils study the samples and examine bits from each sample with a magnifying glass.

2 To show the differences in soil particles

Secure some glass jars that hold about a half gallon or two litres of water. Place several handfuls of soil in a jar. Fill the jar with water and then thoroughly shake up the soil in the water. Let the jar stand for several hours. The heaviest particles will settle out first and the lightest ones last. The layers in the jar after settling will be in the order of the weight of the soil particles. Siphon the water from the jar with a tube. Next examine a small sample from each of the layers with a magnifying glass.

3 To show that soil contains air

Place some soil in a glass jar or bottle and

slowly pour water over it. Observe the air bubbles that rise through the water from the soil.

4 To show how soil is formed from rocks

Carefully heat a piece of glass in a flame and then plunge it into cold water. The sudden cooling of the glass causes it to contract unevenly, and it cracks. Heat some rocks very hot in a fire and then pour cold water on them. The rocks will often break up both when heated and when cooled. One of the stages in the formation of soil is the breaking up of rocks under differences of temperature.

5 What makes streams look muddy?

After a heavy rainfall have pupils take samples of running muddy water in glass jars. Let the water stand for several hours until the sediment has settled and may be observed by the pupils.

6 Making soil from rocks

Find some soft rocks in your locality such as shale or weathered limestone. Bring them into the classroom and have the pupils crush and grind them up into small-sized particles.

7 The effect of soil on growing things

Get samples of a fertile soil from a flower or vegetable garden, from a wood, from a place where a cellar is being dug, from a sandy place, from a clay bank, etc. Place the samples in separate flower pots or glass jars. Plant seeds in each type of soil and give each the same amount of water. Observe in which type of soil the seeds sprout first. After the plants have started to grow, observe the soil sample in which they grow best.

8 To show that soil may contain water

Place some soil in a thin glass dish and heat it cautiously over a small flame. Cover the jar and water will be observed to condense on the cool sides.

9 To study the difference in fertility between topsoil and subsoil

Secure a sample of good topsoil from a flower or truck garden. Secure another sample of soil from a depth of about 50 cm. Place the samples in separate flower pots and plant seeds in each. Keep the amount of water, the temperature and the light equal on each sample. See which soil produces healthier plants.

10 To show the presence of nodules of nitrogen-fixing bacteria on the roots of legumes

Carefully spade up some leguminous plant such as clover, alfalfa, soy-beans, cow peas, etc. Remove the soil from the roots by washing with water. Observe the little white bumps or nodules on the roots. Nitrogen-fixing bacteria are inside these nodules. These bacteria remove nitrogen from the air and fix it in a form that enables plants to get it from the soil.

11 To show how water rises by capillarity

Colour some water in a shallow dish with ink and touch a blotter to the water surface. Observe how the water rises in the blotter.

Touch a lump of sugar to the water surface and observe how the water rises.

Place a lamp wick in the water and observe.

12 To show how water rises in fine tubes

Make some fine hair, or capillary tubes by heating glass tubing in a flame and drawing it out. Cut the tubes and glue them to a piece of cardboard with about 5 cm extending below the edge. Place the ends of these tubes in coloured water and observe how the force of capillary attraction causes the water to rise.

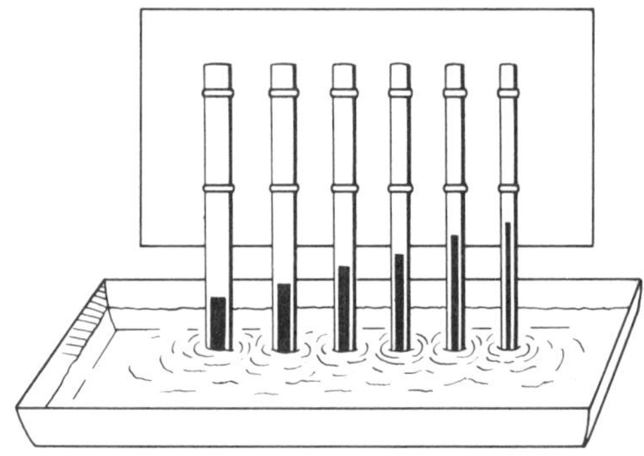

13 To show how water rises in different types of soil

Place about 15 cm of different types of soil in a series of lamp chimneys after tying a piece of cloth over the end of each chimney. Such soil samples as sand, loam, gravel (fine), clay, etc. may be used. Next stand the lamp chimneys in a pan which contains about 3 cm of water. Observe the type of soil in which water rises highest due to capillarity. Clear plastic drinking straws can also be used for this experiment.

14 To show which types of soil hold water best

Tie cloth over the end of several lamp chimneys and then fill each one to within 8 cm of the top with different types of soil. Use sand, clay, loam and soil from the woods. Place dishes under each chimney to catch water which runs through. Next pour measured amounts of water into each chimney until the water begins to run through. Observe the soil type into which the most water can be poured without running through.

15 The effect of rain on loose soil

Make a sprinkling can by punching holes in the bottom of a tin can with a hammer and small nail. Fill several flower pots or cans with loose soil and press it down until it is even with the edges. Place some coins or bottle tops on the surface of the soil. Set each pan in a basin and sprinkle with water from your can to represent rain. First sprinkle lightly and note the effects of a light rain. Continue sprinkling to illustrate a heavy rain. Notice how the unprotected soil is splashed away leaving columns of soil under the bottle caps and coins.

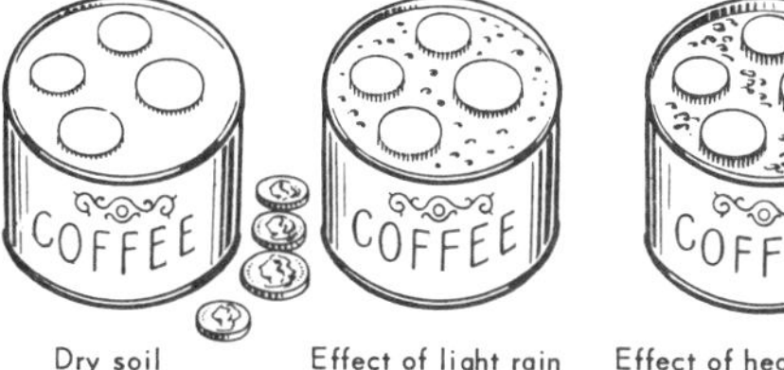

Dry soil Effect of light rain Effect of heavy rain

16 The effect of rain on sloping soil

Fill a shallow pan or box with firmly packed soil. Set the pan outside in the rain with one end raised slightly. Observe how the raindrops splash the soil down toward the lowered end. This experiment can be done inside by using the sprinkling can for rain.

17 To show the impact of a raindrop on soil

Place a saucer or jar lid filled with soil on a piece of white paper. Fill a medicine dropper with water and hold it about a metre above the soil. Release water a drop at a time and observe how much soil is splashed out on the paper. Place a clean sheet of paper under the saucer. Again release drops but hold an obstacle such as a pencil in the path of the drop to break the force of the raindrop. Do plants prevent the wearing away of the soil in this way?

18 How the effect of raindrops on soil varies

Fasten a sheet of white paper to a piece of stiff cardboard with paper clips. Lay it flat on the floor. Drop coloured water on it with a medicine dropper. Note the size and shape of the splashes. Repeat but this time prop up one end of the cardboard. Study the effect on the splashes of varying the height from which the water is dropped, of varying the slope and the size of the drops. Try different combinations of the variables. A record of the results may be kept if a clean sheet of paper and different coloured water is used for each situation.

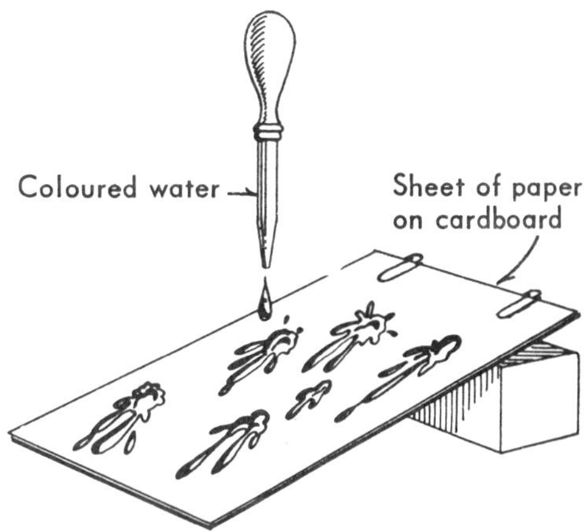

19 The effect of falling water on topsoil

Fill a flower pot with sandy soil or loam. Set the pot under a dripping tap for an hour or more. Observe how the clay and inorganic matter are removed from the surface by falling drops.

20 The effect of rain on unprotected surfaces

Build up a pile of sand and clay in a box or pan. Sprinkle gently near the top with water from the sprinkling can. Note the way the running water transports the rock particles and deposits them near the bottom of the pile.

21 How running water wears away the soil

Construct the two trays as shown in the drawings below. Putty in the cracks will make them water-tight. Pails or glass jugs with funnels may be used to collect the run-off water.

(a) Fill one tray with loose soil and the other with firmly packed soil. With both trays slightly tilted, water each the same amount with a sprinkling can. Observe which soil is moved away faster and the nature of the run-off water.

(b) Fill both trays with soil but cover one with sod. Water equally as before and observe both the erosion and the run-off water.

(c) Fill both trays with soil but give one more slope than the other. Water and observe as before.

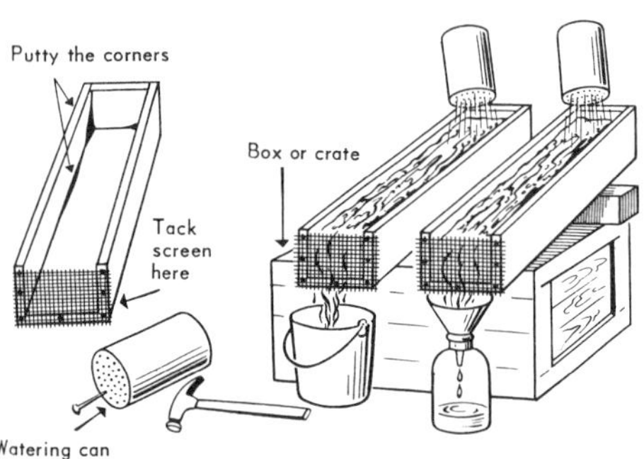

22 How to prevent the erosion of topsoil

Use the trays constructed for the experience above.

(a) Fill the trays with loose soil and tilt each one the same amount. Make furrows with a stick running up and down the hill in one box and across the hill in the other box. Sprinkle each the same amount. Observe the erosion in each case and the run-off water.

(b) Again fill the trays with loose soil. Water them until there are well-defined gulleys formed from the running water. Now block the gulleys at intervals with small stones and twigs. Again water and observe the effect of blocking the gulleys.

23 A field trip to study erosion

Find some place in the locality where running water has done damage by cutting gulleys. Take the class to study the erosion. Why was it caused? How could it have been prevented? What can still be done?

24 Conservation on the school grounds

Almost every school yard will have some place where running water has done damage. Enlist the class in a project to decide upon means for preventing the erosion and then let them carry out their project.

F. FOSSILS

1 Where to find fossils

In some localities fossils may be found in stone quarries or where there are rock outcrops. Try to find someone in the community who knows about fossils and then plan a field trip with the class to collect some of them.

Fossils can often be found by breaking lumps of soft or bituminous coal apart. Break the lumps carefully and examine the broken surfaces for imprints of leaves and ferns.

If there are no fossils in your community, you may have to depend on state or national museums to send you a few. A letter to the state or national museum may prove helpful.

2 How fossils were formed

Cover a leaf with vaseline and place it on a pane of glass or other smooth surface. Place a circular strip of paper or cardboard around the leaf. Press modelling clay against the strip to hold it firmly. Now mix up some plaster of Paris and pour it over the leaf. When the plaster has hardened, you can remove the leaf, and you will have an excellent leaf print. Some fossils were made this way—by having silt deposited over them, which later hardened into sedimentary rock. Repeat this experience using a greased clam or oyster shell to make the imprint.

3 How to mount fossils

If you happen to live in a locality where fossils are plentiful, it will be interesting to have the pupils make a fossil collection for the school museum.

Fossils can be neatly mounted in plaster of Paris by following the instructions given for mounting rocks and minerals in section A 10 of this chapter.

CHAPTER VI

Experiments and materials for astronomy

Astronomy is always an interesting topic for children in the elementary school as well as for young people studying general science. In many places the basic concepts of astronomy are taught descriptively—that is, the children merely read about them. In this chapter many experiments are suggested to enable the teacher to develop some of the concepts from observation and experiment.

No attempt has been made to grade the experiments. It is suggested rather that teachers select those experiments that seem most appropriate for the topics being taught.

A. OBSERVING THE STARS

1 Making a simple refracting telescope

To make a simple telescope, two cardboard tubes will be required, one fitting inside the other.

It is not possible to make a satisfactory telescope unless good lenses are available, a fact which was soon discovered by early experimenters.

A linen tester (sometimes a stamp magnifier also) has lenses which are achromatic, that is corrected for colour distortion. Such a lens of focal length 2 or 3 cm will provide a suitable eye-piece when mounted in a cork with a hole in it.

It is equally important that the object glass should be achromatic for best results. If such a lens is available with a focal length of 25 to 30 cm it should be fixed in the wider cardboard tube by plasticine. A little adjustment is required to get both lenses on the same geometrical axis. When this has been achieved and the focusing done by sliding the tube, it is a superior instrument to the one with which Galileo made all his discoveries.

Jupiter's moons are readily observed with this apparatus, but not Saturn's rings.

2 Making a simple reflecting telescope

A simple reflecting telescope can be made from a concave mirror obtained from a shaving mirror. The mirror is arranged in a wooden box of suitable size in such a way that it can be tilted at different angles. An upright made of wood is attached to the box so that its angle may also be varied. Two short focus lenses are fixed in corks which are then placed in a short length of mailing tube as an eye-piece. Then attach this eye-piece attached to the wood upright exactly at the focal distance away from the mirror.

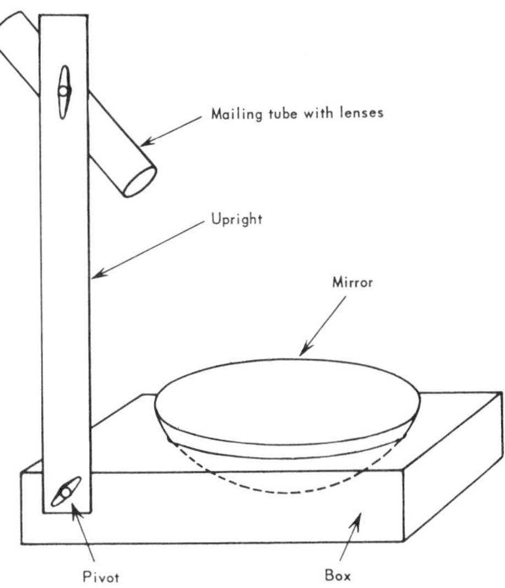

3 Making a precision reflecting telescope

It is quite beyond the scope of this book to include the intricate details for mirror grinding and testing. However, some teachers may wish to have able pupils engage in making a better telescope. Attention is therefore directed to the excellent book called *Amateur Telescope Making* published by the Scientific American Publishing Co., New York City, N.Y.

4 Learning to recognize the main constellations and making a star map

This is a convenient home task, and is best done about the time of a new moon. The moonlight does not then interfere with a good view of the stars. The Pole Star should be identified first, and it is helpful to take outside a piece of brown paper with pinholes pricked through it in the form of a few of the constellations. When the paper is held up to any light the pinholes become visible, and the paper can be rotated until a similar star pattern is recognized. A star map, with the Pole Star as centre, can soon be built up.

After a few constellations have been learnt in this way, it is instructive to make one map in the early evening, and one just before going to bed. Another interesting way of recognizing constellations is to take outside a blackboard and stick into it luminous (phosphorescent) buttons to represent the stars.

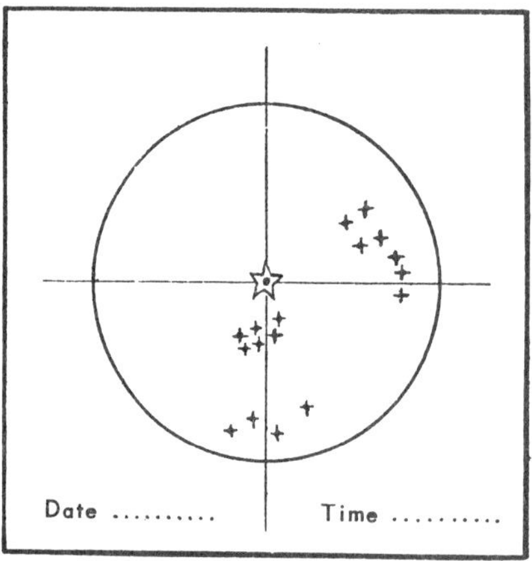

5 Photographing star 'trails'

A very interesting activity for pupils who have cameras is the photographing of star trails as the earth revolves. Select a clear moonless night for this and find a place where there is an unobstructed view of the horizon. The place selected should be away from extraneous light such as automobile headlights, etc. Face the camera as directly at the Pole Star as possible and secure it either with a tripod or with blocks of wood. If the camera is the focusing type, set the lens at infinity and open the diaphragm full. The shutter should be set for a time exposure. When all is ready open the shutter and leave it open any length of time from one to six hours. The longer it is open the longer will be the star trails. Try photographing stars in the Milky Way.

6 How to make a constellarium

A constellarium is a simple device used in teaching the shapes of various constellations. Get a cardboard or wood box and remove one end. Draw the shapes of various constellations on pieces of dark coloured cardboard large enough to cover the end of the box. Punch holes on the diagrams where the stars are located in the constellations. Place an electric lamp inside the box. When the lamp is turned on and various cards are placed over the end of the box, the constellations may be seen clearly.

Another way is to secure several tin cans into which an electric lamp will fit. Holes are punched in the bottoms of the cans to represent the stars in various constellations. When the lamp is placed inside a can and turned on, the light shows through the openings and the shape of the constellations may be observed. The cans may be painted to prevent rusting and kept from year to year.

7 How to make an umbrella planetarium

Since an umbrella has the shape of the inside of a sphere it can be used to illustrate portions of the heavens. Secure an old umbrella that is large. With chalk mark the North Star, or Polaris next to the centre on the inside of the umbrella. Use a star map and mark the star positions for various constellations with crosses. When you have filled in all the polar constellations you can paste white stars made from gummed labels where the crosses are; or you may paint the stars in with white paint. Later you can make dotted lines with white paint or chalk to join the stars in a given constellation.

B. THE SUN AND THE STARS

1 A chart of the constellations of the zodiac

The constellations of the zodiac are found along the ecliptic, in a belt 16 degrees wide. This belt can be subdivided into 12 sections each subtending 30 degrees, and including a constellation called a sign of the zodiac.

The sun has one of these behind it when it rises in each month of the year, e.g. about 21 March Aries is behind the sun at sunrise; a month later, the sun rises in Taurus, etc.

Spring signs	March	1 Aries.
	April	2 Taurus.
	May	3 Gemini.
Summer signs	June	4 Cancer.
	July	5 Leo.
	Aug.	6 Virgo.
Autumn signs	Sept.	7 Libra.
	Oct.	8 Scorpio.
	Nov.	9 Saggitarius.
Winter signs	Dec.	10 Capricorn.
	Jan.	11 Aquarius.
	Feb.	12 Pisces.

The charts display the whole of the constellations. The dates round its edge show when that part of the heavens is due north at midnight. The actual stars visible would be contained in a circle having a diameter slightly less than three-quarters of the whole chart, and so placed on the chart that it is on the opposite edge to the date required. The diameter of the chart being 11 cm, it is a good practice to cut an 8 cm circle of transparent paper, draw a diameter on it as a north to south

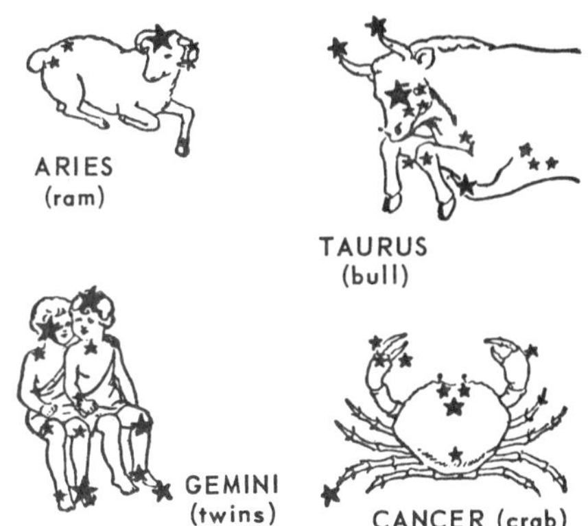

guide, and lay it on the chart to show what area is visible at midnight on a given date. The diameter should cross the Pole Star, and point to the date. There will be a gap between the edge of the paper and the edge of the chart, and it will be found that the Pole Star is always half-way between the centre of the transparent disc and its momentarily northern edge.

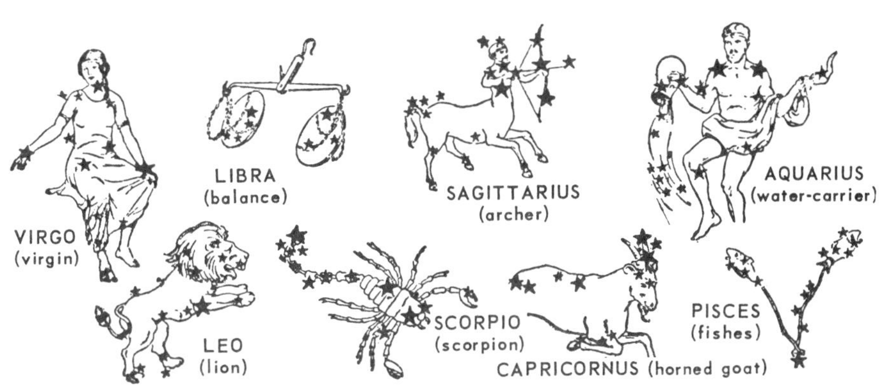

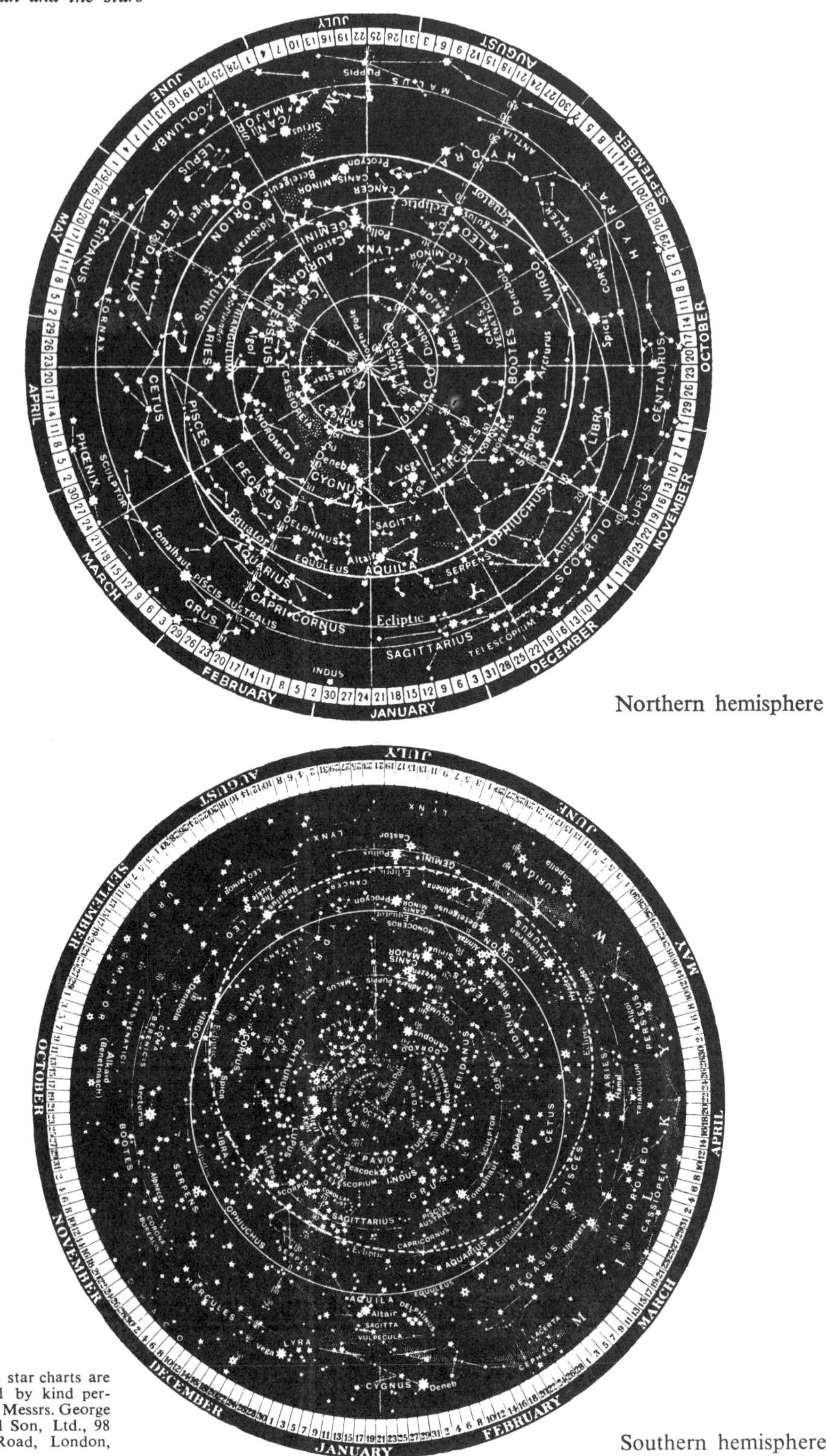

Northern hemisphere

Southern hemisphere

The above star charts are reproduced by kind permission of Messrs. George Philip and Son, Ltd., 98 Victoria Road, London, N.1.

2 A model to show the apparent path of the sun among the stars

The signs of the zodiac are drawn in the correct order on a strip of paper about 60 cm long and 8 cm wide. The ends of the paper are then gummed together making a continuous loop with the zodiacal constellations inside. The loop is then stood edgewise and gummed in a circle about 18 cm diameter to a cardboard base. A short candle placed at the centre represents the sun. The seasons corresponding with the signs of the zodiac are marked on the baseboard outside. A chestnut or other object hung from a piece of cotton will rotate as the cotton unwinds and serve to represent the rotating earth.

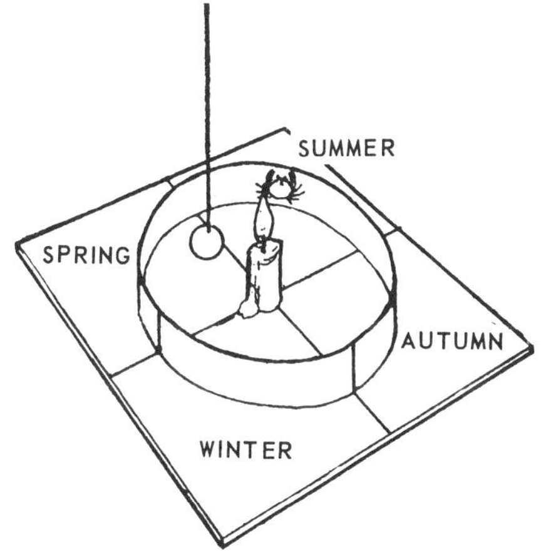

3 A model illustrating how an eclipse appears

The sun is represented by an opal electric bulb shining through a circular hole 5 cm in diameter in a piece of blackened cardboard. The corona is drawn in red crayon around this hole. The moon is a wooden ball 2.5 cm diameter mounted on a knitting needle. The observer views the eclipse through any of several large pin holes in a screen on the front of the apparatus. The corona only becomes visible at the position of total eclipse. The moon's position is adjusted by a stout wire bicycle spoke attached to the front of the apparatus.

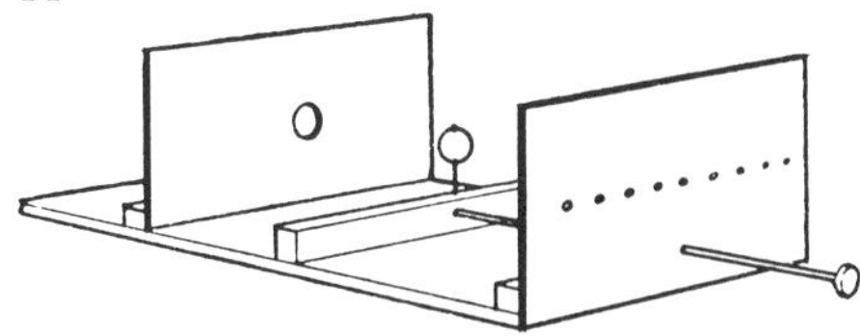

4 Illustrating an eclipse of the sun

Hold a small coin a few inches from one eye and close the other eye while looking at the lighted electric bulb on the ceiling of a room. The large bulb is far away and represents the sun. The small coin is close to your eye and represents the moon coming between the sun and the earth. You will observe that the small coin completely hides the light bulb on the ceiling and casts a shadow on your eye.

5 Observing sun spots

Use the telescope that you made in a previous experiment. Set it up so that it points directly at the sun and focus it so that a clear and bright image of the sun is formed on a piece of white cardboard placed a short distance from the eyepiece lens. If sun spots are present on the surface of the sun you may be able to observe them as small dark spaces of irregular outline on the image.
Caution. Do not look at the sun through the telescope, unless your eyes are protected by a dark glass filter.

6 Observing changes of position of the earth with respect to the sun

Mark a line on the floor or the wall where the sun shines in your room. Note the exact month, day and hour. At the end of each week make another line at exactly the same hour. Repeat this throughout the year and you will have some interesting observations. The variation in position of the line from week to week and from month to month is caused by the movement of the earth around the sun.

C. EXPERIMENTS RELATED TO THE SOLAR SYSTEM

1 Making a model of the solar system

The concepts of the relative size and distance of the planets from the sun can be illustrated by having pupils make a model of the solar system. This can be done by using various sized balls, for the sun and planets, by making clay models or simply by cutting circles of the proper size from cardboard. These can be arranged either on the wall, on the floor or on the blackboard where the orbits of the planets can be marked off with chalk. The table below gives the data necessary for making a model to scale.

Data on planets	*Mercury*	*Venus*	*Earth*	*Mars*	*Jupiter*	*Saturn*	*Uranus*	*Neptune*	*Pluto*
Average distance from the sun in millions of miles	36	67	93	141	489	886	1 782	2 793	3 670
Diameter in miles	3 000	7 600	7 900	4 200	87 000	72 000	31 000	33 000	?

2 Observing visible planets

By using a good star map the planets visible at different times of the year can be easily identified by the teacher. Pupils should be taught to identify the planets and to be able to tell them from the brighter stars. Children always enjoy an evening of observation. Make use of the telescope described on page 67 or a pair of field glasses.

3 Watching for 'shooting stars'

A good time to watch for meteors or 'shooting stars' is in August or November. Have the children keep watch of the evening sky and report any observation they make.

D. EXPERIMENTS RELATED TO THE EARTH

1 A Foucault pendulum to show the rotation of the earth

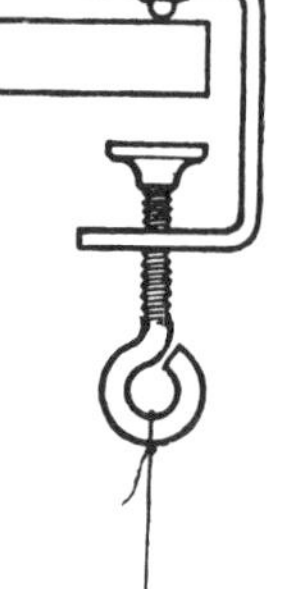

A G-clamp with a ball bearing soldered to the inside of the jaw makes a good support for a Foucault Pendulum.

It is best hung indoors with the ball bearing resting on a stout razor blade or some other hard surface. When such a pendulum is set in motion, the plane of swing is altered after a few hours, as will be noticed if a mark is made on the ground at the time of release. It is, of course, the earth rotating underneath the 'bob' which gives this effect.

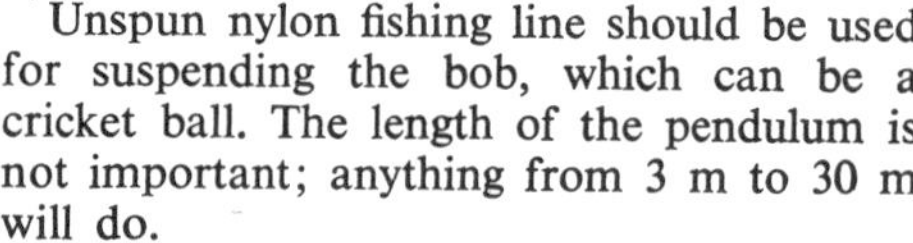

Unspun nylon fishing line should be used for suspending the bob, which can be a cricket ball. The length of the pendulum is not important; anything from 3 m to 30 m will do.

Care must be taken that the pointer, a short knitting needle driven into the ball, is continuous with the suspending thread.

A reference line drawn on a piece of white card can be fastened to the floor with drawing pins. This must be positioned accurately under the pointer when the ball is at rest.

To set the pendulum in motion, attach a long cotton thread to a tintack driven into the bob, and align it so that it lies along the direction of the reference line; then burn the thread near the tack.

It is not easy to get good quantitative results without many refinements, but it is not difficult to observe the effect.

2 A simple theodolite or astrolabe

A simple theodolite or astrolabe is made by fixing a drinking straw to the base line of a protractor with sealing wax or glue.

A plumb line hung from the head of a fixing screw will ensure that the supporting pole is upright and will serve also to measure the angle of the star or any other object.

An improved model for finding latitude, and the bearing of a star from the N.S. meridian can be made by fixing the rod to a

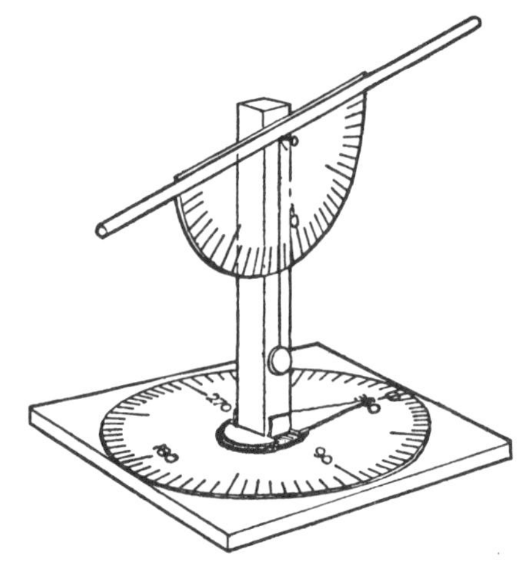

baseboard with a screw. Two coins with holes in the centre can be used as washers and a piece of tin fixed to the rod will indicate the angle on a horizontal scale. It is with such rough apparatus as this that many early discoveries were made.

3 A model sextant

A simple sextant can be devised using cork, glue, pins, glass tube, sealing wax, etc.

The cork is slightly cut away at one end so that the base line of the protractor is parallel to a diameter when in position. A stout pin stuck through the centre of the protractor serves as an axis on which the moving mirror can turn. A piece of glass tubing drawn out to fit the pin serves as a hinge when stuck to the mirror slip (7 cm by 1 cm). The silvering is removed from all except the first centimetre of the mirror slip, and the remaining clear glass acts as an arm to the instrument and indicates the angle on the protractor scale.

The fixed mirror is fastened by wax in a slot made in the protractor with a heated piece of wire or knitting needle. It is convenient to make this slot 45 degrees to the vertical. Half the silvering is scraped off this mirror so that the horizon can be observed through the straw or glass sighting tube which is fixed with wax parallel to the base line of the protractor.

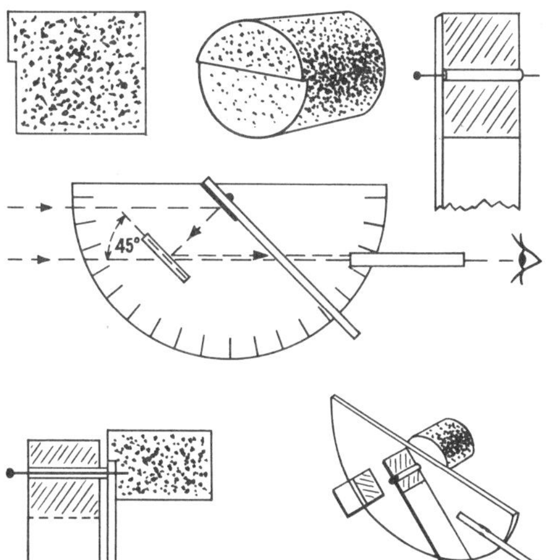

In use the instrument is held by the cork in the right hand, and the arm is adjusted until the two images of the horizon, seen in the clear and silvered half of the fixed mirror, are continuous. The angle indicated by the clear glass arm is then recorded.

The arm is now moved until the image of the sun or other object seen in the silvered half of the mirror rests on the horizon viewed directly through the clear half.

The angle moved through by the arm is half the altitude of the sun. A smoked eyeglass or a piece of gelatine filter may be needed if the sun is too bright.

Similar slips of glass mirror can be supported perpendicular to a drawing board by large pins stuck through the glass tubing. They are then useful for studying the paths of rays of light through the mirror system of a sextant, using beams of light or pins to track down the paths of particular rays.

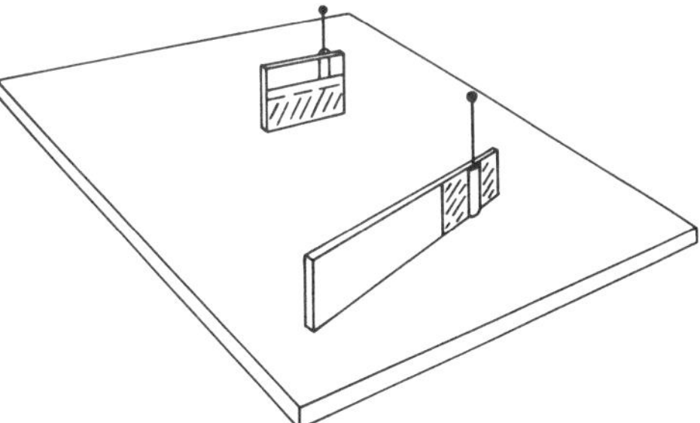

4 Making a sun-dial

To withstand all weather, a sun-dial should be made of metal or painted wood. A cardboard model can be made for simple experiments.

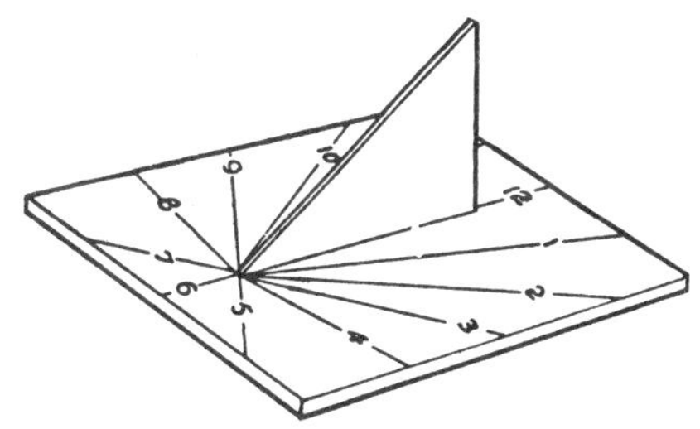

The gnomon which casts the shadow is a right-angled triangle with base angle equal to the latitude of the place at which it is going to be used.

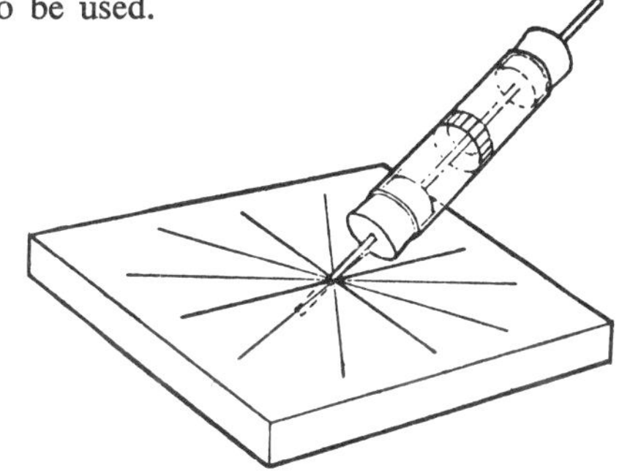

This is glued in position so that the hypotenuse points to the North Star. The hours can then be marked off on the baseboard.

Another pattern can be made if glass tubing about 4 cm in diameter is available.

In this case the gnomon is a stout knitting needle fixed to the base at an appropriate angle. The scale, which is divided into 24 equal parts, is stuck round the circumference of the glass tubing and the shadow of the knitting needle indicates the hour. The glass tubing is held in position by corks.

This type of sundial is not satisfactory in areas lying between latitudes 15° N. and 15° S. of the equator.

5 A simple model of the earth and moon

The earth can be represented by an orange or other round object stuck on a piece of bamboo or a meat skewer. A piece of bent wire or knitting needle stuck through the shaft will support a round chestnut or small nut to represent the moon. The phases of the moon, and the rotation of the earth round the sun, and also the formation of eclipses can be illustrated by holding it in the hand while walking in a circle round a lamp of some sort.

6 Demonstrating the cause of seasons

Use a hollow rubber ball such as a tennis ball to represent the earth. Push a 15-cm length of wire or a knitting needle through the ball to represent the earth's axis. Draw a circle about 40 cm in diameter on a piece of cardboard to represent the earth's orbit.

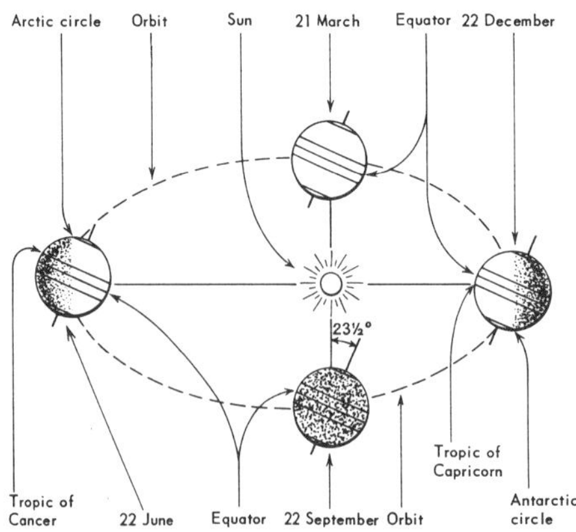

Mark the four quarter points north, south, east and west. Hang an electric lamp about 15 cm above the centre of the cardboard to represent the sun. A lighted candle may also be used. Place the ball representing the earth successively at the four positions with the axis slanted about 23.5 degrees. Observe the amount of the ball that is always illuminated. Observe where the direct rays of the sun strike. In each of the four positions observe which hemisphere receives the slanting rays of the sun.

Repeat the experiment with the needle perpendicular to the table top in each of the four positions and observe what would happen if the axis of the earth were not inclined.

7 Demonstrating the cause of difference in length of day and night in some places

Use the same apparatus as in 6 above. Mark a circle on the ball around its centre to represent the equator. Place dots on the ball to represent cities on the equator, in the northern hemisphere and in the southern hemisphere. Place the ball at each of the four positions again but this time rotate the earth on its axis in each position and observe how long the various city positions you have marked are in the light and how long in shadow. Can you observe when each pole has six months of day and six months of night?

8 Demonstrating the effects of the angle of the sun's rays on the amount of heat and light received by the earth

Bend a piece of cardboard and make a square tube 4 cm² in cross section and 32 cm in length. Secure a piece of very stiff cardboard and cut a strip 23 cm long and 2 cm wide. Paste this to one side of the tube with 15 cm extending. Rest the end of the stiff cardboard on the table and incline the tube at an angle of about 25 degrees. Hold a flashlight or lighted candle at the upper end of the tube and mark off the area on the table that is covered by the light through the tube. Repeat the experiment with the tube at an angle of about 15 degrees. Repeat again with the tube vertical. Compare the size of the three spots and determine the area of each. Is the amount of heat and light received from the sun greater when the rays are slanting or direct?

9 Making a shadow stick

In an open space on the school ground drive a 130 cm stick into the ground and let the children keep a record of the length of the shadow, measured two or three times a day at different seasons of the year.

10 Demonstrating how the angle of the sun's rays changes from day to day at the same hour

Cut a 1-cm round hole in a piece of paper or cardboard. Place this in a south window of your classroom where the sun's rays will shine through the hole and strike a piece of white paper on the floor, the table or window sill. Draw the outline of the spot where the beam of light strikes the paper. Write the date and hour inside the outline. Repeat this on succeeding days at exactly the same hour.

E. EXPERIMENTS RELATED TO THE MOON

1 Observing the surface of the moon

Use the small telescope described on page 67 or a pair of field glasses. Study the surface of the moon and see if you can see any of its craters and mountains.

2 Observing the phases of the moon

Over the period of a lunar month have the children make nightly observations and sketch drawings of the moon. Begin at new moon and continue through the four phases.

3 Demonstrating the cause of the phases of the moon

Place a lighted candle or electric lamp on a table in a darkened room. Paint an 8 cm rubber ball white. Hold the ball in your hand at arm's length with your back to the light. Raise the ball enough above your head to allow the light to strike the ball. Note the part of the ball illuminated by the candle. This represents the full moon. Now turn around slowly from right to left keeping the ball in front of you and above your head. Observe the change in shape of the illuminated part of the ball as you make one complete turn. Do you see the various phases of the moon? Now repeat the turning but stop at each one eighth turn and have someone else draw the shape of the moon (ball) that is illuminated.

4 Demonstrating an eclipse of the moon

Use a flash light or a lighted candle in a darkened room to represent the sun. Hold an 8 cm rubber ball in one hand to represent the earth. Hold a 2-cm ball in the other hand to represent the moon. Hold the ball representing the earth in the beam of light from the flash light and observe the shadow cast by the earth. Next pass the smaller ball or moon behind the earth into the shadow. The moon will be in eclipse while it passes through the earth's shadow.

CHAPTER VII

Experiments and materials for the study of air and air pressure

We live at the bottom of an ocean of air which is one of the essentials for life. Man also makes use of air pressure in many of his daily tasks. Air and air pressure should be a subject of study for every boy and girl.

A. TO SHOW WHERE AIR MAY BE FOUND

1 Plunge a narrow-necked bottle, mouth down into a jar of water. Slowly tip the mouth of the bottle toward the surface of the water. What do you observe? Was the bottle empty?

2 Place a lump of soil in a container of water and observe. Did you see anything that might indicate the presence of air in the soil?

3 Secure a brick and place it in a container of water. Is there any evidence that air was inside the brick?

4 Fill a glass with water and observe it closely. Let the glass stand in a warm place for several hours. Observe again. What difference do you see? Is there any evidence that water contains air?

B. TO SHOW THAT AIR TAKES UP SPACE

1 Secure a bottle and a funnel. Place the funnel in the neck of the bottle. Fill the space around the funnel with modelling clay. Be sure to pack the moist clay tightly in the neck of the bottle. Pour water slowly into the funnel. What do you observe? What does this show about air?

2 Repeat experiment 1 above and pour water into the funnel until it comes nearly to the top. Carefully punch a hole through the modelling clay into the inside of the bottle with a nail. What did you observe? Why did it happen?

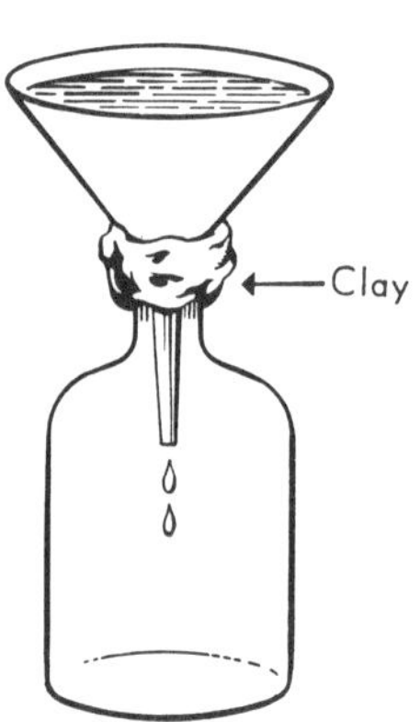

3 Float a cork on a large glass jar half full of water. Lower a drinking glass, mouth downward over the cork. What do you observe? Wedge a piece of paper tightly into the bottom of the glass and repeat. Does the paper get wet?

4 Secure an aquarium or a big water bowl and fill it nearly full of water. Lower a drinking glass, mouth downward into the aquarium. With your other hand lower another glass into the aquarium. Let this glass fill with water by tilting its mouth upward. Now hold the second glass above the first one mouth downward. Slowly tilt the first glass to let the air escape slowly. Fill the second glass with air from the first glass. What does this show about air?

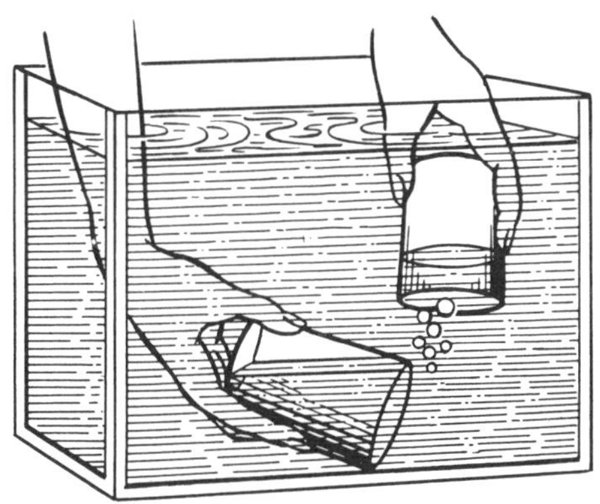

5 Place a tall glass jar in the aquarium. Let it fill with water and stand, mouth down, on the bottom. Place a rubber tube or a soda straw under the edge of the bottle and gently blow into the tube. What does this show about air?

6 Invert a tall glass jar filled with water in a shallow pan of water. This may be done by first filling the jar, placing a piece of glass or cardboard over the mouth and then inverting it in the pan of water. Remove the cover under the water in the pan. Raise

the edge of the jar a little and place the end of a medicine dropper under it. Squeeze the bulb of the medicine dropper and observe what happens. This may be repeated several times. What does this show about air?

7 Secure a bottle with a tightly fitting cork or rubber stopper. Fill the bottle with water except for a small bubble of air. Turn the bottle on its side and try to make the bubble of air disappear by pressing on the cork. What do you observe? What does this show about air?

C. TO SHOW THAT AIR HAS WEIGHT

1 Drive a thin nail through the exact centre of a long rod such as a metre stick or a yard stick. Balance the stick by resting the nail on the rims of two drinking glasses. Make a rider out of a short length of wire and place it on the end of the stick which needs weight to balance. Move the rider until the stick balances perfectly. Hang a rubber balloon and a rubber band on one end of the stick. Now counterbalance the balloon exactly with some weight on the other end of the stick. Mark the place on the stick where the balloon and counter-weight were placed. Remove the balloon and inflate it, using a bicycle pump. Close with the rubber band. Next hang the balloon and counterweight exactly where they were before. What do you observe? What does this show about air? It must be remembered however, that the balloon increases in volume and so *displaces* more air. The resulting increased buoyancy complicates the experiment, but an increase in weight can be observed if the balloon is blown up hard. This difficulty can be avoided if a metal hot-water-bottle fitted with a cycle valve is used instead of the balloon.

D. TO SHOW THAT AIR EXERTS PRESSURE

1 Fill a drinking glass to the brim with water. Place a piece of cardboard over it. Hold the cardboard against the glass and turn the glass upside down. Take away the hand holding the cardboard.

Place the inverted glass on a smooth table

top and carefully slide it off the cardboard on to the table top. Move the glass slowly over the table top. Can you suggest a way to empty the glass without spilling the water on the table top? What does this experiment show about air?

2 Select a tall glass jar and place a few lumps of clay on its rim. Fill the jar with water. Place a saucer on the clay and then invert the tall jar and saucer. This device can be used as a drinking fountain for chickens. Why does the water stay in the jar? Remove a little of the water from the saucer. What happens? Why?

3 Secure a piece of thin board about 5 cm wide and 60 cm long. Place the board on a table with about 25 cm sticking over the edge. Now take a sheet of newspaper and spread it out so that the part of the board on the table is completely covered. Next carefully press all the air from under the paper by stroking with your hands from the centre of the paper toward the edges. The success of this experiment depends on how well you remove the air from under the paper. When this has been done have someone strike a sharp blow with a stick near the extended end of the board. What happens? What does this show about air?

4 Hold a finger over the end of a piece of straight glass tube or soda straw and lower it into a jar of coloured water. Remove the finger and observe what happens. Replace the finger on the top of the tube and then lift the tube from the jar. What happens? Why? What does this show about air?

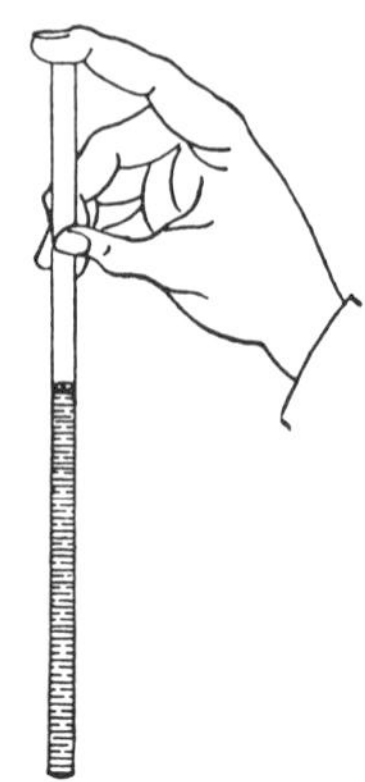

5 Make a hole with a nail near the bottom of a tin can. Fill the can with water. Hold the palm of the hand tightly over the top and water will stop running from the hole. Remove the hand and water runs from the hole. What does this show?

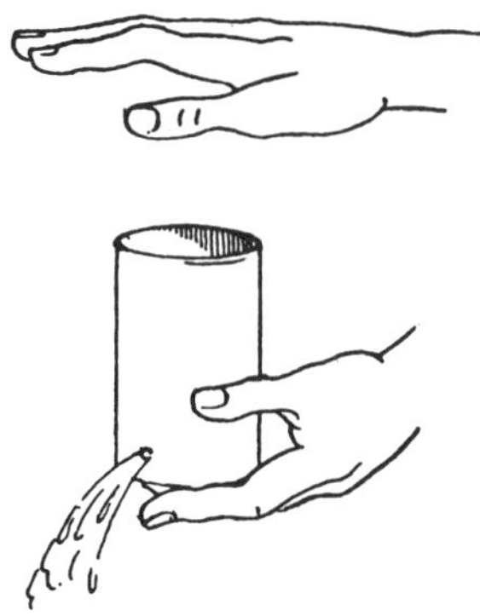

6 Select a tall glass jar or bottle. Screw up some paper, set fire to it and drop it in the container. Quickly stretch a rubber balloon over the mouth of the container or hold a piece of rubber tightly to the top. What do you observe? Can you explain why this happened?

7 Boil an egg for ten minutes or until it is very hard. Remove the shell. Select a bottle with a neck through which the egg can be forced without breaking the hard white of the egg. A quart or litre milk bottle will work very well. Screw up a piece of paper, set fire to it and drop it in the bottle. Quickly place the egg, pointed end down, in the mouth of the bottle. What happens? How do you explain this? To get the egg out, turn the bottle upside down. Let the egg rest, pointed end down, in the neck of the bottle. Now blow hard into the bottle and observe the results.

8 Submerge a drinking glass in a large container of water. Be sure the glass is filled with water. Lift the glass up with the mouth down, until the glass is nearly out of the water. Why does the water not run out of the glass?

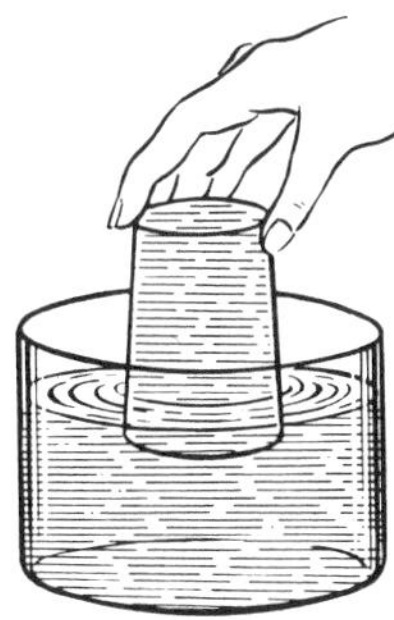

9 Wet the bottom of a plumber's force cup and press it against some flat surface such as the top of a stool. Try to lift the stool with the stopper. Why is this possible?

10 Wet the rims of two plumber's force cups. Press the rubber cups tightly together and then try to separate them. Why is it so difficult to pull them apart? This experiment is similar to the classic Magdeburg Hemispheres experiment.

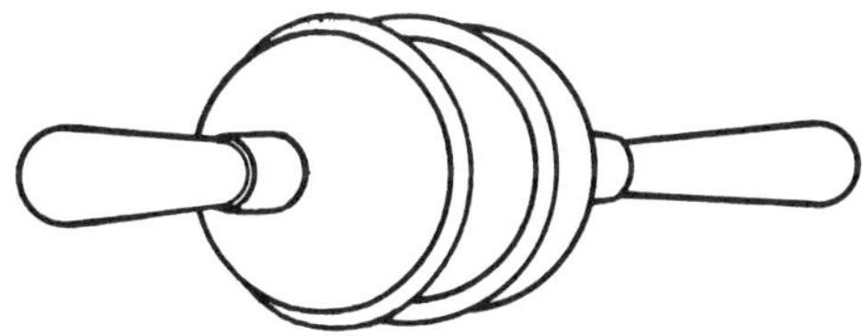

11 Blow a small amount of air into a balloon held in your mouth. Bring the balloon close to a table top and press two tea cups against the sides of the balloon. Blow a little more air into the balloon and then close the mouth of the balloon by pinching it. If the experiment has been carefully done you can lift the two cups with the balloon. What holds the cups to the balloon?

12 Select two thick drinking glasses and fit one of them with a collar of moist blotting paper. Screw up a piece of paper, light it and drop it into one glass standing on the table. Quickly press the other inverted glass tightly to the blotting paper. Can you pick up the bottom glass by lifting the top one? Why?

13 Select two thick drinking glasses. Fill each with water. Place a piece of paper over one and invert it over the other so that the rims fit closely together. Remove the paper. What happens? Why?

14 Place about 3 cm of water in a tin can which has a screw top. Place the can *open* on a stove and heat until the water boils and steam issues from the open stop. Quickly remove from the fire and screw the cap on very tightly. Allow the can to stand and observe the results. The effect can be hastened by running cold water over the can or by immersing it in a dish pan of cold water. Unless the tin has been perforated, it can be blown out for use again by heating it gently.

Plastic bottles or drums used in the home as containers for detergents can be used for a similar experiment. Remove the cap and place the bottle in hot water up to the neck for a few minutes. Replace the cap and plunge the bottle into cold water. Explain what happens.

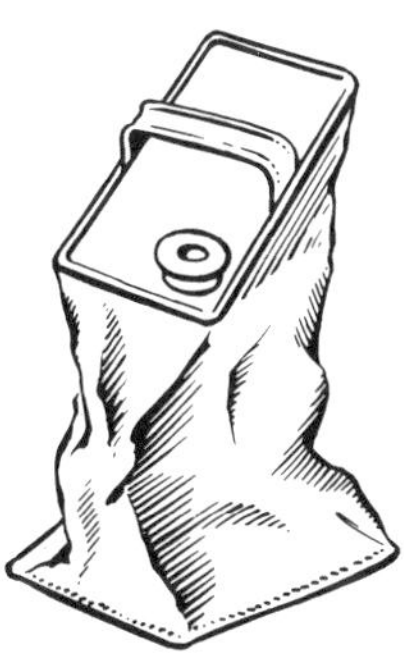

15 Remove the brass shell from a used electric bulb by gently heating it in a gas or alcohol flame. When the sealing wax begins to smoke, grasp the shell with a pair of pliers and twist it away from the glass bulb. Observe the end of the sealed tube, extending from the bulb, through which the air was removed. Place the bulb tube end down in a jar of coloured water. With a pair of pliers, snip the end of the tube (while under water). What happens? How do you explain this?

E. TO MEASURE AIR PRESSURE

1 A simple mercury barometer

Seal one end of a glass tube about 80 cm in length by rotating it in a gas flame. The tube should be held as nearly vertical as possible. Attach a small funnel or thistle tube to the open end of your barometer tube with a short length of rubber tube. Pour mercury into the tube slowly. If air bubbles are trapped they may be removed by gently shaking the mercury in the tube up and down. Fill the tube to within 1 cm of the top. The last part is best filled by using a medicine dropper so that mercury will not be wasted. Fill the tube until a little mercury extends above the tube level. Pour about two centimetres of mercury into a bottle or dish. Place your finger over the end of the tube and place the tube open end down in the jar of mercury. Remove the finger from the tube when it is under the surface of the mercury. When this tube is properly supported it will serve as a mercury barometer. The height of the mercury between the levels in the jar and the tube measures the air pressure in centimetres or inches of mercury.

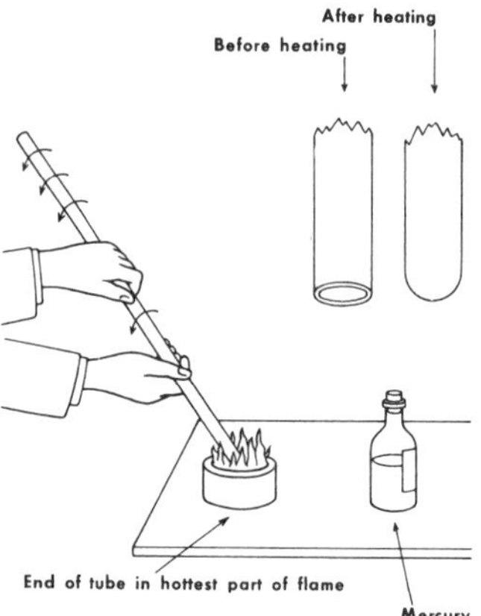

An ink bottle can be used as a container for the mercury in a permanent barometer and will help keep the surface clean. The following procedure may be used to set it up. Before filling the tube with mercury as described, find a cork which fits the barometer tube. Place the cork on the tube at about 15 cm from the open end and cut a small nick along one side. Now stick a rubber cycle patch onto the bottom of the bottle just opposite the mouth. Fill the barometer tube as described and place the bottle neck downwards over the open end, pressing the patch hard onto the top of the tube. Keeping the tube in contact with the patch, turn both over and stand the bottle on the bench. Still pressing on the tube, pour some mercury into the bottle. Now raise the tube a little to allow mercury to run from the tube, and push the cork into the neck of the bottle.

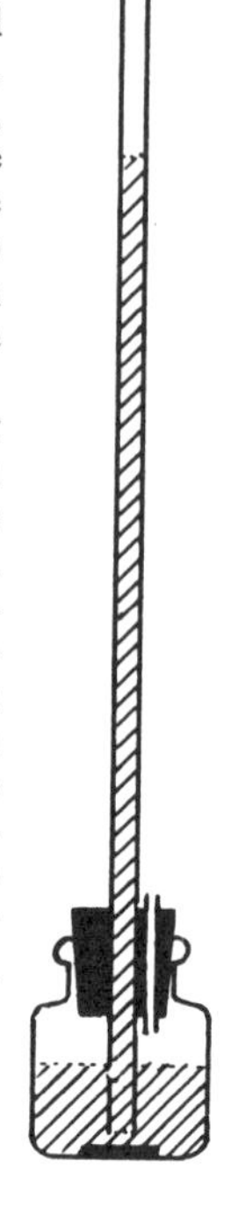

If desired, the barometer may now be supported in a bracket with a metre scale attached to it and hung on a wall. The top of the barometer tube should then be supported, and the ink bottle can be made to fit tightly in a tin fastened to the bracket. The effect of changing the pressure on the surface can be demonstrated by blowing or sucking through the nick in the cork of the mercury reservoir.

2 Fortin type barometer

A simple Fortin type barometer can be improvised for the junior laboratory. The glass tube is held vertically with one end in the reservoir by two curtain-rod holders on wooden blocks, fixed to the back board, which is a piece of 18 cm by 2.5 cm whitewood. The reservoir is a potted meat jar or small beaker, which can be moved bodily up or down by the screw jaw of a G-clamp. This alters the level of the mercury and keeps it in contact with the bottom of the scale. The reservoir is prevented from slipping sideways by a brass collar, fitting loosely and attached to the back board. The scale is cut down so that the first 10 cm can reach the surface of the mercury in the reservoir, or an ivory knitting needle can be substituted. The scale is screwed to the wooden blocks holding the glass tube supports. For setting up, the reservoir should be filled

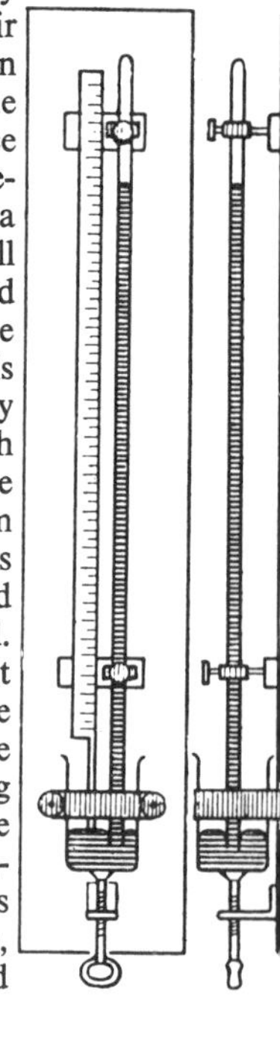

to the top, otherwise it is difficult to get the open end of the tube under the surface. Any excess can then be siphoned off. A carboard disc may be fitted to keep the mercury clean; it also serves to keep out little boys' fingers.

3 A bottle barometer

A bottle, partly filled with water, is inverted with its neck under the surface of more water in a saucer. This is the device used as a chicken feeder, but variations in atmospheric pressure can be recorded approximately on a strip of paper stuck on the outside.

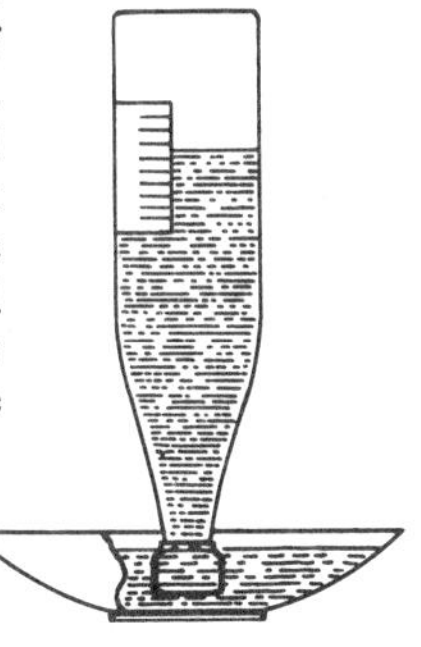

4 An aneroid barometer

The corrugated rubber tube from a gas mask, or a cycle handle grip, can be used to make a model aneroid barometer. No great accuracy is to be expected because of the many possible errors.

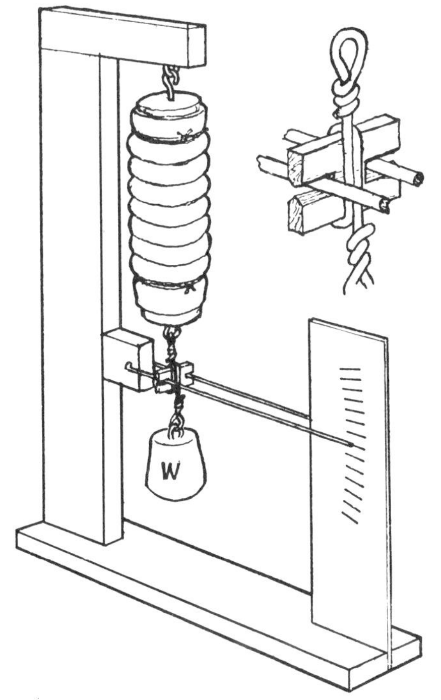

Two good corks or pieces of non-porous wood are needed to close the ends of the tube, which serves as a vacuum box. They are fitted when the rubber is compressed and they should be made airtight with wax and by tying string round the outside of the rubber.

A weight hung from the lower cork will partially counteract the result of atmospheric pressure and extend the bellows.

Variations in atmospheric pressure can be indicated by a magnifying pointer.

5 A balance barometer

This device depends on the fact that dry air is heavier than moist air at the same temperature.

Two equal cylinders (tin cans would do) are mounted, one at each end of the beam of a sensitive balance. Zehnder's arrangement (page 33) is quite satisfactory for this purpose.

One of the cylinders is sealed as a standard specimen of air; the other has a hole in it so that air from the atmosphere can enter. The device would, of course, work on simple buoyancy with one cylinder only, but it is easier to balance it using two cylinders.

It must be mounted in a box to shield it from draughts, and an indicator projecting through the top indicates the position of the beam.

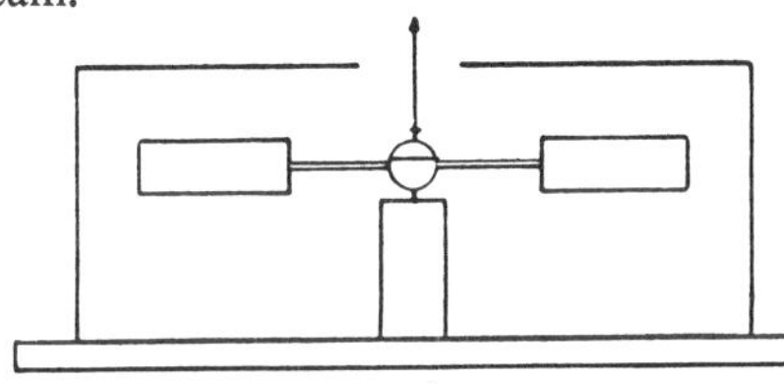

6 Another aneroid barometer

Stretch a piece of thin rubber over the mouth of a small glass jar. Wind thread or string over the rubber to secure it and then put a ring of household cement under the edges of the rubber sheet which have been trimmed off.

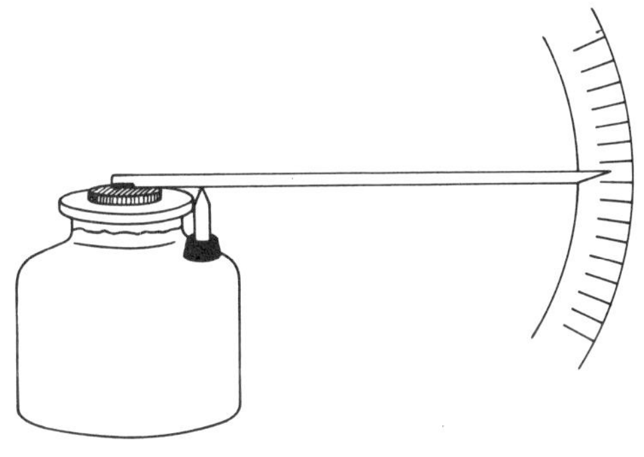

Cut a thin circle from the end of a cork and glue this to the centre of the rubber. Next glue a long broom splint or soda straw to the cork. Cut a little wooden triangle from a match stem and glue to the edge of the bottle so that the splint or soda straw rests on it. A scale can be made and placed behind the end of the splint.

7 Measuring atmospheric pressure with a bicycle pump

A bicycle pump with the washer reversed as shown can be used to measure atmospheric pressure. The piston can be made airtight by adding a little thick oil to the barrel. The area of cross section of the pump barrel can be calculated or measured with squared paper. The pressure of the air can then be calculated in kg/cm^2. The weight supported by the upthrust of atmospheric pressure is found by hanging various loads from a hook, screwed into a wooden plug fitted into the pump handle.

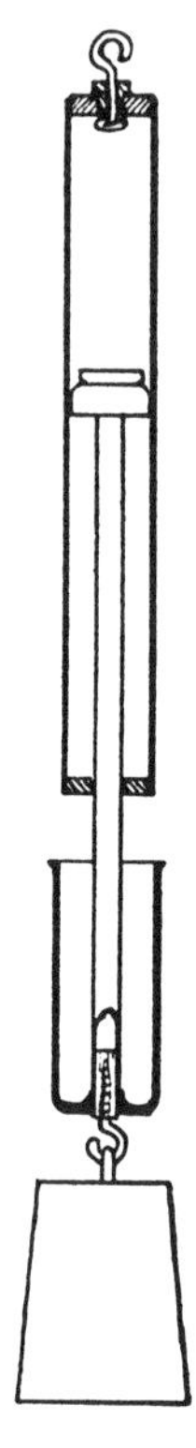

8 Measuring atmospheric pressure with a rubber sucker

The force required to pull the sucker away from a smooth surface can be found by using a spring balance. The area on which the atmospheric pressure is acting can be measured by pressing the sucker on a piece of squared paper.

Use a sucker which has a hook attached. If one is not available, tie some copper wire round the neck and form a loop.

If the laboratory bench is not smooth enough use a piece of plate glass, holding this down with one hand whilst pulling on the spring balance with the other. Make several trials and, if possible, use suckers of different sizes.

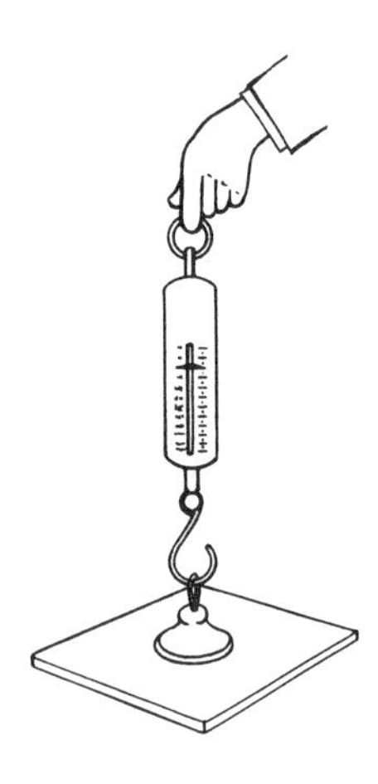

F. TO SHOW HOW PUMPS USE AIR PRESSURE

1 How different pressures of air force water from a container

Fit a test tube with a two-hole stopper. Through one hole place a length of glass tube which extends into the test tube nearly to the bottom. Put water in the test tube and suck on the upper end of the glass tube. Observe what happens. Next tightly close the open hole in the rubber stopper and again suck on the glass tube. Observe what happens. How do you account for the difference?

2 A simple syringe pump

Assemble a simple syringe using glass or metal tubing (iron pipe or conduit tubing is suitable), two corks and a piece of metal rod. The cork which serves as the piston is made to fit tight by wrapping a string round it.

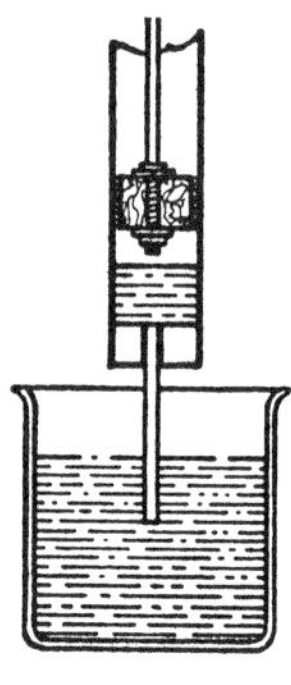

The other cork, with a piece of glass, bamboo or strong straw tubing, acts as an intake.

3 A lift pump

To modify the syringe and make a simple lift pump, burn two holes through the piston with a hot wire and fit a thin piece of leather or rubber above them to act as a valve which closes on the upstroke and yet allows liquid to pass through on the downstroke.

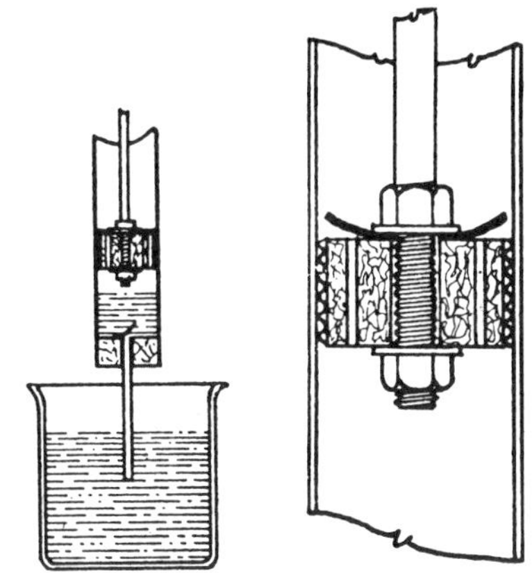

4 A lamp chimney lift pump

Use a straight-sided lamp chimney as a pump cylinder. Fit a two-hole stopper into the chimney for a piston. If the stopper is a little small wrap some string around it to make a tight fit. If it is a little large you can make it smaller with sand paper. Through one hole put an iron or brass rod for a piston rod. Cover the other hole on top of the stopper with a little flap of rubber or soft leather cut from an old shoe. This will be the piston valve. It can be held in place with a tack pushed into the stopper.

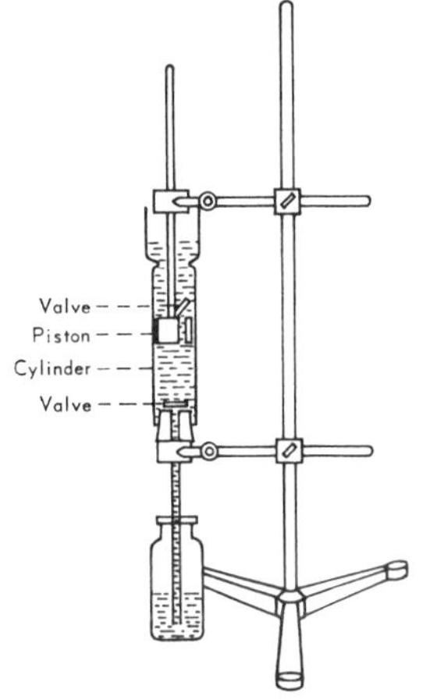

Fit a one-hole stopper carrying a 50-cm length of glass tube into the lower end of the lamp chimney. Over the hole in the stopper place another valve of rubber or soft leather. This is the foot valve. Put water in a pan. Prime the pump by pouring a little water on top of the piston. Observe the valves on the upstroke and on the downstroke of the piston. How does air pressure help the lift pump to work?

5 A lamp chimney force pump

Replace the piston in the lift pump described above with a one-hole stopper. Fit the piston rod through the hole. Fit the bottom of the chimney with a two-hole stopper. Through one hole place a 50-cm length of glass tube and put a valve over it. Through the other hole put a short length of glass tube. Next fit a glass bottle with a two-hole stopper. Put short lengths of glass tube through each hole flush with the underside of the stopper.

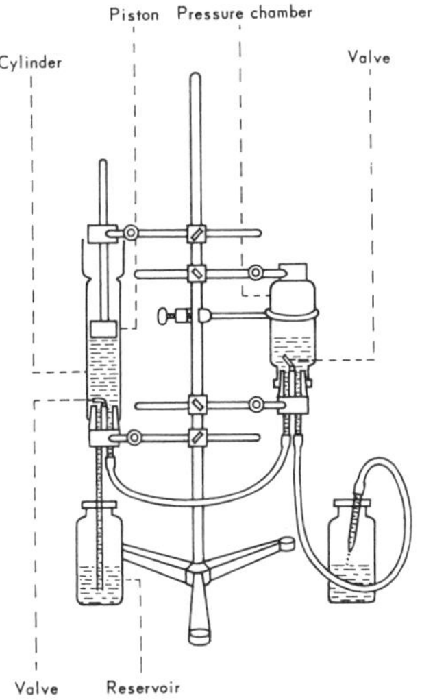

Place a valve over one of the holes. Clamp the pump firmly in a ringstand. Also clamp the bottle to the ringstand upside down. Place a clamp under the stopper and another on top of the bottle to hold it firmly in place. Now connect the outlet tube of the pump (the one without the valve) to the inlet tube of the bottle (the one with the valve). To the outlet tube of the bottle (pressure chamber) connect a length of rubber tube with a nozzle or jet tube (like a medicine dropper) in it. Prime your pump and see how far you can force the water. Observe the valves. How does air play a part in the operation of this pump? How does it differ from the lift pump? For what purpose could this pump be used?

6 A test tube force pump

To make this apparatus, heat the bottom of a test tube with a small flame and blow a hole. Now blow a hole in a larger test tube and fit both with ball bearings or small marbles to act as valves.

If the inner one is made to slide tightly in the outer one by wrapping string round it, and has a cork and tube as shown in the diagram, it will serve as the piston of a force pump.

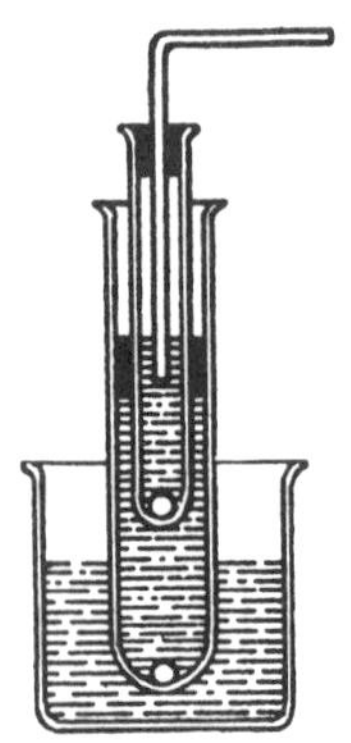

G. TO SHOW HOW SIPHONS USE AIR PRESSURE

1 A simple siphon

Secure two tall glass bottles and fill each about half full of water. Connect two 30-cm lengths of glass tube with a 30-cm length of rubber or plastic tubing. Fill the tube with water and pinch it. Put a glass tube in each bottle of water. Siphon the water back and forth by varying the height of the bottles. The experiment is more interesting if the water is coloured with a little ink. Place the two bottles on a table. Does the siphon flow? Can you explain how air pressure helps the siphon work?

2 A siphon fountain

Fit a glass jar (a flask from a used electric bulb) with a two-hole rubber stopper. Through one hole place a jet tube which will extend about half way to the top of the flask and let about 2 cm extend beyond the stopper. Through the other hole push a short length of glass tube so that it is just flush with the bottom of the stopper. Let about 2 cm of tube extend outside the stopper. Connect a 20-cm length of rubber tube to the jet tube. Connect a 1-m length to the other glass tube. Place some water in the flask, insert the stopper and then invert the siphon. Put the short rubber tube in a container of water on the table and let the longer rubber tube go to a pail on the floor. The fountain can be seen better if the water in the jar on the table is coloured with a little ink. You can make a double siphon fountain by making another flask unit similar to the first one and connecting them together.

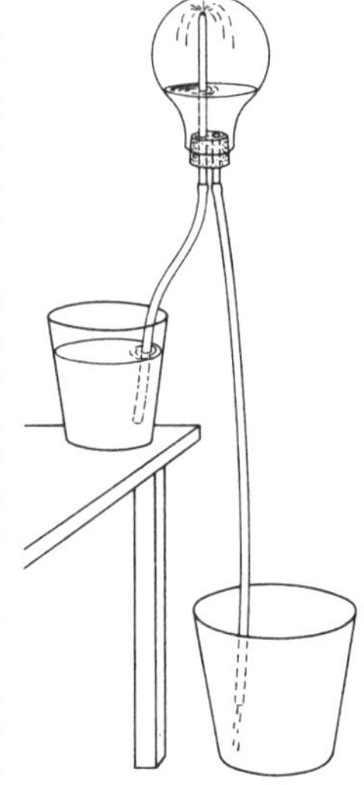

3 A self-starting siphon

Secure a piece of glass or plastic tube about 2.5 cm in diameter and 8 to 10 cm in length. Fit one end with a one-hole stopper, carrying a short length of glass tube that extends about a centimetre below the stopper on the inner side. Fit the other end of the big tube with a two-hole stopper. Through one of the holes in the two-hole stopper place a jet tube which extends up through the larger tube and into the opening of the glass tube in the one-hole stopper. Connect a long rubber tube to the glass tube in the one-hole stopper. Plunge the assembled unit into a pail of water that is standing on a table and direct the longer end of the siphon tube to a container on the floor. The siphon may require some adjustment before it starts to flow.

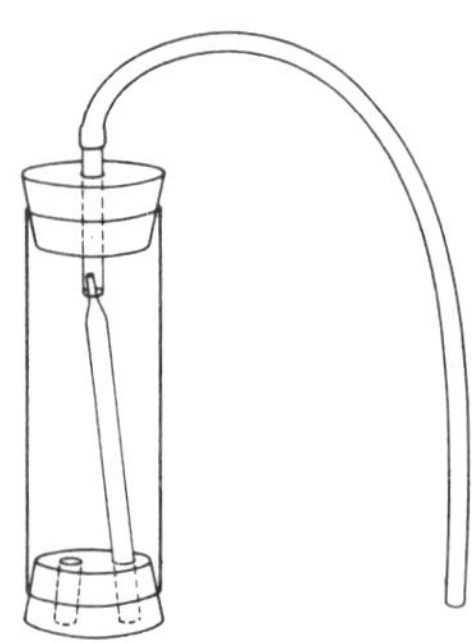

H. TO SHOW SOME EFFECTS OF COMPRESSED AIR

1 To feel the 'spring' of air

Secure a bicycle pump and place your thumb over the end of the outlet tube. Next push the piston in forcibly and quickly let go of it. What happens? How do you account for this?

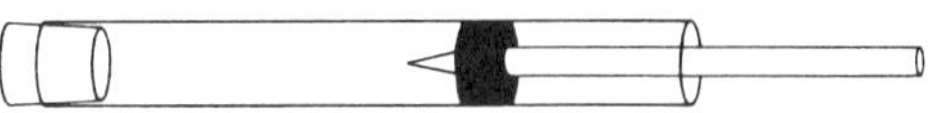

2 Making a 'gusher' with compressed air

Secure a large narrow-necked bottle such as is used for soda water. Place a one-hole stopper in the bottle. Through the stopper put a 10-cm length of glass tube which has been drawn to a jet on the outside end. With a short length of rubber tube attach a length of glass tube that will extend nearly to the bottom of the bottle. Fill the bottle about half full of water. Insert the stopper firmly and hold it in with your fingers. Next blow hard into the bottle; and when you release the pressure, point the bottle away from you. What happens?

3 A compressed air pop-gun

Use a straight piece of glass or plastic tubing of 1 or 2 cm in diameter and 15 or 20 cm in length. Make a piston by winding some string on a pencil till it fits tightly in the tube. Put a small cork in the end of the tube and push the piston in quickly.

4 Lifting things with compressed air

Remove the bladder from a soccer ball or basket ball and place it on a table. Pile some books on the bladder and then blow into it.

5 Making a 'burp' bottle

Fit a bottle or flask with a one-hole stopper which carries a funnel. Put the stopper firmly in the bottle and then pour water into the funnel. The bottle will 'burp' at regular intervals.

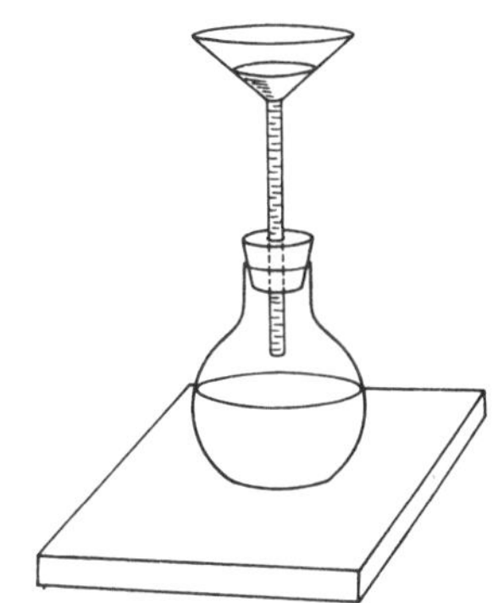

I. TO SHOW SOME RESULTS OF REDUCING AIR PRESSURE

1 Lifting water with air pressure

Fit a test tube with a one-hole cork and glass tube. Drive out the air by boiling a little water in it. Invert it with the open end under the surface of a jar of water. Atmospheric pressure will drive water upwards until it almost completely fills the test tube.

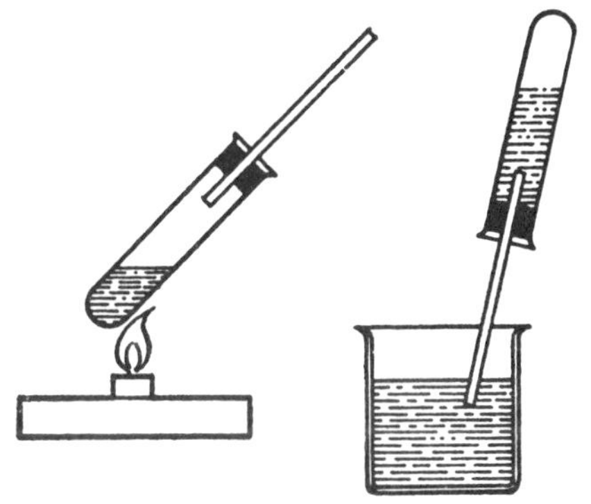

2 How to make a simple vacuum pump

Secure a bicycle or automobile hand pump. Open the pump and remove the piston. Unscrew the bolt that holds the leather washers. Reverse the washers by turning them over. Replace the washers on the piston and insert in the pump cylinder. A pump of this sort will serve to do many simple vacuum experiments.

3 How to make a receiver for vacuum experiments

Secure a large jar with an air-tight screw cap, such as a fruit jar. Drill a hole through the top and have a short metal tube soldered in the hole so that it is air-tight. Solder a tyre valve upside down in the lower end of the tube.

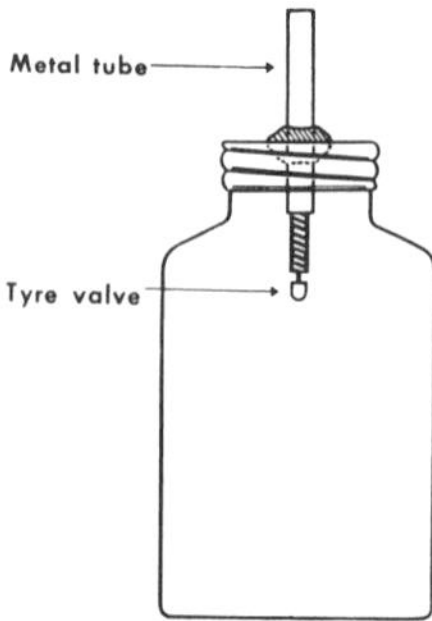

The tyre valve mentioned in this experiment can be fitted into a good cork in the neck of a Winchester bottle with the bottom cut off (page 218). If the edges are ground smooth with carborundum stone or hard rock a sheet of rubber cut from a large tractor tube can be use as a base plate to make an air-tight seal. The baroscope described below can be introduced into this bell jar.

4 Model baroscope

Glue one end of a drinking straw (or better, a strip of balsa wood) so that it forms a beam perpendicular to the surface of a ping-pong ball. Find the point of balance and stick a fine needle through the beam to act as pivot. Rest this on a piece of metal bent into a U shape and supported on a base. Shave away the beam with a razor blade until the balance is perfect. Place this under the bell jar and pump out some of the air. Explain what happens.

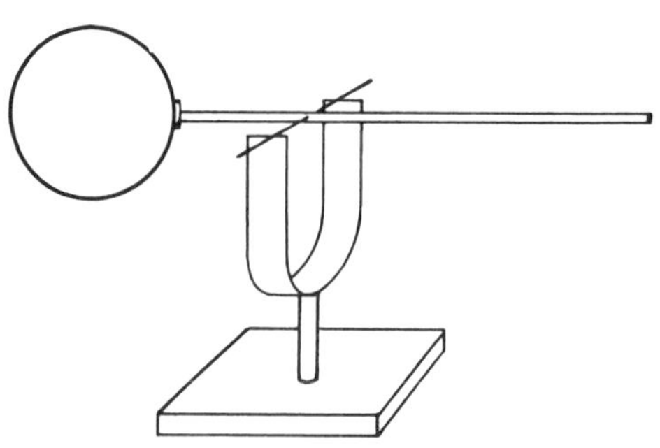

5 An experiment with a balloon

Partially inflate a small rubber balloon and close it with a rubber band. Place the balloon in the receiver and remove some of the air with your pump.

6 An experiment with a bottle and cork

Tightly close a small bottle with a cork or rubber stopper. Place the bottle inside the receiver and remove some of the air with the pump. What happens? How do you account for this?

7 Moving water by reducing air pressure

Secure two small bottles. Fill one about half full of water and close it with a one-hole stopper carrying a length of glass tube that reaches nearly to the bottom of the bottle. Attach a short length of rubber tube which empties into the other bottle. Place these in the receiver jar and remove some of the air with the pump. What happens? How do you account for this? If you wish, you may colour the water with ink.

8 Another balloon experiment

Stretch a rubber balloon over the neck of a small bottle. Place it in the receiver jar and remove some of the air with the pump. What happens? How do you account for this?

9 To study the relation between volume and pressure of air

Obtain a rubber bung or 'door stop' which just fits inside a narrow glass jar or measuring cylinder. Attach it to the lower end of a wooden rod. Fit a tin lid to the upper end of the rod to act as a scale pan. Lubricate the piston so formed with a little vaseline or heavy engine oil. Use the piston to trap air in the jar; put different weights on the pan and measure the volume of air inside the glass cylinder for each weight. Note that the volume is in inverse proportion to the pressure.

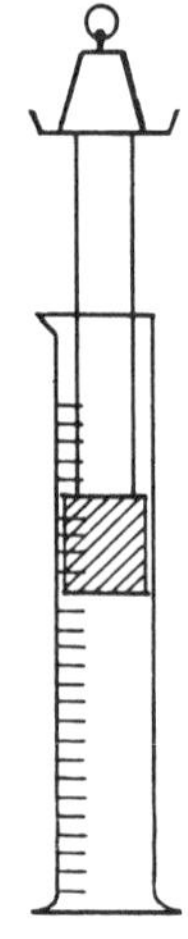

J. AIR IN THE HUMAN BODY

1 How the lungs work

Cut the bottom off a large bottle (see directions, page 218). Fit a cork to the neck with a Y tube in it. On each of the lower limbs of the Y tie a rubber balloon or some small bladder.

Tie a sheet of brown paper or sheet rubber round the bottom of the jar, with a piece of string knotted through a hole and sealed with wax. Pulling this string lowers the diaphragm and air enters the neck of the Y piece causing the balloons to dilate.

Pressing the diaphragm upwards has the opposite effect.

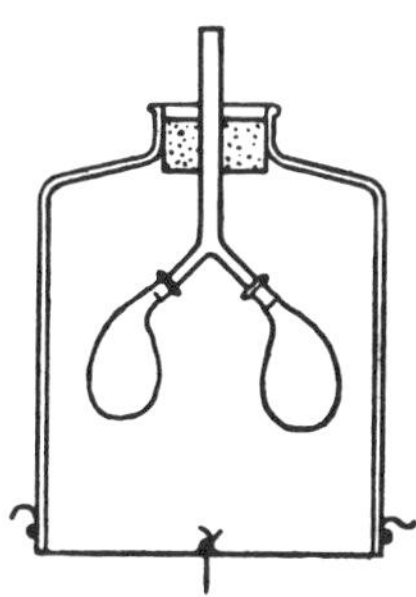

2 To measure the volume of air in the lungs

Invert a bottle full of water so that its neck is under the surface of water in a jar. Introduce a glass or rubber tube into the neck and blow one full breath of your lungs into the bottle.

Adjust the level of the water in the bowl so that the pressure of the air in the bottle is the same as that of the atmosphere, and stick a piece of gummed paper on the side of the bottle. Remove the bottle and measure the volume of water required to fill it to this mark.

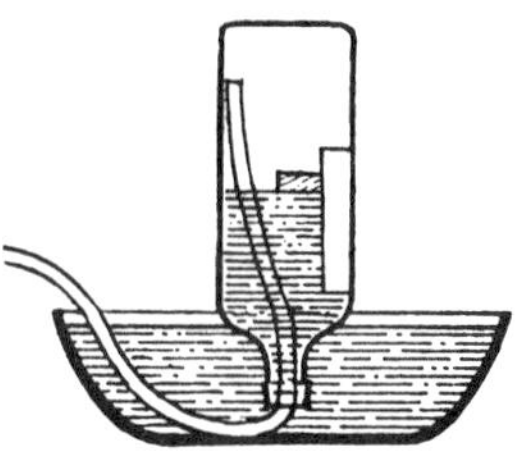

3 To show that expired air contains carbon dioxide

The two flasks are connected so that when you breathe through the T piece, all the air bubbles through the lime water in the flasks. One tube is closed with the finger while the air is drawn in; the other tube is closed when it is expelled.

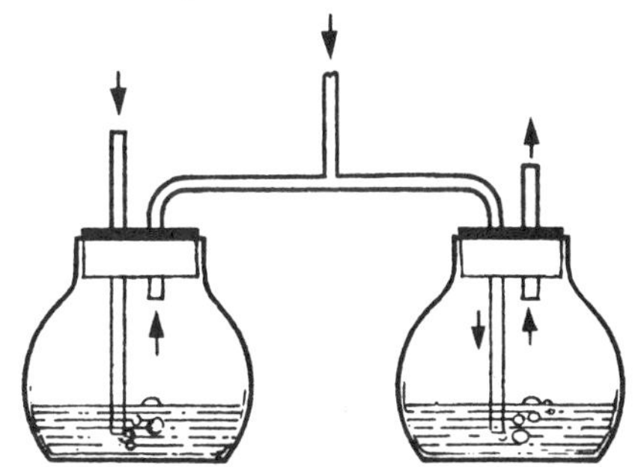

K. TO STUDY SOME CHEMICAL EFFECTS OF AIR

1 Wash a small wad of steel wool in gasoline, benzine or carbon tetrachloride (carbona) to remove any grease. Squeeze it out and then fluff it. As soon as it is dry, place the steel wool in a flask fitted with a one-hole stopper carrying a 40 cm length of glass tube. Stand the flask and tube in a jar of water with the end of the tube under water. Observe for a few hours. What happens? How do you account for it?

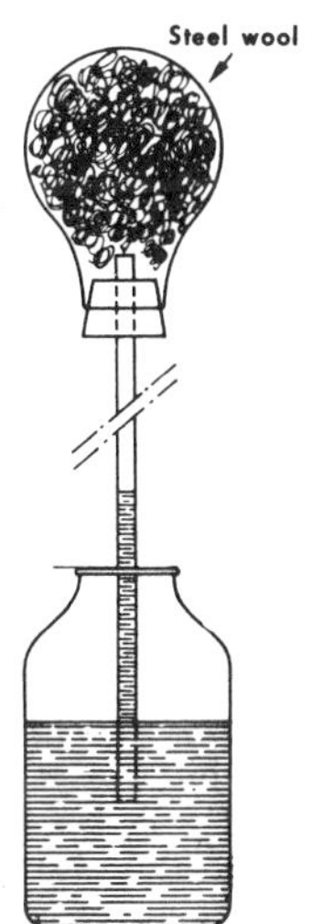

2 Repeat experiment 1, but this time place the steel wool in a small jar or test tube and place in water. Allow to stand for 24 hours. What do you observe? How much of the air in the jar has been replaced? How did the steel wool appear after the experiment? How do you account for what happened?

3 Hang a muslin bag of iron nails, or tin-tacks, from a cork in the top of a lamp chimney. Stand the chimney in a saucer of water. After a time the water will rise up the tube.

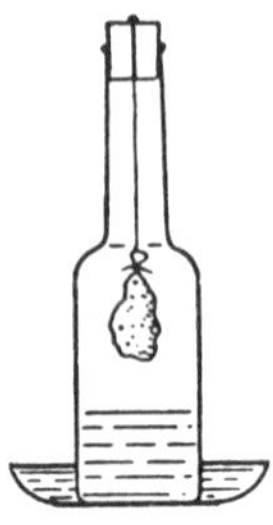

4 Counterpoise a steel rule or a piece of iron on a knife edge using a brass weight or a stone. Leave in moist air or on a window sill for a few days and notice the effect of the rust on the longer arm of the lever.

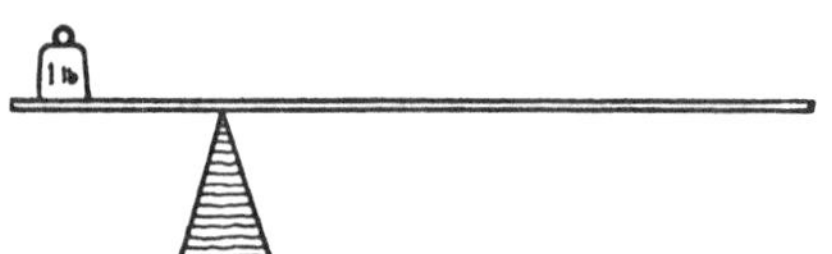

5 Without elaborate equipment it is almost impossible to prove that oxygen is necessary for burning. Yet there are many experiments which show the need for a continuous supply of fresh air to maintain combustion. These experiments will encourage the scientific attitude and help develop habits of critical thinking if carefully drawn conclusions and limited generalizations are made from them. After a suitable background has thus been established, the role of oxygen in burning can be explained.

Attach cardboard bases to several candles so that they stand upright. To do this cut new or used candles into pieces two or three inches long and chip off one end of each so that the wick projects about a quarter of an inch. Ignite a candle and hold it sideways so that melted wax drops off. Drip three or four drops on the centre of several pieces of card-board. Hold the short candles against these until the wax hardens.

Invert a glass jar over a burning candle held upright by the cardboard candle holder. When the flame disappears, ask pupils for conclusions. Accept no conclusions that are not justified by the evidence. Now ask the class to propose conclusions which they can really justify. After several have been sugges-ted, accept the conclusion that a candle will not continue to burn in a small closed space.

6 Direct four pupils to invert, at a given signal, four glass jars over four burning candles. Half-pint, pint, quart and gallon jars or some similar gradation of sizes may be used. Caution should be observed by the teacher as well as by the pupils in drawing conclusions from this experiment.

7 Fix a piece of candle to the bottom of a shallow pan with melted wax. Put water in the pan to a depth of 2.5 cm or 3 cm. Light the candle and invert a small, straight-sided jar over the candle. When the experiment is over, use a ruler and note the distance the water moved up the jar. Repeat the experiment using jars of different sizes. What do you observe? How do you account for this?

8 A small ignition tube (or a piece of ordinary tubing sealed off to make a 5-cm test tube) should be half filled with potassium permanganate. After connecting a delivery tube it should be heated strongly. The oxygen gas given off can be collected over water in a soup plate.

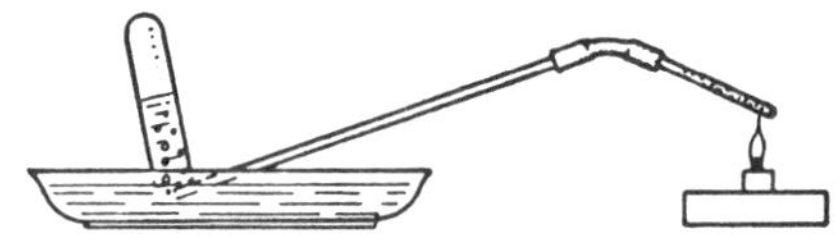

9 Oxygen may also be prepared by heating a mixture of five parts potassium chlorate to one part manganese dioxide in the same apparatus as is used in experiment 8.

10 Into a 100-ml bottle pour about 25 ml of hydrogen peroxide (ordinary drugstore or chain-store peroxide works very well but the kind used for bleaching hair gives off much more oxygen). Add a teaspoonful of manga-nese dioxide, cork the bottle loosely and leave it for a few minutes. The tiny bubbles that escape from the peroxide are bubbles of oxygen.

To test the gas in the bottle for oxygen, light a long wooden splinter and blow out the flame. Remove the cork from the bottle and insert the glowing splinter into the gas inside the bottle. The splinter should burst into flame.

Instead of manganese dioxide, ordinary baking soda may be used to drive off the oxygen from the hydrogen peroxide, but this reaction takes a little longer.

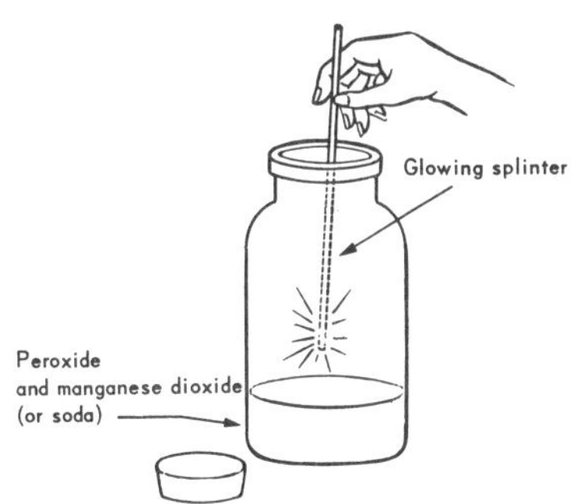

11 Hold the end of a piece of twisted picture wire in a hot flame until it begins to glow. Then quickly lower it into a bottle containing oxygen and watch the iron wire burn. A bit of powdered sulphur on the end of the wire will help.

12 Place a piece of fine steel wool in a metal tray. Ignite the steel wool with a match. The steel burns because it is in very thin strips; the oxygen of the air is in contact with much of the surface.

13 Fasten a strand of steel wool to the end of a wire. Ignite it by holding it in a flame and quickly lower it into a bottle containing oxygen. Notice that it burns more rapidly in oxygen than it does in air.

14 Carbon dioxide may be prepared either from baking soda or marble chips together with a diluted acid. It should be collected by allowing the gas to run into dry bottles or containers which should be covered with glass or cardboard plates.

15 Plunge a burning wood splint into a bottle of carbon dioxide. Does carbon dioxide support burning?

16 Fix a candle in the bottom of a wide glass jar with melted wax. Light the candle and pour carbon dioxide from another jar into the jar with the lighted candle. What does this show about the density of carbon dioxide?

17 Prepare clear lime water by stirring some slaked lime in water (see Chapter XVIII). Let the mixture stand for a day and then siphon the clear liquid into a bottle. This is lime water. Let some carbon dioxide from the generator used in experiment 14 bubble through clear lime water. What do you observe? This is a chemical test for the presence of carbon dioxide.

18 Burn a candle in a glass jar until it goes out. Remove the candle and pour in some clear lime water. Shake well and observe. What did you see? What is one of the products of burning from a candle? Repeat using burning wood and paper.

19 Let a burning candle, a piece of burning wood and some burning paper come into contact with a cool, shiny can. What do you observe? What do you believe this to be? Place a basin of cold water over a gas or kerosene flame. After a moment remove and look at the bottom. What other substance is a product of burning wax, wood and paper? Is the substance produced the same as before?

20 A model fire extinguisher can be made from an old ink bottle fitted with a cork and tube. Half fill it with sodium bicarbonate solution and float in it carefully a small pill bottle of sulphuric acid.

To operate the extinguisher shake the bottle so that the acid mixes with the bicarbonate, releasing CO_2.

Aluminium sulphate used instead of the acid provides a foam, especially if a little soap solution is added.

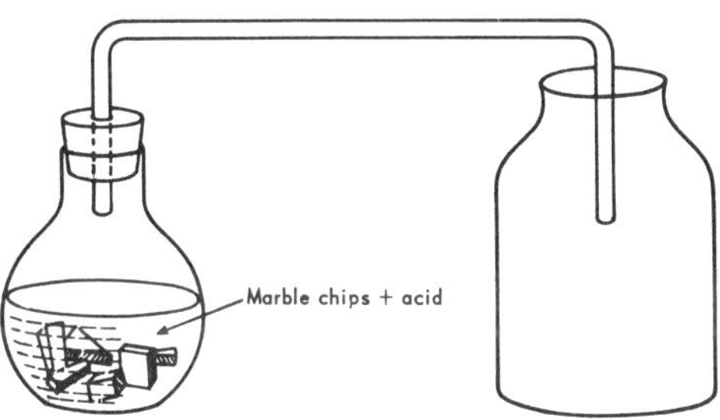

L. EXPERIMENTS WITH AIR STREAMS

When air is moving, air pressure is less where the velocity of the stream is high and greater where the velocity is low. The following experiments apply this principle.

1 Suspend two apples, oranges or ping pong balls on threads at least one metre in length. The suspended objects should be on the same level and should hang about 10 or 15 cm apart. Blow a steady stream of air between the objects and observe what happens. Where was the air stream moving fastest? Where was the pressure reduced? How do you account for what happened?

2 Place a ping pong ball inside a funnel. Blow hard through the stem of the funnel and see if you can blow the ball out of the funnel. Invert the funnel and hold the ping pong ball in the end. Blow hard through the stem and see what happens as you remove your hand holding the ball. Place the ball on a table. Cover it with the funnel. Blow through the stem and see if you pick the ball up from the table. How do you explain your observations?

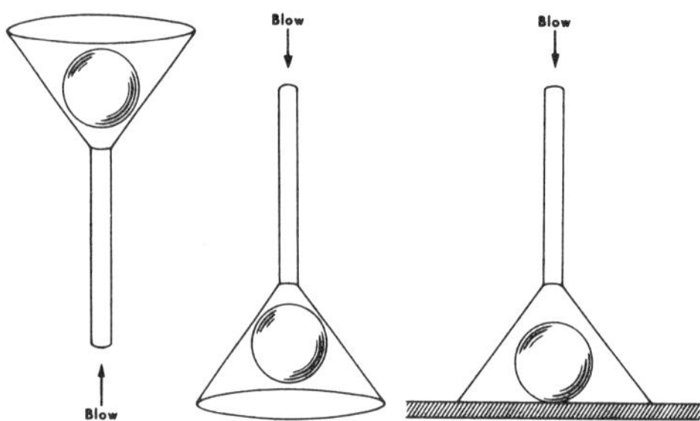

3 Make a bridge from a piece of thin cardboard, 20 cm × 10 cm. Bend down about 2 cm on each end. Place the bridge on the table and try to blow through the arch. The harder you blow the greater the force holding it to the table top.

4 Cut a piece of thin cardboard about 7 cm square. Draw diagonals from each corner and put a common pin through the card where the lines cross at the centre. Secure the head of the pin by covering it with a bit of Scotch tape. Place the pin in the hole of an empty thread spool and try to blow the card from spool by blowing through the hole. Turn the spool and card upside down. Hold the card against the spool lightly with a finger. Blow through the spool, then remove the finger. How do you account for this?

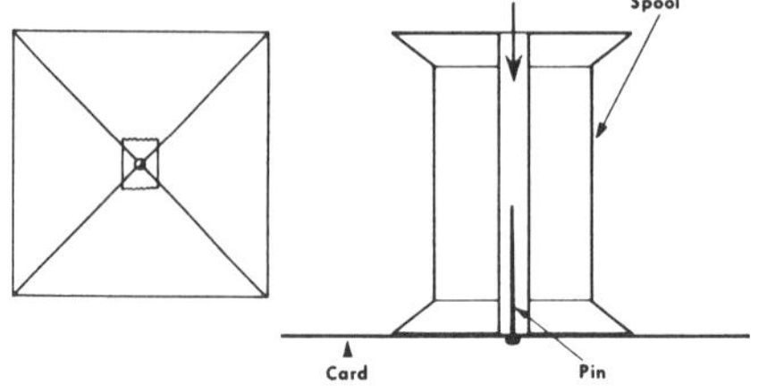

5 Light a candle and hold it behind a card about 5 cm wide. Blow hard toward the card and observe the movement of the flame. How do you account for your observations?

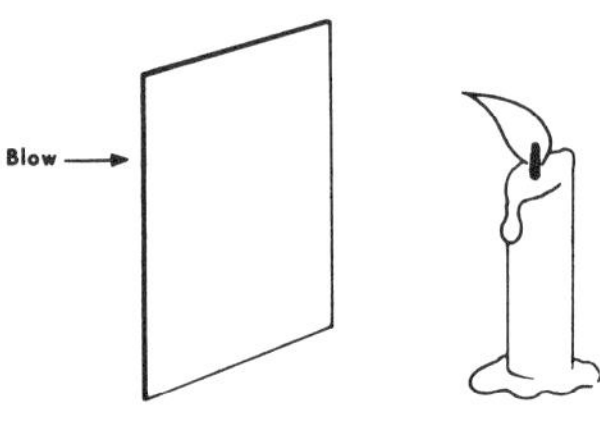

6 Place a lighted candle on a table. Place a bottle in front of the candle. Blow hard against the bottle and observe the flame.

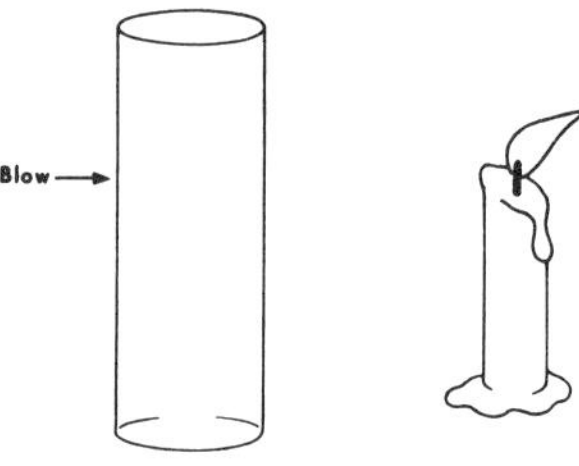

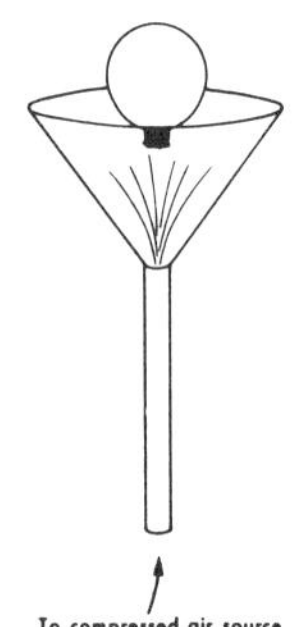

7 Attach a funnel to a source of compressed air such as a vacuum sweeper. Blow up a balloon and place a piece of copper wire around the neck for a weight. Turn on the compressed air and balance the balloon in the air stream. Try also to balance a ping pong ball between the balloon and the funnel.

8 Obtain two glass tubes or two transparent soda straws. Place one tube in a half glass of coloured water. Place the second tube at a

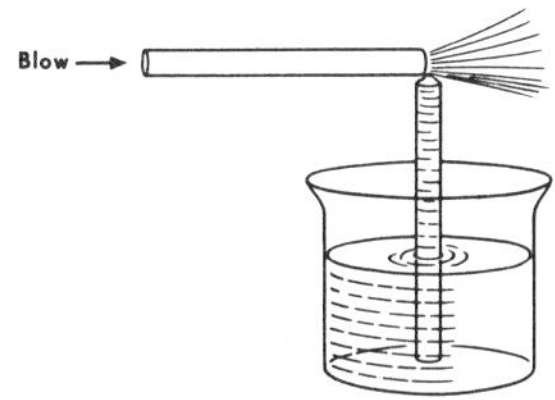

right angle with the first one so that the ends of the two tubes are close together. Blow through the horizontal tube and observe the water level in the second tube. How do you account for the result? Note that the same principle is applied for an atomizer, a DDT or paint sprayer.

9 Take a strip of paper about 30 cm long and 4 cm wide. Fold the paper about 4 cm from one end. Crease the fold well. Now hold the short end of the fold against your chin with the crease about level with your lips. Blow hard across the top surface of the paper and observe what happens. How do you account for this?

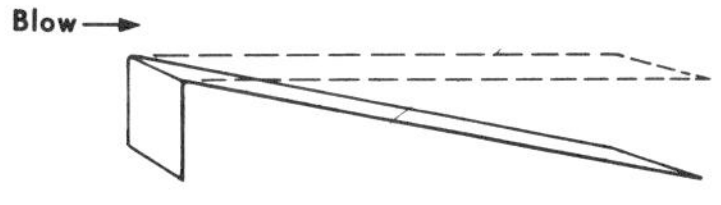

10 Hold your hand flat outside the window of a moving automobile. Then slightly raise the front edge of your hand and notice the lifting effect of the air stream.

11 Make an airfoil section (section of an airplane wing) by folding and glueing a piece of paper as shown in the diagram. Suspend the airfoil section on a pencil or smooth, round rod. Blow a stream of air so that it strikes the leading edge. What do you observe? Can you explain the lift?

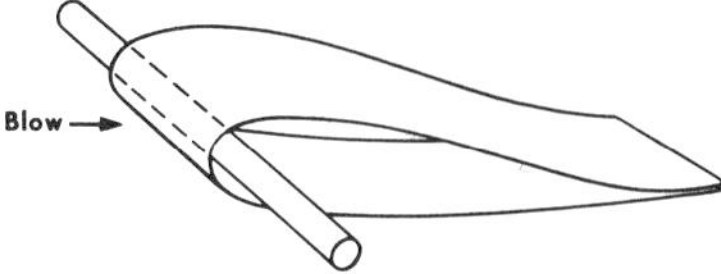

A similar airfoil section can be made from sheet metal. It can be attached to one end of a large knitting needle with a cork or piece of dowelling. A notch cut with a file in the middle of the needle can be used as a balancing point, with a bent pin or nail as its pivot. If the beam is balanced with a counterweight, the lift is very easily shown by blowing on the leading edge of the airfoil through a paper tube.

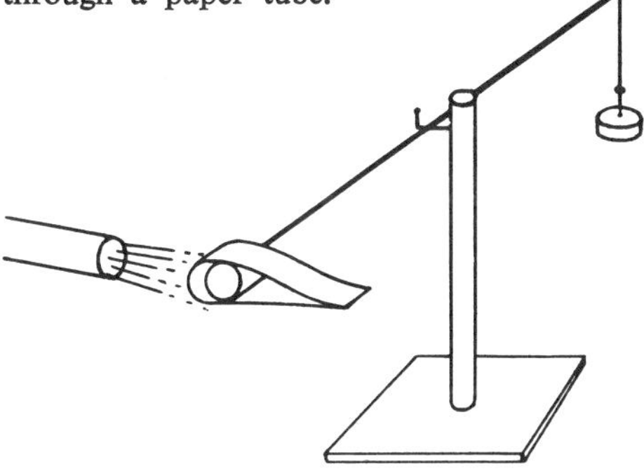

CHAPTER VIII

Experiments and materials for the study of weather

A. MAKING WEATHER INSTRUMENTS AND A WEATHER STATION

Weather is a topic that is close to the life of every child. Even at the lowest levels of primary instruction, observations of the weather may be made from day to day. At the intermediate levels a simple weather station may be set up in the classroom. At the level of general science and later, a more detailed study of the causes of weather phenomena may be made. At all stages of the work it is an advantage to represent readings and observations in graphical form whenever this is possible.

1 An aneroid barometer

A small wooden box such as a cigar box serves well to contain a simple aneroid barometer. Bore a 1-cm hole in the middle of the side to which the cover is hinged. For the pressure mechanism you may use a glass jar with a piece of thin rubber stretched over it and secured as instructed in experiment E 6, page 81. A somewhat better mechanism can be made from a plastic or tin oil-can of the type shown below.

Squeeze the oil-can to force out a little of the air and then seal the end, with plastic cement if a plastic oil-can is used, or solder if it is metal. This pressure mechanism must be absolutely air-tight; so, after the cement or solder has set, try it under water to see if there are any air leaks. If you find some, squeeze out some air and then seal the leaks. Cement the pressure mechanism to the inside of the box so that the centre of the round part falls exactly under the hole you have made in the other side.

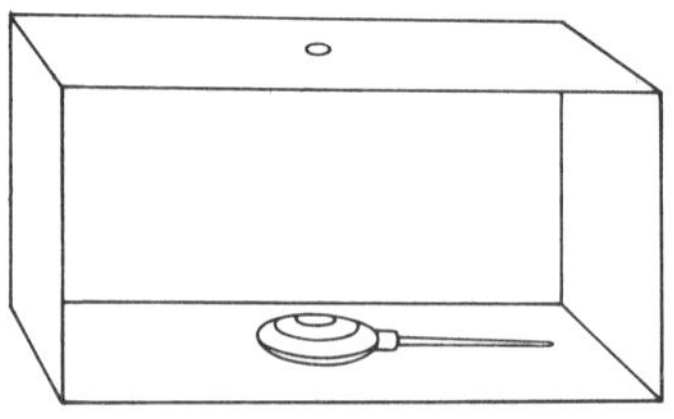

Tie a 30-cm length of thread to a short length of match stem and cement to the centre of the pressure mechanism. Cut a piece of metal from a tin can about 1 cm wide and 9 or 10 cm long. Bend at right angles about 1.5 cm from each end of the piece.

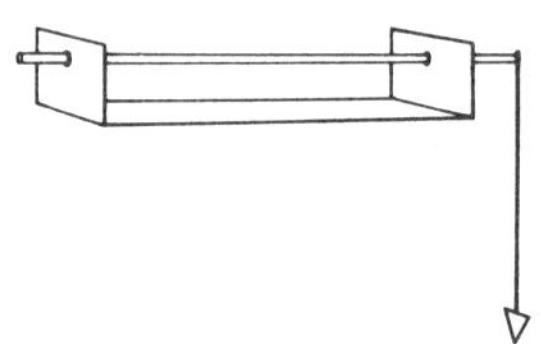

With a nail, punch a small hole in the ends of the piece a little way from the top and in the centre. Enlarge the holes so that they will let a small nail or knitting needle turn easily in them. Glue a broom bristle to one end of the needle to serve as a pointer. Securely fasten the metal piece on top of the box so that the needle-axle is across the centre of the hole. Have the broom splint move over the back of the cigar box but not touch it.

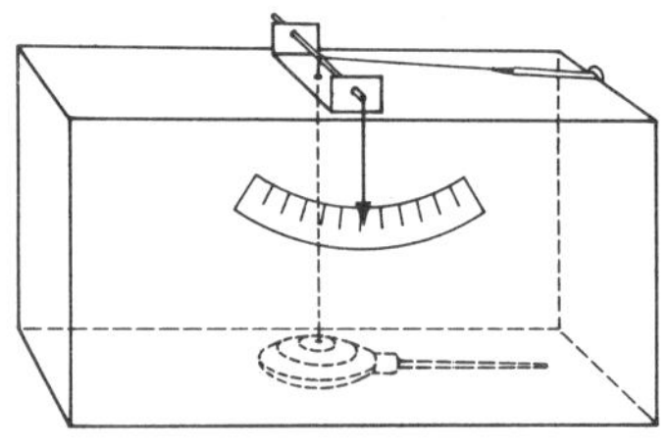

Next put the end of the thread from the pressure mechanism up through the hole. Wind it about the needle axle several times and then tie it to a rubber band. Be sure that the thread from the axle to the pressure mechanism is tight. Stretch the rubber band just enough to place a slight tension on the thread and fasten it to the end of the cigar box with a thumb tack. You may have to change the tension.

Mark off a scale like the one shown and fasten it under the pointer to the back of the cigar box. Arrange the pointer so that it is at the centre of the scale. Set your barometer where you can observe it. As the pointer changes, you can adjust the tension in the rubber band so that it moves properly over the scale. Place the words 'rising' and 'falling' on the proper side of the scale. This is a very sensitive barometer and will clearly indicate changes in air pressure.

Note reference to other types of barometer in Chapter VII, page 80.

2 A wind vane

A wind vane is used to tell the direction of the wind. Secure a piece of wood about 25 cm in length and 1 cm square. With a saw, cut a slot in the centre of each end of the stick, 6 cm deep.

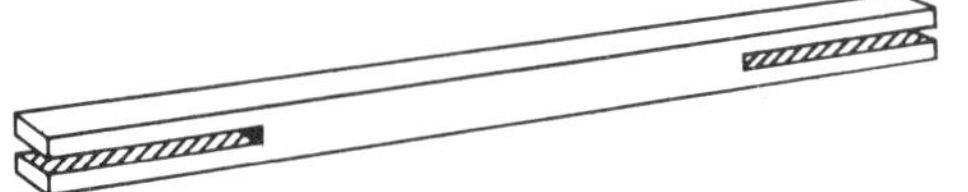

Next select a thin piece of wood about 10 cm wide which will fit tightly in the slots. From this cut two sections, one the head of an arrow and the other the tail, as shown below.

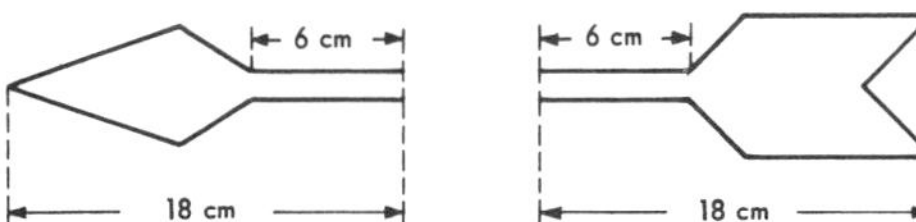

Push the head and tail of the wind vane into the slots and fasten them either with glue or with small nails.

Next balance the wind vane on the blade of a knife and mark the place on the stick where it balances. Secure the glass part of a medicine dropper and close the small end by rotating it in a gas or alcohol flame. At the place where the vane balanced, drill a hole just slightly larger than the medicine-dropper tube about three-quarters of the way through the stick. Put the small end of the tube up in the hole and fasten it securely with glue or putty.

To make a supporting rod for your wind vane select a piece of soft wood about a metre in length and drive a small nail in the top. With a file, sharpen the end of the nail to a point. Place the medicine dropper over

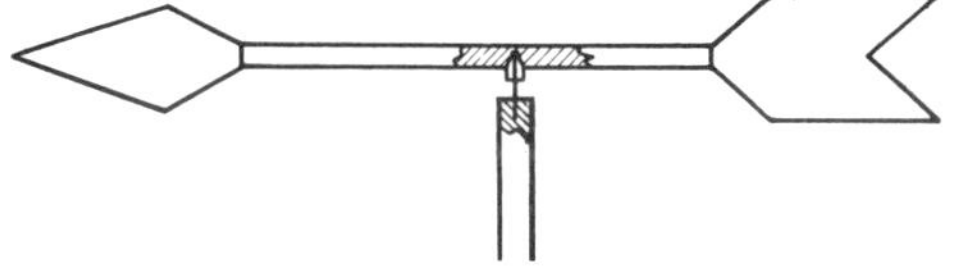

the nail and mount your wind vane on top of a building or on a pole where it is exposed to the wind from all directions.

Fix stout wire arms to the pole and bend the symbols N, E, S, W at the ends, or solder to each free end large letters cut from sheet metal.

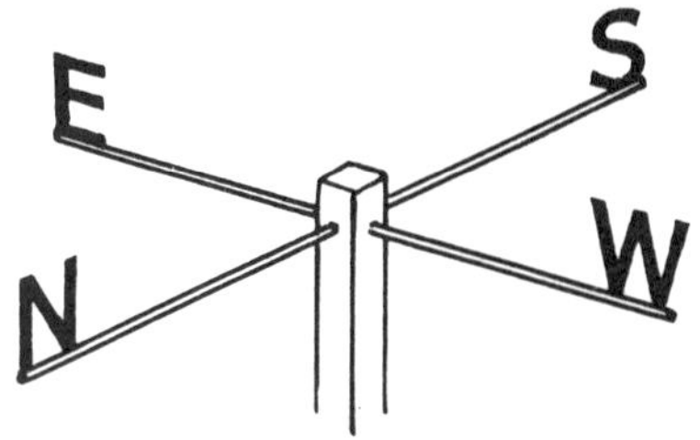

3 A wind speed indicator

Select two pieces of light wood about 50 cm long and 1 cm square. Cut a notch 1 cm wide and about 0.5 cm deep at the exact centre of each piece.

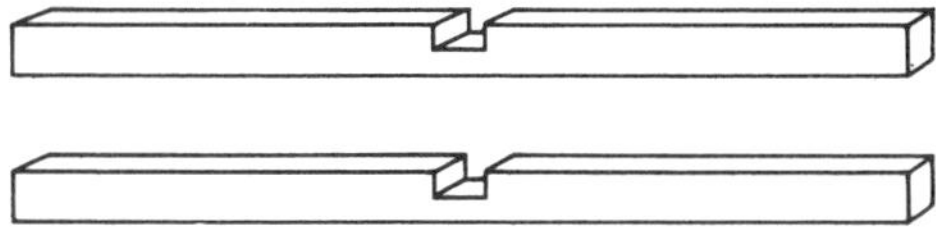

Next fit the sticks together at the notches to form cross arms.

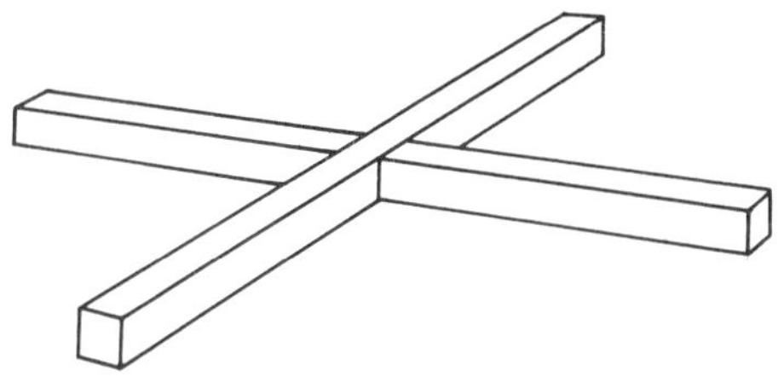

Obtain the glass tube from a medicine dropper and close the small end by rotating in a gas or alcohol flame. At the exact centre of the cross arms drill a hole about three-quarters through the wood and set the medicine-dropper tube securely in the hole with cement or putty. Secure four cigarette tins or small plastic dishes and fasten them to the ends of the cross arms with small nails or screws. Be sure the cups are all facing in the same direction. Prepare a mounting stick for the wind indicator in exactly the same way as you did for the wind vane. Drive a nail in the end of the stick and sharpen it to a point with a file.

Your wind speed indicator will spin in the wind. You can get a rough idea of the speed of the wind in miles per hour by counting the number of turns made in 30 seconds and dividing by 5. If you wish the result in kilometres per hour you divide again by 0.62.

Another way to determine the wind velocity is to have some one drive you in a car on a calm day. Hold your speed indicator out of the front window and have the driver go steadily at five miles per hour. Count the number of turns in 30 seconds for this speed. Repeat with the driver going at 10, 15, 20, 25, 30, 40, etc. miles per hour.

Mount your wind speed indicator in a place that is exposed to the wind from all directions.

4 A rain gauge

It is easy to make a simple rain gauge using a funnel and bottle, with a measuring cylinder to measure the volume of water.

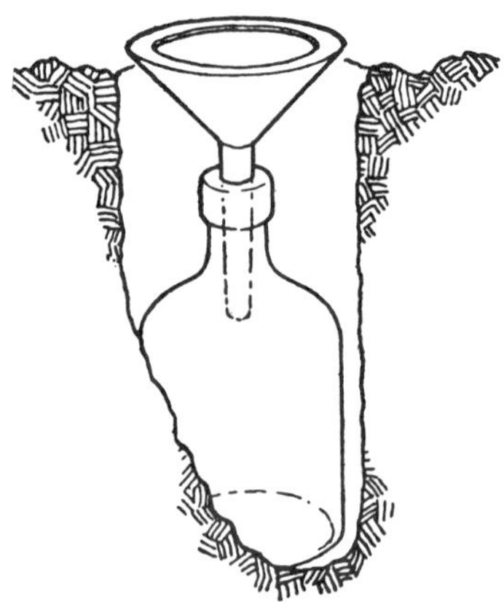

The funnel should have either a very sharp vertical edge, or a horizontal lip to prevent raindrops bouncing out again. The whole apparatus should be buried so that the funnel is a few centimetres above ground level.

5 Another rain gauge

Procure a large tin can about 10 cm in diameter and 14 cm in height. Almost any can will do. Next secure a straight-sided bottle, such as an olive oil bottle about 3 cm in diameter and at least 25 cm high, that will stand inside the larger can. Place the larger can on a level table and pour water into it until the water is exactly 1 cm deep on a ruler. Paste a strip of paper about 1 cm wide the length of the tall straight-sided jar. Next pour the water from the larger can into the tall jar and make a mark on the paper strip at the level where the 1 cm of water from the larger can comes. Measure the distance from the inside bottom of the tall jar to this mark and mark off equal spaces to the top. Divide the distances between the marks into 10 equal parts to measure millimetres. The small jar will measure small amounts of rainfall.

To assemble the rain gauge place a funnel in the tall jar and then place these in the larger can. Set the rain gauge in an open spot where it will not be easily upset. If the rainfall is light it can be measured by the small jar alone. If it is heavy, excess water will overflow into the larger can and may then be measured by pouring it into the bottle. If the rainfall is to be measured in inches, pour 1 in. of water in the large can and then pour this into the tall jar. Mark the depth to which the 1 in. of water reaches and then divide the scale accordingly.

A better way to determine the rainfall in centimetres or inches is to graduate the smaller measuring bottle in terms of its radius and the radius of the collecting funnel by use of the formula:

$$\left.\begin{array}{l}\text{Height in bottle}\\ \text{for cm or inch of}\\ \text{rainfall}\end{array}\right\} = \frac{(\text{Radius of funnel})^2}{(\text{Radius of bottle})^2}$$

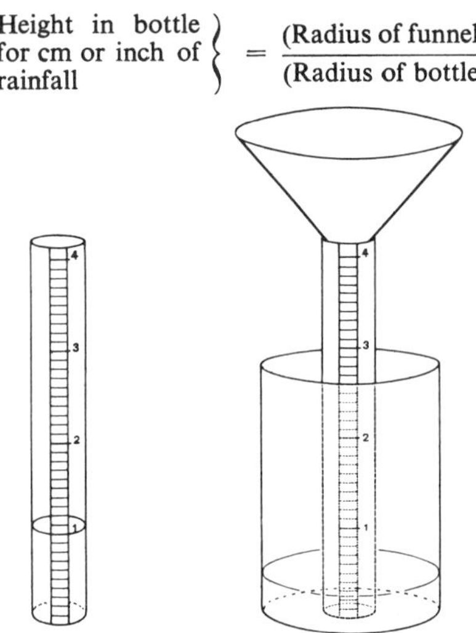

6 A wet and dry bulb hygrometer

Obtain two inexpensive thermometers, and check them in warm water at different temperatures to see that they agree. Attach the two thermometers to a piece of board, about 10 cm apart, with their bulbs projecting and exposed to the air.

Place a small bottle just under the thermometer on the right-hand side. Fasten a wick made from linen cloth or muslin around the exposed bulb and let it dip into the bottle. The bottle should be filled with rain water. This device will help you measure the relative amount of water in the air at any given time.

Hang the instrument where it has free access to the air. Fan the wet bulb until the temperature will go no lower. Make a reading of both the wet bulb and the dry bulb. Subtract the wet bulb reading from the dry bulb reading and then look up Table VI (page 245) to find the relative humidity. If your reading from the table is 40 it means that the air at that time holds only 40 per cent of the water vapour it could hold at the dry bulb temperature.

7 A hair hygrometer

This device will enable you to read the relative humidity directly without the use of tables.

Procure a few human hairs about 30 cm long. Free them from grease with dilute caustic soda solution. Fix one to the upper end of a stand and stretch it with a 50 gm weight. The hair should pass two or three times round a spool fixed to an axle which is free to rotate in bearings made from a piece of tin and fastened two-thirds of the way down the stand. Fix a light pointer of balsa wood to the axle, and arrange a postcard to act as a scale. For greatest sensitivity the diameter of the spool should be small.

Changes in atmospheric humidity will affect the length of the hair and the position of the pointer.

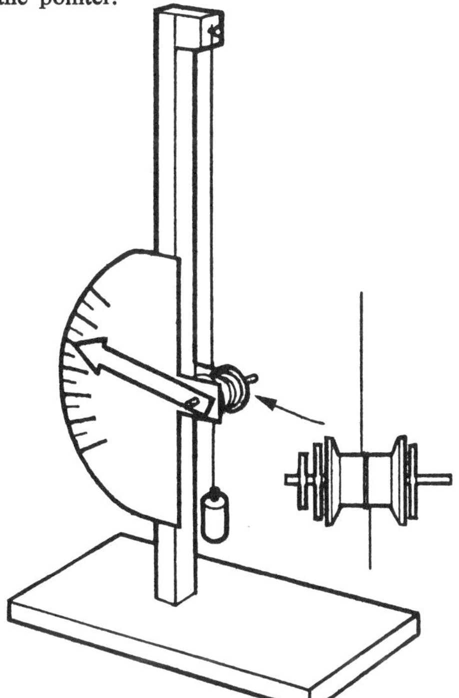

To mark off the scale it is best to compare your hygrometer with a standard one. If one of these is not available place the instrument above some warm water in a pail and cover with a wet towel. When the pointer has moved as far as it will, mark this point 100 on your scale for the air in the pail will be 100 per cent saturated. Other points can be marked by taking readings on your wet and dry bulb hygrometer. Find the relative humidity from Table VI (page 245) and mark the position of the pointer on your scale accordingly. When you have established about three points on your scale you can then divide the rest into equal divisions and mark them off at 5 interval markings from 5 to 100.

8 A weather house

Changes in the amount of water vapour present in the atmosphere can be indicated by variation in tension in a few strands of human hair or by using the hygroscopic properties of a piece of catgut.

The familiar weather house can be constructed from cardboard. One end of the gut is glued to a piece of cork on the roof angle, the other end carries a horizontal platform on which figures can be mounted. The direction of twist of the gut can be found by trial. Two sides of the house should be open to prevent heat accumulation, and the outside should be painted white.

9 A weather picture

A piece of white blotting paper is immersed in a solution containing two parts cobalt chloride to one part common salt. While wet the paper will remain pink, but when dried in the sun or near a bunsen burner it turns blue.

This is the basis of the weather pictures sold in the shops. A home-made one works just as well. A picture containing sky or water can be cut from a book and an inset of this prepared blotting paper made to replace say, the sky. The picture should then be mounted on a card and hung near a window where it will quickly respond to changes in the hygrometric state of the atmosphere.

10 Keeping a weather record

Some kind of scale of intensity is necessary when keeping a record of the weather.

The date, hour, temperature, sky, and wind can all be recorded in a table.

It is better to take the readings at the same time each day.

If no thermometer is available, a suitable temperature scale is: hot, warm, moderate, cool, cold, very cold.

There are international weather symbols, but abbreviated scales can be used unless the records are for some official purpose.

The velocity of the wind can also be recorded.

Light—moves smoke, but not wind vanes.
Moderate—raises dust and just moves twigs.
Strong—large branches move.
High—blows dust, papers and moves whole trees.
Gale—breaks off twigs from trees.

Date	*Time*	*Temperature*	*Sky*	*Wind*	*Rain*

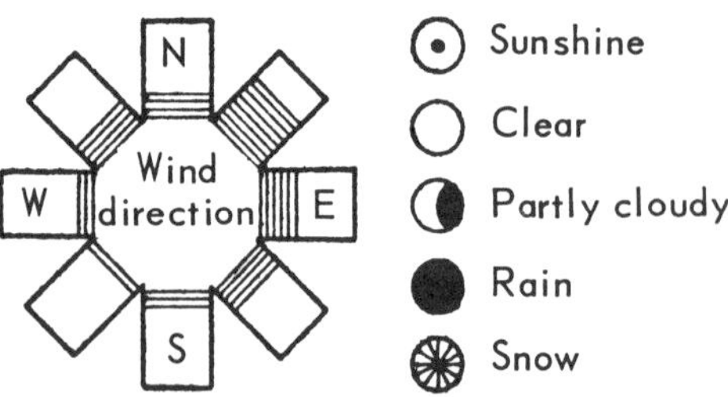

The direction of the wind can be indicated by an arrow in the column, but it is interesting to construct a paper star as shown in the diagram and to draw a line each day along the arm which most nearly coincides with the direction of the wind.

11 Making a housing box for weather instruments

Some of your weather instruments must be exposed to the weather. Among these are the wind vane, the wind speed indicator and the rain gauge. It is wise to protect metal parts of these instruments with either grease or paint. Aluminium paint works very well for this purpose.

Other instruments such as the barometer, the thermometer, and the hygrometer, need to be shielded from rain and wind. These may be placed in a wooden box which has no top. Place the instruments in the box so that one of the closed sides forms a roof and another a floor for your house. The open side should be fitted with louvres, such as are found in a window blind, for best results. This will provide a free access of air but will protect the instruments from wind and precipitation.

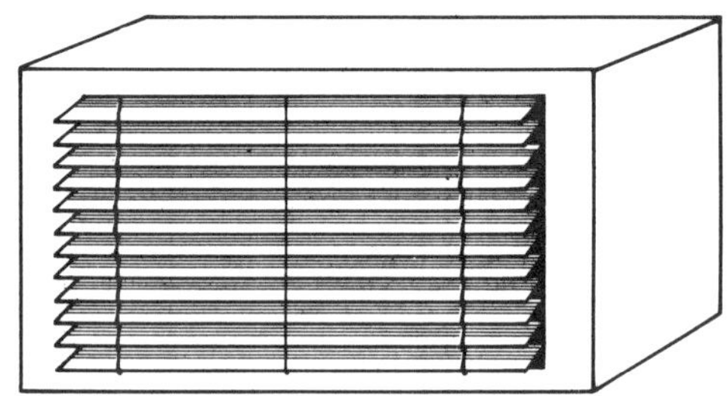

B. WINDS AND WEATHER

1 Air expands when heated

To show that air expands when heated, fit an electric light bulb flask or a bottle with a one-hole stopper or cork which has a 30-cm length of glass tubing or a soda straw through it. Place the end of the tube in a small bottle of water. Heat the flask and observe what happens. Heat the flask until a considerable amount of air has been removed and then cool the flask by pouring cold water over it or by rubbing it with a piece of ice. What do you observe? How do you account for this?

2 Another way to show that air expands when heated

Snap a toy balloon over the neck of a small bottle and place the bottle in a pan of warm water. What do you observe? How do you account for this?

3 Expansion of air

Connect a one-hole rubber stopper carrying a short length of glass tube into a 2 or 3 litre can with a narrow opening. Attach a rubber tube to the glass tube. Invert a bottle of water in a basin of water and put the end of the rubber tube under the edge of the bottle. Heat the can. What do you observe? How do you explain this?

4 Cold air is heavier than warm air

(a) Make a simple balance as you did in experiment C 1, page 77, for showing the weight of air. Secure two paper bags that are the same size. Open the bags and attach a 20 cm thread to the bottom of each one with a piece of Scotch tape or by making a hole in the bottom of the bag, inserting the thread and then tying a knot in the end. Make a loop on the other end of each thread that will go over the ends of the balance rod. Place a bag near each end of the rod. Move the bags in or out until they are in exact balance. With a candle heat the air well below one of the bags. What do you observe? Let the balance stand for several minutes. What happens? Now heat the air under the other bag. Observe what happens. How do you account for this?

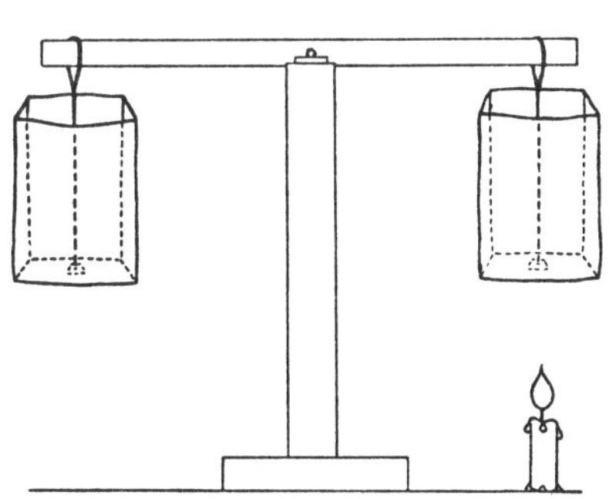

(b) Another way to study the difference in weight between warm and cool air is to use flasks on the balance rather than paper bags. Attach the flasks with loops of string. Move them until they are in perfect balance and then heat one flask gently. Observe the effect. Allow to cool to room temperature. Observe and then heat the other flask. Flasks made from old light bulbs work very well for this experiment.

5 A convection box

A box to show why winds blow may be made easily. Use a wood or pasteboard box for which you can secure a pane of glass, the correct size to make a tight window. A wood chalk box which has grooves for a cover works very well. Cut the glass so that it will slide in the grooves. Next bore two holes in one of the long sides of the box, one near each end. The holes should be from 2.5 to 3 cm in diameter. The box must lie with this side up. Secure two lamp chimneys to place over the holes. If lamp chimneys are not available you can use pieces of mailing tube about 15 cm in length. Place a short piece of candle on the floor of the box just under one of the chimneys. Light the candle. This represents a land area that has been heated by the sun. Close the window and, with a piece of smoking paper, trace the air current in each chimney. Observe the movement of air inside the box. Move the candle under the other chimney and repeat. What do you observe? How do you account for this? This is called a convection current.

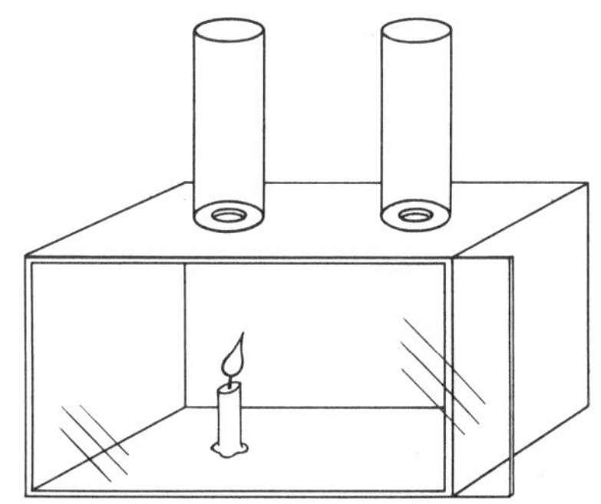

6 Tracing convection currents

(a) Shield a burning candle to protect it from stray air currents. Trace the air currents about it with smoking paper.

(b) Open a door a little way between a warm and a cool room. With a piece of smoking paper explore the air currents about the opening at various levels above the floor.

(c) If you can, explore the air currents in a room that is heated with a radiator or a stove.

(d) Explore the air currents in a room that is ventilated with windows open at the top and at the bottom.

(e) Lower a lighted candle into a milk bottle by means of a wire. Observe what happens. Ventilate the bottle with fresh air. Again place the lighted candle in the bottle but this time separate the warm and cold air currents by a piece of cardboard cut in the shape of the letter T as shown in the diagram. Explore the air currents on each side of the cardboard with smoking paper.

(f) Cut out a metal can top with a rotary opener so as to have a metal disk. Punch a depression in the exact centre. Cut along radial lines almost to the centre and give each of the blades thus formed a twist in the same direction. Mount the wheel on a pointed wire and hold it over a candle or other source of heat. A carefully made wheel of this kind will also turn over a radiator or a lighted electric lamp.

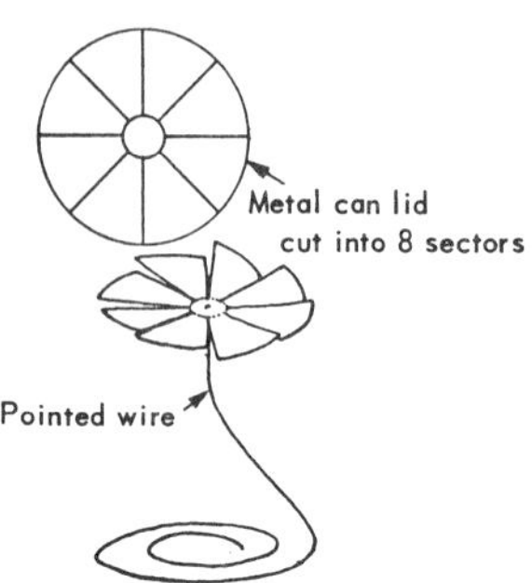

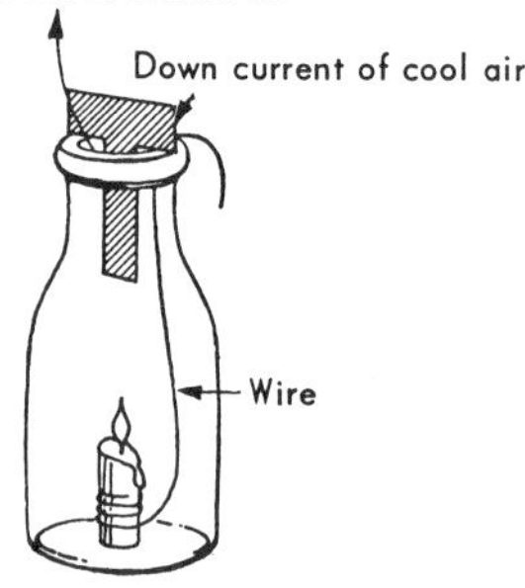

Place a metal foil top from a milk bottle on a piece of blotting paper with the flat side down. Press the point of a ball pen into the middle to make a dent. Cut 'petals' in the turned-up edge to form the vanes of a turbine. Pivot it on a pointed wire or on a needle stuck eye downwards into a cork. This is more sensitive to convection currents than the apparatus described above.

C. HOW MOISTURE GETS INTO THE AIR

1 You cannot see atmospheric moisture

Place some water over a fire in a vessel that has a spout such as a tea kettle or copper pot. If these are not available, fit a flask with a one-hole stopper and place a right-angle bend of glass tubing in it. Place some water in the flask and put it over a flame. When the water is boiling and steam issues from the spout, observe the cloud that is formed. This is not steam, but condensed water. Observe the space next to the spout when the steam comes out. Can you see it? Now hold a candle or a burner in the cloud of condensed steam. What do you observe? Where does the moisture go?

2 The mop weighs less

Put a floor mop in water. Wring it out and then balance it on a triangular file placed on the corner of a table. Be sure you have it carefully balanced. Look at the mop an hour later. What has happened? How do you account for this? Where has the water gone?

3 Weighing moisture again

The same experiment can be done with a bath towel. Wet the towel and wring it out. Hang it on a coat hanger. Hang the coat hanger on one end of a long stick balanced over the corner of a table on a triangular file.

4 Moisture evaporates from soil

Fill a flower pot with moist soil and place it on a pair of scales. Either balance the pot of soil with weights or observe its weight. Observe its weight again after 24 hours.

5 Moisture comes from house plants

Place a cellophane bag over a leaf of some house plant or garden plant and close the end about the stem with a rubber band. Make an observation after one hour. What do you observe? Where did it come from?

6 Moisture comes from other plants

Secure a flower pot which has some bean or pea seedlings that are 10 or 15 cm in height. Cover the top of the pot with cellophane or sheet rubber, pinning it closely around the stems of the plants so no soil is uncovered. Invert a clean, dry glass jar over the plants and observe after an hour. What do you see? Where did it come from?

7 Moisture from breathing

Moisture coming from breathing may be shown by blowing on a cool mirror or into a cool glass or bottle.

8 Moisture from a gas flame

Moisture coming from a flame may be shown by placing a pan of cold water over a gas stove for a few moments. Remove the pan from the fire and observe the bottom.

9 Moisture from other flames

Bring the flame of a candle near a cool blackboard. Repeat using the flame of a gas burner, the flame from an alcohol lamp, the flame from a piece of burning paper, and the flame from a piece of burning wood. What do you observe? Where did it come from?

10 Area affects the rate of evaporation

Measure 50 ml of water and pour it out into a container of much larger diameter than the graduate. Again measure 50 ml in the graduate. Place them side by side where the temperature and air movements will be the same. On the following day measure the amount of water in each container. What causes the difference in evaporation?

11 Temperature affects the rate of evaporation

Warm a spot on a blackboard or slate by using a candle or by placing in the sun. Place water spots of equal size on this warm area and on a cool area. Observe the spots and see what happens.

12 Moving air affects the rate of evaporation

With a moist sponge or cloth, make spots of equal size on a cool blackboard surface at some distance apart. Fan one spot with a piece of cardboard and leave the other to evaporate without fanning.

What causes the difference in rate of evaporation?

13 Moisture in the air affects the rate of evaporation

Fasten some cloth over a wooden hoop or frame that is about 30 cm square and about 3 cm thick. Wet the cloth. Next make two wet spots on a cool blackboard surface with a sponge or cloth. Cover one with the frame carrying the wet cloth and leave the other one open. After a few moments observe both spots. Which has evaporated the faster? How does moist air (under the frame) affect the rate of evaporation?

D. HOW MOISTURE COMES OUT OF THE AIR

1 Moisture condenses on cool surfaces

Place some ice in a shiny tin can. After a little while observe the outside of the can. What do you observe? Where did it come from?

2 The water cycle

Heat some water until it is near the boiling point. Place it in a drinking glass and rotate the glass so as to moisten the sides right to the top. Place some very cold water in a round flask, such as one made from an electric bulb or a Florence flask. Place the flask on the glass at an angle as shown. Water will evaporate from the hot water, condense on the cool surface of the flask and fall back in droplets into the glass. Here

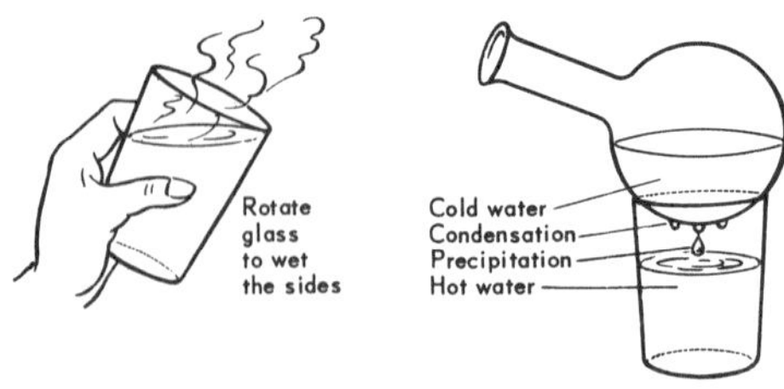

you have evaporation, condensation and precipitation. You have seen the water cycle as it goes on in nature.

3 Dew-point temperature

You can measure the dew-point temperature with a shiny can containing some water, a thermometer and some ice. The dew-point temperature is an important weather observation. It is the temperature at which the moisture in the air begins to condense. The dew-point temperature changes from day to day.

Be sure that the outside of the can is dry and shiny. Place some water inside the can and then stand the can on a page of printing so that the printing is clearly reflected from the can. Place the thermometer in the can. Now add ice, a little at a time, to the water and carefully stir with the thermometer. Keep close watch of the temperature and read the thermometer at the temperature where dew begins to form on the outside of the can. This will be near the dew-point temperature.

4 A cloud in a bottle

You can make a cloud form in a bottle. Obtain a large glass bottle and fit with a rubber stopper carrying a 10-cm length of glass tubing. Place about 2.5 cm of warm water in the bottle and dust a little chalk dust into the air inside. Connect the glass tube to a bicycle pump with a piece of rubber tubing. Hold the stopper in the bottle and have a pupil pump air in. When the air has been compressed inside the bottle let the stopper blow out and observe what happens. If you do not get a good cloud, introduce a little smoke from a smouldering match or cigarette.

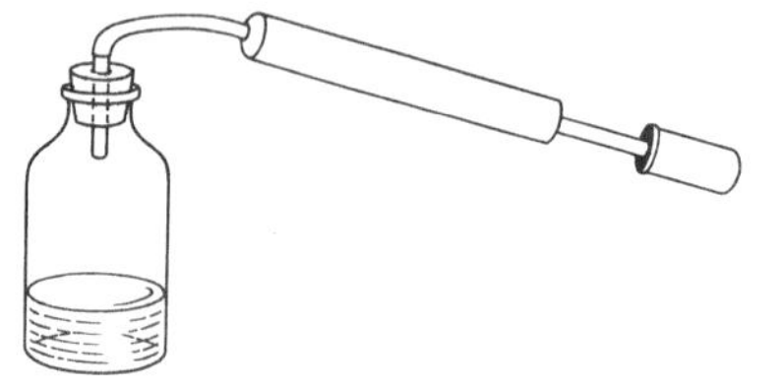

When the air expands it cools, thus reducing the temperature in the bottle below the dew point. The moisture condenses as a cloud. When warm air rises above the earth the air pressure is reduced. The air expands, cools and clouds form when the cooling goes below the dew point.

5 The rain cycle

You can reproduce the rain cycle in miniature in your classroom. Place a box of plant seedlings on the table. Place a metal tray about 35 to 40 cm above the box of seedlings and support it. Strew the top of the tray with pieces of cracked ice. Place a tea kettle or flask containing water over a source of heat so that steam will issue between the seedlings and the tray. You are now ready to study the rain cycle. The tea kettle or flask serves as the earth source of water. This evaporates and rises up to the cool tray which represents the upper layers of air above the earth which have been cooled by expansion. Here the moisture condenses on the tray and drips back on to the seedlings as rain.

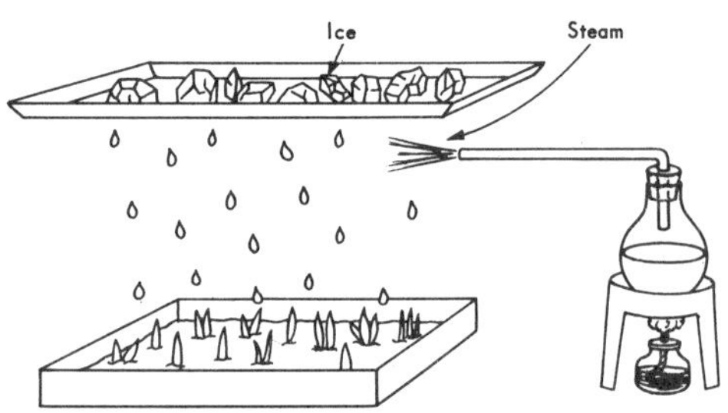

6 Frost in the classroom

Frost can be made in the classroom by using a tall metal container such as a tin can. Pack the can with alternate layers of ice and salt, using about twice as much ice as salt. Tamp the mixture with a stick as you pack it. When it is full, watch the outside of the can. Some dew will form and may freeze, but you should also be able to observe the delicate white frost which forms. When the can has stood for a while it will be covered with a beautiful white frost.

7 To study a hailstone

When it hails, collect some of the hailstones. Cut them in half and observe how the ice of the hailstone has been built up in layers.

8 To study snow-flakes

If you live in a region where snow falls, collect some snow-flakes on a piece of dark wool cloth and look at them with a magnifying glass. You will find them of many, many shapes, but always six-sided. Snow-flakes are among the most beautiful sights in nature.

CHAPTER IX

Experiments and materials for the study of water

A. THE COMPOSITION OF WATER

1 How water can be decomposed

You will need a six-volt storage battery or accumulator or a battery of six dry cells for this interesting experiment.

Remove the insulation from about 6 cm at each end of two lengths of copper wire each at least 30 cm long. Next secure the gold points from two old fountain pens and wrap the uninsulated end of one of the copper wires securely around each one. Cover the joint with sealing wax so that no copper is exposed. Connect one wire to each terminal of the battery. Fill a shallow glass cooking dish about half full of water. Fill two small bottles with water, place a piece of cardboard over the mouth and invert them in the dish of water. Stand each bottle on two thin strips of wood so that the mouth is raised from the bottom of the dish. Now carefully place one of the pen points up in each bottle.

Place about two tablespoonfuls of sulphuric acid in the water and give it a few moments to mix thoroughly. Be very careful in handling the sulphuric acid, as it will burn if it touches your skin, and it will make holes in your clothing if you spill it. You can obtain sulphuric acid at a drug store, a battery service station or from a chemical laboratory.

When all is ready turn on the current. This experiment may take some time to complete. Observe what happens in each bottle. If the bottles are the same size you can measure the results with a ruler. How do these compare?

When the bottles are filled with gas place a glass plate over the mouth of each one. Leave the one which filled more quickly mouth downward on the glass plate. Set the one which filled less quickly mouth upward with the glass plate still covering. Place a glowing splint in the bottle which you placed mouth upward. What happens? This gas is oxygen.

Bring a lighted splint to the mouth of the bottle you left inverted. What happens? This gas is hydrogen. Have you ever heard water called H_2O? Can you explain this from your experiment?

2 How oxygen can be prepared

Directions for preparing oxygen are given in Chapter VII, page 88.

3 Some experiments with oxygen

Directions for experiments with oxygen are given in Chapter VII, page 89.

4 How to prepare hydrogen

Hydrogen can be prepared from a dilute acid, such as hydrochloric or sulphuric, when it is chemically reacted with a metal such as zinc. The acid may be secured from a drug store. It should be handled carefully to avoid spilling acid on hands or clothing. Zinc can be secured from the outside container of an old dry cell. Clean the zinc thoroughly and cut into pieces about 2.5 cm square.

To make the hydrogen place the zinc in a flask or bottle fitted with a two-hole rubber stopper. Through one hole place a funnel tube that reaches nearly to the bottom. In the other hole place a tube with a right-angle bend and attach to it a 30 or 40 cm length of rubber tubing. Fill a pan about half full of water and invert bottles of water in the pan. Place the end of the delivery tube in a bottle to collect

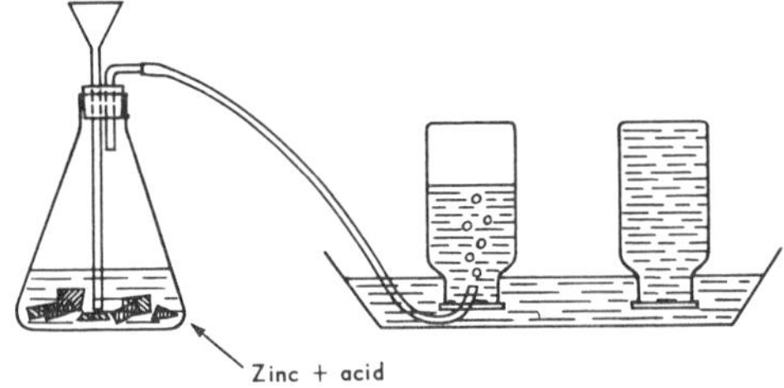

the hydrogen. Pour the dilute acid on the zinc through the funnel tube. Be sure to keep flames away from the generator; hydrogen mixed with air is very explosive. When the bottles are filled with hydrogen, put a glass plate over the mouth and stand them on the table, mouth down.

5 Does hydrogen burn?

Light a wood splint and bring it near one of the bottles of hydrogen as you lift it from the table. Push the wood splint up in the bottle. Now slowly remove the splint. What happens? Does hydrogen burn? Does it support burning like oxygen does?

6 What is produced when hydrogen burns?

Place a short length of glass tubing on the end of the rubber delivery tube and get a good action with zinc and acid in the flask. Bring a smouldering wood splint to the tube. The hydrogen should burn quietly with a pale blue flame. Bring a cold dish or metal plate into contact with the flame. What is formed when hydrogen burns (unites with oxygen)?

7 Blowing soap bubbles with hydrogen

Mix up a strong soap solution that will make good soap bubbles. Place a small funnel tube or a clay pipe on the delivery tube. When you have a good action of acid and zinc in the flask, blow bubbles with the hydrogen. When each bubble has been formed a slight jerk will detach it from the funnel and it will rise to the ceiling. You can have a lot of fun trying to light the bubbles by placing a lighted candle on the end of a stick to reach them near the ceiling.

B. HOW WATER CAN BE PURIFIED

1 How to make a filter

A plant pot with a plug of cotton wool in the bottom and a layer of sand a few inches deep makes a satisfactory filter for many purposes as shown in Chapter II, experiment C 10.

Make some muddy water by stirring earth in a dish of water. Pour the water into the filter and catch it in a clear glass as it drips out. See if you can improve the filter by building it up with alternate layers of sand and powdered charcoal. Such a filter will work very well for clarifying water before it is boiled for drinking purposes.

2 How to make an experimental filter

Fit a one-hole stopper carrying a short length of glass tube into the small end of a lamp chimney. Put a little cotton wool in the bottom and then a layer of small clean pebbles. Wash some coarse sand well and place a layer above the pebbles. Next wash some fine sand and make a thicker layer in the filter. Grind up some wood charcoal and make into a paste with water. Pour the charcoal paste evenly over the surface of the sand. Secure some very muddy water and pour in the top of the filter. Collect the filtrate in a clean glass placed below the filter.

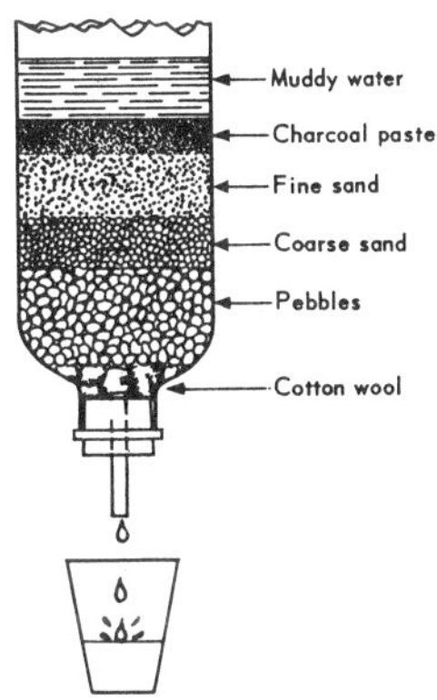

3 Sterilizing water by boiling

The presence of tiny living plants and animals makes water unsuitable for drinking. Such forms of life can only be seen through a microscope. We can study how boiling affects living things in a simple way. White of egg is known to be chemically very similar to the substance that makes up the bodies of living bacteria.

Fill a test tube or flask about half full of water and heat it to boiling. With a medicine dropper put a few drops of egg white in the boiling water. Observe that the egg white is changed completely. It becomes like egg white in a boiled or fried egg. We say it has coagulated. This is probably what happens to the living tissue of harmful bacteria when water containing them is boiled.

4 How to make a simple apparatus for distilling water

You can make a simple water-distilling apparatus from a flask, and a length of glass or rubber tubing. Fit the flask with a one-hole stopper or cork which has a short length of glass tube through it. Either bend a 60 cm length of glass tube as shown in the diagram or use a piece of rubber tube. Attach this tube to the tube in the flask. Use a flask, or drinking glass or jam jar to collect the distilled water. Fill the boiling flask about half full with muddy water containing some ink or other colouring material. Boil the water over a suitable flame.

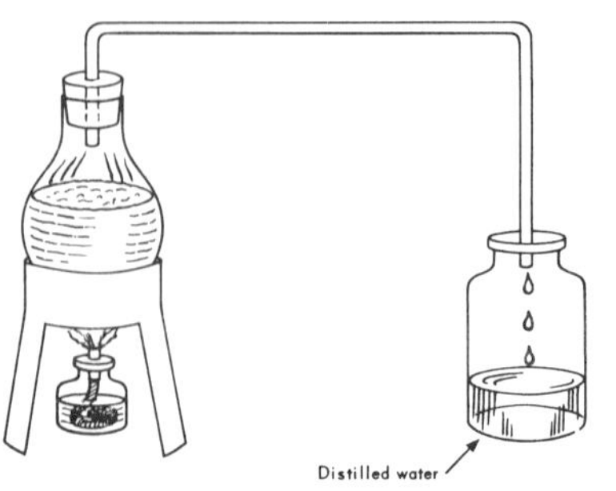

5 How to make a larger distiller

See Chapter II, item C 7, page 36.

6 How to make a Liebig condenser

See Chapter II, item C 9, page 36.

C. HARD WATER AND SOFT WATER

Hard water contains minerals which are dissolved from the rocks as the water runs over and through the earth. Soft water is water that contains little or no dissolved minerals, such as rain water or distilled water.

1 The difference between hard and soft water

Collect some hard water from a stream (or make some as described in the next experiment). Also secure some soft water such as rain water or distilled water. Make some soap solution by dissolving soap shavings or powdered soap in a little warm water. Place equal amounts of hard and soft water in each of two bottles. Add soap solution to the soft water with a dropper, a few drops at a time. Shake the bottle well after each addition. Count the number of drops of soap solution needed to produce suds about 1 cm thick on the top.

Next add the same amount of soap solution to the hard water and shake well for about the same length of time. Observe any differences. Continue to add soap solution to the hard water until you get good suds. How do the amounts of soap used compare?

2 How to make hard water

There are two kinds of hard water, one called temporary and the other called permanent. Temporary hard water can be made as follows: Start with some clear lime water (see Chapter XVIII, item 12, page 214, for directions). Bubble carbon dioxide (see K 14, page 89) through the lime water until the cloudiness first formed disappears and you will have some temporary hard water. Permanent hard water can be prepared by stirring some calcium sulphate or plaster of Paris with water and letting it stand for several hours. After this has been filtered the clear filtrate will be permanently hard. You can also prepare this type of hard water by dissolving magnesium sulphate (Epsom salts) in water.

3 Softening hard water by boiling

Temporary hardness can be removed from water by boiling. Shake a little temporary hard water with a few drops of soap solution and see if you can make suds. Next boil a similar amount of the water that contains temporary hardness. Try making suds with this sample after adding the same amount of soap solution.

4 Softening water with chemicals

Try making suds with a half test tube of hard water and a few drops of soap solution. Next boil a similar sample and again try to make suds by using the same amount of soap solution.

Add some washing soda (sodium carbonate) to a sample of permanent hard water. Try making suds with soap solution. Has the water been softened? Add some borax (sodium pyroborate) to a sample of permanent hard water and test to see if it has been softened.

How soap helps water in cleaning

repare two greasy cloths by smearing itchen fat or vaseline on cloths. Wash one ample in warm water without soap. Wash e other sample in warm water with heavy oap suds. Hang the samples to dry and bserve which one was made cleaner by ashing.

How water acts towards fat

Ialf-fill a tall glass jar with warm water. dd some olive oil or other oil to a epth of about 1 cm. Shake this mixture hard.)bserve how the fat is broken up into tiny roplets or globules. Allow this to stand and bserve that the globules all finally come ogether and collect on the surface. Set this side to compare with the next experiment.

How soap acts towards fat

repare another jar with warm water and oil ust as you did in the experiment above. This ime add about half a cup of either liquid oap or strong soap solution made by dis-olving soap chips in water. Shake this mix-ure vigorously, allow to stand and compare vith the sample from the previous experiment. 'ou should observe that the soap has broken up the globules of fat and they are now distri-buted so that the mixture looks like milk.

8 Hard and soft water in cleaning

Prepare two samples of dirty cloth. Wash one in soft water with soap until it is clean. Wash the other cloth in hard water for the same length of time and with the same amount of soap. Hang the samples to dry and observe the difference.

9 How to make soap

Soap can be made from waste fat. Secure some waste fats and melt in a dish. Strain the fat through several layers of cloth. Weigh the fat and then weigh out about one third as much commercial lye (sodium hydroxide). Dissolve the lye in water. Heat the fat in an iron kettle or dish. When it is melted, pour the lye solution in slowly and stir continu-ously. Keep the flame low to avoid boiling over. Let the fat and lye boil for 30 minutes with frequent stirring. After boiling add com-mon salt—about twice the weight of lye used. Stir well. When this mixture has cooled the soap will appear as a layer at the top. Take only the soap, melt and pour it into match boxes to make little cakes of soap. Is it a good soap?

D. WATER AT REST AND IN MOTION

The meaning of pressure

Stand with muddy feet or boots on a piece of aper and draw an outline of the footprints. Measure the area using squared paper, and alculate the force per square centimetre. Standing on one foot will distribute your veight over about half the area, with a orresponding increase in pressure which can lso be calculated.

2 The difference between weight and pressure

Make two square blocks of wood, one much maller than the other, and join them to-gether as shown in the diagram. Press each of hese faces consecutively into a slab of clay or plasticine using the same force in each case.

The difference in pressure is seen by the different depths of the indentations.

3 To show that liquids exert pressure

Connect two 15 cm lengths of glass tubing or two transparent plastic soda straws with a short length of rubber tubing and attach them to an upright as shown in the diagram.

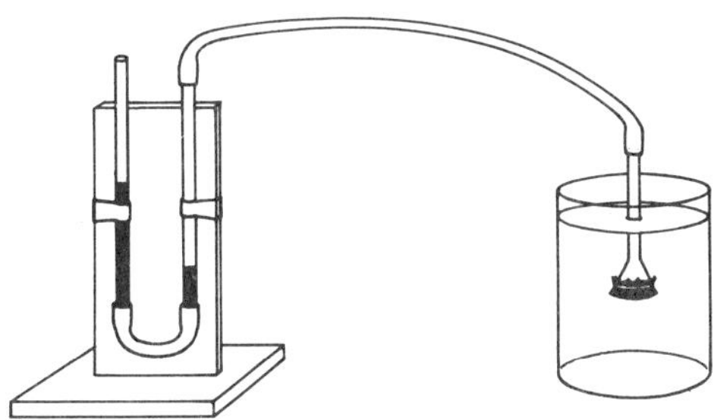

Put some coloured water in the tubes to a depth of about 6 or 8 cm. This is your pressure gauge or manometer. Cover a small funnel with thin rubber stretched tightly and tie it securely with thread or string. Attach the funnel to the manometer with a 30 cm length of rubber tubing. Push the funnel into a pail of water and watch the manometer.

4 Water pressure changes with depth

Use the funnel and manometer which you made in the previous experiment. Fill a tall glass jar or pail with water. Measure the pressure just below the surface with your manometer. Measure the pressure at the bottom. How does pressure change with depth?

5 Pressure depends upon the liquid

Obtain two glass jars into which the funnel will fit. Fill one with water and the other, to the same depth, with a less dense liquid such as alcohol. Measure the pressure at the bottom of the jar of water. Measure the pressure at the bottom of the jar of alcohol. How do they compare for the same depth?

6 Water pressure in a large vessel is the same as in a small one, at the same depth

Use the funnel and manometer from the above experiments. Secure a tall glass jar of small diameter and a glass jar of larger diameter. Fill both jars to the same depth with water. Measure the pressure at the bottom of each jar. How do they compare?

7 Another way to show that water pressure increases with depth

Find a tall tin can. Punch holes up the side of the can about 3 cm apart. Put a strip of adhesive or plastic tape over the row of holes and fill the can with water above the top hole. Hold the can over a sink and strip the tape from the holes beginning at the bottom. Observe the streams and note the distances travelled outwards from the can.

8 Water pressure is the same in all directions

Punch holes around the base of a tall tin can with a nail. Cover the holes as above with a strip of tape. Fill the can with water and strip off the tape while holding it over a sink. Observe and compare the distance the streams shoot out from the holes all around the can.

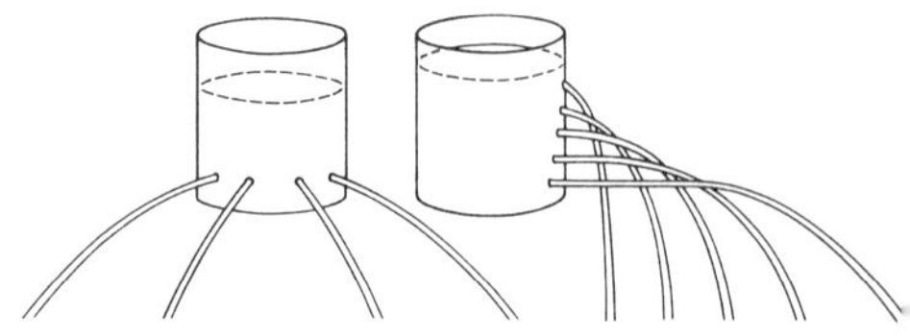

9 Upward and downward pressure are the same at any given depth

Obtain a glass cylinder at least 15 cm long and 4 cm in diameter. Such a length of tube can be made from a straight-sided bottle like an olive oil bottle by removing the bottom (see page 218). A clear plastic tube will do or even a cardboard mailing tube that has been coated with paraffin wax or shellac.

Cut a square of cardboard about 5 cm on one side. Coat it with paraffin or shellac. Attach a length of thread or string to the centre with tape. Put the thread through the tube and hold the cardboard to the bottom with the thread. Plunge the tube, card-end down into a jar of water. Let go of the thread. Now pour coloured water into the tube. Note the depth of water inside the tube when the card falls away.

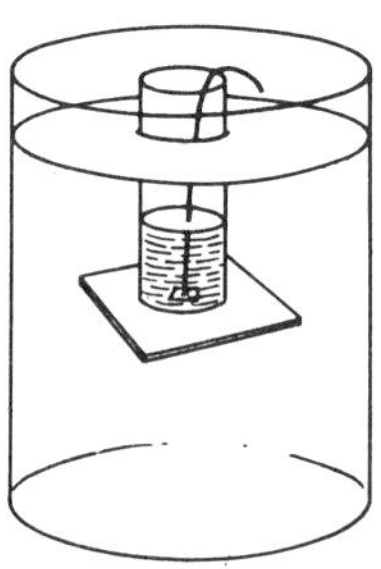

10 Balancing water columns

Remove the bottoms from several glass bottles of different shapes but of about the same height (see page 218 for directions). Fit the bottles with stoppers or corks carrying glass tubes as shown in the diagram. Connect the bottles together as shown. Pour coloured water into the bottles until they are nearly full. This experience again shows that in a given liquid, pressure is independent of the size or shape of the vessel and depends only on the depth.

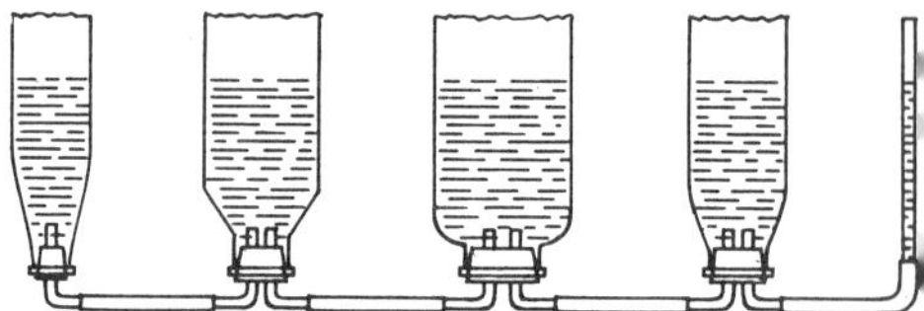

11 Raising heavy weights by water pressure

Obtain a rubber hot-water bottle. Put a one-hole stopper carrying a short glass tube tightly in the neck. Punch a hole in the bottom of a tin can and make it large enough to take a one-hole stopper. Put a short length of glass tube through the stopper. Connect the water bottle and the can with a length of rubber tube at least 1.25 metres in length—it will be wise to wind wire around the connexion at the bottle. Fill the bottle, tube and can with water. Place the bottle on the floor and put a length of board on it. Place books or other heavy objects on the board. Now raise the can above the level of the floor and observe the weights. See how heavy a weight you can lift by raising the can as high above the floor as possible.

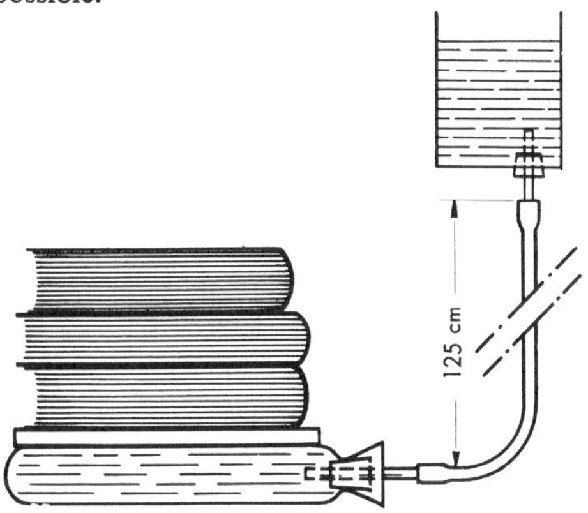

12 Water will not compress

Fit a soda water bottle with a one-hole stopper. Through the stopper place the glass tube from a medicine dropper, narrow end up. Fill the bottle to the top with water. Insert the stopper tightly until the water rises a little way in the medicine dropper. Now grasp the bottle in your hands and squeeze as hard as you can. The water will rise in the tube because you cannot compress it. Can you make the water run over the top of the tube?

Fill a medicine bottle with water. Force in a good cork. Strike the cork sharply with a hammer; the bottle will burst.

13 Making a model hydraulic elevator

Some freight and passenger elevators are raised by water pressure. You can make a model of one of these with an automobile hand pump. Connect the tube from the pump to a length of rubber tube. Bind the connexions with wire so they will not blow out. Now connect the tube to a water tap with a one-hole rubber stopper. Again bind the connexion of the tube and stopper. Steady one of your pupils as he sits on the handle. Turn the water on slowly and see if the water pressure will lift him. You may have to hold the stopper in the tap.

14 Simple hydraulic press

The principle of the hydraulic press is illustrated by the following model.

Half fill a cylindrical jar with water. Pour melted paraffin wax on the surface to form a piston, holding a piece of glass tubing in the wax as it cools. When the wax is solidified it forms a watertight piston. Gently blow down the tube, and the plug will be raised. Considerable weights placed on the piston can be lifted in this way.

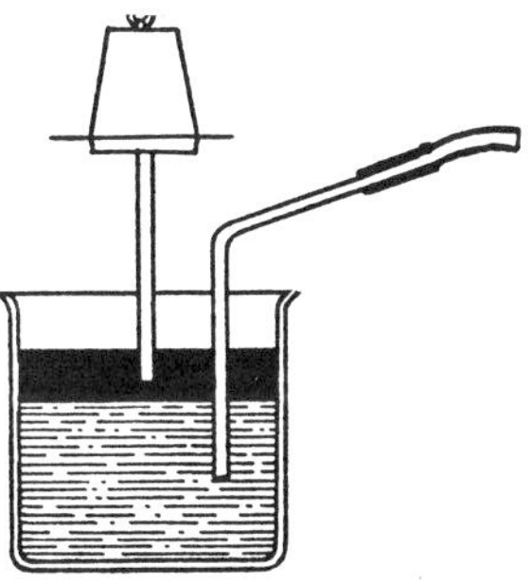

15 A model hydraulic ram

Hydraulic rams are sometimes used to raise water from a low level to a higher level. They are operated by a flowing stream of water.

You can make a model hydraulic ram. Secure a soda water bottle from which the bottom has been removed (see page 218 for directions). Fit the bottle with a one-hole rubber stopper carrying a short length of glass tubing. Connect this to a glass or metal T-tube which has a piece of rubber tubing on one end and a jet tube connected to it with a rubber tube as shown in the diagram. Fill the bottle with water and pinch the tube at the end. Let

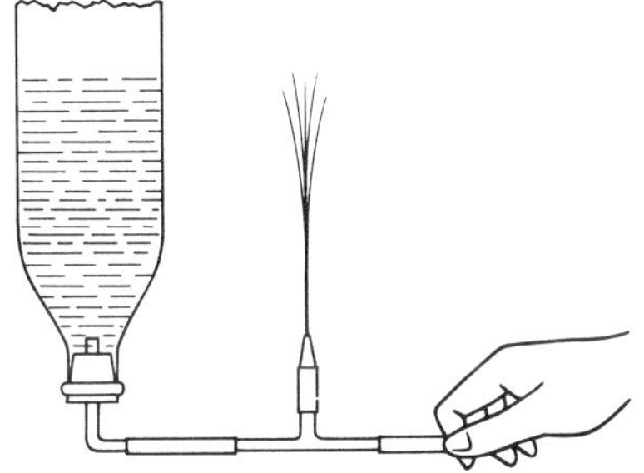

the water run from the end of the tube. Stop the flow suddenly by quickly pinching the tube, and note the height to which the water squirts from the jet tube. Let the water flow and stop alternately, and you have a working model of the hydraulic ram.

16 A model reaction water turbine

Use a soda water bottle from which the bottom has been removed. Wind string around it near the bottom end and suspend it as shown in the diagram. Fit a two-hole stopper to the neck of the bottle. Through the holes place glass tubes that have been bent as shown and have their ends drawn out to jet tubes. Fill the bottle with water and watch the turbine rotate as the water runs from the jets.

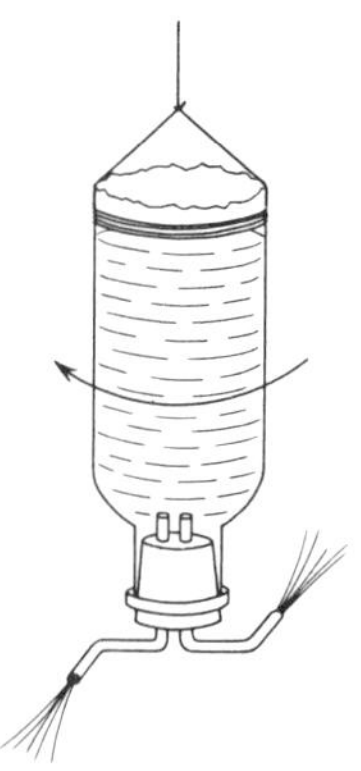

17 Model water wheels

A meat skewer or a knitting needle can be used as an axle. An old typewriter ribbon spool or a sticking plaster reel is useful as a basis for these improvisations. A stream of water from a tap, or guided from a tank along a piece of rainwater spouting is a suitable source of water power.

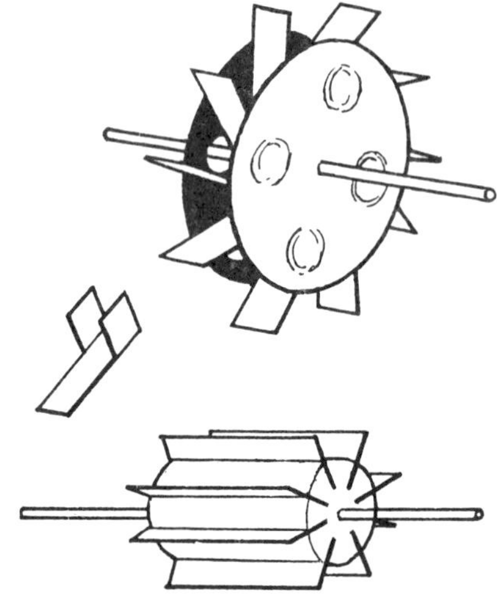

A cotton reel or cork can also be used as the 'nave' of the wheel. Cut slots down the sides, perpendicular to the ends. Slide pieces of wood or tin into these slots to act as paddles.

E. SINKING AND FLOATING

1 What determines sinking and floating?

Shape a piece of lead, tin or aluminium foil into the form of a little boat and float it on the water in a pan; now wad the metal foil from the boat into a small ball and try to float it on the water. What do you observe? What is your best explanation for this?

2 The buoyancy of water

Find a metal can like a coffee can or a cigarette tin which has a tightly fitting cover. With the cover on, push the can into a pail of water, cover end down, and quickly let go of it. Repeat this having the can in different positions. What do you observe? Can you observe the upthrust on the can? Put a little water in the can and repeat the experiment. Keep adding water a little at a time and repeating until the can no longer floats.

3 You can observe the buoyancy of water

Make an equal arm balance (see page 34 for directions). Secure two soda water-bottles and suspend them with loops of string from either side of the arm until they balance exactly. Bring a pail of water up under one of the bottles until the bottle sinks in the water a little way. Observe what happens.

4 Another way to observe the buoyancy of water

Push a large cork to the bottom of a pail of water. Notice the amount of force you have to apply to hold the cork at the bottom. Repeat the experiment using a fairly large empty bottle stopped with a cork. Is there any difference in the force required?

Blow up a toy balloon and push it to the bottom of the pail. How does the force to hold it down compare with the force required for the cork and bottle?

5 Still another way to observe the buoyancy of water

Obtain a can with a tightly fitting cover such as a cigarette tin or a coffee can. Fill the can with water and put the cover on. Put a double loop of string around the side of the can and then attach a large rubber band to the other end of the cord. Lift the can by holding the rubber band and observe how much the band stretches. Now lower the can in a pail of water and observe the stretch in the rubber band. How do you account for the difference?

6 A stone seems to weigh less in water

Weigh a large stone on a pair of kitchen scales. Put a loop of heavy string around the stone and weigh it again suspended in a pail of water. How do you explain the difference?

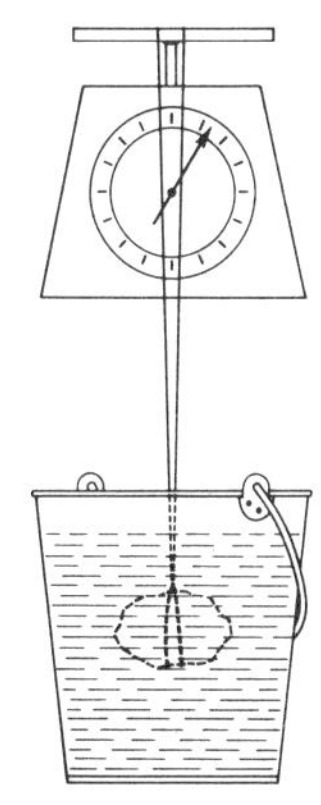

7 How to make a devil diver (cartesian diver)

Find a tall glass jar with a fairly wide mouth. Wrap a few turns of copper wire about the narrow part of the rubber bulb from a medicine dropper. Fill the jar brim full of water. Put a little water in the bulb and float it in the jar of water. The bulb should contain enough water to bring it nearly to the point of sinking. At this point almost all the rubber will be under water. Considerable adjustment will be required. Remove air from the bulb a bubble at a time by pinching the bulb. When you have adjusted the diver, put a solid stopper in the bottle or tie a piece of rubber cut from an old inner tube over it. By pressing on the stopper or rubber, the diver will sink. When the pressure is released it will rise to the surface. If you make the floater from a small glass test tube or a medicine vial you can explain the action of the devil by observing the level of water inside the float when it sinks and when it floats.

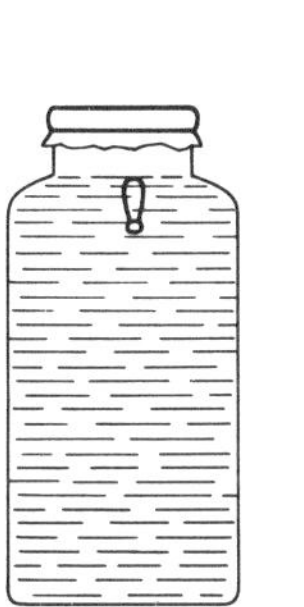

8 How to make an overflow can and catch bucket

These are useful for the study of Archimedes' principle, which controls floating and sinking. To make an overflow can secure a tin can 10 or 12 cm high and 7 or 8 cm in diameter. Make two vertical cuts 2 cm apart and 4 cm down from the top edge. Bend out the tongue so formed into a V-shaped spout.

The catch bucket can be made from a smaller tin can. Punch two holes near the top of the can and on opposite sides. Make a wire bale for the catch bucket.

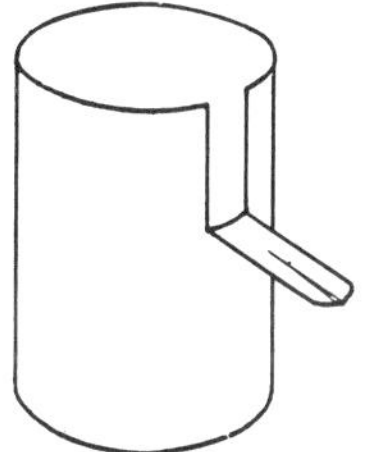

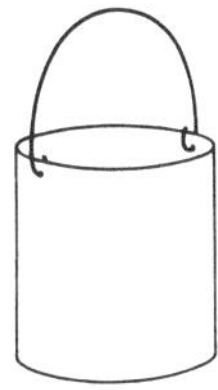

9 Sinking bodies

Fill the overflow can with water to the level of the spout. Select a stone that will go inside the overflow can. Attach a string to the stone and weigh it with a spring balance. Weigh the catch bucket. Place the catch bucket underneath the spout. Immerse the stone in the water and record its weight. Does it weigh the same as in air? Collect the displaced water and determine its weight by subtracting the weight of the bucket from the weight of the catch bucket and water.

How does the apparent loss of weight of the stone from air to water compare with the weight of the displaced water? Try this experiment with other sinking bodies.

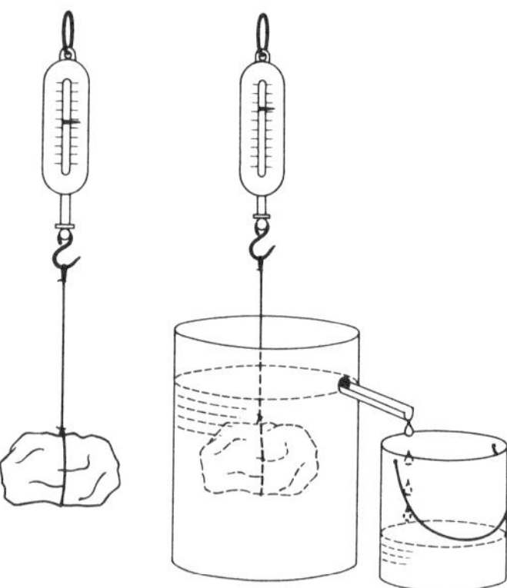

10 Floating bodies

Fill the overflow can with water and let it run out until the surface is level with the spout. Select a piece of wood that floats half or more submerged in the overflow can. Weigh the piece of wood on a spring balance. Weigh the catch bucket. Place the catch bucket under the spout. Put the wood block in the overflow can and note the balance reading. Find the weight of the displaced water by subtracting the weight of the catch bucket from the total weight of catch bucket and water. How does the weight of the floating piece of wood compare with that of the water it displaces? Repeat the experiment with other floating bodies.

11 An experiment with a floating candle

Put a nail in the lower end of a candle. The nail should be just the right weight to make the candle float with its top a little above the surface of the water. Float the candle and nail in a tall glass of water. Light the candle and watch it until it is nearly burned up. The candle constantly loses weight as it burns. Why does it continue to float?

12 A floating experiment with different kinds of wood

Secure a cork, and pieces of wood such as maple, mahogany and ebony. Place them in a pan of water and notice how each one behaves. Can you explain this?

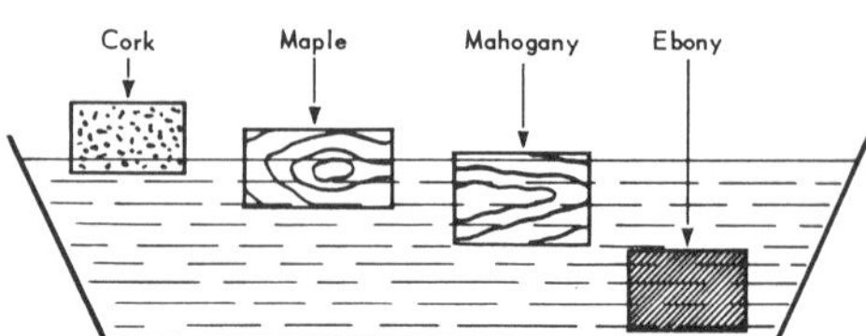

13 An experiment with a floating egg

Place an egg in a glass of fresh water and observe it. Next add salt to the water and see if you can float the egg. Can you explain this? How does this relate to the fact that ships ride higher in ocean water than they do in fresh water?

Egg in salt water

Egg in fresh water

14 Experiment on Archimedes' principle

Solder a cycle valve to one half of a copper ball tap float. Load inside the other half with lead or lead shot until the whole just floats in water. A small quantity of plasticine can be used to make a temporary joint.

After these adjustments solder the two halves of the ball together and make any final changes by winding copper wire round the neck of the valve holder.

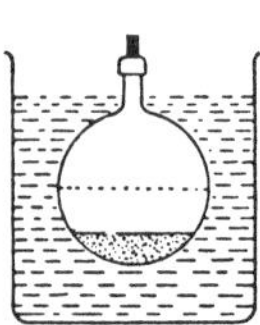

In a discussion on 'why things float', the inevitable answer offered by a class is 'because they have air in them'. Granted this argument, things should float 'better' the more air they have 'in' them. Twenty pumpfuls of air forced into this apparatus causes it to sink.

Try the same experiment with a football or metal water bottle.

15 Drinking straw hydrometer

Procure a drinking straw or a stout natural straw about 20 cm long. If it is not 'water-proof' dip it in melted candle wax and allow it to dry. Seal one end with wax, and introduce some lead shot or fine sand until it floats in a vertical position. Then drop in melted wax to keep the shots or sand in place. Have a thin rubber band or a piece of black cotton tied round the stem so that it can be slid up and down as a marker.

Put a mark on the straw at the water level. Then take the straw out of the water, and measure the length of the straw from the bottom to the water level mark. Let it be x cm. Now let us assume that water has a specific gravity of unity and that the straw has a uniform area of cross-section. Thus we may put a set of markings on the straw for measuring specific gravities of different liquids with ranges, say, from 0.6 to 1.2 by using the formula:

$$\text{length of straw from the bottom to the mark} = \frac{x}{\text{specific gravity of liquid}}$$

16 Specific gravity of a liquid not mixing with water

Pour oil into an open glass tube partially immersed in water until it forces water as far as the lower end. The relative lengths of the total oil column, and of the immersed tube is a measure of the specific gravity of the oil.

For a liquid heavier than water, reverse the procedure, i.e., pour the water into the tube.

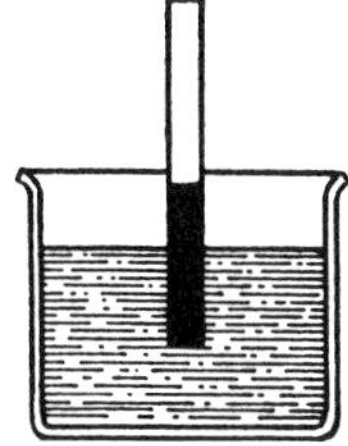

17 Floating in different liquids

Obtain a tall, slender glass jar, test tube or bottle, and the following liquids: mercury, carbon tetrachloride, water and kerosene. You will also need a small iron or steel ball such as a ball bearing, or iron nut or bolt; a small piece of ebony or some other wood that sinks in water; a piece of paraffin wax; and a piece of cork. First pour some mercury into the glass jar, then some carbon tetrachloride, some water and some kerosene. Drop the four solid substances in and you will observe that the iron sinks in the three top liquids but floats on the mercury. The ebony sinks in the two top liquids but floats on the carbon tetrachloride. The paraffin sinks in the kerosene but floats on the water and the cork floats on the kerosene.

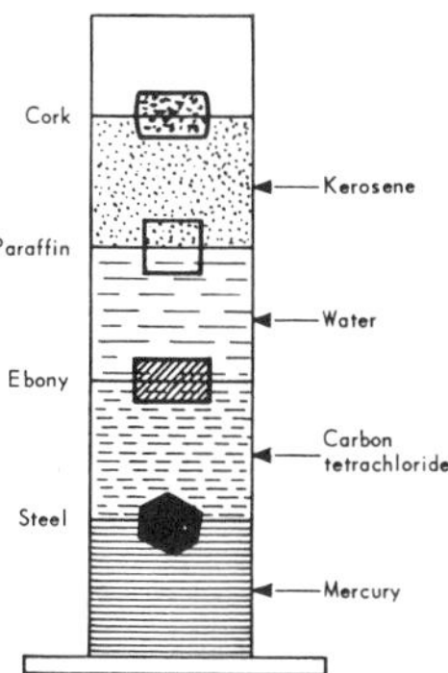

18 How a submarine is raised and lowered

Place pieces of iron or rocks in the bottom of a small wide-mouth bottle and pour a little melted paraffin on them to fasten them down so that the bottle will float in an upright position. Insert a two-hole stopper. In one hole place a U-shaped length of glass tubing which extends to the bottom of the bottle. In the other hole put a short length of glass tube and a rubber tube. Set the bottle in a large vessel of water.

Withdraw some air by sucking on the rubber tube and water will siphon into the

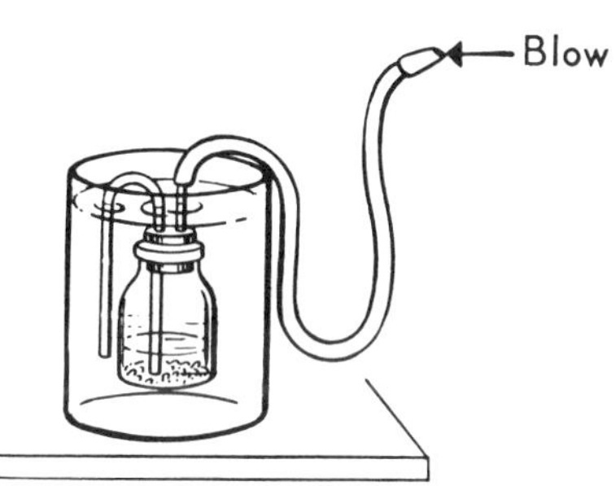

bottle until the bottle sinks. The bottle may be made to rise by blowing out part of the water.

Actually, submarine engineers adjust the buoyancy of the submarine to that of the water and then use the elevators to dive or climb. To remain at the surface they will 'blow' the tanks with surface air after rising. The use of compressed air to empty the tanks is not practical while the submarine is submerged.

The device also illustrates the principle of the tanks or pontoons used to lift sunken ships. Fasten a weight to the bottle, sink both in water and lift the weight by blowing air into the bottle.

F. LIQUID SURFACES

Water and other liquids have a thin film which covers their surfaces. The surface film is pulled tightly over the liquid and this is often spoken of as *surface tension*. Many interesting experiments can be done with liquid surfaces.

1 Floating a needle on water

Thoroughly dry a steel needle. Place it on the tines of a dinner fork and gently break the surface of the water in a dish with the fork. If you are careful the needle will float as you take the fork away. Look at the water surface closely. Can you see how the surface film seems to bend under the weight of the needle?

2 Floating a razor blade

Secure a used razor blade of the double edge type. Try floating it on the surface of water. Again observe the surface and see if the surface film dips under the razor blade.

3 Lifting the water surface

Bend the pointed end of a pin or use a piece of fine wire to make a hook. File the point of the hook until it is very sharp. Put your eye on a level with the surface of the water in a drinking glass. Put the hook under the surface of the water and gently raise the point to the surface. If you are careful the point will not penetrate the surface film but will lift it slightly upwards.

4 Holding water in a sieve

Pour some oil over the wire mesh of a kitchen sieve and shake out the excess so that the holes are open. Carefully pour water into the sieve from a pitcher, letting the water run down the side of the sieve. When the sieve is about half full, hold it over a sink or pail and observe the bottom. You will see the water pushing through the openings but the surface tension keeps it from running through. Touch the bottom of the sieve with your finger and the water should run through.

5 An experiment with a can lid

Punch many holes in a tin can lid with a hammer and very fine nail. Float the lid on the water in a pan. Does water come through the holes? Fill the lid with water from a pitcher. Does water run out of it?

6 Heaping water up in a glass

Place a drinking glass in a shallow pan or on a saucer. Rub the top edge of the glass with a dry cloth. Pour water into the glass until it is full to the brim. You will observe that you can fill the glass several millimetres above the top. Now drop coins or thin metal washers into the water edgewise. See how far you can heap the water up by dropping these in before it runs over.

7 Putting a point on a brush

Secure a paint brush of some sort and observe the bristles. Now dip the brush in water and you will observe that surface tension has drawn the bristles together. An artist's paint brush or a shaving brush will work very well for this experiment.

8 A trick with surface tension

Obtain a used tin can and make five holes in it with a nail. The holes should be very near the bottom of the can and about five millimetres apart. Now fill the can with water and observe that the water comes from the can in five streams. Pinch the jets of water together with your thumb and forefinger and you can make one stream from five. If you brush your hand across the holes in the can the water will again flow in five separate streams.

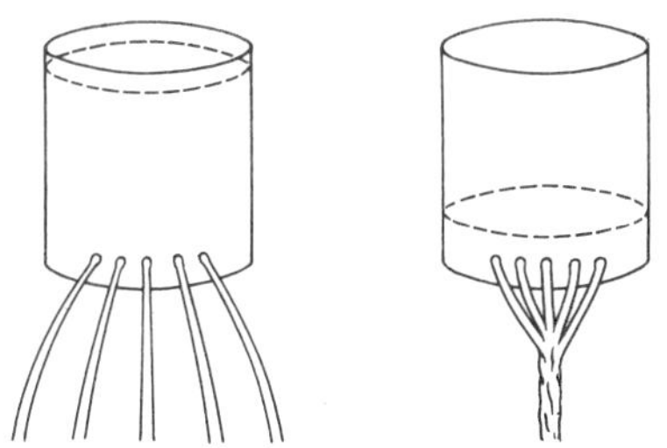

9 The water will not run through the cloth

Select a glass jar and a piece of cloth from an old sheet or handkerchief. Fill the jar with water. Wet the cloth well, stretch it over the mouth of the jar and fasten with a piece of string or thread. Invert the jar over a pail of water and observe that the surface tension keeps the water from coming through the cloth.

10 The effect of soap on surface tension

Select a large plate and rinse it until you are sure that it is very clean. Fill the plate with cold water and let it stand for a time on a table until the water is still. Sprinkle some talcum powder lightly over the surface of the water. Wet a piece of soap in water and touch it to the water near the edge of the plate. The talcum powder will be drawn to the opposite side of the plate at once. The soap reduced the surface tension at one point and the increased surface tension on the other side contracts the surface and pulls the talcum with it.

11 The effect of petrol on surface tension

Repeat the above experiment, being sure that the plate is very clean. It is wise to rinse the plate in cold water for a time before filling it. Instead of soap, place one drop of petrol on the water near the edge of the plate. How does petrol affect the surface tension of water?

12 An experiment with a loop of thread

Rinse a dinner plate thoroughly and then fill it with water. Make a loop with thread, open it a little and float it on the water. Touch the surface inside the loop with a bit of soap and observe the results.

13 Driving a boat by surface tension

Secure some gum camphor at the drug store. Cut two or three boats from stiff paper, each about 2.5 cm in length. Cut a notch in the stern large enough to hold a small lump of gum camphor in contact with the water without letting it fall out. Float your boats in a large pan of water.

You can make an interesting variation by placing the notch in the stern on the right or on the left.

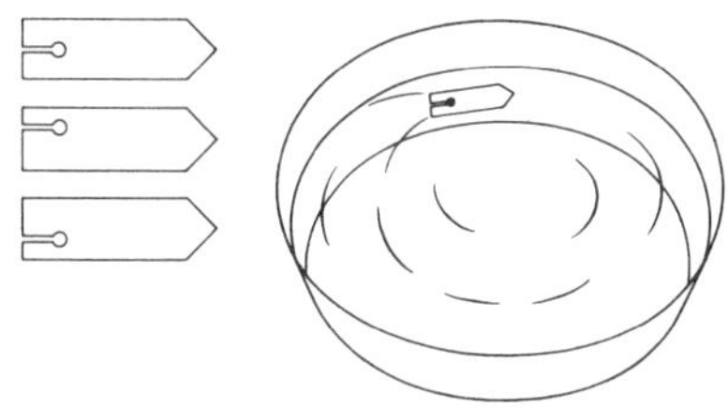

14 A floater to show surface tension

Bend a piece of small copper wire into a ring about 8 cm in diameter. Attach two other pieces of wire rigidly to opposite sides of the ring and join these pieces by twisting them together about 8 cm below. Make the twist about 5 cm long. Attach a flat cork as shown in the diagram and then a wad of tinfoil to keep the floater upright in water.

Now set the floater in a pan of water and press it beneath the surface. When it floats upwards, it does not break through the surface film. Observe how it stretches the surface film.

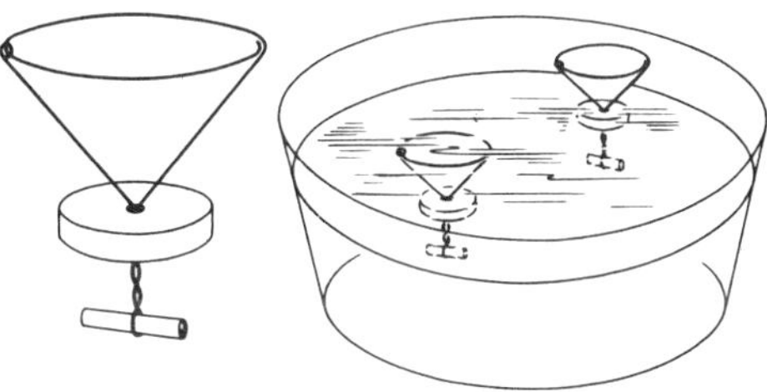

15 Making spheres with surface tension

Find a glass jar and fill it about two-thirds full of commercial alcohol. With a medicine dropper place some drops of oil in the alcohol and then fill the jar with water. If you get the correct mixture, the oil spheres will float down to about the middle of the jar. The oil droplets are pulled into perfect spheres by surface tension.

16 Blowing soap bubbles

Soap films and bubbles serve very well for observations on surface tension. You can make a good soap bubble solution by placing three level tablespoonfuls of soap powder or soap flakes into four cups of hot water. Let the solution stand for three days before using. Try blowing bubbles with a bubble blower, a soda straw, a clay pipe and an old tin horn about 4 cm in diameter.

Another good bubble blower can be made by slitting the end of a soda straw into four parts extending about 1 cm from the end. Bend these pieces outward. A razor blade works well for slitting the end.

17 Making a soap bubble support

Put a round dowel rod about 15 cm long into a wooden spool or a piece of wood suitable for a base. Wind copper or iron wire about the dowel rod and make a loop about 10 cm in diameter. Dip the loop in soap solution.

Blow a large soap bubble and detach it in the loop. Now wet a soda straw in the soap solution and carefully put it through the large bubble. Try to blow a smaller bubble inside the large one. This will take a little practice.

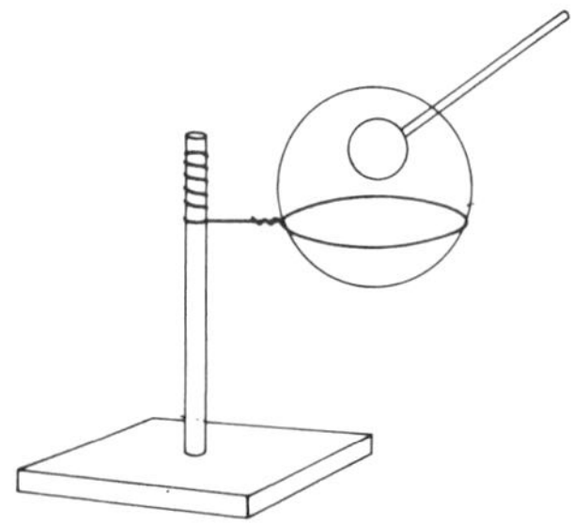

18 Some experiments with soap films

Make the following forms from wire. Dip the various forms in the thick soap solution and observe the films.

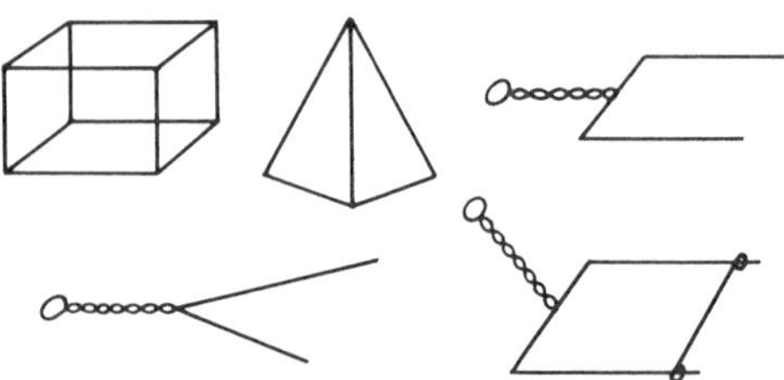

Dip the wire form with the slider in the soap solution. Pull out the slide slightly and watch the film stretch. Release the slider, and it will be pulled back by the contraction of the film.

19 To study the formation of a drop of liquid

Gently pour aniline into a large beaker of cold water until a layer about half an inch deep accumulates at the bottom. Place the beaker on a gauze and tripod and warm it using a small bunsen flame. Aniline expands more than water and after a while it will float to the top. Remove the bunsen and wait for results. As the aniline cools it will sink again to the bottom, but in so doing exhibits the form taken by all drops of liquid when falling. The effects of surface tension are seen in slow motion because the densities of the aniline and water are nearly the same.

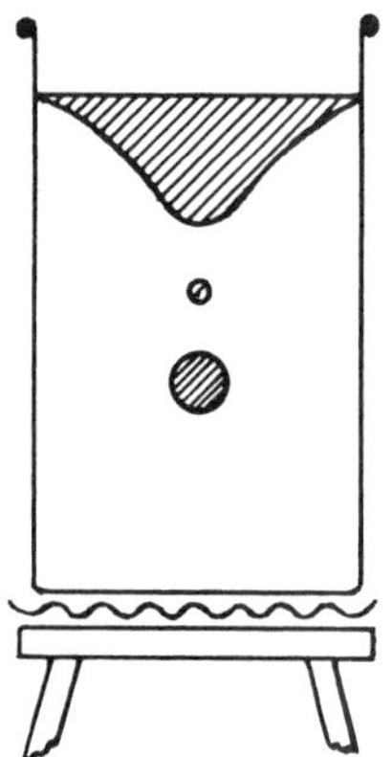

CHAPTER X

Experiments and materials for the study of machines

A. LEVER, WHEEL AND AXLE, PULLEY

1 A simple equal-arm lever

Make a wooden base 15 cm square and 2 cm thick. In the centre of the base fasten another block of wood 4 cm square and 3 cm thick. Fasten to two sides of this block two uprights 15 cm long, 3.5 cm wide and 1 cm thick. These may be fastened to the small block by means of screws. In the top end of each upright cut a narrow slot with a thin blade saw. The slot should be a little less than 2 cm deep or just deep enough to hold a used razor blade with 2 or 3 mm extending above the top of the upright.

For the lever arm use a uniform bar about 1 m in length, 4 cm in width and about 5 mm thick. Balance the bar on a knife edge and locate its exact centre of balance. Put a slender nail through the centre of balance of the bar. The nail should be long enough to rest on the two razor blades at the ends of the uprights and permit the bar to swing freely between them.

Balance the bar on the razor blades, and if it does not balance perfectly cut off a little of the heavy end with a knife or saw.

Mark the bar off in centimetres beginning at the nail (fulcrum) and numbering from 1 in each direction to the end of the bar.

Suspend weights by loops of thread from the balance bar.

1 Hang a 10 g weight 20 cm from the fulcrum and then balance with another 10 g weight on the other side. Observe the distance of this weight when the lever is in balance. Repeat placing the weight nearer the fulcrum; farther from the fulcrum.
2 Repeat 1 above with 100 g weights.
3 Place two weights on one side and balance with one weight on the other side. Can you find the condition for balance here? Suggestion: multiply each weight on one side of the fulcrum by its distance from the fulcrum and add the products. Compare this with the product of weight and distance on the other side.

2 A simple balance

Suspend a ruler by loops of cord a short distance above a table top, as shown in the diagram. When the ruler is in balance, place identical coins in different positions on each side of the fulcrum so that the ruler balances again. Using the simpler combinations of numbers of coins and distances from the fulcrum, develop an elementary understanding of the principle of moments. For instance, two coins placed at one end of the ruler will balance four coins placed halfway between the fulcrum and the opposite end.

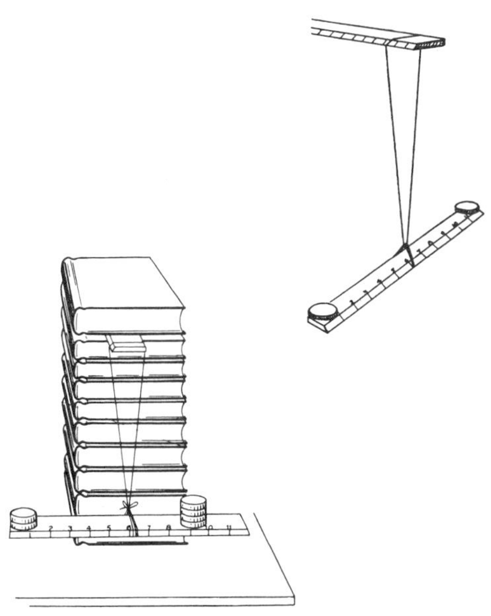

3 A simple beam balance

The beam of a platform balance on which pupils are weighed is really a lever with the fulcrum very close to one end. To show the principle of this type of balance place a stack of eight or ten coins near the fulcrum of the suspended ruler used in 2. Slide a single coin along the opposite end of the ruler until it balances.

4 A lever of the first class

Saw off a stick or board so that it is the same height as a heavy desk or table in the classroom. Place another stick about the same length on this. Place the end of this stick under the edge and use it as a lever to lift the desk or table.

Note that in lifting a heavy object with a lever the longer end travels farther than the shorter end. No energy is really gained but the force exerted by the shorter end of the lever is much greater than the force used to move the longer end.

5 A lever of the second class

Use a uniform wooden bar about 1 m long, 4 cm wide and 5 mm thick. Drill a hole near one end, in the centre of the width dimension. Also drill a hole through both uprights used in experiment 1 above, about 12 cm from the base. Put a nail through the holes in the uprights and the hole in the end of the lever bar so that the lever bar is between the uprights. Place weights along the bar and use a spring balance to lift the end of the bar.

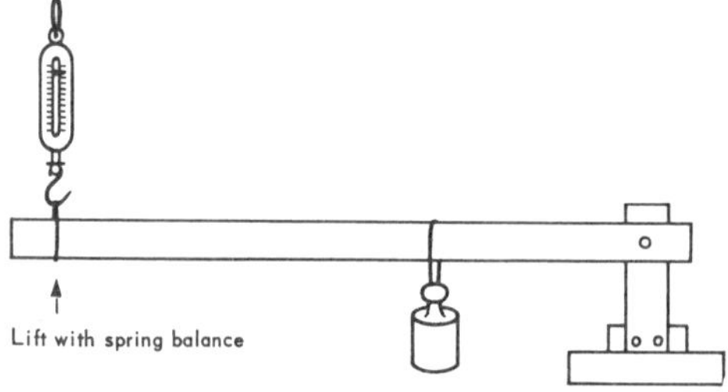

6 A lever of the third class

To make a lever of the third class for simple experiments use the materials which were used in experiment 5 above, but interchange the weight and balance.

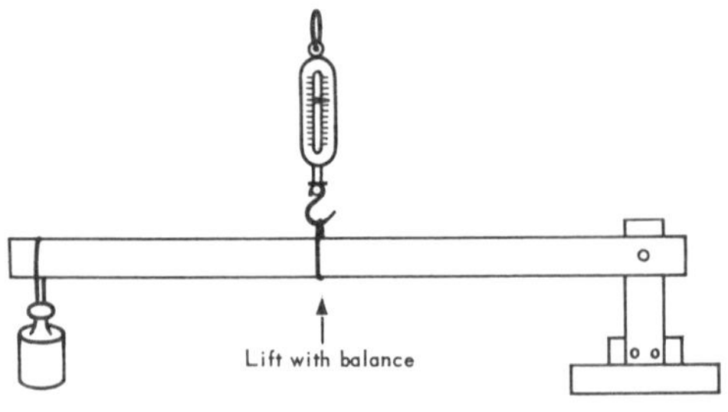

7 A see-saw lever

Obtain a thick plank about 3 m long and bring it into the class room. Balance it over a box or some other convenient device and let the pupils experiment with the see-saw; place different numbers of children on either side of the balance point.

8 A simple wheel and axle

Remove the cover from a pencil sharpener and tie a string tightly around the end of the shaft. Tie a weight of several kilograms to the end of the string and turn the handle. Note that the force needed to turn the handle is much less than the force of gravity on the weight. Point out that the pencil sharpener is used as a wheel and axle in this demonstration.

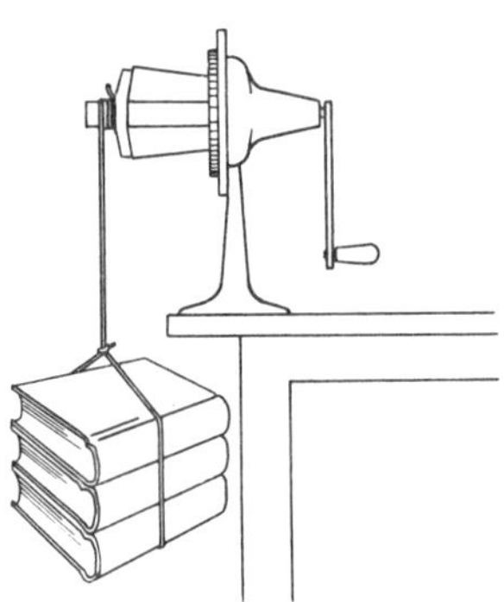

9 Another wheel and axle

Secure some double corrugated cardboard and draw circles of 15, 10 and 5 cm in diameter on it with a compass. Punch through the cardboard with the compass and draw each wheel or circle on the other side. Cut out each of the wheels, cutting cleanly from either side of the cardboard. Punch a nail through the centre of each wheel and then glue or staple the wheels together—with the largest and smallest wheels on the outside—so that they will turn easily on a common axis. Mount them as shown in the diagram. Press gently into the rim of each wheel with a blunt instrument to make a groove. Wind a thread or string over each pulley and attach one end to the groove with a pin. Put a loop in the other end of the thread so that weights may be suspended from it. Use some light weights such as clothes pegs, and you will discover that you can lift weights many times greater, just as you can with a lever. The wheel and axle is a type of lever.

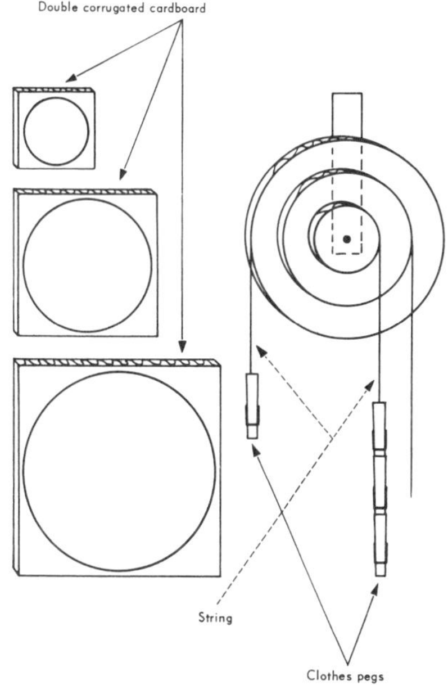

10 How to make a simple pulley

A reasonably satisfactory pulley can be made from a wire clothes hanger and a cotton reel. Cut off both wires of the hanger at a distance of about 20 cm from the hook. Bend the ends at right angles and slip both through a spool. Adjust the wires so that the spool turns easily and then bend the ends down to keep the wires from spreading.

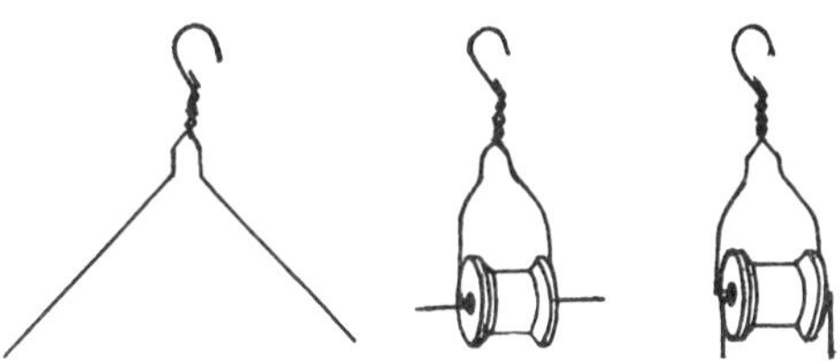

11 A single fixed pulley

Set up a single fixed pulley as shown in the diagram below. By means of weights see how much force is required to lift weights of 25, 50, 75, 100 and 200 g. Measure the distance moved by the effort force when the resistance force (the weight) is moved through 20 cm.

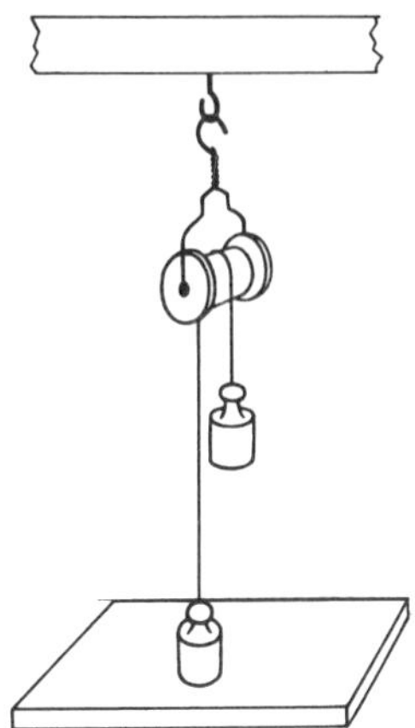

12 A single movable pulley

Suspend two pulleys on a cord from a horizontal support, and load them as shown. If there is no adjustable support on the demonstration desk, a window stick laid across the back of two chairs will serve. Attach a spring balance to the end of the cord and compare the weight of the object with the force required to lift it with the pulley system. Compare also the distances through which the force and the weight are moved.

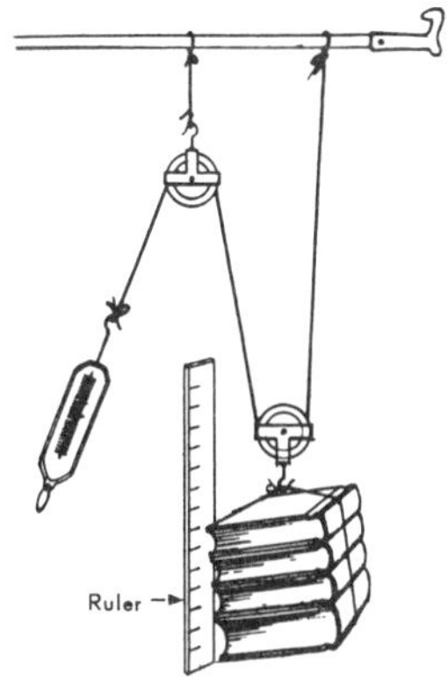

13 The block and tackle

Let two pupils each grasp a round stick, such as a broomstick, and stand several feet apart. Tie a length of clothes line cord to one of the sticks and wrap it several times around both sticks so as to form a combination of pulleys. Ask a third pupil, smaller than the other two to pull on the rope. He can easily pull the two sticks together despite the efforts of the pupils holding the sticks.

Make a list of devices in which pulley combinations are used to increase forces. Tow cars and power shovels are examples. List other devices and machines used to increase forces.

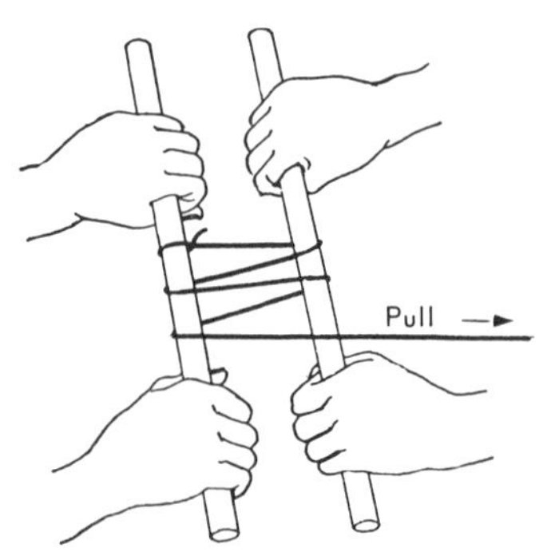

B. INCLINED PLANE, SCREW AND WEDGE

1 A simple inclined plane

Attach a spring balance to a toy car or roller skate and pull it up a slanting board (inclined plane). Note the force required to move the car and compare it with the force needed to lift it vertically. Note also that in moving up the inclined plane, the force is exerted over a greater distance than when the car is lifted vertically to the same height above the table. Neglecting friction, the work required is the same in both cases. Point out that this is also true for other simple machines.

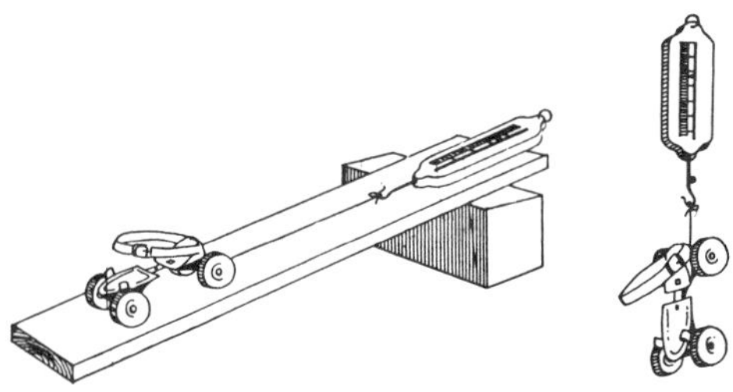

2 The screw is an inclined plane

Mark off and cut out a right angle triangle on a piece of white paper or a piece of wrapping paper. The triangle should be about 30 cm long on its base and about 15 cm long on its shortest side. Secure a round rod about 20 cm long and roll the triangular piece of paper on the rod beginning at the short side and rolling toward the point of the triangle. Keep the base line of the triangle even as it rolls. Observe that the inclined plane (the hypotenuse) spirals up the rod as a thread.

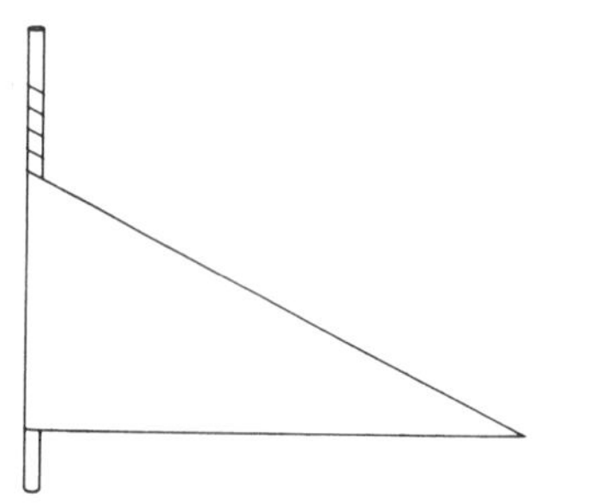

3 A simple jack screw

Bore a hole through a block of wood to fit a carriage bolt. Select a bolt that is threaded nearly its entire length. Sink the head of the bolt in the wood, so that it is flush with the surface and nail a piece of board over it. Over the projecting threads place a nut, then a washer and short piece of metal pipe. The inside diameter of the pipe must be slightly larger than the bolt. By turning the nut with a wrench the device will act as a powerful lifting jack.

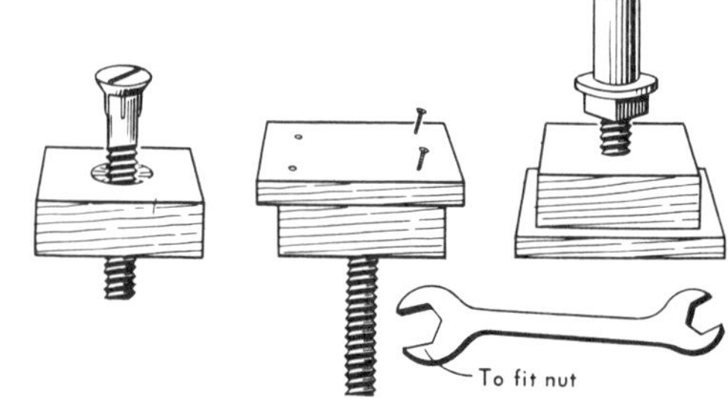

4 The wedge

Make a wedge from a piece of wood and drive it under a table leg or some other heavy object. Observe that the wedge is a double inclined plane.

C. HOW SPEED IS INCREASED BY THE USE OF MACHINES

1 A small spool and a large spool

Using nails for axles fasten a large spool and a smaller spool to a block of wood. Slip a rubber band over both spools. Turn the larger spool one turn and note whether the smaller spool makes more or less than one full turn. Make a list of devices that are driven by belts.

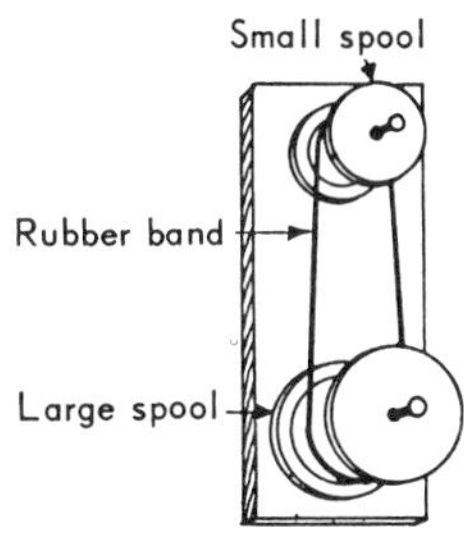

2 Using a bicycle

Turn a bicycle upside down so that it rests on the seat and handlebars. Turn the pedal wheel exactly one turn and note the number of turns made by the rear wheel.

3 An egg beater

Examine an egg beater, hand drill or some other device in which an increase of speed is obtained by means of gears.

4 Using a lever

Show that the longer end of a lever travels farther and faster than the shorter end when the fulcrum is not in the centre. A baseball or cricket bat makes use of this advantage. List other examples of the use of levers and other simple machines to increase speed.

5 Using a pulley

Use the pulley set-up shown in experiment A 12. Apply the force on the movable pulley and observe how rapidly the weight on the other end of the string rises.

6 Using a wheel and axle

Use the pencil sharpener that you used in experiment A 8. Pull on the end of the string that held the books and observe how rapidly the crank turns.

D. HOW MACHINES ARE USED TO CHANGE THE DIRECTION OF FORCES

1 A model elevator

A working model of an elevator can easily be made from simple materials. For the rotating drums or sheaves, metal coffee tins will do. With a hammer and a large nail punch holes in the exact centre of the bottoms and lids. Replace the lids and mount the tins on opposite ends of a board, taking care that they both turn easily.

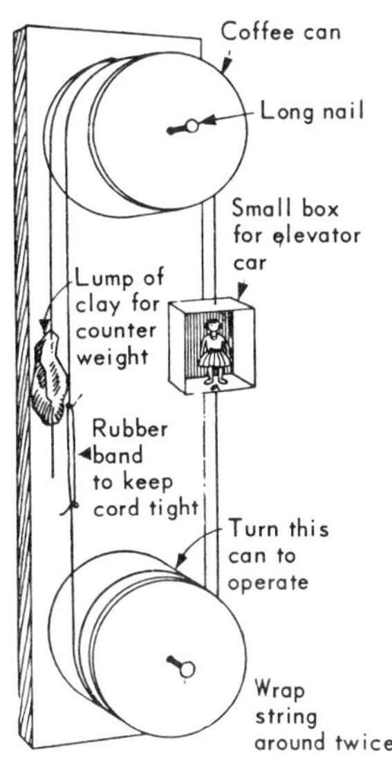

For the elevator car use a small cardboard or wooden box. Attach pieces of string to both ends of the box and wind them round the sheaves as shown. A piece of modelling clay can be used for a counterweight and should just balance the weight of the car. Operate the elevator by turning the sheave that has the double turn of cord. A model of this kind is very similar to real elevators, but the sheave of a real elevator is turned by an electric motor.

2 Simple gears

With a hammer and a medium-sized nail, make holes in the exact centres of several used bottle caps. Straighten the edges of the caps to make them as round as possible.

Lay two of the caps on a block of wood so that the toothlike projections mesh together. Fasten them down with carpet tacks, but make sure that they still turn easily. Turn one of the caps and note the direction tha the other turns. Add a third cap and not the direction that each turns.

3 Using cross belts

Cross the belt on the spool pulleys used i C 1 above and turn one of the pulleys. Not that they now turn in opposite directions

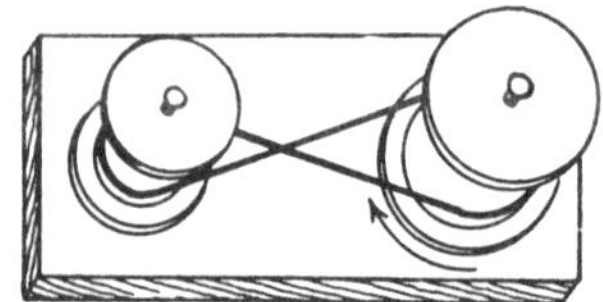

E. USING AND OVERCOMING FRICTION

1 Reducing friction with pencils

Place round pencils under a heavy box. Attach a string to the box and find the force needed to move it across a table. Find the force needed to move the box without the rollers. Summarize the data obtained and suggest explanations for the results.

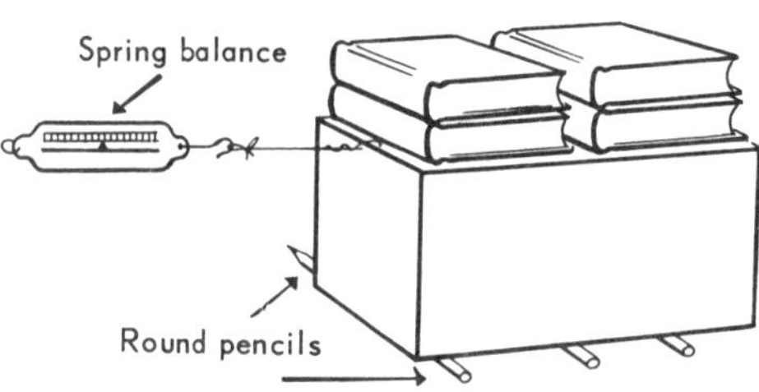

2 Using wheels

Repeat the previous experiment but use a wheeled device such as a roller skate (or several roller skates) instead of rollers. State some advantages that wheels have over rollers for moving things.

3 Sliding friction

Lock the rollers of a roller skate by crisscrossing rubber bands over them on bot sides. Place the roller skate on a slopin board and note how the friction of the rubbe keeps it from sliding.

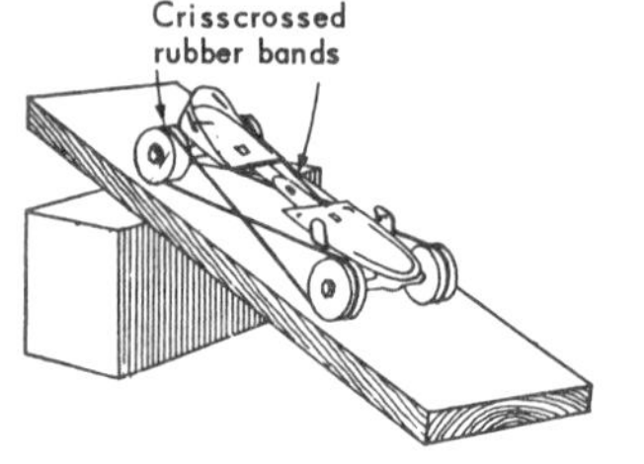

4 Places where friction occurs

Locate the places on various mechanica devices where parts rub together. Rolle skates, pulleys and the wheels of toys ofter need oil. Try to find two similar bearings that need oil, such as those on a roller skate. Oil one and compare the ease with which it turns with the bearing that has not been oiled.

5 Reducing friction with oil

Lay two panes of glass side by side and place a few drops of oil on one. Ask pupils first to rub a finger back and forth on the unoiled pane and then on the oiled pane. Feel the difference.

6 Friction of rough surfaces

Place two pieces of sandpaper together. Notice the friction that is created when one is rubbed against the other. Now put some grease between the pieces of sandpaper. The friction is much reduced because the grease fills up the irregularities on the surface of the sandpaper. Applying grease to the moving parts of a machine acts in a similar way.

7 Reducing friction with ball bearings

Find two tin cans that have a deep groove around the top, such as paint cans. Lay marbles in one groove and invert the other can over the marbles to form a ball bearing.

Place a book on top and note how easily the demonstration bearing turns. Oil the marbles and it will turn still more easily.

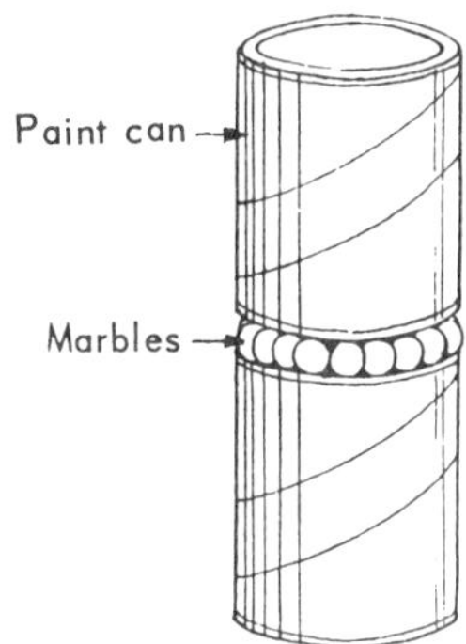

8 Real ball bearings

Examine real ball bearings and roller bearings. Make a list of devices that contain ball bearings or roller bearings.

9 Ball bearings again

Place some marbles in the lid of a tin on the floor. Put one foot on the marbles and notice how easily you can spin round.

10 Reducing friction by an air stream

Cut out a disc of cardboard about 10 cm in diameter. With a red-hot pin, burn a hole through the centre. Saw a small cotton reel in half and glue the original end of one half over the middle of the disc. Find a piece of bamboo or some other tube which just fits the hole in the reel. Push this into the neck of a small balloon, using cotton or a rubber band to secure the joint. Blow up the balloon, pinch the neck, and insert the tube into the hole in the cotton reel. Place the disc on the table and release the air. The expanding air, escaping through the hole in the disc, will lift the card so that, given a flick, it will shoot across the table with practically no friction. This experiment illustrates the principle of the Hovercraft.

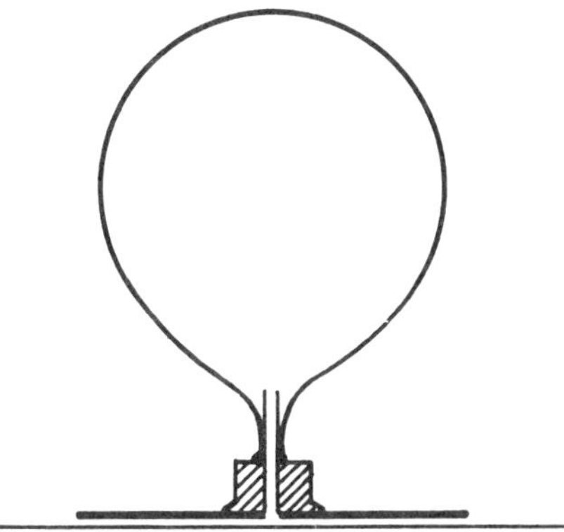

CHAPTER XI

Experiments and materials for the study of forces and inertia

A. BALANCE

1 Making a device for the study of balanced forces

See Chapter X, experiment A 1.

2 Balance with a see-saw

Secure a strong board about 3 m long and a saw horse or box over which the board may be balanced to make a see-saw or teeter-totter. If possible set this up in the classroom. The playground of your school may have a see-saw for the children (see also Chapter X, experiment A 7).

Select two children of equal weight and place them at either end of the board so that they balance. Measure the distance from the balance point to each child.

Next have a heavier child balance himself with a lighter child and observe the changes that have to be made. Next have one child balance two others on the opposite side. Observe the changes. If you measure the distance each time from the balance point to the child and multiply the distance by the child's weight you will discover an interesting thing about balance.

Note: When two children are on the same side, measure the distance of each from the balance point, multiply by the weight of each child and add the products.

3 A balance trick

Obtain a smooth metre stick and let it rest lightly on your two forefingers. Place your fingers near the ends of the stick and then move them toward the centre. Where do your fingers meet on the metre stick? Place the finger of your right hand near the end of the metre stick and the other about half way to the centre on the other side and repeat. Where do your fingers meet this time? Reverse and put the finger of your left hand at the end while the finger of the right hand is about half way to the end on the other side. Where do your fingers meet now? Try other distances. Can you explain this interesting trick?

4 Some simple balance experiments

(a) With a sharp knife cut a slice of some raw vegetable or modelling clay about 2.5 cm thick. Punch the point of a lead pencil through the slice until it protrudes about 2.5 cm on the other side. Insert a dinner fork in the slice of vegetable as shown in the diagram. Now place the pencil point on the edge of a table and adjust the parts until balance is obtained; then give the long end of the pencil a little tap.

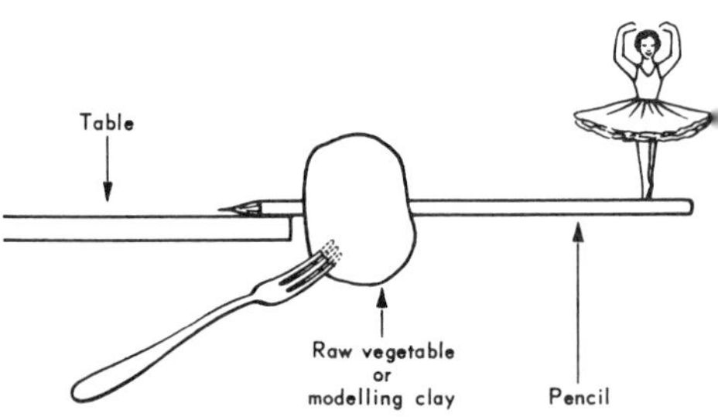

(b) Assemble a slice of raw vegetable or modelling clay, two dinner forks and a pencil as shown in the diagram and balance them on the top of a soda water bottle.

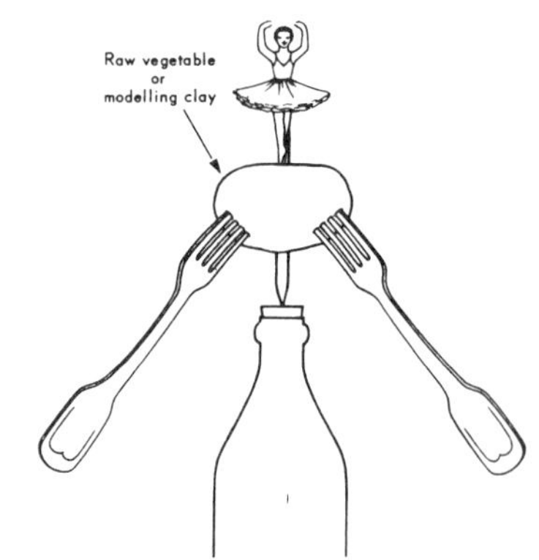

(c) Assemble a slice of raw vegetable or modelling clay, a pencil and two forks as shown in the diagram. This time suspend them with a thread or string. A little experimenting will be required to find the exact point where the string must be placed for balance.

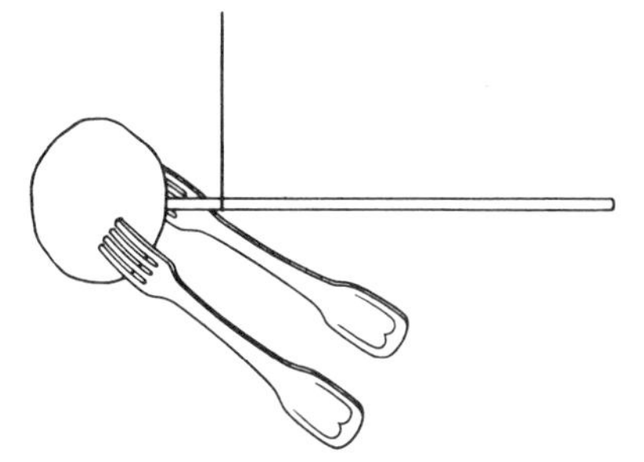

(d) Assemble a coin and two dinner forks as shown in the diagram. Balance on the edge of a bottle or glass.

(e) Try to devise some other simple experiments with balance using common things found about the house or school.

5 Can you straighten the cord?

Obtain a strong cord or small rope about one and a half metres in length. Wrap another cord around a heavy book or other suitable weight. Tie the cord with the weight securely to the centre of the other cord so that it hangs about 15 cm below. Grasp the long end and try to straighten it by pulling your arms apart. Have a pupil pull on one end while you pull on the other. Can you straighten the cord?

6 Finding the centre of gravity of objects

Secure a triangular file and place it on a table as a balancing point. Any sharp-edged device with a flat side may be used. Balance various sticks, rods and devices such as brooms, bats, brushes, etc., on the knife edge and mark the place where they balance with a piece of chalk. Is the centre of gravity of every device you tested at the exact centre of the body? Which objects seem to have the centre of gravity at the centre? Where is the centre of gravity of the others usually found?

B. EXPERIMENTS WITH GRAVITY

1 Falling bodies

If you can find a building that is about 20 m high in your locality you can study how gravity makes bodies fall faster the longer it acts on them. Get a piece of string long enough to reach from a point at least 20 m high to the ground. Fasten the cord so that it forms a straight vertical line. Opposite a window 20 m from the ground tie a piece of coloured cloth or yarn to the string. At about 5 m below this point tie another piece of coloured yarn. Have someone stand on the ground with a watch and call out the seconds. A good way is to beat seconds with the arm and call out 'A thousand and one—a thousand and two—a thousand and three'. This will beat seconds approximately.

Now station someone at the 5 m mark below the starting point and someone on the ground. Drop heavy stones and light stones. Drop small objects and large objects and see how far they have fallen at the end of one second and how far at the end of two seconds.

2 The coins fall together

Place a ruler obliquely on the edge of a table so that one end just projects over the edge and the other end is about 3 cm from the edge. Now place one coin on the projecting end and another on the table, between the other end of the ruler and the edge of the table. With another ruler strike a sharp blow, hitting the projecting end horizontally. One coin falls straight to the floor while the other travels a longer path. Carefully observe when each coin reaches the floor. You will have to repeat this experiment several times. What conclusions do you reach?

3 A simple pendulum

Tie a cord at least 2 m long to some object like a stone or a small metal ball. Suspend this in a doorway or from a hook in the ceiling and start it swinging through a large arc. Count the number of swings it makes in 10 seconds and then multiply by 6 to see how many swings it makes per minute.

Next swing the pendulum through a short arc and determine the number of swings per minute. Repeat each of the above manipulations several times and take the average in each case. Does the length of the arc affect the time of vibration of a pendulum?

Keep the length of the pendulum the same but change the material used for a weight. Repeat the manipulations suggested above.

Does the material in the bob affect the time of vibration of a pendulum?

Repeat each of the above experiments, but use a pendulum that is only half as long. Does the length of the pendulum affect its rate of vibration? How does it affect it?

4 Timing a falling body

The motion of a freely falling body can be examined by attaching it to a strip of paper tape on which marks are made at equal time intervals. This may be done by passing the tape between the armature of an electric bell and a pad of carbon paper. To modify an electric bell mechanism for this purpose, remove the clapper, and extend the armature by soldering to it a strip of metal about 5 cm long. Near the end of this extension, drill a hole to fit a small round-headed screw, and fix it in with the head downwards to act as a marking hammer.

Fasten the mechanism to a piece of wood measuring approximately 5 × 2.5 × 18 cm which will serve as a base. Fix another piece of wood, 5 × 5 × 2.5 cm under the striker to support the disc of carbon paper, and staples to guide the path of the ticker tape. The carbon paper disc should be about 3 cm diameter, held loosely at the centre by a drawing pin so that it can rotate to expose a new surface as the tape passes over it. The staples are easily made from wire paper fasteners pressed into the wood.

The extension to the armature may have to be bent a little so that it does not strike the paper too hard and cause bouncing, which may result in uneven timing. The paper strip is now passed through the staples with the carbon paper underneath and the armature is set in motion. As the strip is released and the body falls, it drags the paper after it. Marks are thus made on the paper at equal time intervals and measurements can be made of the distances travelled from the start.

This timing device can be used for other experiments, e.g., the acceleration of a cyclist can be measured by attaching the tape to the saddle of the machine. For absolute measurements an A.C. bell can be modified, when the time interval is that of the frequency of the mains.

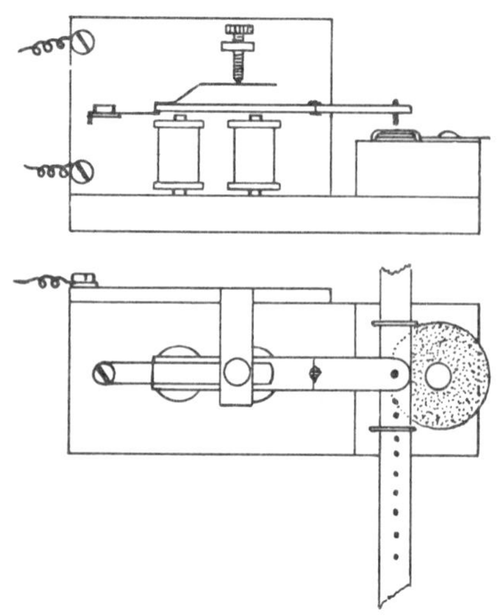

5 Study of a rolling ball

A large ball bearing or 'bagatelle ball' rolling down a smooth track can be timed by a pendulum. To make the track, fasten together two 120 cm lengths of glass tubing (or other smooth rods) with rubber bands. Place them on a length of wood resting on a table, with a matchbox under one end. Set up a simple pendulum to give about quarter second time intervals. A metal nut supported by cotton is suitable. Start the ball rolling down the track and observe its position after successive swings of the pendulum. Make marks along the wood opposite the position of the ball at equal time intervals. Taking the average of several trials, measure the distance travelled from the start. The curve obtained by representing these on a distance-time graph will reveal that the relationship is parabolic, i.e.,

$$s = \tfrac{1}{2}.a.t^2$$

where s is the distance travelled, a the acceleration, and t the time taken.

6 Uniform motion

When a body falls through a fluid, the pull of gravity is soon balanced by the frictional forces set up, and it continues to move at a constant velocity. If this is the case the distances then travelled are proportional to the time taken. The effect can be investigated by the following experiment in which a wax pellet falls in water.

Make a small pear-shaped float out of softened wax and weight it at the tip with lead shot so that it maintains its balance vithout sinking to the bottom or floating on the surface of water contained in a measuring cylinder or large graduated test tube. Take a length of thread measuring exactly 98 cm and attach a small weight to one end, thus making a pendulum which takes exactly one second to swing from side to side. Support this so that it swings near to, and behind, the measuring cylinder. Carefully place the lump of wax on the surface of the water (where it will remain motionless, owing to the resistance of the water at the surface). Push the wax gently with your finger so that it begins to sink through the water and at the same time set the pendulum swinging. Observe the divisions which the wax is opposite each time the pendulum passes the vertical.

Repeat the experiment once or twice, and from the observations find how many divisions the wax falls through per second.

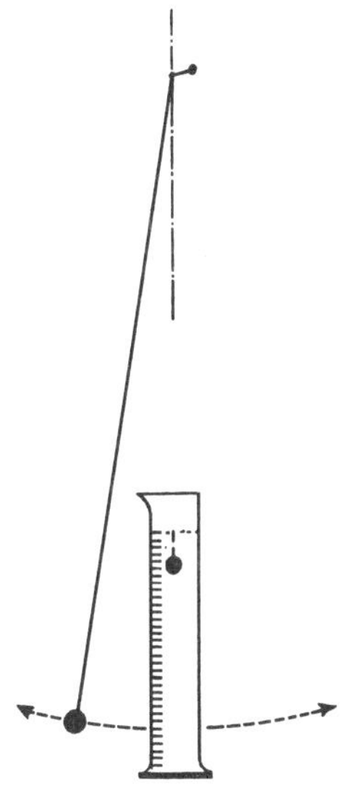

7 The acceleration of a falling ball

The change in speed per second of a moving body is called the acceleration. When it is constant as in the case of a ball falling under the action of the earth's gravity, it can easily be measured. In this particular case it is generally represented by the symbol g. In the following experiment, the fall of a metal ball is intercepted by a lath about 120 cm long swinging from a nail fitting loosely onto a hole near one end.

The period of swing of the pendulum is first found, using a clock to time, say, 100 swings. The ball, which has a small hook attached, is then blackened and hung from a thread which passes over smooth nails and also pulls aside the lath from the vertical position, as shown in the diagram. On burning the thread, the ball and lath are released simultaneously and the ball will hit the lath. From the position of impact, the distance fallen vertically by the ball in one quarter of the period of the lath can be found.

Using the relationship

$$\text{distance fallen} = \tfrac{1}{2}\, g\, (\text{time of fall})^2$$

g can be calculated.

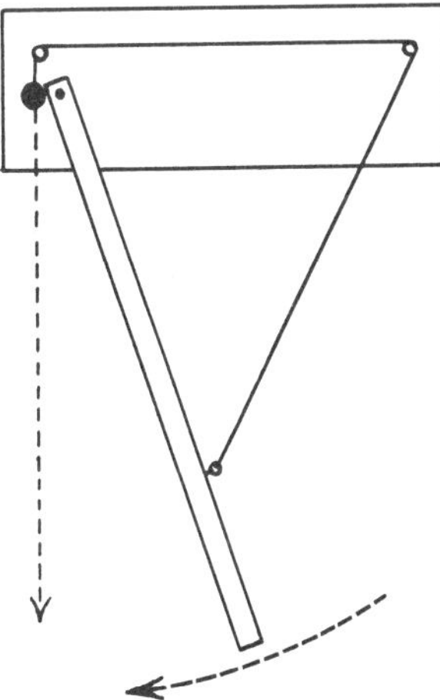

8 Path of a projectile[1]

The apparatus below can be used to show the independence of the horizontal and vertical velocities of a projectile. The projectile is a metal ball, and the target is a small tin can hanging from an electromagnet. The circuit of the electromagnet includes two bared wires which are fixed parallel to and each side of the axis of a cardboard tube, projecting about 2.5 cm beyond the end. An old thermometer case is suitable for this part of the apparatus. A large ball bearing is placed inside the tube, being prevented from falling through by the narrow end. The electrical circuit is completed by a short length of copper wire resting on the projecting wires. Fix the tube in a stand so that it points at the target. Blow up the tube; as the ball passes the muzzle it will displace the copper wire and release the tin can. The ball and target will meet in mid-air. The experiment can be repeated using different angles and distances.

1. Reproduced from *Demonstration Experiments in Physics* by permission of McGraw-Hill Book Co.

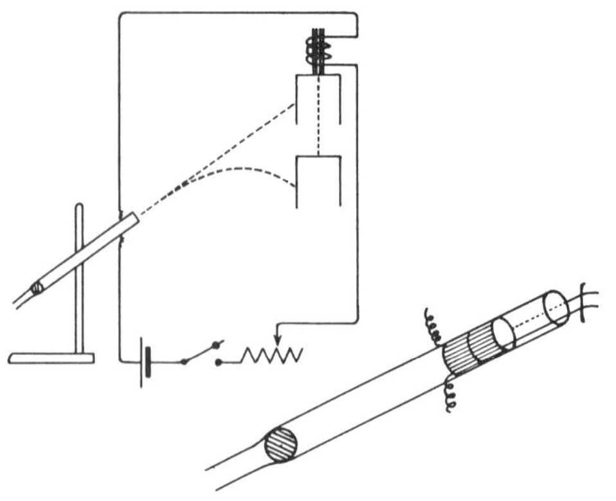

9 Fun with a pendulum

Suspend a hard ball about 8 cm in diameter on a cord over a table. The cord should be at least 1.5 m in length and should be just high enough off the table to hit the top of a pencil which has been placed in a cotton reel and rests on the table. Pull the pendulum and release it in such a way that it misses the pencil on the outward swing and knocks it over on the backward swing. You will find that it requires a great deal of practice to become skilful at this.

10 Shifting pendulums

Obtain two soda water bottles that are exactly the same size. Fill them with water and cork tightly. Place a rod across the back of two chairs. Suspend bottles as pendulums from the rod. Be sure that they are the same length.

Hold one pendulum and start the other swinging; then release the first one to hang at its zero point. Soon the swinging pendulum will slow down, and the one that was quiet will take up the swing.

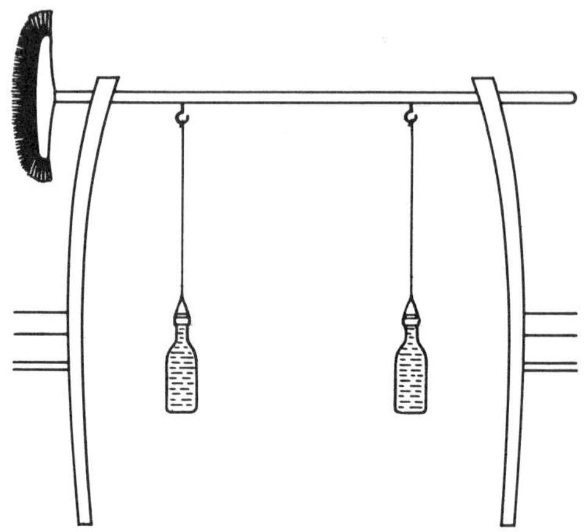

C. CENTRIFUGAL FORCE

1 Feeling centrifugal force

Tie a weight to a string about a metre in length and then whirl the weight around at arm's length. Observe the outward pull on the string. This is centrifugal force.

Replace the string with a strong rubber band. Cautiously whirl the weight on the rubber band. Observe the stretch in the rubber. This is caused by centrifugal force.

2 A simple rotation machine

Secure a breast-drill or hand-drill such as the one shown in the diagram. Clamp a small screw eye or cup hook in the chuck of the drill. Attach a 30 cm length of light string near the point end of a spike. Make a loop in the other end of the string and attach it to the screw eye in the chuck of the drill.

Now rotate the drill steadily by crank. Observe how the centrifugal force affects the suspended spike.

3 An experiment with two spikes

Use the drill for a rotation machine as in the above experiment. Join two spikes by attaching the point end of each to the end of a 15 cm length of cord. Grasp the cord joining the spikes at its centre and attach it to the cord from the drill chuck at this point. Rotate the drill crank steadily and observe the effect of the centrifugal force on the two spikes.

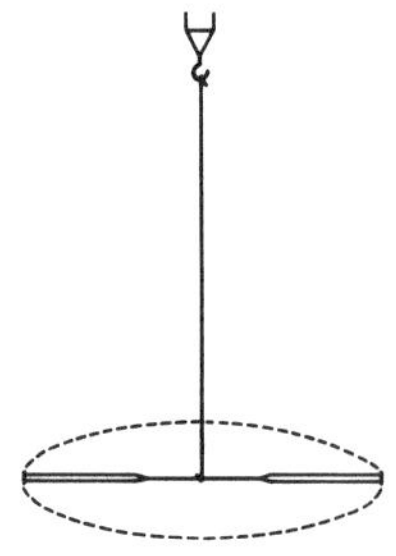

4 Centrifugal force with a ring

Secure an iron ring about 6 cm in diameter and attach it to the cord on the drill. Observe the effects.

5 Centrifugal force with a tin can lid

Punch a hole near the edge of a tin can lid.

Attach it to the cord from the drill and observe the effects of rotation.

6 Centrifugal force with a beaded chain

Secure a length of beaded chain like that frequently used for pull cord on electric light switches or for key chains. Fasten the ends together to make a ring. Attach this to the string from the drill and observe the effects of centrifugal force.

7 Centrifugal force with a liquid

Obtain a small goldfish bowl or glass jar. Fasten a wire securely about the neck. To this wire attach a bale. Attach the cord from the drill chuck to the exact centre of the bale.

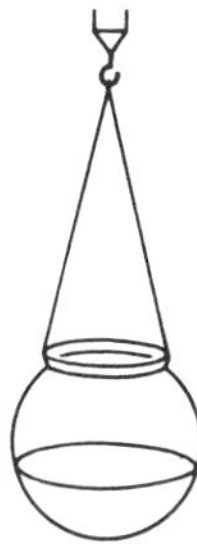

Place about 3 cm of water coloured with ink in the bowl. Turn the drill handle to spin the bowl and water. Observe the effects of centrifugal force on the water.

8 Another experiment with water

Suspend a tin can about 8 cm deep and 12 cm

in diameter as shown in the diagram. Pour about 3 cm of water into the can and spin the drill. Observe what happens to the water.

9 How a centrifugal clothes dryer works

Use a can similar to the one used in the last experiment. Punch the sides full of holes with a nail. Punch three holes equidistant from each other around the top of the can. Suspend with three cords and attach these to the screw eye in the drill chuck. Make a cylinder out of cardboard or find a pail a little deeper than the can and considerably wider. Place a bit of wet cloth in the can attached to

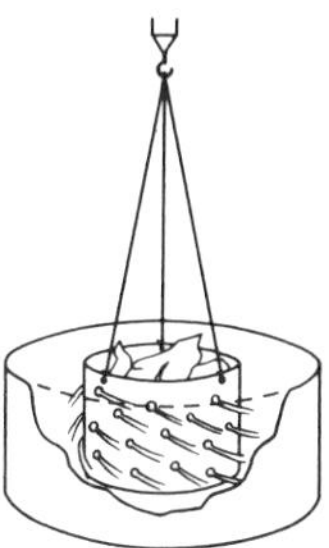

the drill. Lower the can into the cylinder or pail and spin it rapidly with the drill. The water is thrown out of the cloth and can by the centrifugal force.

10 The water will not spill

Obtain a small pail and fill it nearly full with water. Swing it around rapidly at arms' length and the water will not spill because of centrifugal force.

11 Fun with centrifugal force

Find a wire coat hanger and place the hook over the first finger of your hand with the base resting on the table. Carefully balance a small coin on the straight wire at the bottom and directly under the hook. This requires some skill. If you need to, you can flatten a small space on the bar with a file or hammer.

Gently start to swing the hanger and coin on your finger. When it has gained a little motion, and with practice, you can swing the hanger around in a circle, the coin will be held to the wire by centrifugal force.

12 Centripetal force

Sir Isaac Newton first looked at the above effects in another way. He suggested that motion in a straight line is most natural, and that deviations from this type of motion are caused by a force pulling the body out of line. When the force acts on the body from a fixed point, such a body moves in a circle, and the force towards the centre is called a centripetal force.

c. *Centrifugal force*

Circular motion can be studied by the apparatus shown in the diagram. The force producing circular motion with different radii and frequency can be measured. Cut a piece of glass tubing 15 cm long and about 1 cm external diameter. Heat one end in a bunsen flame until the walls of the tube are smoothly rounded. Wrap two layers of adhesive tape round the outside of the tube to provide a grip. Tie a two-holed rubber stopper to the end of about 1.5 m of nylon braided fishing line. Pass the other end of the line down the axis of the tube, and hang half a dozen 1 cm iron washers from it. A wire paper fastener can be used as weight carrier.

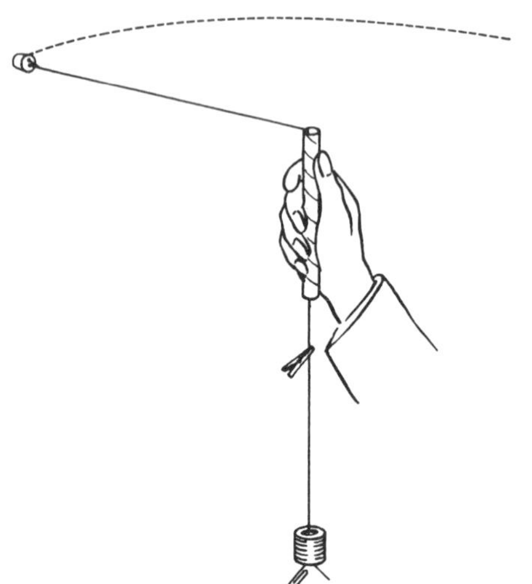

Pull up the line so that the distance from the top of the tube to the cork is 1 m. Grip the glass tube and swing it in a small circle above your head so that the rubber stopper moves in a horizontal circle; the force of gravity on the washers provides the horizontal force needed to keep the stopper moving in a circle. Use a small alligator clip on the vertical fishing line to check that the motion is steady, and record the frequency of revolution required to keep the body moving in a path radius 1 m when different numbers of washers are hung from the carrier.

The relation $F = m\,4\pi^2 f^2 R$ can also be examined, keeping the frequency f constant. This presents a little more experimental difficulty, but a suitable simple pendulum is helpful as a reference in both experiments.

D. EXPERIMENTS ON INERTIA

1 A bottle and marble

Pour some sand into a wide-mouthed bottle. Place a piece of cardboard about 5 cm square over the mouth of the bottle. Set the marble on the cardboard and then tap the edge of the cardboard. If the experiment is successful, and it may require practice, the cardboard will be set in motion and will go flying off while the inertia of the marble causes it to drop into the bottle.

2 Driving nails with the help of inertia

Extend a thin board over the edge of a table and support it well by having someone stand on the part over the table. Try to drive a nail into the board near the end which is not supported by the table. Next have someone hold a heavy hammer or stone under the board. Observe that it is now easy to drive the nail because of the inertia of the weight.

3 Cut an apple in two parts with inertia

Secure a long sharp knife such as a carving knife. Cut into the apple with the knife until you can pick them up together. Be sure to have enough of the end of the knife sticking out to enable you to strike it. Now hold knife and apple securely in one hand and strike the end of the knife a sharp blow with a stick. The knife will move through the apple because of the inertia of the apple.

4 Inertia with a handkerchief and tumbler

Spread a handkerchief out on a smooth table-top. Place a tumbler filled with water near one corner of the handkerchief. Raise the opposite corner and give the handkerchief a sharp jerk. The tumbler will stand still, and no water will spill.

5 Inertia in a pile of books

Stack up a pile of books. Grasp hold of the one at the bottom of the pile and give it a quick jerk. Can you remove it without upsetting the whole pile on top?

6 Break a stick with inertia

Secure a small stick 18 to 20 cm in length. If no other stick is available a lead pencil will do. Fold a newspaper and place it near the edge of a table. Place the stick under the newspaper on the table and let about half the stick extend over the edge. Strike the stick a sharp blow with another. Inertia should cause the one on the table to break in two parts.

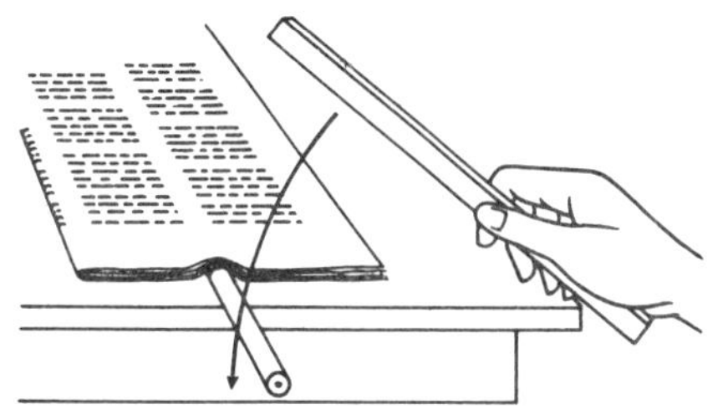

7 Inertia with a spade

Scoop up a spadeful of dry earth. Now pitch the earth away from you. Observe that when the spade stops the earth flies on because of inertia.

8 Inertia on a bicycle

Get your bicycle going and then apply the brakes quickly. Observe the tendency of your body to stay in motion and pitch you over the handlebars. This is the result of the inertia of your body.

9 Inertia in an automobile

You can observe the same effect as in experiment 8 when you are riding in a car that is suddenly stopped. You have to brace yourself to keep from sliding off the seat. Your body is in motion with the car and tends to stay in motion after the car is stopped.

When you are sitting in a car that is at rest and the car is suddenly started, observe that you are thrown backward because of inertia. Your body is at rest and it tends to stay at rest when the car is started.

10 Inertia with a stone

You will need a stone weighing about 1 kg for this experiment. Wrap a length of heavy string about the stone. Now, on opposite sides of the stone, attach half-metre lengths of lighter cord to the heavier cord. The lighter cord should be barely strong enough to support the stone when it is suspended. Next carefully suspend the stone above a table top. Place a length of board on the table under the stone so that the table top will not be dented when the rock strikes it. Grasp the lower end of the string firmly and give it a quick jerk. If you are successful, the lower string will break and leave the stone suspended. The inertia of the stone caused this. Now take hold of the remaining length of the lower string and pull steadily on it. This time the upper string breaks and the stone falls to the table because the steady application of force (rather than the quick jerk) set the stone in motion.

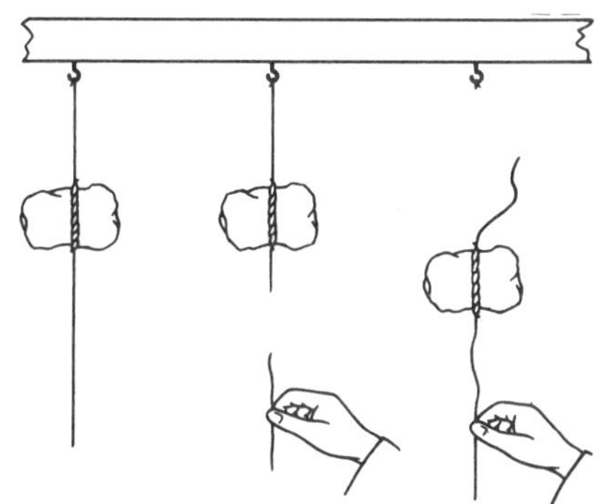

11 How to identify a hard-boiled egg

Secure a fresh egg and a hard-boiled egg. Give each of them a spinning motion in a soup dish or a plate. Observe that the hard-boiled one spins longer. The inertia of the fluid contents of the fresh one brings it to rest sooner.

E. FORCE AND MOTION

1 A light object moves faster

Mark off a half-metre on a table top with chalk. Divide this equally into centimetres. Secure a long rubber band and two spring clothes pegs. Attach a clothes peg to each end of the rubber band. Now grasp the clothes pegs while they rest on the table top. Place them along the marked-off place on the table top. Stretch the rubber band to a distance of about 15 cm and release each clothes peg at the same instant. Observe that they meet half way.

Next, clamp two clothes pegs on one side of the band and one on the other side. Stretch the band to a distance of about

24 cm and release. Where do they meet this time?

Repeat, attaching two clothes pegs on each end of the band. Where do they meet?

Again repeat with two on one side and three on the other. Where do they meet this time?

Can you draw a conclusion from this experiment?

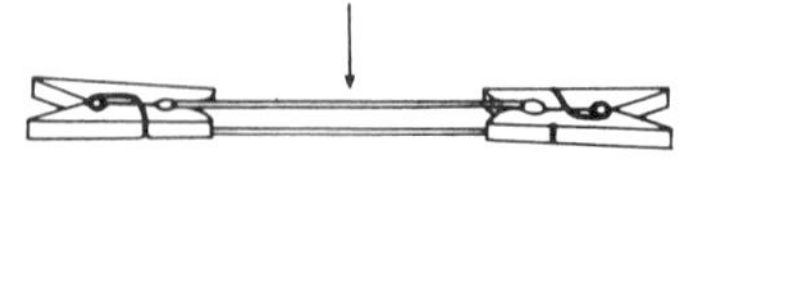

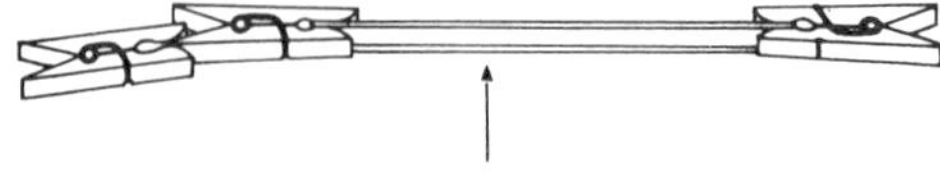

2 An experiment with force and motion

Tie a spring clothes peg open by placing one winding of thread about the long ends. Place the clothes peg in the centre of a long table and put two pencils of about equal size and weight one on either side of, and against the tied end of the clothes peg. Carefully burn the thread and observe the pencils. They are given speeds in opposite directions.

Repeat the experiment, using two larger pencils of about equal weight and size. What do you observe? Compare with the first results.

Repeat, using a large and heavier pencil on one side and a small, lighter pencil on the other side. What do you observe?

If you can secure some metal balls and marbles, repeat, using different combinations of metal balls and marbles.

Can you draw a conclusion from this experiment?

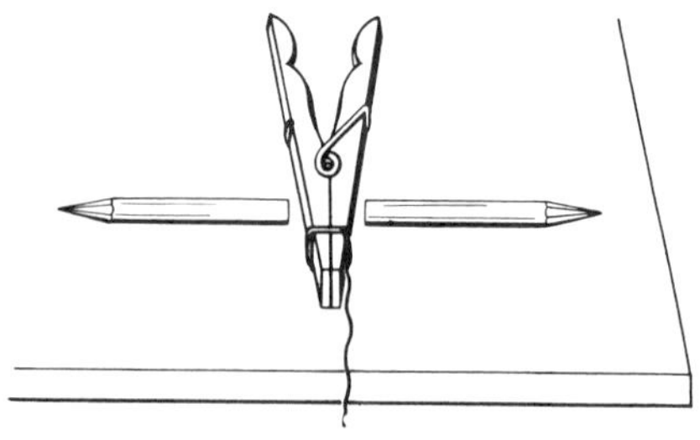

3 Action and reaction in pushing forces

Forces work in pairs. If you push against a wall, the wall pushes with equal force back against you. Secure two kitchen spring balances with square platform tops. Put the tops together with the dial faces up. Have a pupil push on one while you push on the other. Observe that when you push together each balance reads the same.

4 Action and reaction in pulling forces

Secure two spring balances. Make a loop in each end of a short piece of strong cord. Attach a spring balance to each end and have two pupils pull in opposite directions. Make a reading on each balance and compare them.

5 Action and reaction with a roller skate

Place a roller skate on a smooth floor. Step on the roller skate with one foot and take a step forward with the other. Observe that the skate moves backward in the opposite direction.

6 Action and reaction in a boat

Step from a free row boat to land and observe that the boat moves in the opposite direction.

7 Jet propulsion is made possible by action and reaction

Fit a small cardboard stabilizer to the neck of a balloon by means of adhesive tape. Inflate the balloon, and close the mouth with your fingers. When the air contained under pressure in the balloon is allowed to escape, the balloon will be propelled forward by the force of the escaping air. This is the principle used in rockets and jet engines.

CHAPTER XII

Experiments and materials for the study of sound

Children will find fundamental principles and elementary experiments in this chapter on sound interesting and closely related to everyday experiences.

A. HOW SOUND IS PRODUCED AND TRANSMITTED

1 Different sounds

Exercise on naming different sounds from experiments, if possible, such as crash (dish falls and breaks), thud (falling weight), clang (beating sheet of iron with hammer), clatter (falling tin cans), crackle (damp wood on fire), tick (clock), crunch (stepping on gravel), splash (stone falls into water), pop (toy gun), boom (drum), bang (door), patter (rain drops on pavement), tramp (feet), rustle (leaves), rattle (thunder, snake), rumble (far-off thunder; thunder rattles, crashes and rumbles) buzz (bee), tinkle (hitting spoon against drinking glass), neigh (horse), bleat (sheep), cackle or cluck (hen), low (cattle), chirp (bird), hiss (airplane), whistle, moan, etc.

Children will have fun imitating these sounds. Help them to find the exact definitions in dictionaries.

2 Vibrating bodies produce sound

Tie a loop of stout string in a hole near one end of a ruler. Hold the loop with the fingers. Swing the ruler in a vertical circle. Whirl it faster. What sound is produced? Repeat the same experiment with different sizes of rulers and loops. To make it easier, use another ruler or a wood rod instead of your fingers.

3 Say 'Ah'. Prolong it and feel your windpipe. What causes the vibrations? Again feel it when you are speaking, singing and whistling.

4 Place a ruler on a table so that about three-quarters of it juts out from the table edge. Now hold down the end on the table with your hand. Bend the other end and let go quickly. The ruler vibrates up and down. Note what sound you hear. Again place the ruler so that half juts out from the table edge. Repeat the experiment. Note the sound you hear again. Is it different from the last one? Repeat the experiment with different lengths of the ruler jutting out from the table edge.

From these experiences one may conclude that sound is produced by vibrations. The vibrating bodies set up vibrations in the air which strike your ear, and you hear a sound.

5 Meaning of a vibrating object

Secure a small, heavy object, such as a piece of lead or iron or a small ink bottle. Tie the object with one end of a string about 1m in length. Now set up a pendulum by hanging the object from the top of a doorway with the other end of the string. Let the object swing freely like a pendulum. How many swings will it make in one minute? Take many more counts with shorter lengths of string. You will note that shortening the string makes the object swing faster.

Also observe the vibration of a children's swing.

Secure a pendulum clock and a metronome, or a musician's time-piece. Make a study of rates of vibrations with these instruments. Imagine that an object vibrates faster and faster; beyond 16 times per second the surrounding air will be set into vibration, and a very low note will be heard. Higher notes are produced from faster vibrations, up to about 20,000 times per second, which is the highest note man can hear.

Also see Chapter XI, experiments B 3-5, page 123.

6 Run a toy car with a siren. The faster it runs, the higher the note it produces.

7 Blow across the mouth of an empty bottle. Try the same experiment with different-sized bottles.

8 Now replace the vibrating human lips in the last experiment by the wing top of a burner. Air blown through the wing top will pass the opening with great speed and spread out flat like a broad flame. The resonating sounds produced depend on the vibrating air columns in bottles or tubes. Adjust the position of the wing top so that the air stream produces the loudest sound. You will hear the lowest note from a fairly big bottle or a paper mailing tube, up to the highest audible note from the end hole of a very small key.

9 Sympathetic bottles

Have a pupil hold the mouth of one bottle close to his ear without obstructing the opening. Now blow strongly across the mouth of another similar bottle until you produce a strong, clear note. Every time you do this, resonant vibrations are set up in the second bottle. These produce a weaker, though similar, note which your pupil can hear distinctly.

10 Secure a tuning fork and a used petroleum tin can, a violin or any wood box as a sound box. Set the fork into vibration by hitting it against a block of wood. Then press its handle against the sound box. You will hear a very loud humming sound from the box. Repeat the experiment with a dinner fork.

11 Air carries sound

Let one person whistle; other persons in the same room will hear the sound distinctly. Now send the first person into another room, and let him whistle again; it will no longer be possible to hear him distinctly.

12 Sound cannot travel through a vacuum

Make a vacuum pump and receiver (Chapter VII, experiment I 3, page 85).

Tie two small bells inside the vacuum receiver. Start the experiment by shaking the receiver with air inside; you will hear the bells ringing. Then screw in the cap tightly, suck the air out of the receiver with the pump. Shake the receiver again; you will not hear the ringing of the bells as clearly as before. What does this mean?

Repeat the experiment, but create the vacuum by burning pieces of paper in the receiver.

13 Take a long garden hose, open at both ends. Use it as a telephone line for talking and listening to another person. Air inside the hose is the carrier of sound. The principle is still applied within a ship for speaking from one quarter to another.

14 Solids carry sound

Secure two used tin cans with lids neatly cut out. Now punch a small hole in the centre of the bottom of each tin can. Thread several metres of a thin cotton string through the holes. Attach a matchstick at each end of the string so that the matchsticks cannot go through the holes. Now use the cans as telephones: get the string taut and talk and listen to your pupil. Sound travels through the string and through the air inside the tin cans. The bottom part of the tin acts as a diaphragm.

This experiment can also be performed with two empty matchboxes, one side of each being covered tightly with thin pieces of transparent cigarette wrapper paper. The holes may be punched in the paper.

15 Church bell from a spoon

Cut one metre of a cotton cord. With both ends together, balance a teaspoon in the loop. Now hold each end with your fingertips. Press both ends to your ears and bend down so that the string and spoon hang freely. Let someone hit the spoon lightly with a nail or another spoon. You will hear a chime like that of a church bell. Again sound travels right up the string, ending in your ears.

16 Tapping codes through water pipes

Send a code message made up by a pupil and yourself through a water pipe that goes from one room to another on the same floor or on different floors. By striking the water pipe with a piece of iron in one room the sound reaches your pupil in the other. Then interchange messages. Sound travels through the water pipe this time.

17 Hear through your teeth

Set a fork or a tuning fork into vibration. Wait until you cannot hear any sound from the fork, then place the handle between your teeth. The sound will still be heard. Repeat the experiment by placing the handle on the bone at the back of your ear.

18 Liquids carry sound

Place your head under a pool of water so that your ears are immersed. (It may be in a swimming pool, the sea, a river or even a bath tub.) Let somebody else strike a gong or a bell under the water away from you, while your ears are still under water. You will hear the sound coming through the water clearly. It is a fact that sound travels about four times as fast under water as through air.

19 Gas balloon acts as a sound lens

Fill a rubber balloon with air by blowing into it with your mouth until it expands to normal size. Hold the balloon with your fingers. Now the balloon is partly filled with carbon dioxide gas. Hold the balloon between your ear and a watch. You will hear the sound of ticking more clearly than without the balloon. This is because sound waves travel more slowly through heavy carbon dioxide gas than they do through air. The balloon acts as a converging lens to sound waves. Repeat the experiment with a balloon full of hydrogen gas.

20 How waves travel

The way in which energy is carried by waves can be studied by observing how they travel along the surface of water. They can often be seen in lakes, ponds and harbours, and the patterns produced help to explain many of the phenomena of light and radio, as well as of sound.

A more detailed examination of this behaviour can be made in the laboratory by producing ripples on the surface of a shallow dish of water. One way of making the patterns more visible is to place a source of light underneath a shallow tank with a glass bottom. Ripples produced in such a tank behave as cylindrical lenses, and shadows are seen on the ceiling or a screen placed above.

21 Making a ripple tank

Cut a rectangular aperture in the bottom of a photographic developing dish of full plate size, leaving a rim about 2.5 cm wide all round. Fit a sheet of clear glass to the tank and stick it down to the rim using a waterproof glue. Set it aside to dry. Obtain a cardboard box about 30 × 30 × 45 cm in size. Cut a circular hole 15 cm in diameter in the middle of one of the smaller faces, and make a small door in the middle of one of the rectangular sides. Paint the inside of this box a dull black. As a point source of light fit a car bulb and holder to a cube of wood of 7.5 cm side.

Stand the tank over the circular aperture in the box, and pour in water to a depth of about 1 cm. Darken the room and switch on the bulb. Observe the circular pattern produced on the ceiling when a drop of water falls into the water from a pen filler or pipette. If the pattern is distorted by the action of waves reflected from the sides of the tank, fit sloping beaches of picture frame moulding in the water all round the edges. Should there be patterns parallel to the sides caused by vibration of the tank as a whole, stand it on strips of 'sorbo' rubber or felt.

Continuous trains of waves can be produced by a vibrator with one end dipping into the water. Clamp a 30 cm hacksaw blade in the middle and attach a single piece of stout copper wire to one end, using an electrical terminal or a small bolt. Bend the wire at right angles to the plane of the blade and cut it off about 2.5 cm long. Support the blade in a firm retort stand so that the end of the copper wire dips into the water in the tank. Pluck the free end of the blade, and notice the generation of continuous waves.

Cut a T-shaped piece of tin to form a dipper for plane waves and attach it to the free end of the blade as before. Stick a piece of plasticine to the blade near the copper wire so that both ends of the blade carry the same load; in this way the vibration will be maintained for a considerable time.

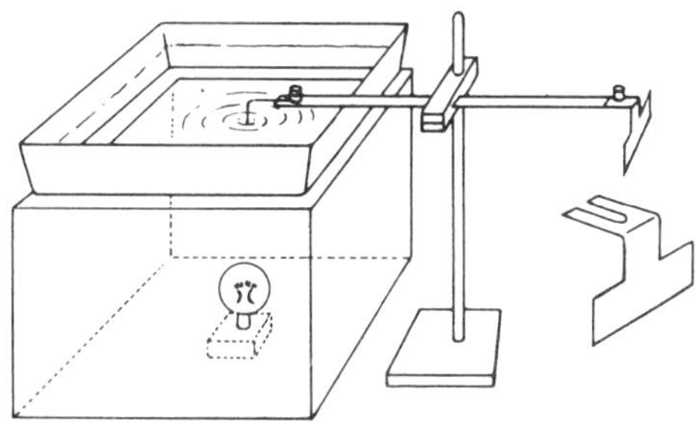

22 To study reflection of waves

Cut strips of tin slightly wider than the depth of the water in the tank and about 8 cm long.

Bend the end of one of them at right angles and stand it in the water near one end of the tank. Adjust the position of the vibrator so that circular waves are reflected from this obstacle. Use both single pulses and continuous waves. Notice that the reflected waves appear to diverge from a spot as far behind the 'mirror' as the vibrating wire is in front. Now replace the point dipper by the flat piece of tin which generates 'plane' waves. Observe the form of the reflected waves when the obstacle makes different angles with the incoming waves. Clearer patterns are obtained with plane waves if the lamp is turned on its side and so placed that the filament is parallel to the dipper. Repeat these experiments using a curved strip of tin which represents a convex or concave reflector when different sides face the waves.

As ripples have a lower velocity in shallow water than in deep water, it is possible to study the transmission of waves as they pass into an apparently 'different' medium. To study, for instance, the action of the 'sound lens' of experiment 19 above, use a circular disc of glass or perspex to form a circular 'shallow' in the tank. Place such a slab in the middle of the tank and use a pipette to adjust the level of the water so that the slab is just covered. Allow a train of plane waves to pass over it and notice that the waves passing over the diameter of the slab are held back and there is a resultant focusing effect. Slabs of different shape can be used to study refraction at a single surface, and the action of prisms and lenses.

B. SOUND AND MUSIC

1 Vibrating box

Cut a hole in the bottom of a used tin can. Put a stout string or a fishing line through it with its end tied tightly to a pencil inside the can. Rub resin on the string. Hold the can with one hand and keep the string taut with two fingers. Now draw your fingers along the line. Sound will come from the can. Repeat the experiment of drawing your fingers along the line at different speeds. Note the different pitches of sound. Can you make music out of the can? Try again with different sizes of tin cans and candy boxes. Will wood boxes give similar sounds?

2 Rubber band harpsichord

Stretch several rubber bands about a cake tin, cigar box, photographic developing dish or wash basin. Arrange them to different tensions with correspondingly different key-notes. Now play on them as on a harpsichord. The principle of this instrument is vibrating strings and a sound box. Repeat the experiment with various sizes of rubber bands on the same box.

3 One-string guitar

Secure a steel wire about 1 m long, a nail, three clothes pegs, a sound box made of thin plywood or of some other material (size about 60 × 15 × 3 cm) and a weight to hold the wire taut. Assemble these parts as shown in the diagram. Can you get music out of this home-made guitar? Repeat the experiment with more strings.

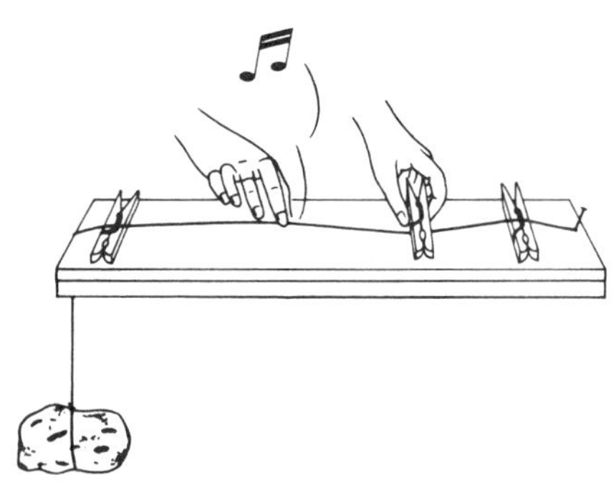

4 Music box with pins

Arrange several pins in a row on the sound box used in the above experiment or on a cigar box. Play music on this music box by plucking the pins with a letter opener. You will get lower notes out of longer pins and higher notes out of shorter ones.

Make another observation using a hair comb having different lengths of teeth.

5 Drinking straw orchestra

Secure 10 drinking straws for five players and a pair of scissors. Flatten one end of a straw and cut both corners of this flat end. Now this flat end acts as the reed of a wind instrument. Blow into it and adjust the reed until you get the best vibrations.

Next, set up an orchestra by making similar reeds out of other drinking straws. Cut off the other ends of the straws bit by bit to tune with different musical notes until you get a complete scale. Each of the five players is responsible for two notes, holding a straw in each hand. To begin with, try to play your National Anthem.

The principle is that the air column inside the straw vibrates because of the vibrating reed.

6 Bottle and glass tube trombone

Secure a glass or metal tube about 1 cm in diameter and 20 cm in length, and a bottle nearly full of water. Hold the bottle in one hand and the glass tube in the other, with the end of the tube dipping in the water. Now blow across the other end of the tube for a note. Next, as you blow, move the bottle up and down. You will hear various notes as you change the length of the column of air vibrating in the tube.

7 Musical bottles

Prepare a set of musical bottles so that each contains an air column tuned to one of the notes of the scale. Select eight similar bottles. Let the first one be empty. If water is added to the others to the proper heights, when they are tapped with a ruler or chopstick they will sound out a complete musical scale. You can do the same experiment with tall drinking glasses. The air columns inside the bottles or glasses take up vibrations from the outsides.

It is fun also, if you happen to possess china vases or bells of many sizes. Pick out those which are tuned to notes of the scale. Arrange them in a row. Hold a chopstick or a fork in each hand and carefully beat out a tune on them.

8 A set of dinner chimes

Secure a straight steel pipe about 3 cm in diameter and about 3.5 m in length. Cut it into four parts, 100 cm, 90 cm, 80 cm and 70 cm. Drill holes through both sides of each pipe near one end, and suspend them. Let them hang freely. Strike each pipe in turn with a rubber hammer and compose a sort of signature chime for your class.

9 Cigar box violin

Procure a cigar box or any similar box, regular strings from a music supply store, bits of wood, a piece of resin and cotter pins. Try to assemble these parts yourself so as to make the cigar box violin shown in the figure. The bow may be made from horsehair and a twig about 70 cm in length.

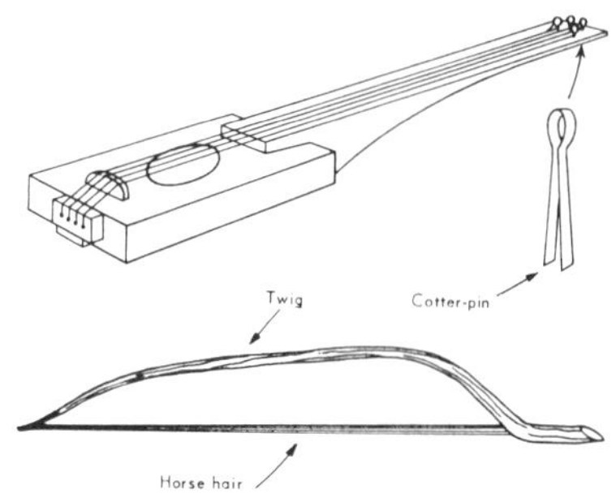

10 Shepherd's pipe

A section of bamboo is suitable for the pipe. Secure a straight bamboo about 1.5 cm in diameter and 30 cm in length, open at both ends and all through its length. Dry it by roasting on a small fire until its skin turns a yellowish brown all over. When it cools, make the mouthpiece and row of holes as shown in the figure. The pipe is similar to a tin whistle but the sound obtained is sweeter. The air column vibrated is measured from the exit hole in the mouthpiece to the first uncovered hole.

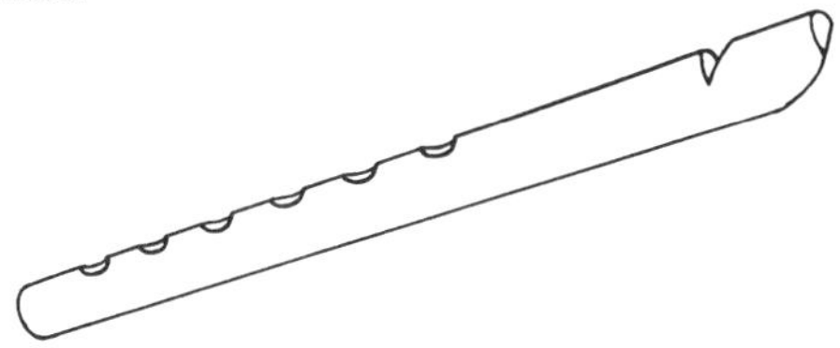

11 Xylophone and marimba

What you need here are strips of hard wood, bamboo, or iron, and a board; 8, 12 or 16 of these strips, cut to the proper lengths to sound out the scale when tapped, are required. For pieces of hardwood 2.5 cm wide and 1 cm thick, lengths of 20.0, 22.8, 24.2, 25.8, 27.2, 28.3, 29.5, 30.5 cm will give the diatonic scale. For the flat board of the xylophone, drill a hole about 2 mm in diameter near the end of each strip. Lay strips of felt on the board and drive small nails through each hole to hold the strips loosely. The strips will vibrate when tapped with a rubber hammer. This can be made from a pencil and a piece of eraser.

For the marimba, pieces of wood are shaped, as shown in the figure, to form the base and act as a sound box. Drill two holes near the end of each strip. Put a stout string through all the holes as shown and suspend the strips over the box.

Now procure two rubber hammers with rather long handles. Tap the strips lightly to obtain music.

Other simple musical instruments can be constructed, e.g., a variety of drums, scale of small gongs, flutes and many string instruments. Try to devise them yourself.

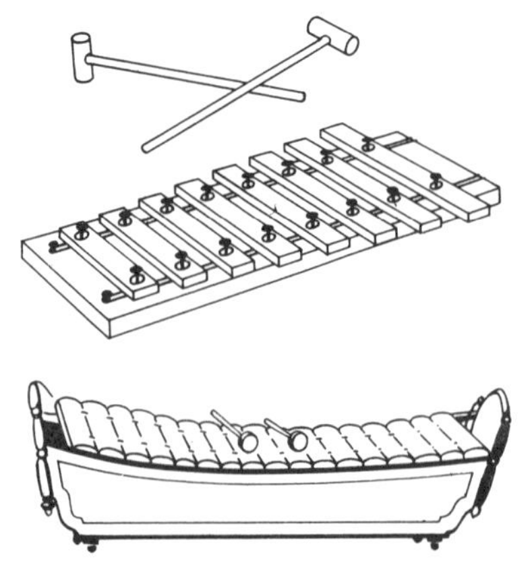

C. RECORDING AND REPRODUCING SOUND

1 How the ear works

Air vibrations enter the ear by the auditory passage formed at the base of the ear by the ear-drum membrane. They set the ear-drum in motion and, in doing so, set in motion the system of three little bones attached to it; by this means they reach a cavity in the bone called the inner ear.

One part of the ear is shaped like a snail shell. Here is found the organ which receives the sound vibrations and is connected with the brain by the auditory nerve. Another part of the inner ear which includes three small semicircular canals and serves to maintain equilibrium plays no part in hearing.

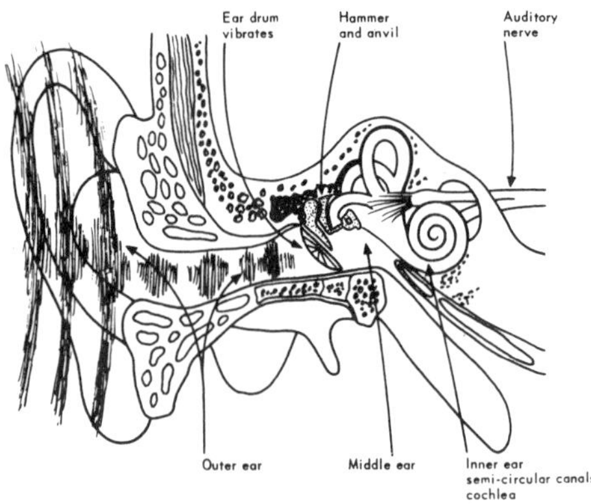

Sound vibrations are normally transmitted to the snail-shell-shaped cochlea by the ear-drum and the small bones (this gives rise to a nerve message which is carried to the brain); but they can also be transmitted by the bones of the skull, and we hear a sound if the waves reach the cochlea by either route.

When a sound reaches our two ears, we can distinguish the direction from which it comes; if it comes from straight ahead, the vibrations reach both ears at the same time and with the same strength; but if the source of the sound is on one side of us, one of our ears is farther away from it and receives the waves less strongly and with a slight delay.

2 How the voice is produced

Mouth, teeth, tongue, throat and lungs are all used in the production of the voice. The sound is produced by vibrations of two thin sheets of membrane called the vocal cords, which are stretched across the sound chamber called the larynx. The larynx is the upper end of the windpipe and is located well back, at the base of the tongue. Here a trap door of cartilage called the epiglottis automatically drops

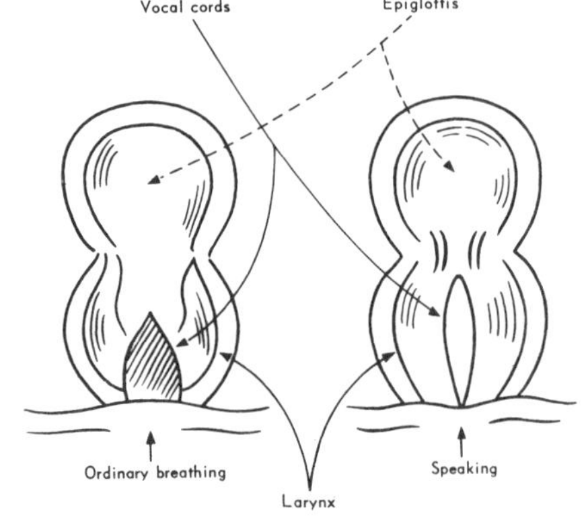

down over the larynx when you swallow, so that no food will go through the windpipe. When the cords are stretched by the contraction of certain muscles in the throat, a narrow slit tends to form between them. It is when the air is forced through this narrow slit that the cords are forced to vibrate. This sets the air vibrating in the windpipe, lungs, mouth and nasal cavities.

3 Sound wave patterns

The number of complete vibrations in one second is the frequency of a particular vibration. The way in which different sound frequencies combine is analogous to water waves. Ocean waves are longest, i.e. of low frequency. Let a small motor-boat pass over these waves. The boat sends out its own waves, which have a shorter frequency than ocean waves. Next, if there is a breeze, it will send tiny ripples across the surface of the motor-boat waves. The ripples usually have an even shorter frequency than the other two. Now these three vibrations combine to form a pattern shown in the figure.

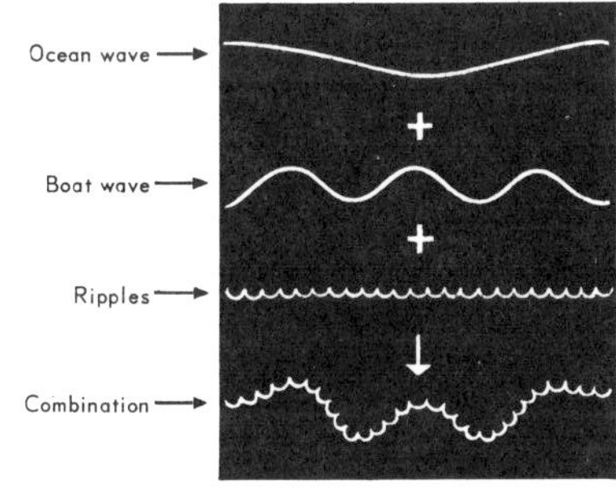

In a similar way, sound waves of different frequencies from various instruments combine and form sound wave patterns.

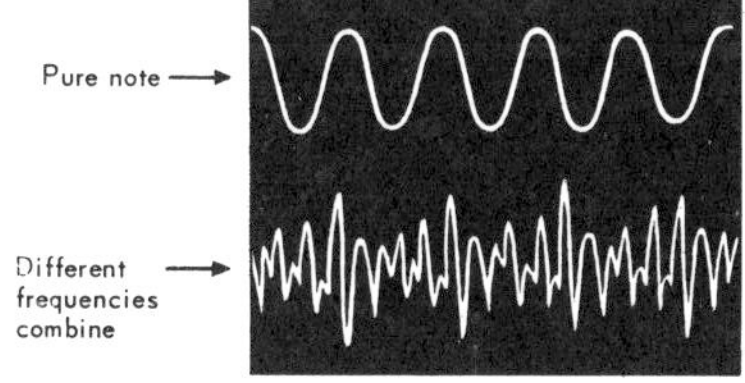

4 Wave pattern of a tuning fork

With a few drops of hot sealing wax attach a piece of fine wire to the prong of a tuning fork. The fork is held rigidly by the handle and placed horizontally just above the table top. Smoke a small pane of glass from the flame of an oil lamp or a candle. Now lay the smoked glass pane under the prong with the fine wire which is bent to touch the glass pane. Start the vibrations with the finger and draw the pane along the table fast enough to make a wavy line on the pane.

Repeat this experiment drawing the pane away at different speeds and using different tuning forks.

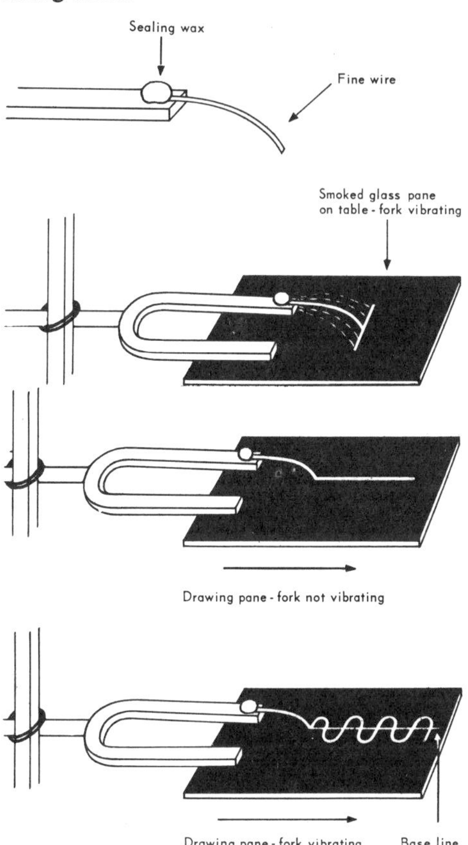

The higher the top of the wave from the base line the louder the sound.

5 A gramophone reproduces sound

Secure a 78 r.p.m. gramophone record and a hand magnifier. Through the magnifier you will notice a great number of wavy lines on the record. If possible, compare the wavy lines of records of different speeds.

Next, set the record turning at its usual speed of rotation. Place the edge of your finger-nail in the groove and listen carefully. Do you hear music coming from your nail? Do you feel your nail vibrate? It is clear that your nail is forced to vibrate as it follows the grooves, and produce the recorded sounds.

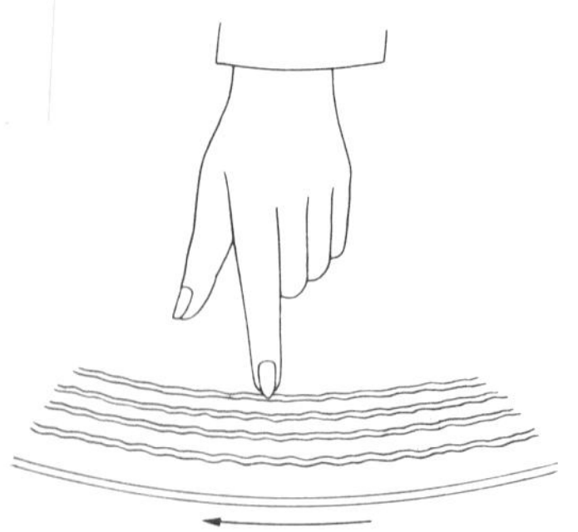

6 A simple reproducer

Thrust a record needle through the corner of a card or an empty matchbox. Now repeat the last experiment. Let the needle replace your fingernail. Has the sound been amplified?

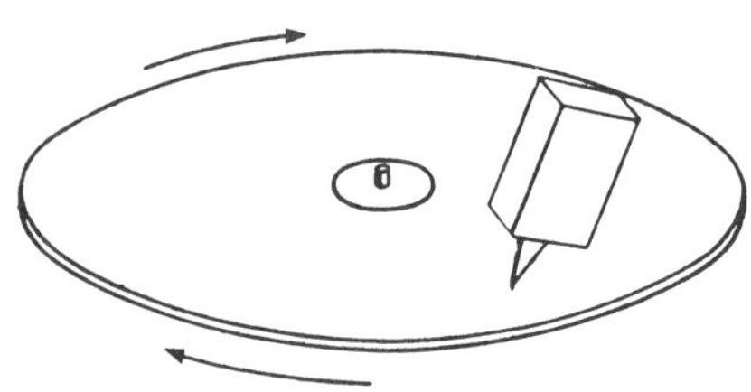

7 Another simple reproducer

For a more effective home-made reproducer you can copy the early phonographs by using a horn. Substitute for the card or the matchbox a horn made out of a square sheet of heavy wrapping paper, about 40 × 40 cm.

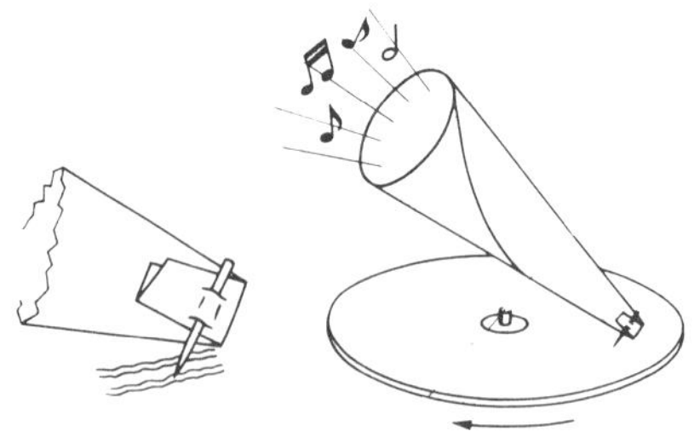

Shape the paper into a cone and fold the small end. Force a needle into all thicknesses as indicated in the diagram. Hold the horn so that the needle will rest lightly in the groove as the record rotates. Now, everybody in the room should hear the music from your simple reproducer.

8 A gramophone for everyone

What you need are two circular pieces of wood about 2.5 cm thick, and 30 cm in diameter, a base board about 80 × 40 × 2.5 cm, a sheet of flannel, 30 cm in diameter, as base, a piece of mica sheet 10 × 10 cm, a tube of Duco cement, gramophone needles, pins, a metal flange as frame of the reproducer, and an adaptor for the needle.

Your gramophone will look roughly like the first figure. Mount the two circular pieces of wood on the base board as illustrated, with the drive wheel and turn-table connected by a suitable length of heavy cotton cord. The flannel or felt pad is glued to the turn-table as the base for the record.

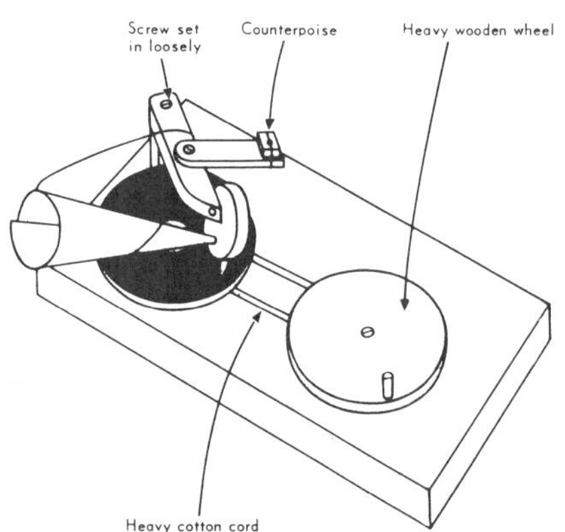

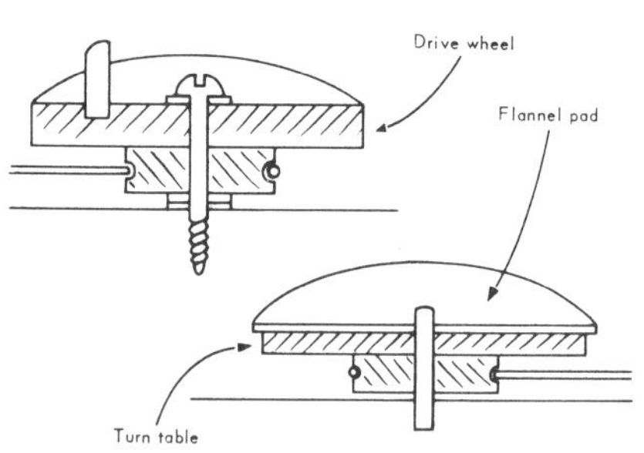

The important part of the machine, i.e., the reproducer and horn, may be made in one of two ways. The paper milk container method is the simpler one. Follow the illustration.

(a) Cement a rubber band neatly around the edge of the metal flange upon which the cap normally rests.

(b) Cut a disk from the mica sheet to fit the milk container opening.

(c) Drill a small hole at the centre and, after bending an oversize pin sharply near the

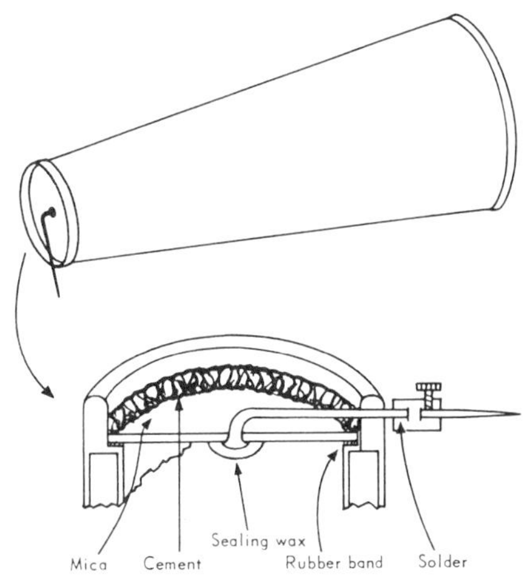

ead, insert it into the hole and then through nother hole in the metal flange.

(d) Cement the diaphragm in place with Duco or a quick-drying cement.

(e) For the adaptor, cut a 6 mm length of small brass rod, drill a small hole all the way through and solder it to the cut-off end of the pin; secure a little set screw and drill a hole in the side a bit smaller than the threaded part of the screw and then force the screw in by turning it strongly so that it is well secured.

(f) Instead of making the adaptor in (e) you can use a brass electric wire fixer in any old lamp socket as the adaptor.

(g) For the horn, remove the bottom of a wax paper ice-cream cup or a paper milk container, and fix it in the hole of the metal flange.

(h) Attach the whole unit to the carrier arm with adhesive tape, and the rest will be up to you.

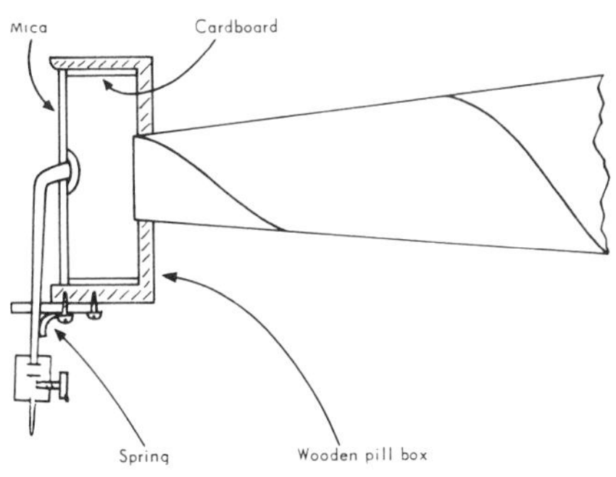

The second way of making the reproducer is illustrated above. This will give you an instrument more on the lines of a regular gramophone.

9 Recording of sound by gramophone

Recording is just the reverse process of reproducing. We have learnt that the voice or any other sound can be used to cause an object to vibrate and to form wavy lines on a smoked glass pane in motion.

Hold a card in front of your mouth and utter sounds against it. Feel the vibrations with your finger tips.

Remove the bottom of an ice-cream cup or a paper milk container and bind a diaphragm of thin paper or rubber over the small end. Hum into it and feel the vibrations again.

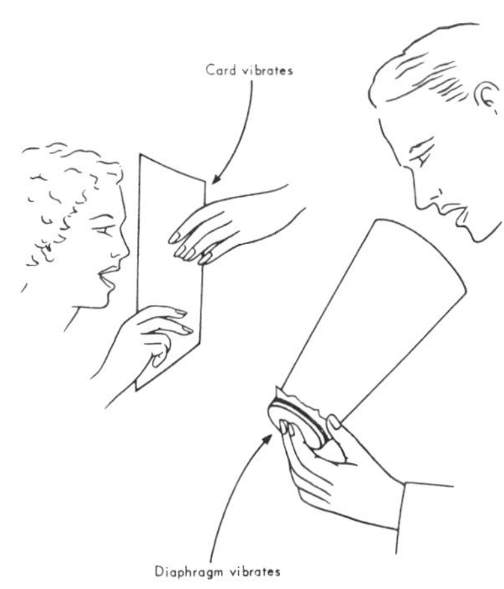

Detach the reproducer you made in the last experiment. Speak into the opening and, while doing so, feel the tip of the needle vibrating.

Now replace the reproducer and put a smoked glass disk of about the same diameter as the usual record on the turn-table. Speak into the horn and at the same time rotate

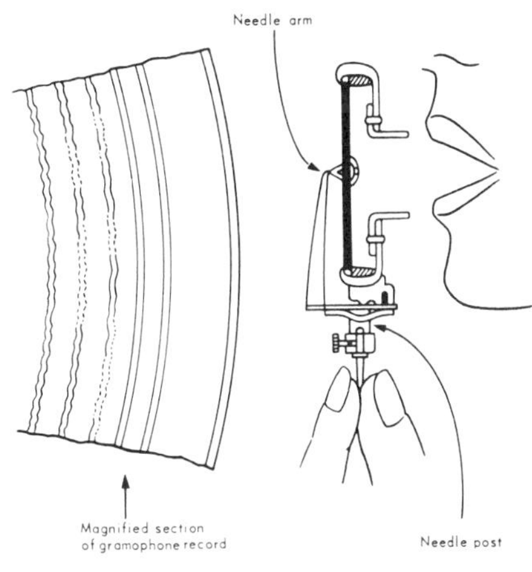

the turn-table. The vibrating needle point will draw wavy lines, a record of your voice. A hard-wax circular sheet might be used in place of a smoked glass disk.

Thomas A. Edison devised the first talking machine, which was a recorder as well as a reproducer. He first recorded the sounds and then played them back. If you are able to visit a science museum, have a look at the old-fashioned type of dictaphone. The parts are shown more clearly than in the newer types.

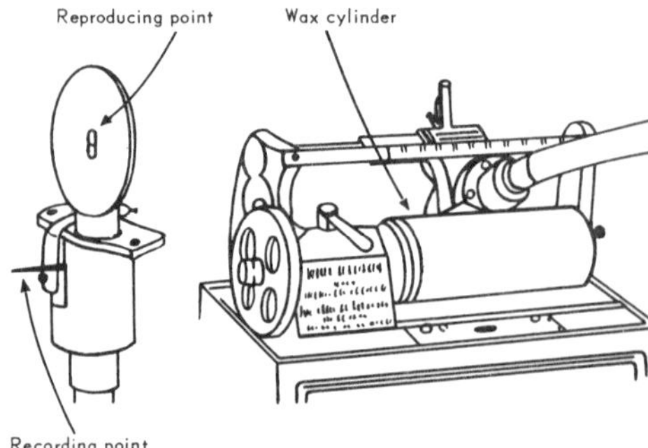

CHAPTER XIII

Experiments and materials for the study of heat

A. THE EXPANSION EFFECT OF HEAT

1 Triangle to show expansion on heating

Bend a piece of stiff metal wire into a triangle. Support it in a horizontal plane and suspend a coin between the two free ends forming one corner. Heat the opposite side of the triangle and the coin will fall out.

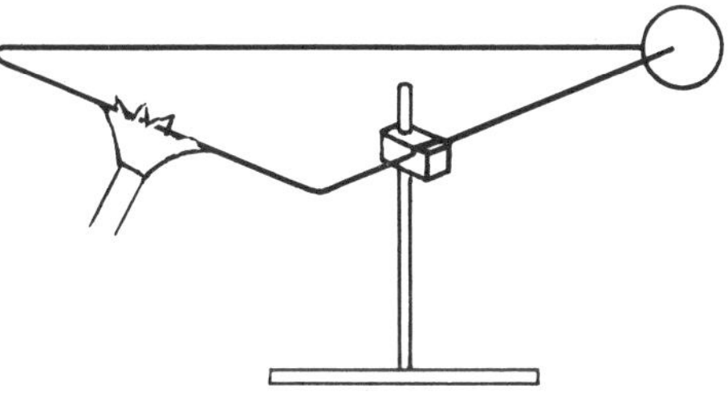

2 To show the expansion of a solid when heated

Get a piece of stout copper tubing about 2 m long. Lay it on a table and fix one end by a clamp. Underneath the other end put a piece of bent knitting needle or bicycle spoke to act as a roller. A thin strip of balsa wood about 1 m long fixed to the roller by sealing wax will show any movement of the rod resting on it. Blow steadily down the tube at the fixed end, and the expansion of the tube caused by the hot breath will be detected by this arrangement. Now pass steam through, and the pointer will make a complete revolution or more, depending on the diameter of the roller. Repeat the experiment after the roller and pointer have been moved nearer to the loose end of the rod. Compare the results.

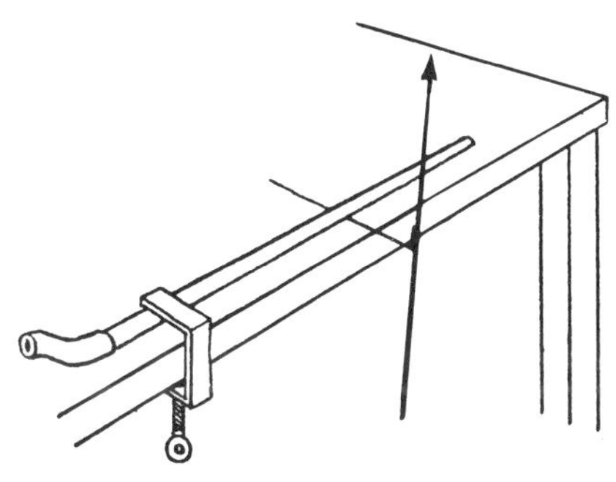

3 The ring and plug experiment

Secure a large wood screw and a screw eye; the head of the screw must just go through the screw eye. Screw each one into the end of a stick, letting at least 2.5 cm of metal protrude. Heat the head of the screw in a flame for a while and then try to put it through the screw eye. Keep the screw hot and heat the screw eye in the flame at the same time. Now try to put the screw head through the screw eye. Keep the screw head in the flame. Cool the screw eye in cold water. Again try to put them together. Next cool the screw head and try again.

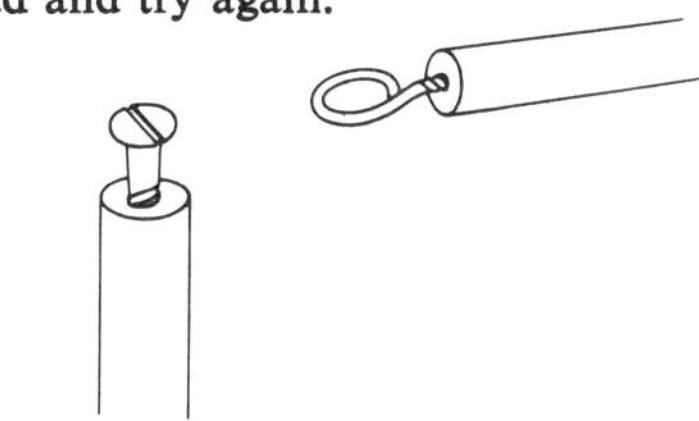

4 A bar and gauge

To construct this traditional apparatus use a cut nail as the bar and a piece of tin as the gauge. Cut the gap in the tin with shears and bend it into an angle girder so that it will stand on the bench with the gap upwards. Wind a piece of iron wire round the nail to serve as a handle.

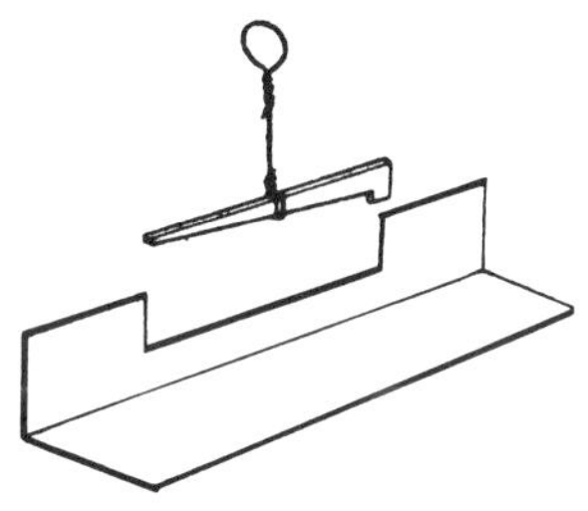

5 Thermal creeper

This model illustrates the creeping of lead roofs etc., under the action of heat. Push a cork onto each end of a knitting needle. Stick two pins through each cork so that the apparatus has four legs. These legs are slanting so that the front pair slide forward as the

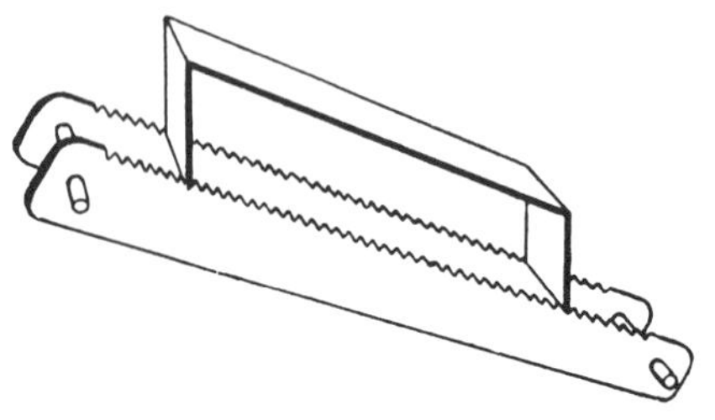

needle expands, but stick in the ground and drag the back 'legs' after them as it contracts. A bridge of brass set on a pair of hacksaw blades will behave in the same way and will, in fact, climb uphill.

6 A bimetallic strip

A pair of iron and brass strips, riveted together, will bend when heated because of the difference of expansion. Make the holes with a nail and use small tacks as rivets.

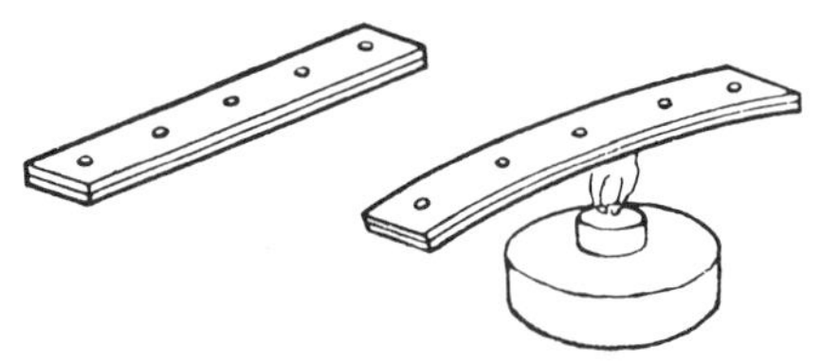

Another way of fastening the strips together is to cut them with projections at equal intervals and bend them over to interlock.

7 A device to measure the rate of expansion

The Liebig's condenser described on page 36 is used as a steam jacket for this experiment. The expansion of the test rod is magnified by a wooden lath acting as a lever. A piece of dowelling rod with a razor blade stuck into the top makes a satisfactory pivot, and X is a counterweight.

First cold water and then steam should be passed through the outer tube. The expansion

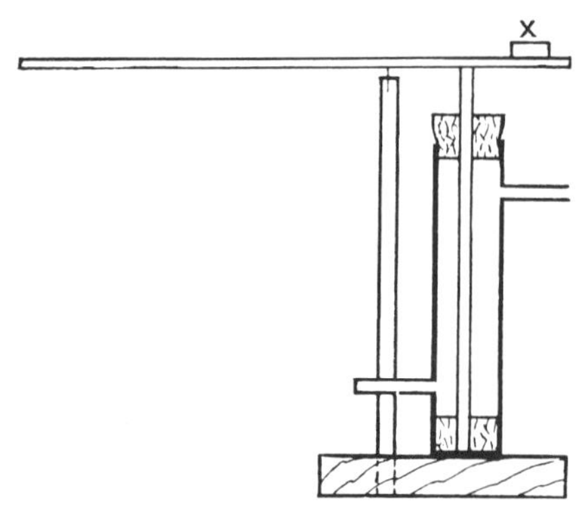

of the rod is calculated from the dimensions of the lever and the movement of the free end.

8 Expansion of liquids

Fit two or three similar medicine bottles with corks and tubes. Fill them with different liquids and immerse them in a pan of hot water. The rise inside the tubes will indicate the difference in expansion rates. If the diameter of the tubes and the capacity of the bottles are known it is possible to calculate the apparent coefficients of expansion.

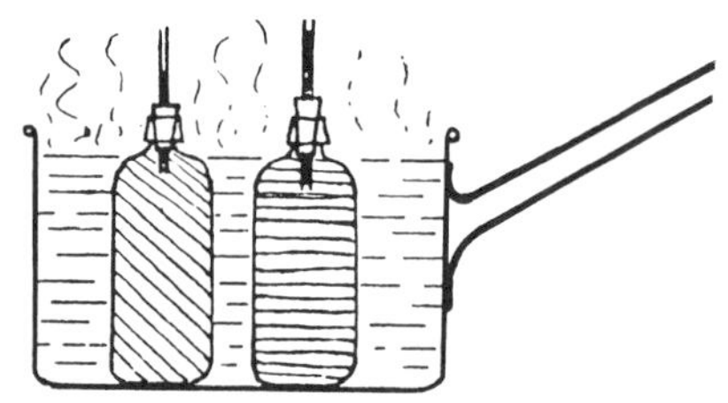

9 Expansion of gases

The medicine bottles can also show the expansion of air or other gases. Push the glass tube through the cork and trap some air. A hand

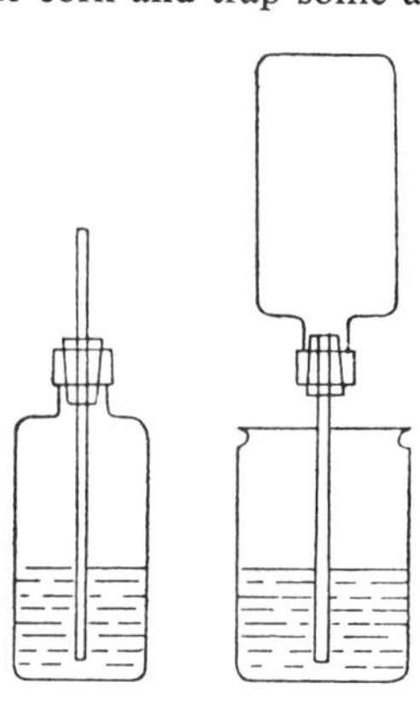

placed on the bottle drives liquid up the tube.

A simple form of air thermometer can be made arranging the tube as shown on the right in the diagram. Also refer to experiment B 2 below.

Warming the bottle causes air to be expelled. This reduces pressure inside. When the bottle cools liquid is forced up the tube.

10 Expansion of gases—soap bubble

A soap bubble stretched over the neck of a medicine bottle will grow larger if warm hands are placed on the bottle.

11 Another way to show the expansion of gases

Stretch a rubber balloon over the neck of a flask which has been made from a used electric bulb. Heat the flask gently with a candle or an alcohol flame.

See also Chapter VIII, experiment B 2, page 97.

12 An expansion experiment with a balloon

Partially inflate a balloon or a basket ball. Hold the balloon or ball over a hot plate or place it in the warm sun for a while and observe the results.

13 Fire balloon

Make a simple fire balloon from a large paper bag similar to those used by milliners.

Open out the mouth with a ring of florist's iron wire having a stay across the diameter. Fix the ring to the bag with strips of gummed paper. Tie a small piece of sponge or cotton wool to the middle of the stay and dip it in methylated spirit. Light the spirit and hold the bag by the ring. There is danger of setting fire to the paper bag in this experiment, which is best performed in the open air.

This paper bag balloon is not very stable in flight. A better one can be made as follows:

Place on a table six sheets of tissue paper, one on top of the other. Cut them in the shape shown in the figure and stick them together at the edges to form a balloon. A circular disk will be needed as cap to close the top. Fix a ring to the neck as before. Such a balloon will rise to great heights and can be flown from a piece of string like a kite. Solid methylated spirit, as employed in some spirit lamps, is easier to use if it can be obtained: it can be placed on a small tin lid attached to the wire ring at the mouth of the balloon.

B. TEMPERATURE

1 Is your temperature sense reliable?

Fill three pans with water. Have one at the highest temperature you can bear your hand in. Fill a second one with ice-cold water. The third should be lukewarm. Put both hands in the lukewarm water and hold them there for about half a minute. Does the water seem to be the same temperature for both hands? Does it feel hot, cold or neither?

Next place your left hand in the hot water and your right hand in the icy water for a minute. Quickly dry your hands and plunge both into the lukewarm water again. How does the right hand feel? How does the left hand feel? Do they feel the same as when in the lukewarm water before? What do you think about your temperature sense?

2 Making an air thermometer

Fit a flask made from a used electric bulb (or a thin-walled bottle or test tube) with a one-hole rubber stopper which has a 60 cm length of glass tubing in it. The stopper must be an air-tight fit in the bulb. You can seal the stopper in by dropping some wax from a candle around the joint. Build a support for your thermometer from wood as shown in the diagram. Paste a strip of paper for a scale behind the tube. Place the lower end of the tube in a small bottle of cold water, coloured with ink. Heat the bulb of the thermometer gently to drive out some of the air. Drive out just enough air so that when the bulb cools to room temperature the coloured water will rise about half way up the tube.

To make your scale, let the thermometer stand in a room for several hours. Have another thermometer near the bulb. Make a line on the paper at the level of the water and mark the reading of the thermometer at this point. Next move your thermometer to a warm place to stand for an hour with the other thermometer near the bulb. Mark the water level and the temperature. Move again to a cool place and again mark the water level and temperature. Divide the space between these marks into equal divisions and mark off the corresponding temperatures.

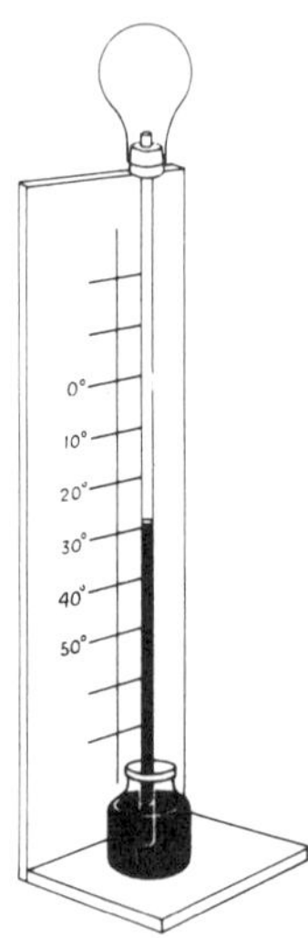

3 How a thermometer works

Fill a flask made from a used electric light bulb with water that has been coloured with ink. Insert a one-hole stopper carrying a 30 cm length of glass tubing until the water rises in the tube a distance of 5 or 6 cm. Place the flask on a tripod over an alcohol burner and observe the water level as you heat it. The water expands more rapidly than the glass and rises up the tube. Some keen observers in the class may notice that just at the moment heating is begun, the water level drops and then begins to rise. This is because the glass bulb starts to expand before the water inside reaches the temperature of the glass.

4 Making a spirit thermometer

To make a simple alcohol thermometer, accurate enough for indicating variations of temperature, use 20-30 cm of glass tubing of about 5 mm external diameter with about 1 mm bore. A bulb of about 1.5 cm external diameter is first blown in one end of the tubing; coloured industrial alcohol is allowed to enter by means of a rubber tube and a thistle funnel till the thermometer is filled and without bubbles. The thermometer is then placed in water at 60° C, which is slightly below the boiling point of alcohol, allowing the excess alcohol to ooze out. Then the open end is sealed off. With water at different temperatures the thermometer is tested and the scales are drawn.

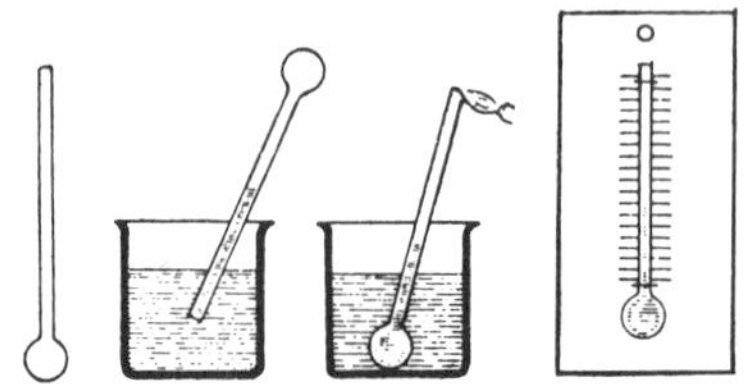

5 Testing a thermometer

Thermometer scales are marked at two fixed points, steam temperature and the temperature of melting ice. Secure a thermometer and place it in steam immediately above the surface of water boiling in a flask. Leave it there for several minutes and notice how closely it registers 100° C, or 212° F.

Note. If you live at a high altitude the temperature of steam may be well below 100° C or 212° F because of the reduced pressure. The thermometer will register exactly only at sea level or where the barometer reading is 760 mm of mercury.

Remove the thermometer from the steam, allow to cool for a few moments and then place it in a jar of melting ice. Observe how nearly it reads 0° C, or 32° F.

6 Heat and temperature—the idea of a calorie

Suspend a tin containing 50 cc of water and a thermometer over a small bunsen flame or a candle. Heat it for two minutes, constantly stirring, and record the final temperature. Empty out the water and repeat the experiment with 100, 150, 200 cc of water, using the same flame. It is sufficiently accurate to count 1 cc of water as 1 g. Find the product of mass of water multiplied by rise in temperature in each case. As the same heat is given out by the flame to each mass of water, the result suggests that a convenient unit of heat would be that absorbed by 1 g of water rising in temperature by 1° C. This unit is called a *gram calorie*.

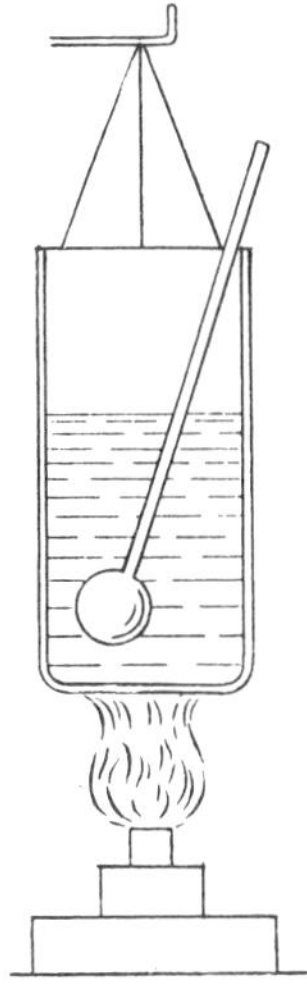

7 Calorific value for fuel

As fuels vary greatly in their heating effect, it is useful to have some way of indicating their relative effectiveness. A suitable index is the number of calories given out when one gram of the substance burns completely away: this is called the *calorific value*.

Hang a small can from a stand by means of fine wires. Pour 100 cc of cold water into it, and take the temperature. Place a small piece of candle on a tin lid and weigh it. Now place it under the can of water and light the wick. Stir the water with the thermometer and when the temperature reaches 60° C blow out the flame and weigh the tin lid and candle again. The mass of water (in cc) multiplied by the rise in temperature (in C°) gives the calories produced, and the mass of candle used can be found from the weighings. The calorific value can be calculated from these two quantities. Solid methylated spirit or a methylated spirit lamp can also be used in this experiment.

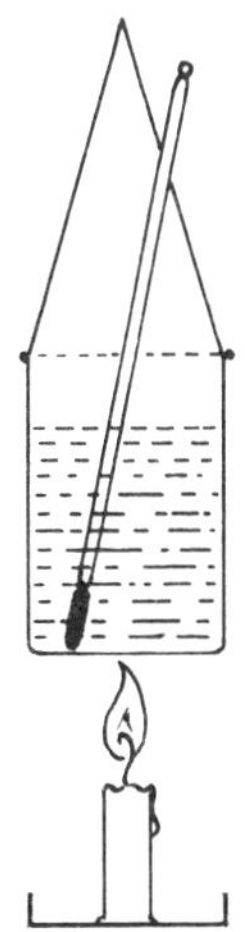

C. THE TRANSFER OF HEAT

1 Conduction in a metal bar

Secure a bar of copper, brass or aluminium at least 30 cm long. Attach tacks or nails to the bar with melted paraffin at intervals of 3 cm. Set the bar above a table top and heat one end with an alcohol or other flame. Observe the evidence that heat moves along the bar by conduction.

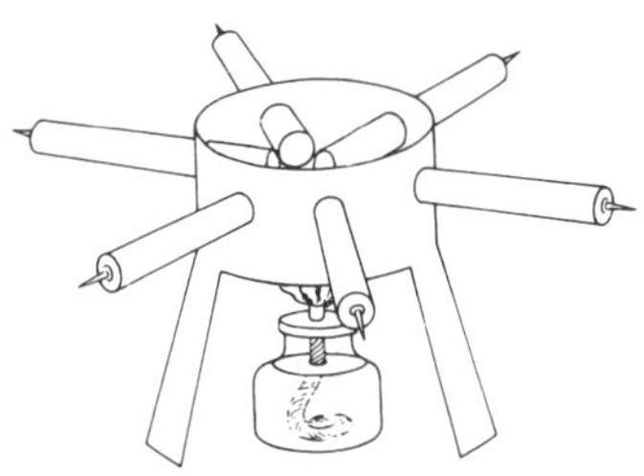

2 Metals conduct heat at different rates

Obtain 15 cm lengths of several metals. The bars should be of approximately the same diameter. Punch holes in the side of a tripod that has been made from a tin can. Insert the metal bars so that they touch at the centre of the can. Attach a tack or nail to the outside end of each bar with some paraffin. Place an alcohol flame under the tripod so that it touches the inner edge of each bar equally. Observe the order in which the tacks fall from the outer end of the bars. Most of the simple experiments on this topic are confusing because they involve specific heat as well as conduction.

3 Measurement of the heat conducted through different substances

The steam can described in Chapter II, C 5, page 36, will serve as a hot plate for experiments in conductivity if it is placed upside down on a tripod. Steam is introduced through the long pipe and condensed in cold water. Place a slab of cardboard on the hot plate and on it a small tin containing 100 cc of water and a thermometer. Measure the rise in temperature after 5 minutes and calculate the heat transmitted. Repeat the experiment using slabs of equal thickness of metal, cloth, cork, etc.

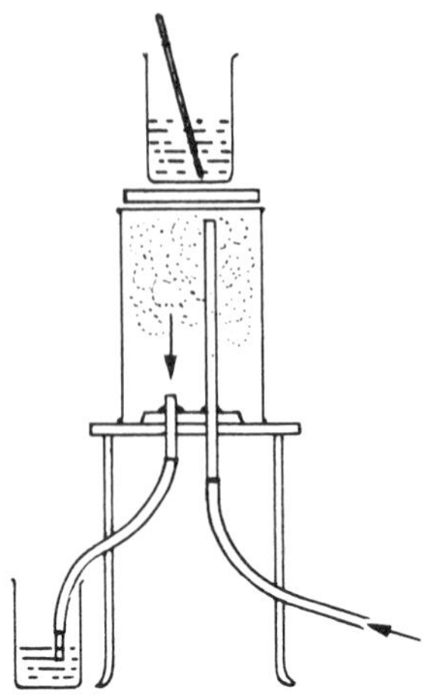

4 Metals are good conductors of heat

Hold a piece of paper above a candle flame: it will char if brought near. Place a metal coin on the paper and repeat the experiment: the metal will conduct away the heat and leave a pattern on the paper.

5 Conductivity of metal and wood

A piece of metal tube with a wooden rod fitted into it shows the same effect: if the wooden rod is held over a flame, it will not burn. A penholder with a metal band at one end can be used for this experiment. The same principle is involved in a simple experiment with a cigarette, a metal coin and a handkerchief. Wrap the coin in the handkerchief, stretching the fabric tightly over it between finger and thumb. Press the red hot ember of the cigarette on this part of the handkerchief; it does not burn.

6 Conduction with a metal gauze

Hold a piece of metal gauze in an alcohol or gas flame. Observe that the flame does not come through the screen as the heat is conducted away from the flame by the wires. If you have gas in your room place a burner under a tripod and cover it with a wire screen. Turn on the gas and light it above the screen. You will observe that the gas burns only above the screen as the heat is conducted away by the screen and keeps the gas below the screen from reaching its kindling temperature. This observation gave Sir Humphrey Davy his idea for making the miners' safety lamp which prevented the explosion of gases in the coal mines.

7 A model Davy lamp

The traditional experiments on the conductivity of wire gauze can be followed by an improvised Davy lamp. A Christmas candle enclosed in a cylinder of wire gauze does not light a jet of gas played on it from a rubber tube.

A block of wood or plasticine is used as a base.

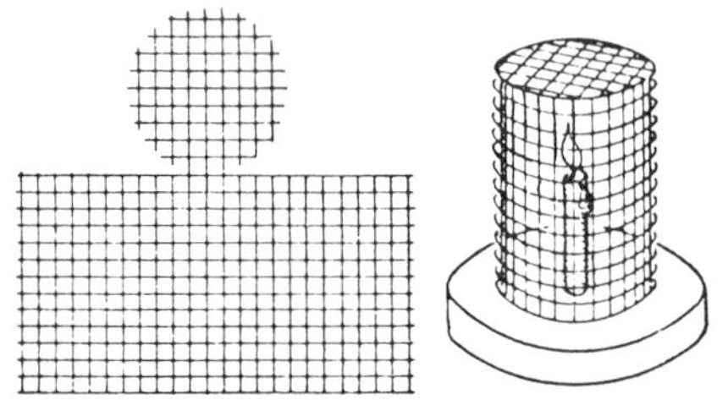

8 Haybox thermos flask

Make a cloth bag to fit loosely round a bottle, and stuff it with kapok and cotton waste. Enclose this in a cardboard or bamboo cylinder fitted with carrying string. Although no vacuum is used, drinks are kept hot or cold for several hours.

9 Water is a poor conductor of heat

Hold the bottom end of a test tube of cold water in the hand. Heat the top in a bunsen flame until it boils. The fact that you can still hold the bottom shows how bad a conductor water is.

10 Heat is transferred by convection in liquids

Secure a large glass jar that can be heated. The bottom part of a glass coffee-maker can be used. Fill the jar with water. Put some grated blotting paper particles or sawdust in the water and give them time to settle to the bottom. Now place the jar over an alcohol lamp and begin to heat it. Observe the paths taken by the particles of paper. The paper particles follow the convection currents set up in the water.

11 What causes convection currents in water?

Fill a large jar with cold water and weigh it accurately on a balance. Fill the jar with exactly the same amount of hot water and weigh. You will observe that the jar of warm water weighs less. Volume for volume cold water is heavier than warm water; so when water is heated convection currents are set up, the warm water being lifted, because of buoyancy, by the cold surrounding water. In other words hot water is less dense than cold, and this is the cause of convection currents in a liquid.

12 Effect of temperature on the density of water

The sensitive balance described on page 34 can be used to demonstrate changes of upthrust when a body is suspended in cold and then warm water. Replace one of the pans of the balance by a key or other suitable metal object hung from the beam. Counterpoise this in a can of water. Now blow steam into the water to raise its temperature and notice that the key apparently becomes heavier owing to reduced upthrust on it. As metals expand much less than liquids the effect is easily seen. If absolute measurements are required, a correction for the expansion of the metal may be made, or an inexpansible alloy such as Invar should be used in place of the key.

13 At what temperature does water attain its maximum density?

Put a piece of ice into a glass of water. Arrange two thermometers so that one measures the temperature near the surface, and the other the temperature near the bottom. It will be noticed that the water cooled by the ice falls to the bottom; this continues until the water at the bottom of the glass reaches a temperature of about 4° C. It will stay at this temperature for a long time, the colder water remaining higher up near the ice. From this it can be deduced that the water at 4° C is denser than the water at 0° C.

This curious behaviour of water is of great practical significance in nature, and explains why a pond freezes from the surface downwards while the bottom surface seldom falls below 4° C.

14 Another way to show convection currents in water

Fit an ink bottle or paste jar with a cork carrying two pieces of glass tubing as shown in the diagram. One piece of tubing should be drawn out to a jet like the end of a medicine dropper. This tube should be put just through the cork and should extend about two inches above. The other tube should be just level with the cork and extend nearly to the bottom of the bottle. Fill the bottle with very hot water that has been coloured deeply with ink.

Now fill a large glass jar such as a battery jar or cookie jar with very cold water. Rinse off the ink bottle and quickly place it on the bottom of the large jar. Observe what happens. Can you explain this?

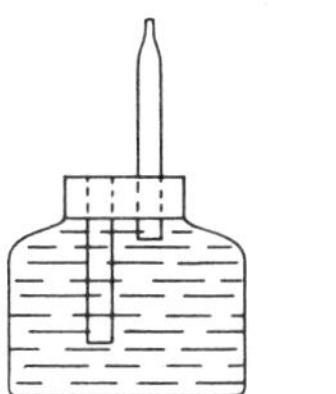

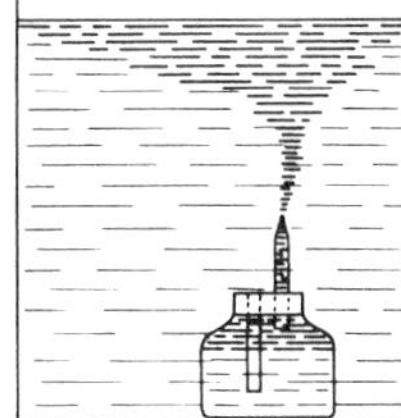

15 How to make a model hot water heating system

Make a flask from a large electric bulb. Secure a wide-mouthed bottle and a funnel. Fit the bottle with a cork carrying three glass tubes arranged as shown in the diagram.

Fit the flask with a two-hole cork carrying two glass tubes, one going just through the cork and the other extending nearly to the bottom. Attach the funnel as shown. This serves as the expansion tank. Fill the system with water and heat. Observe which part of the radiator gets hot first. Can you explain how the water circulates by convection currents?

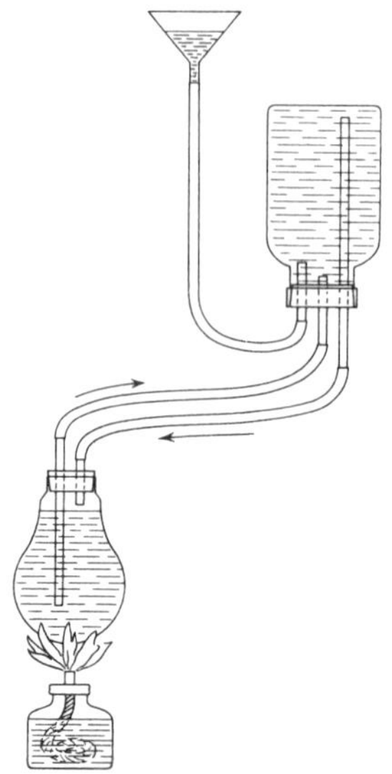

16 Convection currents in air

Obtain a circular disk of thin tin as used to close tobacco containers. Cut teeth in the circumference and pivot it on a bent knitting needle. Hold it above a candle flame, and it will revolve rapidly. A paper spiral supported on a knitting needle will revolve in a similar way.

Bring a piece of red-hot iron into contact with 'solid methylated spirit' (Meta fuel). The vapour immediately recrystallizes and fills the room with a highly diverting snow-storm. The crystals are set in motion by draughts and convection currents already in the room.

Another way of showing these air currents is by making use of the difference in refractive index of warm and cold air. A 12 volt car bulb without reflector will cast 'shadows' of convection currents from an electric heater or even from an ordinary electric lamp bulb.

See also Chapter VIII, experiment B 6, page 97.

17 How convection currents cause winds

See Chapter VIII, experiment B 6, page 97.

18 Convection currents and ventilation

Use the box which you used for a study of winds in Chapter VIII, experiment B 5, page 97. Bore four holes in each end, two above and two below. Put solid corks in all the openings including the two on the top where the lamp chimneys were placed for the other experiment. The holes in the opposite ends represent windows which may be opened or closed at the top and at the bottom. Put four candles in the box and light them. You are now ready to study the best conditions for ventilation. Close all the windows and observe the candles for a little while. Now try different combinations of openings. One window open at top and bottom. One open at the top, the other at the bottom. Both open at the top. One only open at the bottom. Both open at the bottom. One only open at the top. What window openings provide the best ventilation?

19 Heat is transferred by radiation

In the previous experiments you have seen that heat can be transferred by material substances, by solids, liquids and gases. Heat can also be transferred by wave motion, even across a vacuum. This is called radiation. Heat travels by radiation almost instantaneously. This experiment will demonstrate some interesting things about radiation. Hold your hand under an unlighted electric bulb, palm upward. Turn on the electricity. Can you feel the heat almost as soon as you turn on the bulb? The heat could not have reached your hand by conduction because air is a very poor conductor of heat. Neither could it have reached your hand by convection because this would have carried the heat upward away from your hand. It actually came to your hand carried by very short waves. Radiation carries heat in every direction from the source.

20 Radiant heat waves can be focused

Hold a reading glass lens in the sun and focus the rays to a point on a wad of tissue paper. You will observe that the tissue paper catches fire from the focused heat rays. Try the effect of using tissue paper blackened with indian ink or soot. Does it catch alight more readily?

21 Radiant heat waves can be reflected

In the above experiment note the distance from the reading glass to the tissue paper. Place a tilted mirror about half this distance from the lens. Feel about with your hand above the mirror until you find the point where the heat waves are focused. Hold a bit of crumpled tissue paper at this point and see if it will catch alight.

22 Different kinds of surfaces affect radiation

Secure three tin cans of the same size. Paint one white, inside and out, and another one black; leave the third one shiny. Fill the three cans with warm water at the same temperature. Record the temperature. Place cardboard covers on each can, set them on a tray, and then put them in a cool place. Record the temperature of the water in each can at five-minute intervals. Was there a difference in the rate of cooling? Which surface was the best radiator of heat? Which the poorest?

Next fill the cans with very cold water, record the temperature, cover each can and place them in a warm place or in the sun. Record the temperature of the water at five-minute intervals. Which surface was the best absorber of heat? Which the poorest?

23 Another way to show how surfaces affect radiation

Cut two vertical slits opposite each other on the side of a cylindrical tin, so that the surface of the tin is divided into two parts. Blacken the inside of one half leaving the other half shiny. Put a lighted candle inside the tin, in the exact centre of the base.

A difference in temperature of the two outside surfaces can be detected with the fingers.

Matchsticks fastened to the outside with wax can also be used as indicators, and the one behind the black surface will fall off first.

An alternative experiment is to use a coiled cylinder of fine wire gauze wrapped round the top of the tube of a bunsen burner as emitter and blackened thermometers as detectors of radiation.

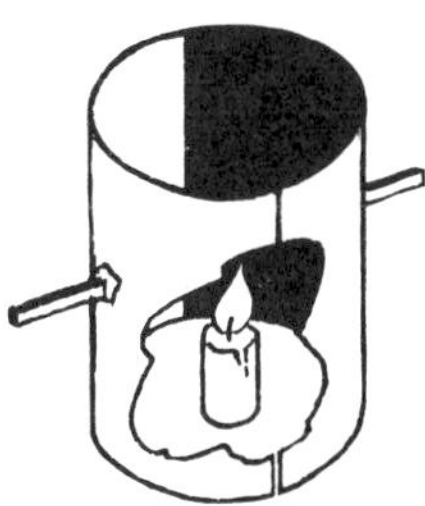

24 A simple thermoscope

Flasks, or cut-off light bulbs, can be used to construct this apparatus. Besides the experiment illustrated with the candle, it works well for other experiments, e.g., the Leslie Cube.

Fit both bulbs with corks and tubes about 15 cm in length. Pass the lower ends of the tubes through flat corks and, having made holes about 22 cm apart in a suitable baseboard, glue the tubes in a vertical position and connect the open ends by rubber tubing. Remove one bulb and blacken the other in a candle flame. Pour liquid into the U tube so formed until the level is about 7.5 cm above the baseboard. Replace the clear bulb and slide the tube in or out a little so that the liquid remains level. Place a candle equidistant between the bulbs and wait for results.

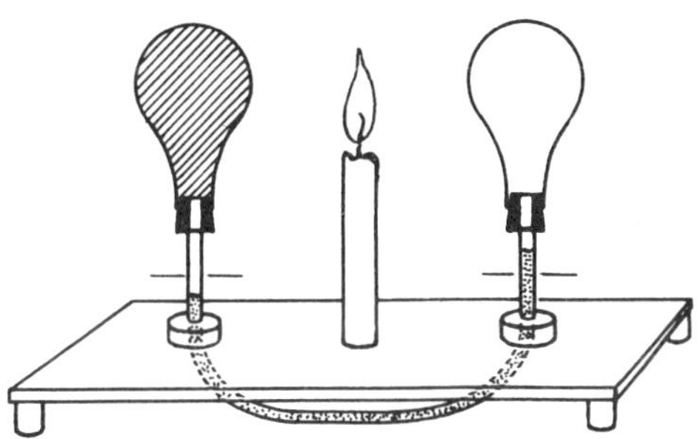

25 How heat losses can be reduced

Secure four large tin cans of the same size and four smaller tin cans of the same size. Put three of the small cans inside three of the larger ones and pack insulating material under and around each of the smaller cans. Pack one with shredded newspaper, the second with sawdust and the third with ground cork (other more convenient insulating materials may be substituted). Inside the fourth large can place the small can resting on two corks. Fit paste board covers to each can. Have a hole in each cover for a thermometer. Now fill each small can to the same depth with water that is nearly boiling. Record the temperature of the water in each can. Take the temperature of the water in each can at five-minute intervals and notice which is the best insulator as indicated by the slowest rate of cooling.

D. MELTING AND BOILING

1 Observing a boiling liquid

Secure a very large pyrex beaker or a large tin can. Fill the vessel nearly full of cold water and place it over a flame. Leave it there until it boils. You will first observe air bubbles coming out of solution in the water and rising to the surface. When the water is near the boiling point, steam bubbles will form and collapse almost at once. As the boiling point is reached, the bubbles will form at the bottom and rise to the surface before bursting.

2 How to boil water in paper

Secure some smooth paper: either wrapping paper or writing paper will do. Make a box about 25 cm square by folding the corners up and pinning them. Fill the box about half full of water and place it on a burner. You can boil the water without burning the paper. The paper conducts heat from the flame to the water and does not catch fire because its kindling temperature is above the boiling point of water (100° C or 212° F).

3 Boiling water by cooling it

Fit a flask with a tight solid stopper. Remove the stopper and fill the flask a little more than half full of warm water. Bring the water to the boiling point over a flame. Put the stopper tightly in the flask and invert it over a pan or sink. Pour cold water over the flask : the water starts boiling again. Put a piece of ice on the flask. Cooling condenses the water vapour above the water and reduces the pressure on the water. When the pressure is reduced, water boils at a lower temperature. This explains why it takes so long to cook things at high altitudes.

4 Boiling ether by reducing the pressure

Obtain a glass bottle or flask, with cork and tube. Pour ether into it to a depth of about 2.5 cm, and add a little powdered glass or sand. Replace the cork and with narrow rubber tubing attach to the glass tube a non-return valve such as the one used in a football pump adaptor. Push over this a length of

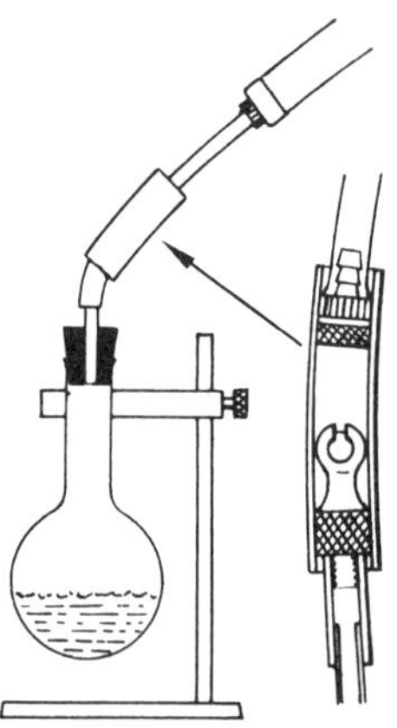

bunsen tubing, and attach the connector of a cycle pump which has previously had the washer reversed. Clamp the flask in a stand so that the liquid can easily be observed. After a few sharp strokes of the pump, the ether will boil vigorously.

5 When liquids evaporate, they absorb heat

Set up an air thermometer like the one in experiment B 2, page 143. Put some rubbing alcohol on the bulb of the thermometer. What do you observe? Where did the heat come from to evaporate the alcohol? Try carbon tetrachloride; try ether.

6 Freezing by rapid evaporation of ether

With a knife cut a depression in a softwood board or block. Place a glass tube in the rubber connector of a bicycle pump. Pour a little water in the depression you have made in the wood block and place a tin can in the water. Pour a little ether in the tin can and force air through it with the pump. As the ether evaporates it absorbs heat from the water and the can will soon be frozen to the wood by a film of ice.

7 The cooling effect of a dry wind

Obtain two similar thermometers and wrap the bulb of one of them in a small piece of wet cloth. Shield them from draughts and wait until they read the same temperature. Now place them on a window sill in a current of air. It will be seen that the thermometer with the wet bulb shows a much lower temperature. This is because the evaporating water takes heat from the bulb.The current of air assists evaporation by bringing dry air to the thermometer. This phenomenon is common in everyday life: the evaporation of sweat from the body on hot and windy days is very refreshing.

8 How heat changes solids to liquids

Place samples of such things as lead, solder, ice, sealing wax, paraffin wax in separate containers that may be heated. Small tin cans or lids will be useful. Experiment with these and see if you can get some information on the relative amount of heat needed to melt each sample.

9 Freezing water with ice and salt

Crack some ice into small lumps and place a layer in the bottom of a large can; cover this with kitchen salt and then add other layers of ice and salt. Put some water in a smaller tin can, and place this tin inside the large can. Then add more layers of ice and salt until the large can is full. Record the time taken to freeze the water in the small tin. Compare this with the time required to freeze the same amount of water if only ice is used in the large can.

10 Water expands when it freezes

Secure a small metal can which has a screw top. Fill it to overflowing with water and then screw the top on so that there is no air space. Bury the can of water in a mixture of ice and salt and leave it for some time until the water freezes. You should obtain some interesting results.

11 Heat is absorbed when solids melt

Secure a small container of chopped ice and find its temperature with a thermometer. Place the container over a flame and observe the temperature until all the ice is melted. When did the temperature begin to rise? Why did it not rise for some time? What became of this heat energy?

12 Melting by pressure and refreezing

When you apply pressure to ice you lower the freezing point. This is why skates move so easily over ice. Hold an ice cube or a piece of broken ice in each hand. Press them together over a piece of paper. Can you make water come from the ice with pressure? Push two ice cubes together forcibly and then release the pressure. Try to separate the ice cubes. The water refreezes when you release the pressure, holding the ice cubes solid.

13 Latent heat of steam found by using a tin

The rate of heat supply of a flame to 100 g of water in a tin may be found by taking the temperature at intervals and plotting a time-temperature graph.

When the water begins to boil there is no further rise in temperature but the rate of heat supply is the same. If one disregards the water lost by evaporation in bringing it to the boil, the heat required to boil 100 g of water completely away (that is until the bottom of the tin is dry), can be found from the time required for this to happen.

14 Latent heat found by using a hollow solid

An alternative way of determining the latent heat of steam is to use a heavy hollow metal solid as a condenser. A teapot can be used for a rough estimate.

The mass of water condensed in the teapot when steam from a kettle is passed into it depends on the heat capacity of the teapot.

If a brass axle cap is used, it should be fitted with a bung having inlet and exit tubes. When steam is passed into the apparatus, some time elapses before any comes out of the exit tube, because it is being condensed by the cold metal. After steam has issued for a few minutes, and the metal is therefore at 100° C, the steam supply should be stopped. The mass of steam condensed is found by taking its volume with a measuring cylinder. Given the specific heat, mass and initial temperature of the metal, the heat absorbed by it in condensing the steam is calculated.

15 Latent heat of ice

A rough value of the latent heat of ice can be obtained by measuring how much ice is melted when a heated solid is buried in ice shavings.

Weigh the solid of known specific heat and raise its temperature to 100° C by suspending it in water from a piece of cotton. Quickly transfer it to a funnel of powdered ice, and collect the resulting water in a test tube or measuring cylinder.

Calculate the heat given up by the metal in cooling to 0° C.

This apparatus can also be used to demonstrate the difference in specific heat of different materials. The volume of water obtained in each case provides a comparison of the specific heats.

16 Specific heat using a teapot

Pour boiling water into a weighed teapot at room temperature. The temperature will remain steady at about 96° C. Measure the mass of hot water used when it has cooled a little, using a measuring cylinder. Assuming there is no loss of heat to the surroundings, the specific heat of the material can be calculated.

This experiment forms an introduction to the subject of specific heat, or might be used as part of an investigation of the qualities of different materials used in teapots.

17 Specific heat comparison

To compare the specific heats of different metals, prepare cylinders of each of them of the same mass. Bring them to the temperature

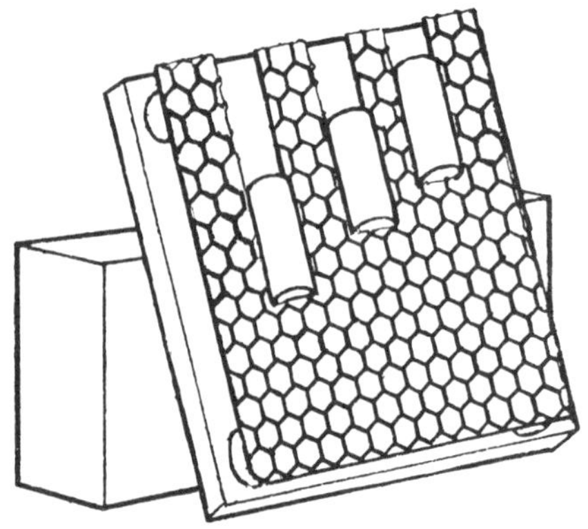

of boiling water and transfer them to a nearly vertical inclined plane, made from a piece of wood, and having a sheet of beeswax cell-former fastened to the front, but held away from the board by corks.

The cylinders will slide down the incline, melting tracks through the wax whose length will depend on the specific heat of the metal used.

18 Measurement of specific heat

Procure a piece of metal (say, 100 g of iron), and a tin containing 100 g of water. Suspend both above similar spirit lamps as in the diagram (a small bunsen flame will do).

The iron weight needs a hole to be drilled in it to fit the bulb of a thermometer loosely; the tin of water also requires a thermometer in it which can be used as a stirrer.

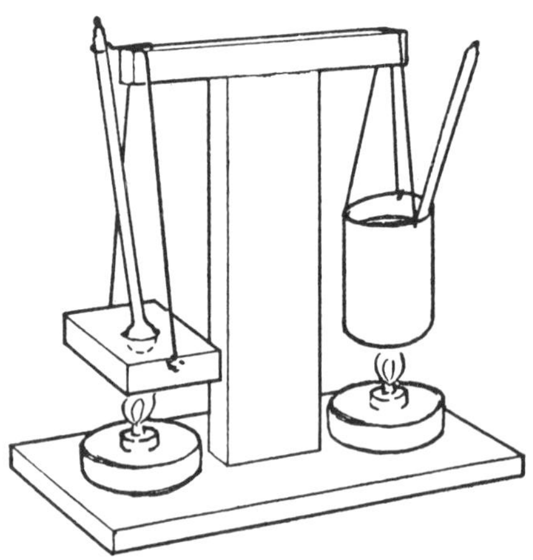

It is assumed that the lamps are supplying heat at the same rate. They are applied to these bodies for the same length of time.

Both lamps should be removed when the thermometer in the iron reaches 80 degrees, as it will probably then overshoot the mark to 100 degrees. The surprising difference in temperature emphasizes the effect of specific heat. Since 1 g of water absorbs 1 calorie for a temperature rise of 1° C, the heat supplied to both iron and water is (100 × rise in temperature of the water). The heat supplied to the iron is (100 × S × rise in temperature of iron). So the specific heat S =

$$\frac{\text{rise in temperature of water}}{\text{rise in temperature of iron}}.$$

19 Specific heat—hollow solids

An experiment somewhat similar to the teapot determination can be carried out using a ɔllow solid such as a brass axle cap or a short ɔnnector for iron tubing. Heat losses can be ıinimized by using a cloth to cover these essels. The procedure is the same as before. oiling water is poured in. The final steady ɜmperature recorded will be much lower than ıat in the case of the teapots.

If a brass object weighs 1 kg the final ɜmperature may be in the region of 60° C.

0 Simple latent heat calorimeter

ı this apparatus the vapour of tetrachlor-thyline, which has a small latent heat, is llowed to condense on a solid (e.g. copper r aluminium) which is suspended in it. The liquid formed is collected in a small graduated test tube. When no more condensation takes place, i.e. when the metal has assumed the temperature of the vapour the liquid collected is measured.

The large test tube is about 20 cm by 4 cm in diameter; the graduated tube is a small aspirin or pill bottle, and is carried in a wire cradle. The solid is pointed, at least at the bottom, so that the liquid streams off it readily.

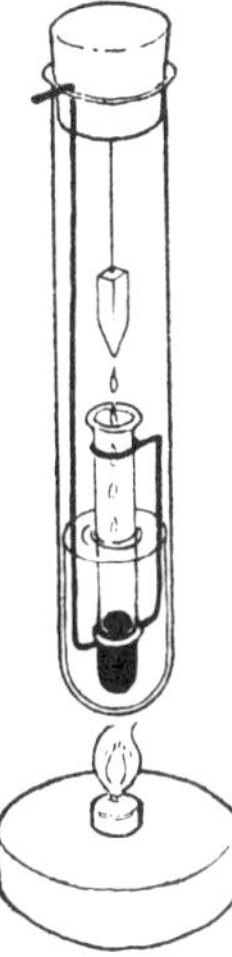

E. HEAT ENGINES

Pressure exerted by steam

ecure a small metal can with a friction top.)o not use a can with a screw top. Place a ttle water in the bottom of the can, press the d on tightly, place over a flame and step back. n a little while you will see the expansive ɔrce of steam.

How a steam engine works

Make a drawing on a blackboard like that hown below. Make the drawing about 60 cm square. Cut from stiff cardboard a piston and a slide valve as shown. You can have pupils move these on the drawing to show the position of the piston and slide valve when the engine is running.

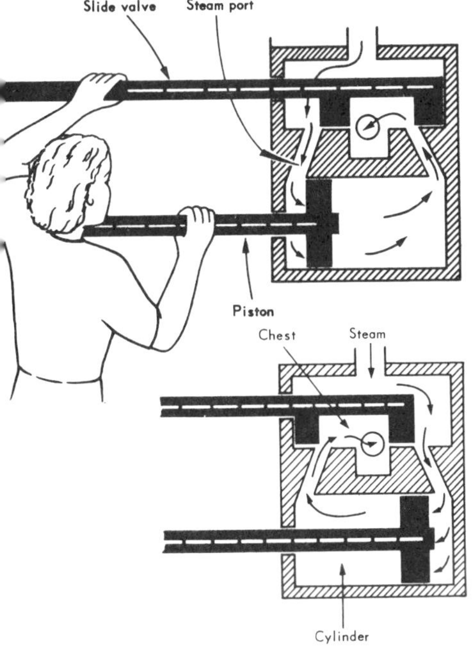

3 How to make a historic steam toy

Hero, scientist of ancient Alexandria in Egypt, made a steam toy which he called the Ball of the Winds. This is how to make a model of the toy. Secure a tin can with a friction top which holds about a pint or half litre. Pierce two holes in the can on opposite sides, large enough to carry small one-hole stoppers. Bend two glass tubes as shown in the diagram. The tubes should be drawn to jets at the end. Insert the tubes in the stoppers so that the jets point in opposite directions. Fasten cord to the stoppers and suspend by a swivel or chain. Pour water in the can to a depth of about 3 cm, put the cover on tightly and place over a flame.

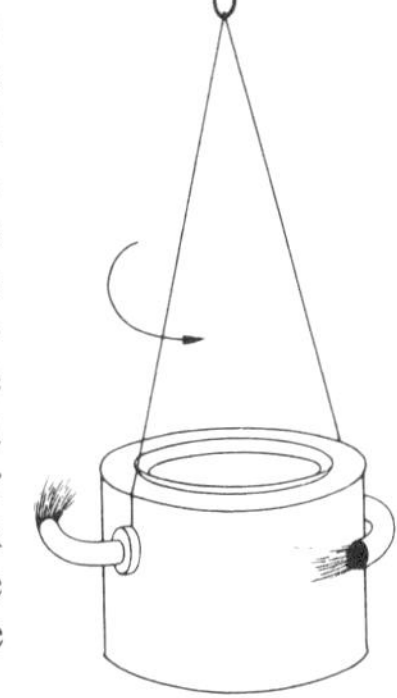

4 How to make a model steam turbine

A turbine model can be made from a tin fitted with a vane wheel. The vanes are made by cutting radial slots from a circular piece of tin, and twisting the blades which remain.

The axle is a piece of knitting needle, and the axle support is made from a strip of tin bent into a U piece and soldered to the top of the can.

A hole for a steam jet should be made opposite the vanes.

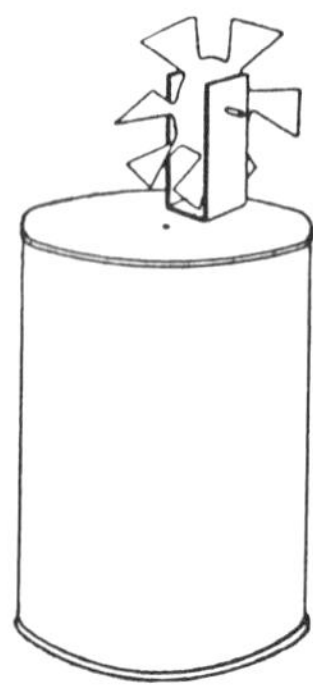

5 How to make a model turbine from glass

Very little glass blowing experience is needed to make this model. Seal one end of an ordinary piece of glass tubing in a flame and blow a bulb about 1.5 cm in diameter.

Soften the bottom of the bulb and press a pencil into it. This will make a depression to serve as a lower bearing for the turbine. Bend the top of the tube over at 90 degrees and draw it out to a jet bent at right angles again. Half fill the bulb with water by heating it and then immersing the open end under the surface of a beaker of water. Make a wire frame to act as a support as shown in the drawing.

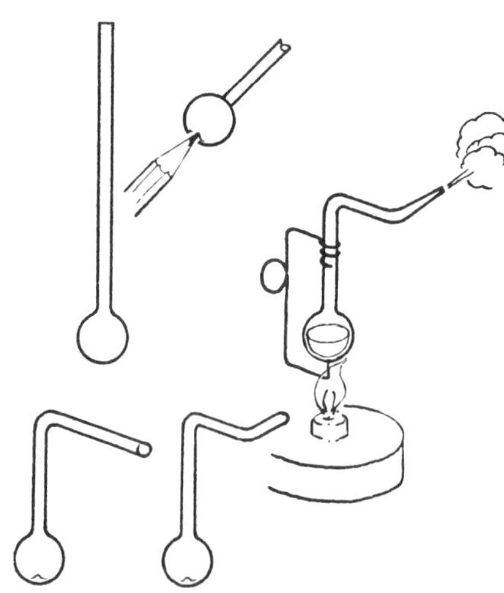

6 Heat engine from an old metal polish tin

The tin is supported horizontally on two copper pipes which serve as exit tubes. The are soldered through the centre of the botton and the cap respectively. The tin is partiall filled with water and rests on two iro brackets screwed to a wooden base.

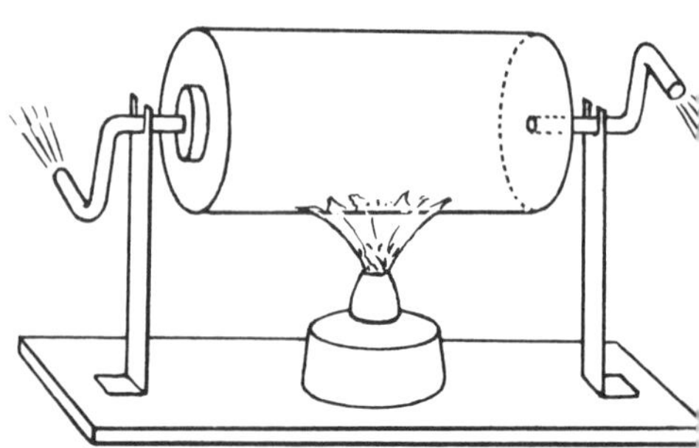

7 To show the force of exploding gas

Secure a metal can with a friction top tha holds about one or two litres. In the centr of the friction top punch a hole about half a centimetre in diameter. Near the bottom o the can punch another hole about 2 cm in diameter. Press the friction top in securely Place a hose from a gas jet in the lower hole and turn on the gas. Allow gas to enter unti the can is full and you can smell gas issuing from the top hole. Remove the hose and ligh the gas at the top hole. Step back and wai for results. Do not go near the can even though the flame seems to have gone out. As the ga burns at the top what comes in at the bottom? When did the mixture become explosive? (How much gas as compared with the amoun of air.)

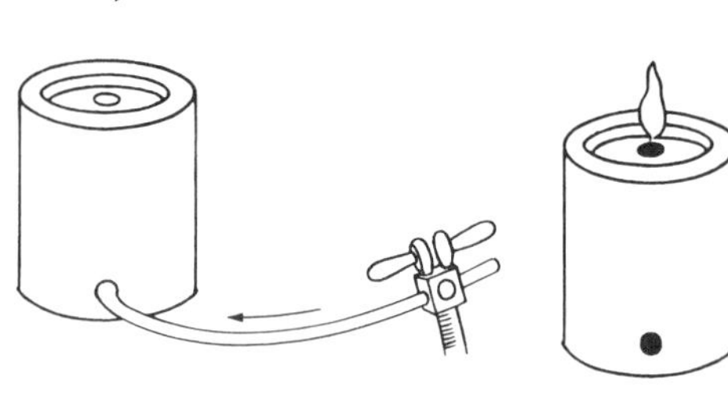

8 How petrol vapour is exploded in an engine

For this experiment you will need a 1 litre metal can with a friction top. Pierce a hole near the bottom into which an ordinary automobile spark plug can be fitted. On the opposite side near the bottom punch a small nail hole. You will need an induction coil with an interruptor in the primary circuit to urnish the high voltage necessary. Connect he primary leads of the induction coil to hree or four dry cells. Connect one secondary ead to the top of the spark plug and the other to the edge of the can. Warm the can. Place about ten drops of petrol in the can. Place the lid on tightly and close the switch n the primary circuit of the induction coil. An automobile ignition coil could also be used to provide the high voltage. The spark occurs when the contacts are opened, due to he sudden collapse of the magnetic field.

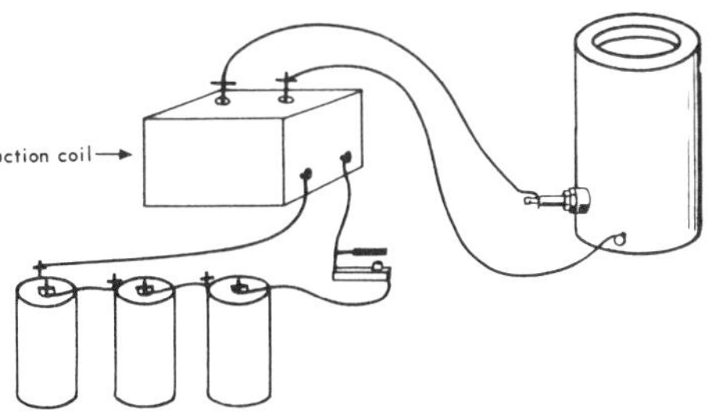

9 How to make a fire syringe

The material usually suggested for use as a fire syringe is amadou, but unless it is very dry it will not ignite. Cotton wool, soaked in carbon disulphide to which a trace of phosphorus has been added, will ignite at the temperatures produced by compression.

It is more effective if a glass fire syringe is used. Fit a piece of hard combustion tube with a good piston (a cycle pump piston will do). Introduce the cotton wool through the open end, and close with a cork. Bring the piston down sharply on a bench or table and a blue flash will be seen when the tinder ignites.

A piece of iron pipe with a slot cut in it can be used as a safety sheath, but the experiment is not really dangerous.

CHAPTER XIV

Experiments and materials for the study of magnetism

1 Natural magnets

Magnetic iron ore is quite common in many parts of the world. If it cannot be obtained locally, any supply house will provide it for a small cost. Secure a piece of such iron ore. This is a natural magnet. Sprinkle some iron filings or finely cut pieces of steel wool on a sheet of white paper and observe how the ore attracts them. Try picking up heavier things made of iron, such as paper clips or carpet tacks. Bring the lump of ore near a compass and observe. Do all parts of the lump affect the compass in the same way?

2 Securing artificial magnets

Strong and useful artificial magnets for the study of magnetism can be obtained from old radio loudspeakers, from old telephone receivers and from old automobile speedometers. Magnets can frequently be purchased in the market and may always be obtained from scientific supply houses. Artificial magnets are made in many shapes such as horseshoe, U-shaped and straight or bar magnets.

3 How to magnetize a steel rod

Use a piece of magnetic iron ore or another magnet to magnetize a steel knitting needle, a darning needle, an iron nail, a piece of clock spring or watch spring. This may be done simply by stroking the bar several times with the magnetized substance. If you wish to make a bar magnet with opposite poles at either end, use an artificial magnet. Begin at the centre of the unmagnetized bar and stroke toward the end using one end of the magnet. After several strokings turn the rod around and stroke from the centre to the other end using the opposite pole of the magnet. Test your results by using the rod to pick up iron filings or by approaching it to a compass.

4 How to make bar magnets

Secure some flat pieces of hard steel. Old hack or metal saw blades are useful. Lengths of steel from a clock spring may be used. Cut the steel into 15 cm lengths. Next stroke the opposite ends of each piece with alternate ends of a strong magnet as instructed in experiment 3 above. Test each bar magnet with a compass. The two ends of the bar magnet should affect the compass in contrary ways. Hard steel is often quite difficult to magnetize. One should place the piece of steel on a table and strike the pole of the magnet against it as you stroke toward the end.

5 How to make a turntable cradle for magnet study

Select a piece of heavy wire. The wire from a coat-hanger will do very nicely. Bend it into the shape shown in the diagram. The distance between the two hooks at the ends should be small enough to cradle the shortest bar magnet that will be used.

Suspend the cradle with fine copper wire or nylon fishing line from a convenient hook or other support. Place a bar magnet in the cradle and bring other magnets near it.

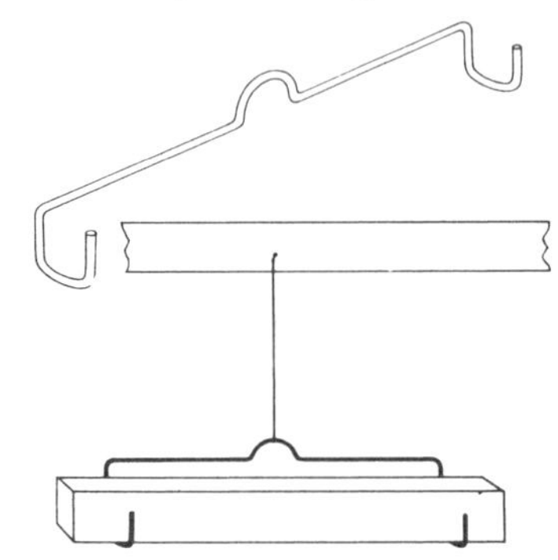

6 The concentration of magnetism in a magnet

Pour a considerable quantity of iron filings on a sheet of paper. Roll a bar magnet in the iron filings and observe that most of the filings stick to points near the ends of the bar. These places on a magnet where the magnetism seems to be concentrated are called magnetic poles. Repeat using magnets of other shapes such as a horseshoe or a U shaped magnet

' Variation of magnetism along a bar magnet tested by spring balance

'lace a bar magnet on a piece of squared aper. Tie a soft iron nail to the hook of a pring balance and test the pull required to ift it away from points along the magnet .5 cm apart. It may be that the hook of the alance will serve instead of the nail, but care hould be taken to see that it does not become ermanently magnetized.

Represent your readings as a graph etween pull required and distance along nagnet from one end. Is the magnet 'strong-st' at the extreme ends?

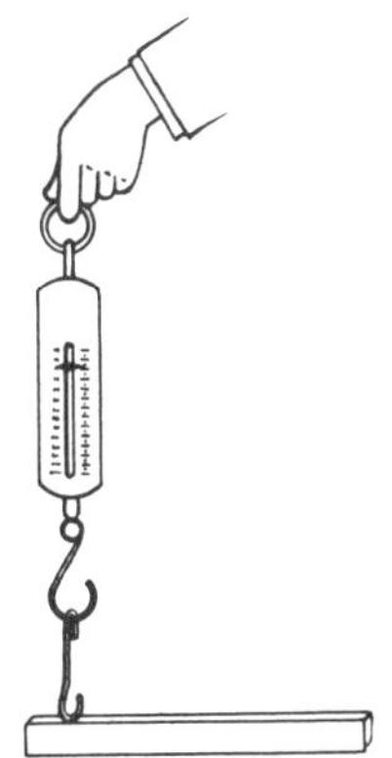

Do magnets act through space?

'uspend a bar magnet in a cradle such as is escribed in experiment 5 above. Bring other nagnets near the suspended magnet and nake observations to answer the question sked in this experiment.

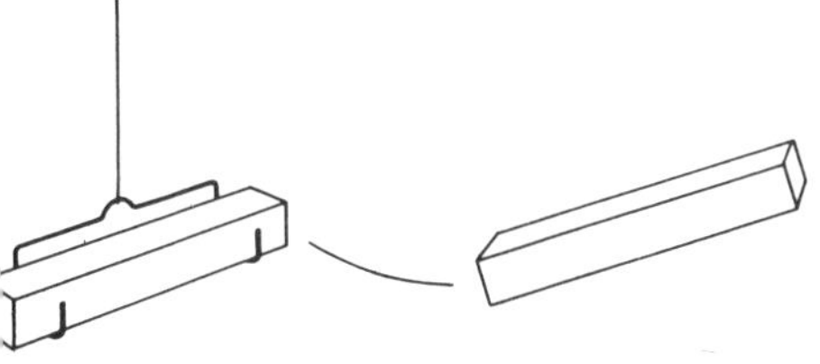

Are the poles of a magnet alike?

Jse the same materials as in experiment 8. Iark one end of the suspended magnet with piece of chalk or paper. Now bring one end f another magnet near the marked pole of ne suspended magnet. Reverse the magnet n your hand and bring the other pole near ne marked pole of the suspended magnet. Do they react in the same way? How would you describe the action in the first case? In the second case?

10 The law of magnetism

Again use the same materials as in experiment 8. Test the magnets with a compass needle. Mark the end of each magnet which repels the north end of the compass needle and attracts the south end of the compass needle. These marked ends of the magnets are called the *north* poles. The unmarked ends are the *south* poles. The south poles of the magnets should repel the south-pointing end of the compass needle and attract the north-pointing end.

Now suspend one of the marked magnets in the turn cradle. Bring the north end of the other magnet near the north end of the suspended magnet. Do you observe attraction or repulsion? Next bring the south ends of the two magnets near each other. What do you observe? Bring the north end of the magnet in your hand near the south pole of the suspended magnet. What do you observe? Bring the south pole near the north pole of the suspended magnet. What do you observe? What can you say about like and unlike magnetic poles? This is the law of magnetism.

11 Making simple compass needles

Magnetize a piece of steel strip or watch spring by stroking it with lodestone or another magnet. To convert it into a compass needle, it must have as frictionless a support as possible. This can be contrived in several ways. Close a short length (2 cm) of glass tubing at the end by heating in a flame. Support the small test tube just made on a pin pushed through a piece of wood or cork. Fix the strip of steel to the tube with sealing wax and adjust it so that it swings freely and evenly.

Another way of supporting the compass needle is to use a metal former from an old cloth-covered button. Clip the magnetized rod to the two projections and place the curved part of the button on a piece of glass or other smooth surface.

Another simple compass needle can be made using two magnetized sewing needles pushed through the holes of a large press

stud. This can be balanced in another needle with its eye pushed into a cork. If a smaller press stud is used the flange must be squeezed between pliers whilst pressing the needles through the small holes.

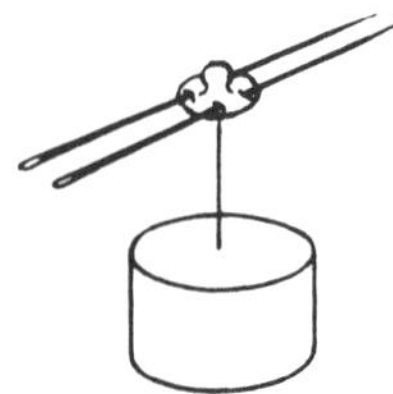

12 A razor blade compass box

Magnetize an old three-hole razor blade by stroking it with a bar magnet. Push an old laundry stud or a piece of closed glass tube through the central hole. Glue a disc of card to the blade and suspend the combined compass on a pin stuck through a slice of cork. Mark the position of north on the top of the card. Enclose the compass in a cardboard box with a circular window in it made of cellophane. Draw a reference line on the box.

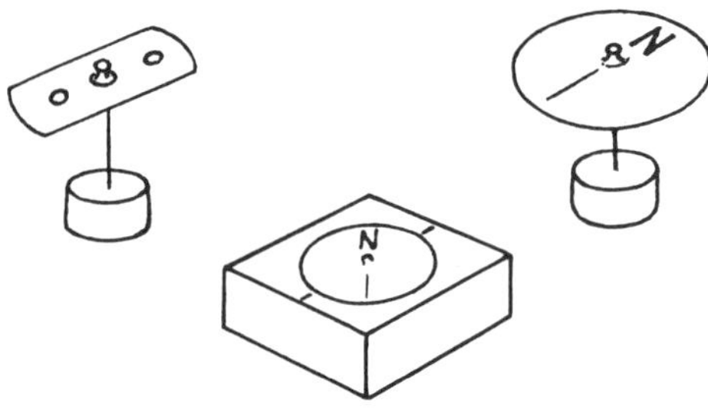

13 To determine magnetic north

Float a piece of flat cork 10 cm by 3 cm in a saucer of water.

Magnetize a short length of hacksaw blade or other steel and fix it to the cork so that its teeth are downwards and its length is along the cork slab. When it comes to rest, sight along its upper edge using two large pins. The line joining the feet of the pins is the Magnetic Meridian.

14 A demonstration compass needle

Rivet together two old hacksaw blades through the holes at each end and then magnetize them. Use a closed piece of glass tube as a support. Push this between the blades at the midpoint and balance it on a knitting needle driven vertically into a block of wood. Fix the bearing in position with sealing wax or other adhesive. Push wire indicators N and S between the blades at the extreme ends.

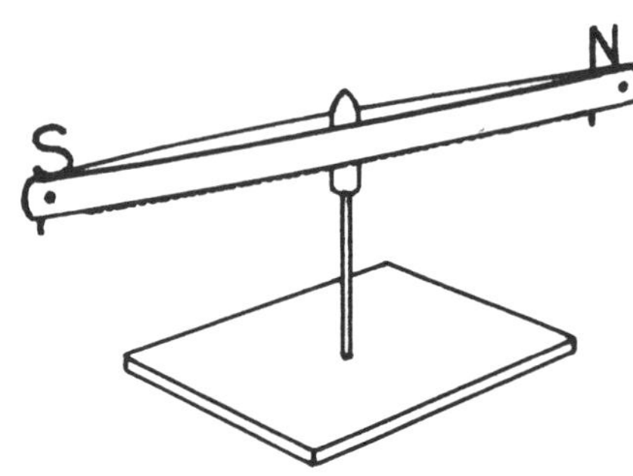

15 A model showing the earth's magnetism

A ball or round fruit is needed to represent the earth in this model. Support it on a wooden meat skewer inclined at an angle. This represents the axis of rotation of the earth.

Pierce the 'earth' with a magnetized knitting needle which will be in the direction of the magnetic axis of the earth.

Examine the external field using a small plotting compass such as is often used as an ornament to a watch chain.

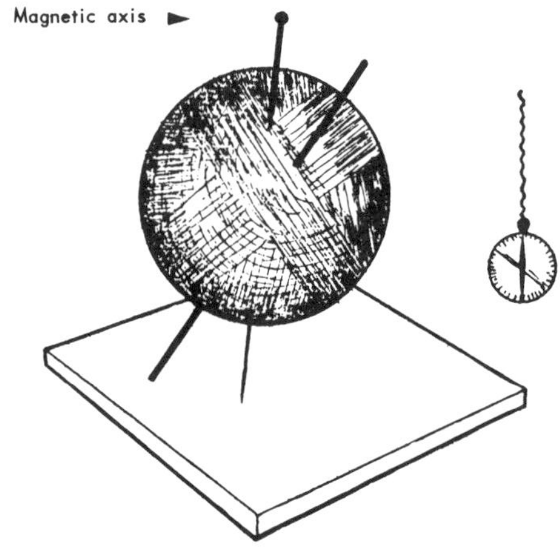

16 How to make a dip circle

Push a knitting needle through a cork in a direction parallel to a diameter of its end. Balance it horizontally on a U piece of brass strip, using pins as an axle. Take it off the knife edges and magnetize without disturbing the cork. When it is replaced on the bearings, one end will be pulled downwards by the earth's magnetic field. The protractor serves to measure this angle of 'dip'.

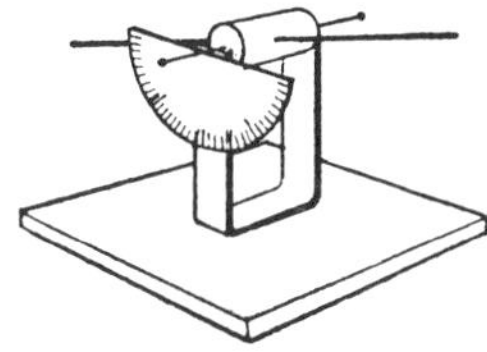

An alternative way of suspending the magnet is to use a piece of cycle valve tubing with a pin pushed through it as a supporting axle. Knife edges can be provided by two postcards held apart by corks maintained in position by drawing pins. The position of dip can then be marked with a pencil and measured later.

If metal 'connectors' are available, a more permanent device can be made by soldering gramophone needles to it.

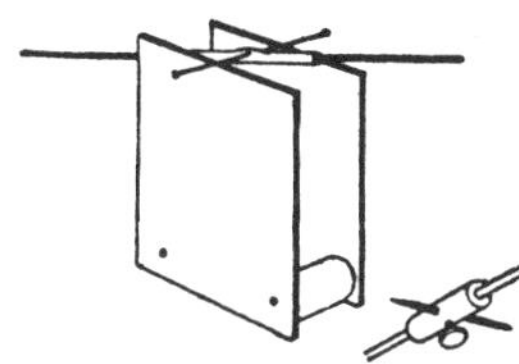

17 A demonstration dip circle

Cut a ring of cardboard with an external diameter of 50 cm. Fasten two laths across a diameter to serve as supports for the dip needle. Cut a model dip needle from card and support it in notches cut in the laths.

Such a model is useful when discussing the various errors of the dip circle.

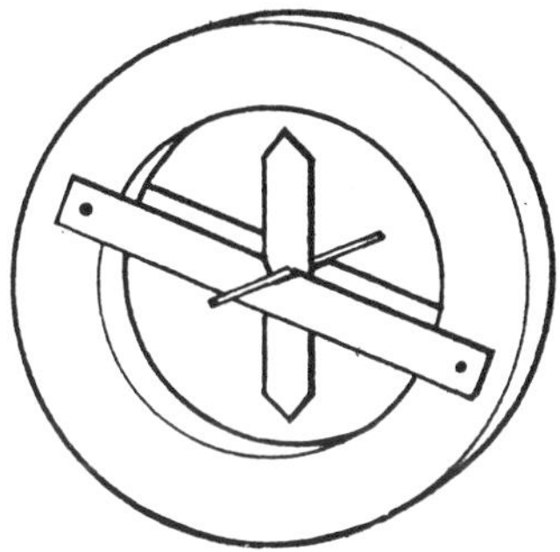

18 Exploring with a compass

Many things made of iron and steel are magnetized by the earth's magnetism. It is interesting to explore iron fence posts, iron bridges, etc., with a compass. Test them at both ends to see if they have magnetic poles. Drive an iron rod into the ground and see if it becomes magnetized. Test it at the top and near the earth. Test things around the school and at home with a compass.

19 What substances are magnetic?

Collect a variety of small objects made of paper, wax, brass, zinc, iron, steel, nickel, glass, cork, rubber, aluminium, copper, gold, silver, wood, tin, etc. Place them in a box and test each object with a magnet to see which ones are attracted and which are not.

20 Magnetizing a bar by hammering

Secure an iron rod about one metre in length. An iron curtain rod will do. Test it with a compass at each end to see if it is magnetized. Hold the bar in a north-south direction and tilt. Strike the rod several sharp blows in this position and then test it again with the compass. A bar can often be demagnetized by holding it in an east-west direction and striking the end several times with a hammer.

21 Lines of force

A piece of plywood with two grooves cut in it to the depth of one ply is useful for holding magnets and magnetic materials while testing the patterns of their lines of force.

Permanent records can be made of such 'filing maps' if the paper used over the magnets is first dipped in hot candle grease and allowed to cool. Place it over the magnets under test, scatter filings on it from a height of 30 cm and tap the paper. Fix the pattern formed by warming the waxed paper with the medium flame of a bunsen burner.

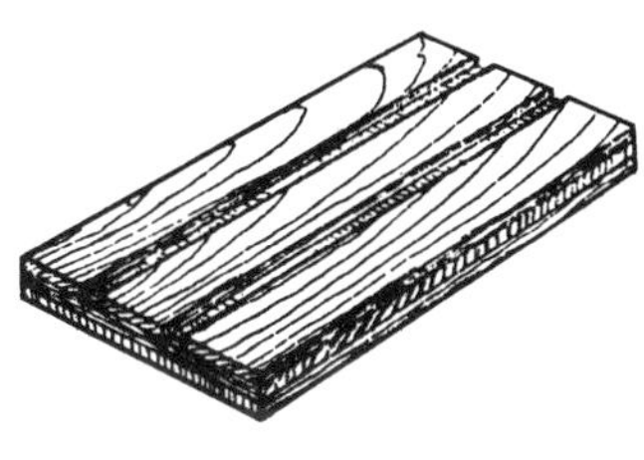

22 Mapping lines of magnetic force

An alternative to the familiar waxed paper method is to use a modern black line paper. This paper, employed by architects in place of the older blue-print paper, can be used in daylight.

Place the magnet in position on the paper and scatter on the filings to produce the required pattern.

Expose to the sun or bright daylight for 10 minutes, or to the light of a small arc for 2 minutes, shake off the filings and mop over with developer on a piece of cotton wool. The prints so made are positives, and the paper can be varnished to form a permanent record.

23 What substances do magnetic lines of force go through?

Secure small pieces of as many of the following substances as possible: wood, glass, copper, brass, zinc, pasteboard, plastic, iron, aluminium, etc. Place some iron filings on one side of the sheet and move a strong magnet on the underside. By observing the iron filings you can tell which substances pass the magnetic lines of force.

24 Magnetic induction

Place a bar of soft iron on a block of wood. Hold a tin-tack near it to test if it is magnetized. While the tack is near one end of the bar, bring a strong magnet near the other end. Is the bar magnetized? Remove the magnet and test again. Is the bar still magnetized? Magnetism produced in a substance in the vicinity of a magnet is called 'induced' magnetism. The effect involved is called 'magnetic induction'.

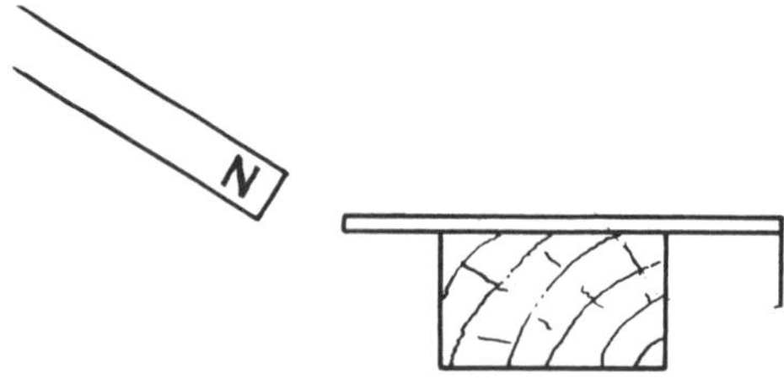

25 Testing for induced polarity

Test a strong magnet with a compass and mark the north pole and the south pole. Place a compass on the table and hold the pointed end of a 15 cm spike or piece of soft iron near it. Next bring the north pole of the tested magnet near the top end of the spike without letting them touch. Is a north or south pole induced in the end of the spike near the compass? What would you guess the polarity of the top end of the spike to be? Test it. Next hold the spike as before, but bring the south pole of the tested magnet near the top end of the spike. Is a north or south pole induced in the end near the compass? In the top end of the spike?

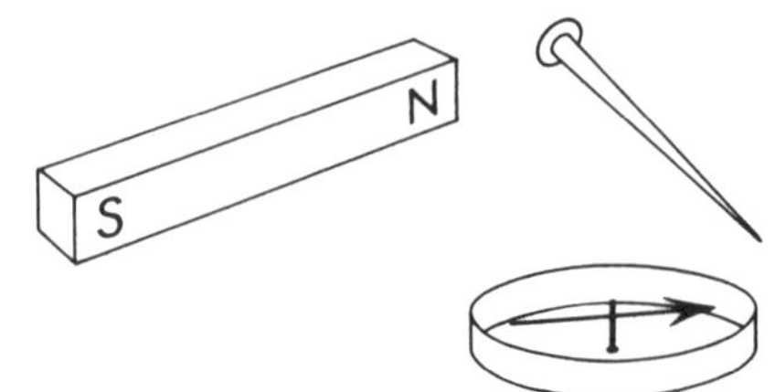

26 What happens when a magnet is broken?

Magnetize a piece of clock spring or a hacksaw blade about 25 cm long as instructed in experiment 3. Test the magnet with a compass to be sure that it has a north pole at one end and a south pole at the other. Mark the poles N and S with chalk. Does the compass show any polarity at the centre of the magnet? Use a pair of pliers and break the long magnet into two parts each about 12.5 cm long. Test the polarity of each end of the two magnets. What do you observe? Mark the poles of each magnet N and S. Now break the two magnets into four magnets. Test each end and mark it N or S. Continue dividing the magnets, as many times as you can. Write a conclusion to the question posed by this experiment.

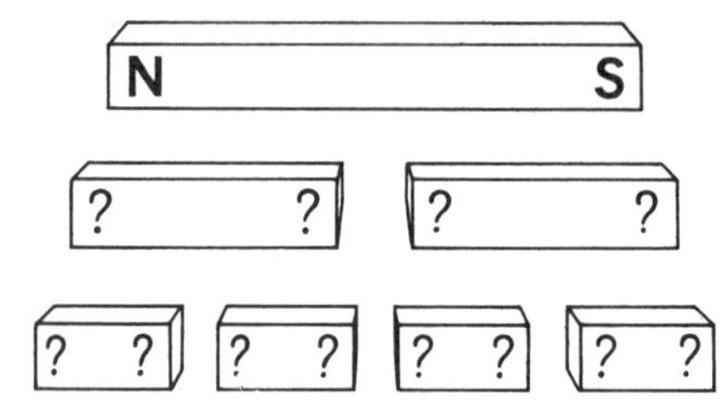

27 Making a magnet with iron filings

Fill a test tube or glass toothbrush tube about two-thirds full of iron filings and stopper the end with a plug of cotton or a cork. Stroke it with the poles of a strong magnet. Be careful not to shake the tube. Bring the tube of filings near a compass, and you will observe that it behaves just like a solid magnet. Shake the tube up well and again bring it near the compass. This time it does not influence the compass. From experiments such as this scientists are led to believe that the magnetism in a magnet is associated with very small particles of matter, perhaps molecules or atoms.

28 How to make floating magnets

Magnetize some used razor blades, being very careful not to cut yourself. Grease the blades lightly with oil, vaseline or kitchen grease. Fill a soup plate with water and float the razor blades on the surface. Now bring a strong magnet under the floating magnets.

29 Some experiments with floating magnets

Magnetize seven or eight steel needles so that their points all have the same polarity and the eyes all have the opposite polarity. Push the needles through small flat corks about 13 mm in diameter so that about 1 cm of the needle is above the cork. Fill a cereal dish or a soup plate with sloping sides nearly full of water. Float the magnets, pointed end down, in the water. Now bring one pole of a strong magnet above the floating needles. Try the other end of the magnet. Such floating magnets can often be arranged in different patterns in the dish. Here are some to try.

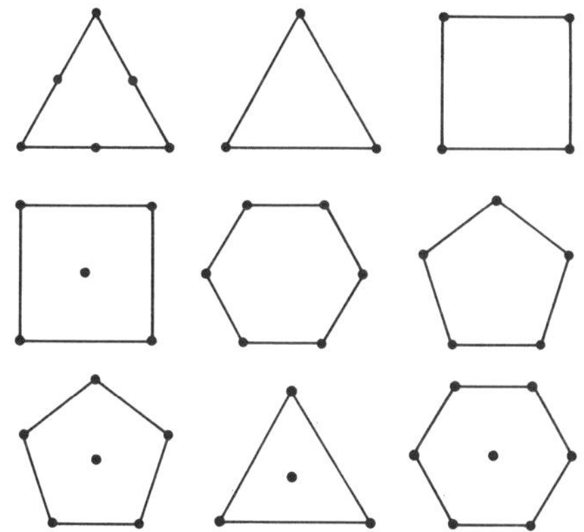

30 A vibrator with a magnet

Set a U-shaped magnet on its side and place a needle or a razor blade on the lower pole. It will stand upright. Strike the free end with a pencil and observe how well it vibrates.

31 Making a needle float in air

Use a threaded needle. Draw the needle over one pole of a magnet resting on the table. Let the needle remain on this pole until it is thoroughly magnetized. Now carefully ease the needle from this pole and lift it by the thread until it is over the other pole. Careful manipulation will make the needle float in the air above the other pole. Can you explain why this happens?

32 How to make a card compass

Secure a wide-mouth glass jar. Fold a length of cardboard or stiff paper so that it will go into the bottle and not be too long to turn inside. Magnetize a steel darning needle (see experiment 3) that is just a little longer than the cardboard. Push the magnetized needle through the cardboard and suspend it on a thread so that the cardboard and needle balance. The needle may be moved in or out to get the exact balance. Tie the end of the thread to a match or longer piece of wood placed across the mouth of the jar.

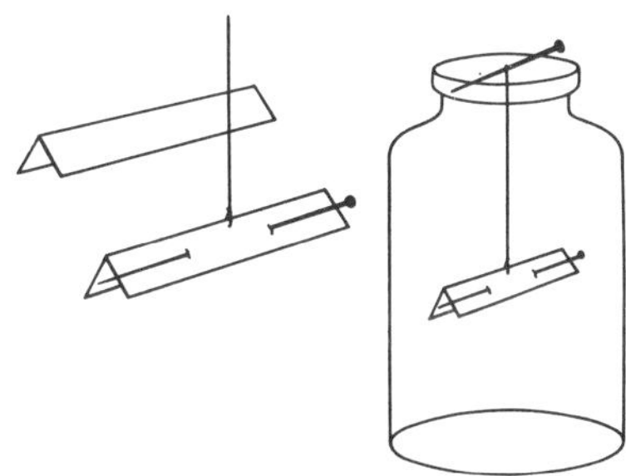

33 A magnetic fishing game

Tie a strong magnet to a string several decimetres long. Attach the string to a short fishing rod or stick. Spread a variety of small objects made of iron on a table behind a screen. Nails, tacks, screws, bolts, nuts, thumb tacks, etc., may be used. To each of the objects assign points, 5 for a large nail, 4 for a screw, 3 for a bolt, etc. The players take turns fishing over the screen with the magnet, and the score of each player is determined by what he picks up with the magnet.

34 A magic magnetic spinner

Make a spinning top from a wooden spool which has been used for thread. The spool is first cut in two. One piece is then shaped to a point like a cone. Find a nail or other piece of iron rod that will fit tightly in the hole of the spool. Cut off a length that will go through the cone and stick out about 1 cm above the top. Grind the lower end, which just sticks out, to a very sharp and evenly rounded point to make a spinning peg.

Magnetize the spindle and insert it in the wooden cone. Form a large S-curve from a piece of soft iron wire. Place this on a smooth surface. If you set the top spinning near one of the curves it will follow the wire to the end.

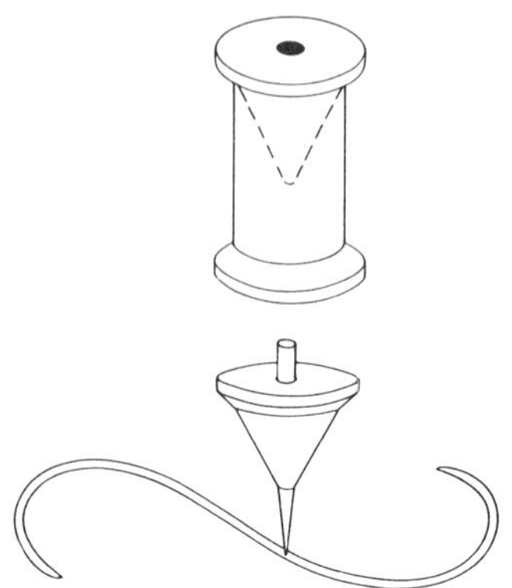

35 A magnetic boat

Fashion a small boat out of some soft wood. You may put a mast and sail on it if you like. Hollow out the inside of the boat or bore a small hole lengthwise in its hull. Magnetize an iron nail and either put it in the hole or simply lay it inside the boat. Use a plastic or aluminium pan for your ocean. You can fashion a shore line from sand or wood. Control your boat by means of a magnet which you move about under the container.

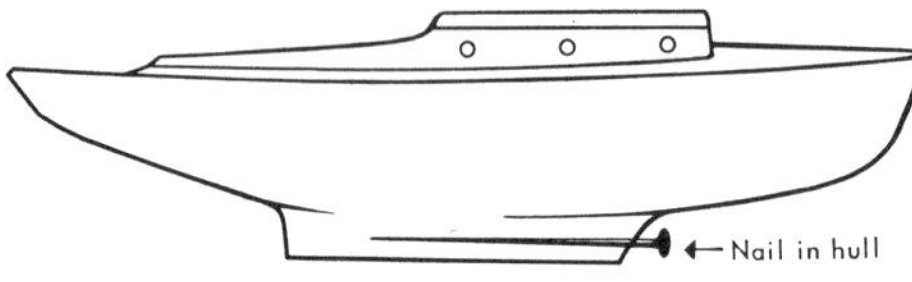

36 A sensitive magnetometer

Push a piece of copper wire through the cork of a test tube to serve as an upper support for the suspension. Make a carrier for the magnet from thin copper wire and solder a small vane to the lower end.

Attach a slip of mirror to the magnet carrier in order to reflect a beam of light. Pour oil into the test tube to a depth of approximately 3 cm. Lower the suspended magnet and carrier into the tube and adjust the upper support until the damping vane just dips into the oil.

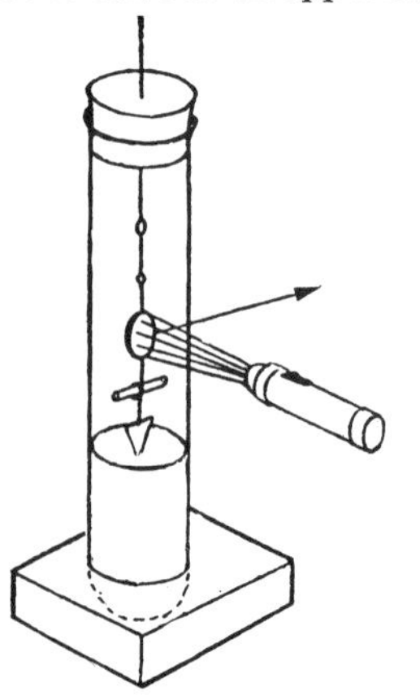

37 A vibration magnetometer

Small, strongly magnetized cobalt or ticonal magnets are now available which, suspended from silk in a specimen tube, are excellent vibration magnetometers. Since there is no 'damping' here, the time of vibration of the 'swing' is a measure of the strength of the magnetic field in which it is placed.

A larger model is easily made by using a preserve jar with a wooden top. A brass connector serves as a suitable clip for the upper support. The magnet can then be lowered to touch the bottom when the instrument is not in use. This precaution increases the life of the suspension.

(N.B. To damp a vibration means to lessen its amplitude.)

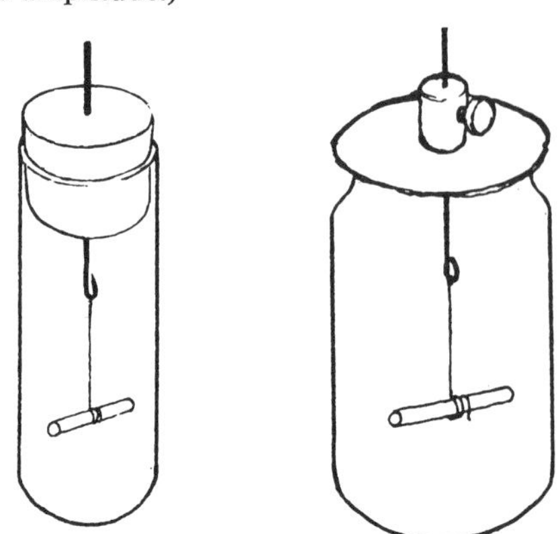

38 Making a magnetizing coil

A piece of ordinary glass tubing wound with close turns of copper wire serves to magnetize knitting needles. A torch battery supplies the current required, but should not be left connected longer than necessary.

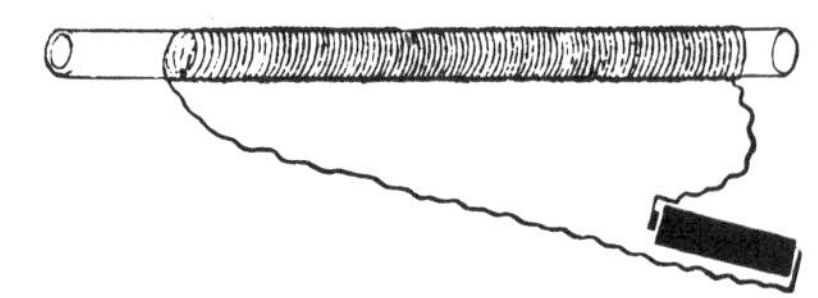

39 To make a magnetizing coil for the electric supply mains

This is just a solenoid through which a heavy current is passed for a short time. The mechanical dimensions are not critical, but the resistance of the wire must be chosen to suit the voltage employed. It will naturally be lower when used with a 12-volt accumulator than with the 230-volt mains. For use with a 12-volt car battery, 4 layers of 22 SWG insulated copper wire are suitable, wound on a cardboard tube about 30 cm long and diameter about 4 cm. If the coil is for use on the 230-volt mains, many more turns are needed. Fifteen layers will give a strong magnetic field, though the number can be reduced if the last four turns are of enamelled 'Euraka' resistance wire. As the current is only needed for a very short time, it is a good plan to include in the circuit a 'press down' switch; a car starter switch is suitable.

Obtain a cardboard tube of the dimensions mentioned. Make two end supports with a hole into which the tube can be glued. Wind on the wire, preferably using a lathe or hand drill. Secure the solenoid by screws passed through a wooden base and into the end supports. Connect the ends of the wire to two insulated terminals with the switch in series. Connect to the source of current, hold the object to be magnetized inside the coil press the switch momentarily if direct current is used. The polarity produced will be the same as that of the coil. With alternating current the polarity must be found afterwards, and the strength of magnetization will depend on the exact instant at which the current is switched off. It may therefore be necessary to make more than one trial.

The coil can be used for demagnetizing with alternating current. The procedure is then to place the magnet inside the coil, switch on the current and, whilst it is still flowing, withdraw the magnet along the axis to a distance of about 2 yards outside the coil before switching off. It is quite safe to use such a coil for demagnetizing a watch, though watchmakers use a much shorter coil.

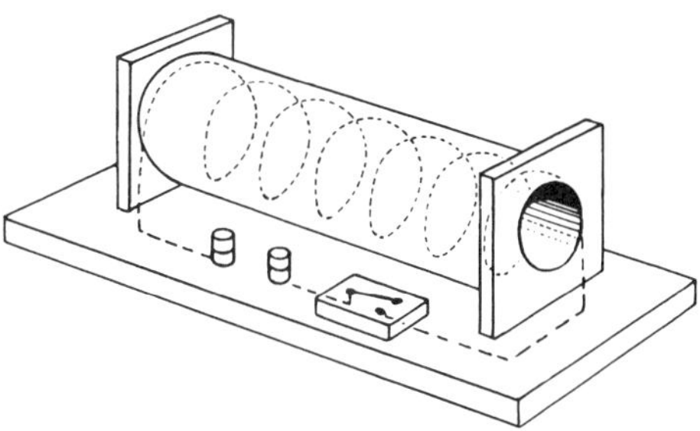

CHAPTER XV

Experiments and materials for the study of electricity

A. STATIC ELECTRICITY

All these experiments work best when the air is dry

1 Electricity can be obtained by rubbing things together

Make a pile of finely divided cork particles by filing a cork. Cut up some thin paper into small pieces. Obtain a plastic comb, a plastic pencil, a plastic fountain pen, a piece of wax, a rubber balloon, a glass or china dish and any other non-metallic objects you may find. Rub each of these things briskly with your hair or a piece of fur and then bring near the pile of cork particles. Rub again and bring near the pile of thin paper. Observe what happens. Repeat the experiment rubbing each article in turn with a silk cloth. Repeat using a piece of flannel.

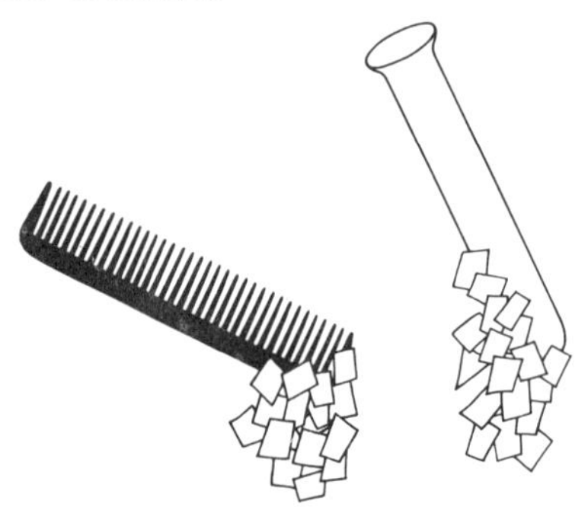

2 Static electricity is everywhere

Rub a blown up balloon on your hair and then bring it near some fine paper or cork particles. Repeat using a comb and a plastic ruler. Rub a fountain pen on your coat sleeve and test it for a static charge. Hold two strips of newspaper, about 5 cm wide and 30 cm long, together. Stroke them lengthwise with the thumb and finger of your free hand. What happens? Try to devise other experiments showing that there is static electricity everywhere.

3 Light from static electricity

Secure a fluorescent light bulb. Rub it briskly with a piece of fur or flannel in a darkened room. What do you observe?

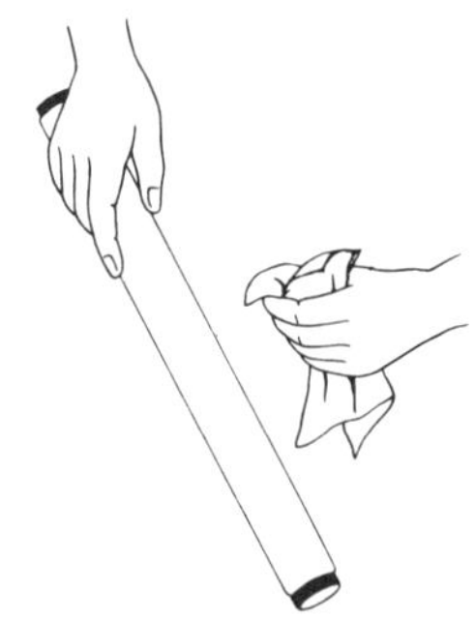

4 Dancing figures with static electricity

Secure an aluminium soup plate, about 2.5 cm deep, and a glass plate to cover it. Cut some little doll figures from thin tissue paper, as shown in the drawing. You may also cut out some other figures like boxers. The figures should be just a little shorter than the depth of the pan. Put the figures on the bottom of the pan and cover with the glass. Rub the top surface of the glass with a piece of fur or soft leather and watch the dance.

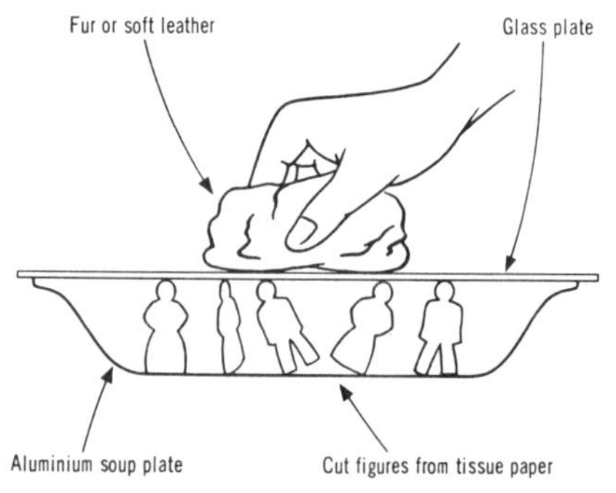

5 How to make the paper jump

Place pieces of paper underneath a sheet of glass resting on two books. Rub the glass with silk or flannel. The papers begin to jump about in an amusing way.

It is the charge induced on them by the charged glass which causes them to be attracted. When they have given up their charge they fall back again. The paper can be cut out in the shape of frogs.

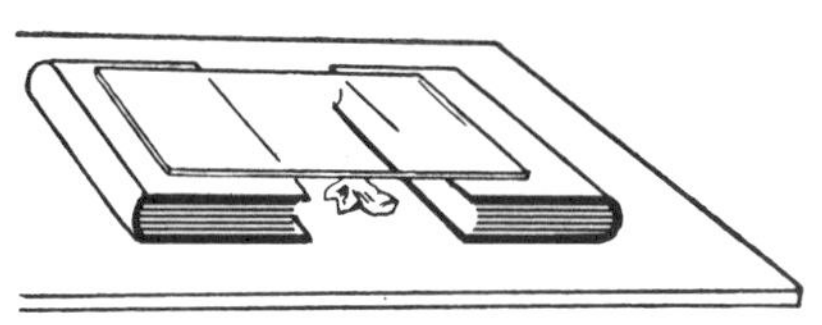

6 An electrostatic airplane

Cut a piece of light aluminium foil into the shape of a small airplane. Bring a charged ebonite or plastic rod near to it. It jumps to the rod and receives the same kind of charge as the rod has, then it jumps away again. It can then be kept in the air as long as is desired, and its direction of flight can be guided by repulsion.

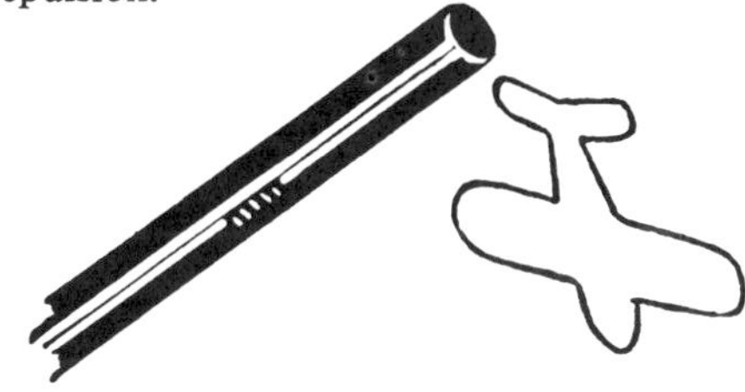

7 Sparks from rubbing

Obtain four water glasses and stand them upside down on the floor, close together. They should be near some metal object such as a water pipe. Have someone stand on the glasses. Brush his clothing for a full minute either with a piece of fur or a piece of folded rubber like a cycle inner tube or a hot water bottle. Have him stick his finger out toward the finger of someone standing on the floor. Repeat and have him bring his finger near the water pipe. Observe the results.

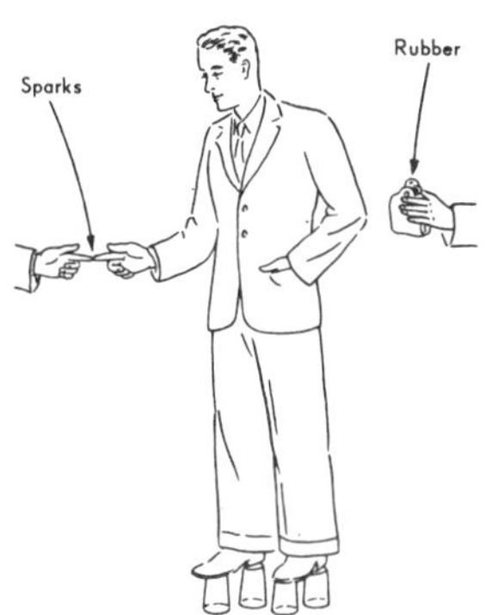

8 The balloon stays put

Blow up a toy balloon and rub it briskly with a piece of fur. Place it against the wall and observe that it stays where you place it. Repeat, rubbing the balloon on your hair. Again repeat, rubbing the balloon on a coat sleeve.

9 The newspaper stays on the wall

Spread out a sheet of newspaper and press it smoothly against a wall. Stroke the newspaper with a pencil all over its surface several times. Pull up one corner of the paper and then let it go. Notice how it is attracted back to the wall. If the air is very dry, you may be able to hear the crackle of the static charges.

10 There are two kinds of static charge

Make a turntable by driving a long nail through a wood base. Push a test tube into a hole made in a large flat cork. File the end of the nail to a sharp point and invert the test tube over it. Set pins in the top surface of the cork; they will brace the objects you place on the turntable. Secure two test tubes or other glass rods, a piece of silk such as a silk stocking, two plastic combs, and a piece of fur or flannel. Rub one glass rod with silk and set it on the turntable. Rub the other glass rod with silk and bring it near the one on the turntable. Repeat this experiment until you are sure of the results.

Again rub the glass rod with silk and place it on the turntable. Now rub a plastic comb with fur and bring it near the glass rod on the turntable. Repeat until you are sure of the results.

Rub a comb with fur and set it on the turntable. Rub the other comb with fur and bring it near the comb on the turntable. Repeat until you are sure your observations are correct.

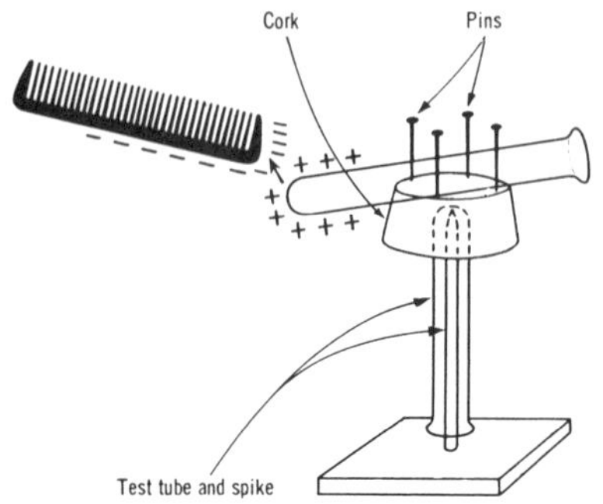

Again rub a comb with fur and place it on the turntable. Rub a glass rod with silk and bring it near. Repeat until you are sure of your observations.

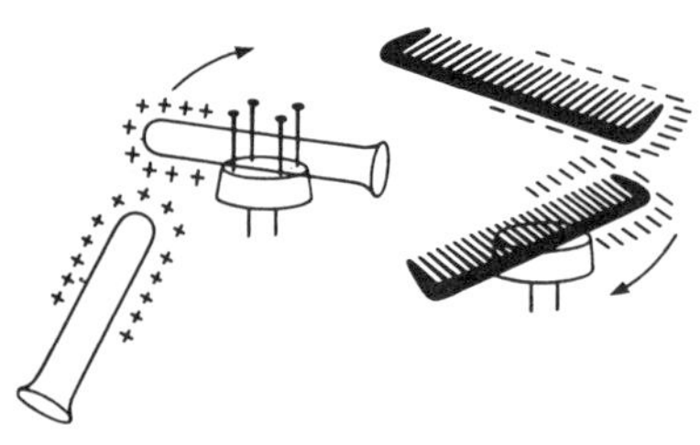

When plastic is rubbed with fur the plastic takes a negative charge of electricity and the fur takes a positive charge. When glass is rubbed with silk the glass takes a positive charge and the silk a negative charge. Your experiment has indicated that like static charges repel while unlike charges attract. This is a basic law of electricity.

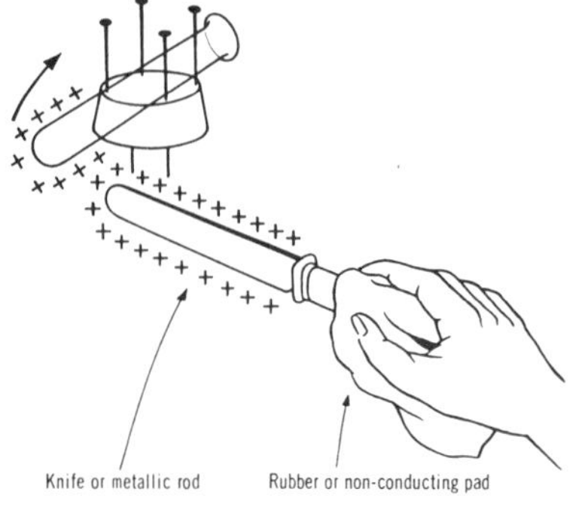

11 How to make a pith ball indicator for static charges

Secure some pith from the inside of a plant stem. Dry the pith thoroughly and then press it tightly into small balls about 5 mm in diameter. Coat the pith balls with aluminium or gold paint. Attach each pith ball to a silk thread about 15 cm in length. Make a wooden stand for the pith ball. Bring objects rubbed with silk, fur or flannel near the pith ball and observe how it behaves. Notice that it is first attracted and then repelled. Such a pith ball system is called an electroscope.

12 Metal foil ball electroscope

Roll up about 6 cm^2 of metal foil from a cigarette packet into a ball of about 6 mm diameter. Use an adhesive to attach it to a piece of silk or nylon thread about 7.5 cm long. Secure the free end to a ball pen or other insulator and rest the pen across the mouth of a jam jar so that the ball hangs clear of the side. Bring any charged body near the ball; it should first be attracted and then jump away. Now rub another plastic pen on a celluloid set square or protractor. Hold the pen near the ball and let it take a charge. Now bring the protractor near the charged ball. What does this tell you about the two kinds of charge produced by rubbing?

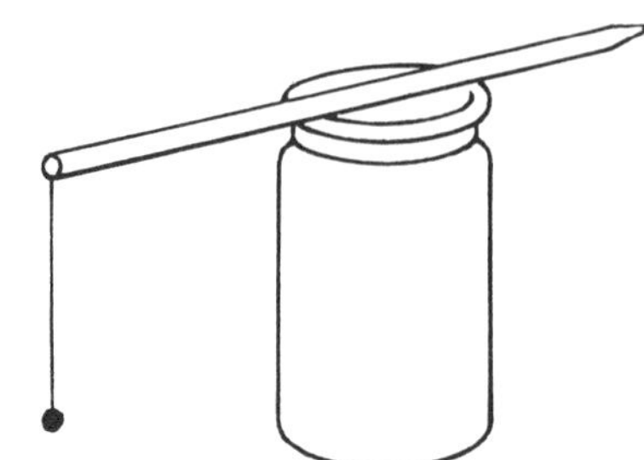

13 How to make an electroscope from newspaper

Cut a strip of newspaper 60 cm long and 10 cm wide. Crease it in the centre and hang it over a ruler as shown in the diagram. Hold it on the table and stroke several times with a piece of fur or flannel. Lift it from the table with the ruler and observe how it acts. Rub a comb or other plastic object with the fur or flannel and bring it between the extended leaves of newspaper. Repeat until you are sure of your results. Now rub a glass bottle with a piece of silk and bring it near the extended leaves of the newspaper. Observe the results and repeat until you are sure they are correct. What does this experiment show?

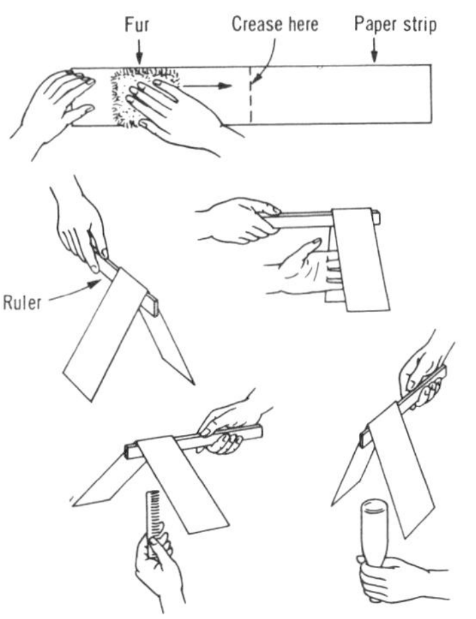

14 How to make a metal leaf electroscope

To make a device for detecting charges of electricity, a jam jar, some wire, and pieces of light foil or paper are needed.

A waxed cork is necessary to prevent the charge from leaking away. Push an L-shaped piece of brass or copper through it, and hang a piece of tissue paper or a strip of aluminium foil from the lower end.

If a charged body is brought near the rod, the leaves of the paper fly apart because they have received the same kind of charge.

Insulating wax (see Chapter XVIII, item 21, page 216) or Perspex are better insulators and therefore more satisfactory than the waxed cork.

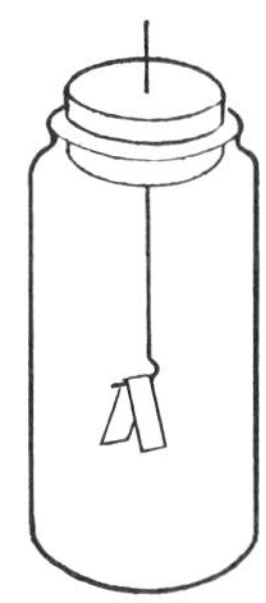

15 How to make a shadow electroscope

A very useful piece of apparatus can be made with a chalk or cigar box. The lid and bottom should be removed and replaced by a piece of clear glass in one side and a piece of linen or paper in the other (front in the diagram). The glass can be kept in position by tin corner plates, and the paper can be glued on. A hole drilled in what is now the top of the apparatus should fit a candle, ebonite or amber insulator with a brass rod down its axis. The top of the brass rod carries a metal disk forming the 'cap' of the electroscope and the other end has a strip of tin soldered to it. The gold or aluminium leaf is attached to the upper part of this tin, but the leaf is shorter. A thin glass thread, easily made in a flame, is stuck to the leaf with glue. It has a small arrow at its lower end. An electric bulb shines a light through the glass side of the apparatus and casts a shadow of the leaf and pointer on the screen. The advantage of this arrangement over the usual projection electroscope is that there is no inversion of the leaf, and movement and position of the leaf can be seen by a large class. It is also possible to put a scale on the paper calibrated in volts.

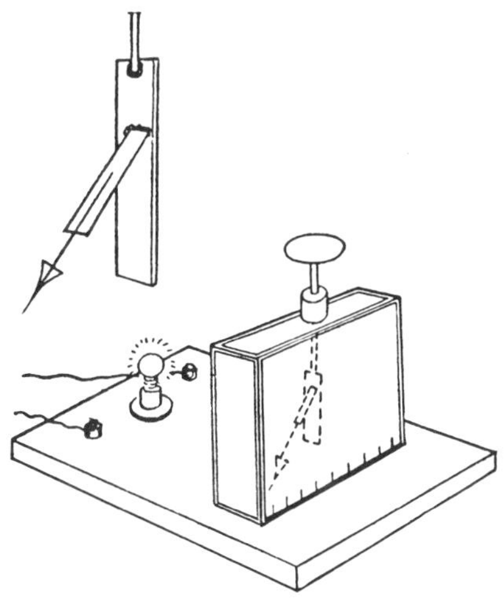

16 Fun with a kissing balloon

Blow up a toy balloon and tie a string to it about one metre long. You can draw faces on it with ink. Use a soft stick dipped in ink. Now hold the string while someone strokes the face on the balloon with a piece of fur or flannel. Let the balloon go and watch it touch everything around.

17 More fun with a balloon

Fix two balloons as in the experiment above. Rub the faces with fur. Hold the strings together and observe how they repel. Put your hand between them and observe what happens. Bring one of the balloons near your face. Repeat, using three balloons.

18 A static horse race

Cut small horses from a piece of folded paper so that they will stand on a table. Rub a hard plastic comb or fountain pen with fur and notice that you can pull the paper horses along the table. With several horses, you can have a horse race.

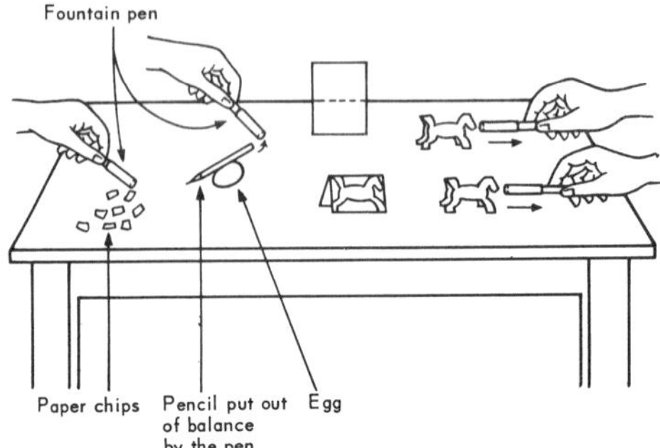

19 How to get many sparks from static electricity

Obtain a piece of aluminium about 24 cm square. An aluminium cake tin will do. Heat the metal evenly over a flame. Touch a stick of sealing wax or a wax candle to the centre of the aluminium until it melts and sticks solidly to it as a handle. If you want a more permanent handle you can punch a hole through the aluminium and screw a plastic or wood handle to it. Unfold an old rubber inner tube from an automobile tyre and place it on a table. Stroke the surface of the rubber briskly with a piece of fur or flannel for half a minute. Now place the aluminium on the rubber and press it down hard with your fingers. Remove your fingers and lift the metal by the handle. Bring your finger near the metal and you should get a spark. You can take many charges from the rubber without further rubbing. Just press the metal against the rubber, press with your fingers and lift by the handle.

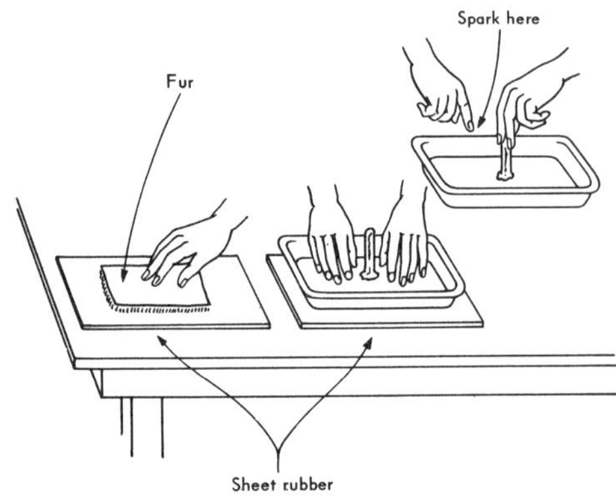

B. SIMPLE ELECTRIC CELLS AND CIRCUITS

1 To show how water flows in a tube

To make water flow from one can tc another the source must be at a higher level. Water flows downhill. You can demonstrate this by using two large tin cans. Punch a hole near the bottom of each and then enlarge the hole so it will take a one-hole cork or stopper. Put a length of rubber tube on one can. Pinch the tube near the end with a spring clothes peg. Place the can on the table and fill it with water. Attach the tube to the other can. Let it also stand on the table. Remove the clothes peg and watch the water flow. When does it stop flowing?

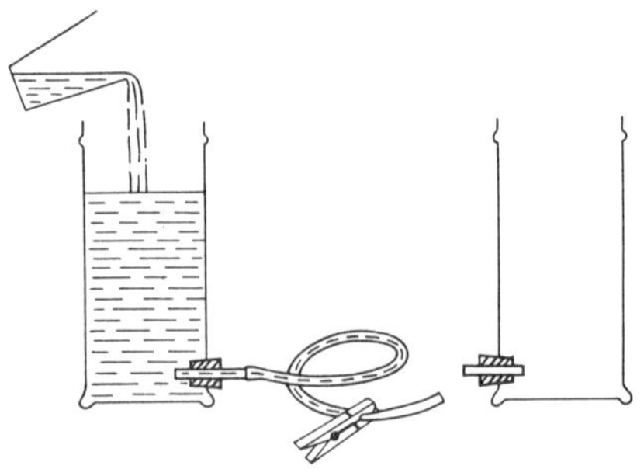

2 To show how electricity flows in a conductor

Use two tin cans as in the experiment above. Fasten the bare end of a wire to one can. Place both cans on plates that have been turned over. Fasten a spring clothes peg near the free end of the wire. Now use the device for getting many sparks which you made in experiment 19 of the previous section. Hook the free end of the wire to the can to which the other end is already attached. Place a charge on the rubber pad and bring the metal plate into contact with the can to which the wire is attached. Repeat this twenty times until you have a good charge on the can.

Place the pith ball electroscope which you made in experiment 11 of the previous section so that it is in contact with the other can. Next unhook the wire from the can, using the clothes peg as a handle and hook it over the other can. Observe the pith ball. If your experiment is successful the electricity will flow from one can to the other, and this will be shown by the pith ball.

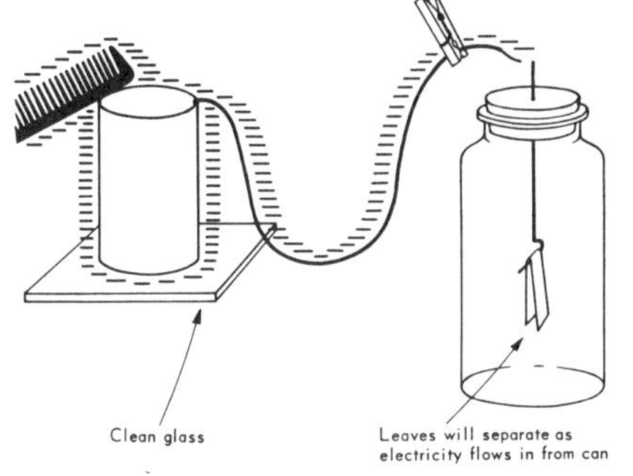

3 Another way to show how electricity flows

Use the can with the wire attached from experiment 2 above. This time attach the other end of the wire to the leaf electroscope which you made in experiment 14 of the previous section. Place a charge on the can with your spark device or from a plastic comb rubbed with fur. Observe the leaf of the electroscope.

4 How to make simple instruments to show electric currents

Procure some cotton-covered bell wire and neatly wrap from 50 to 60 turns to form a coil around a jar that is about 8 cm in diameter. Slip the coil from the jar and fasten it securely with short pieces of wire or with tape. Mount the coil on a wood base. A little platform to hold the compass can be made by cutting a hole in the cork for the coil to go through and

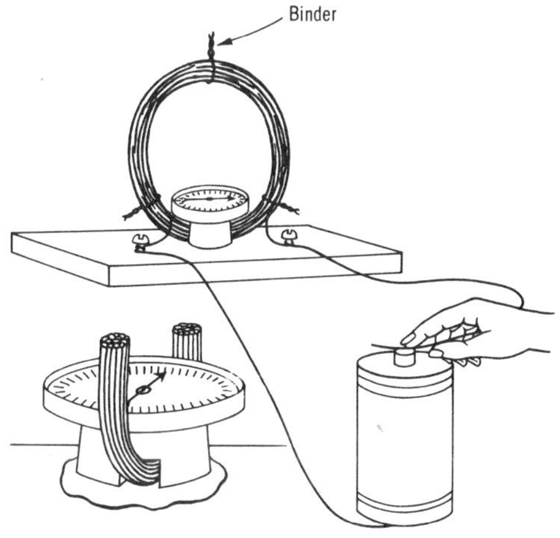

then fastening the cork and coil to the base with melted sealing wax. Place a compass on the cork so that it points parallel with the direction of the coil. Connect a dry cell to the coil and observe the compass needle.

A more sensitive instrument can be made by building a little frame from cigar box wood just large enough to hold the compass. Place the compass in the frame and then wind about 20 turns of bell wire over the frame as shown in the diagram.

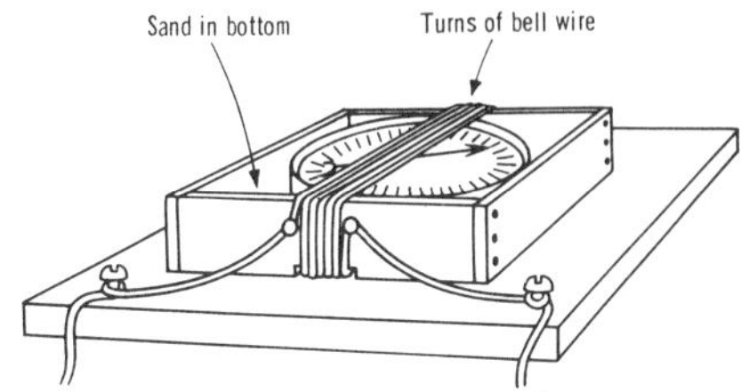

The press-stud compass needle described in Chapter XIV, experiment 11, page 157, can be used in both the above galvanoscopes. A useful model can also be devised using this compass needle in a matchbox. Remove the drawer from the box, and split open the case as shown in the diagram. Wind 20 turns of 26 S.W.G. double cotton-covered wire tightly round the drawer. Support the compass needle on a pin pushed through the bottom of the box.

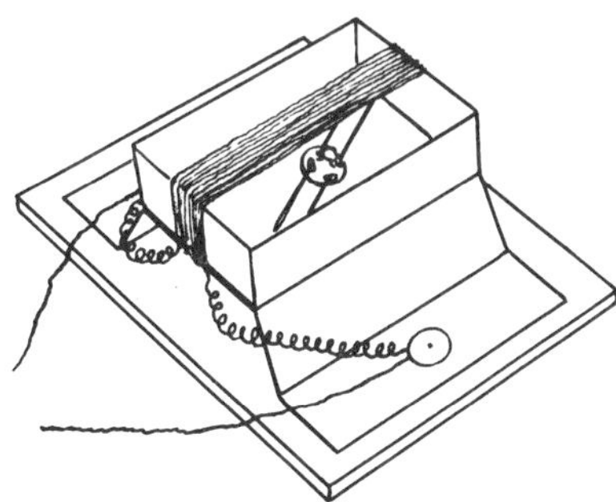

Fix the split-open case to a plywood base with drawing pins. Wind the bared end of the coil round the drawing pins, making electrical contact so that they may be used as terminals.

5 Electrical energy from chemical energy

Take two coins made of different metals. Clean them well with steel wool or fine sand paper. Fold some paper towelling or blotting paper into a pad so that it is slightly larger than the coins. Soak the blotting paper in salt water. Place one coin on top of the pad and the other underneath. Hold them between your thumb and finger. Connect both ends of the coil from your sensitive meter to the coins and watch the compass.

6 Electricity from a lemon

Connect one wire from your sensitive meter to a piece of zinc cut from the can of a used dry cell battery. Connect the other wire to a piece of copper. Roll a lemon on the table, pushing on it with your hand to break up some of the tissue inside. Push the two metal strips through the skin of the lemon, making sure they do not touch. Observe the compass needle.

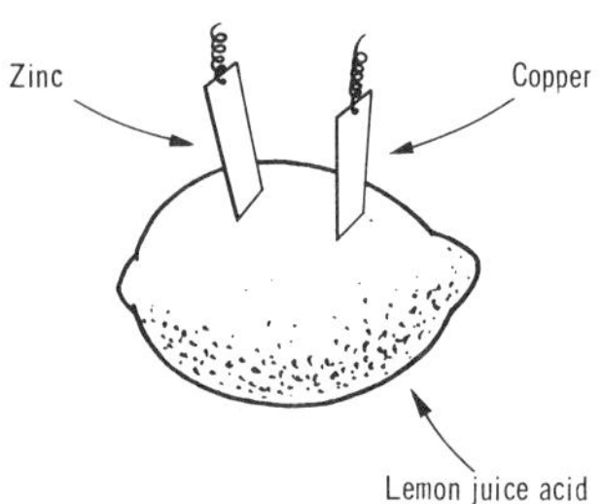

Try this experiment using a potato. Does the distance between the plates affect the meter reading?

7 How to make a simple electric cell

If dry batteries are not available, a simple voltaic cell can be used for many experiments. Copper and zinc plates dipped into dilute sulphuric acid contained in a jar work well, but the plates must be shaken occasionally to remove the gases. A few crystals of potassium dichromate will remove the gases chemically.

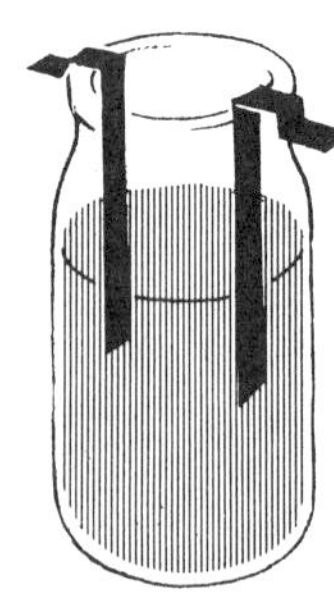

8 Other simple electric cells

You can make a simple Daniell cell for class use with a boot polish or shallow meat jar.

First put in a layer of copper sulphate crystals about 1.5 cm deep, moistened by about 0.5 cm of copper sulphate solution. Bury in this a pancake spiral of copper wire with an insulated lead. Pour in a layer of moist plaster of Paris and allow it to set.

For a negative plate use a strip of zinc sheet with a wire attached to it and fill up the jar with dilute sulphuric acid. This small quantity of acid can be thrown away when the cell is not in use.

A larger cell for supplying current can be improvised from a jam jar and a piece of cardboard tube.

Mix copper sulphate with plaster of Paris to a thin cream and allow to set after pouring it into the space between the jar and the central cardboard tube.

Mix another paste using plaster of Paris and zinc sulphate with a little sulphuric acid added. When the first plaster has set, pour this mixture into the central tube. Insert a copper plate and a zinc rod as electrodes before the pastes are hard.

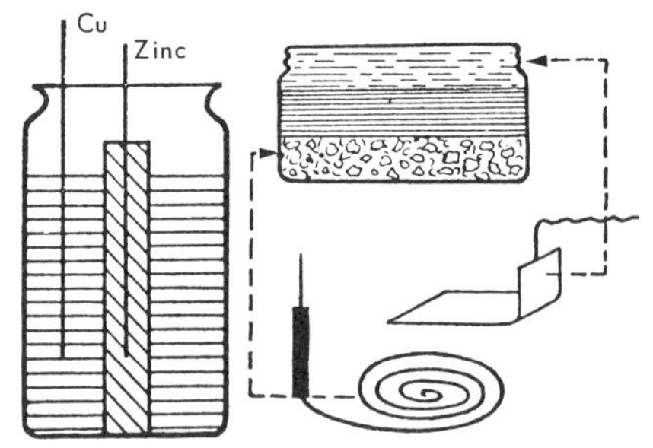

9 How to make a simple accumulator or storage battery

Strip the lead covering from some electric cable. Cut it into pieces, 1.5 cm by 3 cm with a short projection or 'lug' on the short side of each.

Now prepare pieces of thin wood 1.5 cm by 3 cm from a matchbox to act as 'spacers' to separate the plates.

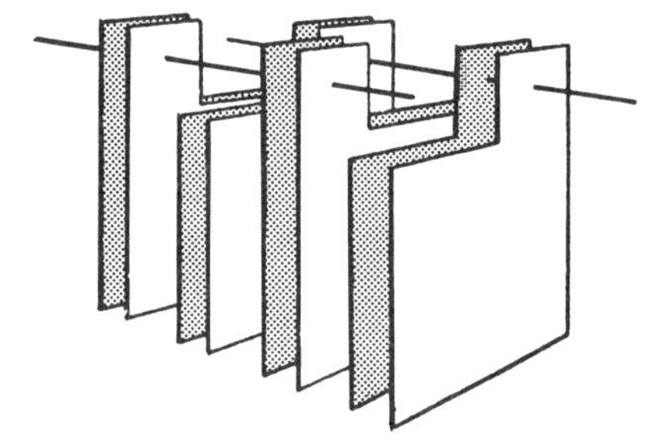

Arrange a pile of plates with lugs placed alternately and separate each plate by a spacer.

Connect the lugs on each side by a copper wire.

Immerse this arrangement in dilute sulphuric acid and pass a current to 'form' the plates. Even after a few minutes the accumulator will light a small torch bulb. Alternate charging and discharging will improve the condition of the plates.

10 How a dry cell is constructed

Remove the outer covering from an old dry cell. With a saw, cut the battery in half and observe its structure. Observe the carbon or positive pole in the centre, the zinc can which is the negative pole and the material between the two poles which is the chemical that acts on the plate of the cell. Notice how the zinc has been eaten away by the chemical. Observe that the chemical materials were sealed into the zinc can with hot pitch.

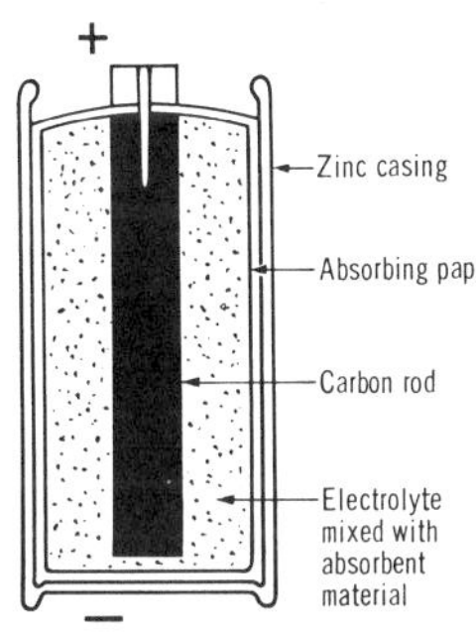

11 Using a dry cell in a circuit

Wrap the end of one of the short pieces of bell wire around the screwlike base of a flashlight bulb so that it holds the bulb tightly. Bend the remainder of the wire in the shape of the letter C. Set the tip of the flashlight bulb on the centre terminal of a flashlight cell and adjust the free end so that the springiness of the wire holds it against the bottom of the cell. If the connexions are tight, the bulb should light. Any flashlight bulb should operate when connected in this way, but the kind made for a single cell flashlight will give a much brighter light.

Look closely at the bulb and notice the fine metal wire held in position by two heavier wires inside. A hand lens will make this easier to see. The fine metal wire is made of wolfram, formerly called tungsten. Passage of the electric current through the wolfram wire causes it to become very hot and give off light.

Turn the cell upside down and reverse the terminals. Note that the lamp still operates, though the electricity is flowing in the opposite direction.

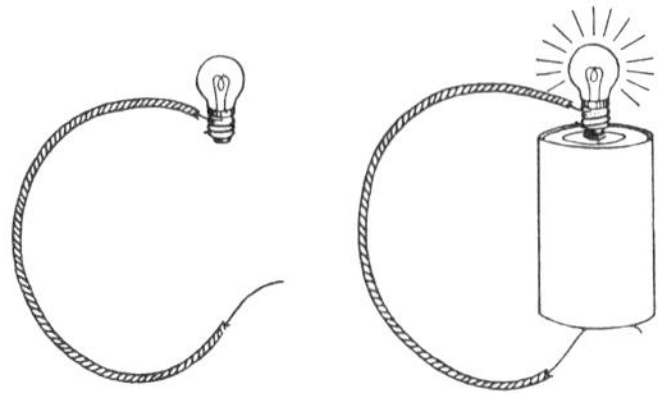

Make a diagram showing the path of the current through the bulb and around to the other end of the cell. Develop the meaning of the term 'electric circuit'.

12 Flashlight bulb holders

Wire nails, screw eyes or staples can be used for supporting flashlight bulbs. Three nails driven into the top of a cork as shown in the diagram will support the bulb. Two more nails or screws in the side of the cork and touching two of the vertical nails serve to make electrical connexions.

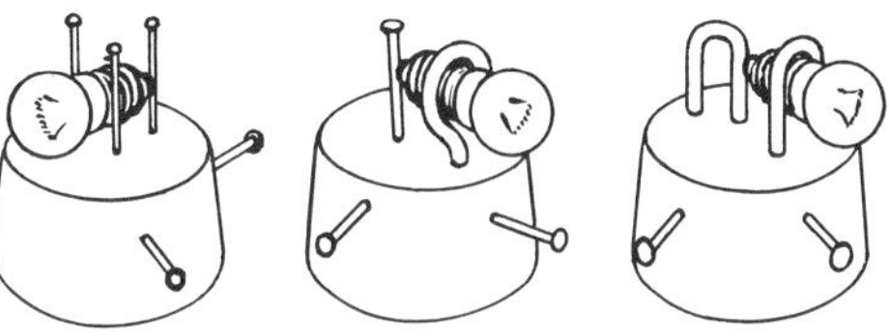

13 How a flashlight works

Bend the bell wire and fasten it to the cell with a piece of friction tape or rubber band. Adjust the wire so that the tip of the bulb touches the centre terminal of the cell. Use the free end of the wire as a switch by pressing it against the bottom of the cell.

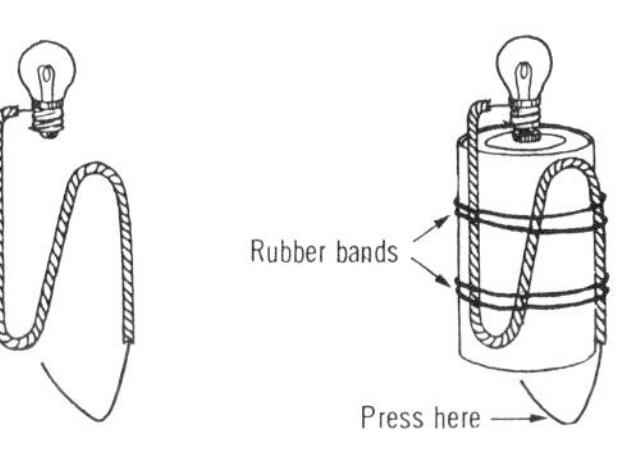

14 How to connect cells in series

Connect three dry cells in series as shown in the diagram. Note that the outside terminal of each cell is connected to the centre terminal of the next cell or vice versa. When the cells are connected in this way, the total voltage or electrical pressure is the sum of the voltages of the cells. In this case, the total voltage is 4.5 volts since the voltage of each cell is 1.5 volts.

Now connect the two lead wires to a lamp for a three-cell flashlight. Disconnect one of the wires and attach the same lamp to a single cell. Note the difference in brightness.

Connect the same lamp to two cells in series and compare the brightness with that produced by one cell and by three cells.

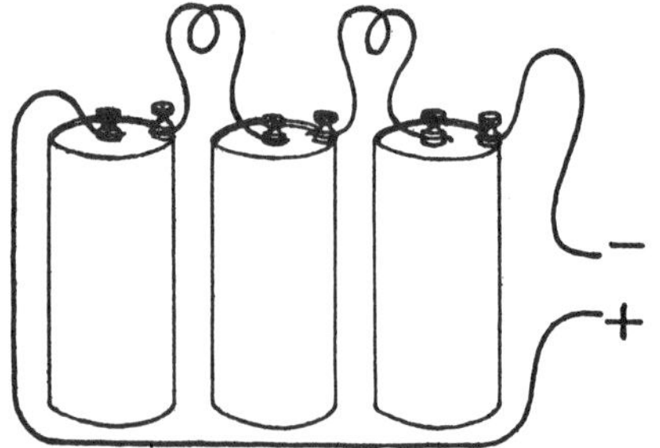

Cells connected in series

15 How to connect cells in parallel

Connect three cells in parallel by attaching all the centre terminals to one wire and all the outside terminals to another wire. Connect the lead wires to a receptacle and insert a bulb for a one-cell flashlight.

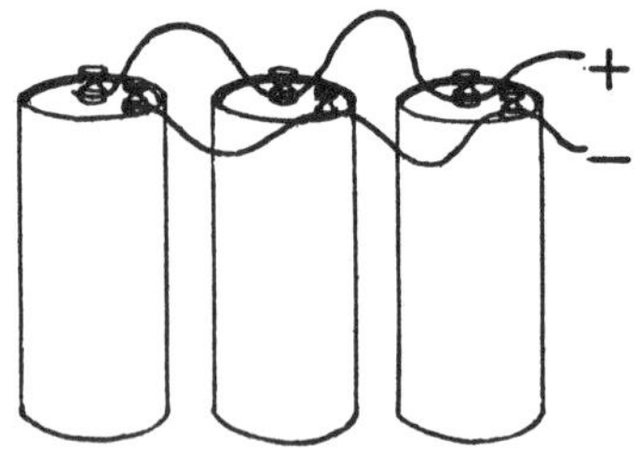

Cells connected in parallel

Disconnect one of the cells and note that there is no difference in the brightness of the lamp. Disconnect two cells and still the brightness does not change. When cells are connected in parallel the total voltage is no greater than that of a single cell.

Develop the distinction between the term ‘cell’ and ‘battery’. A battery is two or more cells in connexion.

16 Torch battery holders

When several torch cells are needed for an experiment they can be held in spring clips fastened to a wooden base. These can be made of steel baling strip bent in the form of an angle bracket and secured by a terminal so that series and parallel arrangements are possible. For greater security, circular clips of standard pattern can be added to grip the cells round the circumference.

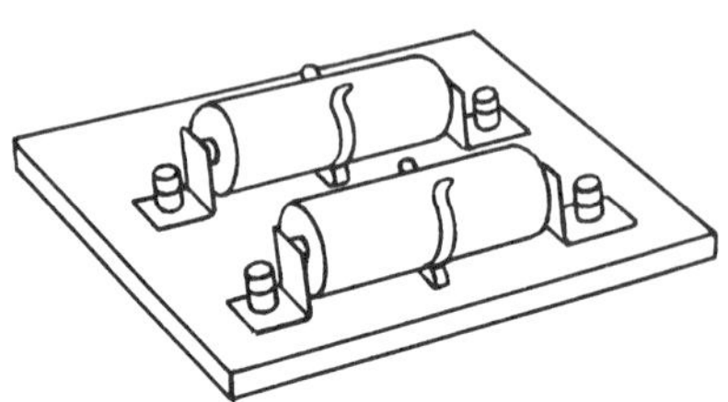

17 How lamps are connected in series

Connect three lamps in series and attach them to a single cell. Connect the same three lamps to two cells in series, then three cells in series. Unscrew one of the bulbs and note that the other two lamps go out, because the circuit is broken. Relate this to Christmas tree lights. In many Christmas tree cords, the lamps are connected in series. If one lamp in the series burns out, all the other lamps go out because the circuit is broken.

Lamps connected in series

18 How lamps are connected in parallel

Connect three lamps in parallel and attach them to a single cell. Unscrew one of the bulbs and note that the other two stay lighted. Increase the brightness of the lamps by adding a second cell in series. Unscrew one bulb, then two bulbs, then three bulbs.

Lamps connected in parallel

19 How a switch is used to control an electric circuit

Place a knife switch in a circuit with a cell and a lamp and turn the light on and off by operating the switch. Replace the lamp with a bell or buzzer and operate the switch. Replace the knife switch with a pushbutton switch. Discuss the appropriateness of each kind of switch for different uses.

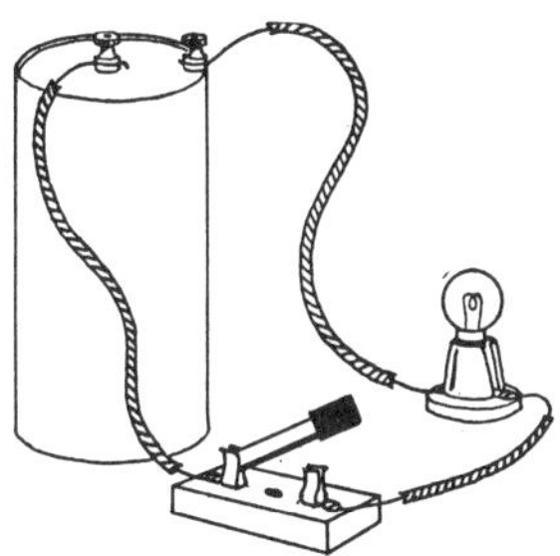

20 How to make a simple switch

A simple switch can be made by fastening the end of a piece of bell wire to a pencil with two rubber bands as shown in the diagram. A second wire spliced under it makes a suitable connexion.

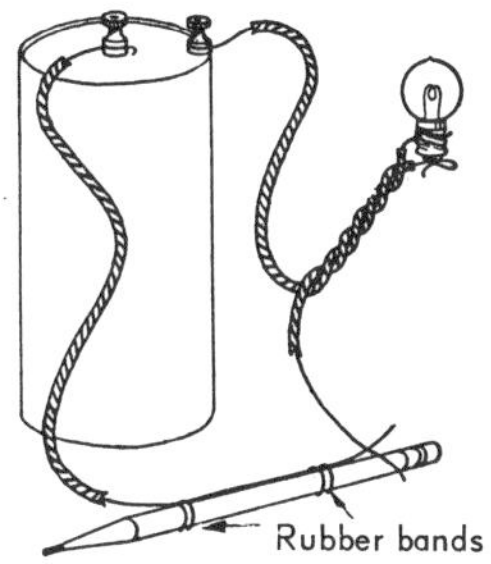

21 Another simple switch

Run a piece of bell wire through a spool (reel) and fasten it. Wind a second piece around the spool (see the second figure).

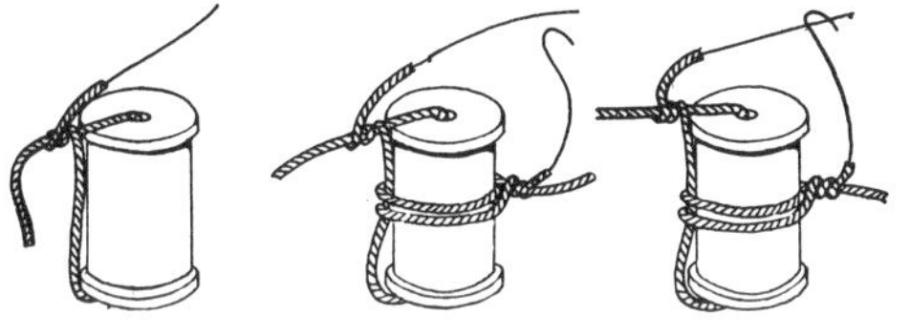

Adjust the free ends of the wires so that the switch can be opened and closed easily.

22 How a door bell can be rung from two pushbuttons

Using two cells, two pushbuttons and a bell, show how a doorbell can be operated from two different points, such as the front door and back door of a house. Lay out the circuit on a table as shown in the diagram. Draw an electrical diagram of the circuit, using standard symbols.

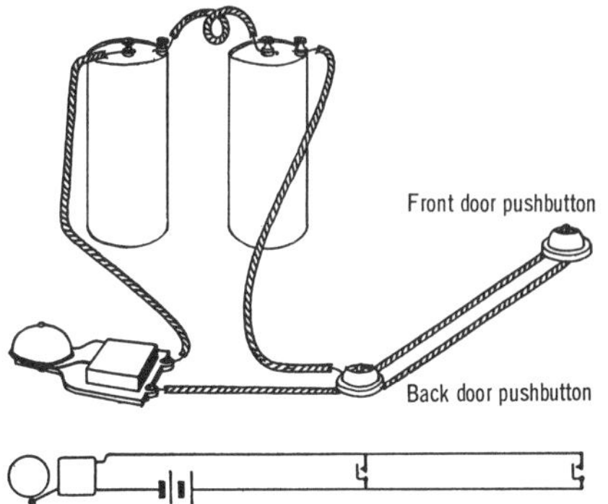

23 How a light is controlled from two switches

With two double throw knife switches, two cells and a lamp, show how a hall light can be operated from either the upstairs or the downstairs switch. Lay out the circuit on a table as shown in the diagram. Draw an electrical diagram of the circuit, using standard symbols.

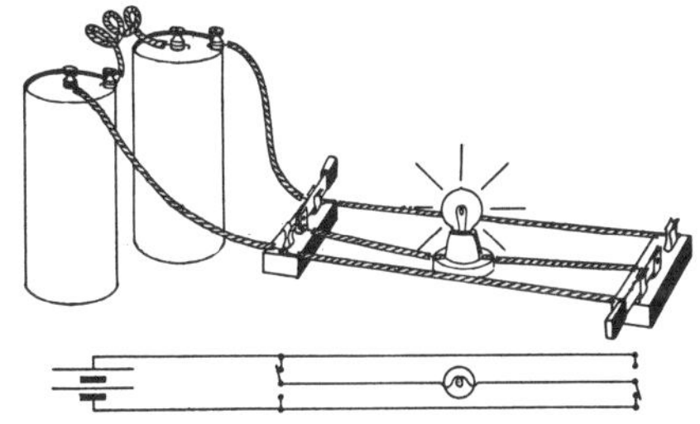

24 A miniature street lighting system

Cut two lengths of insulated bell wire about three metres long. Remove the insulation at six places along each wire and connect miniature light bulb sockets in parallel along them. Fasten the wires between two chairs as shown in the diagram, leaving the wires apart at one end. Connect the wires at the other end with two dry cells. Screw torch light bulbs into the sockets.

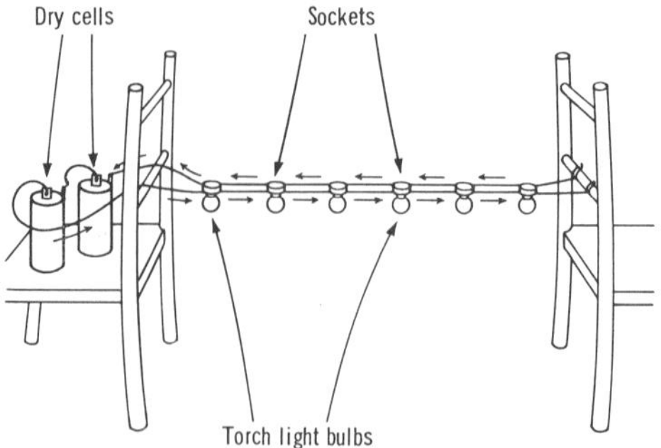

25 How we get heat and light from electricity

Push the ends of two pieces of bell wire through a flat cork that fits a small bottle. A suitable flat cork can be made by cutting off the end of a longer cork, or a two-hole rubber stopper may be used instead. Now untwist a piece of ordinary iron picture cord and cut off a short piece of a single strand. Wind the ends of this short piece of picture wire around the projecting ends of the copper wires and insert the cork into a bottle. The result will serve as a crude model of an electric lamp.

Connect the electric lamp model into a circuit with one or more dry cells and a switch. Close the switch until the fine wire (filament) begins to glow, then open the switch again. With care the lamp can be lighted several times before the filament is consumed, but finally the heated iron wire combines with the oxygen of the air inside the bottle and burns away. Commercially made lamp bulbs contain no oxygen, and the wolfram wire is heated to such a high temperature that it glows brightly. In addition to protecting the filament, the glass bulb also makes an electric lamp safe to use.

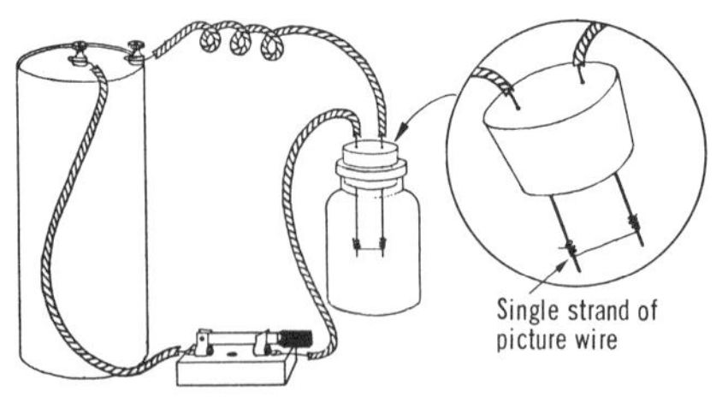

26 How fuses protect electric circuits

Examine normal and burned out fuses. Fuses are safety devices that break an electric circuit when the circuit is overloaded. The fuse wire melts when an unsafe amount of current is flowing through a circuit.

Cut a very thin strip of metal foil from a candy bar or other wrapper and fasten it between the ends of two wires projecting through a cork. This will represent a model of a fuse that should work with dry cells. Experiment with different types and widths of foil until the working model operates satisfactorily.

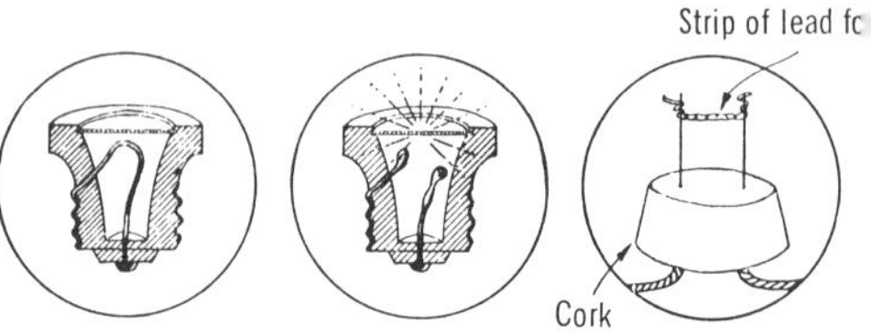

27 How a short circuit burns out a fuse

Place the model fuse shown in a circuit with several cells and a lamp. Then short circuit the lamp. If the fuse does not melt, cut a thinner strip of foil. Experiment with different kinds and widths of foil until the fuse carries the current when connected properly but melts when there is a 'short' in the circuit.

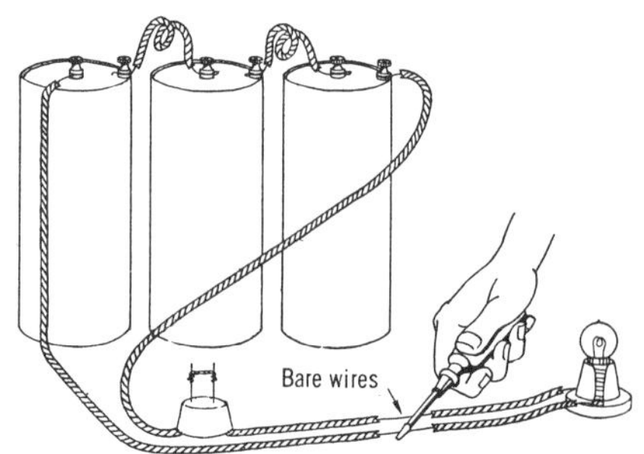

28 How to make a simple fuse holder

Tin foil used for cigarette and packing purposes is useful for experiments on fuses. It can be cut in strips and stuck on a piece of gummed tape which will hold it flat. The metal foil with paper backing which was used during the war for radar camouflage is excellent for the above experiment and can be cut easily with a pair of scissors to give different fusing values.

The ends can be held by bulldog paper clips to a slat of wood or a ruler. The device can then be incorporated with the circuit board set if desired. Different lengths and widths of tin foil should be tried to find the fusing current.

29 How electrical resistance varies with temperature

Connect a coil of about two metres of florist's thin iron wire in series with a torch battery and bulb. Heat the coil with a match; the increase in resistance will reduce the current so that the bulb no longer glows.

C. MAGNETISM AND ELECTRICAL ENERGY

1 An apparatus for building up simple electrical instruments

The different pieces of apparatus used in elementary electricity have so much in common, electromagnets, switches, etc., that it is worth while constructing some multiple sets of apparatus in which they can be used in several different ways. The following arrangements have been found useful for boys of 11-13, and require little more than a penknife to assemble, once the basic parts are made. The devices suggested are not entirely foolproof, because little is learned of the difficulties of a subject if one needs only to follow instructions to the letter.

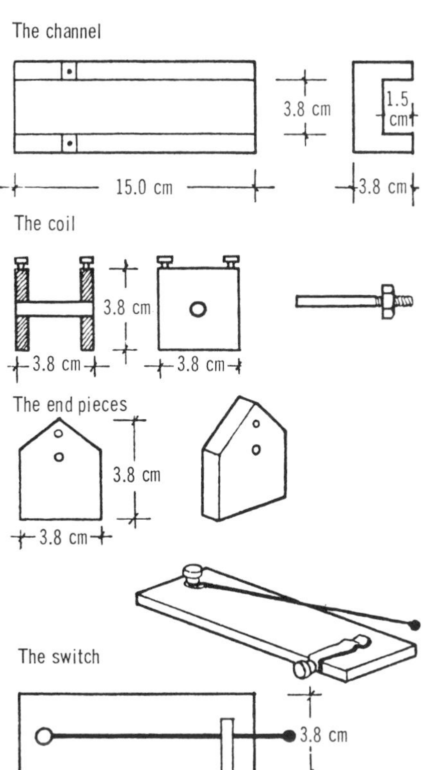

The apparatus consists of a short wooden channel which acts as a base for all experiments; a square-ended former for winding a coil which fits the groove fairly tightly, a few terminals, bits of tin, etc., are all that are required to make a morse sounder, buzzer, bell indicator, electromagnet repulsion meter and attraction meter.

The coil is made of two square end pieces of wood with holes in their centre. They are joined by cardboard tube glued into these holes.

An old carriage bolt with the head cut off makes a convenient iron core.

2 Magnetism from an electric current

Cut two lengths of copper wire and remove the insulation from the ends. Connect the wires to a dry cell and arrange the bare ends as shown in the figure. Place some iron filings on a piece of paper and run one of the bare ends through them. Now let the current flow through the circuit and quickly lift the wire and observe the iron filings. Break the contact and the iron filings will drop from the wire. Do not leave the cell connected long; it will quickly run down when connected this way.

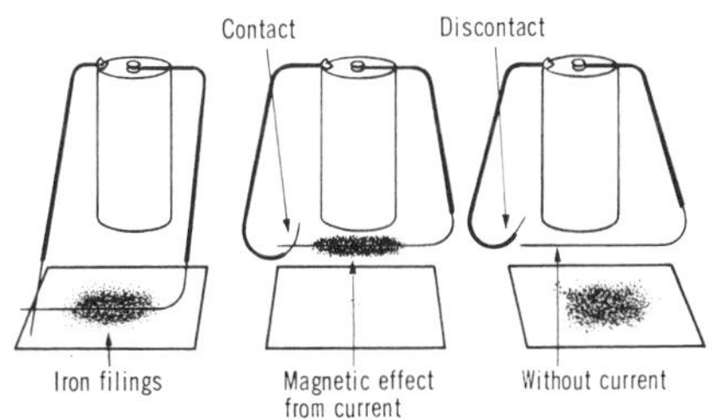

3 Another way to show the magnetic effect of a current

Repeat the experiment above, replacing the iron filings with a magnetic compass. Observe the difference in the compass when it is placed over the wire and under the wire.

4 How to make an electromagnet from a bolt

Secure an iron bolt about 5 cm long which has a nut and two washers. Place a washer at each end and screw the nut just on to the bolt. Wind layers of insulated bell wire on the bolt between the washers, making certain to leave 30 cm of wire sticking out when you start winding the coil. When you have filled the bolt between the washers with several layers of turns of wire, cut the wire, again leaving

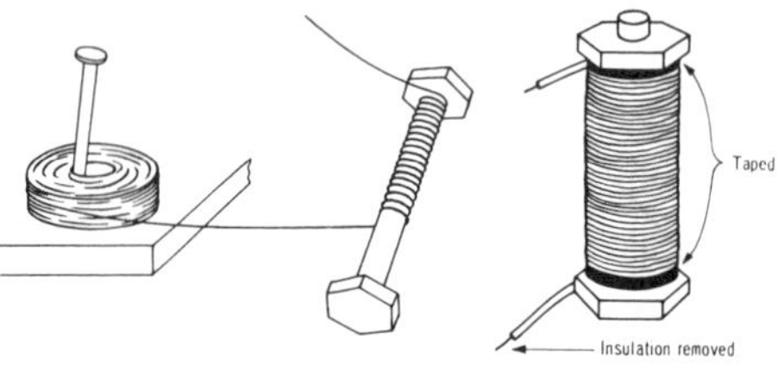

about 30 cm sticking out. Twist the two ends of the wire close to the ends, then wind short lengths of tape at the ends of the bolt to keep the wire from unwinding. Remove the insulation from the two ends of wire. Connect two dry cells in series and attach your electromagnet to them. Pick up some tacks and nails. Disconnect one wire from the battery while the tacks are still attached. Pick up other objects made of iron or steel. Test the poles of each end of the magnet with a compass while the current is turned on.

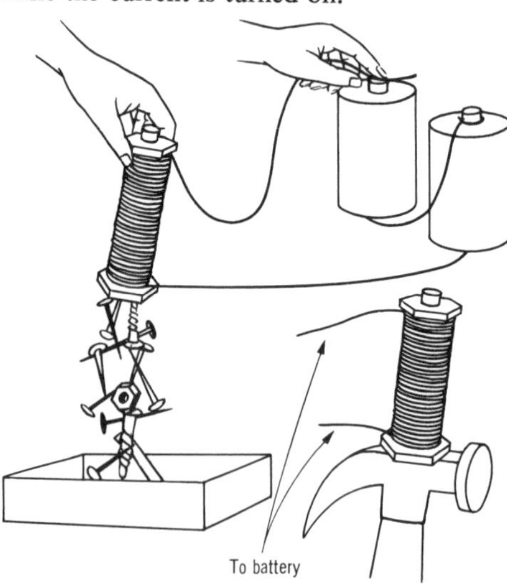

5 How to make a horseshoe electromagnet

Secure a slender bolt or a piece of iron rod about 5 mm in diameter and 30 cm long. Bend this into the shape of the letter U. Wind a coil of several layers of bell wire on each arm of the magnet, leaving the curving part free as shown. Begin at the end of one arm. Leave about 30 cm of wire sticking out for connexions. Wind about three layers on this pole then carry the wire across the top to the other end; be sure to wind this pole exactly as shown in the diagram. Wind about three layers of wire on this pole. When you have finished, tape the wire to keep it from unwinding. Remove the insulation from the ends of the coil, attach to two dry cells, and test the poles of the electromagnet. One should

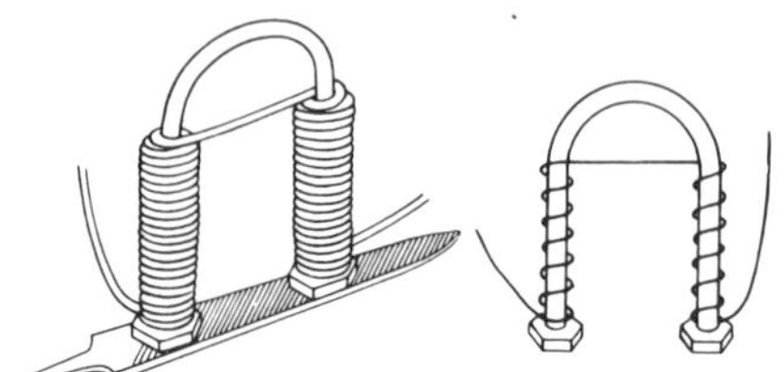

be a north pole and the other a south. If each has the same polarity, you have wound the second coil in the wrong direction. It will be necessary to unwind the coil and rewind it in the opposite direction.

Try picking up different things with the magnet. Compare the strength of this electromagnet with the straight one you made.

6 How to increase the strength of an electromagnet

Wrap 100 turns of bell wire on a straight iron bolt. Connect the ends of the magnet with one dry cell and count the number of tacks you can pick up with the magnet. Make three trials, and take the average as the number that this magnet with one battery will pick up. Next attach two batteries to the magnet and repeat. Count the number of tacks. How is the strength of the magnet affected by increasing the current flowing through it?

Next wrap another 100 turns of wire on the magnet in the same direction. Attach to one battery and see how many tacks you can pick up. Repeat three times and take the average. Compare this number with the number picked up with one battery and a magnet of 100 turns of wire. How does increasing the number of turns of wire affect the strength? Make a statement on increasing the strength of an electromagnet.

7 How to study the magnetic field of a coil

Use the apparatus made in experiment 1 of this section.

A postcard with a square hole cut in it enables the coil to pass through. The card acts as a tray on which the effect of using different cores in the coil can be studied by making iron filing maps.

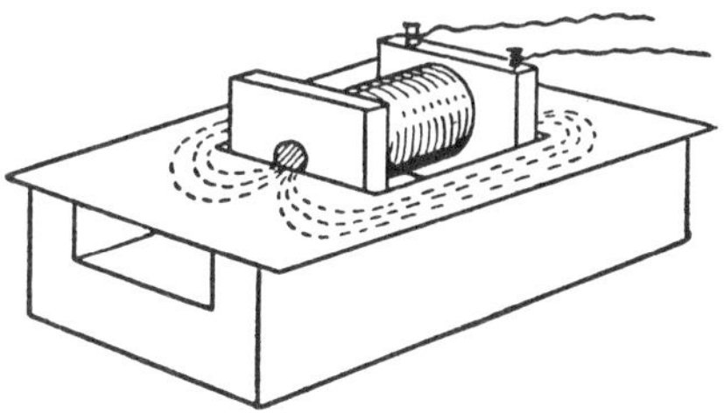

8 How to make a repulsion meter

Use the equipment made in experiment 1 of this section.

A piece of tin can about 4 by 5 cm with a wire soldered to one end is required for the 'movement' of the meter. A blob of solder on the end of the wire acts as a gravity control to the meter.

The coil becomes magnetized when a current is passed. Both the fixed and moving elements are magnetized in the same direction, and repulsion occurs. The fixed element is a soft iron wire held in position by a rubber band. It will give readings 0-5 amps, depending on the wire and the magnetic properties of the metals used.

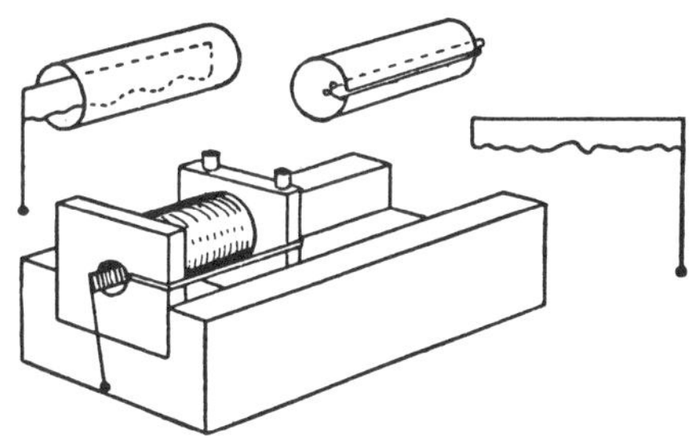

9 How to make an attraction meter

Use the equipment made in experiment 1 of this section.

For this apparatus the channel is laid on its side with the coil fitted as before. The iron core is pushed in and a current is passed. This attracts a pear-shaped piece of tin can pivoted on a pin stuck in the end of the block. A fine wire soldered to the tip of the metal acts as a pointer and graduations can be made on a piece of card held in position by drawing pins.

These are only a few of the devices which can be assembled from the above components. A boy of 12 can discover many more : the electric signal, the sucking bar, the relay, etc.

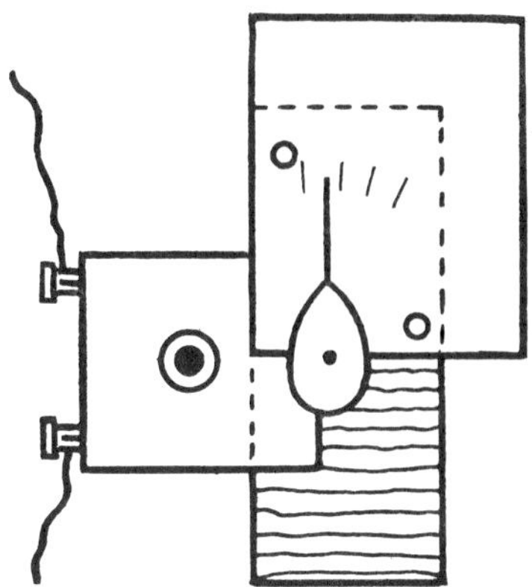

10 How to make a telegraph key and sounder

Again use the equipment made in experiment 1 of this section.

The coil should first be wound with any available copper wire, the ends being fastened under the terminals.

The completed coil is pressed into the groove and the iron core slid in; if necessary, wedge it in place with a piece of paper.

A strip of tin can about 10 cm long is then pressed into the saw cuts in the edge of the channel and secured by a terminal. One of the end pieces with a terminal in its lower hole will act as the sounder.

When the switch is depressed, the coil becomes a magnet, and the piece of tin can is pulled forward to hit the metal core with a 'click': as it springs back at the release of the switch, it hits the terminal on the end piece with a 'clack'.

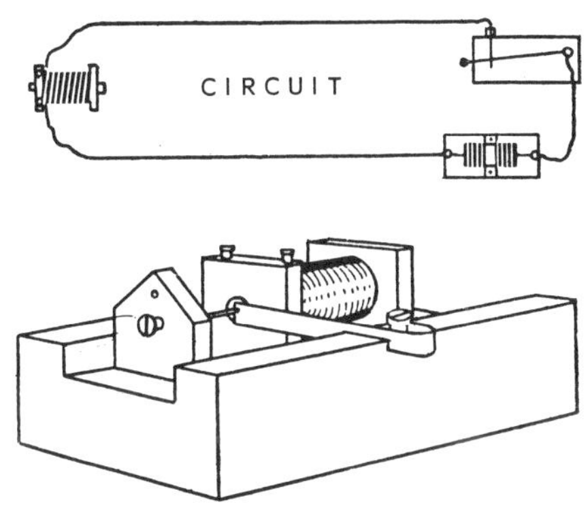

11 How to make an electric buzzer

Use the equipment made in experiment 1 of this section.

A simple rearrangement of the circuit converts the sounder into a buzzer. The contacts soon become fouled, and it is necessary to scrape them with a penknife.

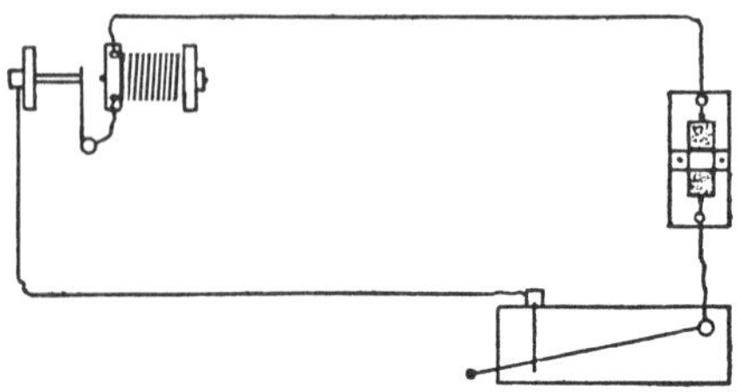

12 How to make a cigar box telegraph and a key

Seventy-five to 100 turns of magnet wire neatly wound on to a 6.5 to 8 cm bolt will serve for the coil. Leave enough of the threaded end for two nuts and the thickness of the box, so that the coil can be fastened to the box. For the armature, a 10 cm bolt, 5 mm in diameter and with a round head, is most satisfactory. Support it between two nuts by a screw-eye fixed to the back of the box so that the head will extend just beneath the coil. A block of wood with a small piece of window glass cemented to it makes an effective anvil. Attach the anvil securely to the box. Hot sealing wax is ideal for both purposes. Any glue, however, will do. The height of the anvil should be such as to allow not less than 3 mm of clearance space for the end of the armature, and it should not exceed this amount by more than a trifle. The remaining feature now is a spring to pull the armature away from the magnet in case it tends to cling after the current is broken. A rubber band will work well. Slip it over the end of the armature and attach it to the box with a thumb tack. Give it just enough tension to prevent the armature from sticking to the magnet.

You are now ready to assemble a key. Secure a small piece of board about 8 cm by 15.5 cm and about 0.5 cm thick. Cut a strip of metal from a can about 2.5 by 13 cm. Go over it thoroughly with sandpaper or steel wool to remove any lacquer or tarnish from its surface. A piece of clock spring is also excellent for this purpose. Holes may be punched with a large nail and a sharp blow from a hammer. Set a screw in one end of the block and attach the metal at the other end so that it will bridge the space when the metal is pressed to the screw head.

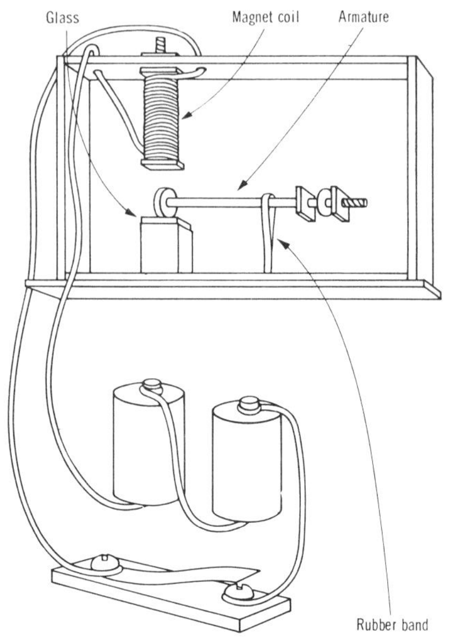

Connect your telegraph sounder, two cells and key in series as shown. You are now ready for your trial message. If, on vibrating the key, you do not get a series of clicks, it means that either your connexions are loose or an adjustment of the rubber band is needed.

13 Another way to make a buzzer

A buzzer is essentially the same as a telegraph instrument except that it produces a buzzing sound instead of a clicking sound when you close the circuit. It is arranged so that it will automatically make and break the circuit many times per second while you hold down the key. The armature vibrates rapidly enough to produce the buzzing sound, which continues as long as the key is down. The buzzer is very fine for sending code—a short buzz for a 'dot' and a longer buzz for a 'dash'. It sounds just like radio code and is therefore better than the telegraph instrument for learning to send and receive by radio.

For the base and mountings, cut out three pieces of board to the following dimensions respectively, 13 by 15.5 cm, 5 by 5 cm and 5 by 7.5 cm. Drill a hole smaller than the bolt through the baseboard about 6.5 cm from one end to hold the magnet. For the magnet coil secure an 8 cm by 4 mm bolt at the hardware store. Put on two washers as collars to hold the wire and a nut leaving a little more than 1.5 cm of the threaded end clear. Wind on 100 turns of bell wire in a neat fashion, leaving about 45 cm of the ends free. Either tie the wire at the last turn or tape it to prevent unwinding. Now mount the coil by turning it into the prepared hole securely.

For the vibrator bend a 10.5 cm strip of thin iron about 2 cm wide into a right angle so that one arm will be 7.5 cm long. A piece of softened clock spring is excellent. To soften the spring bring it to red heat and allow to cool slowly. Punch two holes in the short arm by laying the strip on the end of a block and forcing the point of a large nail through with a sharp blow from a hammer. Attach the strip to the smaller block with screws, and nail the block to the base. Care should be taken to have the vibrator not more than 3 mm above the magnet. If it is not just right, it can be adjusted later by bending the vibrator strip.

For the contact point, secure a small brass bolt about 2.5 cm by 6 mm, and two nuts to fit, and a 5 cm angle iron. Set the brass bolt in one of the holes of the angle iron. Mount this angle iron with screws on the 5 by 7.5 cm block so that when it is nailed in position the horizontal arm of the angle iron will stand about 1.5 cm above the vibrator.

Now connect your buzzer with two cells and a key of your own construction. Be sure

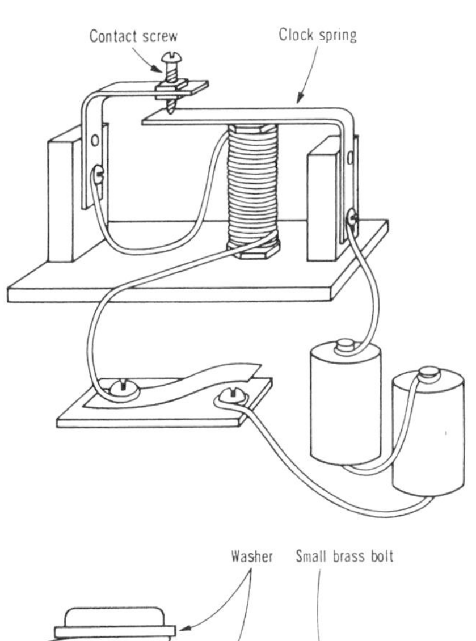

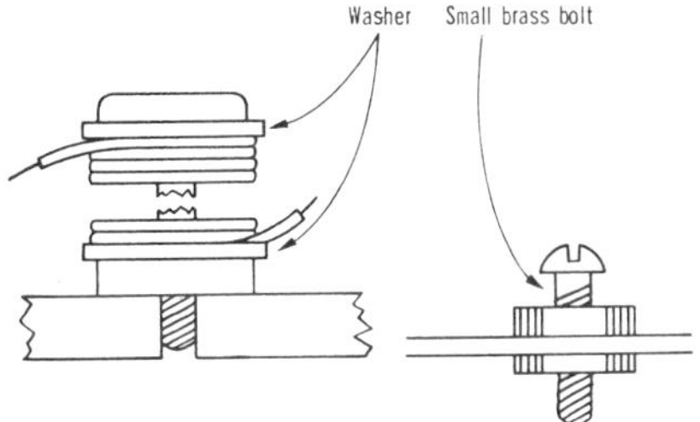

all connexions are tight and that all wire is free from insulation where the connexions are made. Press the key down and hold it while you turn the contact screw down into contact with the vibrator. If it does not vibrate, use sandpaper or steel wool to polish the surface thoroughly under the contact point. As soon as you get it vibrating, you can improve the tone by finer adjustment of the contact screw and also by bending the vibrator to ensure a space about the thickness of a dinner knife between the vibrator and the magnet.

Now you can practice the code. If several buzzers are made, you may connect them to a line in the room, or you may signal between two houses.

14 How to connect up a two-way telegraph system

If you can secure two telegraph sounders and two keys like the ones made in experiment 12

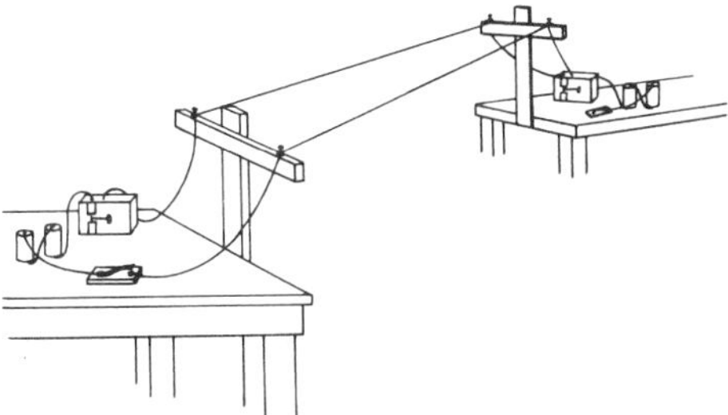

above, you can set up a two-way telegraph system by following the diagrams below.

When one key is being used for sending, the other one must be fastened down so that the electric current will go through it.

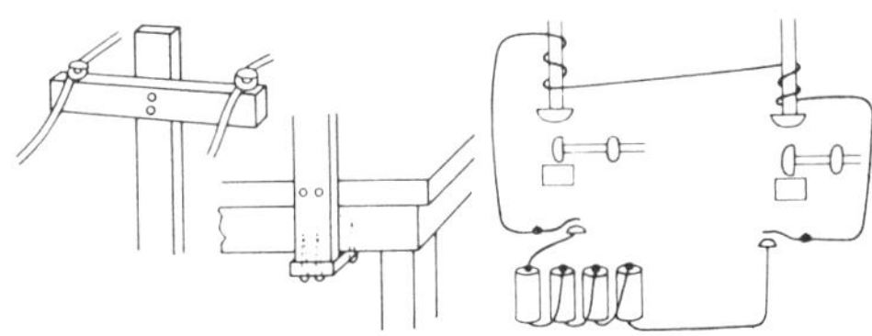

15 How to make an electric bell

If you study the diagrams, you will see how simple it is to adapt a few worthless pieces of material to your purpose of making a bell that will ring nicely on electric dry cells. You will need three pieces of board—one for the base, about 13 by 18 cm, one to hold the magnet, and one to hold the vibrator, each about 5 by 5 cm. Wind not less than 100 turns of cotton-covered magnet wire or bell wire on to an 8 cm bolt for the magnet. Plan to have several centimetres of wire free at the ends when finished. Use a nut and two washers to form the spool. Leave at least 1.5 cm of the threaded end of the bolt free for attaching the magnet to the block as shown in the diagram. Mount the magnet about midway on the base with nails of the proper size.

For the vibrator or clapper, an 18 cm piece of softened clock spring not less than 1.5 cm wide is excellent. The clock repair man in your town should be willing to give you an old spring. Soften a portion of the spring by heating it red hot—over the gas flame of the cook stove, if you do not have a gas burner. Be sure it gets red hot and then let it cool slowly. This takes some of the springiness out of it and softens it so that it will not retain magnetism. Punch a hole very near one end and two more holes about 2.5 cm apart at the other end. In one end set a small bolt, with two nuts to fit, to serve as the hammer. Bend about 4 cm of the other end at right angles and attach it to the wooden block with small screws; attach the block to the base. It should be placed so that the vibrator will stand about 6 mm from the magnet when finally adjusted.

For the contact point, a 2.5 cm angle iron will serve very well as the support, and a small bolt about 10 mm long, preferably of brass, set with two nuts as in the figure, makes a satisfactory contact. Attach to the base with screws at a point about 9 cm from the hammer end of the vibrator, being careful to locate it so that the vibrator can be adjusted correctly, as described above. Before setting, you should spring the vibrator out from the magnet just enough so that when the contact point is set, the vibrator will be pressing against it with a fairly firm pressure.

Before mounting the gong, the wires should be connected and the contacts adjusted, as follows. The plan for connecting the wires is clearly shown. Now connect to two cells and make the proper adjustment of the contact point by setting it in or out. The watch spring should vibrate vigorously.

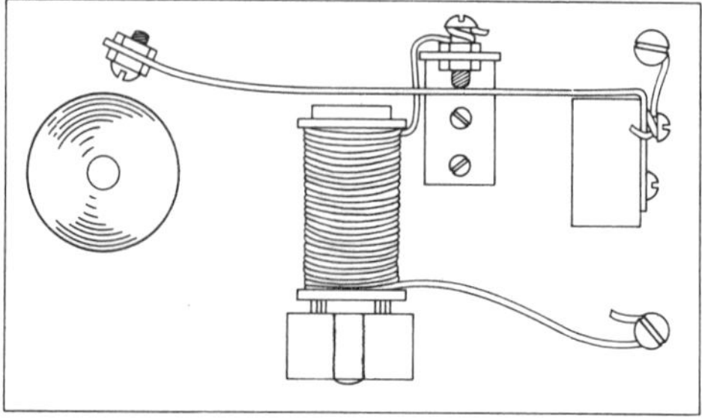

Be sure that all connexions are good and tha the clock spring is sandpapered or scrape down to the clean metal where it presse against the contact point. The end of th contact bolt, too, should be sandpapere While the hammer is vibrating, find the be position for the gong, then fasten it to th baseboard. A little bending of the spring c changing of the pressure at the contact, or th space between the vibrator and magnet, c re-sandpapering the contact points, ma improve its performance.

16 How to set up a simple telephone lin

Secure two copper plates about 10 cr square. Punch a hole in each and attach abou a metre of bell wire after removing insulatio from the ends. It is best to solder the wir to the copper plates. Remove the carbon ro from an old dry cell. Break it up into piece about 5 mm in diameter. Make a selectio of carbon pieces of about the same siz You will need a small handful. Next secur a cigar box and an alarm clock. Place th clock face up on the cigar box. Place on copper plate on the alarm clock. Connec the wire from this plate to two dry cell connected in series. Connect a telephon receiver to the other side of the battery an to the wire of the other copper plate. Nex place the pieces of carbon on the copper plat and then cover them with the other coppe plate. Listen in the receiver, and you will hea the ticking of the clock. You may have t adjust the top copper plate by moving it a little one way or another.

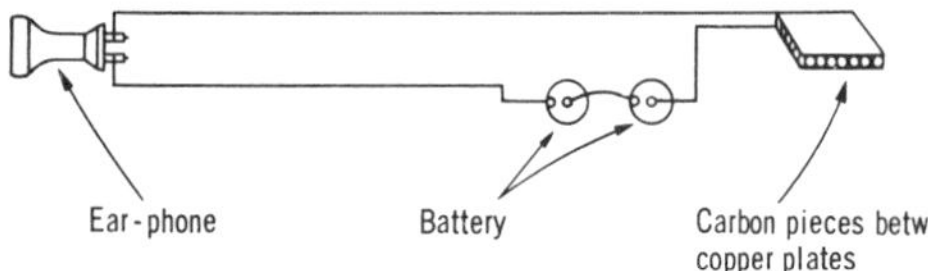

17 How to make a simple telephon transmitter

Cut parallel grooves, about 4 cm apart, int the top surface of a cigar box with the poin of a pocket knife. Force the back of a razo blade firmly into each. This should hold th blades securely in position. If it does not hol them securely, set them in with hot sealin wax (heat the blade and rub it on the wa and, while still hot, force it into the prepare groove). Twist wires into the blades fo connecting purposes. Now sharpen a shor piece of pencil at both ends and set acros the sharp edges of the two blades. Be sur to have the pencil sharpened back far enough, so that the carbon, and not the wood, contacts the blades. Your telephone is now complete.

Obtain a telephone receiver from some convenient source. If you know someone connected with the telephone company, he may be able to get you a discarded one. Connect with dry cells as illustrated in the diagram.

To test your connexions, put the receiver to your ear and raise and lower the pencil. Move it about, and you should hear noise in the 'phone something like static on the radio.

To get your 'phone tuned up for the voice, set a clock on the box and, while listening in the receiver, adjust the position of the rod or pencil until you can hear the clock ticking two or three times louder than ordinary. When a sensitive position is found, remove the clock and speak directly and distinctly into the box. Your friend, with the receiver to his ear, should hear what you say. Of course, he should close his other ear unless you have a long line.

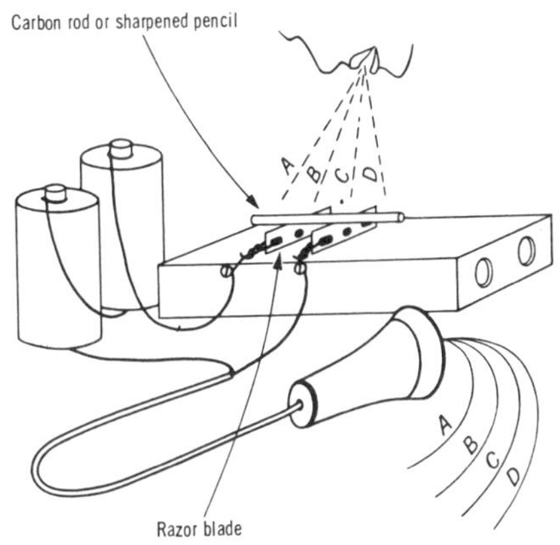

You have now achieved the near magic of making a cigar box reproduce your voice and send it over a wire. Try to figure out how it works. You realize that the sound waves of the voice cause the box to vibrate. Rest your fingers on the box while you make some sounds and feel the vibrations. This vibrating of the box causes the pencil to rattle or vibrate likewise. This, in turn, interrupts the steady current and makes it pulsate as it goes through the electromagnet of the receiver.

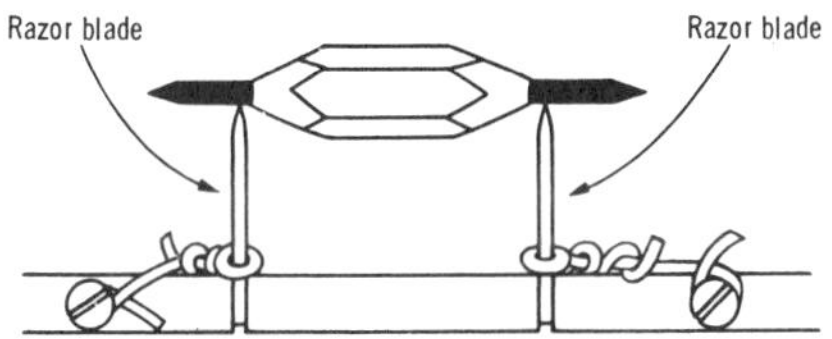

This causes the diaphragm in the rattle or vibrate and produce th of sound waves as those that strike at the other end of the line. Rub the box listen. Drop grains of sand on the box and listen in the phone to hear them strike. Jar the table and listen. Do these tests seem to confirm the above explanation?

18 Producing electricity with a magnet and a coil

You will need to use the sensitive current detector which you made in experiment B 4 above for this experiment. Attach a coil of about fifty turns of bell wire to the current detector, leaving the lead wires long enough so that the magnet is well away from the compass. Move the coil over one pole of a permanent horseshoe magnet. Observe the compass needle. Now remove the coil from the pole and observe the needle. Move the coil on and off the other pole of the magnet. Next hold the coil and plunge the magnet into the coil. Whenever magnetic lines of force are broken by a coil a current is set up in the coil.

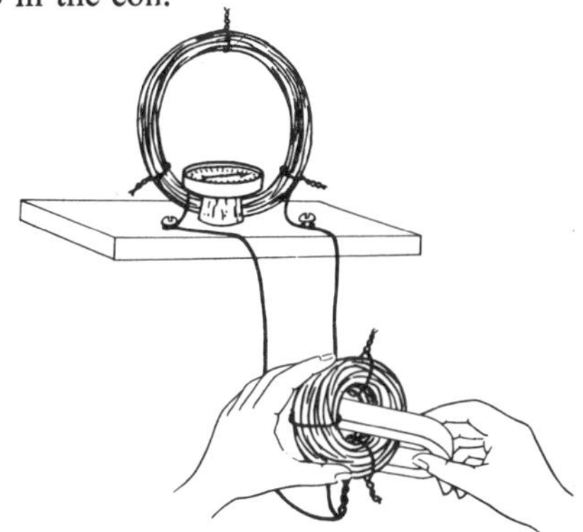

19 Electricity from a hand generator

You will need a magneto from an old-fashioned wall telephone. This type of telephone is still used in some localities. If you have a friend who works for the telephone company, it is very probable that he could get

one for you without cost, because they are often replaced with a more modern type.

Remove the magneto from the cabinet and mount it toward one end of a board about 15.5 by 30 cm. Attach a regular lamp socket near the other end. Connect the socket to the terminals of the generator. Place a 10 watt, 100 volt lamp into the socket.

The machine is now ready to use. Turn the crank and light the lamp. Turn it slowly, and the lamp glows faintly. Turn it fast, and it glows brightly. Why? Close your eyes and while you turn, let someone screw the bulb out and in. Can you tell when the bulb is out and when it is in by the amount of effort you must use to turn the crank? Why is it harder to turn when the lamp is lighted?

20 How to make a pin and cork motor

The armature of this motor is made by winding a coil of thin insulated wire in a groove cut into a cork with a razor blade.

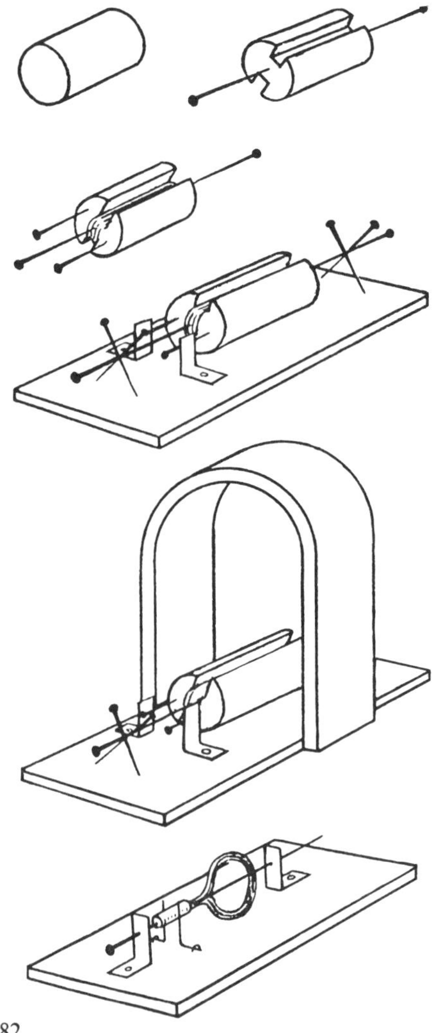

Two pins, one stuck in each end, act as an axle. The ends of the wire (bared) are wrapped round two more pins which serve as terminals through which the current enters and leaves the coil. Strips of thin tin or copper foil are used as brushes, being held to the baseboard by drawing pins.

A horseshoe magnet placed over this arrangement completes the model, which can be driven by a dry cell.

A midget armature can be made by using one pin and no cork. The wire is first wrapped round a pencil and tied into a loop with cotton. The ends are also secured with cotton to a piece of gummed paper rolled round the pin, which serves as commutator.

Small pieces of bent tin act as supports and fine wires lead the current to and from the commutator.

21 How to make an attraction motor

In this motor, a soft iron armature is attracted by an electromagnet. Continuous motion is secured by attaching a current breaker to the armature, so that the various segments of the motor are attracted in turn. The iron parts are 7 cm 'cut' nails; six are required for the armature, and one for the electromagnet.

To make the armature, cut three circles of cardboard 6 cm in diameter. In one of them, cut six equally spaced radial slots to fit the nails, and glue the other two circles to it,

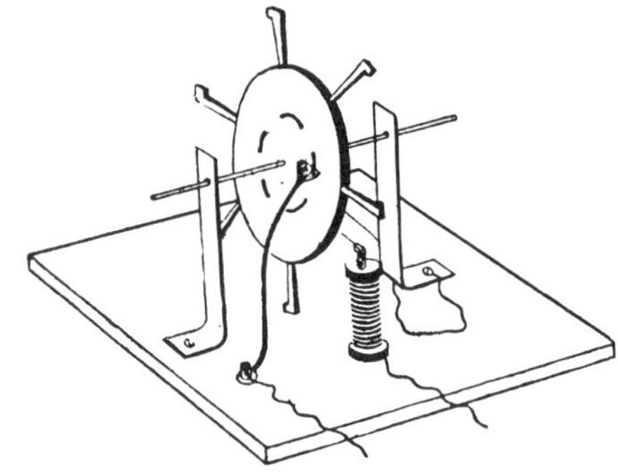

one on each side. Now mark a circle of 2 cm radius on the armature, and thread 18 gauge bare copper wire through 12 holes equally spaced round its circumference. This will provide six contacts which should be connected to the axle by winding the free end of the wire round it. A knitting needle is used for the axle.

To make the electromagnet, drive a nail through two cardboard disks or through two old tap washers, to act as end-pieces for the coil. Wind two layers of insulated bell wire on the nail and drive the completed electromagnet into a piece of wood which will serve as the baseboard.

Make the armature supports from two strips of tin cut from an ordinary can; punch holes for the axle and for fixing it to the base, using a pointed nail.

The method of assembly and the remaining details, including the bare wire to act as contact breaker, can be seen from the drawing.

If low voltage alternating current, say from a bell transformer, is available, the contact breaker can be dispensed with. The alternating current is then fed straight to the electromagnet, and after a little practice the armature can be spun at just the right speed to keep in step with the alternations of the current. This illustrates the action of the mains electric clock motor.

22 Another simple motor

This simple model will give you real satisfaction. It uses current from the battery to excite the field magnets as well as the armature coil.

Prepare a board 20 by 25.5 cm for the base. Drill a small hole through the centre and drive a 15.5 cm spike up through it. Wind 100 turns of insulated bell wire neatly onto two other 15 cm spikes, leaving about 30 cm for free ends. Drive these spikes into the base 15.5 cm apart. Drive two small nails on the diagonal and 5 cm from the spike at the centre. Strip the free ends of each coil and twist them several times around the nails and bend them so that they will rest in contact with the central spike. These ends will serve as brushes. Care must be taken to have the field coils wound in the proper direction. The diagram is a complete plan for the direction of windings. It will work in no other way. The other ends of the coils may be fastened to screws in the corners of the base.

Your field magnets and brushes, two of the four essential parts of a motor, are now complete. The armature coil and commutator remain to be constructed. Drill a hole crosswise through the top of a 4 cm cork and force a 13 cm spike through it. Wind about 40 turns of insulated bell wire on to each end, being sure the direction of windings is as shown. Scrape the free ends. Now gouge out the centre of the cork neatly; round with a penknife and insert the closed end of a 10.5 cm or 13 cm test tube. This completes the armature coil.

You are now ready to make the commutator. Cut out two rectangular pieces of sheet copper about 4 cm long, and wide enough

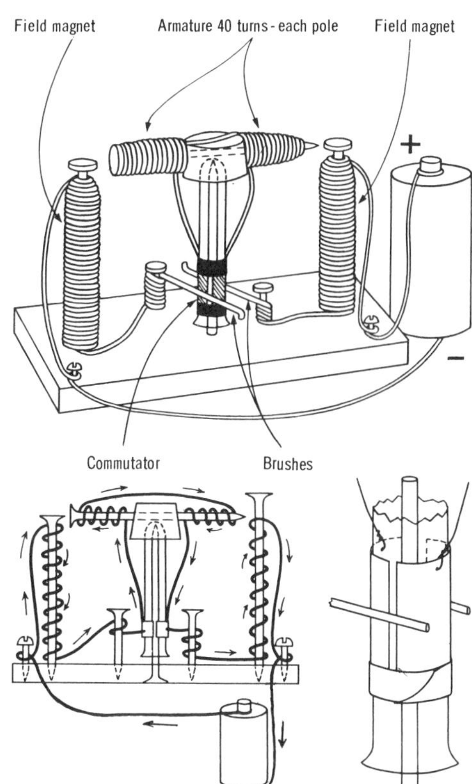

to reach around the test tube with about 6 mm space between. Curve these to fit the tube. Punch small holes and into each twist one of the scraped free ends of the armature windings. Then bind these commutator plates securely into position at top and bottom with adhesive tape.

Your rotor, consisting of armature and commutator, is now complete. Set it into position on the vertical bearing and bring the brushes into contact with the commutator. Now if your windings and connexions are all as shown, connect to one or two cells and with a slight push of the armature it should start off at a lively speed. If it does not go, examine the brushes to see whether they make a light, but certain contact. It may also help to change the angle of the brushes. To test this point, untwist the brushes from the nails and hold them lightly against the commutator plates with the fingers. While holding them, always parallel, swing them around at different angles while a helper turns the armature with his hand. Note the point at which the armature picks up most speed and set the brushes at that point. With a little patience you will be successful and will be well rewarded for your efforts in making this interesting and instructive toy.

D. HEAT AND LIGHT FROM ELECTRICAL ENERGY

1 How to get heat and light from electrical energy

See experiment B 25 of this chapter.

2 How to make a simple rheostat

In some of the experiments which follow, you will need to reduce the strength of the electric current.

This can be done by causing the current to flow through a poor conductor, called a resistance or rheostat, at some point in the circuit. There are several different kinds of rheostats possible. You will find it easier to use what is know as a water rheostat. Water is a poor conductor of electricity. Therefore, allowing a container of water to constitute one stretch of the path through which the current must travel will cut down the strength of the current. Pure water would conduct almost no current. A few grains of salt added to the water will make it sufficiently conducting to serve your purpose. Now, the farther the current has to flow through this salt water, the more its strength will be reduced. So, if you can arrange a scheme that will permit you to vary this distance at will, you will be able to increase or decrease the strength of current as needed.

A convenient way to set up such a rheostat is illustrated. Secure a Pyrex glass bake dish or an earthen tray about 25 or 30 cm across. (Caution: do not use a metal tray or container.)

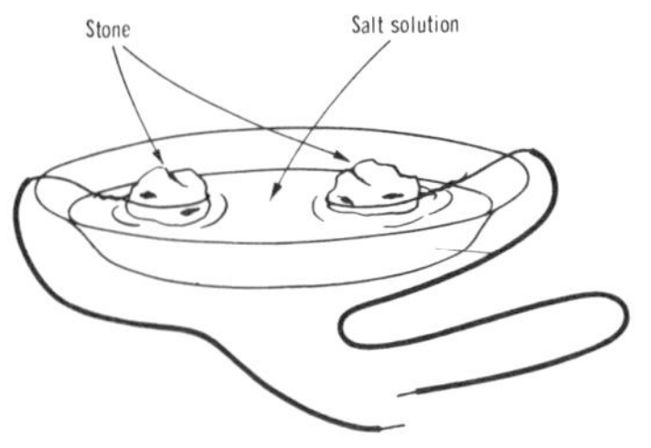

Secure two metal can covers of any kind about 8 cm in diameter. Punch a hole in the side of each and attach the clean ends of insulated wire for connectors. Set the covers into the dish a few centimetres apart and place in each a fair-sized cobble-stone to weight it down. Now dissolve a level teaspoonful of table salt in two litres of water. Pour enough of this into the bake dish to submerge the covers. Your water rheostat is now complete. You can connect it into any circuit and regulate the strength of current at will merely by changing the distance between the covers. Use insulating material for moving the covers, and do not put your hands into the water. Instead of the can covers, carbon rods may be used as shown in the second figure.

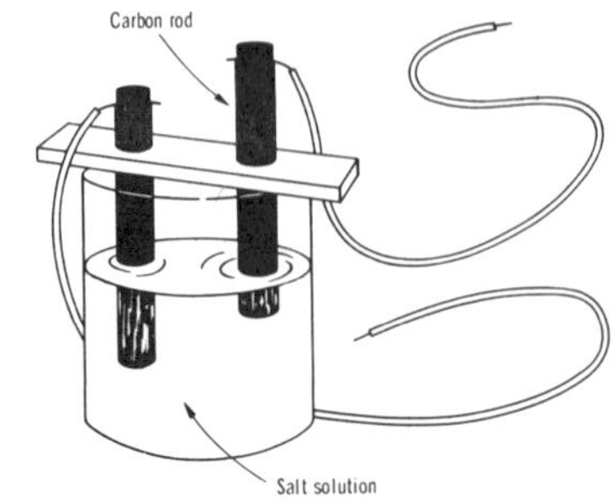

3 A resistance wire dimmer

A small rheostat for controlling model stage lighting or dimming electric torch bulbs can be made from 30 SWG bare nichrome wire. Wind about 100 turns around a pencil and anchor one end to two or three turns of thick copper wire which will serve as one terminal. Hold the other end of the resistance wire down by a strip of adhesive tape. Solder a piece of connecting wire to a midget spring clip and fit it over the resistance wire.

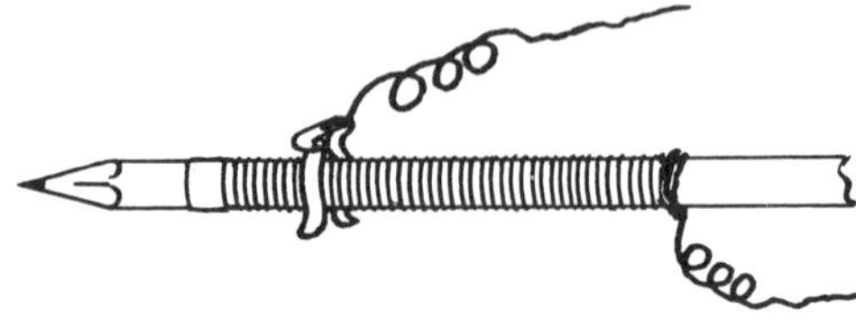

4 How to heat a wire red hot with electricity

This experiment will give you an opportunity to study how electricity will heat different kinds of wire. Build a wooden support with baseboard 15 by 15 cm and two vertical strips about 20 cm high. Drive a screw or nail part-way into the upper end of each support. Now to prepare a spiral-form element, wind about 1.5 metres of iron wire, size between No. 30 and 24, in one layer neatly onto a pencil. Slip this off and stretch it long enough to reach from nail to nail and twist the ends to support it. Connect this with a water rheostat and lamp socket (but be careful!). Be sure the rheostat is wide open before plugging into the socket. Then gradually reduce the resistance and notice how the wire gets hotter until it glows bright red. Hold your hand close to it. Touch a piece of paper or a splinter of wood to the wire and kindle it. Now increase the current until the wire burns or melts off.

Try to secure a piece of nichrome wire and use it instead of the iron. Nichrome wire is the kind that is used for electric heater elements. Can you get this much hotter than the others before it burns apart?

Does this experiment suggest a way to make an electric heater?

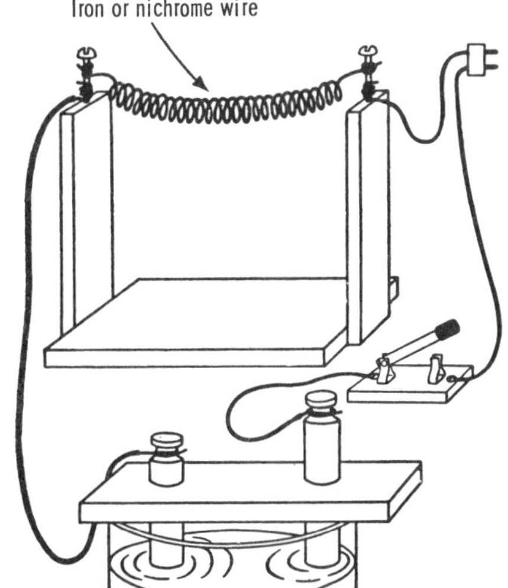

5 How to make an electric arc heater

The electric arc is not only the brightest light known but also almost the most intense source of heat known to man. The brightest point at the end of the carbon rod gets as hot as 3760 degrees Centigrade! Boiling water is 100 degrees Centigrade. Iron melts at 1535 degrees Centigrade.

You certainly will not want to miss the opportunity of making an electric arc heater or furnace, especially when it requires only a small plant jar, two carbons from discarded flashlight batteries, two pieces of hollow curtain rod and some bits of wood.

Secure an ordinary 8 cm unglazed plant jar. Drill two holes directly opposite each other and a bit more than 2.5 cm from the bottom. If you do not have a drill, you can work a hole through with the end of a triangular file in your hand, or with almost any sharp-pointed metal object. When you get the holes broken through, ream them large enough with the file or other appropriate object to allow the carbon rods to slip thr(Now cut off two pieces of hollow about 12 cm long. If you have no b of cutting metal, this thin metal can be cut easily by filing a groove all the way around with a triangular file and then breaking it off. Insert the carbon rods into the ends of the metal tubes, and you have all the essential parts of your furnace complete.

You now need a rack to support these parts. Nail two vertical strips of wood about 15 cm long to a baseboard about 15 by 15 cm. Place half a brick or even a small piece of flat stone onto the baseboard and put the prepared plant jar onto this. It will improve your heater to cement the brick to the base, and the jar to the brick, with black asbestos furnace cement. Obtain this from the hardware store or the plumbing shop. Just smear a bit of the cement onto the bottom and press the jar into place. Determine the height at which the holes shall be drilled in the vertical wooden supports in order to have the rods project through them and into the jar so that both will be in horizontal alignment. Bore the holes large enough to allow the metal tubes to slide easily. This done, insert the rods, and your furnace is ready to go.

Connect the furnace into the circuit with water rheostat and lamp socket as shown in the diagram. Establish the arc as described in D 7 below. (Caution: Do not take hold of the rods unless you have their ends covered with tape, or keep gloves on your hands.) It is advisable to wear dark glasses when using your furnace.

6 How to make an electric toaster

Your problem is to find a convenient way to mount 5 metres (no less!) of nichrome wire in a space not much larger than a slice of bread. Nichrome wire is the kind of wire used in all electric heating devices you ordinarily buy for home use. The wire can be obtained at the electric repair shop. You should use No. 24 gauge wire (0.559 mm diameter) for 110 volts. For other voltages, ask the electrician to tell you the length and gauge of wire for a 500-watt element.

The method of winding the wire into a spiral is shown in the figures. Measure off the wire and wind it neatly onto a round rod about 5 mm in diameter. Keep the turns pushed over into close contact each time you wind on a few. This keeps them regular. You should of course leave about 10 or 12 cm at each end. Now slip the coil off the rod and slowly draw it out far enough so that it will remain in the form of a spiral about 75 cm long. Now twist about 10 cm of copper wire tightly on to each end of the element close to where it begins to spiral to serve as lead-in wires.

To prepare your mount for the element, secure a 30 cm square of asbestos board from the lumber dealer. Cut out one piece 15 by 20 cm for the base and cut four strips 2.5 by 15 cm each for the sides. Put these together as shown. They may be put together by drilling holes and using small screws or by using furnace cement. Asbestos furnace cement is excellent. It may be obtained at the hardware store or plumbing shop. Now cut a piece of board to fit the base; with two narrow strips of asbestos board to furnish air space, attach the frame to the board.

You are now ready to instal your element. At the front end drill four small holes equally spaced and three holes equally spaced at the opposite end. Turn small screws about 2.5 cm long partly into the holes. Drill two holes through the front of the frame for the copper lead-in wires. Also set two screws into the front corners of the base for terminals. Now loop your element back and forth onto the screws. Plan this part so there will be equal amounts of the element in each segment. Set each segment into a thread of its screw support so that they will all be supported about 5 mm above the base. Bring the copper lead-ins through the holes prepared for them and twist them around the terminals. This completes your toaster, except for a grill to hold the toast. Cut out a square piece of wire screen with a 1 cm mesh for this or use some small grill from the kitchen. Make sure that the grill can never touch the element or the terminals.

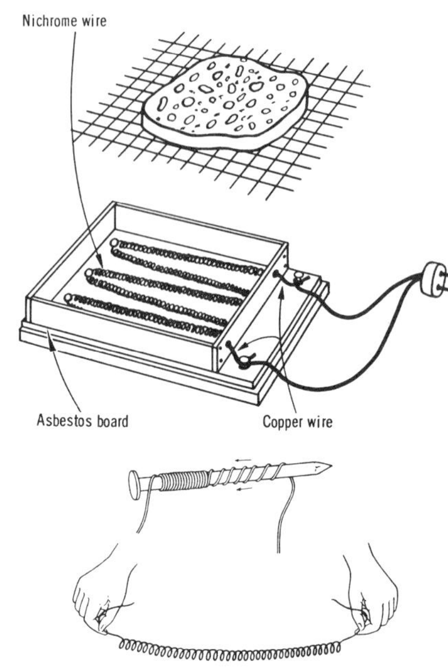

For a connecting cord you may be able to find a broken flat iron cord. Strip the ends of the wires and twist them around the terminals. Plug the other end of the cord into a lamp socket or baseboard receptacle and proceed to toast bread and cook or heat any food you desire. (Caution: Keep pupils' fingers well away from the exposed wires. Take out the plug if any water is spilled onto the toaster.)

7 How to make an arc lamp

Use the carbons from two discarded flashlight batteries to serve as the electrodes. Connect the carbons, salt water rheostat, and an ordinary double wire electric lead. An old flat-iron cord with some of the outer fabric stripped off the lower end is good for the purpose. Set the rheostat plates wide apart and plug into the socket.

Now pick up the carbons with clothes pegs, one in each hand, or if you wear dry heavy gloves you may hold them in the fingers. (Caution: Never pick up the carbon rods directly with the bare fingers. Why?) Touch the ends together lightly while someone else slowly reduces rheostat resistance. Never close the rheostat far enough to cause the metal covers to touch each other. Why?

Touch and then barely separate the carbon rods repeatedly while the rheostat is being closed. You should notice the ends heating to a glow and flashes of white light each time you separate them. (Caution: It is highly advisable to wear dark sun glasses when doing this part of the experiment.) At this stage supply just a little more current by closing the rheostat more, and you should have a steady and very brilliant light as you hold the rods steadily with about a 3 mm gap. Practice this until you succeed.

You have now been able to produce a very brilliant light with electricity. Does any of the carbon seem to be consumed? What carries the electricity across the gap? What do you think of this type of lamp as a means of lighting homes?

E. ELECTRICITY AND CHEMISTRY

In Chapter IX, experiment A 1, page 102, it was shown how water is decomposed when an electric current passes through it. This is just one example of a general phenomenon: many liquids are similarly affected by an electric current. The process is called electrolysis, and substances which behave in this way are called electrolytes. The effects are often complicated by interaction of the products of electrolysis with the electrodes by which the current is led into the electrolyte, but some of the principles can be studied in the following experiments.

1 Conduction effects in different types of liquids

Liquids can be divided into different chemical classes. The following can easily be studied: (a) distilled water, oils, methylated spirit; (b) acids and alkalis, e.g. dilute sulphuric acid, dilute hydrochloric sulphate and silver nitrate.

Obtain two small carbon rods from an old torch battery and pass them through holes about 2.5 cm apart in a strip of wood 2.5 cm wide and 10 cm long. Solder copper wires to the brass caps and join up a series circuit as shown in the diagram, using a 6 volt dry battery as current supply and a 2.5 volt bulb as current detector.

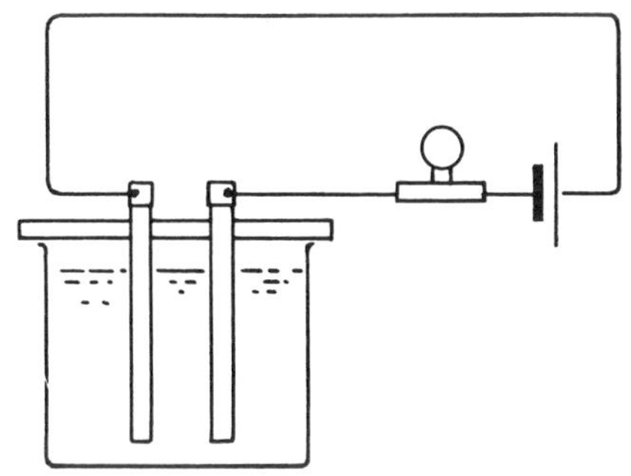

Put the liquid under test in a small jar and immerse the rods. You will find that some of the liquids do not conduct electricity, gases are released from others, and that in some cases changes take place on the surfaces of the rods.

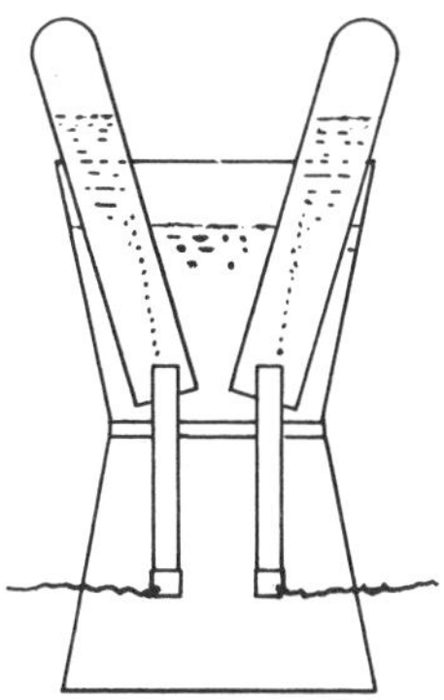

2 Collecting the gaseous products of electrolysis

If the gases released by electrolysis are collected separately they can be identified. A simple apparatus for doing this, called a voltameter, can be constructed using an ice-cream carton as container for the liquid, carbon rods as electrodes, and small glass test tubes or tubular pill bottles for collecting the gases. Solder copper wires to the carbon rods as before, and fit them through the holes made with a cork borer in the bottom of two cartons; the second carton is used as a stand for the apparatus. Hold the two carton bottoms together, and using balsa wood or other cement, seal the rods in position with about 2.5 cm protruding into the upper cup. Pass connecting wires through holes in the side of the lower cup. Pour dilute hydrochloric acid into the upper cup and fill the glass tubes with it, inverting one over each carbon rod. Connect the wires to a 6-volt dry battery as before and wait for results. As chlorine is soluble, it is necessary to wait until the solution is saturated, but finally equal volumes of hydrogen and chlorine will be collected.

3 To make a bleaching solution by electrolysis

Make a strong solution of common salt by dissolving as much as possible in half a tumbler of water. Fit a cardboard wedge between the carbon rods of the voltameter used in the last experiment, thus dividing it into two equal compartments. Pour in the salt solution, and put a piece of red litmus paper in each compartment. Connect the rods to a grid bias battery, using 7.5 volts. Bubbles of *hydrogen* will immediately be released at the cathode (negative) but no chlorine will appear at the anode (positive) for the reason given in the last section. After about twenty minutes, however, the litmus paper in the anode compartment will be bleached, while in the cathode compartment the paper will turn blue owing to the formation of sodium hydroxide.

When bubbles of chlorine appear, stop the current, remove the wedge, and stir up the liquid. Sodium hypochlorite will then be produced. This is the compound contained in commercial bleaching fluids; examine its effect on a test tube of water coloured with a drop of ink.

4 To examine the electrolysis of special solutions: (a) zinc sulphate; (b) lead acetate

(a) Pour a weak solution of zinc sulphate into the voltameter and electrolyse it, using a 9-volt grid bias battery. Almost immediately a spongy mass of zinc appears on the cathode.

(b) Add a few grams of lead acetate to half a tumbler of water. To remove cloudiness, stir the solution with a glass rod which has been dipped in acetic acid. Pour the liquid into the voltameter and connect to a battery as before. Lead quickly deposits on the cathode in the form of a 'tree' which is fascinating to watch as it grows.

5 To study the action of a simple lead accumulator

From a sheet of lead about 1.5 mm thick cut strips 15 cm long and about 15 mm wide for use as plates of the cell. Punch holes near the end of each plate and thread through copper connecting wires. Wash the plates in water and clean them with steel wool or emery cloth. Put them into a boiling tube containing a little dilute sulphuric acid and separate them by a wooden splint. Also bend over the tops of the plates so that they can never touch one other. First transform these plates into spongy lead and lead peroxide respectively by passing current from a 6-volt dry battery. After a few minutes one of the plates becomes a red-brown colour, whilst the other remains grey. When this has happened disconnect the battery and connect in its place a 2 volt torch bulb. If the bulb does not light, join the plates to the battery again for a few more minutes and then carry out the test.

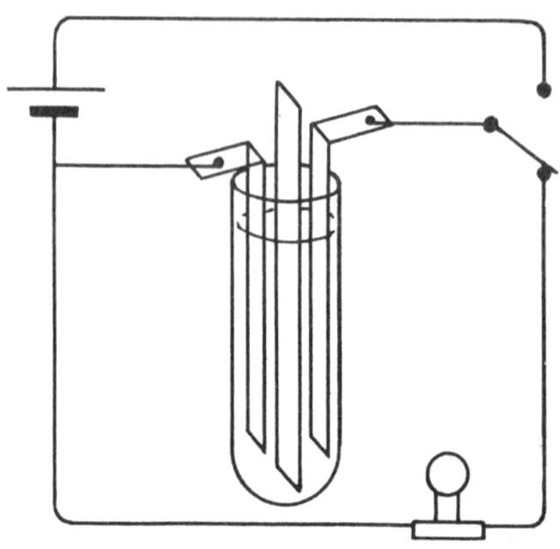

Now arrange a circuit as shown so that the plates can be charged and discharged through the bulb at the turn of a switch. Connect the battery for one minute, then discharge through the bulb, noticing the time in seconds that the bulb remains alight. Repeat this experiment, charging in turn for 2, 3, and 4 minutes and recording the time taken to discharge through the bulb.

As a further test take a few more readings with the plates half immersed in acid. Put a thermometer in the acid and notice if there is any change in temperature after charging for some time. If facilities are available, try to detect any change in the density of the acid after charging for half an hour.

6 How to make a more serviceable accumulator

The preceding way of forming the plates is only suitable for demonstration purposes.

To make a working accumulator, larger and thicker plates must be used, and chemicals must be embedded in holes drilled in the plates.

Use lead sheet about 5 mm thick—old gas or water pipe hammered out will do. Prepare plates of the dimensions shown, with holes drilled in them, and fill up the holes with the following pastes:

Positive plate	*Negative plate*
1 part litharge.	6 parts litharge.
4 parts red lead.	1 part sulphuric acid.
1 part sulphuric acid.	

Separators of wood, about 5 mm thick, the same as before but with holes drilled in them, will be required.

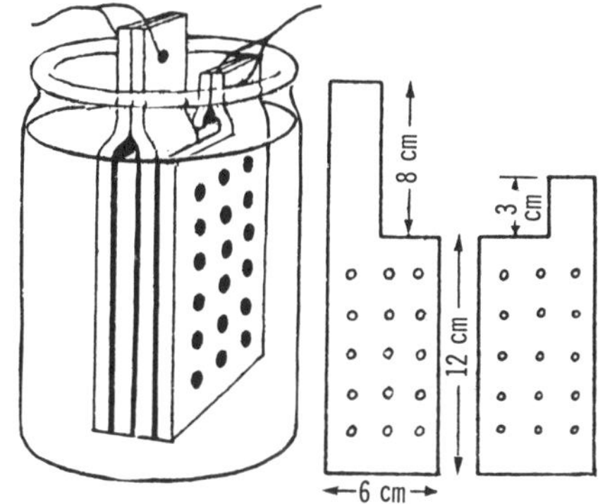

Assemble the plates by fastening the two negative plates together and holding in the separators, etc., by a rubber band, or a piece of string. Insert the whole into a jam jar filled with dilute sulphuric acid (S.G. 1.5), so as to just cover the plates.

The cell should be charged as before. When charged, the positive plate will be a red-chocolate colour, and the negative plate a light grey.

7 Electro-plating nickel and copper

Electro-plating is now familiar to everyone. It is done by forming a layer of metal on the object which is used as a cathode in a voltameter containing a salt of the metal to be deposited. To get lasting results the object must be carefully cleaned and degreased; the correct anode must be used, and the solution must be carefully prepared and used at a temperature of about 5° C. The copper anode used for copper plating and the nickel anode for nickel plating need only be degreased. The following baths have proved satisfactory.

Copper		*Nickel*	
Cupric sulphate	200 g	Nickel sulphate	240 g
Sulphuric acid	60 g	Nickel chloride	54 g
Water up to	1000 ml	Boric acid	30 g
		Water up to	1000 ml

Copper plating. Pour the electrolyte into a jar and immerse in it a strip of copper which serves as an anode. Clean a sheet of brass with fine emery cloth, and degrease it with a mixture of magnesia and water on a wad of cotton wool. Rinse it in water, immerse it in the bath and connect it to the negative terminal of a 3-volt torch battery. Complete the circuit by joining the anode to the positive pole of the battery. Note the deposit of copper produced. Too heavy a current may result in a spongy deposit; the correct value for a hard deposit is 4 amperes per 100 cm² of area.

Nickel plating. Use a strip of copper as a cathode, cleaning and degreasing it as before. A nickel spatula can be used as an anode, but if this is not available a strip of lead may be used; this will mean that the electrolyte becomes weaker during use. Join up to the battery as before, when a good deposit of nickel will be obtained. The surface, after washing, can be polished using jewellers' rouge or cigarette ash on a piece of soft cloth.

8 To copy a scout badge or medal by electrolysis

This process, called electrotyping, is much used in industry. A mould is made of the object to be copied. This is then made conductive by various methods and a shell of this impression is made by depositing copper on it electrolytically. The object is removed from the mould, and the copy is strengthened by pouring typemetal into it.

First warm the badge in a clean bunsen flame and make an impression on the end of a short piece of candle or alkathine rod. Make the surface of the mould conducting by scraping some lead from a pencil over it, or by coating it with colloidal graphite. Another way to do this is to scatter some iron filings over it after moistening it with copper sulphate; the copper will displace the iron and cover the surface of the mould with a layer of copper. Now heat a piece of copper wire and press it into the wax in such a way that connexion is made to the conducting surface without disfiguring the shape. Use the wire to hang the mould in a copper-plating bath. Also suspend a strip of copper in the

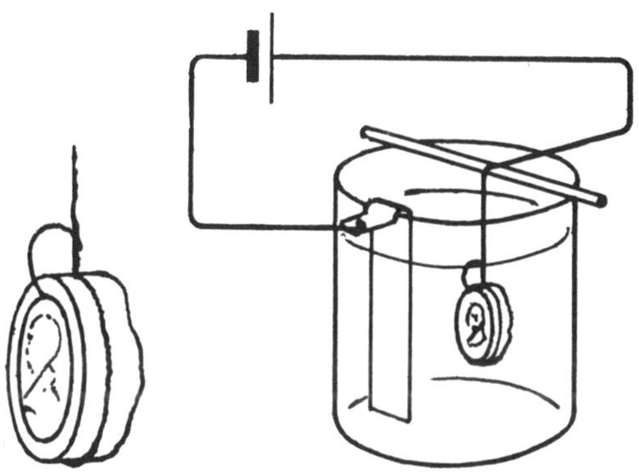

solution to serve as an anode, facing the mould. Connect to a 3-volt torch battery through a small rheostat and leave it overnight. The next day a good strong layer of copper will have been deposited. Strip this from the mould, and if necessary strengthen it by pouring molten solder into the back of the shell. Trim the badge with a pocket knife and solder a safety pin to the back. If desired it can now be plated as in the last experiment.

CHAPTER XVI

Experiments and materials for the study of light

A. LIGHT TRAVELS IN A STRAIGHT LINE

1 Making tracks

Find a dusty road or a sandy beach. Fix your yes on a distant object and walk towards t without changing your line of vision. Now observe the tracks you have made, and you will see that you have been following a straight ine.

2 With a string

Obtain a piece of string that is at least 25 metres in length. Fasten one end of the string to a post or a tree. Pull the string taut and hold it to the eye. Look along the string, and you will see the object to which it is fastened. Now look in another direction, not along the string, and you do not see the object. This shows that light comes to the eye from such objects in a straight line.

3 An experiment with cards

Cut four pieces of cardboard about 10 cm square. Tack them to small wood blocks so hat they will stand upright. Punch a small hole through each card at exactly the same place so that when the cards are set up and arranged in a straight line you can look straight through all four holes. Place a candle flame so that it can be seen by looking through all the cards spaced about 30 cm apart. Now pull one of the cards a little out of line with he others and try to look through them at he candle flame. Can you see it? Why not? What does this show?

4 A pinhole camera

A simple pinhole camera can be made by making a fine hole in the bottom of a tin and receiving the image on tissue paper, stretched across the top of the tin. Roll a sheet of brown paper round the tin so that a tube projects and shields the tissue paper. This will keep daylight from the screen, and enable an image of a window or candle flame to be observed. What do you notice about the image? How does this show that light travels in straight lines?

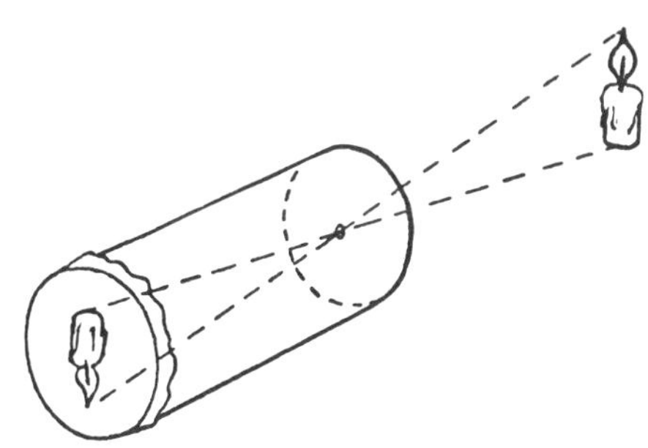

5 Making a smoke box to study light rays

Obtain or construct a wooden box about 30 cm wide and about 60 cm in length. Fit panes of window glass in the top and front of the box. Leave the back open, as shown in the diagram, and cover with loosely hung black cloth which drapes like a curtain. Hang this curtain in two sections making about a 10 cm overlap at the centre of the box. Paint the inside of the box with matt black paint. About midway between the top and bottom of one end and about 8 or 10 cm from the glass front, cut a window 10 cm long and 5 cm wide. This is to let in light rays. You can cover the window with different kinds of openings cut from cardboard and fastened with drawing pins.

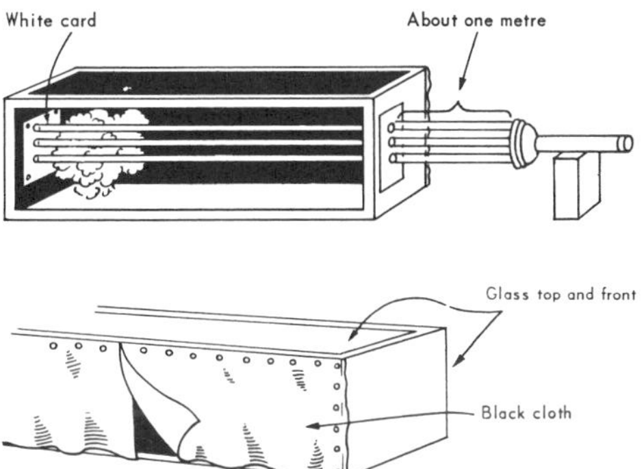

For the first experiment cut a piece of black cardboard with three equidistant holes about 5 mm in diameter. Fix over the window with drawing pins. Fill your box with smoke. This can be done with dry rotten wood, incense candles or smouldering cigarettes placed in a dish and set in one corner of the box. Next set up an electric torch about one metre from the window. Focus the light down to a parallel beam and direct it at the holes in the window. Observe the light rays in the box made visible by the smoke. Does this experiment show that light travels in straight lines?

B. THE REFLECTION OF LIGHT

1 Regular reflection with the smoke box

Fill the smoke box with smoke. Shine the torch beam on the three holes in the window as in the last experiment. Now hold a plane mirror inside the box and observe how clearly the rays are still defined after reflection from the mirror. When light rays are thus reflected without scattering they are said to be *regularly reflected.*

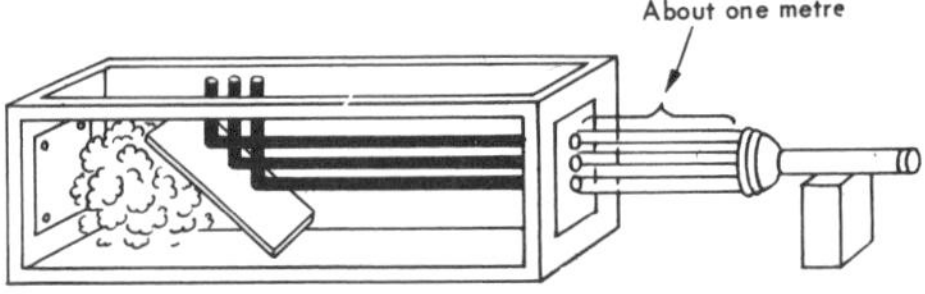

2 Diffuse reflection with the smoke box

Place a piece of clear cellophane on a pane of glass and roughen it by rubbing with a piece of steel wool until the surface has a uniformly dull appearance. Fix the piece of dulled cellophane to the glass with glue or rubber bands. Hold in the beam of the torch inside the smoke box and observe the results.

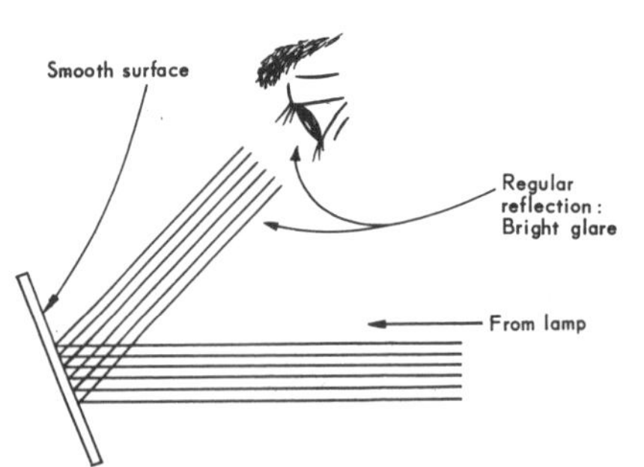

Compare with the regular reflection in the previous experiment. When light is scattered by reflection from an irregular surface it is called *diffuse* reflection. Place your eye in direct line with the reflected beam from a mirror. Repeat, using the dulled cellophane reflector. Observe and describe the differences.

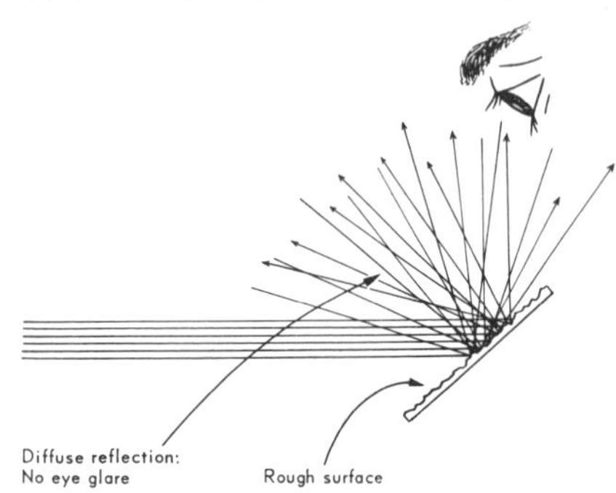

3 Reflection with a rubber ball

Study reflection from a floor or wall by bouncing a rubber ball straight and at angles to the reflecting surface. Try to observe and compare the angle at which the ball strikes the surface with the angle at which it is reflected.

4 Reflection with a mirror

Place a plane mirror on the floor where a beam of sunlight will strike it and be reflected. Stand a drinking straw upright at the place where the beam strikes the mirror. Compare the angle made by the incident beam and the straw with the angle made by the reflected beam and the straw.

5 Making reflected beams of light

Hold a comb in a sunbeam falling on a piece of white cardboard. Tilt the cardboard so that

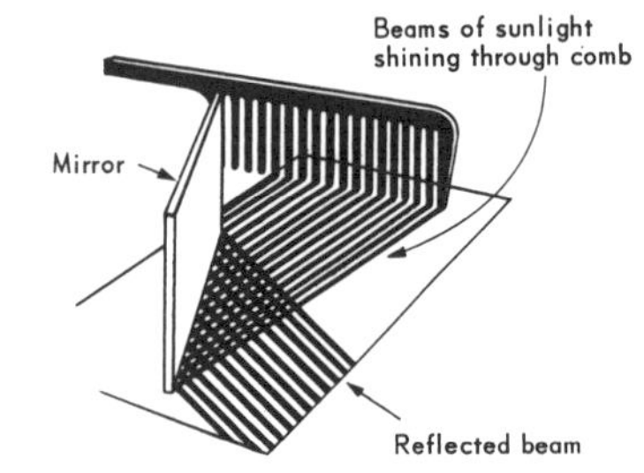

the beams of light are several centimetres long. Place a mirror diagonally in the path. Observe that the beams which strike the mirror are reflected at the same angle. Turn the mirror and observe how the reflected beams turn.

6 How to make a sighting stool for the study of reflected light

Though 'pin optics' are rather out of fashion at the moment, this method is capable of yielding accurate results. Confusion often arises with juniors because pins are used both as object and to track rays of light. This confusion is avoided if sighting stools are used in the first experiments. A piece of tin, 12 by 1.5 cm, is bent in the form of a stool; the ends form legs and a slit is cut with a hacksaw blade in each of them. A pin is used as object, and its image is sighted through the slits. Pencil marks are then made to track down the path of the light.

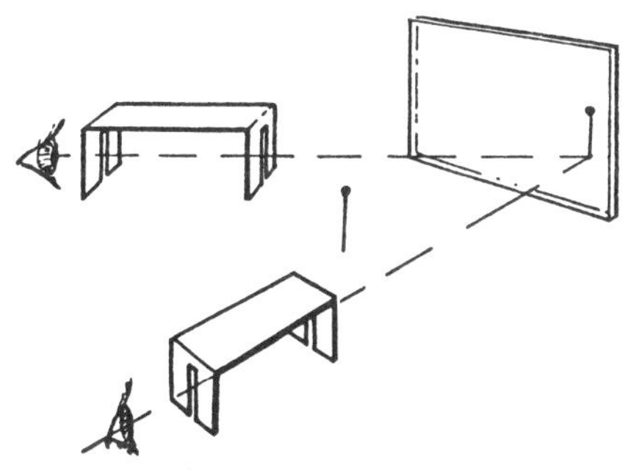

7 The laws of reflection

Draw a broken line on a piece of paper with a ruler. Next draw a straight line from it at any angle. Set a small mirror upright at the point where the two lines meet. Turn the mirror until the reflection of the dotted line is in line with the real dotted line. Now look into the mirror and line up one edge of your ruler with the reflection of the straight line. Draw this line with your pencil and measure the angles on each side of the broken line with a protractor.

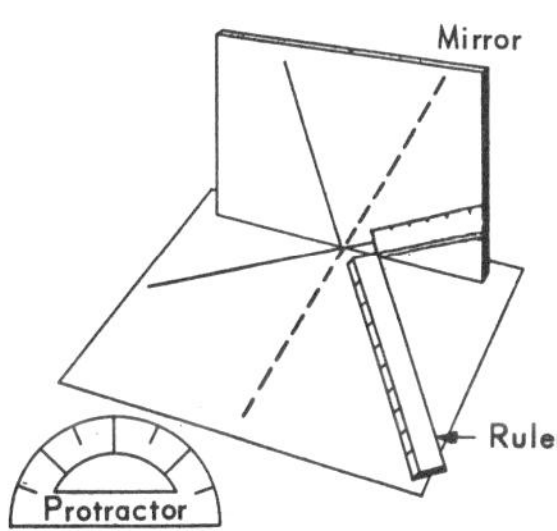

Repeat this experiment several times, changing the size of the angle each time. The evidence should show that light is always reflected at the angle at which it strikes the mirror.

8 How to make a cylindrical lens for a ray box

File down the edges of a piece of perspex or lucite 5 by 3 by 6 cm. Grind it by using the inside of a can with a layer of emery paper glued inside.

Final polishing is done with metal polish and cotton wool.

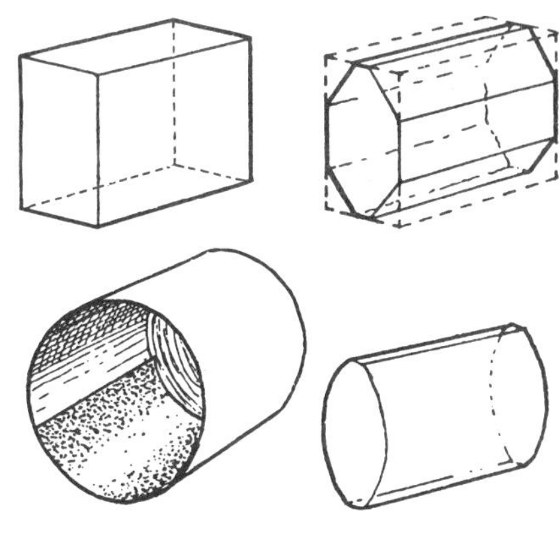

9 How to make a ray box for beams of light

The cylindrical lens described in experiment B 8 above can be used in a ray box. This apparatus consists of two sides of an oblong box 22 by 6 cm held together in this case by 2 BA rod, with the lens placed at one end of the box. The box has no bottom, and in use rests on paper pinned to a drawing board. The light source is a 12-volt 24-watt automobile lamp. The lampholder has a sleeve of brass tubing just fitting in a hole in a wooden slide, which forms the top of the box. The groove in front of the lens is for screens and filters. A piece of card with a slit in it provides narrow rays and a painter's graining comb will give a bundle of rays. Convergent, parallel or divergent beams are obtained by adjusting the position of the slider. All the usual experiments with rays can be performed using slips of plane mirror, glass blocks and prisms. A curved piece of tin will show a caustic curve.

In experiments with lenses and in refraction, the lamp should be pushed down as far as possible so that the light does not pass over the top of the obstacle. A card with a hole and cross wires can be used in front of the lens, as a source for optical bench experiments.

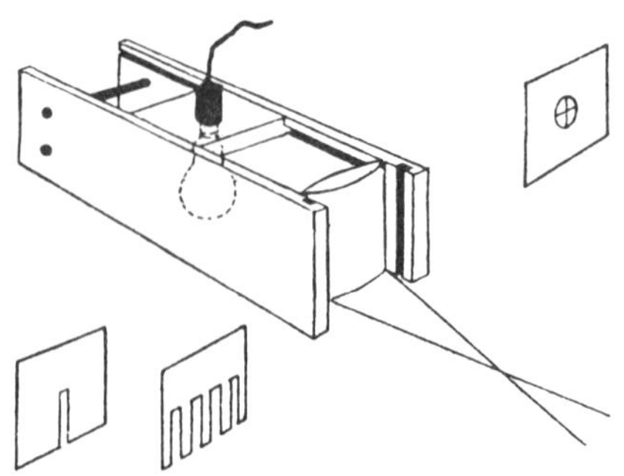

10 Laws of reflection with a ray box

A slip of mirror can be made to stand vertical by inserting one end in a piece of cork with a groove in it, or in a paperclip. Beams of light shone along the paper are marked by crosses. The incident, and reflected rays, and the normal, are recorded by joining up the crosses by pencil lines.

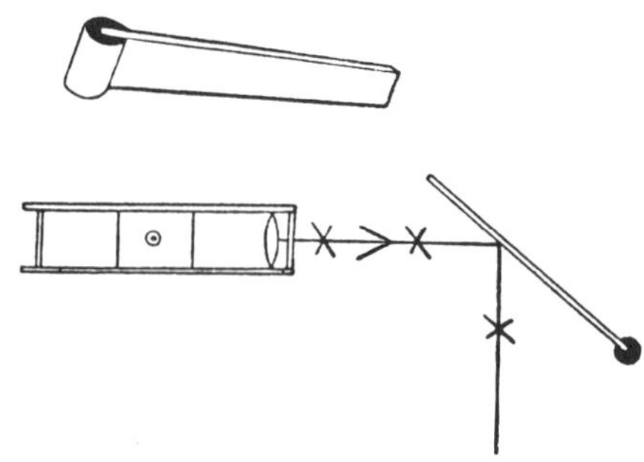

11 A simple optical disc

Obtain a shallow can of roughly the same diameter as an ordinary protractor. Cut out a piece of white card to put on the top of the can: glue it down and mark degrees on it. Fix a strip of mirror to a small block of wood and mount it on a nail which fits loosely through a hole in the centre of the scale and the can. Cut a narrow slit in a rectangular sheet of metal as shown in the diagram, and bend the sheet round the circumference of the can, fixing it in position so that the slit is opposite the 90° mark on the circular scale. Place the can on the bench so that the sun or a distant source of light throws a ray which passes through the slit to the centre of the scale. Adjust the mirror so that the light is reflected along its own path. Now rotate the mirror through 10°. What do you notice about the angle through which the reflected ray is turned?

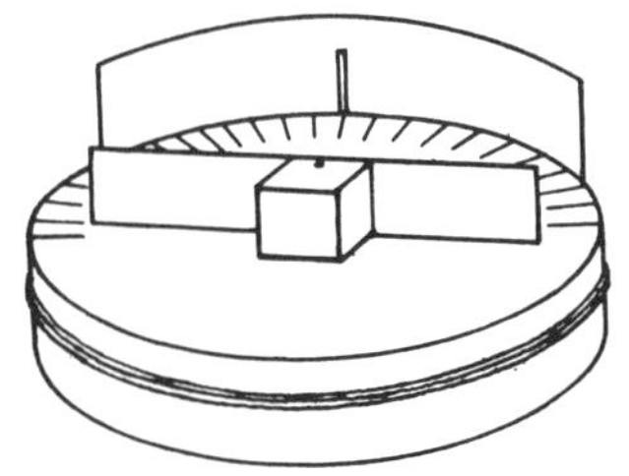

12 A mirror on a stick

Fasten a mirror to the end of a ruler with a paperclip. Stand on one side of a door and hold the mirror outside the door opening. Explain how reflected light enables you to see around the corner.

13 How to make a model periscope

Score three lines parallel to the long side of a postcard and 2 cm apart. These will divide the card into four strips. Cut away pieces from the ends 2 cm wide as shown in the diagram. Cut holes in the positions shown, using a cork borer, and then fold up the card into a rectangular box. Stick small pieces of mirror opposite the apertures, using plasticine or gummed paper.

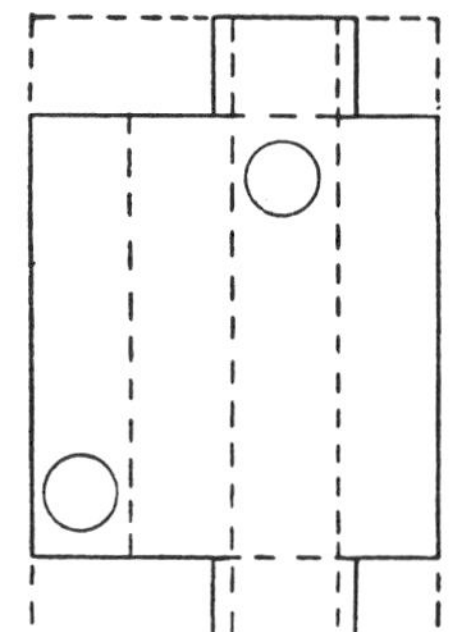

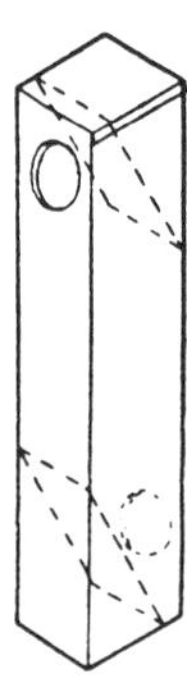

14 How to make a kaleidoscope

Fasten together two slips of mirror about 10 cm by 3 cm and a piece of card the same size, with a rubber band or gummed paper. Look down the axis of the triangular prism so formed. Objects viewed through it will form a regular pattern. If silvered glass is not available, black paint on the outer side of plain glass will give quite good results.

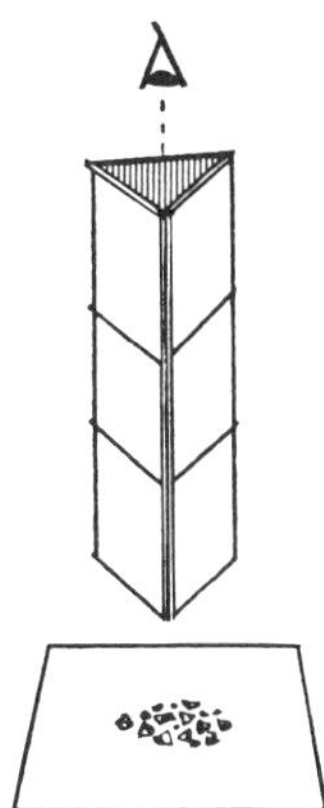

15 Double reflection

Cut a slit about 1 cm wide in one end of a small cardboard box. Be sure to cut the slit all the way to the bottom of the box. Set the box on one side and place it in bright sunlight. Adjust the box so that the beam of sunlight falls along the bottom of the box and place mirrors as shown in the diagram.

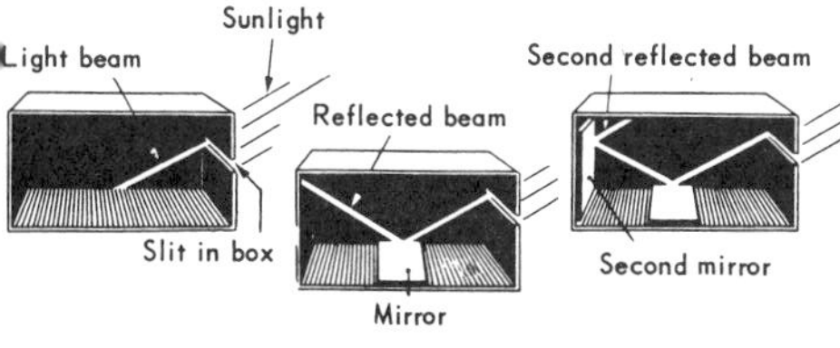

16 Reversed writing

Produce reversed writing by placing a piece of carbon paper, carbon side up, under a sheet of plain paper. Write something on the paper and you will have reversed writing on the other side. Read the reversed writing by holding it in front of a mirror. Write something while you look in the mirror at the paper and watch the pencil.

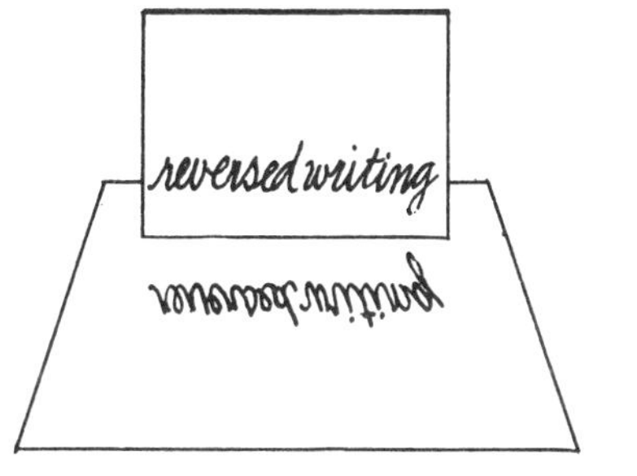

17 Copying drawings by reflection

Use a wooden clothes peg to support a sheet of clear glass vertically on the bench. Place the drawing to be copied on one side of the glass and a piece of white paper on the other. Look through the glass at the white paper and draw over the reflection of the drawing. Why must the glass be vertical? How does the copy differ from the original? Why is it an improvement to shield daylight from the paper you are drawing on?

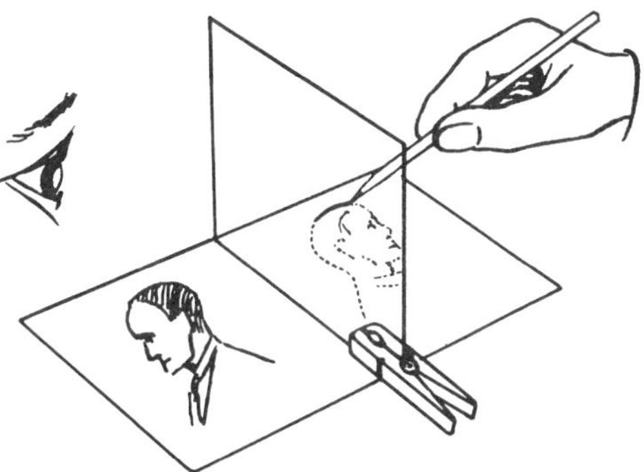

18 The clock face and a mirror

Stand two mirrors at right angles to each other with their edges touching. These edges may be joined with strips of tape. Place a clock in front of the mirror with the midline of its face opposite the junction of the two mirrors. Observe the image and compare with the image seen with a single mirror.

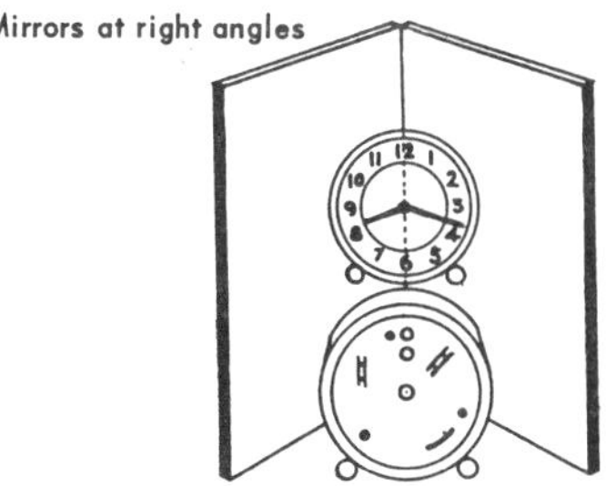

19 Making money with reflection

Hinge two mirrors together with a piece of tape and set them up as shown in the diagram.

Place a coin between the mirrors and observe the number of images formed. See if you can increase the number of images by varying the angle of the mirrors. Place a lighted candle between the mirrors and observe the images.

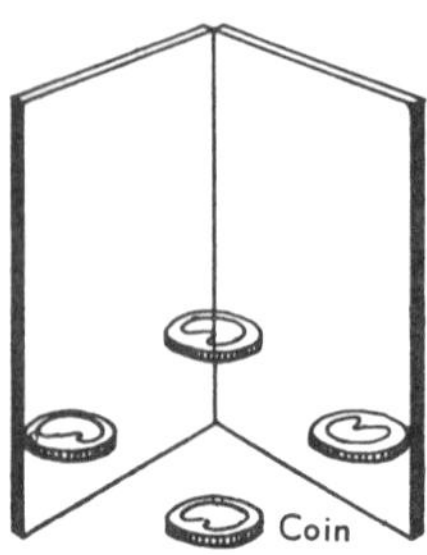

20 Reflection with parallel mirrors

Stand two mirrors on edge with the reflecting surfaces facing each other. Place a coin or a lighted candle between the mirrors. Look in one mirror and see how many images are formed. Look in the other mirror.

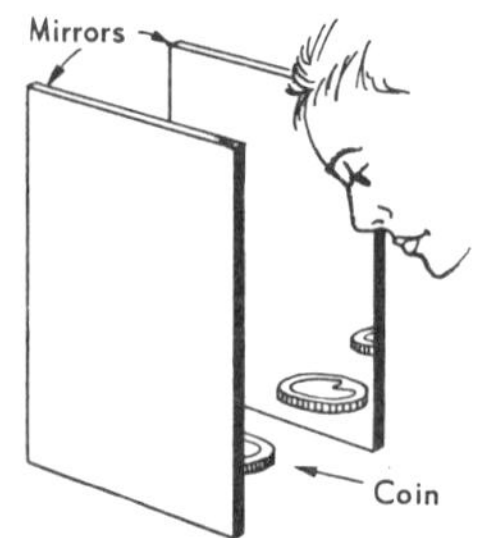

21 Reflection from a concave mirror with a ray box

Use the ray box constructed in experiment B 9 above. The focal length can be measured directly by directing a parallel beam of light on to a curved strip of tin, or a part of a metal ring.

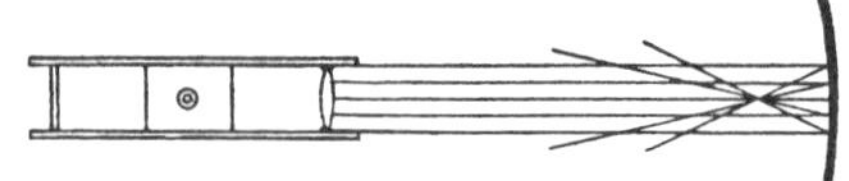

22 Reflection from a convex surface

Obtain a convex mirror such as an automobile wing mirror. Use this with the ray box and observe the reflected rays of light. Compare with the reflection from a plane mirror and a concave mirror.

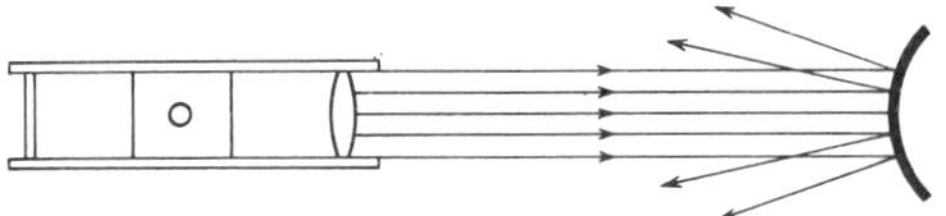

C. THE REFRACTION OF LIGHT AND ITS USES

1 The stick appears to bend

Place a stick in a tall jar of water, so that part of the stick is above the surface. Observe where the stick enters the water and appears to be bent. This is caused by the bending or refracting of the light rays as they reach the air from the water. Light travels faster in air than in water and so is bent slightly when it passes from one medium to the other.

2 Refraction in a beam of light

Pour a few drops of milk into a glass of water in order to cloud the water. Punch a small hole in a piece of dark paper or cardboard. Place the glass in direct sunlight. Hold the card in front of the glass. A beam of sunlight will shine through the hole. Hold the

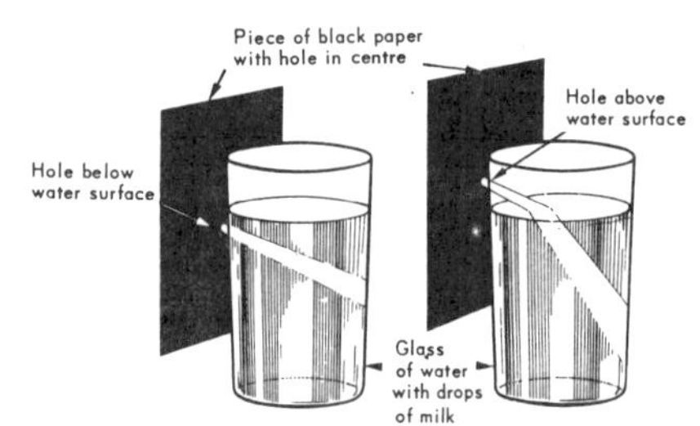

card so that the hole is just below the water level and observe the direction of the beam in the water. Now raise the card until the beam strikes the surface. Observe the direction of the beam of light. Experiment to find out how the angle at which the beam strikes the water affects the direction of the beam in the water.

3 How to make a refraction bottle

Paint the outside of a medicine bottle black. Scratch a circle off one side and fill the bottle with water until the surface is just level with the centre of this circle. Shine a beam of light through the top of the bottle (the paint should be removed from a small area). A drop of milk in the water will make the beam show up better. The angles of incidence and refraction are now measured with a protractor.

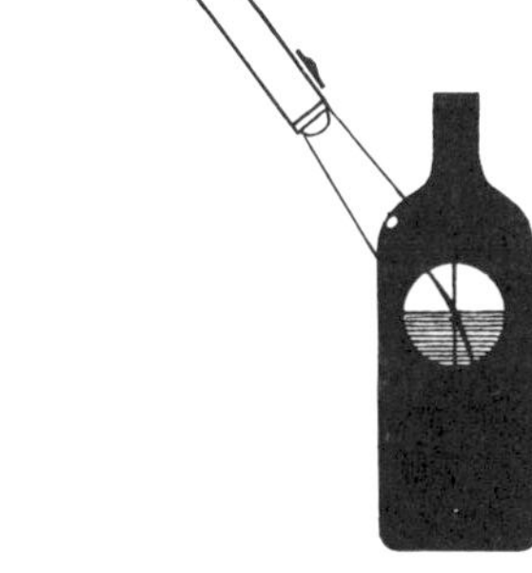

4 Refraction shown with the smoke box

Over the window of the smoke box (see experiment A 5 above) fasten a piece of black cardboard with a single hole in it about 8 mm square. Arrange the torch to shine a beam of light into the box as in previous experiments. Fill a large rectangular bottle with water and add a few drops of milk or a pinch of starch or flour to make the water cloudy. Cork the bottle. Fill the box with smoke. Hold the bottle at right angles to the beam of light and observe the direction of the light through the water. Next tilt the bottle at different angles to the beam of light and observe how the path of light through the bottle is affected.

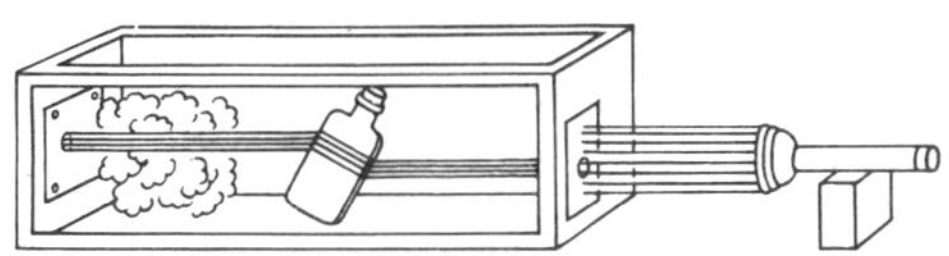

5 Making a coin appear with refraction

Place a coin in the bottom of a teacup on a table. Stand away and arrange your line of vision so that the edge of the cup just interferes with your seeing the coin in the bottom. Hold this position while another person pours water carefully into the cup. What do you observe? How do you account for this?

6 How a prism affects light rays

Use the smoke box exactly as you did for experiment C 4 above. Hold a glass prism in the single beam of light and observe how the beam is refracted.

7 How lenses affect light rays

For these experiments, you can take the lenses from an old pair of spectacles or used optical instruments, or purchase reading glass lenses and hand magnifiers.

Cover the window of the smoke box with a piece of black cardboard in which you have punched three holes. The holes should be the same distance apart, but the distance between the two outside holes should be a little less than the diameter of your lens. Arrange the torch to supply the light rays as in previous experiments. Fill the box with smoke and hold a double convex lens in the path of the three beams of light so that the middle beam strikes the centre of the lens. Observe the beams on the opposite side of the lens from the source of light. How are they affected?

Repeat the experiment using a double concave lens. Compare the observations made in this experiment with those made in experiment C 6 above. Think of the double convex lens as made up of two prisms put together base to base and the double concave lens as two prisms put together tip to tip.

8 Rough lenses from bottle bottoms

Bottles can be found with convex or concave bottoms. These can be cut off by any of the methods indicated (page 218) and the rough edges removed by rubbing on a stone surface. Whilst rarely good enough to provide a clear image, they can be used to illustrate how bush fires may be started by old bottles lying in dry grass, etc., and focusing the sun's rays.

9 How lenses magnify

Dip a pencil (or your finger) into a glass of water, and look at it from the side. Is it magnified? Observe a fish in a fish bowl, looking at it from the top and from the side. Do the bowl and the water magnify the fish? Observe olives or other things placed in circular jars. Are they magnified? Clear glass marbles act as lenses also.

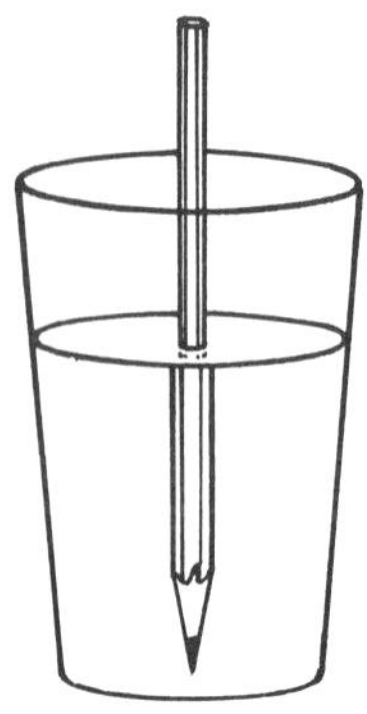

10 How to measure the magnifying power of a lens

Focus a hand lens over some lined paper. Compare the number of spaces seen outside

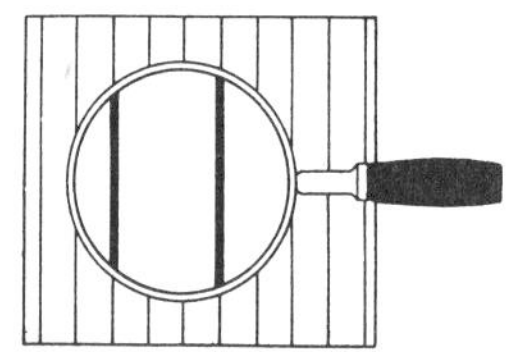

the lens with a single space seen through the lens. The lens shown in the diagram magnifies three times.

11 How a convex lens forms a picture image

Darken all the windows in a room but one. Have a pupil hold a lens in the window directed at the scene outside. Bring a piece of white paper slowly near the lens until the image picture is formed. What do you observe about the position of the image?

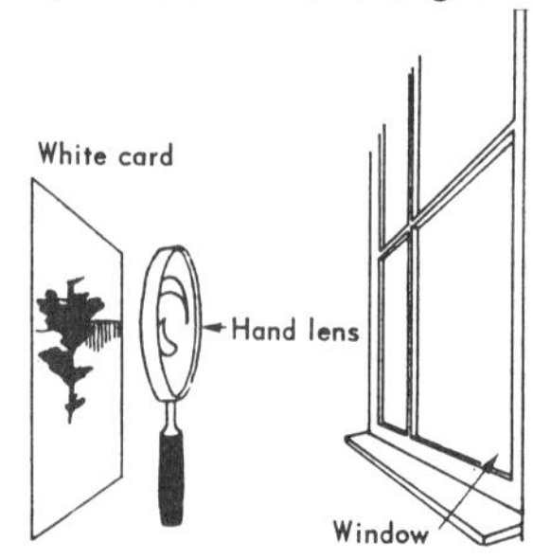

12 How to make a simple apparatus to study lenses

All that is needed for an optical bench is a firm surface, a way of holding mirrors and lenses, and a convenient way of measuring distances.

A metre scale laid flat on the bench serves as the basis of this simple apparatus. Wooden blocks, with grooves that just fit over the scale, can be adapted as holders. A layer of cork or soft cardboard glued on the top makes it easy to stick pins, such as object and search pins, into each block; strips of tin screwed to

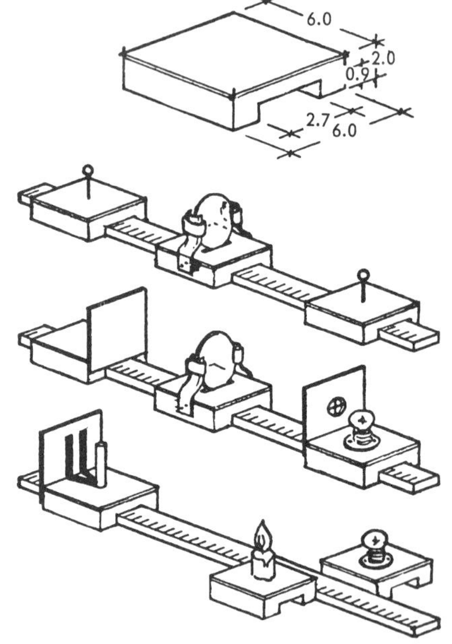

the side make convenient lens holders. A groove in the top of a block helps to keep the lens in position, and rubber tubing over the tin increases the grip.

Light sources and screens can be improvised with card and torch bulbs fastened to the blocks. It is worth while to make complete sets of this apparatus so that individual work on lenses can be attempted. The groove is easy to make with a chisel after two sawcuts have been made in the wood.

Many other experiments, for instance on interference and diffraction, can be attempted using this apparatus.

13 A simple microscope

Make a single turn of copper wire around a nail to form a loop. Dip the loop into water and look through it. You will have a microscope like the earliest ones used. Often such a lens will magnify four or five times.

If you tap the wire sharply against the edge of the glass a drop of water will fall off. Because of adhesion between the wire and the water, the liquid remaining will form a lens which is very thin at the centre, i.e., a concave lens.

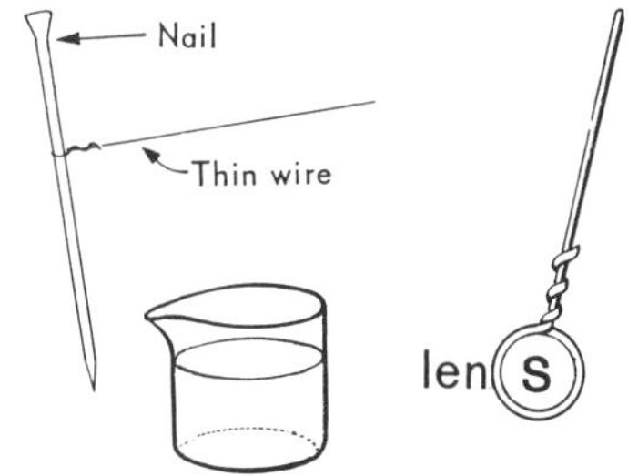

14 A water drop microscope

Place a drop of water carefully on a plate of glass. Bring your eye close to the drop and look at something small through the water drop and glass. This serves as a simple microscope.

15 A model compound microscope

Arrange a short focus lens on the optical bench made in experiment C 12. Place a lighted candle behind a piece of window screen on one side of the lens. On the other side of the lens place a white cardboard sheet at the point where the clearest image of the screen is formed. Remove the cardboard sheet and place another double convex lens slightly farther away than where the cardboard was. Look through both lenses at the screen. It will appear enlarged.

16 A model refracting telescope

Arrange a long focus lens on the end of the optical bench pointing at some scene through a window. As in the previous experiment, bring a white cardboard up on the opposite side of the lens to the place where the sharpest image of the scene is formed. Now bring a short focus lens up behind the cardboard until the cardboard is a little nearer the lens than its focal length. Remove the cardboard and look through the two lenses at the scene.

17 How to make a line light source

A bulb as used in direction indicators and interior car lights provides a useful line source of light for optical experiments. A convenient holder can be made from a piece of plywood. Strips of tin tacked to the wood, or held by screw terminals, can be used to make electrical connexion to the caps.

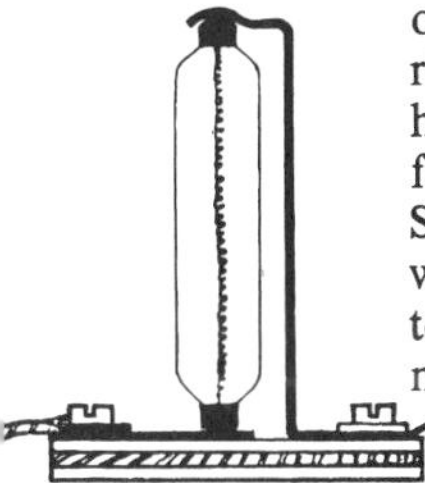

18 Image and object relationships for a lens

The lens can be fastened to the front of a wooden block with plasticine. The image position is where the rays cross. It is interesting to plot u against v and test the formula

$$\frac{1}{u}+\frac{1}{v}=\frac{1}{f}.$$

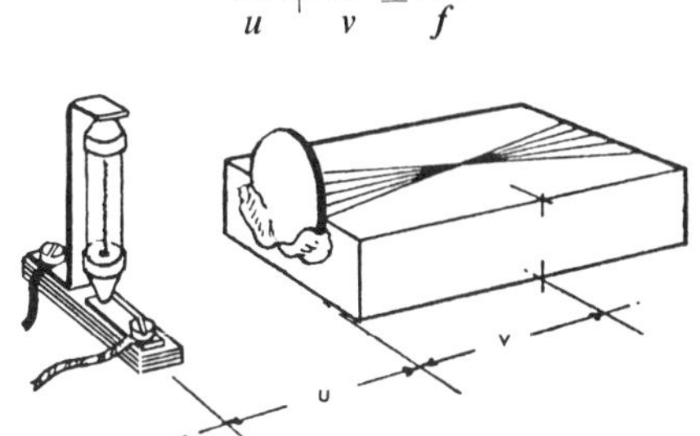

19 Image and object relation for a lens (without source)

A piece of mirror about 5 cm square can replace a source of light. The object is then a 1 cm square at the centre of the mirror from which the silvering has been removed.

The mirror should face the light, when the image can be caught on a piece of cardboard on the side away from the light.

The relationship $\frac{\text{image size}}{\text{object size}}$ can also be tested.

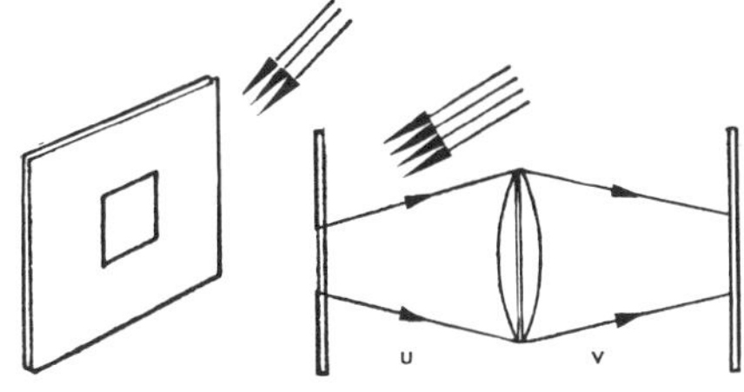

20 Critical angle

Make an air cell from two microscope slides by cutting a tinfoil frame and sticking it between the slides with Canada balsam or Bostik cement.

Fit this in a slot in a piece of wood about 20 cm long. Push knitting needles through the ends of the wood to act as pointers, indicating the position of the lath.

When this rod rests on a beaker of water with the air cell inside it, the needles should just touch the paper on which the beaker stands. This is the critical angle apparatus.

In use a base line of three pins is used, a diameter of the beaker. The rod is moved until total reflection occurs. There will be two positions for this, and the points of the needle should be marked in each case.

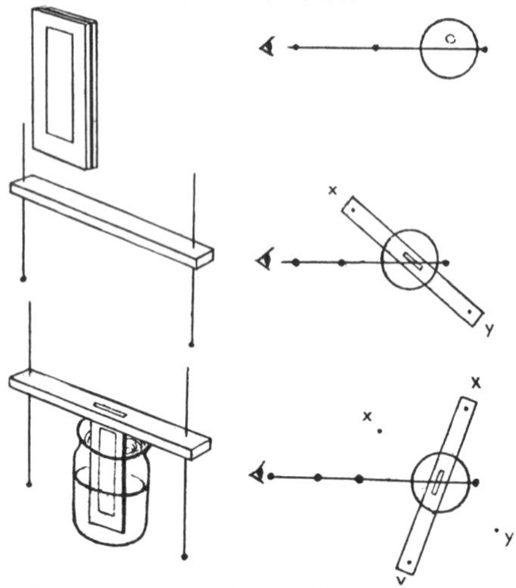

21 To measure the critical angle for water

Cut a disk 4 cm in diameter from a piece of waxed cardboard.

Pass a long pin through the centre of the card and float it head downwards in a vessel of water. Viewing the pinhead from above the surface it will be found that its position can be adjusted until it just disappears behind the card. In this position, a ray of light from the pinhead is refracted so that it passes along the surface and cannot reach the eye.

The angle θ can be measured directly or by measuring $\frac{CE}{CH}$ and using tangent tables.

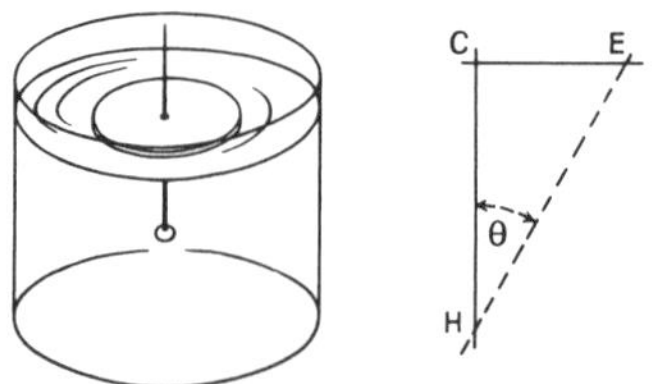

22 Another critical angle experiment

Put a small specimen tube or pill bottle in a rectangular glass tank, and look through the sides. The centre part of the tube will act as a cylindrical diverging lens, but the edges will appear to be silvered.

From the ray diagram it will be seen that $\sin C = \frac{d}{r}$.

These two distances can be measured by using sighting stools with their ends against a ruler parallel to the face of the tank.

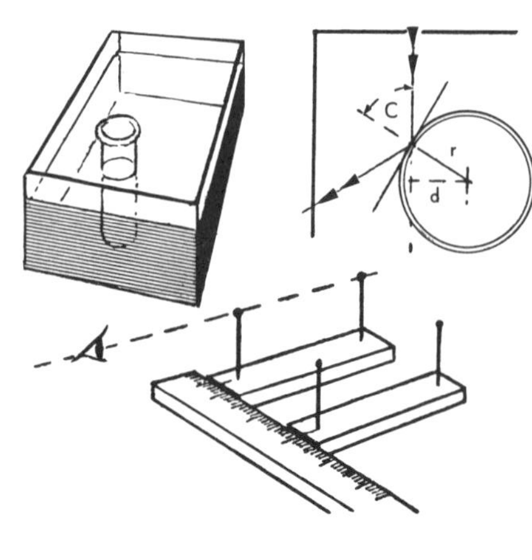

23 How a camera works

Secure two boxes which will telescope over one another rather tightly. Cut one end out of each box and slip the boxes over each other, with the cut ends together. Now cut the back end from one box and fit a piece of grease-proof or tissue paper over it. Cut a hole the size of a lens in the other end and fix a convex lens in the hole. Now move the boxes in and out until the lens focuses an image of an outside scene on the paper screen. In a camera the sensitive film is placed where the paper is on the model.

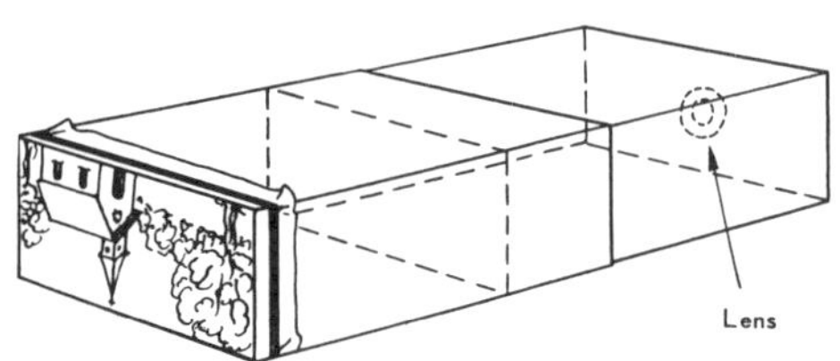

24 How to take a picture with a pin-hole camera

Make a pinhole camera (see experiment A 4 of this chapter) from a wooden box such as a chalk box. Paint the inside black. Bore a 1 cm hole in the centre of one end. On the inside of the box cover the hole with a piece of thin metal foil. With a needle punch a hole in the centre of the metal foil and be sure that the hole is very neat. Inside the opposite end of the box fit some guides, into which you can slide sections of cut film. Fit a cork tightly in the hole to cover the pinhole. In a dark room cut some photographic film to the proper size to slide into the guides. Cover the top of the box and take your camera outside. Point it at the scene you wish to take a picture of. Remove the cork for a second or two and replace it. In the dark room remove the exposed film and develop it or wrap it in black paper and take it to a photographic shop for developing.

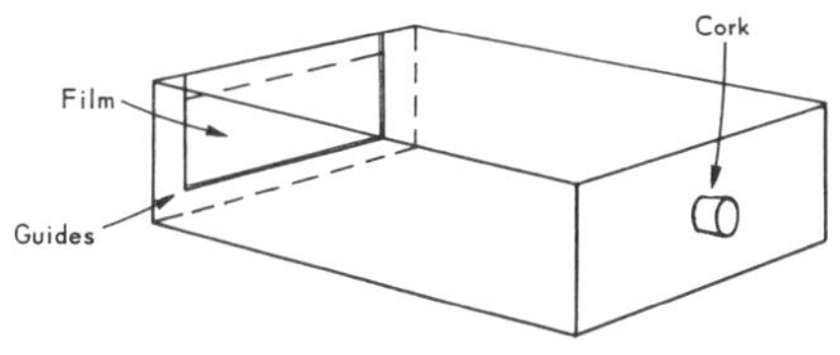

25 A simple view camera

A simple view camera can be made as follows. With a hand lens focus the image of a distant hill or tree on a card. Measure the distance between the lens and the card and cut down a small carton so that its height equals this distance. In the centre of the bottom cut a hole a little smaller than the lens. Fix the lens over this hole with a piece of cardboard

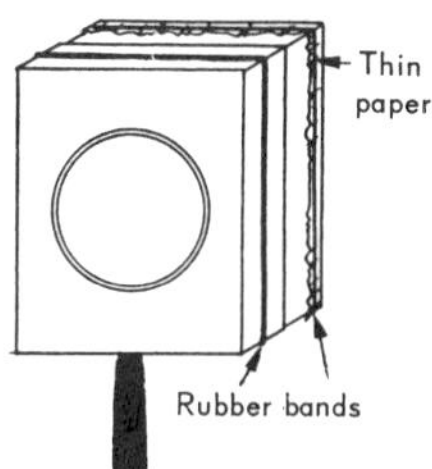

containing a hole the same size as the first. Tie a sheet of thin tissue paper over the open top of the box. This view camera may be used in a darkened room with the lens directed towards a window.

26 A focusing view camera

A focusing view camera can be made in much the same way as one described in experiment C 25. A second box telescopes into the first to allow focusing. The brighter the object viewed and the darker the screen of tissue paper, the better the results will be.

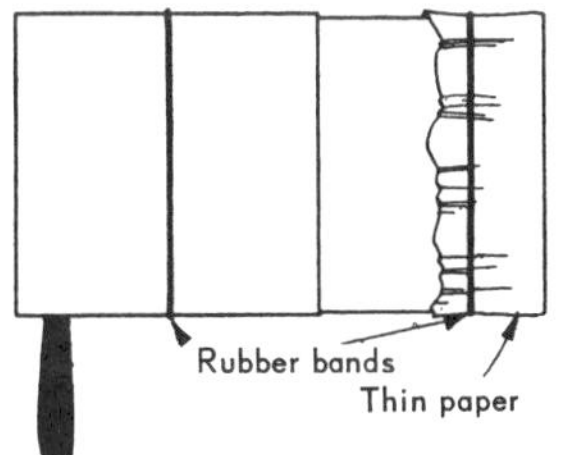

D. EXPERIMENTS WITH COLOUR

1 What is the colour of sunlight?

Darken a room into which the sun is shining. Punch a small hole in the window shade to admit a thin beam of light. Hold a glass prism in the beam of light and observe the band of colours, called a spectrum, on the opposite wall or ceiling. Can you name the colours thus found in a spectrum of the sun?

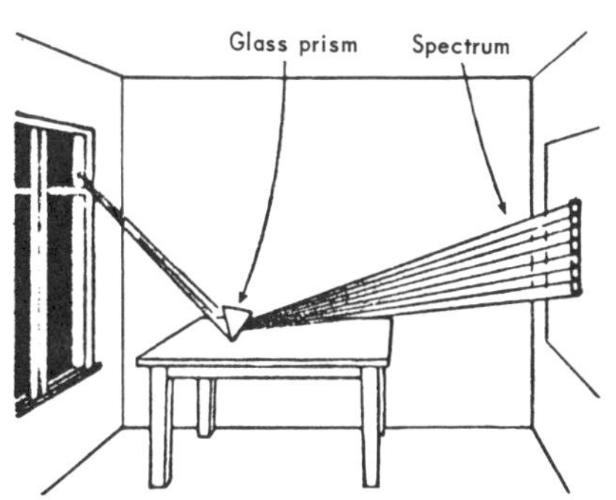

2 Putting spectrum colours together

Hold a reading glass lens in the colour band on the opposite side of the prism from the white sunlight. What happens to the colour band on the wall?

3 Another way to make a spectrum

Set a tray of water in bright sunlight. Lean a rectangular pocket mirror against an inside edge and adjust it so that a colour band or spectrum appears on the wall.

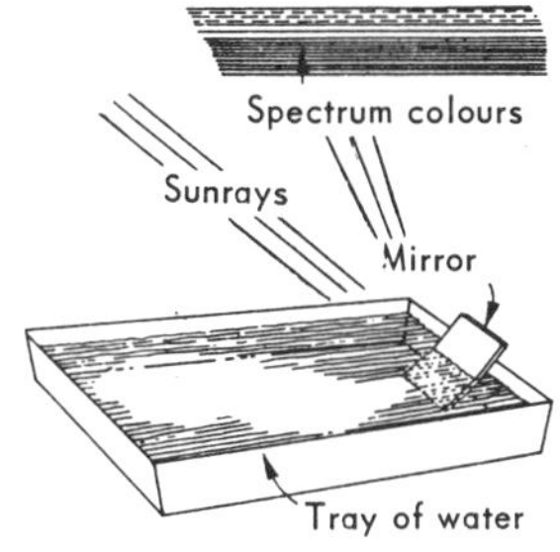

4 Studying a spectrum with the ray box

A glass prism will produce a good spectrum from a parallel beam of light using a ray box. In front of the lens the ray box should have

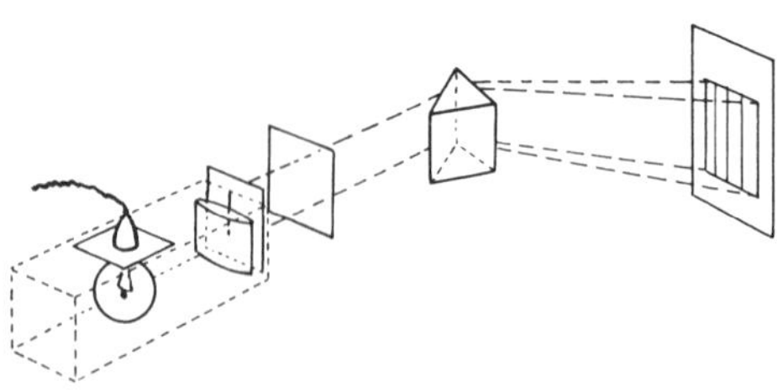

a narrow slit, which can be cut from a piece of card. Interposing coloured gelatine filters and packing papers in the beam will suppress certain colours. For instance, when a transparent purple paper is used, only red and blue lines will be seen on the screen.

5 How to see a line spectrum

To make a simple optical slit scratch some silver off the back of a mirror with a needle, or remove in the same way some of the emulsion from a fogged photographic plate. For viewing a line spectrum, the slit can be replaced by a needle held parallel to the refracting edge of the prism, and illuminated by the light under examination.

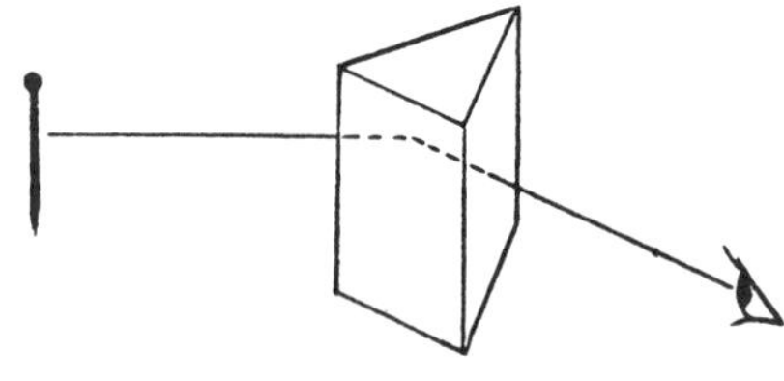

6 How to make a rainbow

Stand a tumbler very full of water on a window ledge in bright sunlight. Let it project a little over the inside edge of the window ledge. Place a sheet of white paper on the floor and you will be able to see a rainbow or spectrum band.

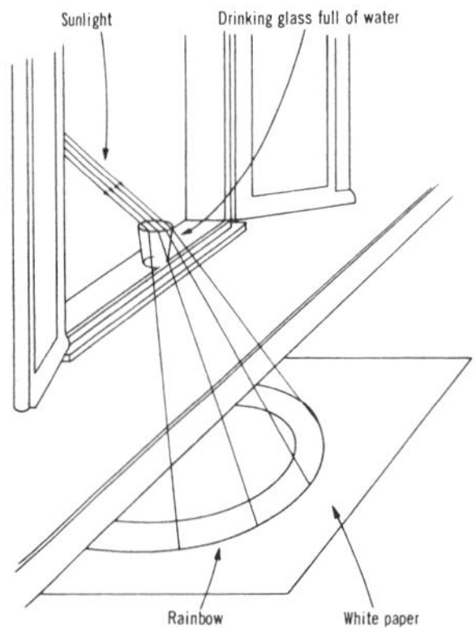

7 Another way to make a rainbow

Early in the morning or late in the afternoon of a bright sunny day, spray water from a hose against a dark background of trees with your back toward the sun. You will see a lovely rainbow.

8 The colour of transparent objects

Use the smoke box (see experiment A 5 above) as in previous experiments. Have a single ray of light enter the box. Hold a clear sheet of glass or cellophane in the beam of light and note that the beam on the white screen in the box is white. Next hold a sheet of red glass or cellophane in the white beam and observe that the beam which reaches the white screen is red. All the other colours of the white light have been absorbed by the red. Experiment with other coloured transparent sheets. You will observe that such objects have colour due to the colours they transmit and that they absorb other colours.

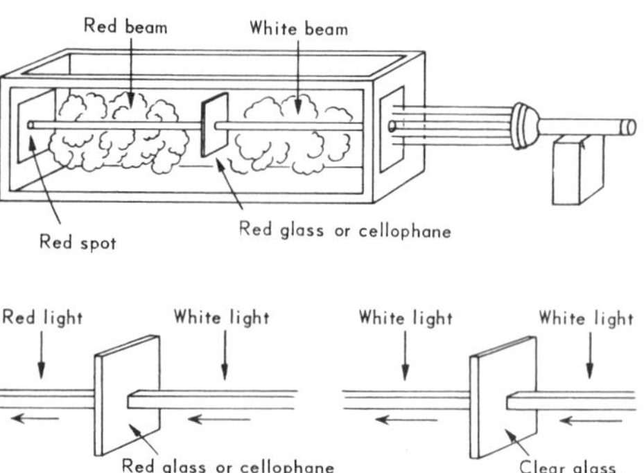

9 The colour of opaque objects

Get a good spectrum on a wall or a sheet of white paper in a darkened room. Place a piece of red cloth in the blue light of the spectrum. What colour is it? Place it in the green and in the yellow. How does it appear? Place it in the red light. How does it appear? Repeat using blue, green and yellow coloured cloth. You will observe that they appear black except when placed in the same coloured light. Thus opaque objects have colour because of the light they reflect; they absorb the other colours of the spectrum.

10 Mixing coloured pigments

Take a piece of blue chalk and a piece of yellow chalk. Crush them and mix them. The resulting colour is green. These are not pure colour pigments. Notice that green is between yellow and blue in the spectrum. The yellow absorbs all colours but yellow and green. The blue absorbs all colours but blue and green; thus the yellow and blue absorb each other, and the green is reflected to the eye.

Try the same experiment by mixing paints from a painter's box.

11 Mixing coloured lights

(a) Mixing of coloured lights can be achieved by using water colours painted on disks of cardboard.

One suggestion is to paint a yellow 'egg yolk' on one side of a 10 cm disk, and a blue 'yolk' on the other side. When the disk is suspended by short pieces of string, and twirled between the fingers and thumbs, the result is nearly white, if the colours are carefully chosen.

Other colour mixtures can be investigated in a way similar to that used on the toy 'colour tops'. Radial segments are painted, say, alternately red and green. The resulting mixture of red and green lights reflected to the eye by spinning the disk on string is, of course, yellow in this case.

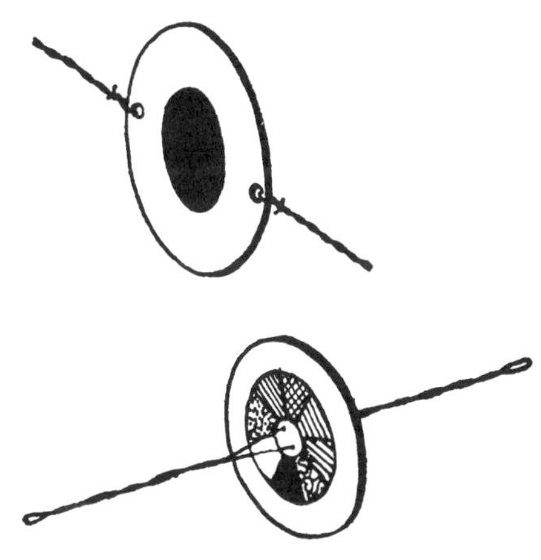

(b) Three of the boxes described for experiments on rays in elementary optics can also be used for mixing coloured lights. Any similar box containing a car bulb will serve the same purpose.

Place red, green and blue theatrical filters in the front of the box and cast rectangular patches of light on a white screen.

Red and green give *yellow*.
Blue and red give *purple*.
Green and blue give *peacock blue*.
Red, green and blue give *white*.

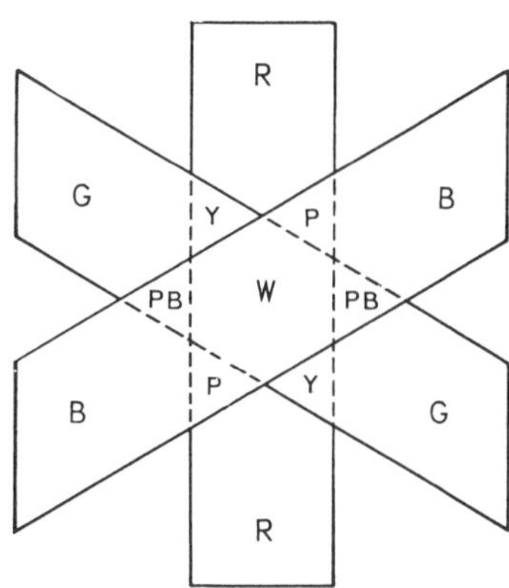

12 Colours in a soap film

Make a strong soap solution such as would be used for blowing soap bubbles. Fill a flat dish with the solution and dip an egg cup or a tea cup into the solution until a film forms across the cup. Hold this in a strong light and observe the colours you can see. Thin films often have colours.

13 Colours in an oil film

Fill a shallow dish with water. Colour the water with black ink until it is very dark. Put the dish in a window where light from the sky is very bright, but not in direct sunlight. Look into the water so that light from the sky is reflected to your eye. While looking at the water place a drop of oil or gasoline on the surface at the edge of the dish nearest to you. You should see a brilliant rainbow of colours flash away from you toward the opposite edge. By blowing on the surface you will observe a change in the colours.

14 Colours from a feather

Look at a distant candle flame through the end of a feather. You should see two or three candle flames on each side of the actual flame and a flattened X with four coloured arms. If the feather is good you will see two blue and red bands in each of the four arms.

15 How colours change

Paste some coloured illustrations from a magazine on a piece of cardboard. Pour three tablespoonfuls of salt in a saucer and add several tablespoonfuls of alcohol. Mix and light. This produces a very brilliant light that gives out only yellow. View the picture in this light in a darkened room and observe how all colours but the yellow change.

E. OPTICAL PROJECTION

In order to produce a good image or picture on a screen, a lens must be of good quality. A magnifying glass may be used, but better results are obtained with an old camera lens. Used in this way the lens is called the 'objective' or object lens, and the magnification obtained depends on its focal length.

Opaque objects must be strongly illuminated because only the light reflected from the surface will pass through the lens. Transparencies can be illuminated from behind; in this case an extra 'condensing' lens is used behind the slide or film to ensure even illumination of the image produced on the screen.

1 How to make a projector for coloured pictures

A projector for coloured pictures can be made from simple materials as shown in the diagram. Use a box slightly longer than the focal length of the lens to be used. For most lenses the box should be between 30 and 100 cm long. Use a small candy box as light shield for the lens as shown. Connect two lamp sockets in parallel and put one on either side of the shield. Two 50-watt lamps should provide sufficient illumination. Use gummed tape to fasten down the front portion of the top of the larger box and hinge the rear portion.

Place a picture upside down in the back of the box, focusing by moving it back and forth until a clear image appears on the wall or screen in front of the projector.

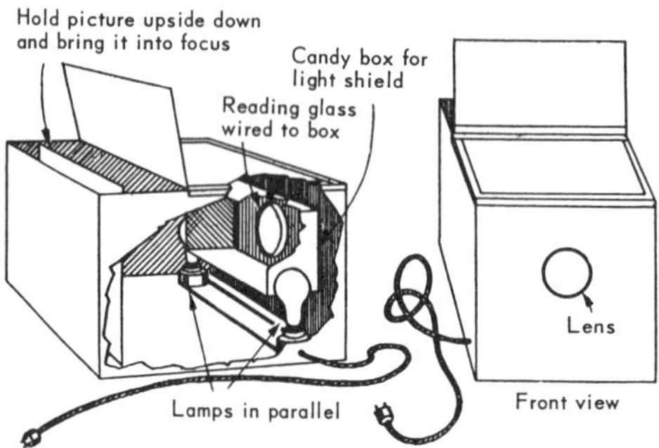

2 To construct a projector for filmslides or strips

The base of the instrument is a piece of wood 40 by 10 by 3 cm. A plywood board 10 cm wide and 25 cm long fits into a groove cut across the base, and serves as filmstrip carrier. A hole 35 by 23 mm cut in this wood serves as an 'aperture' or gate to limit the light passing to one frame of the strip. The strip itself is held close to the gate. in a vertical position, by staples made from wire paper fasteners. These are easily bent to the width of the film; the ends are cut off short and sharpened with a file, and they can then be pressed into position on the plywood board. No reels are necessary. The strip can be moved on from one frame to the next by pulling on the end of the film; there is sufficient 'curl' to hold it stationary.

The lamp, which is an automobile head-lamp in a holder mounted on a block, is adjustable; it can be slid between two strips of wood nailed to the base. A carafe or flask of water can be used as condensing lens and should be placed so that the whole of the gate is illuminated by the image of the lamp. When it has been so positioned, the lamp and condensing flask are fixed in place with glue.

The object lens is mounted on a piece of wooden dowelling which is a fairly tight fit in a hole drilled into a block of wood arranged, like the lamp support, to slide between two wooden guides. The lens can then be adjusted for height by sliding the rod in or out of the hole so that the centre of the lamp, condenser and objective are all the same distance from the baseboard.

A plywood, metal or cardboard case is required to enclose the lamp and the condenser as shown by the dotted line in the diagram. A darkened room is necessary for this apparatus. Commercial instruments using 100 watt bulbs can be used in a semi-darkened room, but the problem of dissipating the heat from the lamp is then considerable.

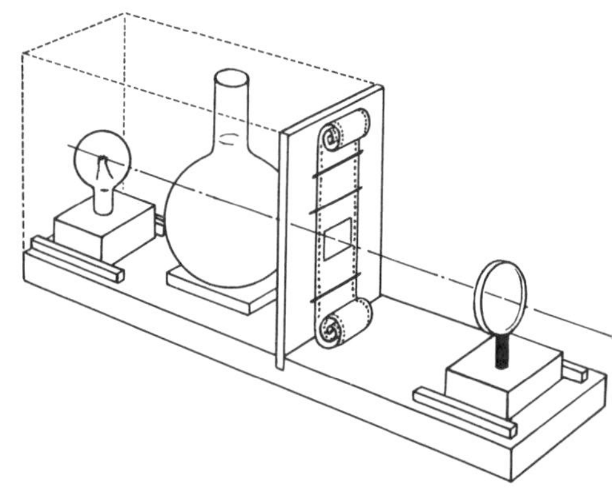

3 A simple microprojector

The optical system of this instrument is the same as that of the strip projector. The differences in construction are necessary because of the size of the objects (microscope slides or small objects similarly mounted), and the need to use a very short focus objective to obtain high magnification. The lamp is a 12-volt car bulb, the condenser is a small glass bulb 1.5 to 2 cm in diameter blown on a piece of quill tubing, and the object lens is the objective of a commercial microscope.

The base of the apparatus is a small wooden trough 10 by 7 by 4 cm made by nailing two strips of wood 4 cm wide to the sides of a piece measuring 10 by 5 by 1 cm. These sizes are not critical, and may be varied to suit the other available materials. A support for this objective is provided by closing one end of the trough by a piece of plywood 9 by 7 cm with a 2.5 cm hole in it.

Into the channel fits a rectangular lamphouse; this is easily improvised by fixing a car bulb and holder inside a household mustard or other rectangular tin. Holes drilled round the top provide ventilation, and a hole 1.5 cm in diameter serves to support the condenser. Copper wire passing round the stem of the bulb and through holes punched through the tin hold the condenser firmly in position.

The slide holding the object to be projected fits into grooves cut across the edges of the channel, and is thus held in a vertical plane so that the light from the condenser passes through it. The position of the grooves is determined in the way indicated below.

The microscope objective fits tightly into a hole in a piece of plywood, 7 by 4 cm, which is held in contact with the end plate by a trouser cycle clip in such a position that the lens can be adjusted to be on the axis of the optical system.

The diagram shows the components mounted further apart than in actual practice; this is done to show the relative positions more clearly. In adjusting this apparatus the slide, lamphouse and condenser are moved forward together until the light passes through the objective and forms an image (of, say, a botanical specimen) on a ground glass screen 30 cm square placed about 60 cm away from the end of the trough. Once the correct position for the slide has been found, the sawcuts are made in the edge of the trough and serve for all other slides used. This apparatus can also be used for projecting Newton's rings and diffraction phenomena.

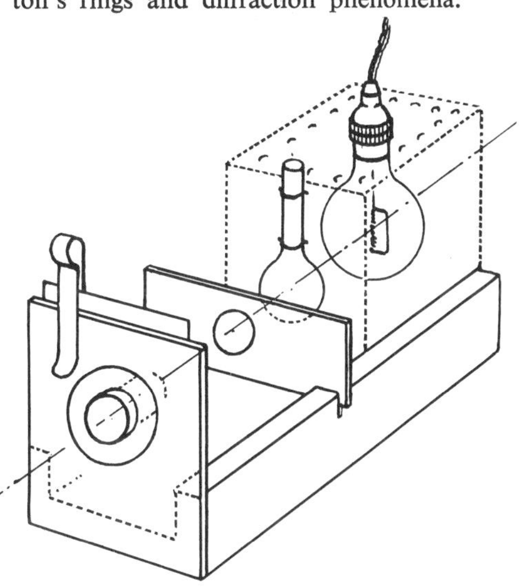

CHAPTER XVII

Experiments and materials for the study of the human body

A. THE BONES AND MUSCLES

1 A model of the arm

Obtain two pieces of wood about 5 to 8 mm thick (plywood will work very well), 5 cm wide and 30 cm long. Drill a hole in the upper corner of one piece of wood. Round the ends of the other piece and drill a hole near each end as shown in the diagram:

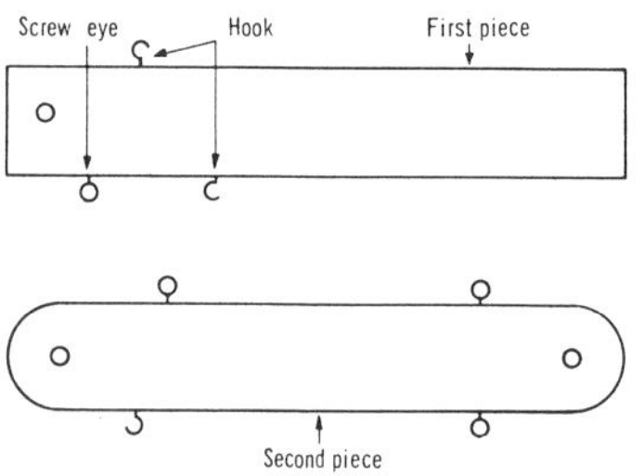

Next, put two cup hooks and a screw eye in the first piece of wood approximately at the places indicated. In a similar way place one cup hook and three screw eyes in the second piece. Put the two pieces together with a short bolt and nut as shown in the diagram below.

Cut some long strands of rubber from old bicycle or automobile inner tubes and fasten them to the cup hooks on the under side of the two pieces after threading them through the screw eyes. Thread a strong cord through the screw eyes on the upper side and attach to the hook. When the string is pulled, you will have a good representation of the way the bones and muscles of the arm work.

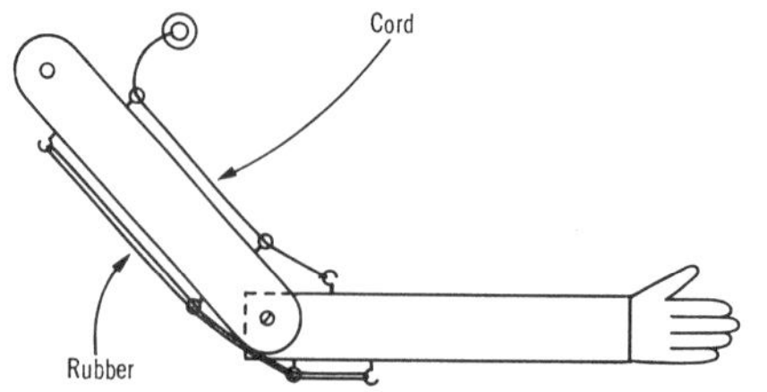

2 A model of the foot

Cut, from thin wood or cardboard, sections to represent the foot and leg as shown in the diagram. Attach rubber strands cut from old inner tubes, as indicated.

3 A model of the head and neck

The diagram indicates how this model may be improvised from wood or cardboard.

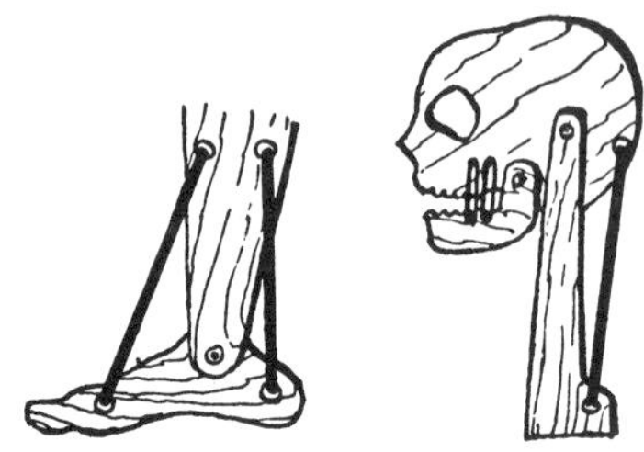

4 The walking hairpin

Hold a dinner knife tightly in your hand. Place a hairpin astride the knife and lift it just enough for the legs of the hairpin to rest lightly on the table with the pin in a slanting position. Observe that the pin walks along the knife blade. This is caused by the slight movement of the arm muscles.

B. YOUR SENSES

1 Your sense of smell

With pupils sitting perfectly still and evenly distributed in the room, release, in one corner, some substance with a penetrating odour. A little ether or ammonia poured on a cloth works well for this purpose.

Ask pupils to raise their hands as soon as the odour is detected. Note the progress of the diffusion of the odour through the air across the room.

Quote examples of ways in which the sense of smell protects us from danger.

2 The best reading distance

Ask pupils to read something and to hold their books at the distance where reading is most comfortable; 35 to 40 cm is normal. If the most comfortable distance is greater or less than this, spectacles may be needed to correct the vision.

3 Proper illumination

With the curtains or blinds drawn, hold a lighted 40-watt electric lamp exactly 60 cm above an open book. This amount of illumination is about right for comfortable reading. Show that the illumination rapidly diminishes as the lamp is moved farther away. At a distance of a little under 1 m, a 100-watt bulb is needed to provide the same illumination that a 40-watt bulb gives at 60 cm.

Demonstrate proper reading positions to prevent glare. Decide whether there is proper lighting in all parts of the classroom. If not, discuss methods of correcting the unsatisfactory conditions.

4 The adjustment of the eye

Roll 10 or 12 sheets of white paper into a hollow roll so that each sheet extends twice around the roll. Slip a rubber band around the roll. Set the roll on the page of a book and press one eye against the top so that no light is admitted at the bottom or the top. It should be impossible at first to read any of the words. If any of the words can be read immediately, add a few more sheets of paper to the roll.

With the other eye closed, keep looking through the roll for a minute or two without admitting any light. The print will slowly become legible in the dim light diffused through the paper.

As soon as the print can be read clearly, look quickly into a mirror and note the size of the pupils of the eyes. Keep watching the pupils for a minute and see how they change in size as the bright light of the classroom enters the eyes. Each of the children should have the opportunity to perform this experiment for himself.

Suggest some advantages of this ability of the pupils of the eye to change in size: contraction of the pupils protects the eyes against very bright light; enlargement helps us to see in very dim light; adjustment of the pupils helps us avoid danger.

5 Can you find your blind spot?

At the place where the optic nerve enters the eyeball there is a little blind spot only a few millimetres in diameter. You can find this blind spot by a very simple experiment. Draw a black dot on a white sheet of paper and about 5 cm to the right draw a black cross. Close your left eye and stare steadily at the black dot with your right eye, while the sheet rests on the table. Now pick the sheet up and move it slowly towards your eye while still staring at the dot. You will find a point where the image of the cross to the right will disappear. You can find the blind spot of your left eye by closing the right one and staring at the cross. When the book is brought near your eye, the black spot will disappear.

6 Optical illusions

There are several very striking optical illusions in everyday life. When near the horizon, the sun and moon appear to be much larger than when seen high in the heavens. When seen rising behind a hill, they seem to move much more rapidly than they do when they are above us. Measurement of the sun's or moon's regular diameter by an instrument or of their bearing when rising and setting does not confirm our first impressions. Our estimates of sizes and distances near the horizon are inaccurate because we adopt comparatively near terrestrial objects as our standard of comparison.

Make use of the theodolite or astrolabe and sextant made in Chapter VI, in measuring the speed of the sun or the moon during its setting or rising. Compare its movement when it is above us.

Vision is not merely a static copy of the changing world. We have to learn to use our eyes as we have to learn to use any other instrument. Our estimates of distance, direction and position do not merely depend on what the retina of the eye (see experiment C 1 below) tells us. They involve complex movements of the muscles that move the lens of the eye, of the muscles that change its curvature and of the muscles that move the eye itself in its socket, together with the movements of the muscles of the neck and limbs and all the signals which these muscles send to the brain when they move. We learn to co-ordinate our bodily movements with those of our eye muscles and with the pattern of light on the retina from the common experience of everyday life.

Part of our everyday experience is that light travels in straight lines. We learn to put things *in line*. The delicate adjustment which makes us able to grasp a thing by seeing it, or to direct our gaze to the thing we touch, is easily upset.

The following diagrams are of some well-know optical illusions. See that accurate measurements do not confirm your impressions.

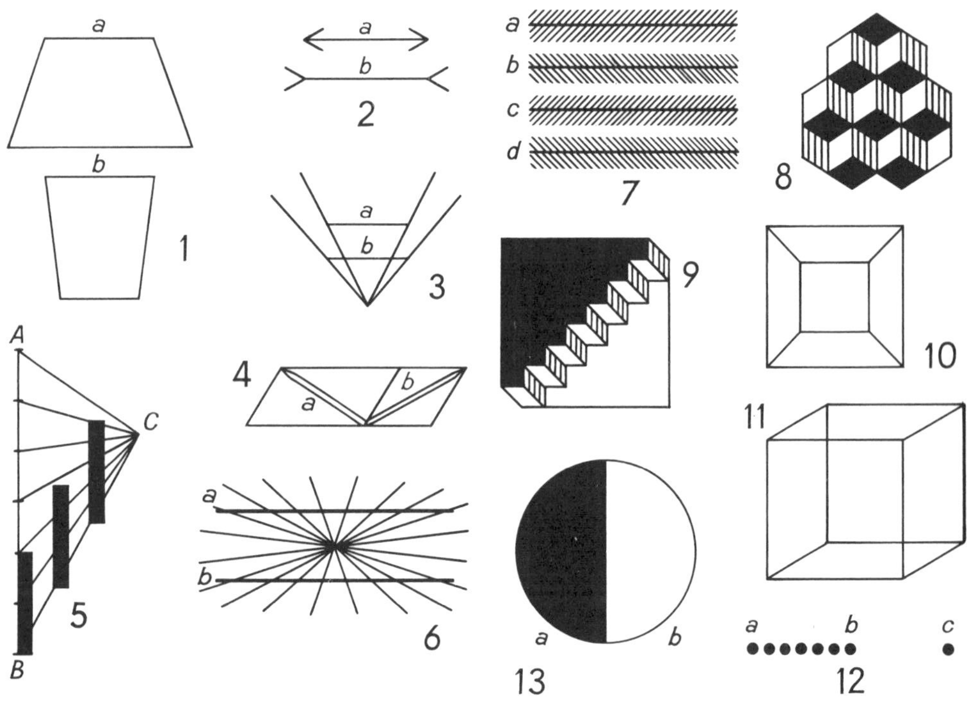

Nos. 1, 2, 3, 4. Look at lines *a* and *b* and compare their lengths.

No. 5. The black fence-posts appear to differ in height.

Nos. 6, 7. Look at the horizontal lines; are they parallel?

No. 8. Count the cubes and then carefully recount them.

No. 9. Look steadily at the staircase. Then turn your book slowly so that the staircase becomes inverted.

No. 10. The inside square appears to shift back and forth.

No. 11. Sometimes you appear to be looking at the top of the cube and sometimes at the bottom.

No. 12. Look at the figure and compare the distances *ab* and *bc*.

No. 13. Glance at the figure; is it a true circle?

7 Your sense of feeling

With a pencil mark off a 1 cm square on the back of the first joint of the middle finger. Sharpen the pencil and press the point firmly against the skin at many places within the square. Nerve endings that register sensations of touch, heat, cold and pain are located in the skin. Find the points within the square that produce each of these sensations.

Quote examples of situations in which the sensations of touch, heat, cold and pain might help us avoid harm or danger.

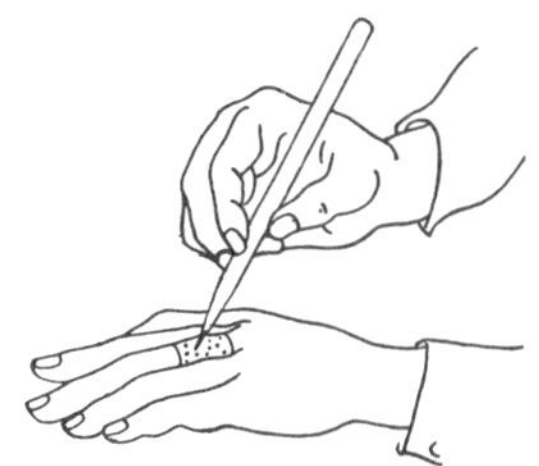

8 Testing your temperature sense

See Chapter XIII, experiment B 1, page 143.

C. SOME ORGANS OF THE HUMAN BODY

I The eye

1 How to dissect an eye

A bull's or a sheep's eye can be used. Remove the clear front skin or cornea. This will reveal the iris, and behind it the crystalline lens.

This lens divides the eye into two parts, the front containing a thin liquid called 'aqueous humour' and the back a jelly-like liquid, the 'vitreous humour'.

Removing the lens and vitreous humour, the retina or sensitive surface can be seen. It is more richly served with sensitive cells at a spot opposite the lens called the yellow spot. The nerves carrying the sensations pass out through a hole in the outer sclerotic membrane; this spot is therefore not sensitive to light and is called the blind spot.

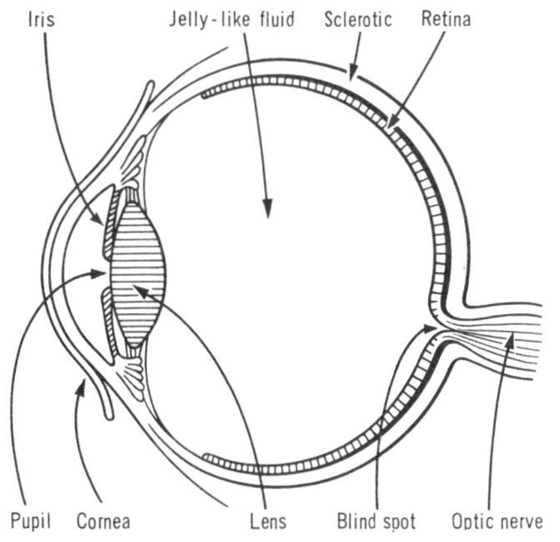

2 How an image of an object appears on the retina

See Chapter XVI, experiment A 4, page 191, on the pinhole camera.

3 How the lens of the eye forms an image on the retina

See Chapter XVI, experiment C 11, page 198, on image formation by a convex lens.

II The heart

1 Making a simple device for listening to the heart beat

Make a stethoscope and have pupils use it to listen to the heart action.

A very satisfactory demonstration stethoscope can be made from a small funnel, a glass T-tube or Y-tube, and some rubber tubing. Slip a piece of rubber tubing 7 or 8 cm long over the tip of the funnel. (Any kind of small funnel will do, such as a glass laboratory funnel or the kind used to fill babies' milk bottles.) Insert the T-tube into the other end of the short piece of rubber tubing and attach longer pieces of tubing to both arms of the T-tube.

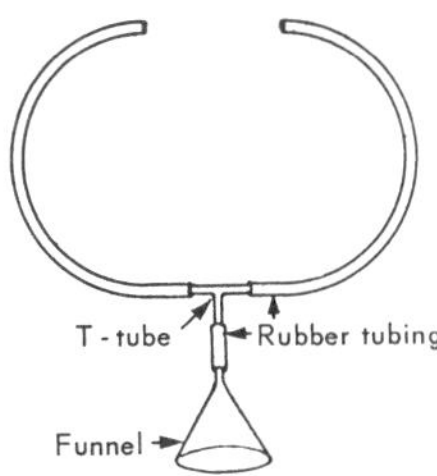

To use the stethoscope, have one pupil hold the funnel firmly over his heart while another holds the ends of the long tubes in his ears. Heart sounds will be heard very clearly though of course, pupils will not be able to interpret them. A doctor uses a stethoscope to find out if the heart action is normal.

This experiment will naturally lead to a discussion of what the heart does and its importance in maintaining good health. Dangerous activities that might injure the heart and diseases that sometimes result in heart impairment might also be discussed.

2 Taking the pulse rate

Demonstrate the proper method of taking the pulse rate by placing two fingers on the wrist and applying slight pressure by pushing against the back of the wrist with the thumb. Practise finding the pulse rate by counting for 15 and 30 seconds.

3 The effect of exercise on the pulse

Have several pupils take their pulse rate at rest and after vigorous exercise. Summarize the results in a table.

4 Watching the pulse beat of the heart

Stick a drawing pin into the end of a kitchen match. Hold your hand out with the inside of the wrist up and level. Place the head of the drawing-pin on your wrist at the point where you can feel the heartbeat. Observe the match as it sways each time the heart beats.

III The lungs

1 How the lungs work

Demonstrate the action of the diaphragm by means of the apparatus shown in the accompanying diagram. The rubber balloons represent the lungs, the tube represents the windpipe and the open bottom jar represents the bony thoracic girdle. Lowering the diaphragm reduces the pressure inside the chest cavity and air flows into the lungs. Raising the diaphragm reverses the flow of air. Try moving the diaphragm with the clamp closed.

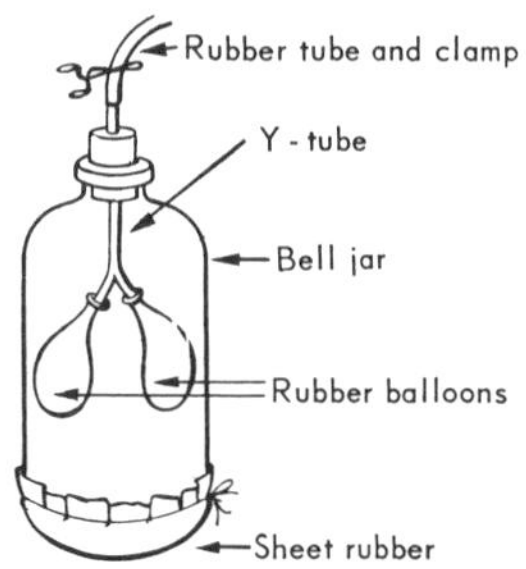

2 What is your lung capacity?

Pupils may be interested in finding the volume of air that the lungs can displace. This can be determined quite easily.

Fill a jar with water and fit a two-hole stopper. Insert a rubber tube through one hole; the other hole serves as an outlet. Invert the jar in a larger vessel and have a pupil make one exhalation through the tube. Place the fingers over the outlet and remove it from the large vessel. Use the graduate to measure the amount of water needed to refill the jug. The amount of water needed will equal the volume of air that was exhaled.

CHAPTER XVIII

Some useful notes for teachers

1 Cleaning of glassware

Dissolve 100 g of potassium dichromate in a solution of 100 g of concentrated sulphuric acid in 1 litre of water. Glassware can be soaked in the solution, which may be used over and over again.

Caution: Great care should be taken to avoid getting this very corrosive solution on skin or clothes. When diluting concentrated sulphuric acid use a stone or earthenware vessel. Pour the acid very slowly into the water as a great amount of heat is given out in the process.

The teacher should use his knowledge of chemistry to remove stains of know origin. If dirty vessels have contained alkalis, or salts with alkaline reactions, then obviously the cleaning effect of a little dilute acid should first be tried; if the stain is due to potassium permanganate, then the effect of sodium sulphite solution, acidified with dilute sulphuric acid, should be tried, etc.

Alkalis slowly attack glass, and bottles which have contained caustic soda, etc., for a long time, will never recover their original transparency.

2 Cleaning of mercury

When mercury, flowing over a surface, begins to leave 'tails', it should be cleaned. It is allowed to drip into a tall cylinder containing nitric acid slightly more dilute than the usual bench reagent. If the mercury falls through the acid in a fine stream, as it does when made to pass through a capillary tube attached to the end of a funnel, so much the better. The mercury is then shaken up with water in a strong bottle to wash it free from acid. Finally it is allowed to pass through a pinhole made in the middle of a filter paper, which is folded in a funnel in the usual way. The last drops of mercury remaining in the funnel should be kept for the next occasion when mercury is cleaned. The mercury may be warmed in an air oven before the final filtering, if required particularly dry.

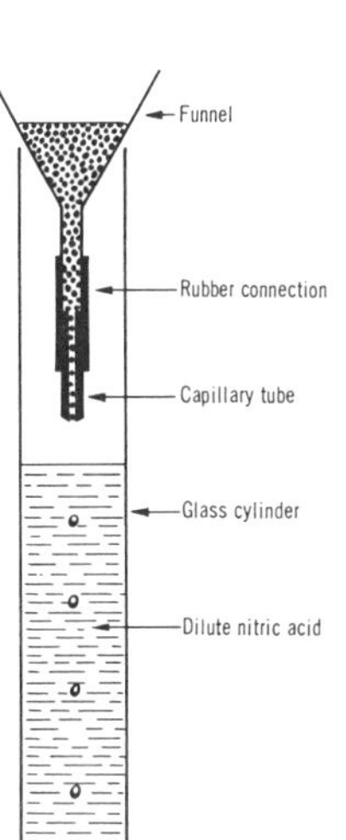

3 Removal of air bubbles from, and the recovery of, spilt mercury[1]

Air bubbles appear in a tube which is being filled with mercury. To remove them the tube is closed with the finger, before it is quite full, and inverted to allow a large air bubble to travel up it. As it moves upwards, the large bubble collects the smaller ones. When the tube is turned up again the large bubble reverses its track, moves upwards and escapes. The small amount of mercury needed to fill the tube is then added.

Mercury spilt on tray, bench or floor, may be recovered by sucking it into a small 'wash-bottle'.

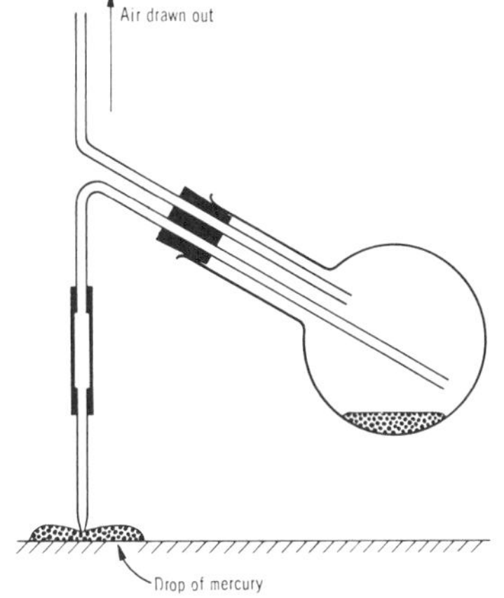

4 Collections of biological materials

These have little value unless they are kept in good condition, and the various kinds require different treatment.

1. Note taken from H. N. Saunders, *The Teaching of General Science in Tropical Secondary Schools*, London, Oxford University Press, 1955. (Unesco Handbooks on the Teaching of Science in Tropical Countries, vol. 7.)

Flowers and plants: A collection of dried specimens is called a herbarium. Its main purpose is to provide a supply of identified plants for general reference and to facilitate the naming of freshly collected specimens. The teacher must always have at hand a supply of material with which to illustrate the various kinds of flowers, leaves, fruit and roots. A specimen is not complete until all the parts of a plant are present. As flowers and fruits do not always appear at the same time, it may be necessary to collect specimens of a plant on more than one occasion.

Plants can be dried by pressing between sheets of newspaper. Special paper can be purchased for the purpose, but newspaper makes a satisfactory substitute if two or three sheets are put on each side of the specimen. A number of layers of specimens can be pressed at the same time. Drying is assisted by inserting sheets of stiff corrugated paper between every few layers. The pressing can be carried out by putting the sheets on a table under a heavily weighted drawing board. But drying is quicker between two wire frames pressed together by spring fasteners, adjustable screw fasteners, or straps. For the first few days the specimens should be removed and placed between fresh dry paper every day, but as they become drier the changes need be made less frequently.

Specimens are less subject to the growth of mould if brushed over gently with a solution of 0.5 g of mercuric chloride in 100 ml of methylated spirit (methyl alcohol). The specimens should then be gummed, or glued, to sheets of stiff drawing paper, or to cards (about 25 × 45 cm) specially made for the purpose. The gum, or glue, should be made up with a little mercuric chloride, which also helps to repel insects. Alternatively, or in addition, the specimen can be sewn to the card, or fastened to it with transparent adhesive tape.

Each specimen should be labelled with at least: (a) the name and family of the species; (b) the name of the person, or group, which has identified the specimen; (c) the place and date of finding; and (d) the name of the finder.

Fruits or other bulky material associated with the specimen may have to be labelled and stored separately, but small seeds can be put in an envelope and attached to the mounting card.

Insects: These are best killed in a wide-mouthed bottle containing a suitable poison. A killing bottle is easily made as follows. Some plaster of Paris is stirred to a thin paste with a 20 per cent solution of potassium cyanide (the 'commercial' mixture of potassium and sodium cyanides is satisfactory) and quickly poured, to a depth of about 1 cm, into the bottom of the bottle, where it soon sets hard. Cut a piece of blotting paper to place over the cyanide and plaster of Paris. Punch the circle full of holes. The bottle should have a screw-cap or a well-fitting air-tight stopper, when it will remain effective for some months.

Caution: The cyanides of potassium and sodium are deadly poisonous and should be handled with the utmost care.

A captured insect becomes merely insensitive when first put into a killing bottle; so it should be left for a few hours until it is dead. It may then be removed to a setting board. A good substitute for the usual 'board' with a half-round groove consists of two sheets of compressed cork, or thick cardboard, with a gap between their edges, fixed on a third sheet, as shown in the figure. The setting board should be just large enough to hold the insect satisfactorily. A long thin pin, of the 'entomological' type, is then pushed through the middle of the insect's thorax, securing it in position in the groove. The wings, legs and antennae are then spread out carefully by means of seekers or fine tweezers, and kept in place by narrow strips of paper. (The strips are held down by pins, which must not touch the insect.) The specimen must now be dried thoroughly—not always an easy matter, in the tropics, unless the setting board can be left in a desiccator for some days. When it is dry the strips of paper are removed, as the various parts of the insect will now remain in place. It tends to be brittle, so no attempt should be made to move the thorax pin. By means of this pin the insect is lifted from the setting board and pinned in a suitable position on the mounting card. This is a sheet of cardboard or compressed cork previously cut to fit the bottom of a flat tin or other suitable box, the lid of which may be replaced by a glass top.

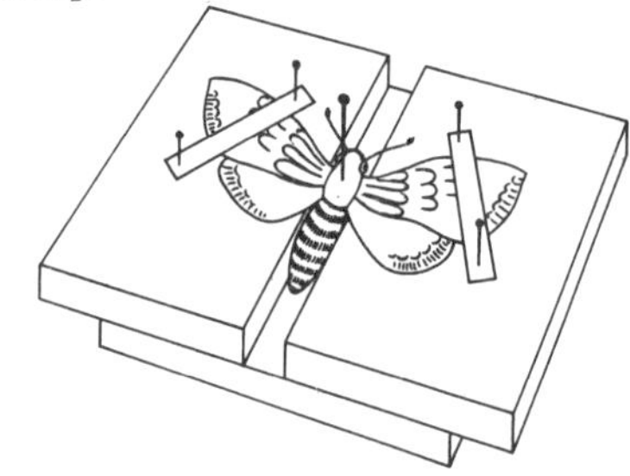

The preservation of specimens in the tropics is somewhat difficult, the chief problem being to prevent the attack of various kinds of ants.

Some minute species seem eager for viscera, fresh or dried, and determined to remove everything except head, thorax and wings. The specimens must be kept, therefore, either in ant-tight cases, or in cases on some support completely surrounded by liquid. (Water requires frequent replacement owing to evaporation, and a layer of oil or disinfectant to prevent mosquitoes from breeding. Used engine oil, from a car sump, needs less attention and is just as effective as water.) Probably the best answer to the problem is to keep the insect boxes on a table with its legs standing in tins of oil or disinfectant. The legs remain clean and dry if they stand on smaller tins inverted in the middle of the liquid. Ants and other harmful insects are unable to cross the liquid surface.

Other biological specimens: Amphibians, reptiles, birds and mammals are killed with chloroform, a pad of cotton wool, soaked in the liquid, being placed in the containing box. Mammals can be preserved in either 70 per cent alcohol or 4 per cent formalin. Amphibians, reptiles, molluscs and crustaceans are most suitably preserved in alcohol.

The cleaning of small skeletons, and the removal of viscera from large horny beetles, are jobs which, in the tropics, can be left to ants. The dead creatures are exposed in a suitable place. Their presence is soon detected by various ants, and before long a perfectly cleaned specimen remains. Bones can be scrubbed with an old toothbrush; bleaching powder should first be applied, and then hydrogen peroxide.

5 Botanical specimens

To keep these fresh until there is time to press them, they may be put in a closed tin in a refrigerator, where they readily remain stiff and fresh for a week.

6 Hand lens

Young pupils find difficulty in holding lens and object steady, and so fail to keep the image in focus. Control is much easier if the thumb and forefinger of one hand hold the object, and those of the other hand hold the lens, and the tips of the middle fingers are pressed together.

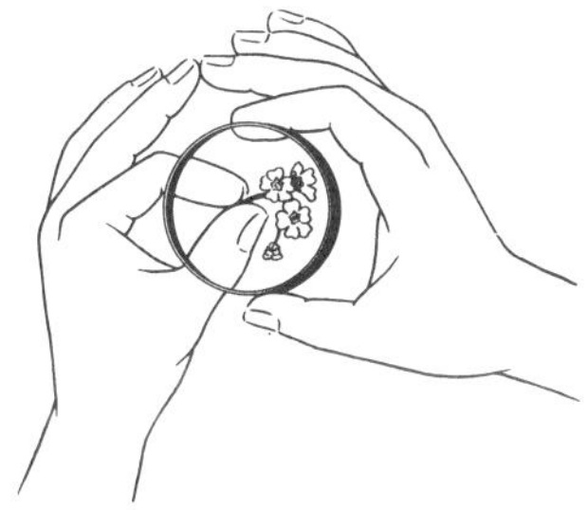

7 Hydrogen balloons[1]

In filling a toy balloon with hydrogen, the usual thistle funnel can be replaced by a funnel fitted with a tap. The delivery tube should be of as large a diameter as possible. The end of the balloon tube should be tied to the very end of the glass tube. This allows the final tying-off of the balloon to be done without first removing it from the glass tube. The acid is run into the vessel and the tap closed. The vessel should be a stout flask or bottle.

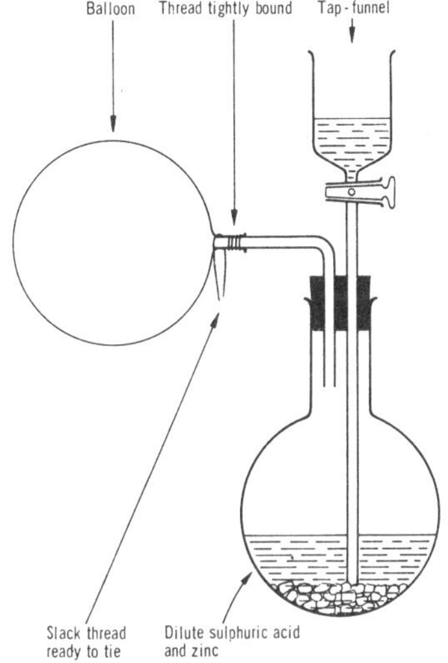

8 Tropical conditions

There are many causes of trouble in a laboratory, especially during a wet season, in the tropics. Materials perish, papers stick together, instruments rust, specimens go mouldy, lenses develop a fungus which quickly renders them useless and ruins their accurately ground surfaces. In addition, ants, termites and other insects continue their endless work of destruction.

Whatever can be kept in an air-tight container should be so kept. Glass jars, such as specimen jars with lids well greased, are ideal. Screw-capped bottles, e.g. those which

1. Note taken from H. N. Saunders, *The Teaching of General Science in Tropical Secondary Schools*, London, Oxford University Press, 1955. (Unesco Handbooks on the Teaching of Science in Tropical Countries, vol. 7.)

have contained sweets, are very useful. Metal containers, such as biscuit tins, cake tins, etc., can be rendered fairly air-tight by strapping the joint between the lid and container with insulating tape.

Lenses of microscopes should be kept in a desiccator when not in use. A piece of string soaked in creosote and placed with the eyepiece in the lens container has been found useful for retarding the growth of mould.

During the rainy season, microscopes, galvanometers and other sensitive instruments should if possible be stored in an air-tight cupboard with a 50-watt electric bulb continuously burning. Needles can be inserted in a piece of material in which some vaseline has been rubbed. Metal instruments such as screw gauges, vernier callipers, tuning forks, etc., should be greased. The screws of retort stand bases, rings and clamps should be oiled frequently. Scalpels should be smeared with vaseline and kept in a case. The metal parts of tools should be rubbed over with an oily rag.

Paste, gum and glue should contain some chemical to make them repellant to insects. Such adhesives are sold specially prepared for the tropics. But, if the teacher makes his own, the addition of a very small quantity of a solution of mercuric chloride, during the preparation, is generally effective. (Also, consult a pamphlet on *It's Easy to Reduce Humidity*, published by the Calcium Chloride Institute, 909 Ring Building, Washington, D.C., U.S.A.)

9 Culture solution (for plants)

The following salts, of *purest* quality, should be dissolved together in 1 litre of distilled water:

- 0.70 g potassium nitrate
- 0.25 g calcium sulphate (hydrated)
- 0.25 g calcium hydrogen phosphate (hydrated)
- 0.25 g magnesium sulphate (hydrated)
- 0.08 g sodium chloride
- 0.005 g iron (ferric) chloride (hydrated)

To the solution should then be added:

- 1 ml 0.06 per cent boric acid solution
- 1 ml 0.04 per cent manganese chloride solution.

10 Stains

In general it is preferable to buy stains ready made up in solution, but the following are useful recipes:

(a) *Aniline sulphate.* A few drops of dilute sulphuric acid are added to a saturated solution.

(b) *Borax carmine.* 4 g of borax are dissolved in 100 ml of water; 3 g of carmine are added and the solution warmed until the carmine is dissolved; 100 ml of 70 per cent ethyl alcohol are then added and the solution filtered.

(c) *Safranin.* 1 g is dissolved in 100 ml of water *or* 100 ml of 50 per cent aqueous ethyl alcohol.

11 Sea water

A useful substitute for sea water can be obtained by dissolving the following in 2 litres of water:

- 45.0 g sodium chloride
- 3.5 g magnesium sulphate
- 5.0 g magnesium chloride
- 2.0 g potassium sulphate

12 Lime water

Lime is not very soluble in water, but the solution required for class use is easily made by adding 10 g of slaked lime to 1000 cc distilled water. After shaking, allow it to settle before use.

13 Litmus solution

Litmus decomposes on heating; it should therefore be prepared by extracting the solid litmus with cold distilled water. It should also be stored in bottles which allow access to air, otherwise the colour will disappear.

14 Accumulator solutions

(a) *Lead accumulator.* The specific gravity of the sulphuric acid in various conditions of the battery is as follows:

Fully charged 1.28
Half charged 1.21
Discharged 1.15

The above figures are approximate. The recommendations of the makers, usually printed on the battery, should be followed. A rough guide to the making of a solution of sulphuric acid of specific gravity 1.28 is as follows:

Concentrated sulphuric acid is added slowly, with stirring, to a beaker two-thirds full of distilled water, until the solution is almost boiling. The solution is allowed to cool, and more acid is added, with similar precautions, until the solution is again almost boiling. After cooling to room temperature, the specific gravity is adjusted by the addition of more acid or more water, according to the hydrometer reading.

(b) *Nickel-iron* (*Nife*) *accumulator.* The specific gravity of the caustic soda solution is as follows:

Specific gravity when the battery is	*Temperature*		
	60°C	*80°C*	*100°C*
First filled	1.190	1.185	1.180
Working and fully charged	1.170	1.165	1.160

Four pounds (2 kg) of caustic soda are dissolved in 1 gal (5 l) of water to provide a solution of the approximate strength required. It can then be diluted with water as necessary.

15 Pole finding paper

Blotting paper is soaked in a solution of sodium sulphate to which a few drops of phenolphthalein has been added. Damp the paper before use, and apply the wires to it a short distance apart. The paper touched by the negative pole becomes red.

16 Electroplating solutions

(a) *Copper.* About 100 g of copper sulphate crystals are dissolved in about 300 ml of water; 6 g of potassium bisulphate and 5 g of potassium cyanide are then added. The solution is made up to 450 ml. (The solution should be kept cold while it is being made.)

(b) *Silver.* About 20 g of sodium cyanide (poison) and 40 g of crystalline sodium carbonate are dissolved in about 500 ml of water. About 20 g of silver nitrate are dissolved separately in 250 ml of water. The second solution is added slowly to the first, and the mixture made up to 1 litre.

(The *current* to be passed through the solutions depends on the area of the electrode upon which the metal is to be deposited. It should not exceed about 2 amps for 100 cm^2 of surface. It should be proportionately less if the electrode is smaller. The deposited metal will appear dull. It will not present the expected bright and shining appearance until it has been burnished, by rubbing, for instance, with a bone spatula or some other hard, smooth, non-metallic surface.)

17 Silvering solution (for depositing a bright silver mirror on glass)

First, 12.5 g of silver nitrate are dissolved in 100 ml of water, and 32.5 g of sodium potassium tartrate are dissolved separately in 100 ml of water. The two solutions are mixed, warmed to 55° C, and kept at that temperature for 5 minutes. The mixture is then cooled and the clear liquid poured off from the precipitate and made up to 200 ml for solution A. Second, 1.5 g of silver nitrate are dissolved in 12 ml of water. Dilute ammonium hydroxide solution is added until the precipitate first formed is almost entirely redissolved. The liquid is made up to 200 ml for solution B. The solutions A and B are then mixed. (The surface to be silvered, having been cleaned very carefully to free it from all traces of grease, should be suspended upside down in the solution, just below the surface. The solution can be put into a clean test-tube, or small flask, and a mirror deposited on the inside of the vessel. The solution can be slightly warmed to hasten the deposition of the silver.)

18 Heat sensitive paper

A solution of cobalt chloride in water is added to a solution of ammonium chloride in water. (The proportions do not matter.) The solution is diluted until it is pale pink. Filter paper soaked in the solution and allowed to dry appears to be almost colourless, but on heating it will turn a bright green colour.

19 Cements for general purposes

Many special cements are now available on the market. Where they are not available the following can easily be made up in the laboratory:

Acid-proof cement

1 part rubber solution
2 parts linseed oil
3 parts powdered pipeclay

Aquarium cement

(a) Equal parts of powdered sulphur, ammonium chloride, and iron filings are mixed. Boiled linseed oil is then added and all are mixed thoroughly. White lead is added to form a thick paste. The cement should be applied while fluid.

(b) Mix red lead with sufficient gold size to make a smooth paste and apply immediately. Allow a few days to set and rinse the aquarium before using.

Celluloid cement

Celluloid scraps can be dissolved in acetone or amyl acetate. This cement is useful when making up small accumulators.

Cement for iron

90 parts fine iron filings
1 part flowers of sulphur
1 part ammonium chloride
Mix to a paste with water immediately before use.

Waxes

Chatterton's compound
1 part Archangel pitch
1 part resin
Melt these together and add three parts of crêpe rubber in small pieces.

Faraday's cement
5 parts resin
1 part beeswax
1 part yellow ochre
Melt the resin and wax together in a tin and stir in the ochre.

Wood's alloy (melting point 70° C)
2 parts lead
4 parts tin
8 parts bismuth
2 parts cadmium

Darcet's alloy (melting point 70° C)
5 parts lead
3 parts tin
8 parts bismuth

20 Commercial adhesives

Many glues are now available for special purposes and it is worth selecting them carefully. China, glass and metal can all be stuck by china cements. But if the mended articles are likely to be put into hot water the only completely satisfactory results are from the new epoxy resins such as araldite. Paper and card can be stuck with almost anything. Cleanest and easiest to use are the vegetable glues, such as Croid No.22; Gripfix; Ste-fix; and Gloy. Textiles, leather and carpets are best stuck by the rubber lattice glues including Copydex; Fabrex; and Jiffytex.

To stick plastics is very difficult, or even, as in the case of polythene, impossible. Best results are normally obtained with a cement of the same base as the plastic, e.g. PVC sheeting with a PVC cement such as Pac or Plastitex. The impact adhesives are very suitable for sticking laminated plastics to other materials.

Evostick and Formica Adhesive are rubber solutions, and can be removed from the hands by petrol. Most other domestic adhesives yield to soap and water.

There are many types of adhesive suitable for wood, of which the following are good examples:

Hot animal glues: Cake Glue, Pearl Glue, Croid Aero.

Cold animal and fish glues: Croid Universal, Duroglue, Seccotine, Le Page's Fish Glue.

Casein cold water glues: Casco, Croid Insol, Neverpart.

Urea Resins: Aerolite, Cascamite.

PVA Emulsions: Casco PVA, Croid Polystic, Le Page's Suregrip, Unibond.

Animal glue and the emulsions are not resistant to cold water; resin glues are, and—for a time—to hot water. Casein glues are less strong, have a fair resistance to heat and damp, but stain some woods.

Sticking things takes time. The more trouble taken in preparing and applying the glue the better the result.

21 Insulating material for electrostatics experiments

Melt some paraffin wax in a can surrounded by a water bath. Add flowers of sulphur and stir until a pasty mass is formed. This can then be moulded to fit the neck of a flask or cast into slabs as required.

22 Replacing eyepiece cross-wires

Drawn out glass tubing, monofilament nylon (obtained by unravelling a piece of nylon material) or spider web can all be used for this purpose. Remove the supporting ring from the instrument. To make a frame for holding the fibre, bend a U-piece of copper wire so that the arms are about 1 cm further apart than the diameter of the ring. Place the arms under the fibre and stick it to them with a strong adhesive before breaking off the ends. Now lift the frame and place the fibre in position over the supporting ring. Fix it down with adhesive, and allow it to dry before trimming the ends.

If spider web is to be used, it is better to apply the adhesive to the frame before taking the filament from the web, and to the supporting ring before placing it in position.

Satisfactory threads can also be made from Durofix, Centofix and Seccotine by making a blob on a piece of paper and allowing it to dry partially. Very fine filaments of glue can then be drawn from the blob by touching it with a pin or the nozzle of the tube. These can then be fitted as before, though with some practice the operation can be carried out in the supporting ring, and the cross-wires fitted directly.

23 Soldering

Solder is an alloy of 66 per cent tin and 34 per cent lead which is used for making mechanical and electrical joints between two metals. It is generally obtained in the form of rods or sticks. It is applied in the molten state from a pointed block of copper known as a 'bit'. This may be heated electrically (in which case a 75 watt heater is sufficient for general purposes) or it may be heated in a bunsen flame.

Whatever method of heating is used, the surface of the bit must be cleaned by scraping or dipping in a liquid flux, or the solder will not stick to it. When the right temperature has been reached, a little solder applied from the stick will flow all over the bit. This process, a preliminary to the actual making of the joint, is known as 'tinning'.

The surfaces to be joined must also be cleaned and tinned. In this case the heat is supplied by holding the hot copper bit on the object. When the solder begins to flow, it can be spread over the required area by rubbing gently with the tip of the bit.

When both surfaces have been tinned, they should be brought together and heat applied again by the bit while they are held in the required position. The solder from the two surfaces runs together, and on cooling makes a strong joint. Naturally large surfaces require more heat, and it may be necessary to use a flame to bring the object to the required temperature.

The three essentials to successful soldering are cleanliness, flux and heat.

Fluxes

Rosin is the most useful flux, especially for copper, brass, and tinplate, but it is not satisfactory for iron and steel.

'Dead' zinc chloride or 'killed spirits' is the easiest flux to use, but it is corrosive, and it is best to avoid it in electrical work. It is easily made by pouring hydrochloric acid on scraps of zinc and waiting until all action has ceased. The liquid can then be filtered off into a wide-necked container.

There are many commercial fluxes for special purposes. Fluxite is perhaps the best for all general purposes.

Soldering paste is now obtainable. A combination of solder and flux, it is applied with a brush and only needs the heat of a soldering iron to make a satisfactory joint.

Tallow is used for joining lead to lead, or brass to lead, and rosin or killed spirits for joints in brass, copper, tinplate, zinc; killed spirits are suitable for iron and silver. After soldering, killed spirits should be washed off with water, and rosin or Fluxite with methylated spirit.

24 Blackboard dressing

A satisfactory dressing can be made using:

100 g shellac
1000 ml alcohol
100 g powdered pumice
100 g crushed lamp black

The alcohol and shellac should be mixed first, as the shellac takes some time to dissolve. Some of the alcohol should be set aside for mixing with the lamp black. This mixture should be added later through a muslin strainer, and the whole should be well shaken before use.

25 'Dead black'

This is useful for painting the inside of 'light' apparatus, so that unwanted reflected light may be eliminated, rays made less diffused, and images made sharper. Lamp black is mixed with gold size, and turpentine added, with constant stirring, until the mixture is sufficiently thin for use as a paint.

26 Fluorescin solution

(This is useful because the track of a ray of light travelling through a dilute solution of fluorescin can be seen very clearly.) One gram of fluorescin is dissolved in 100 ml of industrial, or methylated, spirit.

27 Cutting glass

(a) *Sheet glass*. First prepare a firm, flat surface on which to lay the glass: a table with a blanket or felt thrown over it is satisfactory.

Using a rule and with a firm grip on the diamond or glass cutter, make a scratch along the required line. Turn the sheet over and tap gently along the line of the scratch with the wooden end of the cutter. If this does not result in a crack spreading along the line, turn the sheet over again and grasp it with one hand on each side of the scratch and boldly bend it about, using this line as a hinge.

(b) *Glass tubing*. Tubing is best cut with a glass knife, and 'everlasting' knives are now available. A file, though often used, makes a rounded valley in the glass instead of a crevice.

Make a scratch at the required point and holding between the thumb and finger each side of the cut, pull the tubing apart, flexing slightly upwards.

To cut off a very short piece, hold in one hand and place the scratch over some firm pivot such as a gas tap. Strike the short end a smart blow with some hard object.

Wide tubing must be scratched all round to make a neat cut. A molten piece of glass rod placed carefully on one part of the scratch will cause a crack to run round the circumference in each direction. If the two cracks do not exactly join, the tube should be bent about the uncracked part as hinge in order to separate the two pieces.

(c) *To cut the bottom off a bottle.* Make a scratch round the bottle at the required level. Wrap strips of damp blotting paper on either side of this scratch. Play a fine gas flame on the cut, rotating slowly as the glass begins to crack at this point.

If no gas flame is available the crack can be made in another way. See that the bottle is dry and well corked. Then tie a length of very absorbent cotton around it horizontally, keeping the knot as flat as possible and cutting off the loose ends. Level off carefully, so that the thread is exactly the same height up the bottle all round. Turn the bottle on its side and soak the thread with kerosene from an eye-dropper. See that no kerosene runs on the glass; if any does, wipe it off with cotton wool or filter paper. With the bottle still on its side and resting on two wood blocks with a gap between them, set fire to the thread and rotate the bottle on its axis with both hands until the whole thread is burning uniformly. Set the bottle upright on the table until the thread is burnt out, at which stage the bottle may split in two of its own accord along the line of the burn. If this does not happen as the flame goes out, gently lower the bottle upside down and vertically into cold water. It must be kept absolutely vertical and must not be immersed beyond the line of the thread.

Smooth off the raw edge with a file, or by rubbing on a flat ground-glass plate on which has been smeared a paste of carborundum powder.

(These bottles are useful for electrolysis experiments and as bell jars. In the latter case, a ring of soft rubber can be used to make an air-tight seal.)

(d) For (a) and (c), if electricity, either AC or DC, is available, it is also possible to place a round of wire, german silver or nichrome on the scratch. Switch on the current; the red hot wire will crack the glass along the scratch. This method is also found useful in cutting used electric bulbs.

28 Extinguisher

Materials for putting out a fire must be kept handy in definite places. Teacher and pupils should know how to use them quickly and correctly.

First-aid kit

A first-aid kit should be kept in each laboratory or adjoining preparation room, preferably in a separate cupboard. It must be kept in good condition, and the teacher must know how to use its contents.

29 Blueprinting

Solution 1: potassium ferricyanide 10 g; water 50 ml.

Solution 2: ferric ammonium citrate 10 g; water 50 ml.

The solutions are prepared separately and kept in a dark room or in subdued light. For use, mix equal quantities in subdued light and place in a shallow glass or enamelled tray. The paper is sensitized by brushing the mixed solution over it with a soft, wide brush, or the paper may be placed on the surface of the solution and allowed to float there for a few seconds. After sensitizing, the paper should be hung to dry in the dark room.

An opaque object, a drawing in black ink on tracing paper or any material to be printed is placed and fixed (on frame) on the paper. It should be exposed to sunlight (or artificial light) for several minutes and then washed thoroughly in running water.

30 Shellac coating

Dissolve 1 part of shellac in 5 parts of alcohol, and apply with a soft brush.

31 Preparation of common alloys

Lower melting alloys

These may, in general, be produced by using a bunsen burner as a source of heat. The bismuth and lead are melted together, and then the other ingredients added. The temperature should not be higher than necessary to prevent excess oxidation. The parts indicated are by weight.

Alloy	*Lead*	*Tin*	*Bismuth*	*Cadmium*
Wood's metal	4	2	7	1
Solder	1	1	0	0
Electric fuse alloy	8.5	2.5	1.3	0

Higher melting alloys

These may be produced using a furnace. The copper should be melted first, and the other metals added to it.

Alloy	*Copper*	*Tin*	*Zinc*
Bronze	80	5	15
Brass, malleable	58	0	42
Brass, casting	72	4	24

32 Dyeing

(a) *Direct.* The dyeing of cotton should be preceded by removing the sizing from the fabric. This is accomplished by boiling it for 5 minutes in a dilute solution of HCl (hydrochloric acid). This solution is made by adding 1 part of concentrated HCl to 10 parts of water. The following formula makes a satisfactory dye:

Congo red 0.5 g
$NaHCO_3$ (sodium bicarbonate) 2.0 g
Na_2SO_4 (sodium sulphate) 1.0 g
H_2O (distilled) 200.0 ml

The fabric should be boiled for 4 to 5 minutes and then rinsed in cold water and dried.

Instead of the congo red, methylene blue or primuline brown may be used. The dye and salts should be mixed together first and then added slowly, with stirring, to the water. White silk, rayon or wool may be dyed in the same way.

(b) *Use of a mordant.* Show the use of a mordant by heating a piece of white cotton fabric for 10 minutes in a dilute solution of $(NH_4)_2SO_4$ (ammonium sulphate). It should stand for a few minutes in dilute NH_4OH (ammonium hydroxide), after which it is rinsed. White silk may be mordanted by boiling for 5 minutes in a tannic acid solution. It should then stand for a few minutes in a solution of tartar emetic. The effect of the mordant may be studied by boiling the mordanted and unmordanted pieces of cotton and silk in alizarin solution for a few minutes, after which they are rinsed and dried.

(c) *Basic dyes.* Show the use of basic dyes using malachite green. Boil samples of mordanted and unmordanted cotton and mordanted and unmordanted silk in a solution of malachite green (or methylene blue) for 5 minutes. They are then rinsed and dried. The malachite green solution is made by dissolving 1 g of dye in 200 g of water. Two hundred grams of water are acidified with acetic acid. Forty grams of the dye solution are added to the acidified water.

(d) *Ingrain or developed dyes.* The development in the fibres of colours known as ingrain or developed dyes requires the use of three solutions. The first consists of 0.1 g of primuline and 0.1g of $NaHCO_3$ (sodium bicarbonate) dissolved in 100 ml of water. Boil a strip of unsized cotton in this solution for 1 minute, then transfer it to the second solution. This solution is made by adding 0.5 g of $NaNO_2$ (sodium nitrite) and 3 ml of HCl to 100 ml of water. The strip is permitted to remain in this bath for 15 minutes and is then transferred to the developing bath. The developing bath is made by dissolving 0.05 g of NaOH (sodium hydroxide) and 0.05 g of phenol in 100 ml of water. (Instead of phenol, alpha naphthol or resorcinol may be used.) The solution should be kept warm and the cloth allowed to remain in it for 20 minutes, after which it is rinsed and dried. The results of various types of dyeing may be studied for quality.

33 Making matches

Make small splints of wood or use matchsticks from which the heads have been cut before they are used. The ends of these sticks are dipped in melted paraffin wax. A mixture of 2 g of powdered $KClO_3$ (potassium chlorate) and 1 g of red Sb_2S_3 (antimony trisulphide) is made. *Do not grind.* The two solids should be mixed with the fingers. A thin mucilage is added to make a paste. The paraffined end of the matchstick is dipped in this mixture, and it is hung head down to harden for a day. A surface for igniting the matches is prepared by adding mucilage to equal volumes of red phosphorus and fine white sand. This is spread on a cardboard or wooden surface and permitted to dry. The matches ignite when rubbed on this surface.

The matches so prepared should be compared with commercially-made safety matches and with those that are not of the safety variety.

34 Chemical 'flower gardens'

Chemical 'flower gardens' are the result of osmotic action. A water glass (sodium silicate) solution of specific gravity of 1.1 is desirable. Into 400 ml of this solution in a beaker are dropped pieces of the sulphates of copper, iron, nickel and aluminium; the chlorides of copper and iron; and the nitrates of copper, iron, cobalt, nickel and calcium. From these pieces the 'flowers' grow rapidly. The silicates form membranous sacs which have a high concentration on the inside, thus promoting the rapid growth of the sac.

35 Winding a spiral spring

Phosphor bronze or steel wire (SWG 26) is suitable for an average spring. Choose a nail 15 cm long and clamp the point in the jaws of a hand drill. Trap the end of the wire in the jaws also. Fix the drill horizontally in a vice. Turn the handle of the drill, and pull hard on the free wire, using a piece of cloth or a leather glove to protect your hand. When you have made the spring as long as you need, use a pair of pliers to bend the free end round the nail, and cut the wire. The wire will uncoil a little, but this does not matter. Release the wire from the jaws of the drill, cut off the ends of the spring so formed and remove the nail. Using pliers, grip the two end turns of the spring together and bend them at right angles to form a loop. Repeat this at the other end of the spring.

CHAPTER XIX

Some new tendencies in science teaching

Science has been taught in schools for approximately a hundred years. It began as natural philosophy, and by about fifty years ago had settled down to become a course of scientific knowledge which was mainly factual and descriptive. During the last few years the science programmes of many countries have been under scrutiny. The rapid progress of scientific knowledge during this century has brought with it many new concepts, and a new unity of ideas. The manner as well as the matter of science has changed: individual research has been replaced by team work; new techniques have appeared, and the apparatus in use has become much more elaborate. The science taught in schools has become divorced from everyday life, and many teachers have begun to feel that it is no longer sufficient to teach the science of even a generation ago, but that matter should be included in the courses which is more relevant to a modern age. There is nothing essentially new in this—sooner or later the skills and achievements of society have always been reflected in the curriculum of the schools. But the great advances that have been made in science and mathematics, and in the associated technology, seem to have outstripped the progress of educational theory and practice.

For this reason, many countries are rethinking their educational programmes, and because physics is the most advanced of the sciences, and possibly produces the most far-reaching effects on human life, it is this subject which has received first consideration. The conclusions reached bear equally on the other science subjects, but in what follows physics will be stressed because in this subject some complete syllabuses and schemes have been worked out and tried as pilot schemes. In a short survey it is not possible to give in detail the educational schemes of different countries, and in what follows the emphasis is on the principles involved in the construction of the courses. Mention will be made of the work done by the Physical Sciences Study Committee in the United States of America, by the Science Masters' Association in the United Kingdom, and by the International Union of Pure and Applied Physics, and a brief note is added on physics teaching in the Union of Soviet Socialist Republics.

The work of the Physical Sciences Study Committee

The Physical Sciences Study Committee is a group of university and secondary school physics teachers, who undertook in 1956 the task of developing an improved physics course for American secondary schools. Its work has been administered by Educational Services Incorporated, a non-profit making corporation. It has stimulated a general movement in the United States to improve secondary school science education; similar groups are now working in the areas of biology, chemistry and mathematics.

A critical examination of school textbooks, apparatus, visual aids and library material revealed the following deficiencies:

1 Textbooks in general reflected a scientific outlook which dated back half a century, and was no longer representative of the views of the scientific community.
2 Genuine attempts to remain abreast of scientific developments had given even the best textbooks a patchwork quality in which the unity of the subject had disappeared. The sheer mass of the material had become unreasonably great.
3 With the increasing application of science to everyday life the books had become further overloaded by more and more attention to technology.
4 The laboratory manuals suffered the same defects.
5 The potentialities of audio-visual aids were not being adequately exploited.

It was then decided to formulate a new physics course in which the unity of the subject would be preserved, and modern ideas would fall naturally into place. This has now been embodied in a textbook entitled *PSSC Physics*. Naturally, this book is designed to fit the educational schemes of the United States, and in fact is intended to be a one-year course for the last year of the secondary school. But the outline of the syllabus, the ingenious experiments which have been incorporated in the laboratory manual, and the supporting films and library books are of interest to teachers in all countries.

The syllabus divides naturally into four parts. The first is an introduction to time, space, matter and motion. The second includes optics and waves. A particle model of light is developed to explain wave behaviour. When the particle model is found inadequate, a kinematic picture of wave behaviour is introduced as an alternative. In the third part, mechanics is presented through the dynamics of Galileo and Newton, leading to a study of momentum, energy, and the conservation laws. The fourth part begins with an introduction to electricity and magnetism, and the behaviour of particles in fields. Discovery of the photo-electric effect leads back once more to a more subtle consideration of the nature of light. The synthesis of wave behaviour and particle mechanics in a description of the atom bring the course to a conclusion.

In close relation to the ideas developed in the textbook, a laboratory programme was then conceived; in this the following considerations were used as a guide:

1 Experiments should be true experiments, and not routine accumulation of data to agree with a result well known in advance.
2 They should be performed with simple apparatus that can be quickly assembled by the student.
3 They should encourage further work along suggested lines, and should lead to the consideration of theoretical ideas growing from the experiment, and be guided by those already mentioned in the textbook.

It was originally the intention of the committee to develop laboratory apparatus of a type which could be constructed by the teachers and students themselves, but it was soon discovered that although there would be obvious advantages in this, the burden on the teachers would be too great. The apparatus described in the laboratory manual is now manufactured commercially to designs which have made it possible to set the commercial price at a minimum.

Visual aids were then considered, and an examination of the many educational films available showed that there were few which in manner and content furthered the ideas outlined in the textbook. Accordingly, a new set of about sixty films was planned. The intention of these films is: (a) to ease the load on the teacher; (b) to provide visual presentation of operations too difficult to carry out in the laboratory or to show by demonstration experiments; (c) to present a new subject, or to summarize and integrate a field of study; (d) to show, where possible, real scientists at work in real situations, and speaking directly to the students.

A further activity of the committee has been the production of a set of paperback books about science and scientists. Their primary purpose is to take the load off the textbook, leaving it free for the elucidation of general principles. Sixty books are at present envisaged, which will provide a survey of physics within the grasp of those following the main course. Some tell of the role of physics in the service of man, others are biographical in nature and tell the stories of discoverers and their great discoveries. It is hoped, too, that besides supplementing the course, they may be comprehensible to the layman, and perhaps help to bridge the gap between the science and arts student.

Trials of the course outlined above showed that some teachers would find a guide to the textbook helpful. The final effort of the committee was therefore to produce a set of teachers' notes for this purpose, including solutions to the problems in the text, and suggestions for teaching the subject. This comprehensive guide is now available, and will prove invaluable to all attempting to adopt the course, or to adapt it to their own special needs.

Further information

The Physical Science Study Committee is interested in rendering whatever services may be of use to those individuals and schools who wish to know exactly what the new course is, and how it has come into being in its present form. Such information, as well as advice on the present status of foreign translations and adaptations, may be obtained from:

Physical Science Study Committee, Educational Services Incorporated, 164 Main Street, Watertown 72, Mass.

Copies of the textbook and laboratory guide and teacher's guide may be obtained from:

D. C. Heath and Co., 285 Columbus Avenue, Boston 16, Mass.

A catalogue of the laboratory apparatus may be obtained from:

Macalaster-Bicknell Co., 253 Norfolk Street, Cambridge 39, Mass.

A film catalogue, and information on previewing the films, may be obtained from:

Modern Talking Picture Service, Inc., 3 East 54th Street, New York 22, N.Y.

The Science Study Series—a library of paperback books for outside reading in fields related to the PSSC course—may be obtained from:

Doubleday and Company, Inc., 575 Madison Avenue, New York 22, N.Y.

Up to the present time, arrangements have been completed for the translation of the Science Study Series into Arabic, Bengali, Dutch, Finnish, German, Indonesian, Italian, Japanese, Persian, Polish, Spanish, Swedish and Urdu, and for the publication of the series in the British Commonwealth.

References

Modern high school physics: A recommended course of study. Bureau of Publications, Teachers' College, Columbia University, New York, N.Y.

Science in your school. American Association of Science Teachers.

Education for an age of science, by President Eisenhower's Science Advisory Committee. United States Information Service, 1959.

International education in physics, by Brown and Clark. John Wiley and Sons, 440 Park Avenue S., New York 16, N.Y.

The work of the Science Masters' Association and the Association of Women Science Teachers in the United Kingdom

In 1957, motivated by the considerations mentioned earlier, the above associations issued a policy statement on science teaching in schools. Subject panels later compiled syllabuses for the biological, chemical and physical parts of the science course below the sixth forms, as well as for the specialist teaching which follows.

The general recommendations were that science should be the 'core' subject in grammar schools in much the same way for example as English and mathematics are at present, and as classics used to be. Believing that all students should study science up to the fifth form years, and that all specialists should study some science, the authors of the statement laid down the following principles. Teaching should be divided into three phases: an introductory phase covering the first two years, an intermediate phase up to about sixteen years of age, and an advanced phase to include some specialization.

In 1960 the committee issued syllabuses for physics, chemistry and biology covering these three phases. To make it possible to include material more closely connected with modern life, difficult concepts, ideas and numerical problems on energy, magnetism, and certain aspects of heat and light were omitted from the early and intermediate phases of the physics course. The criterion for the inclusion of any item at the advanced phase was, 'Is it fundamental to physics today?' Subjects more properly included under the heading of applied physics or technology have also been excluded. These have been replaced by substantive sections on mechanics, the understanding of which is so essential and fundamental to an appreciation of modern physics. The same general principles have been applied to chemistry. Although it can be claimed that the teaching of chemistry in British schools has at its best been as good as any in the world, some modifications are necessary to meet the new situation. The past syllabuses have been too heavily weighted with facts, preparation, and details of procedure.

The general plan of the early stages in chemistry, it is suggested, should be visualized as a series of empirical investigations, with the emphasis on experimentation and observation. Speculations in the light of ascertained facts will then arise, and opportunities will be provided for the invention of simple theories. These in turn will lead to new theories and the discovery of new facts. In the second phase, it is suggested that the pupil should learn to appreciate the nature of scientific laws, the inter-relationship between facts and theories, and the intimate relation between matter and electricity. Some ideas, too, should be formed concerning the need to assume a particle structure of atoms when considering the reactions in which matter takes part, as well as the factors which can affect chemical reactions in general. On the sound basis of the first two phases of teaching, it should now be possible to discuss the material basis of chemistry, types of materials and changes, and their full explanation in terms of molecules and ions.

The committee, reviewing the teaching of biology, emphasized that this term implies not a single science, but a whole group of sciences. It was further realized that biology can be used to unite all the sciences, and to link them with psychology, the social sciences, and with history and the arts. To achieve this linking effect, biology should be centred on the study of whole organisms, and not on anatomical, physiological, cytological or biochemical abstractions.

In the introductory and intermediate phases biology should be part of an introduction to science as a whole. Personal observations on live organisms should be made, and prominence given to practical work. The organisms studied should be selected from easily available local flora and fauna, and simple habitat studies are eminently suitable. Nutrition and respiration can be studied as parts of wider science topics with physical, chemical and biological aspects. At the intermediate phase an advance should be made in greater depth and on a narrower front than at the introductory phase. A further suggestion was that a syllabus based on that of the level of the Cambridge Local Examinations Syndicate meets the above requirements, and contains more useful suggestions to teachers than many of the other syllabuses. The syllabus at the advanced stage grows out of that of the earlier phases. Sixth formers approach the subject with more mature minds: more advanced practical work is possible. Individual dissections of animals can take the place of the previous demonstrations. The staining and mounting of some microscopical preparations can also be undertaken. Teachers can develop particular sections according to their own outlook and interests, and to the local conditions, especially as regards field work. The syllabus would therefore include further study of the mammal and of flowering plants; a variety of patterns of life; elementary ecology, and a number of general biological topics under the general title of 'The nature, continuance and diversification of life'.

The work of all these planning committees is not complete, but the suggestions outlined have been embodied in detailed syllabuses published by the associations. The great freedom allowed to British teachers allows them to be interpreted in many different ways. Pilot schemes are in operation in the schools, and in the next few years much will be learnt of how best to achieve the desired objectives.

Publications

The following publications of the Science Masters' Association and the Association of Women Science Teachers are obtainable at 2s. each from the Librarian, Science Masters' Association, 52 Bateman Street, Cambridge:
A policy statement on science education.
Physics for grammar schools.
Chemistry for grammar schools.
Biology for grammar schools.

The work of the International Union of Pure and Applied Physics

In July 1960 an international conference on physics teaching took place in Paris. It was sponsored by the Organization for European Economic Co-operation (now OECD), Unesco and the International Union of Pure and Applied Physics, and was part of a wider study of the teaching of science, mathematics and chemistry being undertaken by OEEC. Delegates from the Netherlands, Switzerland, Italy, Denmark, France, the United States of America, Japan, Poland, Germany and the United Kingdom considered topics including examinations, laboratory work, the training of teachers, and the use of films and television in science teaching. They further considered the defects of the present systems, the approach to the teaching of physics and the supply of physics teachers.

The diversity of conditions and facilities in the various countries made it very difficult to arrive at general conclusions. Some countries were inevitably criticised for over-emphasizing the theoretical aspects of the subject, and others for the inclusion of too much practical work. But all were agreed that drastic changes in the method and content of physics teaching were necessary. General agreement was however found in an agreed syllabus, and suggestions were made for its implementation. These are to be found in a full report of the conference. This is now published under the title *International Education in Physics*, John Wiley and Sons Inc., 440 Park Avenue S., New York 16, N.Y.

Science teaching in the Union of Soviet Socialist Republics

The revision of the science teaching programme in the Soviet Union began as early as 1919, when a State Council was set up to provide, amongst other things, general and methodological guidance and curricula for the higher schools. In 1921 a further special commission declared the aim of the Soviet high schools, and set up schemes for the training of scientists and teachers.

But the greatest step forward was made in 1957, when the regulations of the Ministry of Education required all scientists in postgraduate training to study pedagogics, psychology, logic, and methods of teaching special subjects, as well as the skill of conducting classes. This resulted in a great increase in the numbers of scientists available for teaching.

The Academy of Pedagogical Science set up in 1943 has rendered great help to the teachers. It provides information on new teaching methods, and promotes constructive co-operation between teachers and educational authorities, and furthers the production of textbooks. It is also responsible for the syllabuses and supply of apparatus, as well as for the textbooks to be used. The syllabus thus includes a full list of the demonstration experiments to be shown, the topics to be discussed, the films to be shown, and the expeditions and factory visits to be made. Regional training institutes set up in all areas supplement the work in the academy by organizing courses, lectures and seminars.

Education is now compulsory from 7 to 18 years of age, and all pupils have the same basic course for the first eight years. The schools are co-educational, and classes must not exceed 30 in number, though more usually they do not exceed 24. There is no 'streaming'; all pupils go through this same basic course. For the last three years the pupils proceed to a type of school suited to their abilities.

Biology is the first science to be taught, but in the last three years gives way to physics. The syllabus here includes advanced work on atomic structure; nuclear energy; isotopes; the physics of light; supersonics; the photo-electric effect, semi-conductors, as well as work on three-phase alternating current. There is a great emphasis on practical work by the students, and also on good demonstration experiments. Most schools possess an oscilloscope and the necessary apparatus for teaching alternating current. As mentioned, the apparatus is supplied by the academy, and is thus of a type most suitable for the purpose.

The syllabus outlined is only a minimum; sufficient time is allowed for individual teachers to follow their own ideas. The intention of the syllabus, the suggestions and the provision of apparatus is merely to ensure that all pupils are adequately taught, even by the less gifted teachers.

This brief outline shows what consistent effort, immense energy and resources have been directed towards science teaching during the last 40 years. The result is seen in the outstanding position of Soviet science today.

References

The training of scientists in the Soviet Union, by G. Galkin.

Education in the USSR, by M. I. Kondakov.

APPENDIX A

BOOKS FROM A SCIENCE MASTER'S LIBRARY

France

Anatomie végétale, by Bourceau. 3 volumes, Presses Universitaires de France.
Biologie végétale, by Cannefort and Paniel. Doin
Cours de physique générale, by Bruhat. 4 volumes, Masson.
Cours de physique, by Lemoine and Guyot. 5 volumes, Bordas.
Cours de physique, by Moussa and Ponsonnet. 2 volumes, Desvignes.
Cours de physique, by Faivre, Dupaigre and Lamirand. 3 volumes, Masson.
Chimie générale, by Rumeau and Gallais. Delagrave.
Chimie générale, by Pascal. 4 volumes, Masson.
Cours de chimie, by Lamirand, Brunold and Pariselle. 4 volumes, Masson.
Chimie propédeutique, by Lombard. Gauthier-Villars.
Encyclopédie française: tome II: Physique, by Dubois. Larousse.
Flore complète, 120 fascicules et table, by Bonnier. Orlhac.
Géologie générale et pétrographie, by Theobald and Gama. Doin.
Manuel de paléontologie animale. Masson.
Manuel de paléontologie végétale. Masson.
Minéraux et les roches (Les), by Buttgenbach. Dunod.
Monde vivant (Le), by Gautière. 3 volumes, Béranger.
Morphologie et physiologie animales, by Bresse. Larousse.
Nouveau traité de chimie minérale. 10 volumes parus, Masson.
Paléontologie, by Theobald and Gama. Doin.
Physique générale et experimentale, by Fleury and Mathieu. 6 volumes, Eyrolles.
Physique de base, by Llibantry. Masson.
Précis de biologie animale: PCB-Licence, by Aron and Grasse. Masson.
Précis de biologie végétale: PCB, by Guilliermond and Mangenot. Masson.
Précis de géologie, by Moret. Masson.
Précis de minéralogie, by Lapadu and Hargues. Masson.
Principes de géologie, by Fourmarier. 2 volumes, Masson.
Tableaux des minéraux des roches, by Christophe, Michel and Lévy. Éditions du CNRS.
Technique générale du laboratoire de physique, by Surugue. 3 volumes, Éditions du CNRS.
Traité de botanique (systématique), by Chadefaud and Emberger. 2 volumes, Masson.

Union of Soviet Socialist Republics

The following books in English are obtainable from Foreign Languages Publishing House, 21 Zubovsky Boulevard, Moscow:
Archaeology in the USSR, by Mongait. £2 5s. (Survey ranging from Stone-Age Russia to the Middle Ages.)
Astronomy for entertainment, by Perelman. 7s. 6d.
Bees, by Khalifman. 7s. 6d. (Complete guide to bees and bee-keeping.)
Celestial mechanics, by Ryabov. 7s. (Simplified explanation of the calculation of the movements of the heavenly bodies and earth satellites.)
Cerebal cortex and the internal organs (The), by Bykov. £1 1s.
Control of communicable diseases in the USSR, by Zhdanov. 1s. 3d.
Cosmic rays, by Zhdanov. 6s.
Fundamentals of geology, by Obruchev. 12s. 6d.
General chemistry: a text book, by Glinka. 4s. 6d.

Geochemistry for everyone, by Fersman. 12s. 6d.
Life of the plant (*The*), by Timiryazev. 7s. 6d.
Origin of man (*The*), by Nesturkh. £1 10s.
Pavlov: his life and work, by Asratyn. 3s. 6d.
Pavlov: selected works. 10s. 6d.
Sea bed (*The*), by Zenkovich. 4s. 6d.
Soviet medicine in the fight against mental diseases. 5s.
Sun (*The*), by Severney. 6s.
Textbook of physiology, by Bykov. £2 5s.
Theoretical physics, by Kompanyets. £1 17s. 6d.
Theory of the origin of the earth (*A*), by Schmidt. 4s. 6d.
Training of scientists in the Soviet Union (*The*), by Galkin. 6s.
Universe (*The*), by Oparin and Fesenkov. £1 17s. 6d. (Examination of the possibility of life in neighbouring planets and throughout the universe.)

United Kingdom

Alternating currents, by Dance, Savage and Ghey. John Murray. (Modern Science Memoirs.)
Atom and its energy (*The*), by Andrade. Nelson.
Dictionary of physics, by Gray. Longmans, Green.
Dictionary of science, by Uvarov and Chapman. Penguin Books.
Introduction to laboratory techniques, by Ansley. Macmillan.
Lecture experiments in chemistry, by Fowles. Bell.
Rural science and school gardening, by Hilton. Batsford.
School experiments with alternating current, by Pearce. Bell.
School laboratory management, by Sutcliffe. John Murray.
Science books for the school library. Science Masters' Association. (Supplements are issued with the *School science review* and are available from the librarian. price 6d. each.)
Science data, by Friend. Griffin.
Science master's book (*The*). (Experiments selected from the *School science review*.)
Series I
Part I *Physics*.
Part II *Chemistry and biology*.
Series II
Part I *Physics*.
Part II *Chemistry and biology*.
Series III
Part I *Physics*.
Part II *Chemistry*.
Part III *Biology*.
Part IV *Experiments for the modern school*.
Series IV
Part I *Physics*.
Secondary modern science teaching. Parts I and II, by John Murray.
Simple experiments in biology, by Bibby. Heinemann.
Simple experiments with insects, by Kalmus. Heinemann.
Tables of physical and chemical constants, by Kaye and Laby. Longmans, Green.
Teaching of astronomy in schools (*The*), by Beet. Cambridge University Press.
Teaching and learning of biology in secondary schools (*The*), by Green. Allman.
Teaching chemistry, by White. University of London Press.
Teaching of chemistry (*The*), by Newbury. Heinemann.
Teaching of colour in elementary science courses (*The*), by Savage. John Murray. (Modern Science Memoirs.)
Teaching of science in secondary schools (*The*). John Murray.
Teaching science to the ordinary pupil, by Laybourn and Bailey. University of London Press.

The following titles appear in the series of Unesco handbooks on the teaching of science in tropical countries :

Teaching of science in tropical primary schools (*The*), by Joseph. Oxford University Press.

Teaching of general science in tropical secondary schools (*The*), by Saunders. Oxford University Press.
Teaching of physics in tropical secondary schools (*The*), by Boulind. Oxford University Press.
Teaching of chemistry in tropical secondary schools (*The*), by Newbury. Oxford University Press.

United States of America

Animals without backbones, by Buchsbaum. University of Chicago Press.
Biology investigations, by Oho, Blanc and Towle. Henry Holt and Co.
Chemistry, by Sienko and Plane. McGraw Hill Book Co.
College zoology, by Hegner and Stiles. Macmillan.
Condensed chemical dictionary, by Rose and Rose. Reinhold Publishing Co.
Demonstration experiments in physics, by Sutton. McGraw Hill Book Co.
Fundamentals of microbiology, by Frobisher. W. B. Saunders Co.
General chemistry, by Pauling. W. L. Freeman and Co.
Handbook of chemistry and physics. 42nd edition. Chemical Rubber Co.
Introduction to concepts and theories of physical science, by Holton. Addison-Wesley Publishing Co.
Laboratory and field studies in biology, by Lawson. Holt, Rinehart and Winston.
Laboratory exercises in animal biology, by Braungart. C. V. Mosby Co.
Laboratory introduction to chemistry, by Weaver and Weaver. McGraw Hill Book Co.
Machinery of the body, by Carlsen, Apton and Johnson. University of Chicago Press.
Matter and light, by L. de Broglie. Dover.
Organic chemistry, by Morrison and Boyd. Allyn and Bacon.
Physical chemistry, by Daniels and Alberty. John Wiley and Sons.
Physics, by the Physical Sciences Study Committee. Educational Services Inc.
Physics in your school, by the American Institute of Physics. McGraw Hill Book Co.
Plant physiology, by Meyer and Anderson. Van Nostrand Co.
Plant world (*The*), by Fuller. Holt, Reinhart and Winston.
Saturday science, by Blumle. E. P. Dutton and Co.
Science education for the elementary school teacher, by Tannheim. Ginn and Co.
Science teaching in secondary schools, by Richardson. Prentice-Hall.
'Scientific American' book of projects for the amateur scientist, by Strong. Simon and Shuster.
Scientific experiments in chemistry, by De Bruyne, Kirk and Beers. Henry Holt Co.
Semi-micro chemistry, by De Bruyne, Kirk and Beers. Henry Holt Co.
Source book for biological science, by Marholt, Evelyn and others. Harcourt Brace.
Source book for physical science, by Moreholt. Harcourt, Brace and World.
Textbook of physiology, by Zoethout and Tuttle. C. V. Mosby Co.
Universe and Dr. Einstein (*The*), by Barnett. New American.
Van Nostrand's scientific encyclopedia. D. Van Nostrand Co.

APPENDIX B

PERIODICALS FOR SCIENCE TEACHING AND SCIENCE CLUB LIBRARIES

Australia

Australian journal of science, six issues per year, 25s. The Australian and New Zealand Association for the Advancement of Science, Science House, 157 Gloucester Street, Sydney.

Australian science teachers' journal, 1s. per issue. 156 Pelham Street, Melbourne, N.3.

Science education news. Science Teachers' Association of New South Wales, Box 3328 PP, GPO Sydney.

Science Teachers' Association of Queensland's newsletter. Mr. F. T. Barrell, The Cavendish Road High School, Holland Park, Brisbane.

Austria

Natur und Technik, monthly. Wien VII. Burggasse 28-32.

Der Osterreichische Schulfunk, monthly. Prof. Franz Gregora, Wien IV, Argentinierstrasse (Funkhaus).

Universum Natur und Technik, fortnightly, DM 0.90 per copy. R. Spies and Co., Wien V, Straussengasse 16.

Belgium

Bulletin, International Union for the Conservation of Nature and Natural Resources, 31 rue Vautier, Brussels.

Ciel et terre, 25 frs per copy. Av. Circulaire 3, Uccle, Brussels.

Dia-Revue: enseignement et vulgarisation des sciences par la diapòsitive et la photo, bimonthly. 125 Belgian francs per annum, 17 Belle-Voie, Wavre.

Brazil

Matemática, Técnica e Ciêcia, monthly. Praia de Botafogo 244-A, 1º ander-Rio de Janeiro.

Canada

Canadian nature, bimonthly, 35 cents per copy. Audubon Society of Canada, 177 Jarvis Street, Toronto 2, Ontario.

Ceylon

Young scientist, 3 issues, Rs. 1.90 Gotami Rd., Colombo 8.

Czechoslovakia

Ochrana Prirody (nature study), bimonthly, 48 Kcs. Praha II, Ostrovini ul c 30.

Denmark

Naturviden-Ungdommens naturvidenskabelige forening, Denmarks tekniske Hojskole, Oster Voldgade 10 N, Kobenhavn K.

Finland

Maatalouskerho-neuvoja (4-H Club), Bulevadi 28, Helsinki.
Molekyyli, Postilokero 252, Helsinki.

France

Air et l'espace (*L'*), monthly, year's subscription 27 NF; 2.50 NF per copy. 51, avenue des Ternes, Paris-17e.
Atomes, monthly, year's subscription 21 NF; 1.80 NF per copy. 4, place de l'Odéon, Paris-6e.
Bulletin du Musée national d'histoire naturelle, bimonthly, year's subscription 20 NF; 2.50 NF per copy. 57, rue Cuvier, Paris-5e.
Électricien, monthly, year's subscription 18 NF; 1.80 NF per copy. Librairie Dunod, 92, rue Bonaparte, Paris-6e.
Énergie nucléaire, monthly, year's subscription 53 NF. 28, rue Saint-Dominique, Paris-7e.
Enseignement des sciences, five issues per year, year's subscription 12 NF. Librairie Hermann, 115, boulevard Saint-Germain, Paris-6e.
Humanités scientifiques, monthly, year's subscription 22 NF. Librairie Hatier, 59, boulevard Raspail, Paris-6e.
Information scientifique, monthly, year's subscription 19 NF. Librairie Baillière, 19, rue Hautefeuille, Paris-6e.
Ingénieurs et techniciens, monthly, year's subscription 25 NF; 2.50 NF per copy. 30, rue Tronchet, Paris-9e.
Naturalia, monthly, year's subscription 25 NF; 2 NF per copy. 122, rue des Rosiers, Saint-Ouen (Seine).
Mathématiques élémentaires, monthly, year's subscription 10 NF. Librairie Vuibert, 63, boulevard Saint-Germain, Paris-5e.
Nature (*La*), monthly, year's subscription 33 NF; 2.80 NF per copy. 92, rue Bonaparte, Paris-6e.
Nucleus, monthly, year's subscription 45 NF. Librairie Dunod, 92, rue Bonaparte, Paris-6e.
Oiseaux de France, quarterly, 2 NF per copy. 129, boulevard Saint-Germain, Paris-6e.
Radio et TV, monthly, year's subscription 17 NF; 1.80 NF per copy. Éditions Chiron, 40, rue de Seine, Paris-6e.
Revue du son (Arts et techniques sonores), 2.50 NF per copy. Éditions Chiron, 40, rue de Seine, Paris-6e.
Science et nature, bimonthly, year's subscription 18 NF; 2.80 NF per copy. 12 *bis*, place Henri-Bergson, Paris-8e.
Sciences et avenir, monthly, year's subscription 18 NF; 1.50 NF per copy. 14, rue de la Baume, Paris-8e.
Terre des jeunes, monthly, year's subscription 9 NF; 0.70 NF per copy. 5, rue Palatine, Paris-6e.

Federal Republic of Germany

Deutscher Jugendbund für Naturbeobachtung, Hamburg, Volksdorf, Wiesenhöfen 7.
Hobby, Das Magazin der Technik, Stuttgart-W, Paulinenstr. 44.
Kosmos, Monatsschrift für Naturfreunde, Stuttgart-O, Pfizerstr. 5/7.
Lupe, Dieter Koenig, Premervörde, Zevenerstr. 3.
Naturwissenschaftliche Rundschau, quarterly, DM 4.80, Stuttgart, Tübingen Str. 53.
Orion, Naturwissenschaftliche Zeitschrift für jedermann, Murnau/München, Seidlpark.
Schulfunk, Hessischer Rundfunk, monthly, Prof. Gottfried Hausmann, Frankfurt am Main, Liebfrauenberg 37.
Die Umschau in Wissenschaft und Technik, fortnightly, DM 42, Frankfurt am Main, Stuttgarter Str. 20/22.

Ghana

Bulletin of the Ghana Association of Science Teachers, J. K. Lamptey (Editor), Fijai Secondary School, Sekondi.

Indonesia

Mimbar teruma, monthly, Djl. Karangtinggal 23, Pos Hegarmanah, Bandung.

Pengantar pengetahuan, monthly, Jajasan Pendidikan Masjarakat, Djl. Karangtinggal 2 Pos Hegarmanah, Bandung.

Italy

Scienza e lavoro, monthly, 1,500 lire, La Scuola, Brescia.

Japan

Bulletin of the National Science Museum, monthly. Ueno Park, Tokyo.

Netherlands

Amoeba, N.J.N., monthly. Aart van Rossum, Sassenheimstraat 49 I, Amsterdam W.
Hobby club, quarterly, F.5. Van Miereveldstraat 1, Amsterdam Z.
Natuur en Landschap, quarterly, F.5. Herengracht 540, Amsterdam C.

New Zealand

Science review, monthly, 25s. G.P.O. Box 3001, Wellington.

Spain

Aldea—Revista para la juventud del campo, monthly, 2.50 pesetas per copy. Alcala, 44 6º, Madrid.
Matualidades y cotos escolares de previsión, monthly, 2 pesetas per copy. Manuel Silvela 4, Madrid.

Sweden

Fältbiologen, 4 Kr., Riddargatan, Stockholm Ö.

Switzerland

Jeunesse magazine, monthly, 6 frs. Jordils 5, Lausanne.
Jugend Woche, monthly. Jenatschstrasse 4, Zürich 2.
Leben und Umwelt, monthly, 5.20 frs. Oberalpstrasse 13, Basel.
Lehrerzeitung, weekly. Zürich 4, Stauffacherquai 36.

Thailand

Science, monthly, 30 bahts. Science Society of Thailand, Physics Building, Chulalongkorn University, Bangkok.

Union of Soviet Socialist Republics

The following periodicals are obtainable from Mezhdunarodnaja Kniga, Moscow, G-200, at the annual subscription rate indicated:

Pedagogical

Biology in school, bimonthly, 18s.
Chemistry in school, bimonthly, 18s.
Information bulletin of higher and specialized education, monthly, 18s.
Physics in school, bimonthly, 18s.
School and industry, monthly, £1 2s.
Teacher's gazette, 156 issues per year, £1 5s.

Scientific

Astronomical journal, bimonthly, £5 15s.
Atomic energy, monthly, £5 16s.
Biochemistry, bimonthly, £5.

Biophysics, bimonthly, £4 7s.
Journal of acoustics, quarterly, £2 6s.
Journal of botany, monthly, £10 16s.
Journal of scientific and applied photography and cinematography, bimonthly, £2 14s.
Radio and electronics abstracts, 24 issues per year, £4 13s.

Bulletins of higher schools (Ministry of Higher and Specialized Secondary Education)
Colloids, bimonthly, £3 16s.
Crystallography, bimonthly, £5 7s.
Instruments and techniques of experiments, bimonthly, £5 7s.
Physics, bimonthly, £3 16s.
Radiophysics, bimonthly, £3 16s.

Magazines for the young
Science and life, monthly, £1 2s.
Young naturalist, monthly, 12s.
Young technician, monthly, £1 7s. (With supplement *For skilful hands*.)

United Kingdom

Advancement of science, quarterly, 7s. 6d. per copy. British Association, 18 John Adam Street, London, W.C.2.
Aeromodeller, monthly, 2s. per copy. Argus Press, 8-10 Temple Avenue, London, E.C.4.
Atom, monthly. Information bulletin of the UK Atomic Energy Authority, 11 Charles II Street, London, S.W.1.
Bird notes, quarterly, 2s. per copy. 25 Eccleston Square, London, S.W.1. (Journal of the Royal Society for the Protection of Birds.)
British trade alphabet, yearly. Lofthouse, Wakefield, Yorkshire.
Bulletin of amateur entomologists, monthly, 1s. 3d. per copy. 3 Salcombe Drive, Morden, Surrey.
Contemporary physics, bimonthly, 5s. per copy. Taylor and Francis, Red Lion Court, London, E.C.4.
Discovery, monthly, 2s.6d. per copy. Jarrold and Sons, Norwich.
Endeavour, quarterly. Imperial Chemical Industries, Millbank, London, S.W.1.
Farming, monthly, year's subscription, 19s. Jarrold and Sons, Norwich.
Journal of the East Kent Science Teachers' Association, 1s. 3d. (post free). Miss C. E. Groves, Glebe Corner Cottage, St. Martin's Hill, Canterbury.
Journal of the Royal Society of Arts, monthly, 5s. per copy. 6 John Adam Street, London, W.C.2.
London science teacher, quarterly, 2s. 6d. per copy. H. E. Knock, Esq., 17 Salcombe Gardens, North Side, London, S.W.4. (Journal of the London Science Teachers' Association.)
Meccano magazine, monthly, 1s. per copy. Meccano, Binns Rd., Liverpool, 13.
Model aircraft, weekly, 1s. 6d. per copy. Percival Marshall, 19-20 Noels Street, London, W.1.
Model engineer, weekly, 1s. per copy. Percival Marshall, 19-20 Noels Street, London, W.1.
Mond magazine, monthly. The Mond Nickel Co., Thames House, Millbank, London, S.W.1.
Model railway news, monthly, 2s. per copy. Percival Marshall, 19-20 Noels Street, London, W.1.
Nature, weekly, 2s. 6d. per copy. Macmillan and Co., St. Martin's Lane, London, W.C.2.
New era in home and school, year's subscription (10 issues), £1. 1 Park Crescent, London, W.1.
New scientist, weekly, 1s. per copy. Cromwell House, Fulwood Place, High Holborn, London, W.C.1.
Observatory. Royal Observatory, Greenwich, London, S.E.10.
Practical mechanics, monthly, 1s. 6d. per copy. George Newnes, Tower House, Southampton Street, London, W.C.2.
Practical wireless, monthly, 1s. per copy. George Newnes, Tower House, Southampton Street, London, W.C.2.
Proceedings of the Royal Institute, quarterly, 8s. 6d. per copy. 21 Albemarle Street, London, W.1.
Railway magazine, bimonthly, 2s. 6d. per copy. 33 Tothill Street, London, S.W.1.
School nature study, quarterly, 3s. 6d. per copy. 5 Dartmouth Chambers, Theobalds Road, London, W.C.1.
School nature study union, 1s. per copy. 23 Crystal Palace Road, East Dulwich, London, S.E.22.

School science review, 3 issues per year, 12s. 6d. per copy. 52 Bateman Street, Cambridge
Science club, fortnightly, year's subscription £1 2s. 6d. Junior Clubs Publications, 5 St. Jame Street, London, W.C.1.
Science Museum bulletin. Science Museum, South Kensington, London, S.W.7.
Scientific film, bimonthly, 3s. 6d. per copy. 55a Welbeck Street, London, W.1. (Journal o the Scientific Films Association.)
Science progress, quarterly, year's subscription £2 12s. Edward Arnold, 41 Maddox Street London, W.C.1.
Science teacher, fortnightly, year's subscription 5s. Junior Clubs Publications, 5 St. Jame Street, London, W.C.1.
Short wave magazine, monthly, year's subscription £1 13s. 55 Victoria Street, London, S.W.1
Space flight, monthly, 3s. 6d. per copy. 3 Cork Street, London, W.1.
Technology, weekly, 1s. per copy. The Times, Printing House Square, London, E.C.4.
Times science review, quarterly, 1s. per copy. The Times, Printing House Square, London E.C.4.
Trains illustrated, monthly, 2s. per copy. Ian Allen, Hampton Court, Surrey.
Trees, quarterly, 2s. 6d. per copy. The Men of Trees, Stansted Park Estate Office, Rowland Castle, Hants.
World science review, 2s. 6d. per copy. 11 Eaton Place, London, S.W.1.

United States of America

American biology teacher, monthly (Oct.-May), $6 (abroad $6.75). National Associatio of Biology Teachers, P. Webster, Bryan City Schools, Bryan, Ohio, *or* Herman C. Kranzer College of Education, Temple University, Philadelphia 22, Pa.
American journal of physics, monthly (Sept.-May), $10. American Association of Physic Teachers, American Institute of Physics, 335 East 45th Street, New York 17, N.Y.
Audubon junior membership leaflet. National Audubon Society, 1130 Fifth Avenue, New York 28, N.Y.
Bausch and Lomb focus. Bausch and Lomb, Rochester 2, N.Y.
Bi-weekly newsletter. US National Commission for Unesco, Department of State, Washington 25, D.C.
Chemical and engineering news, weekly, $6 (abroad $20). American Chemical Society, 115 16th Street, N.W. Washington, D.C.
Film news, bimonthly, $4 (abroad $5). 54 West 40th Street, New York 18, N.Y.
Geographic school bulletins, 30 issues per year, $2 (USA), $2.25 (Canada), $2.50 (elsewhere) National Geographic Society, Washington 6, D.C.
Illinois Junior Academy of Science year book, Illinois State Academy of Science, Donald G Hopkins, State Chairman of the Junior Academy, Carl Sandburg High School, Orland Park, Ill.
Industrial research newsletter, monthly. Armour Research Foundation of Illinois, Institut of Technology, Technology Center, Chicago 16, Ill.
Journal of chemical education, monthly, $4 (abroad $5). American Chemical Society, Divisio of Chemical Education, American Chemical Society, 20th and Northampton Streets Easton, Pa.
Laboratory, Fisher Scientific Co., 711 Forbes Avenue, Pittsburgh 19, Pa.
Metropolitan Detroit science review, quarterly, $2. Metropolitan Detroit Science Club, 1470 Wilfred, Detroit 13, Mich.
Monsanto magazine. 800 North Lindberg Boulevard, St. Louis 66, Mo.
Physics today, monthly, $4 (abroad $5). American Institute of Physics, 335 East 45th Street New York 17, N.Y.
SCA sponsor handbook, *Science projects handbook*, etc. Science Clubs of America, 1719 N Street, N.W. Washington 6, D.C.
School science and mathematics, monthly (Oct.-June), $6 (abroad $6.50). Central Associatio of Science and Mathematics Teachers, P.O. Box 108, Bluffton, Ohio. (Journal for all scienc and mathematics teachers.)
Science, weekly, $8.50. American Association for the Advancement of Science, 1515 Massachusetts Avenue, N.W., Washington 5, D.C.
Science counselor, quarterly. Duquesne University Press, Pittsburgh 19, Pa.

Science digest, monthly, $3.50 (abroad $4.50). 200 East Ontario Street, Chicago 11, Ill.

Science education, 5 issues per year, $5 (abroad $6). National Association for Research in Science Teaching, Council of Elementary Science International, C. M. Pruitt, University of Tampa, Tampa, Fla.

Science newsletter, weekly, $5.50. Science Service, 1719 'N' Street, N.W. Washington 6, D.C. (Weekly summary of current science.)

Science on the march (formerly *Hobbies*), 5 issues per year, year's subscription $1, $0.25 per copy. Buffalo Museum of Science, Humboldt Park, Buffalo 11, N.Y.

Science teacher, 8 issues per year, $6. National Science Teacher's Association, 1201 16th Street, N.W., Washington 6, D.C.

Science world, biweekly, $1.50. Scholastic Magazine, 33 West 42nd Street, New York 36, N.Y.

Scientific American, monthly, $6. 415 Madison Avenue, New York 17, N.Y.

Sky and telescope, monthly, $5 (abroad $7). Sky Publishing Corporation, Harvard College Observatory, Cambridge 38, Mass.

Sponsor's guide book, $5 (inc. annual supplement services). Future Scientists of America, NSTA, 1201 Sixteenth Street, N.W., Washington 6, D.C.

Weatherwise, bimonthly, $4. American Meteorological Society, 45 Beacom Street, Boston 8, Mass.

Welch. 1515 Sedgwick Street, Chicago 10, Ill.

Unesco[1]

Education abstracts, monthly, year's subscription $2 *or* 10s. *or* 6 NF; $0.25 *or* 1s. 3d. *or* 0.75 NF per copy.

Impact of science on society, quarterly, year's subscription $1.75 *or* 9s. 6d. *or* 4.50 NF; $0.50 *or* 2s. 6d. *or* 1.25 NF per copy.

International journal of adult and youth education (formerly *Fundamental and adult education*), quarterly, year's subscription $1.50 *or* 7s. 6d. *or* 4.50 NF; $0.50 *or* 2s. 3d. *or* 1.25 NF per copy.

Museum, quarterly, year's subscription $6.50 *or* £1 12s. 6d. *or* 20 NF; $2 *or* 10s. *or* 6 NF per copy.

Unesco Courier, monthly, year's subscription $3 *or* 10s. *or* 7 NF; $0.30 *or* 1s. *or* 0.70 NF per copy.

1. Place de Fontenoy, Paris-7e. France. Copies may also be obtained in most countries from Unesco's national distributors.

APPENDIX C

ROCKS AND MINERALS

A *mineral* is a natural inorganic[1] substance, having a nearly constant chemical composition and fairly definite physical characteristics.

An *ore* is a rock or mineral that contains enough of one or more metals to make mining profitable. The amount of metal in ores varies greatly. Some iron and lead ores will run as high as 50 to 75 per cent metal. On the other hand, an ounce of gold per ton of rock is considered good gold ore. Metals rarely occur in their native state. Many valuable ores are oxides, sulphides, or carbonates.

Identification of minerals

A mineral may be identified by certain properties or characteristics. Some minerals are easily identified; others require careful examination and often chemical analysis. Properties of minerals are as follows:

1. The *colour* of some minerals is very definite. For example, azurite has a deep blue colour. Certain other minerals, however, such as quartz, may occur in several colours.

2. The *streak* of a mineral is the colour of a mark that it makes on unglazed porcelain. Examples: graphite, black; hematite, reddish brown; malachite, light green.

3. Certain minerals break so that smooth plane surfaces are produced. This is called *cleavage*. Galena, for example, cleaves in three planes. These are at right angles to each other, so that a large piece of galena may be broken into many cubes.

4. The *lustre* of a mineral is the appearance of its surface, as affected by the peculiarities of its reflecting qualities. Many ores have a metallic lustre. The diamond has a brilliant lustre called *adamantine*. Chrysotile, the chief source of asbestos, has a silky lustre; kaolin, a form of hard clay, a dull lustre.

5. The *hardness* of minerals ranges from 1 to 10. Talc, which can be easily scratched with the fingernail, has a hardness of 1. The opposite extreme is represented by the diamond, the hardest known substance, which has a hardness of 10. The fingernail has a hardness of about 2½, and a knife blade, about 5½. The hardness of a specimen is ascertained by comparison with the standard series of minerals given below. Care should be exercised in testing for hardness. If one mineral scratches another, the scratch cannot be rubbed off. If it can be rubbed off, it indicates that the powder of the softer mineral has formed on the harder one and no scratch has been made.

1. Talc
2. Gypsum
3. Calcite
4. Fluorite
5. Apatite
6. Orthoclase feldspar
7. Quartz
8. Topaze
9. Corundum
10. Diamond

6. *Specific gravity* is a number that represents the weight ratio between 1 cubic centimetre (or other unit of volume) of a substance and 1 cubic centimetre of water. If 1 cubic centimetre of sphalerite (zinc ore) weighs 4 times as much as 1 cubic centimetre of water, then the specific gravity of sphalerite is said to be 4. The specific gravity of most minerals ranges between 2 and 4. Liquid petroleum, since it floats on water, has a specific gravity of less than 1. Pure gold has a specific gravity of 19.

7. *Effervescence in acid* is a property of some minerals. If a drop of hydrochloric acid is put on a piece of limestone, marble, or calcite, chemical reaction will result in bubbles of gas being given off. This is called *effervescence*. It can be used as a test for certain minerals known to possess this property.

8. The *crystalline form* of minerals varies greatly. Only four crystalline forms will be mentioned here: cubical crystal, represented by galena and halite (common salt); hexagonal (six-sided), by quartz; octahedron, by pyrite and the diamond; rhombohedron, by calcite.

Classes of rock

A *rock* is defined as a combination of two or more minerals, although some rocks are

1. Coal and petroleum are derived from substances that were originally organic, but they have been so changed by time that they are now considered to belong to the mineral kingdom. They are always spoken of as 'the mineral fuels'.

composed almost entirely of one mineral. Granite is composed mainly of three minerals: quartz, feldspar and mica. On the other hand, sandstone and quartzite are mainly quartz; limestone and marble, mainly calcite. It is important to remember that minerals have definite chemical compositions, but rocks have not.

Rocks are classified as igneous, sedimentary, or metamorphic.

Igneous rocks are formed when molten rock cools and solidifies. Examples:

1 Granite: red or grey; composed principally of quartz, feldspar and mica; the speckled appearance is due to different mineral crystals being visible.
2 Basalt: dark greenish black; sometimes shows small cavities, probably caused by steam; a common form of solidified lava.
3 Obsidian: volcanic glass; black, brown, green, etc.
4 Pumice stone: white to grey; porous; floats on water.
5 Scoria: black, grey, dark red; resembles cinders.

Sedimentary rocks are formed of sediment deposited by water. Examples:

1 Limestone: white to grey; composed mainly of calcite; often contains many fossils of marine animals; effervesces in acid; may be coloured yellow brown by limonite (iron oxide).
2 Sandstone: grey or red; mainly quartz; sand particles visible.
3 Shale: dark grey, black, red; can usually be broken into thin layers; clay odour when wet; oil shale is black.
4 Bituminous coal: black; composed of carbon and carbon compounds; may contain impurities such as hard shale.
5 Conglomerate: rounded pebbles cemented together.

Metamorphic rocks are other types that have been altered by pressure and heat. Examples:

1 Gneiss: mainly a metamorphosed granite; the minerals quartz, feldspar and mica often occur in layers; the mica may be the white variety (muscovite) or the black (biotite).
2 Marble: metamorphosed limestone; many colours; a beautiful rock when polished; effervesces in acid.
3 Quartzite: metamorphosed sandstone; extremely hard and compact; grey or red; sand particles firmly cemented together.
4 Slate: metamorphosed shale; usually black; splits into thin layers; harder than shale.
5 Anthracite: harder and not so dusty as bituminous coal; a superior fuel.

TABLE I

WEIGHTS AND MEASURES

Linear measure

12 inches (in) = 1 foot (ft)
3 feet = 1 yard (yd)
5½ yards = 1 rod (rd)
16½ feet = 1 rod
320 rods = 1 mile (mi)
1,760 yards = 1 mile
5,280 feet = 1 mile
6 feet = 1 fathom

Square measure

144 square inches (sq.in) = 1 square foot (sq.ft)
9 square feet = 1 square yard (sq.yd)
30¼ square yards = 1 square rod (sq.rd)
160 square rods = 1 acre (A)
640 acres = 1 square mile (sq.mi)
1 square mile = 1 section (US)
36 square miles = 1 township (US)

Cubic measure

1,728 cubic inches (cu.in) = 1 cubic foot (cu.ft)
27 cubic feet = 1 cubic yard (cu.yd)

Wood measure

16 cubic feet = 1 cord foot (cd.ft)
128 cubic feet, 8 cord feet = 1 cord (cd)

Table of counting

12 units = 1 dozen (doz)
12 dozen = 1 gross (gro)
12 gross = 1 great gross (gt.gro)
24 sheets of paper = 1 quire
20 quires or 480 sheets = 1 ream

Avoirdupois weight

7,000 grains (gr) = 1 pound (lb)
16 ounces (oz) = 1 pound
100 pounds = 1 US hundredweight(cwt)
112 pounds = 1 British hundredweight (cwt)
2,000 pounds = 1 US ton (T)
2,240 pounds = 1 US gross ton, 1 British ton

Troy weight (for precious metals, jewels, etc.)

24 grains = 1 pennyweight (dwt)
20 pennyweights = 1 ounce
12 ounces = 1 pound
437½ grains = 1 ounce, 7,000 grains = 1 pound } Av.
480 grains = 1 ounce, 5,760 grains = 1 pound } Troy

Apothecaries' weight

20 grains = 1 scruple
3 scruples = 1 dram
8 drams = 1 ounce
12 ounces, 5,760 grains = 1 pound

Apothecaries' liquid measure

60 minims = 1 fluid dram
8 fluid drams = 1 fluid ounce
16 fluid ounces = 1 pint
8 pints = 1 gallon

Measure of time

60 seconds (sec) = 1 minute (min)
60 minutes = 1 hour (hr)
24 hours = 1 day (da)
7 days = 1 week (wk)
365 days or 12 months (mo) = 1 year (yr)
10 years = 1 decade
10 decades = 1 century

Liquid measure (US)

4 gills (gi) = 1 pint (pt)
2 pints = 1 quart (qt)
4 quarts = 1 gallon (gal)
231 cu. in. = 1 gallon
31½ gal. = 1 barrel
1 liquid quart = 57.7 cubic inches

ry measure (U S)

pints (pt)	=	1 quart (qt)
quarts	=	1 peck (pk)
pecks	=	1 bushel (bu)
2 quarts	=	1 bushel
,150.4 cubic inches	=	1 bushel

iquid and dry measure (British)

pints (pt)	=	1 quart (qt)
quarts	=	1 gallon (gal)
gallons	=	1 peck (pk)
pecks	=	1 bushel (bu)
bushels	=	1 quarter (qr)
quart	=	69.318 cubic inches
gallon	=	277.274 cubic inches

Household measures

1 teaspoon	=	5 cc
3 teaspoons	=	1 tablespoon
16 tablespoons	=	1 cup
2 cups	=	1 pint

Miscellaneous

1 US gallon of water weighs 8.33 lb
1 British gallon of water weighs 10 lb
1 cubic foot of water weighs 62.3 lb
1 British billion means 1 million millions
1 US billion means 1 thousand millions
1 British trillion means 1 million billions
1 US trillion means 1 thousand billions, or
1 US trillion = 1 British billion

THE METRIC SYSTEM

easures of length

0 millimetres (mm)	=	1 centimetre (cm)
0 centimetres	=	1 decimetre (dm)
0 decimetres	=	1 metre (m)
0 metres	=	1 decametre (dam)
0 decametres	=	1 hectometre (hm)
0 hectometres	=	1 kilometre (km)
0 kilometres	=	1 myriametre (mn)

easures of surface

00 sq.millimetres (mm^2)	=	1 sq.centimetre (cm^2)
00 sq.centimetres	=	1 sq.decimetre (dm^2)
00 sq.decimetres	=	1 sq.metre (m^2)
00 sq.metres	=	1 sq.decametre (dam^2)
00 sq.decametres	=	1 sq.hectometre (hm^2)
00 sq.hectometres	=	1 sq.kilometre (km^2)

easures of volume

,000 cu. millimetres (mm^3)	=	1 cu. centimetre (cm^3)
1,000 cu.centimetres	=	1 cu. decimetre (dm^3)
1,000 cu. decimetres	=	1 cu. metre (m^3)

Measures of capacity

10 millilitres (ml)	=	1 centilitre (cl)
10 centilitres	=	1 decilitre (dl)
10 decilitres	=	1 litre (l)
10 litres	=	1 decalitre (dal)
10 decalitres	=	1 hectolitre (hl)
10 hectolitres	=	1 kilolitre (kl)
Note: 1 cc	=	1 ml

Measures of weight

10 milligrams	=	1 centigram
10 centigrams	=	1 decigram
10 decigrams	=	1 gram
10 grams	=	1 decagram
10 decagrams	=	1 hectogram
10 hectograms	=	1 kilogram
1,000 kilograms	=	1 metric ton

EQUIVALENTS

inch	=	2.54 centimetres
foot	=	30.48 centimetres
quart (US liq.)	=	0.9464 litre
quart (US dry)	=	1.101 litres
quart (British)	=	1.1351 litres
pound av.	=	0.4536 kilogram
1 centimetre	=	0.3937 inch
1 metre	=	39.37 inches
1 litre	=	1.051 quarts (US liq.)
1 litre	=	0.9081 quart (US dry)
1 litre	=	0.8809 quart (British)
1 kilogram	=	2.205 pounds

TABLE II

STARS AND PLANETS

A. Stars in descending order of brightness

Star	Constellation	Time of northing or southing		N or S of sun's position at noon
		8 p.m. Month	10 p.m. Month	
(a)	(b)	(c)	(d)	(e)
Sirius	Big Dog	February	January	10° S
Canopus	Ship Argo	February	January	40° S
α-Centauri	Centaur	June	May	80° S
Vega	Lyre	August	July	30° N
Capella	Charioteer	January	December	70° N
Arcturus	Herdsman	June	May	0°
Rigel	Orion	January	December	10° N
Procyon	Little Dog	February	January	20° N
Achernar	River Eridanus	December	November	30° S
β-Centauri	Centaur	June	May	80° S
Altair	Eagle	September	August	10° N
Betelgeuse	Orion	February	January	20° N
α-Crucis	Southern Cross	May	April	80° S
Aldebaran	BULL	January	December	40° N
Pollux	HEAVENLY TWINS	March	February	30° N
Spica	VIRGIN	May	April	30° S
Antares	SCORPION	July	June	50° S
Formalhaut	Southern Fish	October	September	20° S
Deneb	Swan	September	August	40° N
Regulus	LION	April	March	0°
β-Crucis	Southern Cross	May	April	80° S
Castor	HEAVENLY TWINS	March	February	30° N

The columns of Table A give the following data: (a) The names of the brightest stars in descending order of brightness. (b) The name of the constellation in which the star appears (the *signs of the zodiac* are printed in capitals). (c) The month when the star reaches its highest point above the horizon at about 8 p.m. local time. (d) The month when the star reaches its highest point above the horizon at about 10 p.m. local time. (e) The angle between the elevation of the star, when it is at its highest in the sky, and the elevation of the sun at *noon*, local time, during the month given in column (c). For example, to find Capella during January at 8 p.m., the observer should first look toward the place where the sun appeared to be at *noon* by local time, and then turn his gaze *northward* through 70° (approximately). Of course, all these stars are not visible from any one point of the earth. For instance, a star immediately above an observer at a point 60° N will appear on the horizon to an observer at a point 30° S, and will be below the horizon (i.e. invisible) to an observer at any point further south.

Notes: α-Centauri and β-Centauri are the 'pointers' for the Southern Cross. α-Centauri is the farthest from the Cross. It is the nearest bright star to the Earth, which its light takes about four years to reach.

Of the four bright stars which outline the Southern Cross, α-Crucis is the farthest south and β-Crucis the farthest east.

In the Heavenly Twins, Castor is to the north of Pollux.

B. Planets in increasing order of distance from the sun

Planet	Distance from sun (millions of miles)	Diameter (thousands of miles)	Time taken to complete orbit (years)
Mercury	36	3.2	0.24
Venus	67	7.85	0.62
Earth	93	7.9	1.00
Mars	142	4.25	1.88
Jupiter	483	89	11.9
Saturn	887	75	29.5
Uranus	1,785	31	84
Neptune	2,797	33	165
Pluto	3,675	4	248

The columns of Table B show the names of the planets, their distances from the sun, their diameters, and the times taken for their orbits.

The positions of the planets relative to the stars vary during the course of the year, and the brightness of each is also variable. (The positions of the planets in the sky at a particular time must be found from an appropriate almanac.)

Notes: Mercury is visible for only half an hour at most, either before sunrise or after sunset.

Venus is visible for not more than three hours either before sunrise or after sunset.

Mars, *Jupiter* and *Saturn* are often very conspicuous objects in the sky.

Of the remainder, only *Uranus* is visible to the naked eye; it has the appearance of a faint star.

C. Latitudes and dates when the sun is directly overhead at noon

Latitude	Dates		Latitude	Dates	
23.5° N	June 21 [1]	June 21 [1]	23.5° S	Dec. 22 [2]	Dec. 22 [2]
23° N	July 3	10	23° S	Jan. 2	11
22° N	12	1	22° S	10	3
21° N	19	May 26	21° S	16	Nov. 27
20° N	24	21	20° S	21	22
19° N	29	16	19° S	25	18
18° N	Aug. 2	12	18° S	29	14
17° N	6	8	17° S	Feb. 2	10
16° N	9	5	16° S	5	7
15° N	12	1	15° S	9	3
14° N	16	Apr. 28	14° S	12	Oct. 31
13° N	19	25	13° S	15	28
12° N	22	22	12° S	17	25
11° N	25	19	11° S	20	22
10° N	28	16	10° S	23	20
9° N	31	13	9° S	26	17
8° N	Sept. 2	11	8° S	28	14
7° N	5	8	7° S	Mar. 3	12
6° N	8	5	6° S	6	9
5° N	10	3	5° S	8	6
4° N	13	Mar. 31	4° S	11	4
3° N	16	29	3° S	13	1
2° N	18	26	2° S	16	Sept. 29
1° N	21 [4]	23 [3]	1° S	18	26
Equator	23 [4]	21 [3]	Equator	21 [3]	23 [4]

1. Summer solstice.
2. Winter solstice.
3. Spring equinox.
4. Autumn equinox.

TABLE III

ATOMIC NUMBERS OF THE ELEMENTS

Actinium	89	Europium	63	Mendelevium	101	Samarium	62
Aluminium	13			Mercury	80	Scandium	21
Americium	95	Fermium	100	Molybdenum	42	Selenium	34
Antimony	51	Fluorine	9			Silicon	14
Argon	18	Francium	87	Neodymium	60	Silver	47
Arsenic	33			Neon	10	Sodium	11
Astatine	85	Gadolinium	64	Neptunium	93	Strontium	38
		Gallium	31	Nickel	28	Sulphur	16
Barium	56	Germanium	32	Niobium	41		
Berkelium	97	Gold	79	Nitrogen	7	Tantalum	73
Beryllium	4			Nobelium	102	Technetium	43
Bismuth	83	Hafnium	72			Tellurium	52
Boron	5	Helium	2	Osmium	76	Terbium	65
Bromine	35	Holmium	67	Oxygen	8	Thallium	81
		Hydrogen	1			Thorium	90
Cadmium	48			Palladium	46	Thulium	69
Calcium	20	Indium	49	Phosphorus	15	Tin	50
Californium	98	Iodine	53	Platinum	78	Titanium	22
Carbon	6	Iridium	77	Plutonium	94	Tungsten	74
Cerium	58	Iron	26	Polonium	84		
Cesium	55			Potassium	19	Uranium	92
Chlorine	17	Krypton	36	Praseodymium	59		
Chromium	24			Promethium	61	Vanadium	23
Cobalt	27	Lanthanum	57	Protoactinium	91		
Copper	29	Lawrencium	103			Xenon	54
Curium	96	Lead	82	Radium	88		
		Lithium	3	Radon	86	Ytterbium	70
Dysprosium	66	Lutecium	71	Rhenium	75	Yttrium	39
				Rhodium	45		
Einsteinium	99	Magnesium	12	Rubidium	37	Zinc	30
Erbium	68	Manganese	25	Ruthenium	44	Zirconium	40

THE ELEMENTS

Atomic number	*Name of element*	*Symbol*	*Atomic weight*	*Atomic number*	*Name of element*	*Symbol*	*Atomic weight*
1	Hydrogen	H	1.0080	10	Neon	Ne	20.183
2	Helium	He	4.003	11	Sodium	Na	22.997
3	Lithium	Li	6.940	12	Magnesium	Mg	24.32
4	Beryllium	Be	9.013	13	Aluminium	Al	26.98
5	Boron	B	10.82	14	Silicon	Si	28.09
6	Carbon	C	12.010	15	Phosphorus	P	30.975
7	Nitrogen	N	14.008	16	Sulphur	S	32.066
8	Oxygen	O	16.0000	17	Chlorine	Cl	35.457
9	Fluorine	F	19.000	18	Argon	A	39.944

Atomic number	*Name of element*	*Symbol*	*Atomic weight*
19	Potassium	K	39.096
20	Calcium	Ca	40.08
21	Scandium	Sc	44.96
22	Titanium	Ti	47.90
23	Vanadium	V	50.95
24	Chromium	Cr	52.01
25	Manganese	Mn	54.93
26	Iron	Fe	55.85
27	Cobalt	Co	58.94
28	Nickel	Ni	58.69
29	Copper	Cu	63.54
30	Zinc	Zn	65.38
31	Gallium	Ga	69.72
32	Germanium	Ge	72.60
33	Arsenic	As	74.91
34	Selenium	Se	78.96
35	Bromine	Br	79.916
36	Krypton	Kr	83.80
37	Rubidium	Rb	85.48
38	Strontium	Sr	87.63
39	Yttrium	Y	88.92
40	Zirconium	Zr	91.22
41	Niobium	Nb	92.91
42	Molybdenum	Mo	95.95
43	Technetium	Tc	99
44	Ruthenium	Ru	101.7
45	Rhodium	Rh	102.91
46	Palladium	Pd	106.7
47	Silver	Ag	107.880
48	Cadmium	Cd	112.41
49	Indium	In	114.76
50	Tin	Sn	118.70
51	Antimony	Sb	121.76
52	Tellurium	Te	127.61
53	Iodine	I	126.92
54	Xenon	Xe	131.3
55	Cesium	Cs	132.91
56	Barium	Ba	137.36
57	Lanthanum	La	138.92
58	Cerium	Ce	140.13
59	Praseodymium	Pr	140.92
60	Neodymium	Nd	144.27
61	Promethium	Pm	145
62	Samarium	Sm	150.43
63	Europium	Eu	152.0
64	Gadolinium	Gd	156.9
65	Terbium	Tb	159.2
66	Dysprosium	Dy	162.46
67	Holmium	Ho	164.94
68	Erbium	Er	167.2
69	Thulium	Tm	169.4
70	Ytterbium	Yb	173.04
71	Lutecium	Lu	174.99
72	Hafnium	Hf	178.6
73	Tantalum	Ta	180.88
74	Tungsten	W	183.92
75	Rhenium	Re	186.31
76	Osmium	Os	190.2
77	Iridium	Ir	193.1
78	Platinum	Pt	195.23
79	Gold	Au	197.2
80	Mercury	Hg	200.61
81	Thallium	Tl	204.39
82	Lead	Pb	207.21
83	Bismuth	Bi	209.00
84	Polonium	Po	210
85	Astatine	At	211
86	Radon	Rn	222
87	Francium	Fr	223
88	Radium	Ra	226.05
89	Actinium	Ac	227
90	Thorium	Th	232.12
91	Protoactinium	Pa	231
92	Uranium	U	238.07
93	Neptunium	Np	237.07
94	Plutonium	Pu	239.08
95	Americium	Am	243
96	Curium	Cm	244
97	Berkelium	Bk	245
98	Californium	Cf	(246) [1]
99	Einsteinium	E	(253) [1]
100	Fermium	Fm	(254) [1]
101	Mendelevium	Me	(256) [1]
102	Nobelium	No	(—) [1]
103	Lawrencium	Lw	(—) [1]

1. Transuranic elements—atomic weights are not yet fixed. *Physical Review* or other scientific publications should be consulted. Mass numbers of the abundances in parentheses.

TABLE IV

DENSITIES

(In grams per cubic centimetre)

Substance	Density	Substance	Density
Alcohol, 95%	0.807	Marble	2.5-2.8
Aluminium	2.7	Mercury	13.6
Brass	8.4	Milk	1.03
Carbon tetrachloride	1.6	Nickel	8.9
Coal (anthracite)	1.4-1.8	Paraffin	0.824-0.94
Copper	8.93	Platinum	21.5
Gasoline	0.75	Sea water	1.03
Glass (flint)	3.0-3.6	Silver	10.5
Glass (crown)	2.4-2.7	Tin	7.3
Gold	19.3	Wood — Ebony	1.2
Ice	0.917	Oak	0.7-0.9
Iron	7.1-7.9	Pine	0.4-0.6
Lead	11.4	Lignum vitae	1.33
Magnesium	1.74	Zinc	7.1

Stones, Brick, Cement (Kent)

Substance	Density	Substance	Density
Agate	2.615	Gravel	1.600-1.920
Asphaltum	1.390	Gypsum	2.080-2.400
Brick (soft)	1.600	Hornblende	3.200-3.520
Brick (common)	1.790	Lime (quick)	0.800-0.880
Brick (hard)	2.000	Limestone	2.720-3.200
Brick (pressed)	2.160	Magnesia (carbonate)	2.400
Brick (fire)	2.250-2.400	Marble	2.560-2.880
Brickwork in mortar	1.600	Masonry (dry rubble)	2.240-2.560
Brickwork in cement	1.790	Masonry (dressed)	2.240-2.880
Cement (Rosendale)	0.960	Mortar	1.440-1.600
Cement (Portland)	1.250	Pitch	1.150
Clay	1.920-2.400	Plaster of Paris	1.180-1.280
Concrete	1.920-2.240	Porcelain	2.380
Diamond	3.530	Quartz	2.640
Earth (loose)	1.150-1.280	Sand	1.440-1.760
Earth (rammed)	1.440-1.760	Sandstone	2.240-2.400
Emery	4.000	Slate	2.720-2.880
Glass (crown)	2.520	Soapstone	2.650-2.800
Glass (flint)	3.000-3.600	Trap	2.720-3.400
Glass (green)	2.640	Tile	1.760-1.920
Granite	2.560-2.720		

TABLE V

HEAT CONSTANTS

Substances	*Specific heat*	*Melting point (°C)*	*Boiling point (°C)*	*Coefficient of linear expansion (per °C)*
Solids				
Aluminium	0.22	658	2,200	0.000023
Brass	0.092	900		0.0000189
Copper	0.092	1,083	2,300	0.0000167
Glass, ordinary	0.16	1,100		0.000085
Ice	0.50	0		
Iron	0.12	1,530	3,000	00.00012
Lead	0.031	327	1,755	00.00029
Mercury.	0.033	—39	356.7	
Tin.	0.055	232	2,260	0.000023
Zinc	0.093	419	907	0.000029
Liquids				
Alcohol, ethyl	0.58	—130	78.3	
Glycerine	0.576	17	290	
Kerosene	0.5-0.6			
Mercury.	0.033		357	
Sulphuric acid.	0.34	10.5	330	
Water.	1.00		100	
Gases				
Air.	0.24		—190	
Alcohol, ethyl	0.41			
Ammonia gas	0.52	—78	—33	
Carbon dioxide	0.20	—56.6	—79	
Hydrogen	3.38			
Nitrogen	0.25			
Oxygen	0.22			
Steam.	0.48			

EQUIVALENT TEMPERATURES IN DIFFERENT SCALES

	Absolute	*Centigrade*	*Fahrenheit*	*Reaumur*
Absolute zero	0° A	—273° C	—459° F	—218° R
Fahrenheit zero.	255° A	—18° C	0° F	—14° R
Freezing point of water	273° A	0° C	32° F	0° R
Boiling point of water.	373° A	100° C	212° F	80° R

Table V

CENTIGRADE TO FAHRENHEIT CONVERSION TABLE

°C	°F	°C	°F	°C	°F	°C	°F
0	32						
1	34	26	79	51	124	76	169
2	36	27	81	52	126	77	171
3	37	28	82	53	127	78	172
4	39	29	84	54	129	79	174
5	41	30	86	55	131	80	176
6	43	31	88	56	133	81	178
7	45	32	90	57	135	82	180
8	46	33	91	58	136	83	181
9	48	34	93	59	138	84	183
10	50	35	95	60	140	85	185
11	52	36	97	61	142	86	187
12	54	37	99	62	144	87	189
13	55	38	100	63	145	88	190
14	57	39	102	64	147	89	192
15	59	40	104	65	149	90	194
16	61	41	106	66	151	91	196
17	63	42	108	67	153	92	198
18	64	43	109	68	154	93	199
19	66	44	111	69	156	94	201
20	68	45	113	70	158	95	203
21	70	46	115	71	160	96	205
22	72	47	117	72	162	97	207
23	73	48	118	73	163	98	208
24	75	49	120	74	165	99	210
25	77	50	122	75	167	100	212

TABLE VI

RELATIVE HUMIDITY (PERCENTAGE)—°F

Temperature of dry bulb (°F)	*Depression of the wet bulb (°F) i.e. difference between wet and dry bulb readings*																			
	1	2	3	4	5	6	7	8	9	10	11	12	13	14	15	16	17	18	19	20
120	97	94	91	88	85	82	79	77	74	72	69	67	64	62	59	57	55	53	51	48
118	97	94	91	88	85	82	79	76	74	71	69	66	63	61	59	56	54	52	50	48
116	97	94	90	87	84	82	79	76	73	71	68	65	63	61	58	56	54	51	49	47
114	97	94	90	87	84	81	79	76	73	70	68	65	63	60	58	55	53	51	48	46
112	97	94	90	87	84	81	78	75	73	70	67	65	62	59	57	55	52	50	48	46
110	97	93	90	87	84	81	78	75	72	69	67	64	61	59	56	54	51	49	47	45
108	97	93	90	87	84	81	78	75	72	69	66	63	61	58	56	53	51	49	46	44
106	96	93	90	87	84	80	77	74	71	68	66	63	60	58	55	52	50	48	45	43
104	96	93	90	86	83	80	77	74	71	68	65	62	60	57	54	52	49	47	44	42
102	96	93	90	86	83	80	77	73	70	67	65	62	59	56	54	51	48	46	43	41
100	96	93	89	86	82	79	76	73	70	67	64	61	58	55	53	50	47	45	42	40
	99	*98*	*96*	*95*	*94*	*93*	*91*	*90*	*89*	*87*	*86*	*85*	*83*	*82*	*80*	*79*		*76*		*72*
98	96	93	89	86	82	79	76	72	69	66	63	60	57	54	52	49	46	44	41	39
96	96	93	89	85	82	78	75	72	68	65	62	59	57	54	51	48	45	43	40	38
94	96	93	89	85	81	78	75	71	68	65	62	59	56	53	50	47	44	42	39	36
92	96	92	88	85	81	78	74	71	67	64	61	58	55	52	49	46	43	40	38	35
90	96	92	88	84	81	77	74	70	67	63	60	57	54	51	48	45	42	39	36	34
	89	*87*	*86*	*85*	*83*	*82*	*81*	*79*	*78*	*76*	*75*	*73*	*72*	*70*	*69*	*67*		*63*		*59*
88	96	92	88	84	80	77	73	69	66	63	59	56	53	50	47	44	41	38	35	32
86	96	92	88	84	80	76	72	69	65	62	58	55	52	49	45	42	39	36	33	31
84	96	92	87	83	79	76	72	68	64	61	57	54	51	47	44	41	38	35	32	29
82	96	91	87	83	79	75	71	67	64	60	56	53	49	46	43	40	36	33	30	27
80	96	91	87	83	79	74	70	66	63	59	55	52	48	45	41	38	35	31	28	25
	79	*77*	*76*	*74*	*73*	*72*	*70*	*68*	*67*	*65*	*63*	*62*	*60*	*58*	*56*	*54*		*50*		*44*
78	95	91	86	82	78	74	70	66	62	58	54	50	47	43	40	36	33	30	26	23
76	95	91	86	82	78	73	69	65	61	57	53	49	45	42	38	34	31	28	24	21
74	95	90	86	81	77	72	68	64	60	56	52	48	44	40	36	33	29	26	22	19
72	95	90	85	80	76	71	67	63	58	54	50	46	42	38	34	31	27	23	20	16
70	95	90	85	80	75	71	66	62	57	53	49	44	40	36	32	28	24	21	17	14
	69	*67*	*66*	*64*	*62*	*61*	*59*	*57*	*55*	*53*	*51*	*49*	*47*	*44*	*42*	*39*		*33*		*26*
68	95	90	84	79	75	70	65	60	56	51	47	43	38	34	30	26	22	18	15	11
66	95	89	84	79	74	69	64	59	54	50	45	41	36	32	28	23	20	16	12	8
64	94	89	83	78	73	68	63	58	53	48	43	39	34	30	25	21	17	13	9	5
62	94	88	83	77	72	67	61	56	51	46	41	37	32	27	23	18	14	10	5	
60	94	88	82	77	71	65	60	55	50	44	39	34	29	25	20	15	11	6	2	
	58	*57*	*55*	*53*	*51*	*49*	*47*	*45*	*43*	*40*	*38*	*35*	*32*	*29*	*25*	*21*				
58	94	88	82	76	70	64	59	53	48	42	37	31	26	22	17	12	7	2		
56	94	87	81	75	69	63	57	51	46	40	35	29	24	19	13	8	3			
54	93	87	80	74	68	61	55	49	43	38	32	26	21	15	10	5				
52	93	86	79	73	66	60	54	47	41	35	29	23	17	12	6					
50	93	86	79	72	65	59	52	45	38	32	26	20	14	8	2					
	48	*46*	*44*	*42*	*40*	*37*	*34*	*32*	*29*	*26*	*22*	*18*								
48	92	85	77	70	63	56	49	42	36	29	22	16	10	4						
46	92	84	77	69	62	54	47	40	33	26	19	12	6							
44	92	84	75	68	60	52	45	37	29	22	15	8								
42	91	83	74	66	58	50	42	34	26	18										
40	91	82	73	65	56	47	39	30												
	38	*35*	*33*	*30*	*28*	*25*														

Note: In this table, the dew points are in italics

Table VI

RELATIVE HUMIDITY (PERCENTAGE)—^{0}C

Temperature of dry bulb (^0C)	*Depression of the wet bulb (^0C)*														
	1	2	3	4	5	6	7	8	9	10	12	14	16	18	20
50	94	89	84	79	74	70	65	61	57	53	46	40	33	28	22
45	94	88	83	78	73	68	63	59	55	51	42	35	28	22	16
40	93	88	82	77	71	65	61	56	52	47	38	31	23	16	10
35	93	87	80	75	68	62	57	52	47	42	33	24	16	8	
30	92	86	78	72	65	59	53	47	41	36	26	16	8		
25	91	84	76	69	61	54	47	41	35	29	17	6			
20	90	81	73	64	56	47	40	32	26	18	5				
15	89	79	68	59	49	39	30	21	12	4					
10	87	75	62	51	38	27	17	5							

TABLE VII

PRESSURE OF SATURATED WATER VAPOUR IN MILLIMETRES OF MERCURY AT DIFFERENT TEMPERATURES

°C	+0	+1	+2	+3	+4	+5	+6	+7	+8	+9
0	4.6	4.9	5.3	5.7	6.1	6.5	7.0	7.5	8.0	8.6
10	9.2	9.8	10.5	11.2	12.0	12.8	13.6	14.5	15.5	16.5
20	17.5	18.6	19.8	21.0	22.3	23.7	25.1	26.7	28.3	29.9
30	31.7	33.6	35.5	37.6	39.8	42.0	44.4	46.9	49.5	52.3
	+0	+2	+4	+6	+8	+10	+12	+14	+16	+18
40	55.1	61.3	68.1	75.4	83.5	92.3	102	112	123	135
60	149	163	179	195	214	233	255	277	301	327
80	355	384	416	450	487	525	567	611	657	707
100	760	815	875	938	1004	1075	1149	1227	1310	1397

Examples: Pressure of saturated water vapour at 12° C (= 10° + 2°) is 10.5 mm; at 94° C (= 80° + 14°) it is 611 mm.

TABLE VIII

GREEK ALPHABET

Alpha (a)	Α α	Nu (n)	Ν ν
Beta (b)	Β β	Xi (x)	Ξ ξ
Gamma (g)	Γ γ	Omicron (o)	Ο ο
Delta (d)	Δ δ *or* ᵹ	Pi (p)	Π π
Epsilon (e)	Ε ε	Rho (r)	Ρ ϱ
Zeta (z)	Ζ ζ	Sigma (s)	Σ σ *or* ς
Eta (h)	Η η	Tau (t)	Τ τ
Theta (th)	Θ θ	Upsilon (u)	Υ υ
Iota (i)	Ι ι	Phi (ph)	Φ φ *or* ϕ
Kappa (k)	Κ ϰ	Chi (ch)	Χ χ
Lambda (l)	Λ λ	Psi (ps)	Ψ ψ
Mu (m)	Μ μ	Omega (o)	Ω ω

	0	1	2	3	4	5	6	7	8	9	1	2	3	4	5	6	7	8	9
10	0000	0043	0086	0128	0170						4	9	13	17	21	26	30	34	38
						0212	0253	0294	0334	0374	4	8	12	16	20	24	28	32	37
11	0414	0453	0492	0531	0569						4	8	12	15	19	23	27	31	35
						0607	0645	0682	0719	0755	4	7	11	15	19	22	26	30	33
12	0792	0828	0864	0899	0934	0969					3	7	11	14	18	21	25	28	32
							1004	1038	1072	1106	3	7	10	14	17	20	24	27	31
13	1189	1173	1206	1239	1271						3	7	10	13	16	20	23	26	80
						1303	1335	1367	1399	1430	3	7	10	12	16	19	22	25	29
14	1461	1492	1523	1553							3	6	9	12	15	18	21	24	28
					1584	1614	1644	1673	1703	1732	3	6	9	12	15	17	20	23	26
15	1761	1790	1818	1847	1875	1903					3	6	9	11	14	17	20	23	26
							1931	1959	1987	2014	3	5	8	11	14	16	19	22	25
16	2041	2068	2095	2122	2148						3	5	8	11	14	16	19	22	24
						2175	2201	2227	2253	2279	3	5	8	10	13	15	18	21	23
17	2304	2330	2355	2380	2405	2430					3	5	8	10	13	15	18	20	23
							2455	2480	2504	2529	2	5	7	10	12	15	17	19	22
18	2553	2577	2601	2625	2648						2	5	7	9	12	14	16	19	21
						2672	2695	2718	2742	2765	2	5	7	9	11	14	16	18	21
19	2788	2810	2833	2856	2878						2	4	7	9	11	13	16	18	20
						2900	2923	2945	2967	2989	2	4	6	8	11	13	15	17	19
20	3010	3032	3054	3075	3096	3118	3139	3160	3181	3201	2	4	6	8	11	13	15	17	19
21	3222	3243	3263	3284	3304	3324	3345	3365	3385	3404	2	4	6	8	10	12	14	16	18
22	3424	3444	3464	3483	3502	3522	3541	3560	3579	3598	2	4	6	8	10	12	14	15	17
23	3617	3636	3655	3674	3692	3711	3729	3747	3766	3784	2	4	6	7	9	11	13	15	17
24	3802	3820	3838	3856	3874	3892	3909	3927	3945	3962	2	4	5	7	9	11	12	14	16
25	3979	3997	4014	4031	4048	4065	4082	4099	4116	4133	2	3	5	7	9	10	12	14	15
26	4150	4166	4183	4200	4216	4232	4249	4265	4281	4298	2	3	5	7	8	10	11	13	15
27	4314	4330	4346	4362	4378	4393	4409	4425	4440	4456	2	3	5	6	8	9	11	13	14
28	4472	4487	4502	4518	4533	4548	4564	4579	4594	4609	2	3	5	6	8	9	11	12	14
29	4624	4639	4654	4669	4683	4698	4713	4728	4742	4757	1	3	4	6	7	9	10	12	13
30	4771	4786	4800	4814	4829	4843	4857	4871	4886	4900	1	3	4	6	7	9	10	11	13
31	4914	4928	4942	4955	4969	4983	4997	5011	5024	5038	1	3	4	6	7	8	10	11	12
32	5051	5065	5079	5092	5105	5119	5132	5145	5159	5172	1	3	4	5	7	8	9	11	12
33	5185	5198	5211	5224	5237	5250	5263	5276	5289	5302	1	3	4	5	6	8	9	10	12
34	5315	5328	5340	5353	5366	5378	5391	5403	5416	5428	1	3	4	5	6	8	9	10	11
35	5441	5453	5465	5478	5490	5502	5514	5527	5539	5551	1	2	4	5	6	7	9	10	11
36	5563	5575	5587	5599	5611	5623	5635	5647	5658	5670	1	2	4	5	6	7	8	10	11
37	5682	5694	5705	5717	5729	5740	5752	5763	5775	5786	1	2	3	5	6	7	8	9	10
38	5798	5809	5821	5832	5843	5855	5866	5877	5888	5899	1	2	3	5	6	7	8	9	10
39	5911	5922	5933	5944	5955	5966	5977	5988	5999	6010	1	2	3	4	5	7	8	9	10
40	6021	6031	6042	6053	6064	6075	6085	6096	6107	6117	1	2	3	4	5	6	8	9	10
41	6128	6138	6149	6160	6170	6180	6191	6201	6212	6222	1	2	3	4	5	6	7	8	9
42	6232	6243	6253	6263	6274	6284	6294	6304	6314	6325	1	2	3	4	5	6	7	8	9
43	6335	6345	6355	6365	6375	6385	6395	6405	6415	6425	1	2	3	4	5	6	7	8	9
44	6435	6444	6454	6464	6474	6484	6493	6503	6513	6522	1	2	3	4	5	6	7	8	9
45	6532	6542	6551	6561	6571	6580	6590	6599	6609	6618	1	2	3	4	5	6	7	8	9
46	6628	6637	6646	6656	6665	6675	6684	6693	6702	6712	1	2	3	4	5	6	7	7	8
47	6721	6730	6739	6749	6758	6767	6776	6785	6794	6803	1	2	3	4	5	5	6	7	8
48	6812	6821	6830	6839	6848	6857	6866	6875	6884	6893	1	2	3	4	4	5	6	7	8
49	6902	6911	6920	6928	6937	6946	6955	6964	6972	6981	1	2	3	4	4	5	6	7	8
50	6990	6998	7007	7016	7024	7033	7042	7050	7059	7067	1	2	3	3	4	5	6	7	8

	0	1	2	3	4	5	6	7	8	9	1	2	3	4	5	6	7	8	9
51	7076	7084	7093	7101	7110	7118	7126	7135	7143	7152	1	2	3	3	4	5	6	7	8
52	7160	7168	7177	7185	7193	7202	7210	7218	7226	7235	1	2	2	3	4	5	6	7	7
53	7243	7251	7259	7267	7275	7284	7292	7300	7308	7316	1	2	2	3	4	5	6	6	7
54	7324	7332	7340	7348	7356	7364	7372	7380	7388	7396	1	2	2	3	4	5	6	6	7
55	7404	7412	7419	7427	7435	7443	7451	7459	7466	7474	1	2	2	3	4	5	5	6	7
56	7482	7490	7497	7505	7513	7520	7528	7536	7543	7551	1	2	2	3	4	5	5	6	7
57	7559	7566	7574	7582	7589	7597	7604	7612	7619	7627	1	2	2	3	4	5	5	6	7
58	7634	7642	7649	7657	7664	7672	7679	7686	7694	7701	1	1	2	3	4	4	5	6	7
59	7709	7716	7723	7731	7738	7745	7752	7760	7767	7774	1	1	2	3	4	4	5	6	7
60	7782	7789	7796	7803	7810	7818	7825	7832	7839	7846	1	1	2	3	4	4	5	6	6
61	7853	7860	7868	7875	7882	7889	7896	7903	7910	7917	1	1	2	3	4	4	5	6	6
62	7924	7931	7938	7945	7952	7959	7966	7973	7980	7987	1	1	2	3	3	4	5	6	6
63	7993	8000	8007	8014	8021	8028	8035	8041	8048	8055	1	1	2	3	3	4	5	5	6
64	8062	8069	8075	8082	8089	8096	8102	8109	8116	8122	1	1	2	3	3	4	5	5	6
65	8129	8136	8142	8149	8156	8162	8169	8176	8182	8189	1	1	2	3	3	4	5	5	6
66	8195	8202	8209	8215	8222	8228	8235	8241	8248	8254	1	1	2	3	3	4	5	5	6
67	8261	8267	8274	8280	8287	8293	8299	8306	8312	8319	1	1	2	3	3	4	5	5	6
68	8325	8331	8338	8344	8351	8357	8363	8370	8376	8382	1	1	2	3	3	4	4	5	6
69	8388	8395	8401	8407	8414	8420	8426	8432	8439	8445	1	1	2	2	3	4	4	5	6
70	8451	8457	8463	8470	8476	8482	8488	8494	8500	8506	1	1	2	2	3	4	4	5	6
71	8513	8519	8525	8531	8537	8543	8549	8555	8561	8567	1	1	2	2	3	4	4	5	5
72	8573	8579	8585	8591	8597	8603	8609	8615	8621	8627	1	1	2	2	3	4	4	5	5
73	8633	8639	8645	8651	8657	8663	8669	8675	8681	8686	1	1	2	2	3	4	4	5	5
74	8692	8698	8704	8710	8716	8722	8727	8733	8739	8745	1	1	2	2	3	4	4	5	5
75	8751	8756	8762	8768	8774	8779	8785	8791	8797	8802	1	1	2	2	3	3	4	5	5
76	8808	8814	8820	8825	8831	8837	8842	8848	8854	8859	1	1	2	2	3	3	4	5	5
77	8865	8871	8876	8882	8887	8893	8899	8904	8910	8915	1	1	2	2	3	3	4	4	5
78	8921	8927	8932	8938	8943	8949	8954	8960	8965	8971	1	1	2	2	3	3	4	4	5
79	8976	8982	8987	8993	8998	9004	9009	9015	9020	9025	1	1	2	2	3	3	4	4	5
80	9031	9036	9042	9047	9053	9058	9063	9069	9074	9079	1	1	2	2	3	3	4	4	5
81	9085	9090	9096	9101	9106	9112	9117	9122	9128	9133	1	1	2	2	3	3	4	4	5
82	9138	9143	9149	9154	9159	9165	9170	9175	9180	9186	1	1	2	2	3	3	4	4	5
83	9191	9196	9201	9206	9212	9217	9222	9227	9232	9238	1	1	2	2	3	3	4	4	5
84	9243	9248	9253	9258	9263	9269	9274	9279	9284	9289	1	1	2	2	3	3	4	4	5
85	9294	9299	9304	9309	9315	9320	9325	9330	9335	9340	1	1	2	2	3	3	4	4	5
86	9345	9350	9355	9360	9365	9370	9375	9380	9385	9390	1	1	2	2	3	3	4	4	5
87	9395	9400	9405	9410	9415	9420	9425	9430	9435	9440	0	1	1	2	2	3	3	4	4
88	9445	9450	9455	9460	9465	9469	9474	9479	9484	9489	0	1	1	2	2	3	3	4	4
89	9494	9499	9504	9509	9513	9518	9523	9528	9533	9538	0	1	1	2	2	3	3	4	4
90	9542	9547	9552	9557	9562	9566	9571	9576	9581	9586	0	1	1	2	2	3	3	4	4
91	9590	9595	9600	9605	9609	9614	9619	9624	9628	9633	0	1	1	2	2	3	3	4	4
92	9638	9643	9647	9652	9657	9661	9666	9671	9675	9680	0	1	1	2	2	3	3	4	4
93	9685	9689	9694	9699	9703	9708	9713	9717	9722	9727	0	1	1	2	2	3	3	4	4
94	9731	9736	9741	9745	9750	9754	9759	9763	9768	9773	0	1	1	2	2	3	3	4	4
95	9777	9782	9786	9791	9795	9800	9805	9809	9814	9818	0	1	1	2	2	3	3	4	4
96	9823	9827	9832	9836	9841	9845	9850	9854	9859	9868	0	1	1	2	2	3	3	4	4
97	9868	9872	9877	9881	9886	9890	9894	9899	9903	9908	0	1	1	2	2	3	3	4	4
98	9912	9917	9921	9926	9930	9934	9939	9943	9948	9952	0	1	1	2	2	3	3	4	4
99	9956	9961	9965	9969	9974	9978	9983	9987	9991	9996	0	1	1	2	2	3	3	3	4

Note: These tables are so constructed that the fourth figure of a logarithm obtained by their use is never more than one unit above or below the best 4-figure approximation. E.g. if the logarithm found is 0.5014 the best 4-figure approximation may be 0.5013, 0.5014 or 0.5015. Greater accuracy than this cannot be obtained by the use of a uniform table of differences of this kind.

10 10
9 9
8 8
7 7
6 6
5 5
4 4
3 3
2 2
1 1

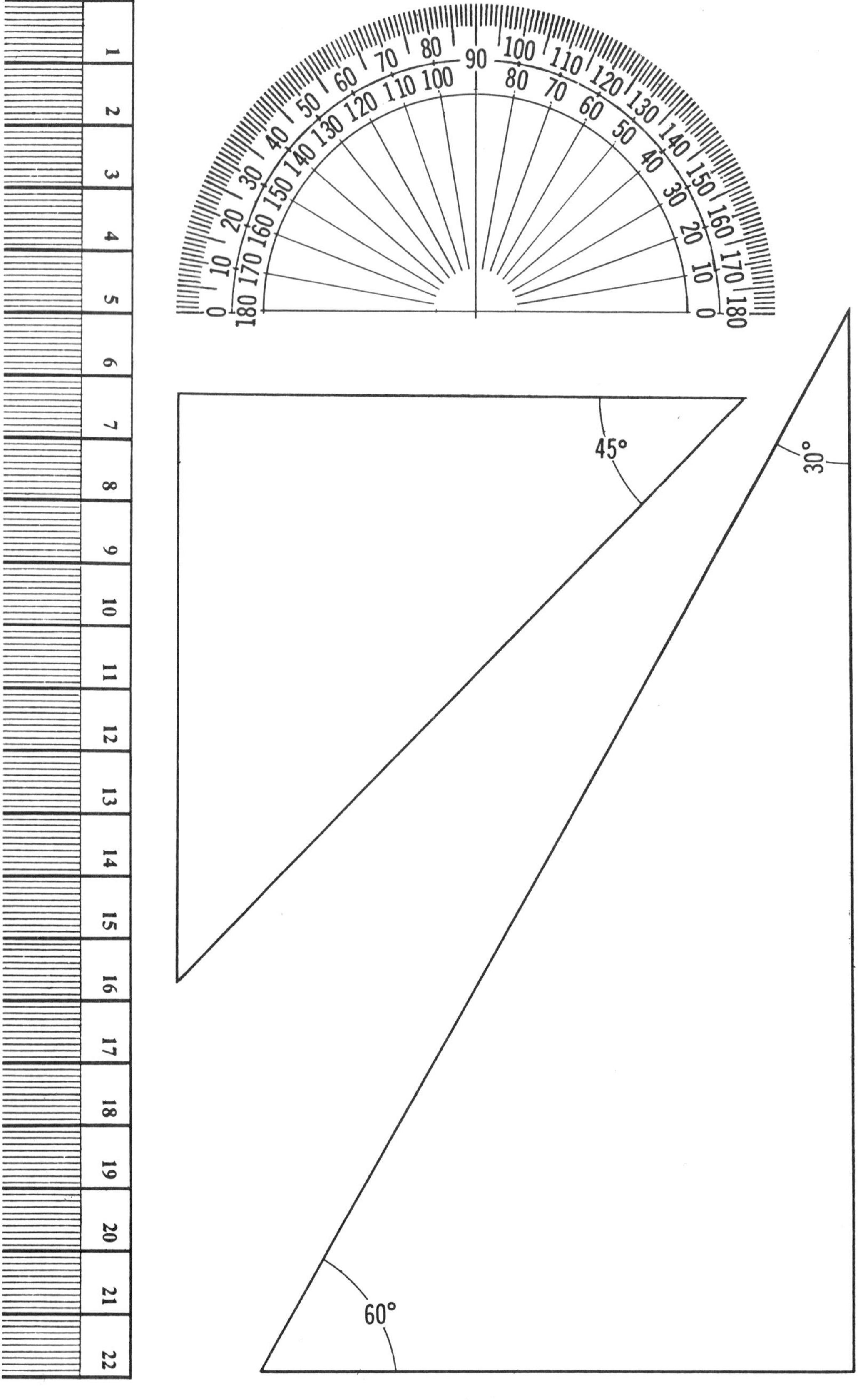
45°
30°
60°

This book was a gift from:
P.T.A. Campbell Soup Label Program
May 1989